AF348673

PAUL GAUGUIN

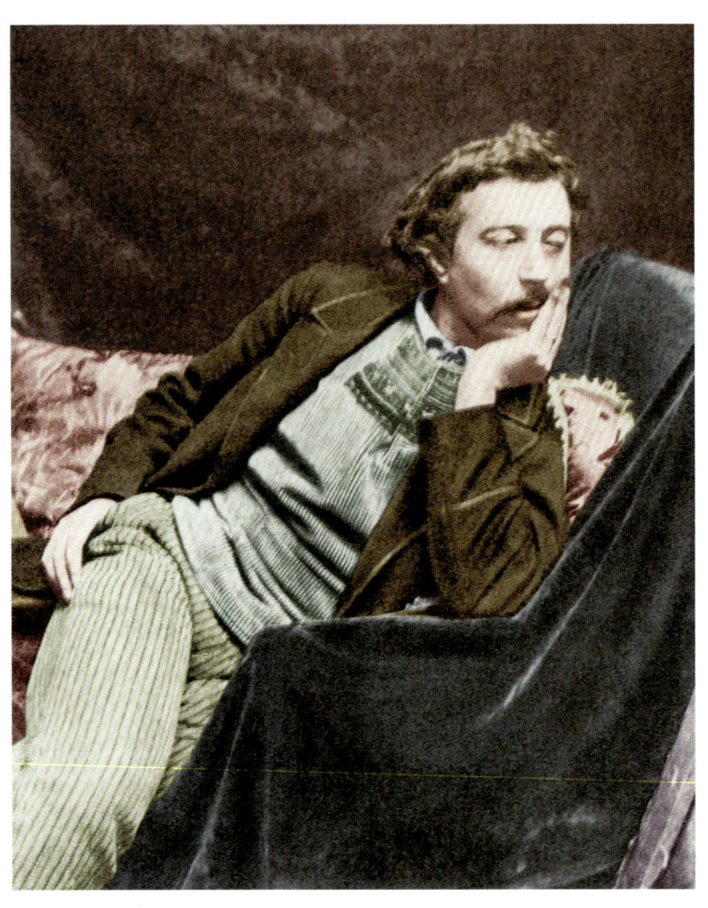

PAUL GAUGUIN

ARMELLE FÉMELAT

p. 2
Paul Gauguin

1891

KÖNEMANN

© 2017 koenemann.com GmbH
www.koenemann.com

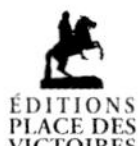

ÉDITIONS
PLACE DES
VICTOIRES

© Éditions Place des Victoires
6, rue du Mail – 75002 Paris
www.victoires.com
ISBN: 978-2-8099-1462-7
Dépôt légal: 3e trimestre 2017

Concept, Project Management: koenemann.com GmbH
Text: Armelle Fémelat

Translations into English, German, Spanish, Italian and Dutch:

TEXTCASE
Translation Agency

Art Direction: Oliver Hessmann
Layout: Beate Lennartz
Picture credits: akg-images gmbh

ISBN: 978-3-95588-628-8 (international)

Printed in China by Shenzhen Hua Xin Colour-printing & Platemaking Co., Ltd

Contents   Sommaire   Inhalt   Índice   Indice   Inhoud

À propos

Freedom and authenticity
An avant-garde artist fully recognised as such, since the great Parisian exhibition of 1949, Paul Gauguin (1848–1903) remained marginal all of his life because of his atypical career, his extreme character and his polymorphic and innovative art. Although he did not enjoy fortune during his life, but only success among critics, he was aware of his talent. He wrote to his wife Mette Sophie on March 1892: "I am a great artist and I know it. It is because I know it, that I have endured so many sufferances in order to follow my path." A self-proclaimed "savage", nostalgic for his Peruvian childhood, he was on a perpetual quest for authenticity and freedom.

Liberté et authenticité
Artiste avant-gardiste pleinement reconnu en tant que tel depuis la grande exposition parisienne de 1949, Paul Gauguin (1848–1903) est resté en marge toute sa vie du fait de son parcours atypique, de son caractère extrême et de son art, polymorphe et novateur. Bien qu'il n'ait pas connu la fortune de son vivant, tout juste un succès d'estime, il est conscient de son talent. « Je suis un grand artiste et je le sais. C'est parce que je le sais que j'ai tellement enduré de souffrances, pour poursuivre ma voie » écrit-il à sa femme Mette Sophie, en mars 1892. « Sauvage » autoproclamé, nostalgique de sa petite enfance péruvienne, il fut en quête perpétuelle d'authenticité et de liberté.

Freiheit und Authentizität
Wenngleich er seit der großen Pariser Ausstellung von 1949 voll und ganz als Avantgardekünstler anerkannt ist, bleibt Paul Gauguin (1848–1903) zu Lebzeiten stets eine Randfigur – wegen seines ungewöhnlichen Lebenswegs, seines extremen Charakters und nicht zuletzt seiner Kunst, polymorph und zugleich innovativ. Obwohl das Glück ihm zeitlebens abhold ist und er es nur mit größter Mühe zu Ansehen und Erfolg bringt, ist er sich seines Talents bewusst. „Ich bin ein großer Künstler und ich weiß es. Das kommt daher, dass ich so viel Leid ertragen musste, um meinen Weg fortzusetzen", schreibt er seiner Frau Mette Sophie im März 1892. Der „Wilde", zu dem er sich selbst ausgerufen hatte, erfüllt von Sehnsucht nach seiner frühen Kindheit in Peru, war fortwährend auf der Suche nach Authentizität und Freiheit.

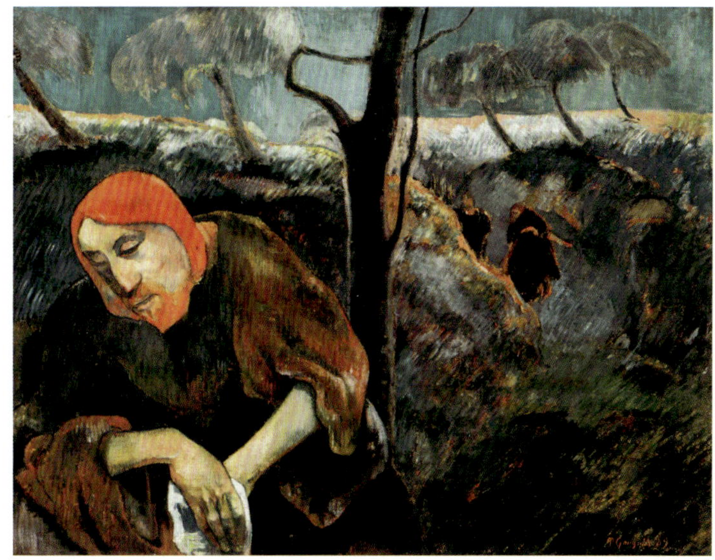

1889, Oil on canvas/Huile sur toile, 73 × 92 cm,
Norton Museum of Art, West Palm Beach

La libertad y la autenticidad

Artista vanguardista plenamente reconocido como tal desde la gran exposición parisina de 1949, Paul Gauguin (1848–1903) se mantuvo toda su vida al margen debido a su trayectoria atípica, a su carácter extremo y a su arte, polimorfo e innovador. Aunque no conociera la fortuna en vida, solo se le tuvo en buena consideración, fue consciente de su talento. "Soy un gran artista y lo sé. Por eso he soportado tanto sufrimiento para seguir mi camino" escribió a su mujer, Mette Sophie, en marzo de 1892. "Salvaje" autoproclamado, nostálgico de su primera infancia peruana, se mantuvo siempre a la búsqueda perpetua de autenticidad y libertad.

Libertà e autenticità

Artista d'avanguardia pienamente riconosciuto come tale dal momento della grande esposizione parigina del 1949, Paul Gaugin (1848–1903), è rimasto in disparte per tutta la sua vita a causa del suo percorso atipico, per la sua natura estrema e per la sua arte, polimorfa e innovativa. Sebbene non abbia conosciuto la sua fortuna in vita, solamente un successo da parte della critica, egli è cosciente del suo talento. "Io sono un grande artista e ne sono consapevole. Questo è il perché per perseguire la mia strada ho sopportato una tale sofferenza", scrisse a sua moglie Mette Sophie, nel Marzo 1892. Autoproclamatosi "Selvaggio", nostalgico della sua prima infanzia peruviana, fu alla ricerca costante dell'autenticità e della libertà.

Vrijheid en authenticiteit

Paul Gauguin (1848–1903) wordt sinds de grote Parijse tentoonstelling van 1949 zonder meer als avant-garde kunstenaar erkend, maar is vanwege zijn atypische carrière, extreme karakter en veelvormige en vernieuwende kunst zijn leven lang in de marge gebleven. Hoewel hij tijdens zijn leven geen rijkdom heeft gekend, alleen respect afdwong, is hij zich bewust van zijn talent. "Ik ben een groot kunstenaar en dat weet ik. En omdat ik dat weet, heb ik zoveel geleden, om voort te gaan op mijn weg", schreef hij zijn vrouw Mette Sophie, in maart 1892. Als zelfverklaarde 'wilde' en weemoedig terugdenkend aan zijn jeugd in Peru, was hij voortdurend op zoek naar authenticiteit en vrijheid.

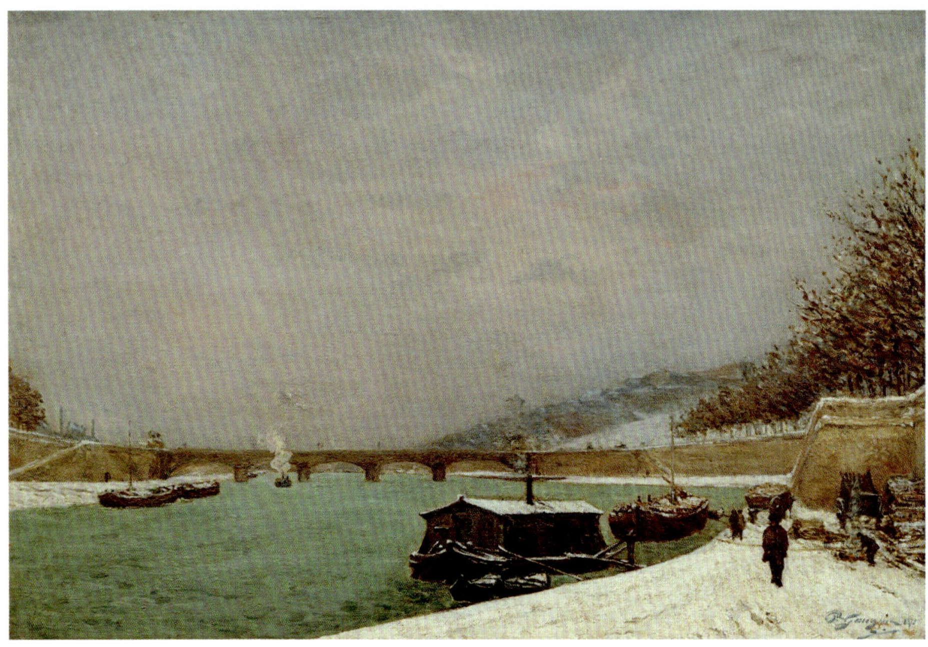

The art amateur, a dilettante painter

Paul Gauguin was born in Paris on 7 June 1848. During the following summer, he set off for Peru together with his family, and they would remain there for 5 years. Engaged with the navy between 1865 and 1871, Paul travelled the globe, from Latin America to India via the Mediterranean and the North Sea. He was then employed by a Paris stockbroker where he became friends with Émile Schuffenecker (1851–1934). An amateur painter and collector during his spare time, he followed painting courses together with his colleague. In 1873 he wed Danoise Mette Sophie Gad, with whom he would have five children.

L'amateur d'art, peintre dilettante

Paul Gauguin est né à Paris le 7 juin 1848. Avec sa famille, il embarque pour le Pérou l'été suivant où ils resteront cinq ans. Engagé dans la marine entre 1865 et 1871, Paul sillonne le globe, de l'Amérique latine aux Indes en passant par la Méditerranée et la mer du Nord. Il est ensuite employé dans un bureau d'agent de change parisien où il se lie d'amitié avec Émile Schuffenecker (1851–1934). Peintre amateur et collectionneur à ses heures perdues, il suit des cours de peinture en compagnie de son collègue. En 1873, il se marie avec la Danoise Mette Sophie Gad, avec laquelle il aura cinq enfants.

Kunstliebhaber und Amateurmaler

Paul Gauguin wird am 7. Juni 1848 in Paris geboren. Im darauf folgenden Sommer schifft sich die gesamte Familie nach Peru ein, wo sie fünf Jahre bleiben wird. Gaugin heuert bei der Marine an und reist von 1865 bis 1871 um die Welt, von Lateinamerika bis nach Indien, er befährt das Mittelmeer wie die Nordsee. Danach wird er Angestellter im Büro eines Börsenmaklers, in dem er Freundschaft schließt mit Émile Schuffenecker (1851–1934). In seiner Freizeit ist er Amateurmaler und Sammler und besucht gemeinsam mit seinem Kollegen einen Malkurs. 1873 heiratet er die Dänin Mette Sophie Gad, mit der er fünf Kinder haben wird.

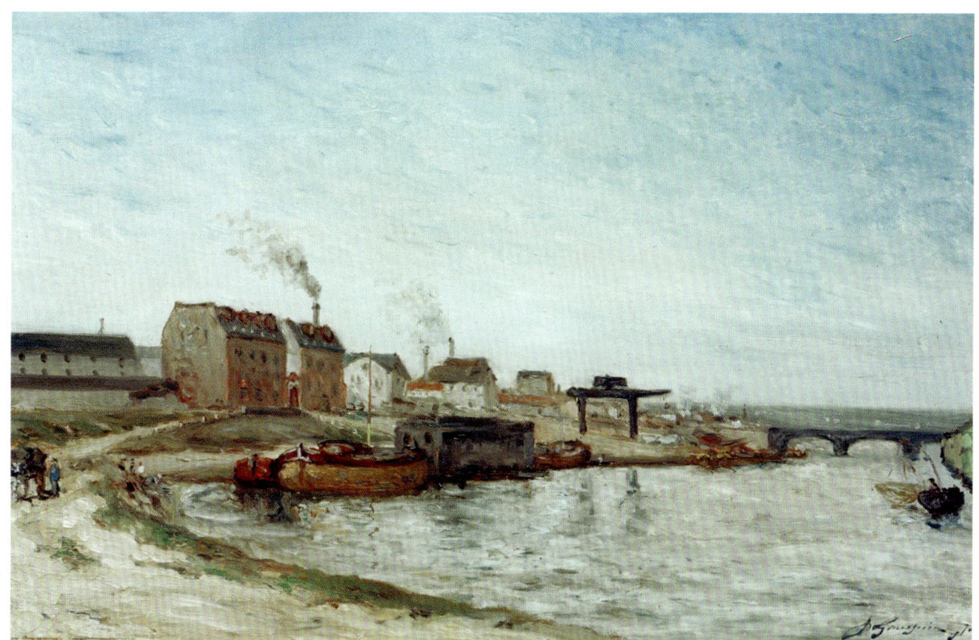

El amante del arte, pintor diletante

Paul Gauguin nació en París el 7 de junio de 1848. Junto a su familia, se embarcó hacia Perú al año siguiente, donde permanecieron cinco años. Estuvo en la marina entre 1865 y 1871, Paul recorrió el mundo de punta a punta, de América latina a la India, pasando por el Mediterráneo y el mar del Norte. Después de eso fue contratado en una oficina como agente de cambio parisino, donde trabó amistad con Émile Schuffenecker (1851–1934). Pintor aficionado y coleccionista en sus horas libres, realizó cursos de pintura en compañía de su colega. En 1873, se casó con la danesa Mette Sophie Gad, con quien tuvo cinco hijos.

L'amante dell'arte, pittore dilettante

Paul Gauguin nasce a Parigi il 7 Giugno 1848. Con la sua famiglia, si imbarca per il Perù l'estate successiva e li resteranno 5 anni. Arruolato in marina tra il 1865 e il 1871, Paul gira per il mondo, dall'America Latina alle Indie, passando per il Mediterraneo e il Mare del Nord. Egli è subito impiegato in un'agenzia di cambio parigina dove diviene amico di Emile Schuffenecker (1851–1934). Pittore dilettante e collezionista nel tempo libero, segue dei corsi di pittura in compagnia del suo collega. Nel 1873, si sposa con la danese Mette Sophie Gad, con la quale avrà cinque figli.

E' il suo tutore, Gustave Arosa, che lo introduce nel vivo dell'arte, e gli

Kunstliefhebber, amateurschilder

Paul Gauguin wordt op 7 juni 1848 in Parijs geboren. In de zomer van 1849 vertrekt het gezin naar Peru en blijft daar vijf jaar. In dienst van de marine, van 1865 tot 1871, zwerft Gauguin over de wereld, van Latijns-Amerika naar Indië, via de Middellandse Zee en de Noordzee. Als hij daarna in Parijs als beursmakelaar werkt, raakt hij bevriend met Émile Schuffenecker (1851–1934). In zijn vrije uurtjes is hij amateurschilder en kunstverzamelaar. Samen met zijn collega volgt hij schilderlessen. In 1873 trouwt hij met de Deense Mette Sophie Gad. Ze zullen vijf kinderen krijgen.

Zijn mecenas, Gustave Arosa, introduceert hem in kunstenaarskringen

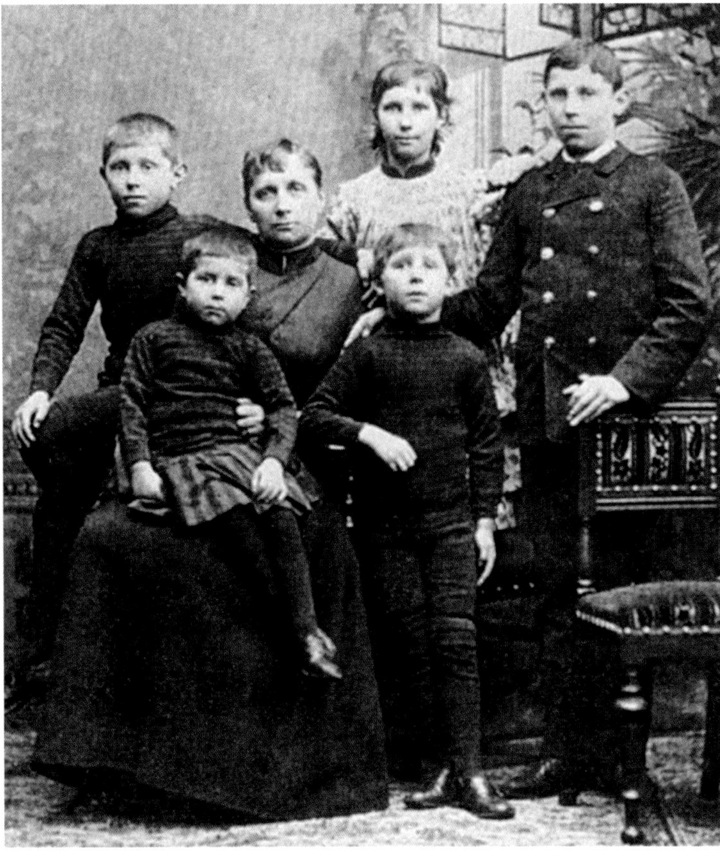

It is his tutor, Gustave Arosa, who introduced him to artist circles, particularly by introducing him to Camille Pissarro (1830–1903). The latter advised him, encouraged him to participate in the expositions of the impressionists—which he did from 1879 to 1886—and allowed him to work alongside Paul Cézanne (1839–1906) and Armand Guillaumin (1841–1927). During this period, Gauguin

C'est son tuteur, Gustave Arosa qui l'introduit dans le milieu l'art, notamment en lui présentant Camille Pissarro (1830–1903). Ce dernier le conseille, l'encourage à participer aux expositions impressionnistes – ce qu'il fera de 1879 à 1886 – et lui permet de travailler aux côtés de Paul Cézanne (1839–1906) et d'Armand Guillaumin (1841–1927). À cette époque, Gauguin

Sein Lehrer Gustave Arosa führt ihn in das Künstlermilieu ein und stellt ihn vor allem Camille Pissarro (1830–1903) vor. Dieser berät ihn, ermutigt ihn zur Teilnahme an Ausstellungen der Impressionisten – was er auch von 1879 bis 1886 tun wird – und ermöglicht es ihm, an der Seite von Paul Cézanne (1839–1906) und Armand Guillaumin (1841–1927) zu arbeiten. Damals malt

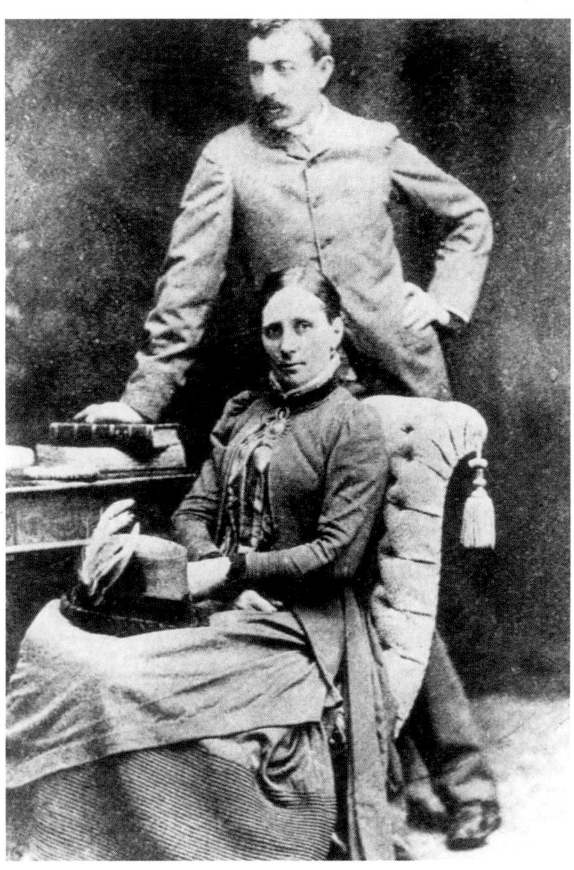

Fue su tutor, Gustave Arosa, quien le introdujo en el ambiente del arte, principalmente presentándole a Camille Pissarro (1830–1903). Este último le aconsejó, le animó a participar en las exposiciones impresionistas, lo que hizo de 1879 a 1886, y le permitió trabajar junto a Paul Cézanne (1839–1906) y Armand Guillaumin (1841–1927). En aquella época, Gauguin pintó paisajes

presenta Camille Pissarro (1830–1903). Quest'ultimo lo consiglia, lo incoraggia a partecipare alle esposizioni impressioniste e gli permette di lavorare al fianco di Paul Cézanne (1839–1906) e Armand Guillaumin (1841–1927). A quel tempo, Gauguin dipinge paesaggi e ritratti, influenzato da Pissarro e Edgar Degas (1834–1917), i suoi due mentori impressionisti. Rovinato dal crollo del

en stelt hem voor aan Camille Pissarro (1830–1903), die zijn raadgever wordt en hem stimuleert deel te nemen aan de tentoonstellingen van de impressionisten – wat hij van 1879 tot 1886 ook doet – en hem in de gelegenheid stelt om aan de zijde van Paul Cézanne (1839–1906) en Armand Guillaumin (1841–1927) te werken. De landschappen en portretten die

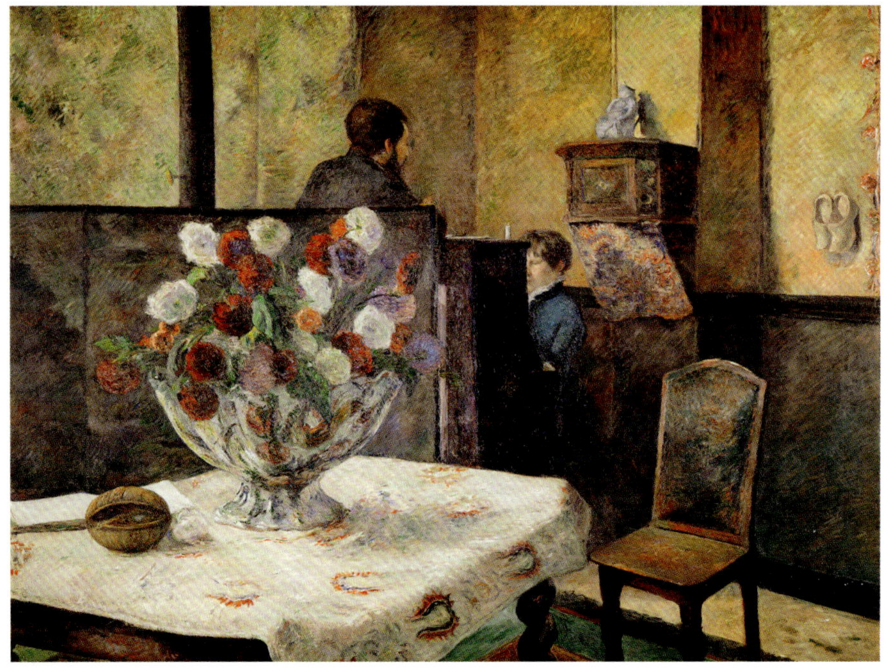

painted landscapes and portraits in a manner influenced by Pissarro and Edgar Degas (1834–1917), his two impressionist mentors. Ruined by the stock market crash of 1882, he quit his job as a stockbroker in the following year. Having lost part of his collection, he tried to live from his painting in Rouen, and then launched into a commercial venture in Denmark—without success. Leaving his family in Copenhagen, he returned to Paris in 1885 with his son Clovis, ill and penniless, alone in the face of his artistic ambition—this also being an existential quest.

peint des paysages et des portraits influencés par Pissarro et Edgar Degas (1834–1917), ses deux mentors impressionnistes. Ruiné par le krach boursier de 1882, il quitte son emploi d'agent de change l'année suivante. Ayant vendu une partie de sa collection, il tente de vivre de sa peinture à Rouen, puis se lance dans une aventure commerciale au Danemark. Sans succès. Laissant sa famille à Copenhague, il revient à Paris en 1885, avec son fils Clovis, malade, sans le sou. Seul face à son ambition artistique qui est aussi une quête existentielle.

Gauguin Landschaften und Porträts, beeinflusst von Pissarro und Edgar Degas (1834–1917), seinen beiden impressionistischen Mentoren. Ruiniert durch den Börsenkrach von 1882 kündigt er seine Stelle als Börsenmakler im Jahr darauf. Nach dem Verkauf eines Teils seiner Sammlung versucht er in Rouen, von seiner Malerei zu leben. Anschließend stürzt er sich in ein geschäftliches Abenteuer in Dänemark, aber ohne Erfolg. Er lässt seine Familie in Kopenhagen zurück und kehrt 1885 mit seinem Sohn Clovis nach Paris zurück, krank und völlig mittellos. Allein mit seinem künstlerischen Ehrgeiz, der auch eine existenzielle Suche ist.

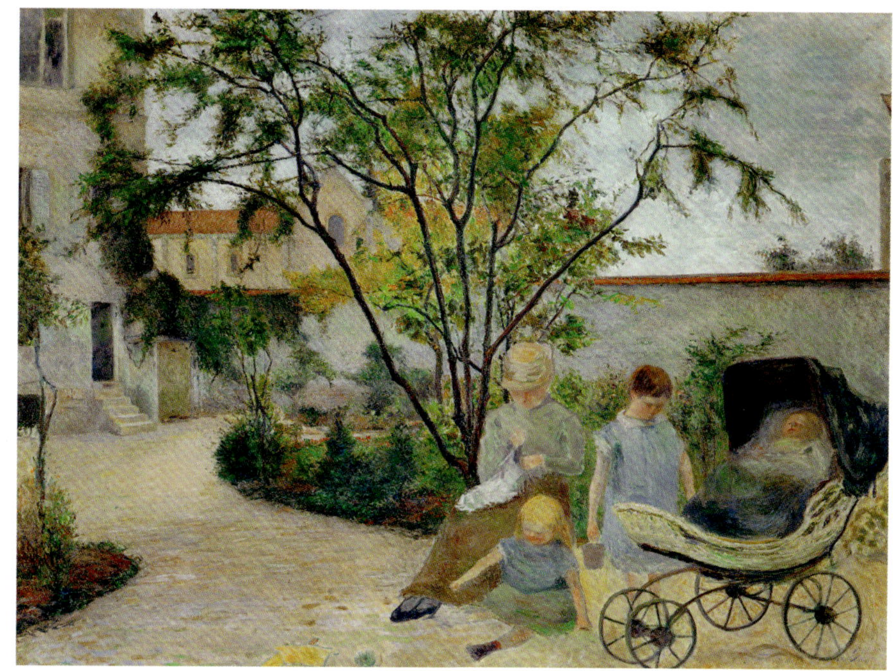

y retratos influenciados por Pissarro y Edgar Degas (1834–1917), sus dos mentores impresionistas. Arruinado por la crisis económica de 1882, abandonó su empleo de agente de cambio al año siguiente. Vendió una parte de su colección e intentó vivir de su pintura en Rouen; posteriormente se embarcó en una aventura comercial en Dinamarca. Sin éxito. Dejó a su familia en Copenhague y regresó a París en 1885, con su hijo Clovis, enfermo, con las manos vacías... Solo frente a su ambición artística que era a la vez una búsqueda existencial.

mercato azionario del 1882, lascia il suo lavoro come agente di cambio l'anno successivo. Avendo venduto parte della sua collezione, cerca di vivere della sua pittura a Rouen, poi si imbarca in un'impresa commerciale in Danimarca. Senza successo. Lasciando la sua famiglia a Copenhagen, torna a Parigi nel 1885 con il figlio Clovis, malato, senza un soldo ... Solo con la sua ambizione artistica che è anche ricerca esistenziale

Gauguin in die tijd schildert, zijn duidelijk beïnvloed door Pissarro en Edgar Degas (1834–1917), zijn twee impressionistische mentoren. Geruïneerd door de beurskrach van 1882 zegt hij in 1883 zijn baan op. Hij verkoopt een deel van zijn schilderijenverzameling en probeert in Rouen de kost te verdienen met schilderen. Vervolgens stort hij zich in een commercieel avontuur in Denemarken. Zonder succes. Hij laat zijn familie in Kopenhagen achter en keert in 1885 samen met zoon Clovis terug naar Parijs, ziek en platzak... Moederziel alleen met zijn artistieke ambitie, die tevens een existentiële zoektocht is.

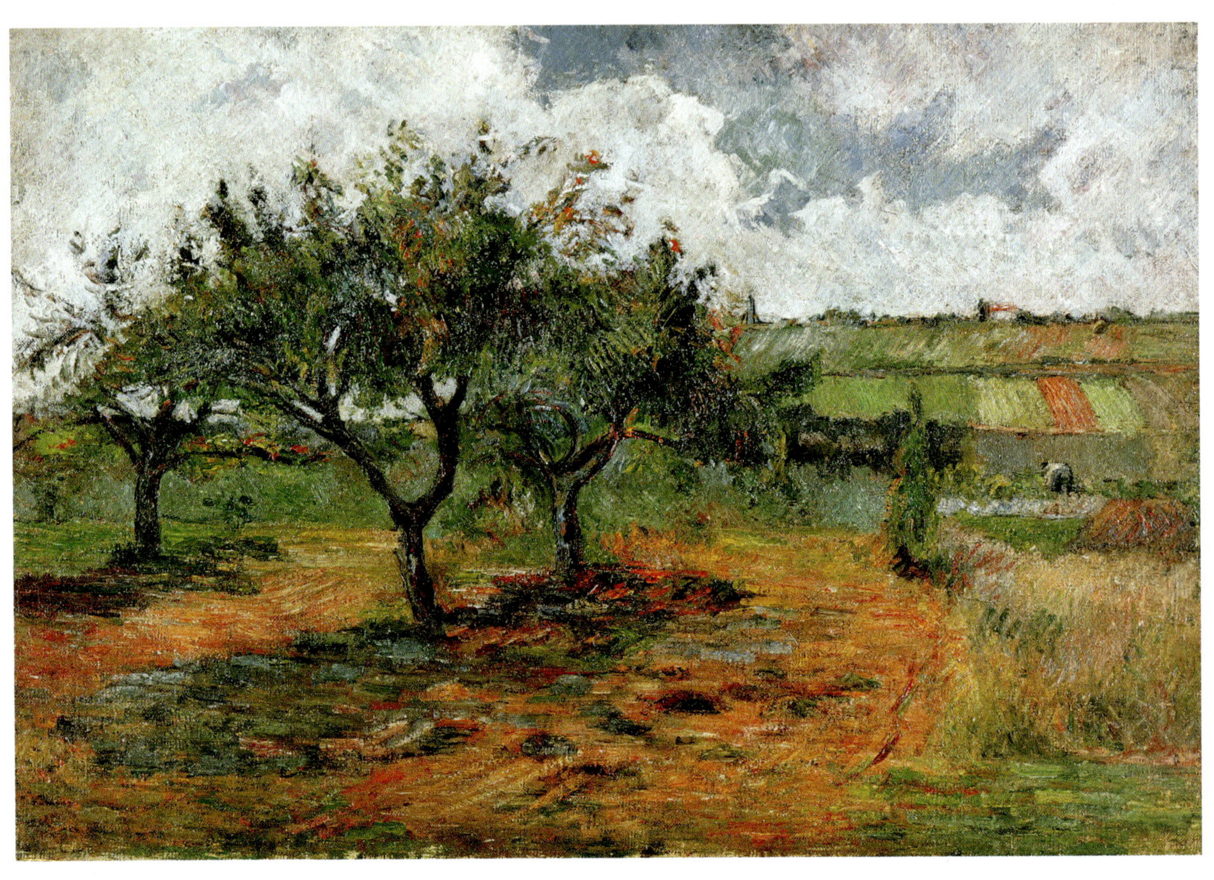

Apple Trees, Hermitage, Pontoise

Pommiers, Ermitage, Pontoise

Blühende Apfelbäume

Manzanos, Ermita, Pontoise

Meli, Eremo, Pontoise

Appelbomen, Hermitage, Pontoise

1878, Oil on canvas/Huile sur toile, 46 × 65 cm, Private collection

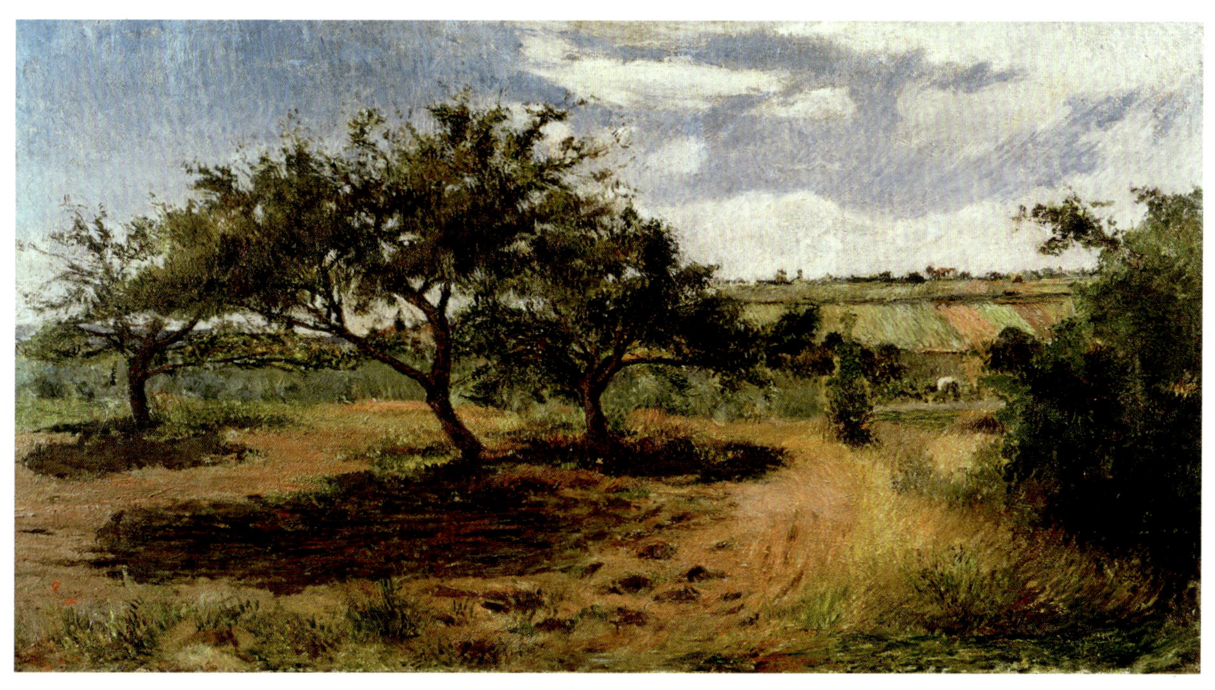

Apple Trees, Hermitage, Pontoise

Pommiers, Ermitage, Pontoise

Blühende Apfelbäume

Manzanos, Ermita, Pontoise

Meli, Eremo, Pontoise

Appelbomen, Hermitage, Pontoise

1879, Oil on canvas/Huile sur toile, 65 × 100 cm, Aargauer Kunsthaus, Aarau

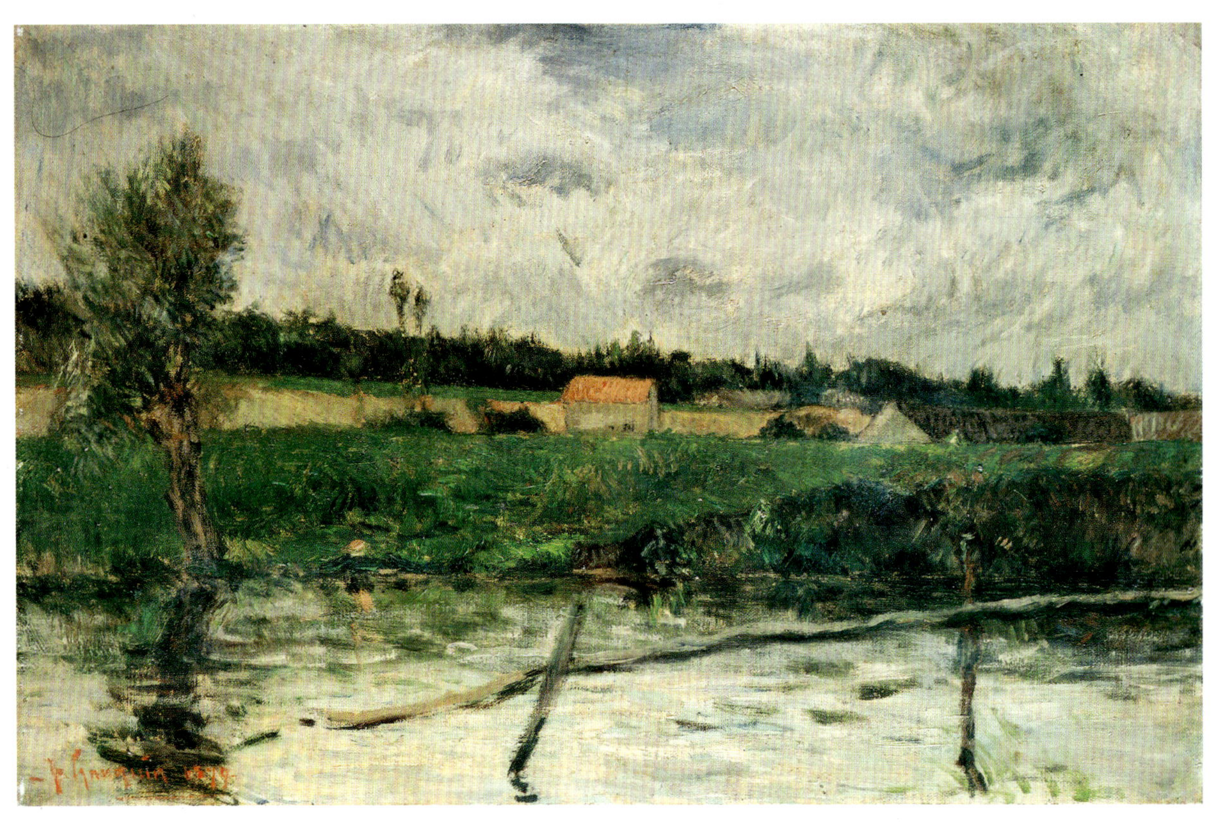

Breton Landscape

Paysage breton

Landschaft in der Bretagne

Paisaje bretón

Paesaggio bretone

Bretons landschap

1879

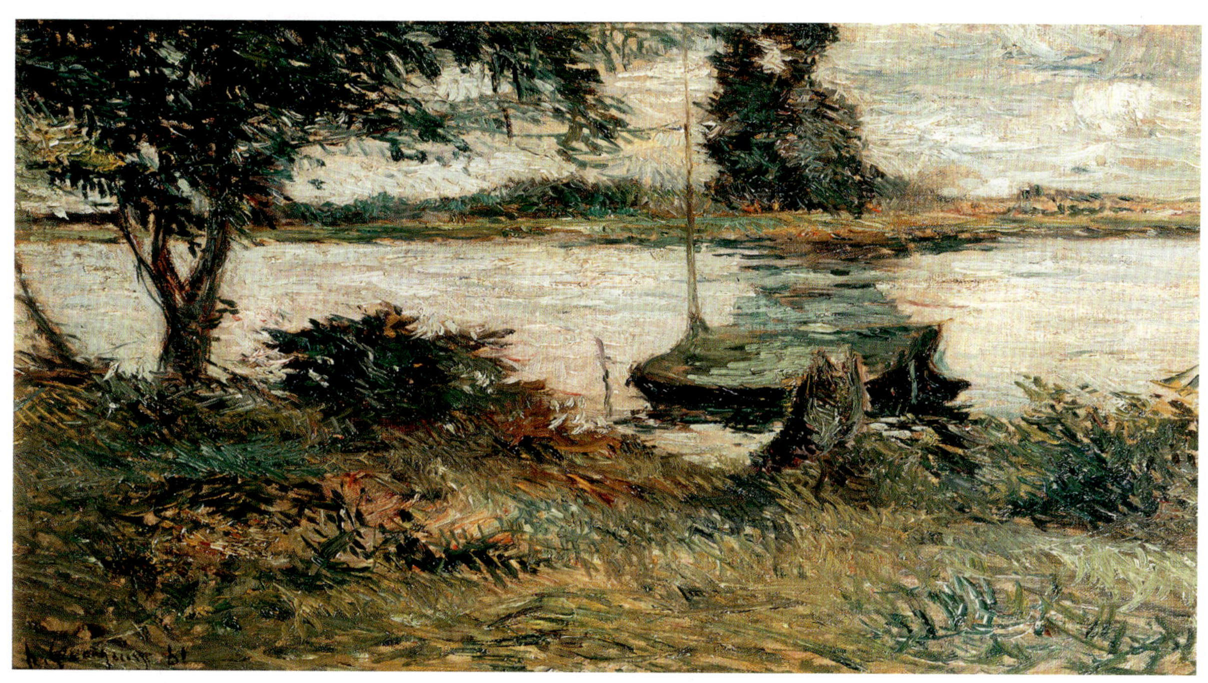

Riverbank
Berge de rivière
Flussufer
Orilla del río
Montagne di riviera
Rivieroever
1881, 31 × 47 cm, Private collection

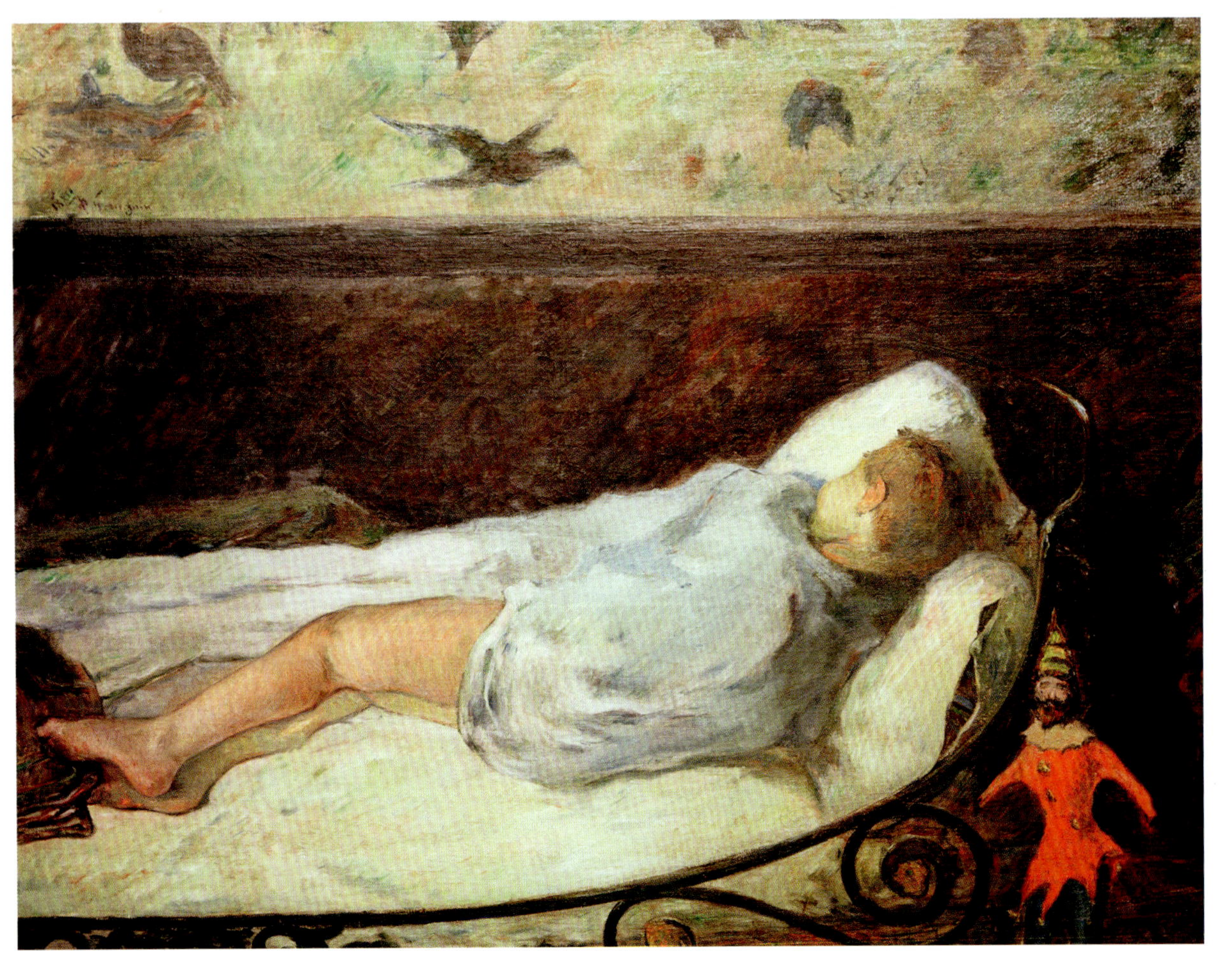

Little Dream (Aline Gauguin)

La Petite rêve (Aline Gauguin)

Die kleine Träumerin (Aline Gauguin)

La pequeña sueña (Aline Gauguin)

Il piccolo sogno (Aline Gauguin)

De kleine droom (Aline Gauguin)

1881, Oil on canvas/Huile sur toile, 59,5 × 73,5 cm, Ordrupgaard, København

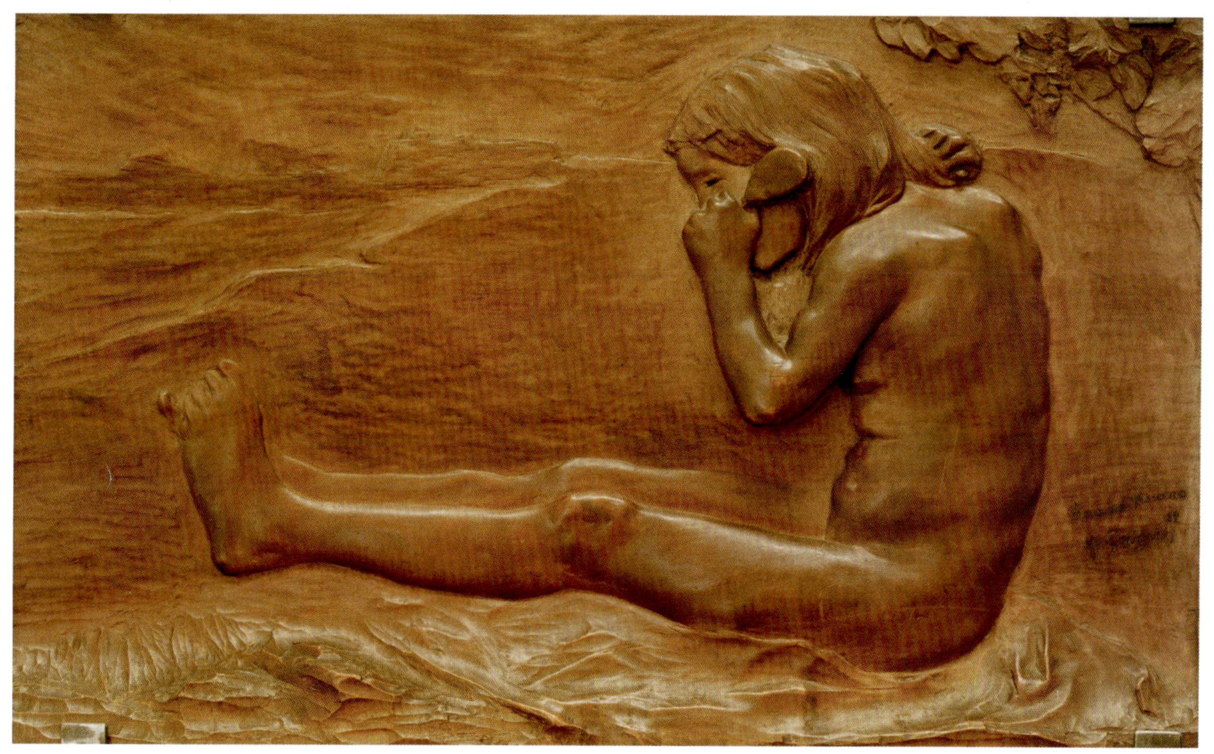

The Toilet

La Toilette

Die Toilette

El aseo

La Toilette

Het toilet

1882, Wood/Bois, 34,1 × 55 × 7 cm, Musée d'art moderne et contemporain, Strasbourg

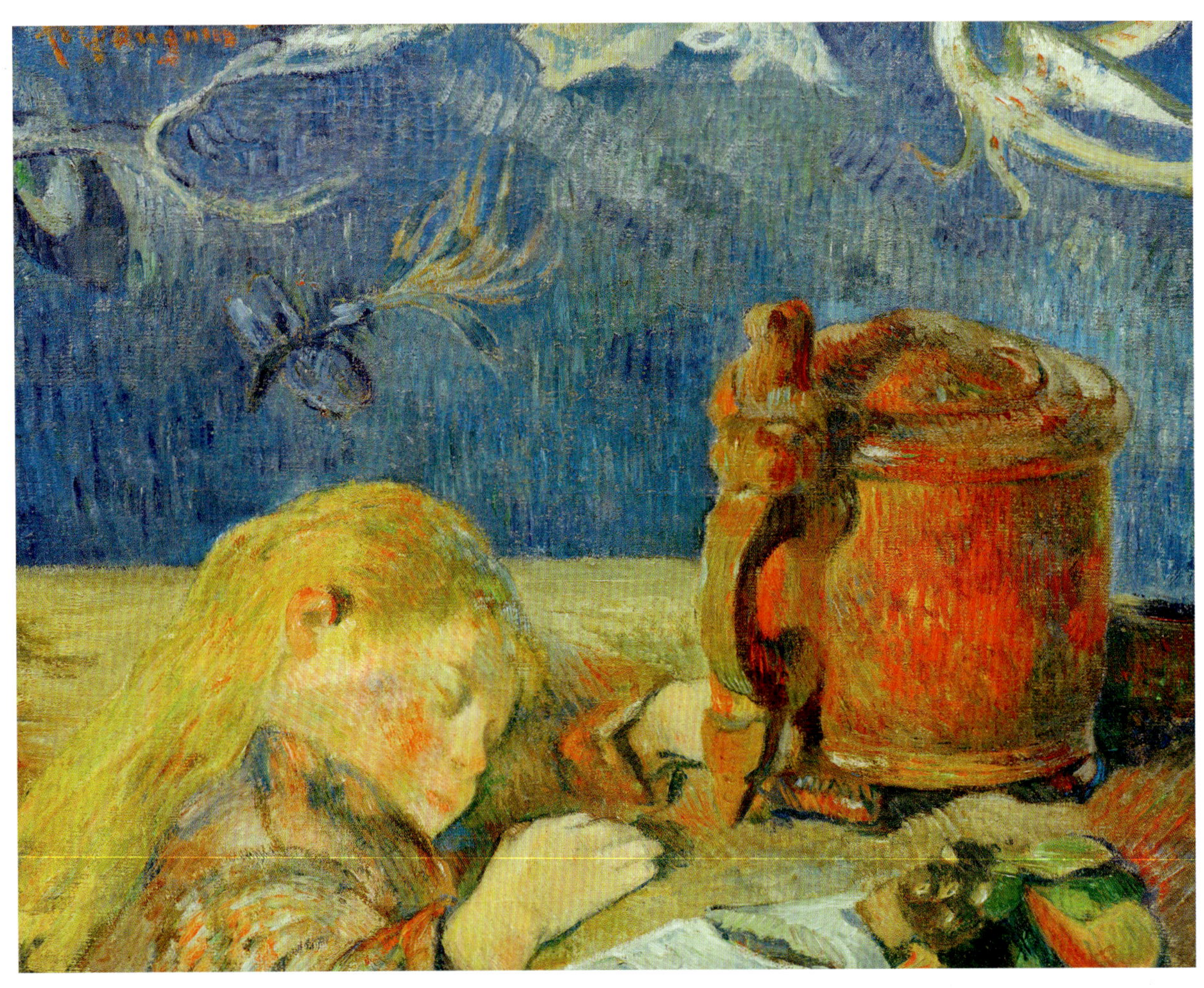

Sleeping Child (Clovis Gauguin)
L'Enfant endormi (Clovis Gauguin)

Schlafendes Kind (Clovis Gauguin)
El niño dormido (Clovis Gauguin)

Il bambino che dorme (Clovis Gauguin)
Het slapende kind (Clovis Gauguin)

1884, Oil on canvas/Huile sur toile, 46 × 55,5 cm, Private collection

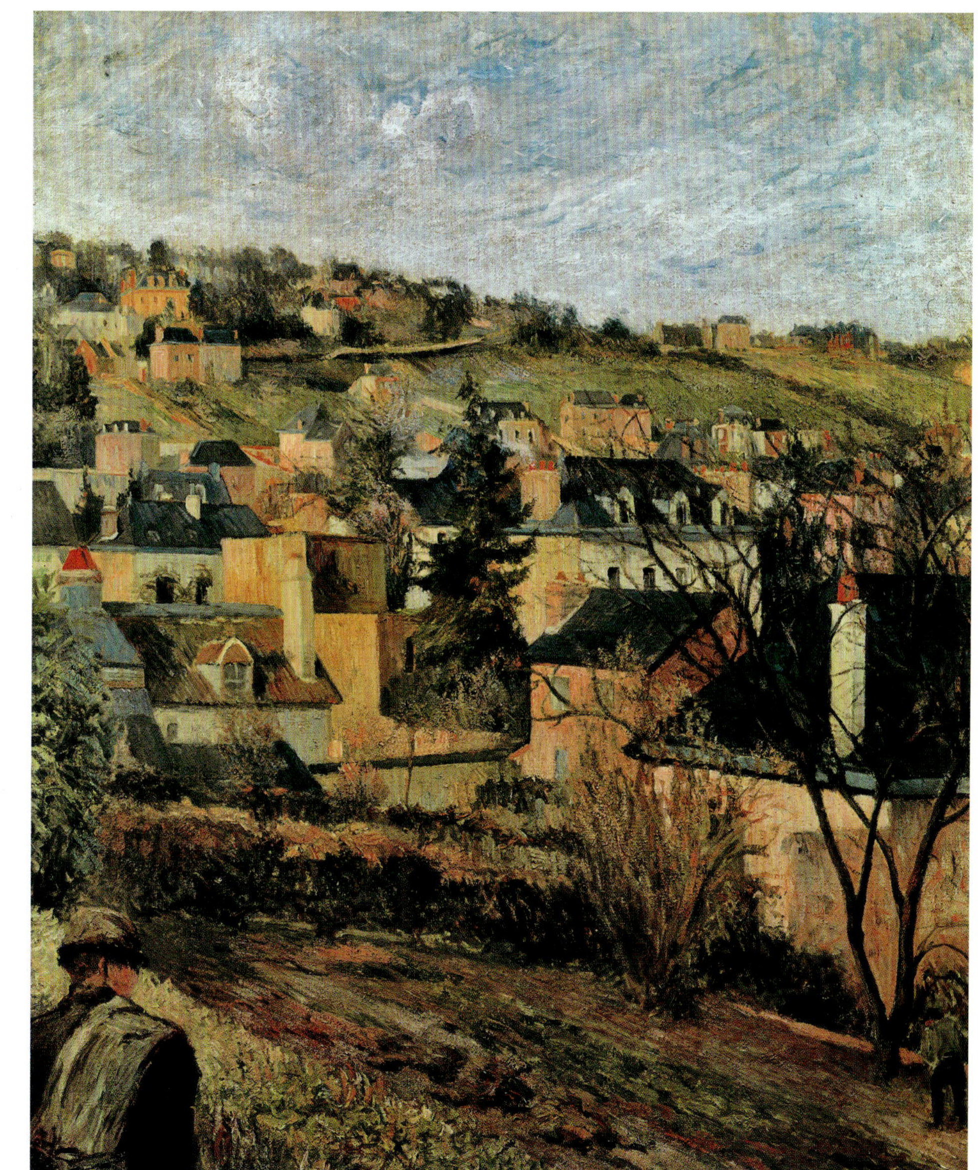

Blue Roofs of Rouen
Les Toits bleus (Rouen)
Die blauen Dächer (Rouen)
Los tejados azules (Rouen)
I tetti blu (Rouen)
De blauwe daken (Rouen)

1884, Oil on canvas/Huile sur toile, 74 × 60 cm, Museum Oskar Reinhart, Winterthur

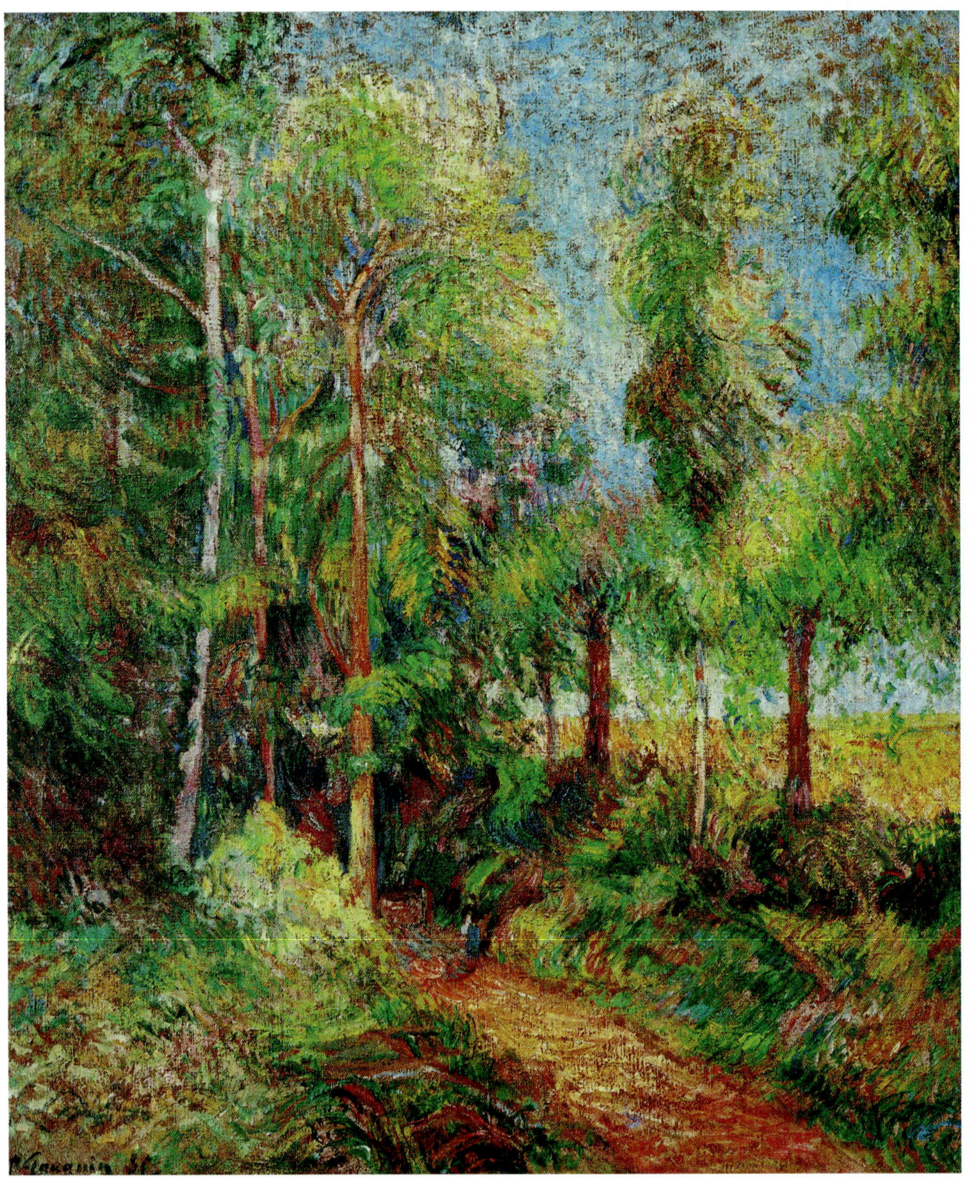

The Edge of the Forest (I)

La Lisière de la forêt (I)

Waldrand (I)

La linde del bosque (I)

La vegetazione della foresta (I)

De bosrand (I)

1885, Oil on canvas/Huile sur toile, 55,5 × 46 cm, Aargauer Kunsthaus, Aarau

The Beach at Dieppe

Plage de Dieppe

Strand bei Dieppe

Playa de Dieppe

La spiaggia di Dieppe

Strand van Dieppe

1885, Oil on canvas/Huile sur toile, 71,5 × 71,5 cm, Ny Carlsberg Glyptotek, København

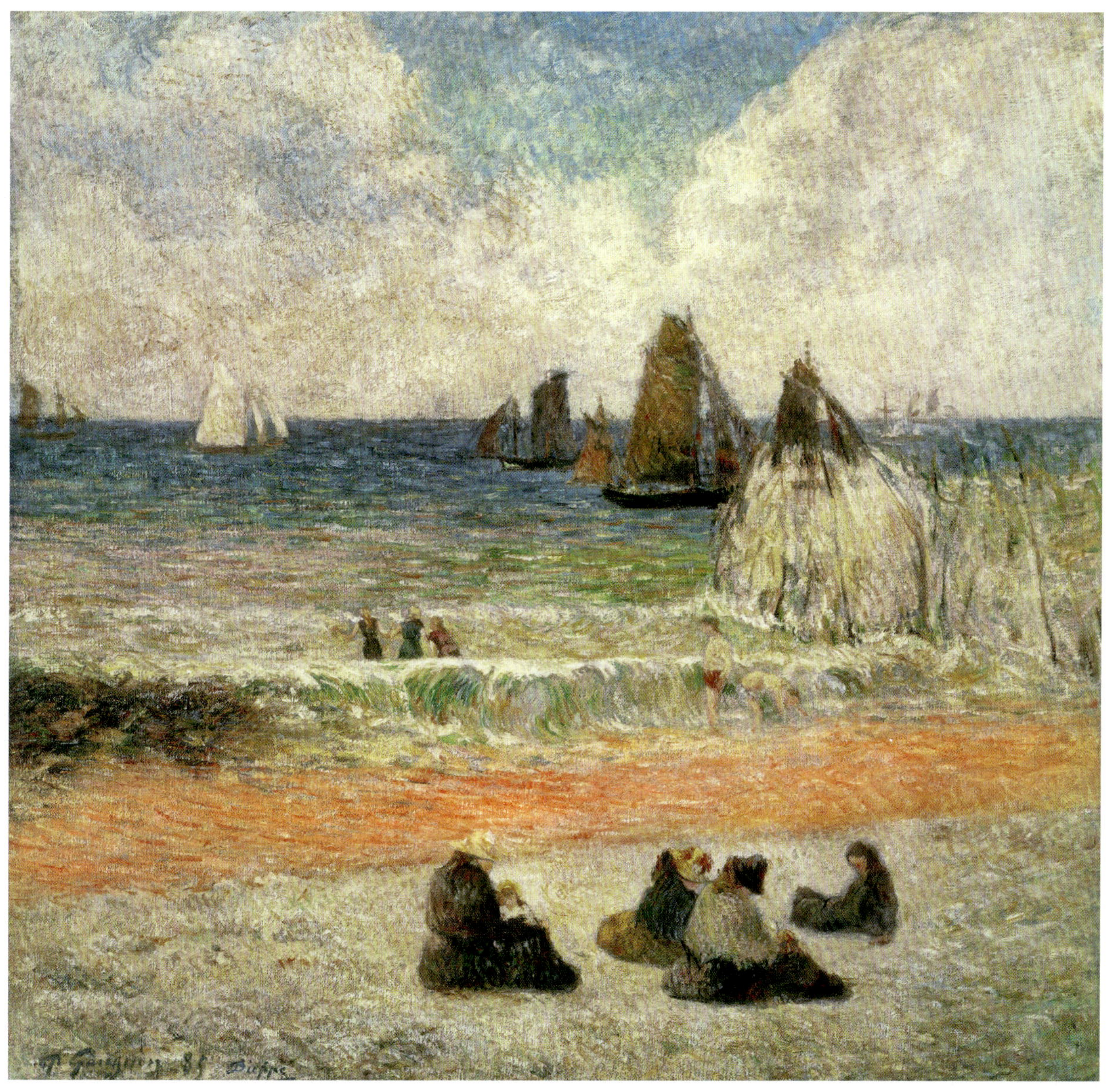

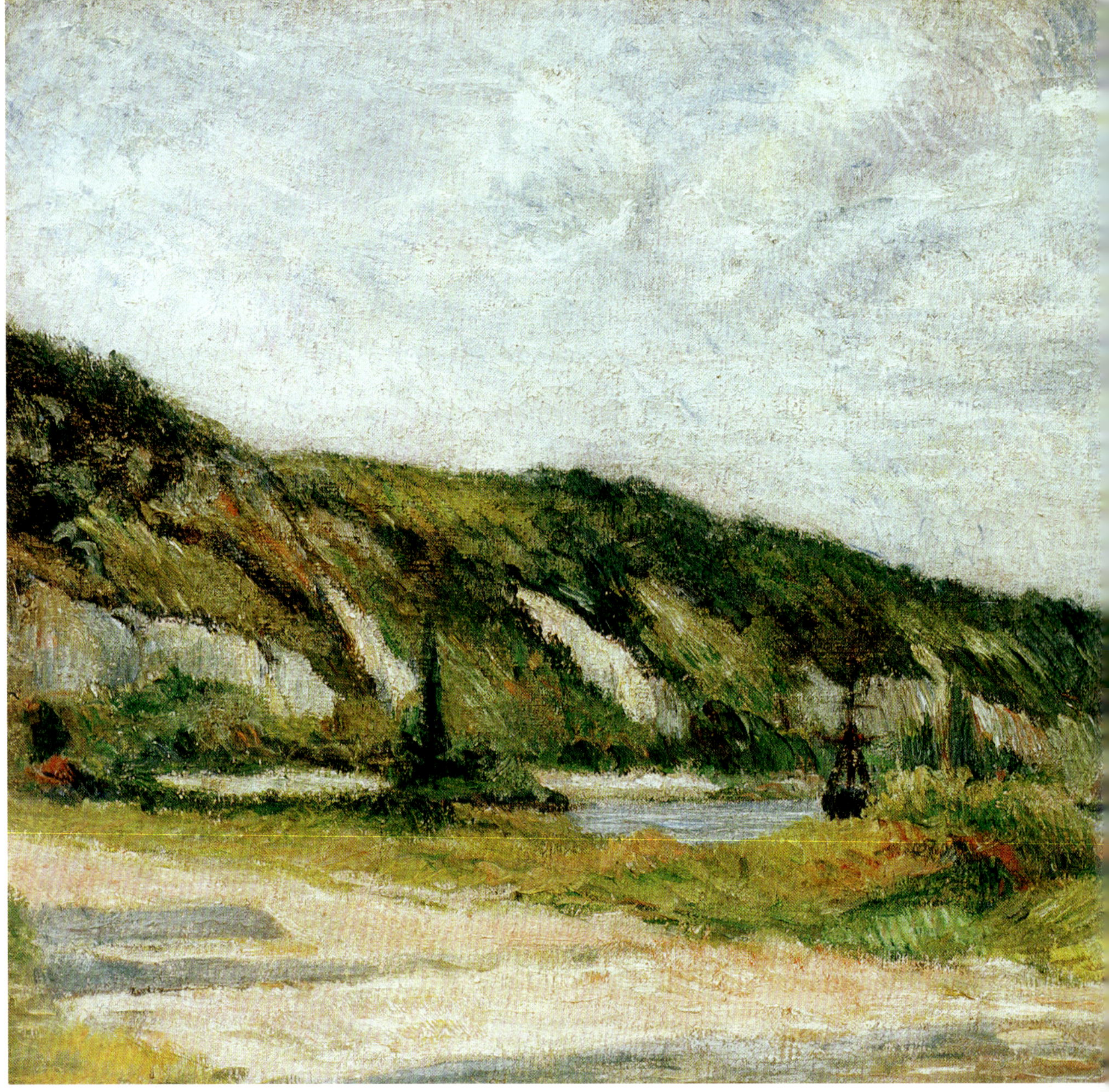

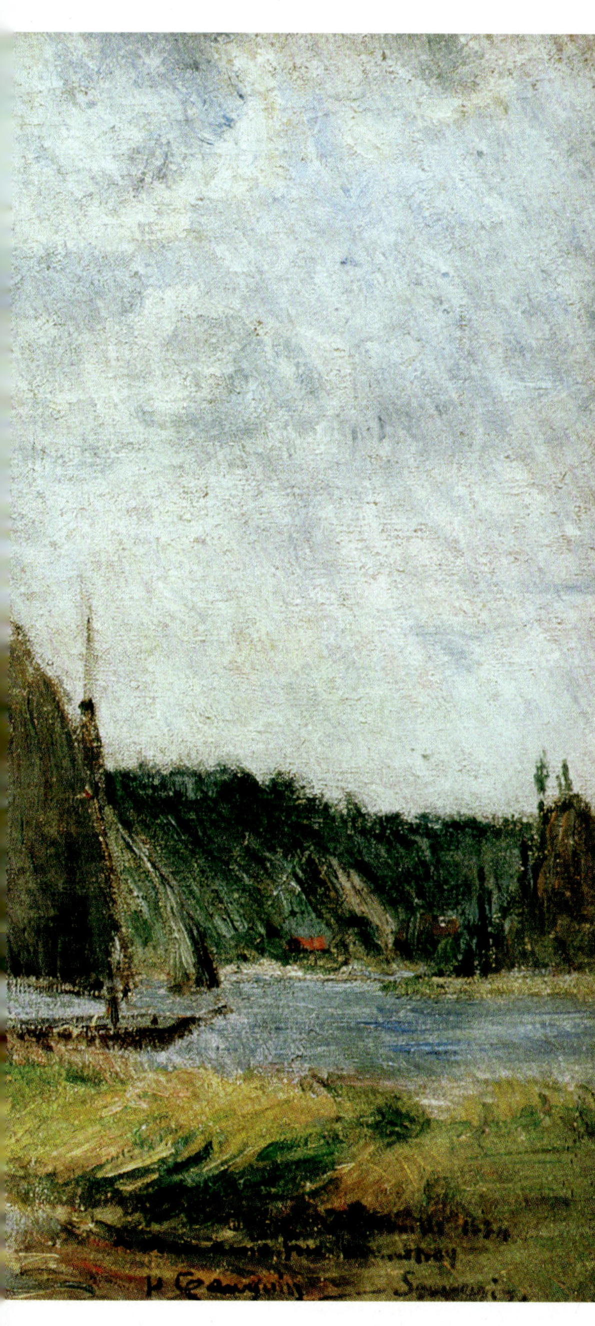

The Sailboats

Les Voiliers

Segelboote

Los veleros

Le Vele

De zeilboten

1884, Oil on canvas/Huile sur toile, 38 × 56 cm, Private collection

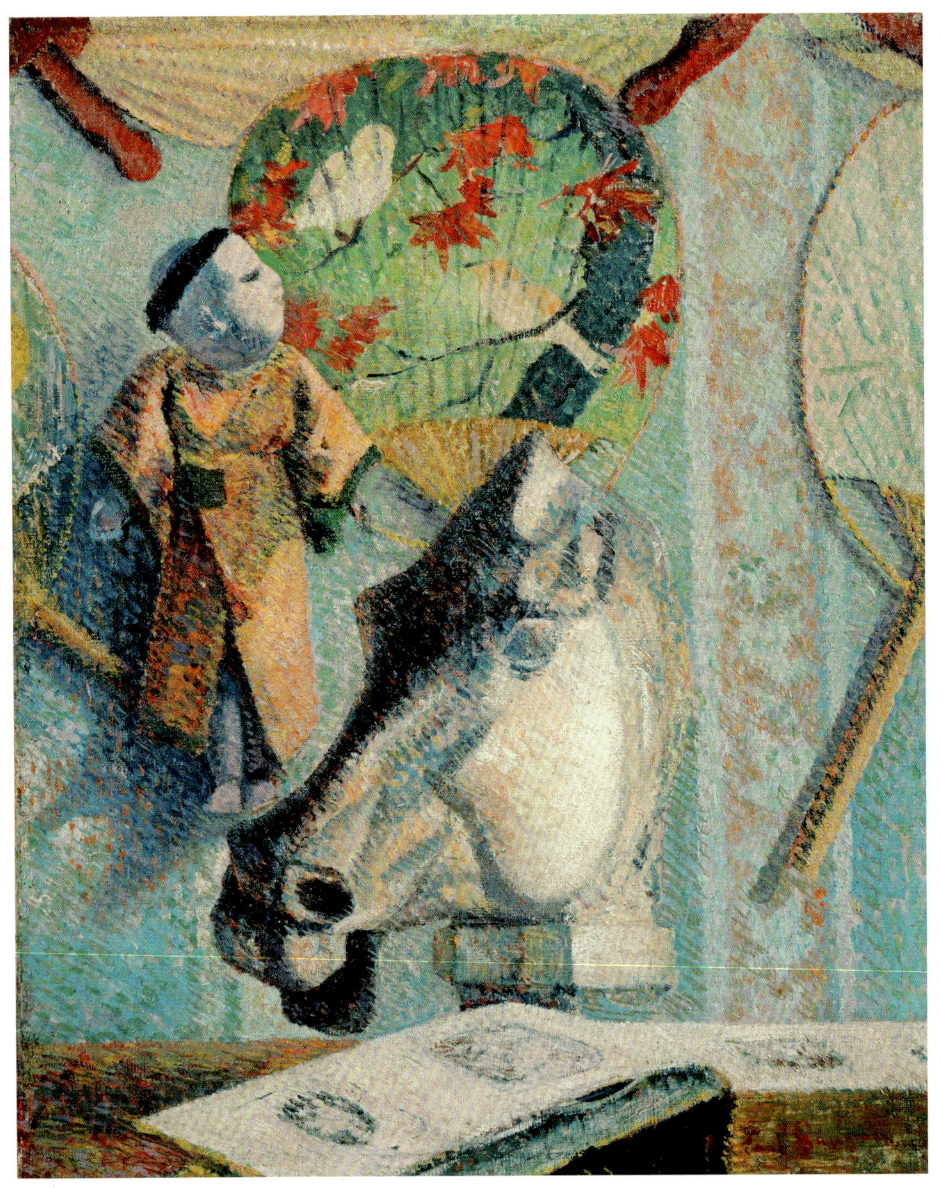

Still Life with Horse's Head

Nature morte à la tête de cheval

Stillleben mit Pferdekopf

Naturaleza muerta con cabeza de caballo

Natura morta sulla testa di cavallo

Stilleven met paardenhoofd

1886, Oil on canvas/Huile sur toile, 49 × 38,5 cm, Bridgestone Museum of Art, Tokyo

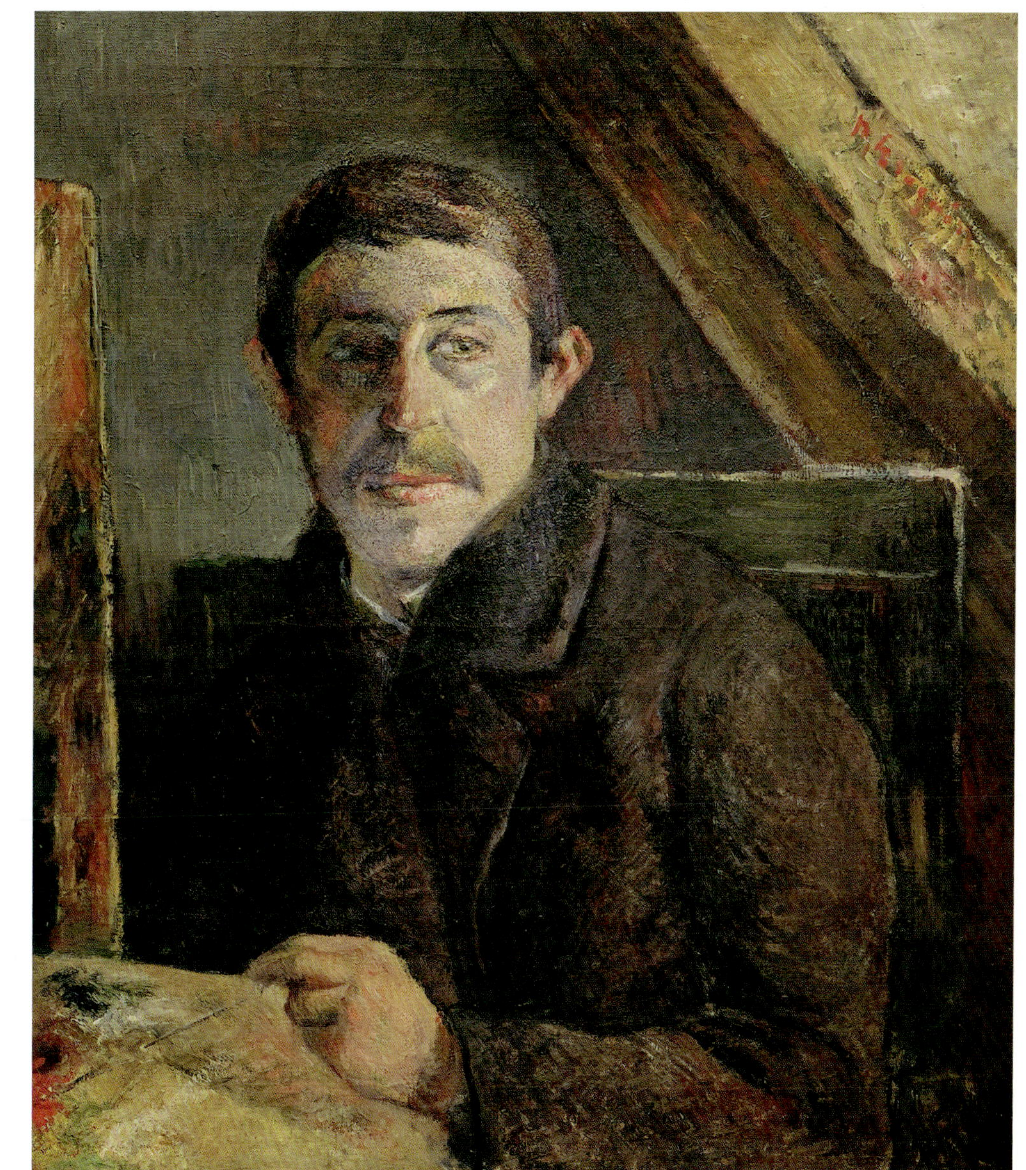

Self Portrait
Autoportrait
Selbstbildnis
Autorretrato
Autoritratto
Zelfportret

*1885, Oil on canvas/
Huile sur toile,
65 × 54 cm, Kimbell Art
Museum, Fort Worth*

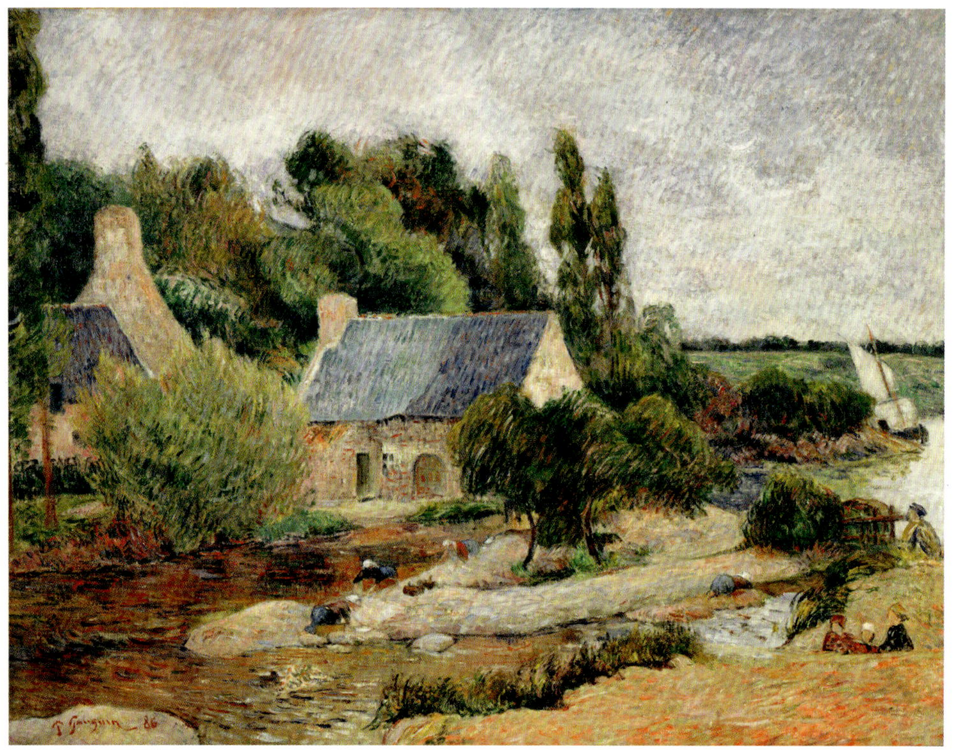

*Washerwomen
At Pont-Aven*

*Les Lavandières
de Pont-Aven*

*Die Wäscherinnen
von Pont-Aven*

*Las lavanderas
de Pont-Aven*

Le lavandaie di Pont Aven

Wasvrouwen in Pont-Aven

*1886, Oil on canvas/Huile
sur toile, 71 × 90 cm, Musée
d'Orsay, Paris*

The revelation of Pont-Aven

Between 1886 and 1890, the artist made
four decisive stays in Brittany. The first
one took him to Pont-Aven in July 1886,
to which was drawn by the favourable
rates for the Gloanec boarding house.
He stayed for three months in that small
Brittany village which had gathered a
small colony of cosmopolitan artists since
1866. He was seduced by the simple and
authentic life that he led there, far from
the Parisian agitation and the irritations
of industrial civilisation. He met many
younger painters—by then he was 38—

La révélation de Pont-Aven

Entre 1886 et 1890, l'artiste fait quatre
séjours décisifs en Bretagne. Le premier
l'amène à Pont-Aven, en juillet 1886, où
il est attiré par les prix bon marché de la
pension Gloanec. Il reste trois mois dans
ce petit village breton, qui accueille une
colonie cosmopolite d'artistes depuis
1866. La vie simple et authentique qu'il y
mène, loin de l'agitation parisienne et des
travers de la civilisation industrielle, le
séduit. Il y rencontre quantité de peintres
plus jeunes que lui – il a alors 38 ans –,
dont certains avec lesquels il lie une

Die Offenbarung von Pont-Aven

Zwischen 1886 und 1890 unternimmt
der Künstler vier prägende Reisen in
die Bretagne. Die erste führt ihn im
Juni 1886 nach Pont-Aven, wo er für
wenig Geld in der Pension Gloanec
unterkommt. Drei Monate bleibt er in
dem kleinen bretonischen Dorf, das
bereits seit 1866 eine kosmopolitische
Künstlerkolonie beherbergt. Das
einfache und authentische Leben, das
er dort führt, weitab von der Hektik in
Paris und der industriellen Zivilisation,
lockt ihn. Er lernt zahlreiche Künstler

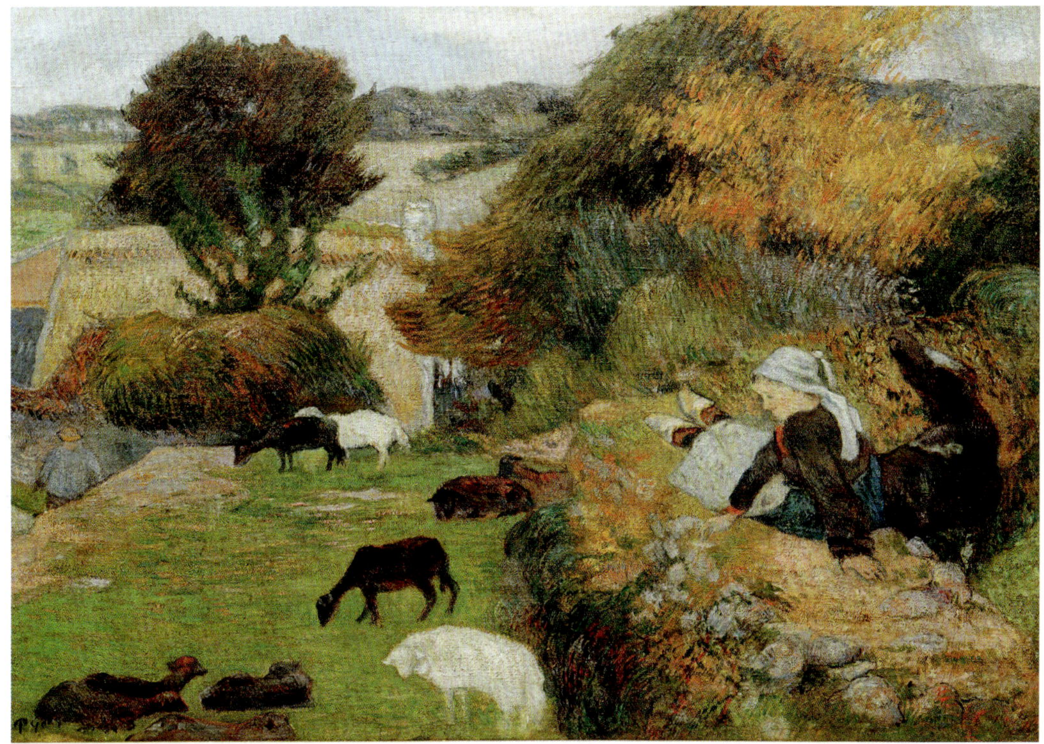

La revelación de Pont-Aven

Entre 1886 y 1890, el artista realizó cuatro viajes decisivos a Bretaña. El primero le llevó a Pont-Aven, en julio de 1886, donde se sintió atraído por los competitivos precios de la pensión Gloanec. Se quedó tres meses en este pueblecito bretón, que alberga una colonia cosmopolita de artistas desde 1866. La vida sencilla y auténtica que llevó allí, lejos de la agitación parisina y de los reveses de la civilización industrial, le sedujo. Allí se reunió con gran cantidad de pintores más jóvenes que él (por aquel entonces

La rivelazione di Pont-Aven

Tra il 1886 e il 1890, l'artista fa quattro soggiorni cruciali in Bretagna. Il primo lo porta a Pont-Aven, nel luglio 1886, dove è attratto dal prezzo a buon mercato della pensione Gloanec. Rimane tre mesi in questo piccolo villaggio bretone che ospita una colonia di artisti cosmopolita dal 1866. La vita semplice e genuina che lì conduce lontano dal trambusto di Parigi e attraverso la civiltà industriale lo seduce. Incontra molti pittori più giovani - aveva allora 38 anni – tra cui alcuni a cui lo lega una duratura amicizia,

De openbaring van Pont-Aven

De vier keer dat Gauguin tussen 1886 en 1890 in Bretagne verblijft, zijn beslissend voor de rest van zijn leven. In juli 1886 is hij in Pont-Aven, waar hij besluit te blijven omdat Auberge Gloanec zo goed betaalbaar is. Hij blijft drie maanden in het Bretonse dorp, waar sinds 1866 een kosmopoliete kunstenaarskolonie is gevestigd. Het eenvoudige boerenleven in Pont-Aven, ver van de drukte van Parijs en de uitwassen van de industriële beschaving, bevalt hem. Hij ontmoet er veel schilders die jonger zijn dan hij – hij

29

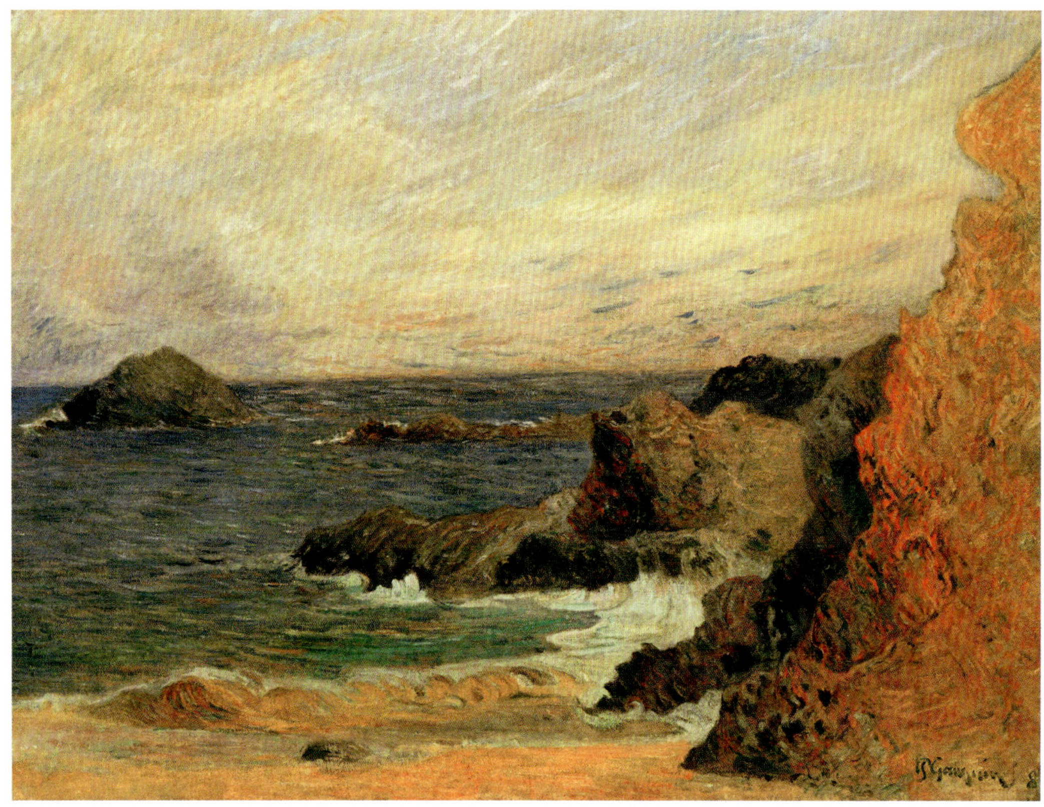

some with whom he established a lasting friendship, such as Charles Laval (1861–1894) and Émile Bernard (1868–1941). A few days were enough to establish his reputation, nourished by his whole temperament and artistic aspirations.

Upon his return to Paris, Gauguin produced some vases in Ernst Chaplet's (1835–1909) studio, but these did not have the expected success.

amitié durable, à l'instar de Charles Laval (1861–1894) et Émile Bernard (1868–1941). Quelques jours suffisent à établir sa réputation, nourrie par son tempérament entier et par ses aspirations artistiques.

De retour à Paris, Gauguin produit des vases en céramique dans l'atelier d'Ernst Chaplet (1835–1909), qui n'auront pas le succès escompté.

kennen, die jünger sind als er – er ist inzwischen 38 Jahre alt. Mit einigen, zum Beispiel Charles Laval (1861–1894) und Émile Bernard (1868–1941), schließt er dauerhaft Freundschaft. In nur wenigen Tagen erwirbt er sich Ansehen durch sein ganzes Wesen und sein künstlerisches Streben.

Zurück in Paris stellt Gauguin im Atelier von Ernst Chaplet (1835–1909) keramische Vasen her, die jedoch nicht den erhofften Erfolg haben sollen.

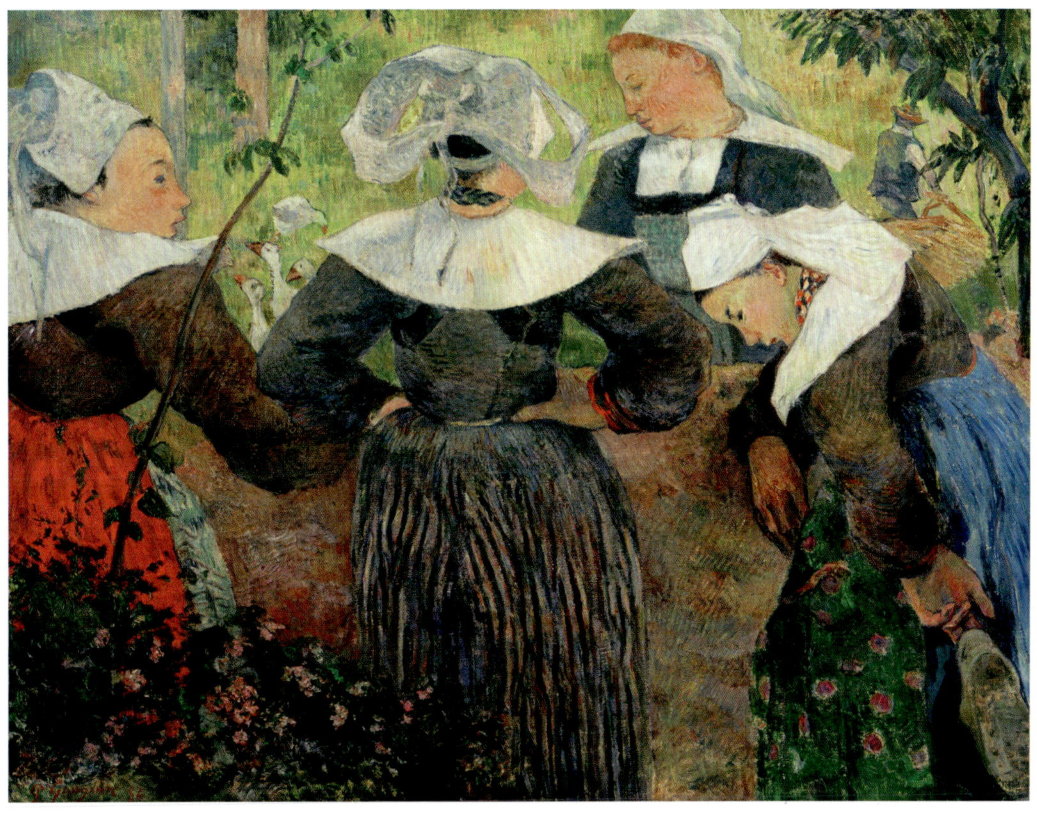

tenía 38 años) con algunos de los cuales entabló una amistad duradera, como con Charles Laval (1861–1894) y Émile Bernard (1868–1941). Unos días fueron suficientes para afianzar su reputación, alimentada por su temperamento sólido y por sus aspiraciones artísticas.

De regreso a París, Gauguin fabricó jarrones de cerámica en el taller de Ernst Chaplet (1835–1909), que no obtuvieron el éxito esperado.

come Charles Laval (1861–1894) ed Émile Bernard (1868–1941). Pochi giorni sono sufficienti per stabilire la sua reputazione, nutrita dal pieno temperamento e per le sue aspirazioni artistiche.

Di ritorno a Parigi, Gauguin inizia a produrre vasi di ceramica nell'atelier di Ernst Chaplet (1835–1909), che però non avranno il successo desiderato

is dan 38. Met een paar van hen blijft hij lang bevriend, onder wie Charles Laval (1861–1894) en Émile Bernard (1868–1941). Door zijn vurige temperament en zijn kunstzinnige aspiraties is de naam Gauguin binnen een paar dagen bij iedereen bekend.

Terug in Parijs maakt Gauguin keramieken vazen in het atelier van Ernst Chaplet (1835–1909), maar het verwachte succes bleef uit.

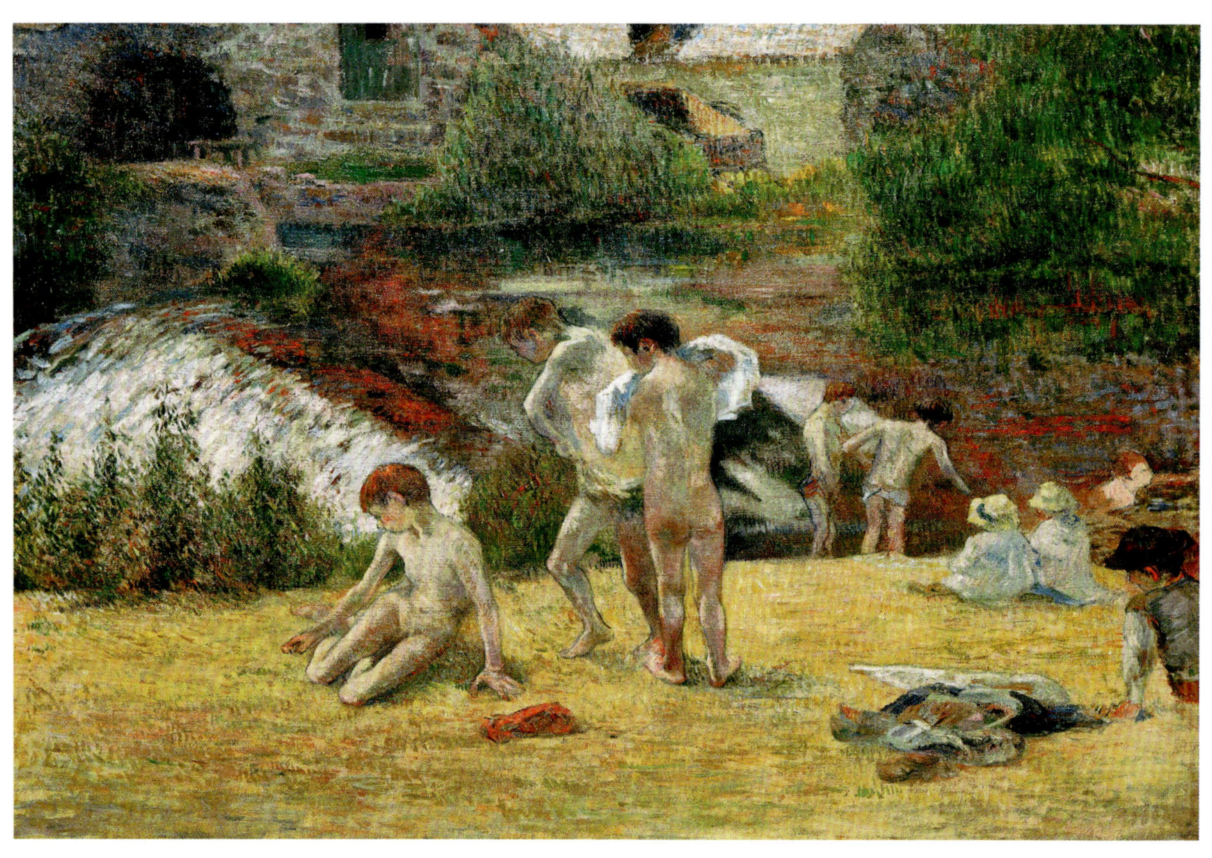

Young Breton Boys Bathing or *The Bathing by the Bois d'Amour*

Jeunes Bretons au bain ou *La Baignade au bois d'amour*

Junge Bretonen im Bad oder *Das Bad bei der Mühle im Bois d'Amour*

Jóvenes bretones bañándose o *El baño en el bosque del amor*

Giovani bretoni ai bagni o *La bagnante nel bosco d'amore*

Jonge Bretons aan het zwemmen, of *De zwempartij bij de molen in het Bois d'Amour*

1886, Oil on canvas/Huile sur toile, 60 × 73 cm, Museum of Art, Hiroshima

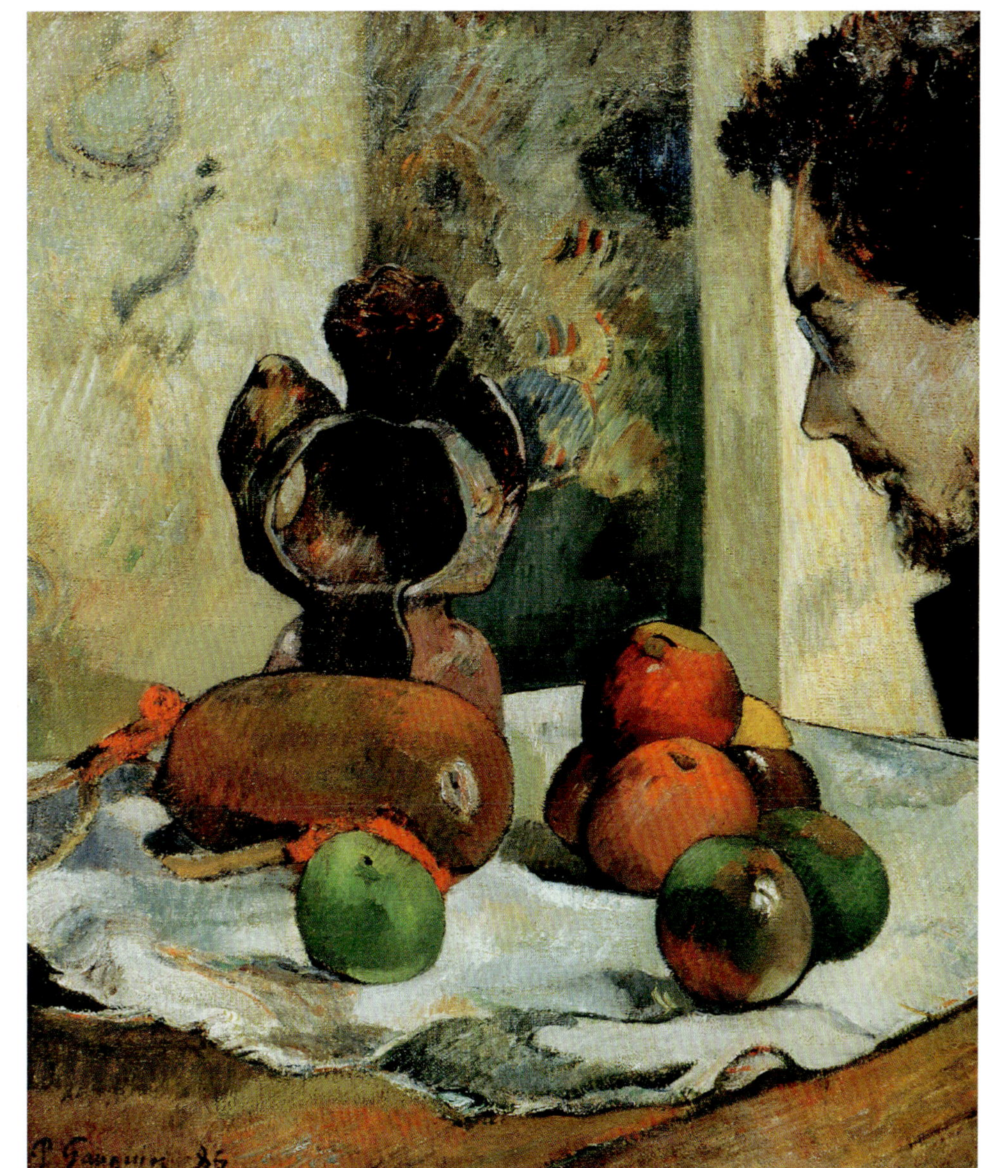

Still Life with Profile of Laval

Nature morte au profil de Laval

Stillleben mit dem Profil von Laval

Naturaleza muerta y perfil de Laval

Natura morta sul profilo di Laval

Stilleven met het profiel van Laval

1886, Oil on canvas/Huile sur toile, 46 × 38 cm, Indianapolis Museum of Art, Indianapolis

Dreams of the edge of the world

His Peruvian infancy and marine peregrinations seem to have left indelible traces. All of his life, Gauguin would be haunted by the idea of travelling far, very far away—no doubt also fleeing a stifling society —a quest for wild nature in the form of original paradise where freedom rhymes with authenticity. He planned to settle at the edge of the world in 1887, doing his best to enlist his painting friends Ferdinand du Puigaudeau (1864–1930) and Charles Laval. In the end, only Laval accompanied him to make fortune in Panama and to "live wild" as Paul explained to his spouse in April 1887. On the spot, the artists fled a nightmarish Panama and headed for Martinique. After being floored by dysentery and malaria, Gauguin succeeded in painting during the last weeks of his stay, inspired by rustic motifs, the light and contrasting shades of the rich Caribbean island nature.

The return to Paris was rather more bitter than his scenes of life in Martinique, and his landscapes of the bay of Saint-Pierre sold poorly. In vain they aroused the admiration of the merchant Theo van Gogh and the critic Octave Mirbeau—the purse remained desperately empty … Far from being idyllic, this first trip strengthened the artist's firm conviction that he had to work in the tropics, that it was there where he would find his human and artistic truth.

Des rêves de bout du monde

Son enfance péruvienne et ses pérégrinations de marin semblent avoir laissé des traces indélébiles. Toute sa vie, Gauguin sera hanté par l'idée de voyager, loin, très loin – fuyant sans doute aussi un peu une société contraignante –, en quête de nature sauvage et d'une forme de paradis originel où liberté rime avec authenticité. Il projette de partir s'installer au bout du monde dès 1887, faisant son possible pour enrôler ses jeunes amis peintres Ferdinand du Puigaudeau (1864–1930) et Charles Laval. Finalement, seul Laval l'accompagne pour faire fortune au Panamá et « vivre en sauvage », comme l'explique Paul à son épouse en avril 1887. Sur place, les deux artistes quittent rapidement le Panamá, cauchemardesque, pour la Martinique. Après avoir été anéanti par la dysenterie et le paludisme, Gauguin parvient à peindre durant les dernières semaines de son séjour, inspiré par les motifs rustiques, la lumière et les tons contrastés de la nature luxuriante de l'île des Caraïbes.

Le retour à Paris est d'autant plus rude que ses scènes de vie martiniquaises et ses paysages de la baie de Saint-Pierre se vendent mal. Elles ont beau susciter l'admiration du marchand Théo Van Gogh et du critique Octave Mirbeau, la bourse reste désespérément vide. Loin d'avoir été idyllique, ce premier voyage renforce cependant l'intime conviction de l'artiste qu'il lui faut aller travailler sous les tropiques, que c'est là qu'il trouvera sa vérité humaine et artistique.

Träume vom Ende der Welt

Die Kindheit in Peru und seine Fahrten über die Weltmeere scheinen unauslöschliche Spuren hinterlassen zu haben. Zeitlebens wird Gauguin vom Wunsch beherrscht sein, weit zu reisen, sehr weit – wohl auch ein wenig auf der Flucht vor gesellschaftlichen Zwängen –, auf der Suche nach unberührter Natur und einer Art ursprünglichen Paradieses, in dem Freiheit und Echtheit Hand in Hand gehen. Ab 1887 schmiedet er Pläne, sich am Ende der Welt niederzulassen, und er versucht auch, seine jungen Künstlerfreunde Ferdinand du Puigaudeau (1864–1930) und Charles Laval für diesen Plan zu gewinnen. Nach Panama begleitet ihn schließlich nur Laval – auf der Suche nach dem Glück und um „in der Wildnis zu leben", wie Paul es seiner Gemahlin im April 1887 erklärt. Vor Ort verlassen die beiden Künstler eilends das albtraumhafte Panama und reisen weiter zur Insel Martinique. Von Ruhr und Malaria geschwächt findet Gauguin trotzdem in den letzten Wochen des Aufenthaltes zur Malerei zurück, inspiriert von den ländlichen Motiven, dem Licht und den kontrastierenden Farbtönen der üppigen Natur der karibischen Insel.

Die Rückkehr nach Paris ist umso enttäuschender, als sich seine Szenen des Lebens auf Martinique und die Landschaftsbilder der Bucht von Saint-Pierre nur schlecht verkaufen. Seine Bilder finden im Kunsthändler Théo van Gogh und im Kritiker Octave Mirbeau Bewunderer, doch der Geldbeutel bleibt hoffnungslos leer. Obwohl diese erste Reise keineswegs idyllisch verlief, bestärkt sie seine innere Überzeugung, in den Tropen arbeiten zu müssen und dort menschliche und künstlerische Wahrhaftigkeit zu finden.

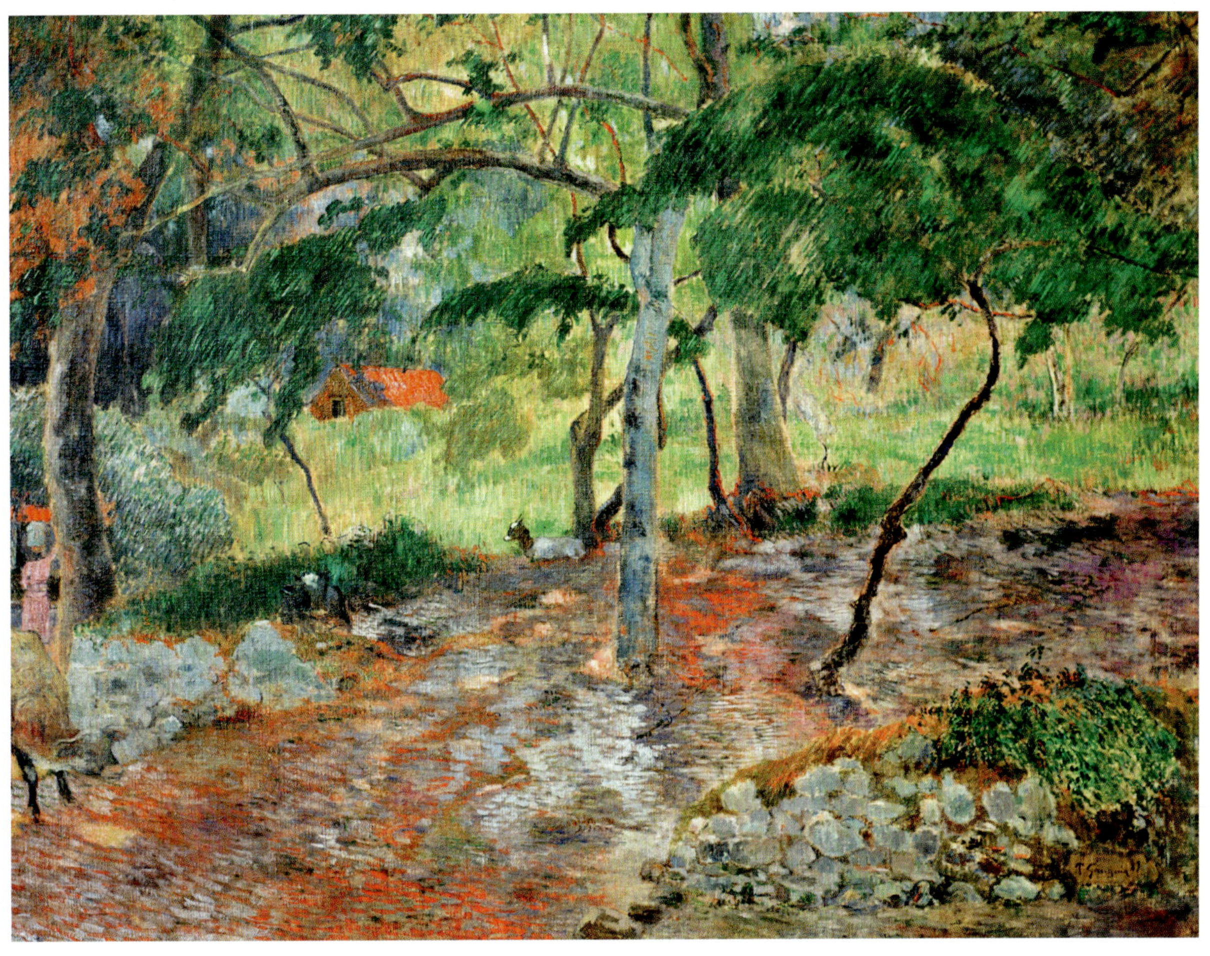

Tropical landscape on Martinique

Paysage tropical de Martinique

Tropische Landschaft auf Martinique

Paisaje tropical de Martinica

Paesaggio tropicale di Martinique

Tropisch landschap op Martinique

1887, Oil on canvas/Huile sur toile, 90,2 × 116 cm, Neue Pinakothek, München

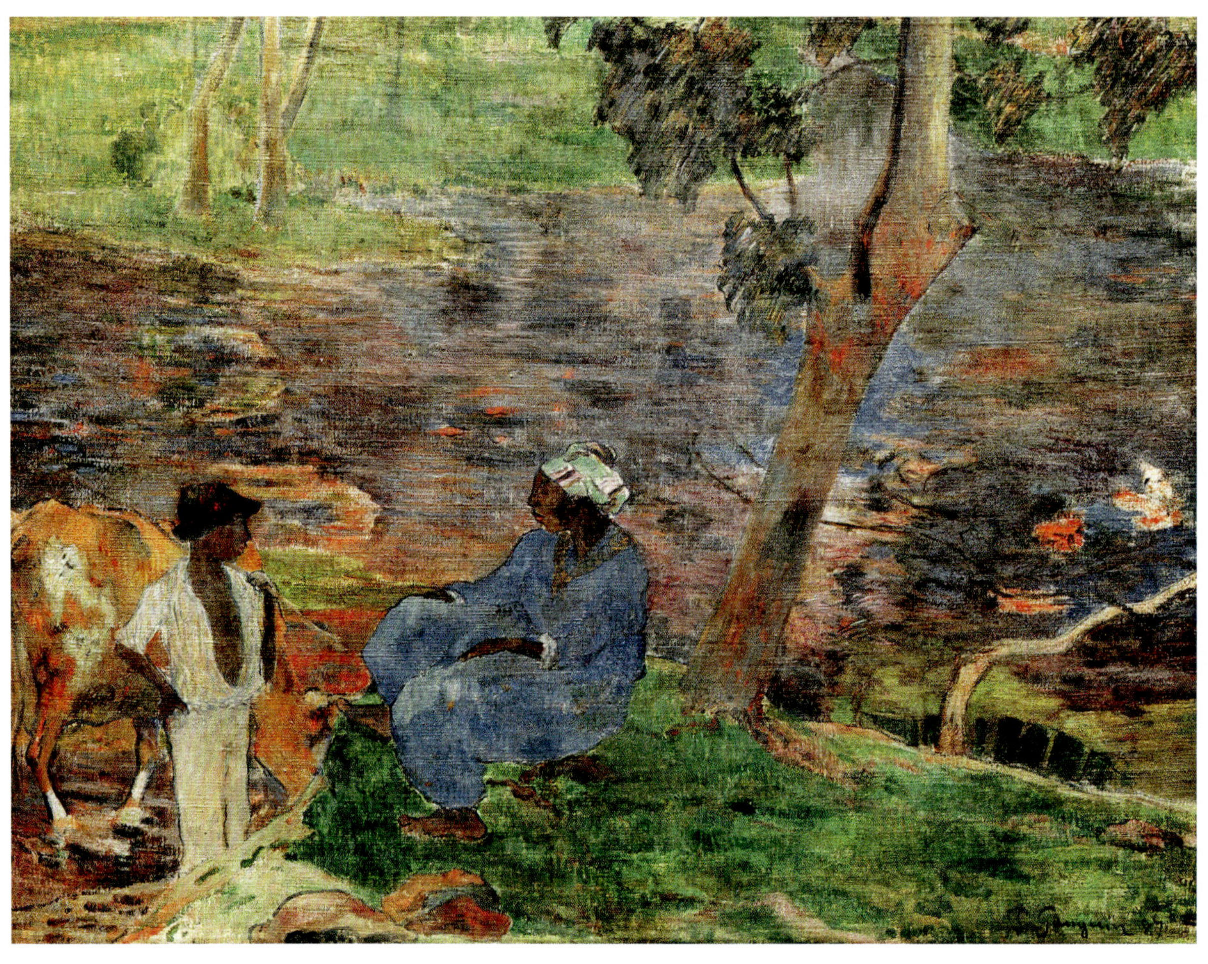

On the Banks of a River in Martinique

Sur les berges d'une rivière de Martinique

Am Ufer eines Flusses auf Martinique

A orillas de un río de Martinica

Sui monti di una riviera di Martinica

Op een rivieroever op Martinique

1887, Oil on canvas/Huile sur toile, 54,5 × 56,5 cm, Van Gogh Museum, Amsterdam

Sueños del fin del mundo

Su infancia peruana y sus peregrinaciones de marino parecen haber dejado una huella imborrable. Toda su vida, Gauguin se vio perseguido por la idea de viajar, lejos, muy lejos, huyendo sin duda también en parte de una sociedad agobiante, en busca de naturaleza salvaje y de una forma de paraíso original en el que libertad rima con autenticidad. Desde 1887, planeó marcharse para instalarse en el fin del mundo, haciendo todo lo posible para que sus jóvenes amigos pintores Ferdinand du Puigaudeau (1864–1930) y Charles Laval se unieran a él. Finalmente, solo Laval le acompañó para hacer fortuna en Panamá–y "vivir como un salvaje", como le explica Paul a su esposa en abril de 1887. Allí, los dos artistas abandonaron rápidamente un Panamá de pesadilla, en dirección a Martinica. Después de quedar destrozado por la disentería y el paludismo, Gauguin llegó a pintar durante las últimas semanas de su viaje, inspirado por motivos rústicos, la luz y los tonos en contraste con la lujuriosa naturaleza de la isla caribeña.

El regreso a París es aún más difícil que sus escenas de vida en Martinica y sus paisajes de la bahía de San Pedro se vendieron mal. A pesar de suscitar la admiración del comerciante Théo van Gogh y del crítico Octave Mirbeau, su cartera seguía desesperadamente vacía… Sin embargo, lejos de ser idílico, este primer viaje reforzó el íntimo convencimiento del artista sobre la necesidad de ir a trabajar a los trópicos, que era allí donde encontraría la verdad humana y artística.

Sogni dei confini del mondo

La sua infanzia peruviana e le sue peregrinazioni da marinaio sembrano aver lasciato segni indelebili. Durante tutta la sua vita, Gauguin sarà ossessionato dall'idea di viaggiare, lontano, molto lontano – in fuga, probabilmente, anche un po' da una società vincolante – in cerca di natura selvaggia e di una forma di paradiso originale dove la libertà fa rima con autenticità. Ha intenzione di partire per la fine del mondo nel 1887, facendo del suo meglio per arruolare i suoi giovani amici pittori Ferdinand du Puigaudeau (1864–1930) e Charles Laval. Alla fine, solo Laval lo accompagna a fare fortuna in Panama e "vivono allo stato selvaggio", come Paul spiega a sua moglie nel mese di aprile 1887. Lì, i due artisti rapidamente lasciano Panama, che considerano da incubo, per la Martinica. Dopo essere stato provato da dissenteria e malaria, Gauguin riesce a dipingere durante le ultime settimane della sua permanenza, ispirato da motivi rustici, luce e colori contrastanti dei dintorni lussureggianti dell'isola caraibica.

Il ritorno a Parigi è ancora più duro in quanto le sue scene di vita di paesaggi della Martinica e la baia di Saint-Pierre vendono poco. Destano viva ammirazione nel commerciante Theo van Gogh e nel critico Octave Mirbeau, ma il mercato azionario rimane disperatamente vuoto. Lungi dall'essere idilliaco, questo primo viaggio, però rafforza la ferma convinzione dell'artista che doveva andare a lavorare nei tropici; è lì che egli troverà la sua verità umana e artistica.

Dromen over het andere eind van de wereld

Zijn jeugd in Peru en zijn omzwervingen als marinier lijken een onuitwisbaar stempel te hebben gedrukt. De kunstenaar blijft zijn leven lang geobsedeerd door het idee van reizen. Hij wil weg, verweg, waarschijnlijk ook een beetje om de benauwende maatschappij te ontvluchten. Hij gaat op zoek naar ongerepte natuur en een oerparadijs waar vrijheid en authenticiteit hand in hand gaan. Vanaf 1887 maakt hij plannen om aan de andere kant van de wereld te gaan wonen. Zijn jonge vrienden en collega-schilders Ferdinand du Puigaudeau (1864–1930) en Charles Laval probeert hij over te halen dat ook te doen. Uiteindelijk gaat alleen Laval mee om zijn geluk in Panama te beproeven en "als een wilde te leven", zoals Gauguin in april 1887 aan zijn echtgenote schrijft. Bij aankomst blijkt Panama een nachtmerrie te zijn en reizen de twee door naar Martinique. Gauguin wordt door dysenterie en malaria geveld, maar kan de laatste weken van zijn verblijf toch schilderen, geïnspireerd door de rustieke motieven, het licht en de contrastrijke kleuren van de weelderige natuur op het Caribische eiland.

De terugkeer in Parijs is nog moeilijker dan gedacht als blijkt dat zijn schilderijen met scènes uit het leven op Martinique en zijn landschapsschilderijen van de Baai van Saint-Pierre slecht verkopen. Kunsthandelaar Theo van Gogh en criticus Octave Mirbeau zijn lovend, maar Gauguins portemonnee blijft leeg. Toch versterkt deze verre van idyllische eerste reis de kunstenaar in zijn diepgevoelde overtuiging dat hij in de tropen moet gaan werken. Alleen daar zal hij als mens en als kunstenaar zijn ware zelf kunnen vinden.

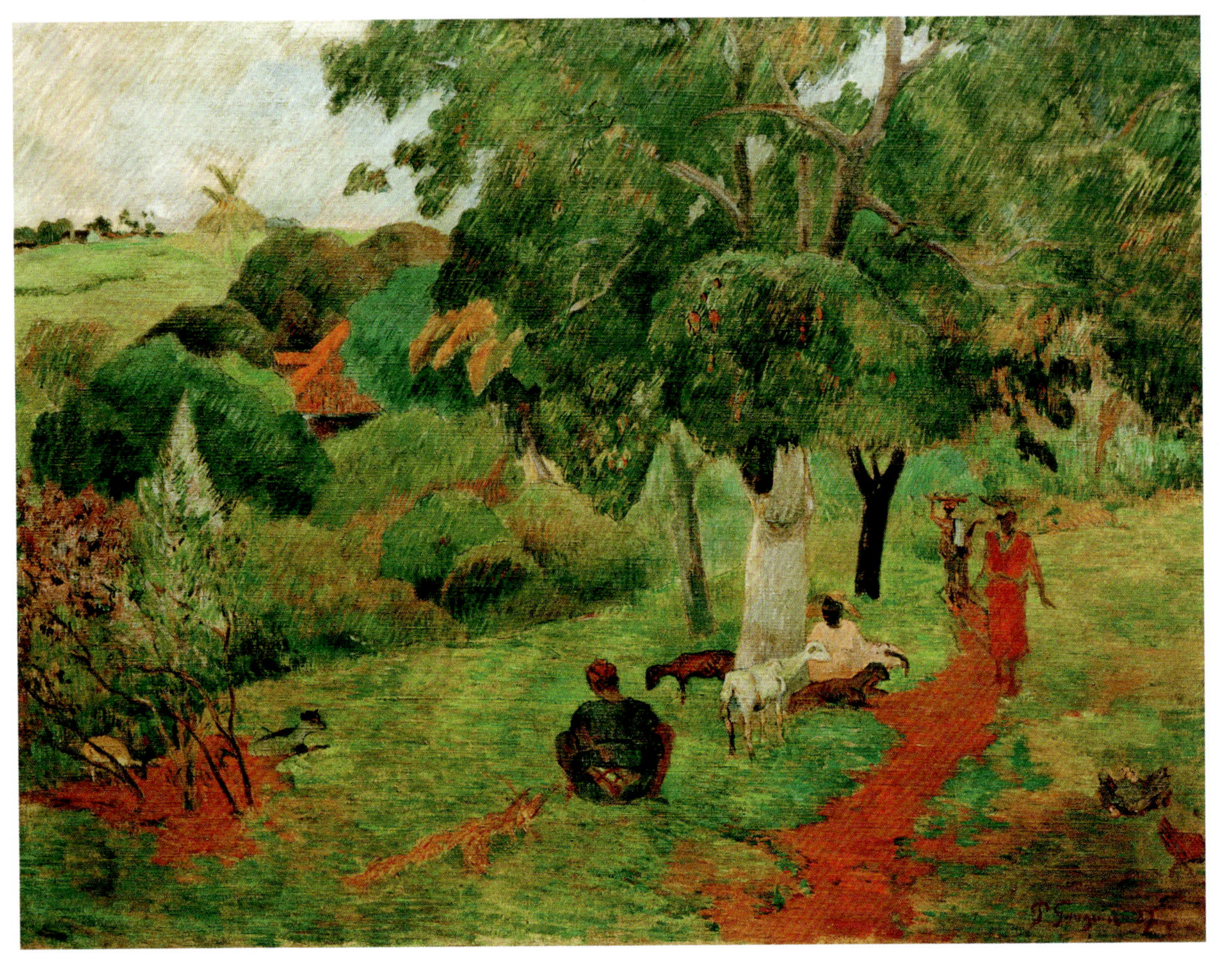

Coming and Going, Martinique
Allées et venues, Martinique
Kommen und Gehen, Martinique
Idas y venidas, Martinica
Strade e viali, Martinica
Komen en gaan, Martinique

1887, Oil on canvas/Huile sur toile, 72,6 × 92 cm, Museo Thyssen-Bornemisza, Madrid

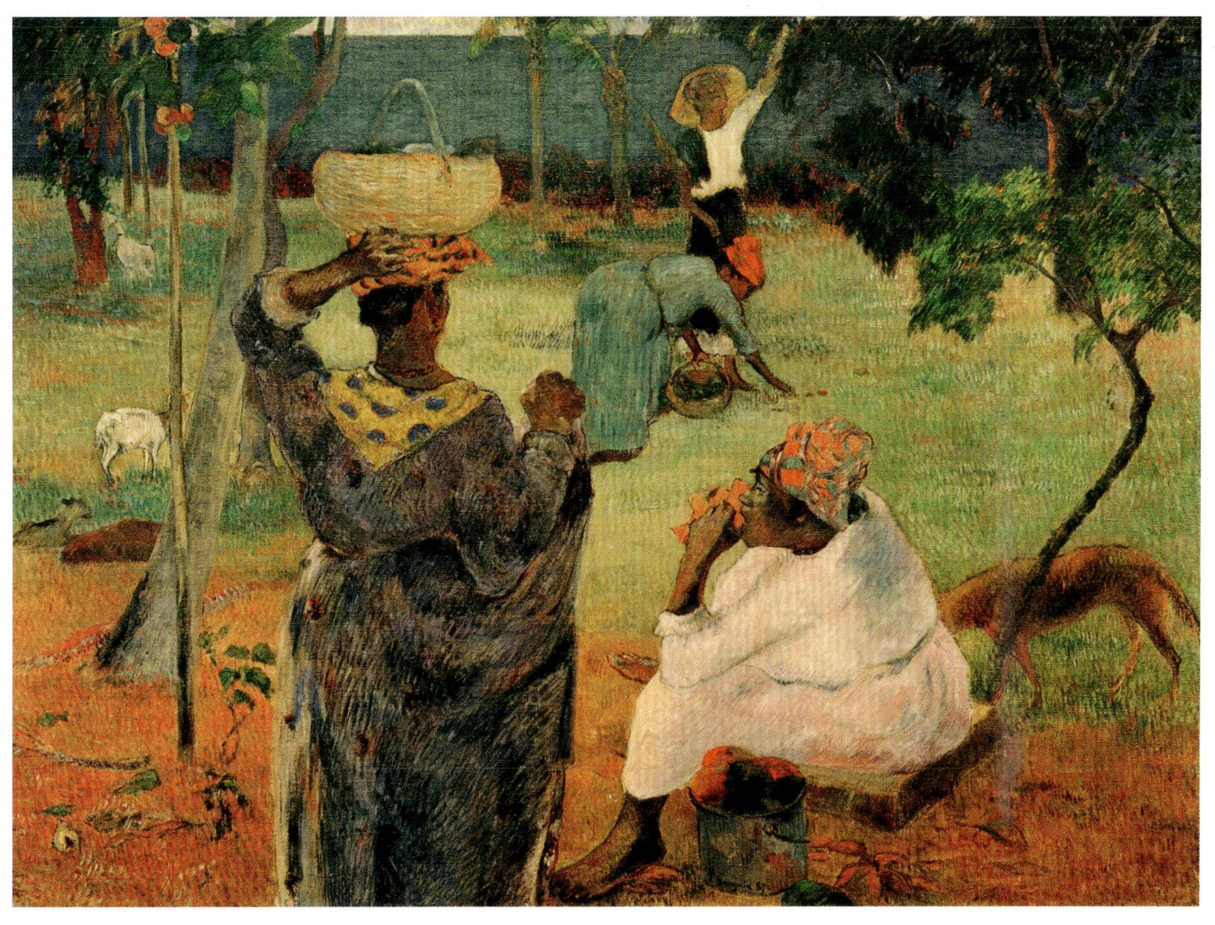

Fruit Picking, Martinique or *Mango Pickers*
La Cueillette des fruits, Martinique ou *Les Mangues*
Obsternte, Martinique oder *Die Mangopflücker*
Cosechadoras de frutas, Martinica o *Los mangos*
La raccolta di frutta, Martinica o *I Manghi*
De fruitoogst, Martinique of *De mango's (De mangoplukkers)*
1887, Oil on canvas/Huile sur toile, 86 × 116 cm, Van Gogh Museum, Amsterdam

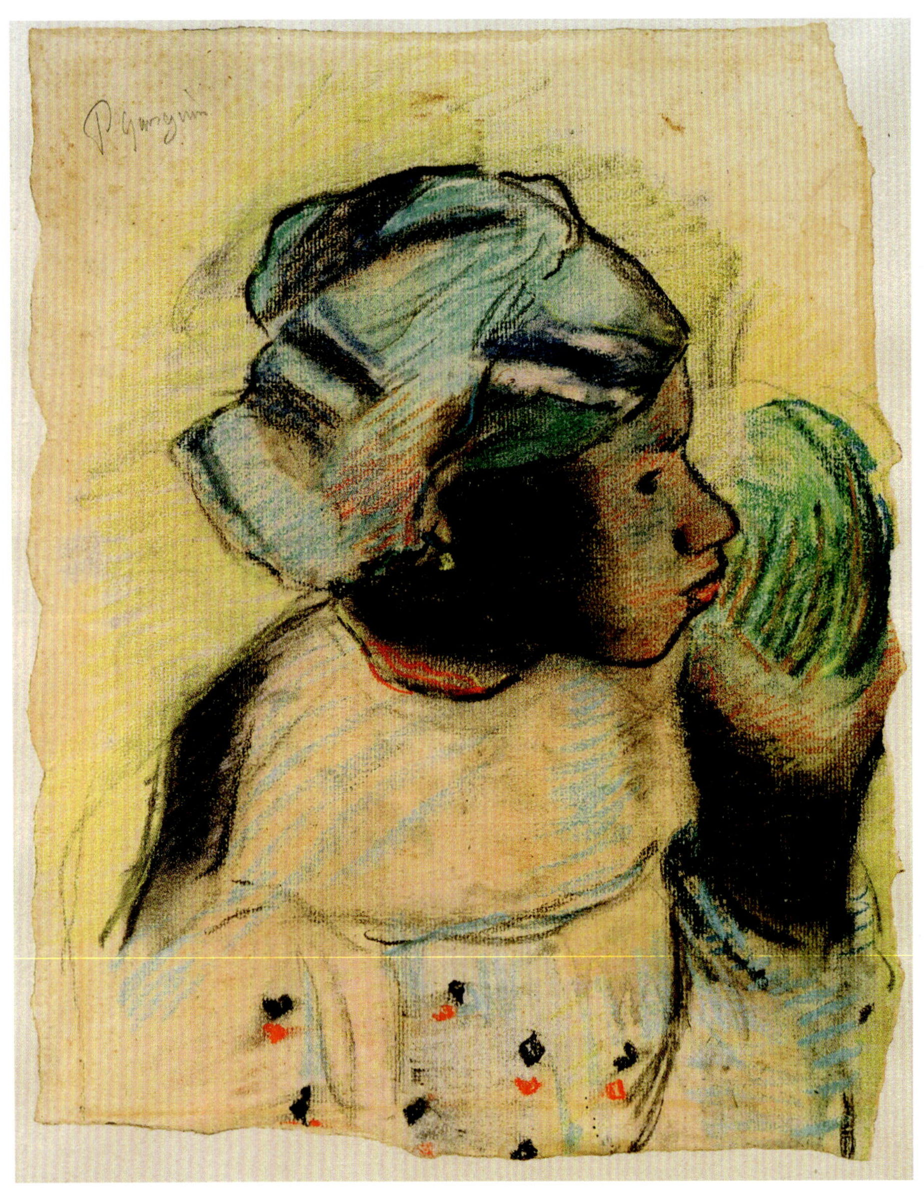

Head of Woman, Martinique
Tête de femme, Martinique
Kopf einer Frau, Martinique
Cabeza de mujer, Martinica
Testa di donna, Martinique
Hoofd van een vrouw, Martinique

1887, Chalk and pastel/Craie et pastel, 36 × 26 cm, Van Gogh Museum, Amsterdam

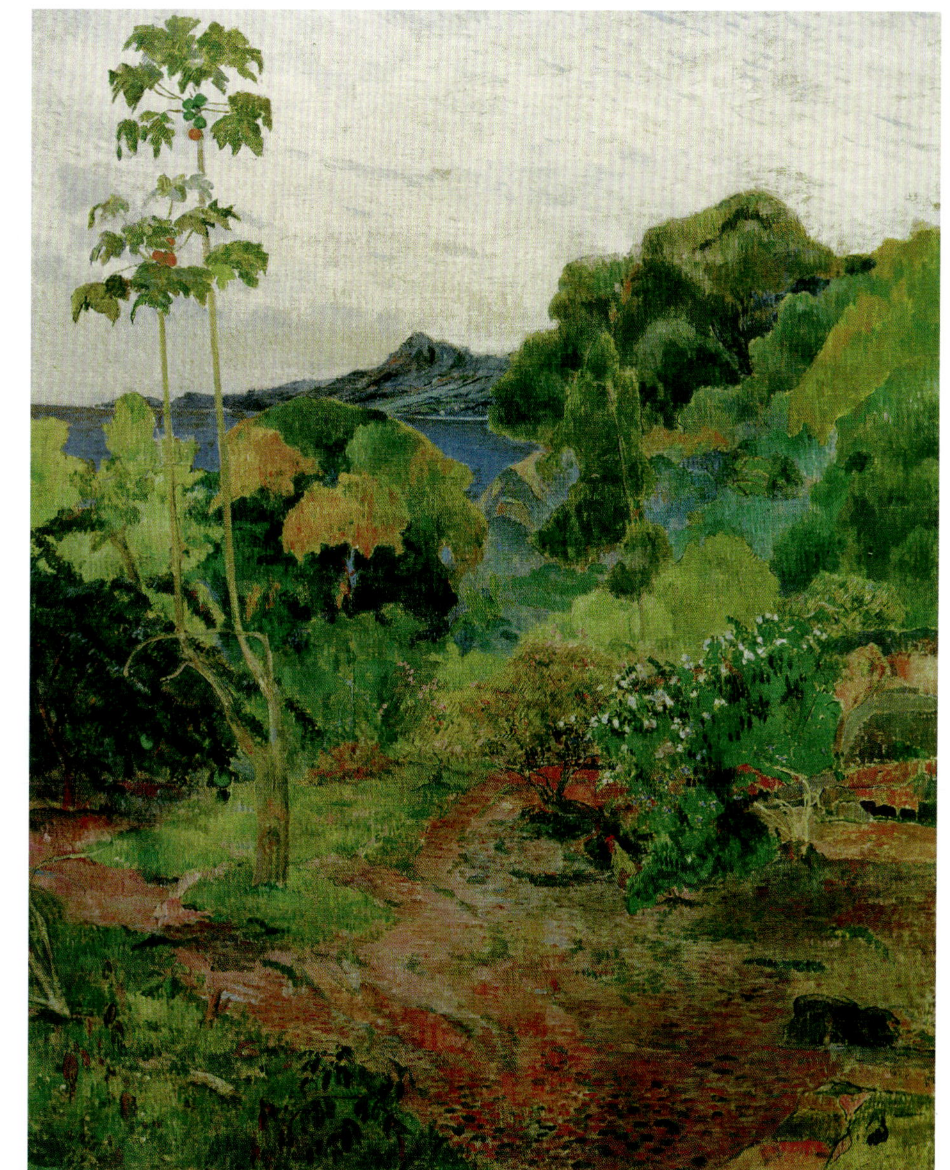

Martinique Landscape

*Paysage tropical
de Martinique*

*Tropische Landschaft
auf Martinique*

Paisaje tropical de Martinica

*Paesaggio tropicale
di Martinique*

*Tropisch landschap
op Martinique*

*1887, Oil on canvas/Huile sur
toile, 117 × 89 cm, Scottish
National Gallery of Modern Art,
Edinburgh*

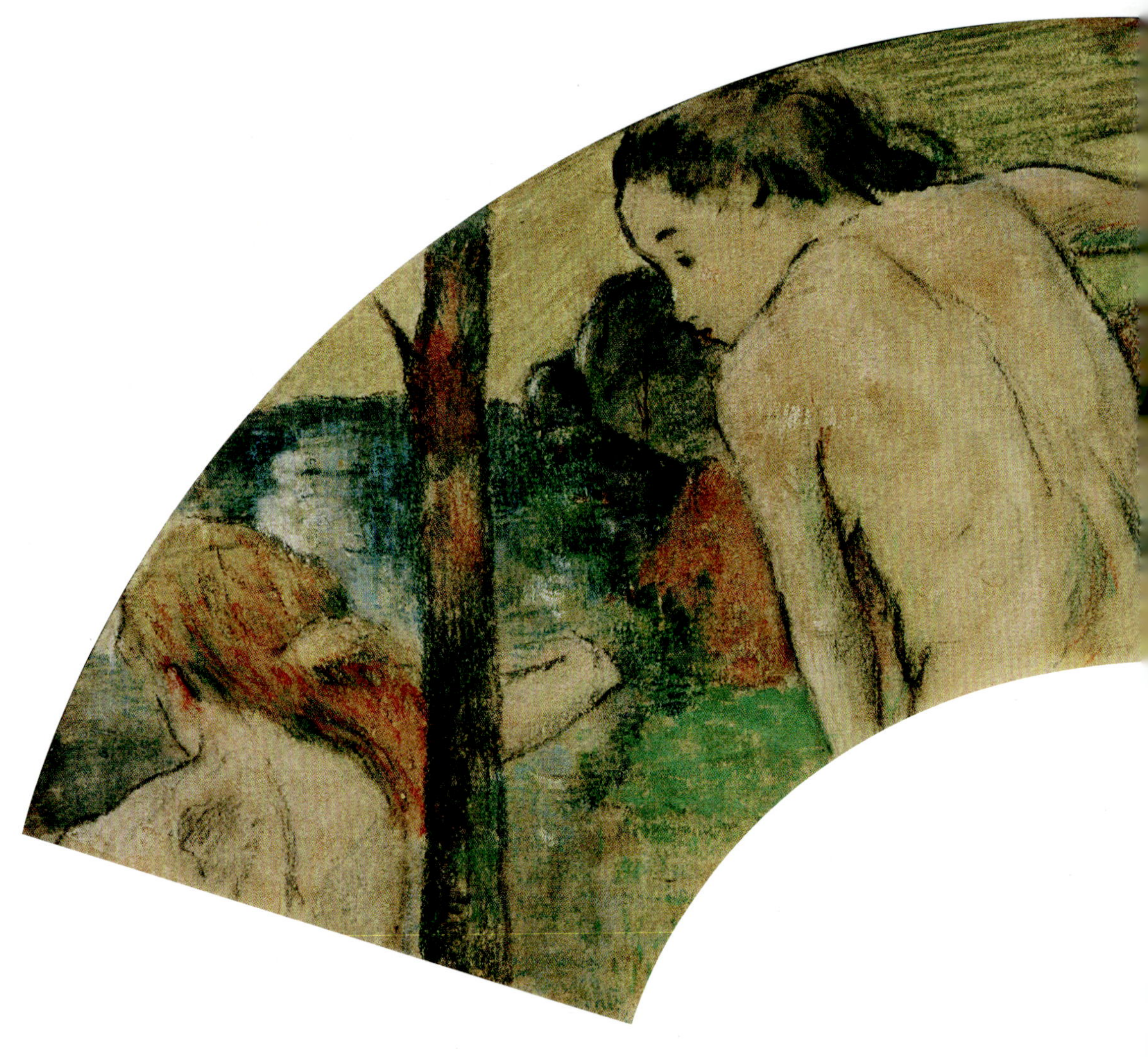

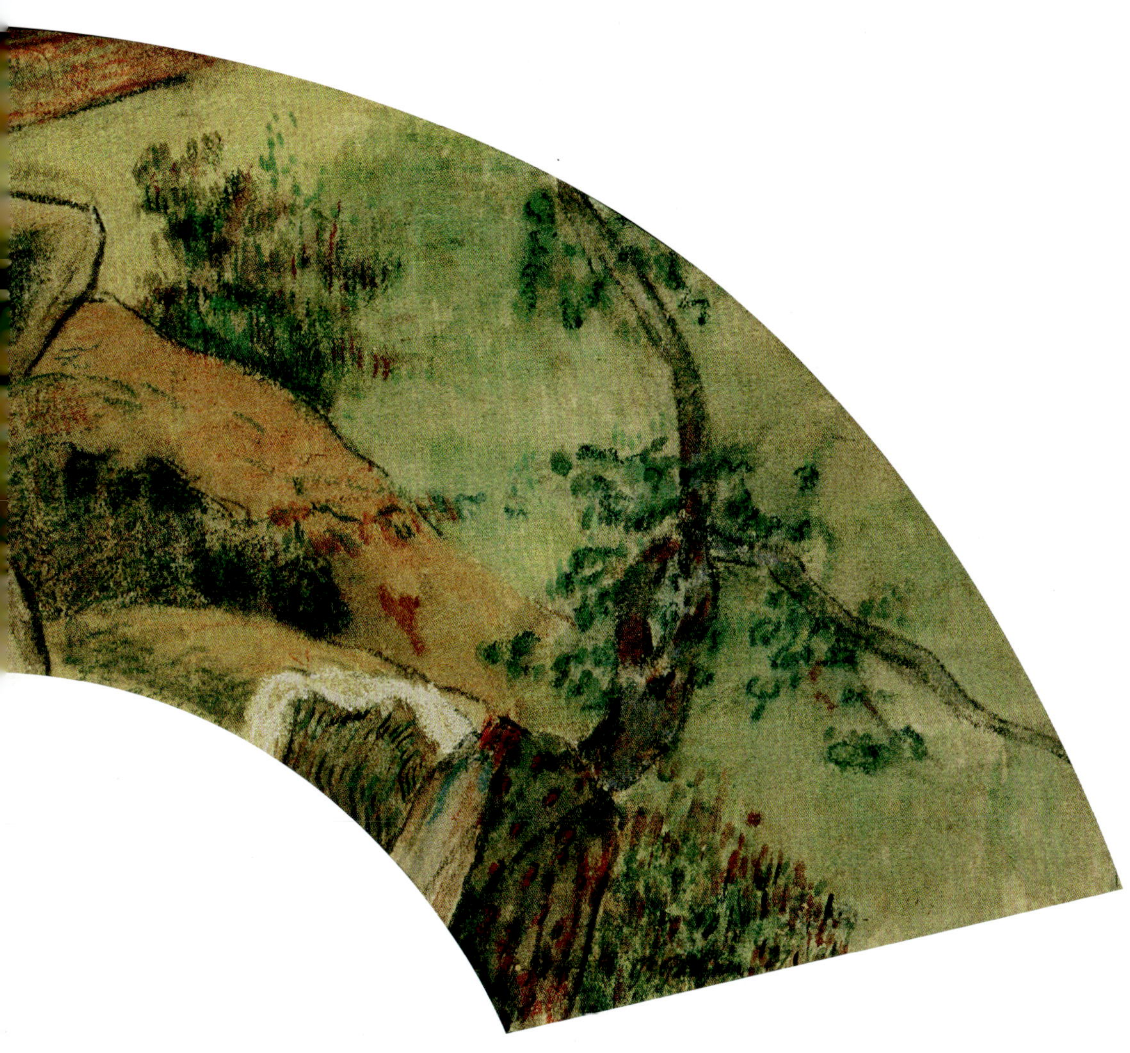

Bathing

Baignade

Badende

Baño

Nuotata

Zwempartij

1887, Pastel, chalk, gouache, wash and graphite/Pastel, craie, gouache, lavis et graphite, 11,5 × 40,5 cm, The Kelton Foundation, Santa Monica

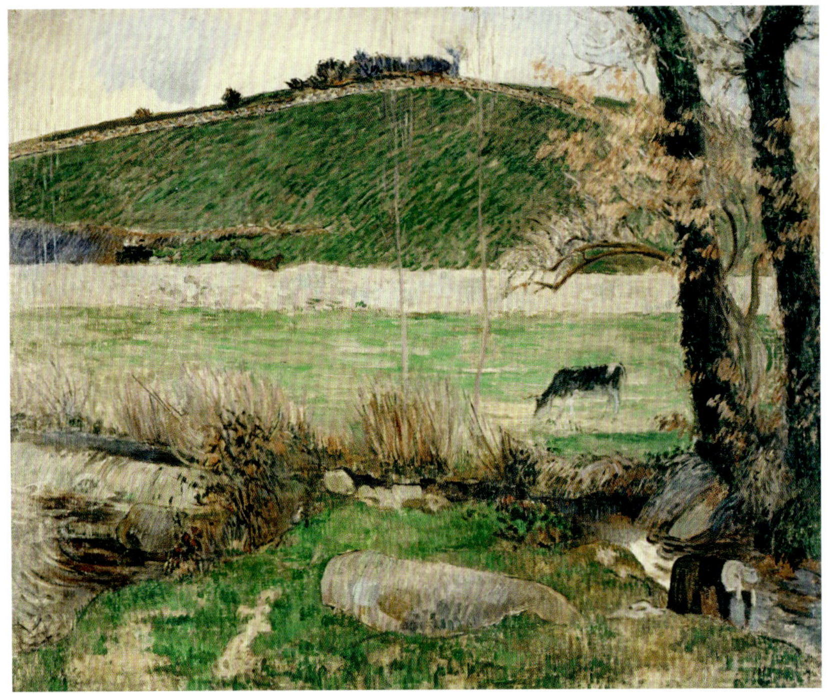

1888, a decisive year

It is during his second stay at Pont-Aven in 1888, that the stylistic revolution took place, the fruit of his interactions with Émile Bernard and Vincent van Gogh. The first stayed, as he did, at the Gloanec boarding house, while the second, whom he met in Paris two years earlier, lodged at Arles. All three shared the taste for pure colour, Japanese prints, and a radical conception of art.

Symbols of their friendship and their artistic aspirations, their self-portraits—the *Self-portrait "Les Misérables"* by Gauguin, the *Self-portrait "au copaing Vincent"* by Bernard and the *Self-portrait*

1888, année décisive

C'est lors du deuxième séjour de Gauguin à Pont-Aven, en 1888, que s'opère la révolution stylistique, fruit de ses échanges avec Émile Bernard et Vincent Van Gogh. Le premier vit, comme lui, à la pension Gloanec tandis que le second, rencontré à Paris deux ans auparavant, demeure à Arles. Tous trois partagent le goût de la couleur pure, des estampes japonaises et une conception radicale de l'art.

Symboles de leur amitié et de leurs aspirations artistiques, leurs autoportraits – *Autoportrait « Les Misérables »* de Gauguin, *Autoportrait*

1888, Jahr der Entscheidung

Während des zweiten Aufenthalts in Pont-Aven im Jahre 1888 vollzieht sich eine stilistische Revolution in Gauguins Schaffen – Ergebnis seines Austausches mit Émile Bernard und Vincent van Gogh. Ersterer lebt wie er in der Pension Gloanec, letzterer – er hatte ihn zwei Jahre zuvor in Paris kennengelernt – bleibt in Arles. Alle drei teilen sie den Sinn für ursprüngliche Farben, eine Vorliebe für japanische Drucke sowie eine radikale Kunstauffassung.

Zeichen ihrer Freundschaft und ihres künstlerischen Strebens sind ihre Selbstporträts – *Selbstbildnis mit*

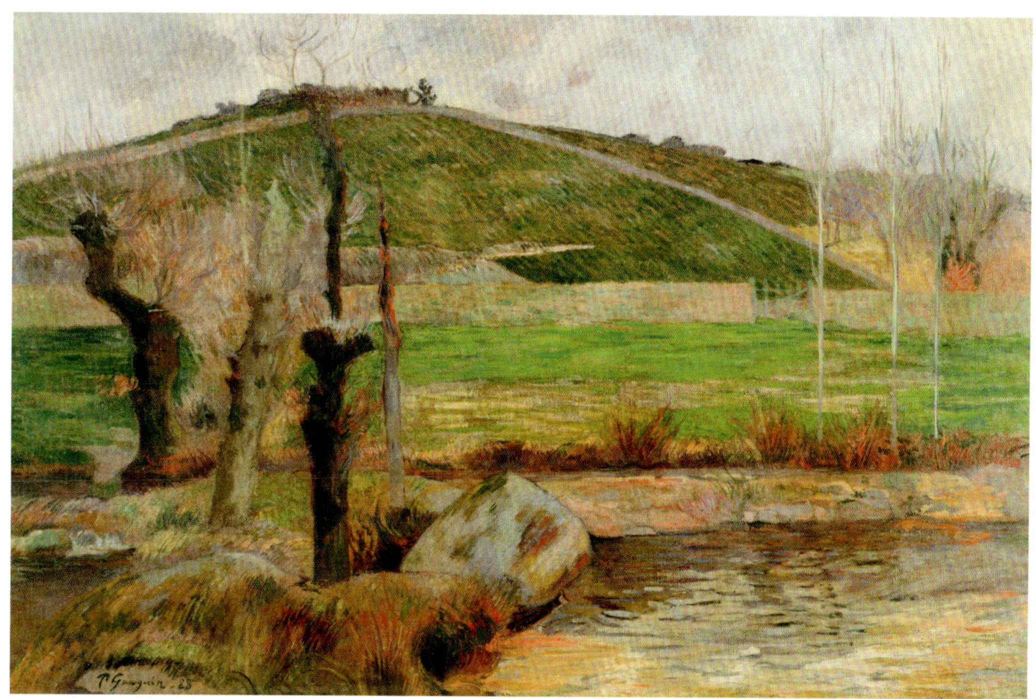

1888, el año decisivo

Fue durante el segundo viaje de Gauguin
a Pont-Aven, en 1888, cuando se operó
la revolución estilística, fruto de sus
intercambios con Émile Bernard y Vincent
van Gogh. El primero vivía, como él,
en la pensión Gloanec mientras que el
segundo, con quién se encontró en París
dos años antes, vivía en Arles. Los tres
compartían el gusto por el color puro, las
estampas japonesas y una concepción
radical del arte.

Símbolos de su amistad y de sus
aspiraciones artísticas, sus autorretratos,
Autorretrato "Los Miserables" de Gauguin,
Autorretrato "al amigo Vincent" de Bernard

1888, l'anno decisivo

E' durante il secondo soggiorno di
Gauguin a Pont-Aven, nel 1888, che
avviene la rivoluzione stilistica, frutto
degli scambi con Émile Bernard e Vincent
van Gogh. Il primo vive come lui nella
pensione Gloanec, mentre il secondo,
con cui si è incontrato a Parigi due
anni prima, dimora ad Arles. Tutti e tre
condividono il gusto del colore puro,
stampe giapponesi ed una concezione
radicale dell'arte.

Simboli della loro amicizia e delle loro
aspirazioni artistiche, gli autoritratti –
Autoritratto "I Miserabili" di Gauguin,
Autoritratto "al compagno Vincent"

Het beslissende jaar 1888

Tijdens zijn tweede verblijf in Pont-Aven,
in 1888, ontwikkelt Gauguin onder invloed
van zijn contacten met Émile Bernard
en Vincent van Gogh een totaal andere
schilderstijl. Bernard verblijft net als
Gauguin in Auberge Gloanec; Van Gogh,
die Gauguin twee jaar eerder in Parijs
heeft ontmoet, woont en werkt in Arles.
De drie delen een voorliefde voor zuivere
kleuren, Japanse prenten en radicale
kunstopvattingen.

Hun zelfportretten – *Zelfportret 'Les
Misérables'* van Gauguin, *Zelfportret
'voor vriend Vincent'* van Bernard en
Zelfportret, opgedragen aan Gauguin van

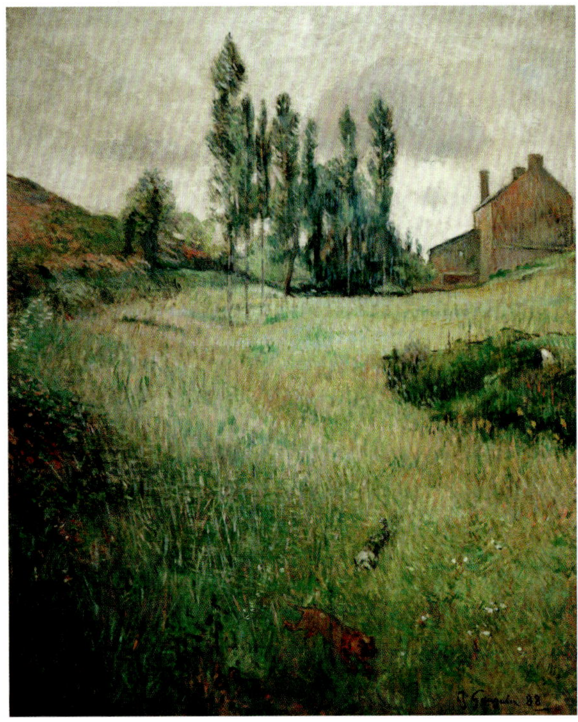

dédicacé à Gauguin by Van Gogh—constituted the relics of an idyll of short duration. Gauguin left Arles after Van Gogh cut off his own ear on the night of 23 December; he had spent only two months at his side, abandoning the project to build an artistic community together. As for Emile Bernard, he would always reproach him for having left him in the shadows.

Together they developed synthetism—a style characterised by chromatic expression, a simplification of forms and thick contours—along with other young artists developing

« *au copaing Vincent* » de Bernard et *Autoportrait dédicacé à Gauguin* de Van Gogh – constituent les reliquats d'une idylle de courte durée. Gauguin quitte Arles après que Van Gogh se soit coupé l'oreille la nuit du 23 décembre ; il n'aura passé que deux mois à ses côtés, abandonnant le projet d'une communauté artistique à bâtir ensemble. Quant à Émile Bernard, il lui reprochera toujours de l'avoir laissé dans l'ombre...

Ensemble, ils élaborent le synthétisme – un style caractérisé par un chromatisme expressif, une simplification des formes et des contours

dem *Porträt Bernards*, Vincent van Gogh gewidmet („*Les Misérables*") von Gauguin, *Selbstporträt „mit Freund Vincent"* von Bernard und *Selbstbildnis, Paul Gauguin gewidmet* von van Gogh – Spuren einer kurzlebigen Idylle. Gauguin verlässt Arles, nachdem van Gogh sich in der Nacht des 23. Dezembers das Ohr abgeschnitten hat. Er sollte nur zwei Monate an ihrer Seite bleiben und gibt das Projekt einer Künstlergemeinschaft auf. Emile Bernard wird Gauguin stets vorwerfen, ihn im Ungewissen gelassen zu haben.

Landscape at Pont-Aven

Paysage à Pont-Aven

Landschaft bei Pont-Aven

Paisaje de Pont-Aven

Paesaggio a Pont-Aven

Landschap bij Pont-Aven

1888, Oil on canvas/Huile sur toile, 90,5 × 71 cm, Ny Carlsberg Glyptotek, København

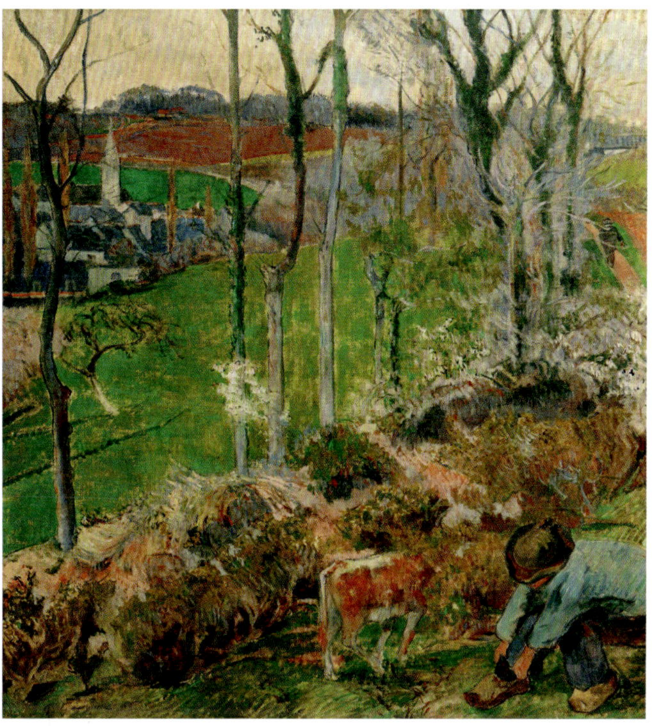

y *Autorretrato dedicatoria a Gauguin* de van Gogh, constituyen los remanentes de un idilio de corta duración. Gauguin dejó Arles después de que van Gogh se cortara la oreja la noche del 23 de diciembre, solo habrán pasado un par de meses a su ado, abandonando el proyecto de una comunidad artística a construir juntos. En lo que respecta a Émile Bernard, le reprochará siempre el haberlo dejado en la oscuridad...

Juntos, crearon el sintetismo, un estilo caracterizado por un cromatismo expresivo, una simplificación de las formas y de los contornos gruesos, con

di Bernard e *Autoritratto dedicato a Gauguin* di van Gogh – sono le reliquie di un breve idillio. Gauguin lascia Arles dopo che van Gogh si era tagliato l'orecchio la notte del 23 dicembre; non aveva che trascorso due mesi con lui, abbandonando il progetto di una comunità artistica da costruire insieme. Per quanto riguarda Émile Bernard, gli rimprovererà di averlo lasciato sempre nell'ombra.

Insieme, essi sviluppano il sintetismo – uno stile caratterizzato da cromatismo espressivo, semplificazione delle forme e contorni di spessore – con altri giovani

Van Gogh – staan symbool voor hun vriendschap en hun artistieke aspiraties. Niettemin was hun idyllische verhouding maar van korte duur. Gauguin verlaat Arles nadat van Gogh in de nacht van 23 december een stuk van zijn oor sneed. Ze hebben dan pas twee maanden met elkaar opgetrokken. Het plan om een leefgemeenschap van kunstenaars te stichten eindigt voordat het is begonnen. Émile Bernard zou Gauguin altijd blijven verwijten dat hij alle eer voor zichzelf opstreek...

Samen met andere jonge schilders die tussen Parijs en Pont-Aven heen en weer

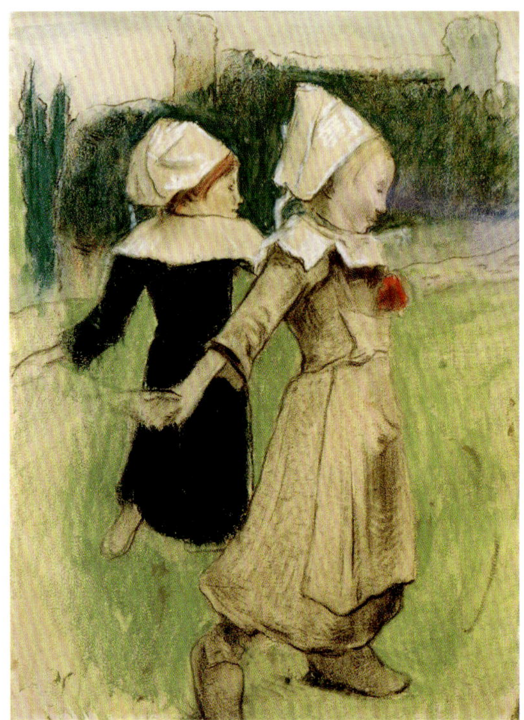

Sketch of *Breton Girls Dancing*

Étude pour *La Ronde des petites Bretonnes*

Studie zu *Tanzende bretonische Mädchen*

Estudio para *el corro de las pequeñas bretonas*

Studio per *la ronda dei piccoli bretoni*

Studie voor *De rondedans van de Bretonse meisjes*

*1888, Pastel and charcoal, watercolor and gouache
on cream-coloured paper/Pastel et fusain, aquarelle
et gouache sur papier crème, 58,4 × 41,9 cm, Pierpont
Morgan Library, New York*

themselves around Paris and Pont-Aven.
Self-proclaimed as "nabis", meaning
"prophets" in Hebrew, the members
of this group, which formed in the
summer of 1888 and whose theorists
were to be Paul Sérusier (1864–1927)
and Maurice Denis (1870–1943), would
be commemorated the next year at an
exposition in the Volpini café in Paris.

épais – avec d'autres jeunes artistes
évoluant entre Paris et Pont-Aven.
Autoproclamés « nabis », signifiant
« prophètes » en hébreu, les membres
de ce groupe, formé durant l'été 1888
dont les théoriciens seront Paul Sérusier
(1864–1927) et Maurice Denis (1870–1943),
se verront consacrés l'année suivante,
lors d'une exposition au café Volpini,
à Paris.

Zusammen mit anderen jungen
Künstlern, die sich zwischen Paris und
Pont-Aven bewegen, erschaffen sie
gemeinsam den Synthetismus – einen Stil
geprägt von ausdrucksstarker Chromatik,
Vereinfachung der Formen und derben
Konturen. Die Mitglieder dieser im
Sommer 1888 gegründeten Gruppe –
unter ihnen als Theoretiker Paul
Sérusier (1864–1927) und Maurice Denis
(1870–1943) – nennen sich selbst „Nabis",
was aus dem Hebräischen kommt und
„Propheten" bedeutet. Im Jahr darauf
erfahren sie Anerkennung bei einer
Ausstellung im Café Volpini in Paris.

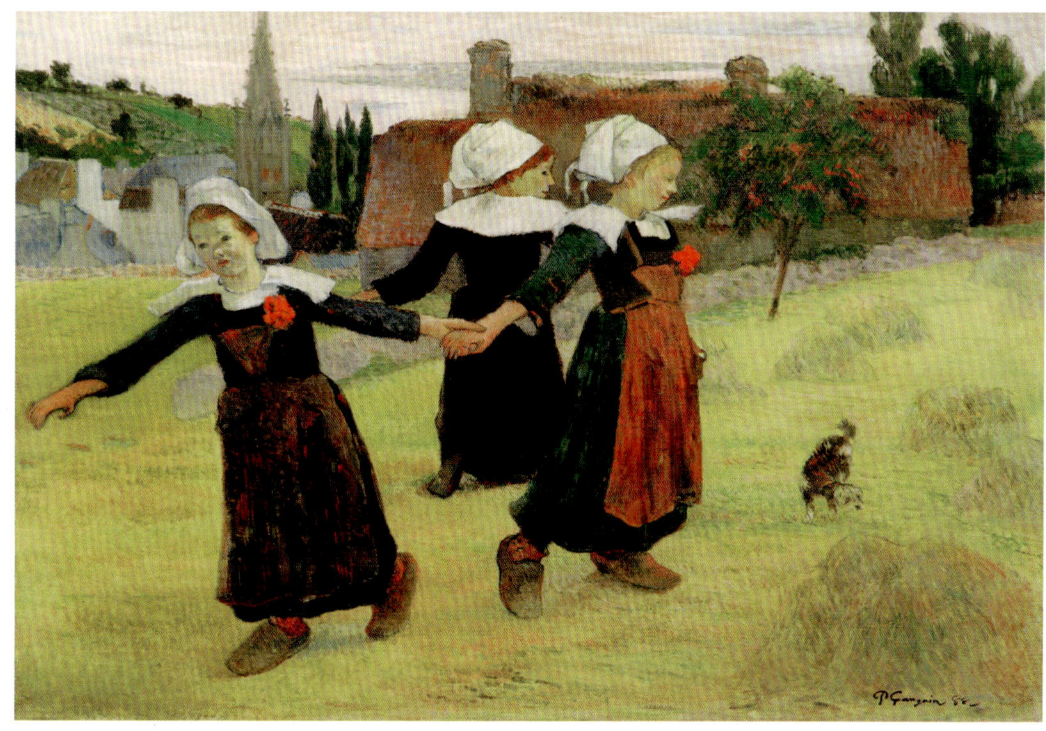

otros jóvenes artistas que trabajan entre París y Pont-Aven. Autoproclamados "nabis", que significa "profetas" en hebreo, los miembros de este grupo, formado durante el verano de 1888 cuyos teóricos fueron Paul Sérusier (1864–1927) y Maurice Denis (1870–1943), se vieron consagrados al año siguiente, durante una exposición en el café Volpini, de París.

artisti che lavorano tra Parigi e Pont-Aven. Autoproclamati "Nabis", che significa "profeti" in ebraico, i membri di questo gruppo, costituito durante l'estate del 1888, e di cui i teorici sono Paul Sérusier (1864–1927) e Maurice Denis (1870–1943), saranno consacrati l'anno successivo, durante una mostra al caffè Volpini di Parigi.

reizen, ontwikkelen ze het synthetisme – een stijl die wordt gekenmerkt door expressief kleurgebruik, vereenvoudigde vormen en donkere contourlijnen. In de zomer van 1888 besluiten de leden zich de Nabis te noemen – naar het Hebreeuwse nabi, 'profeet'. De groep, waarvan Paul Sérusier (1864–1927) en Maurice Denis (1870–1943) de theoretici waren, trad in 1889 in de openbaarheid met een tentoonstelling in Café Volpini, in Parijs.

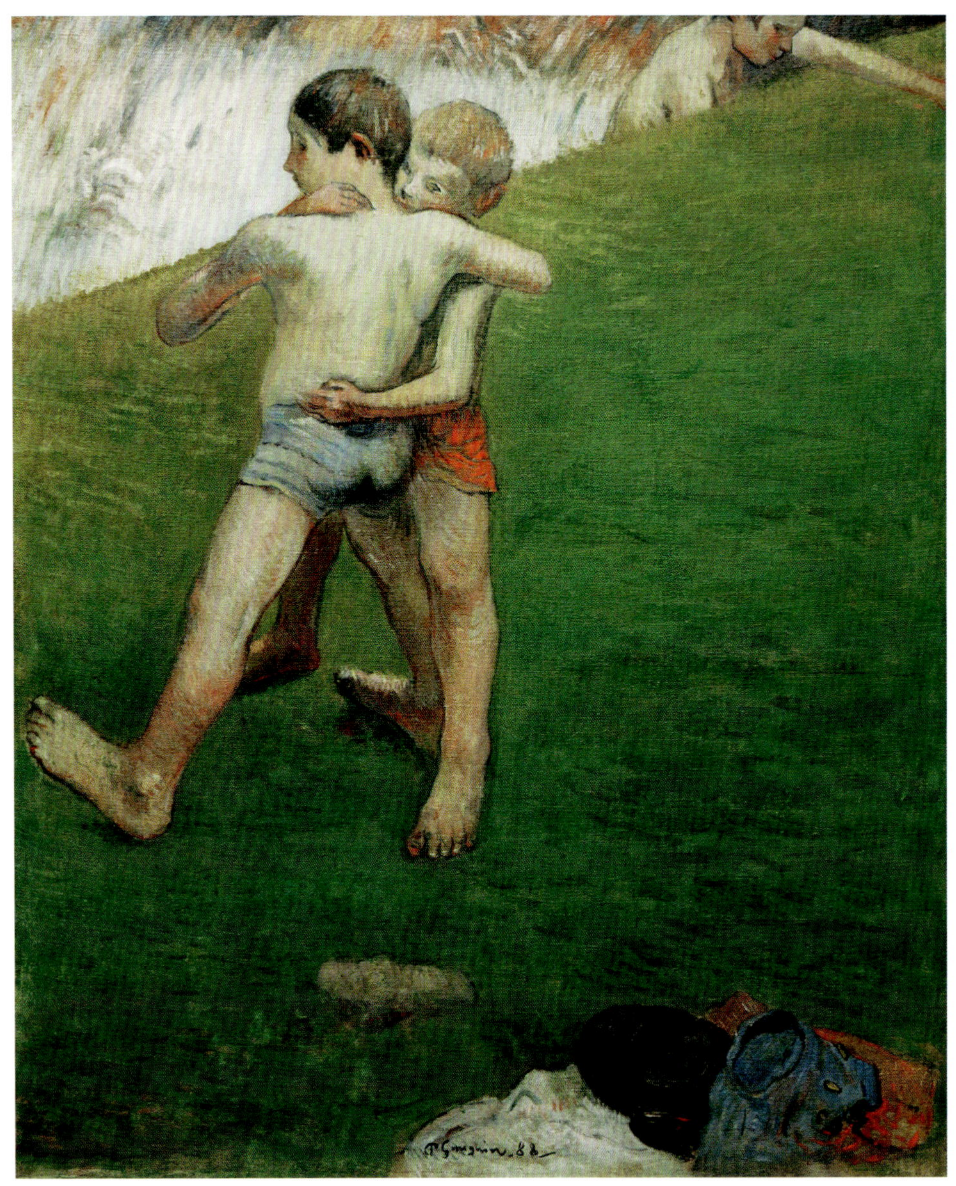

Young Wrestlers
Jeunes lutteurs
Junge Ringkämpfer
Jóvenes luchadores
Giovani lottatori
Jonge vechtersbazen

1888, Oil on canvas/Huile sur toile, 93 × 73 cm, Louvre Abu Dhabi, Abu Dhabi

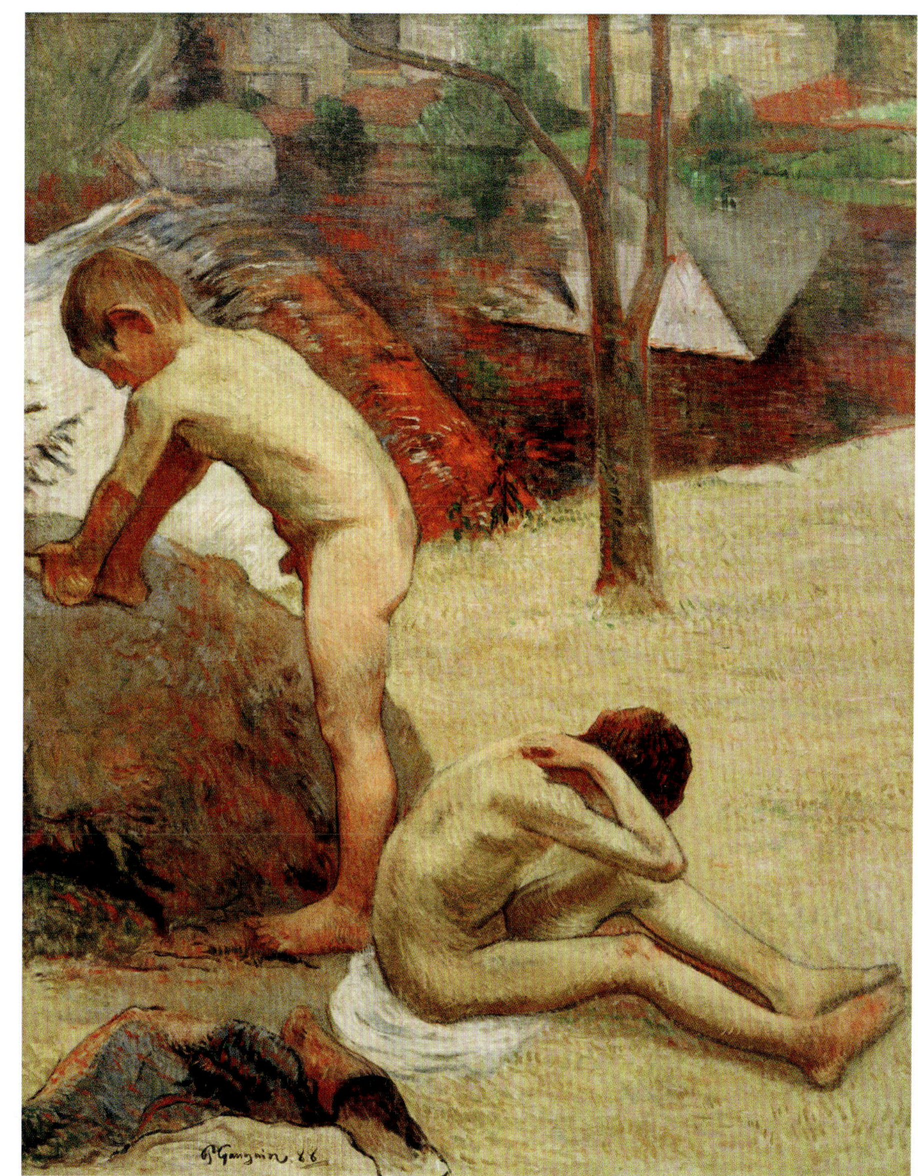

Young Breton Bathers
Jeunes baigneurs bretons
Badende bretonische Knaben
Jóvenes bañistas bretones
Giovani bagnanti bretoni
Jonge Bretonse zwemmers

1888, Oil on canvas/Huile sur toile,
92 × 72 cm, Kunsthalle, Hamburg

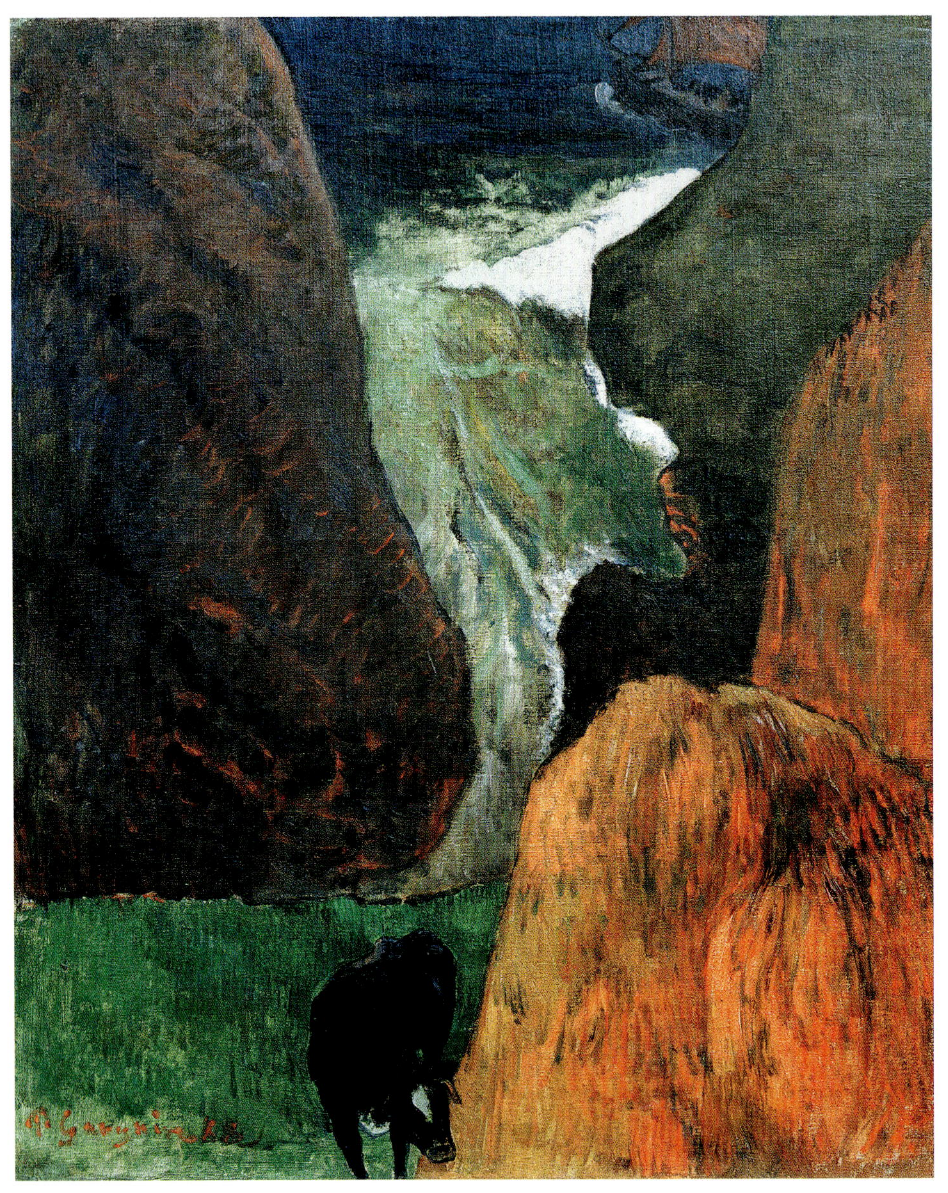

**Seascape with Cow.
On the Edge of a Cliff**

**Marine avec vache.
Au bord du gouffre**

**Landschaft mit Kuh
zwischen Klippen**

**Marina con vaca.
Al borde del abismo**

**Marina con vacche.
Al bordo della voragine**

**Zeegezicht met koe.
Aan de rand van de afgrond**

*1888, Oil on canvas/Huile
sur toile, 72,5 × 61 cm, Musée
d'Orsay, Paris*

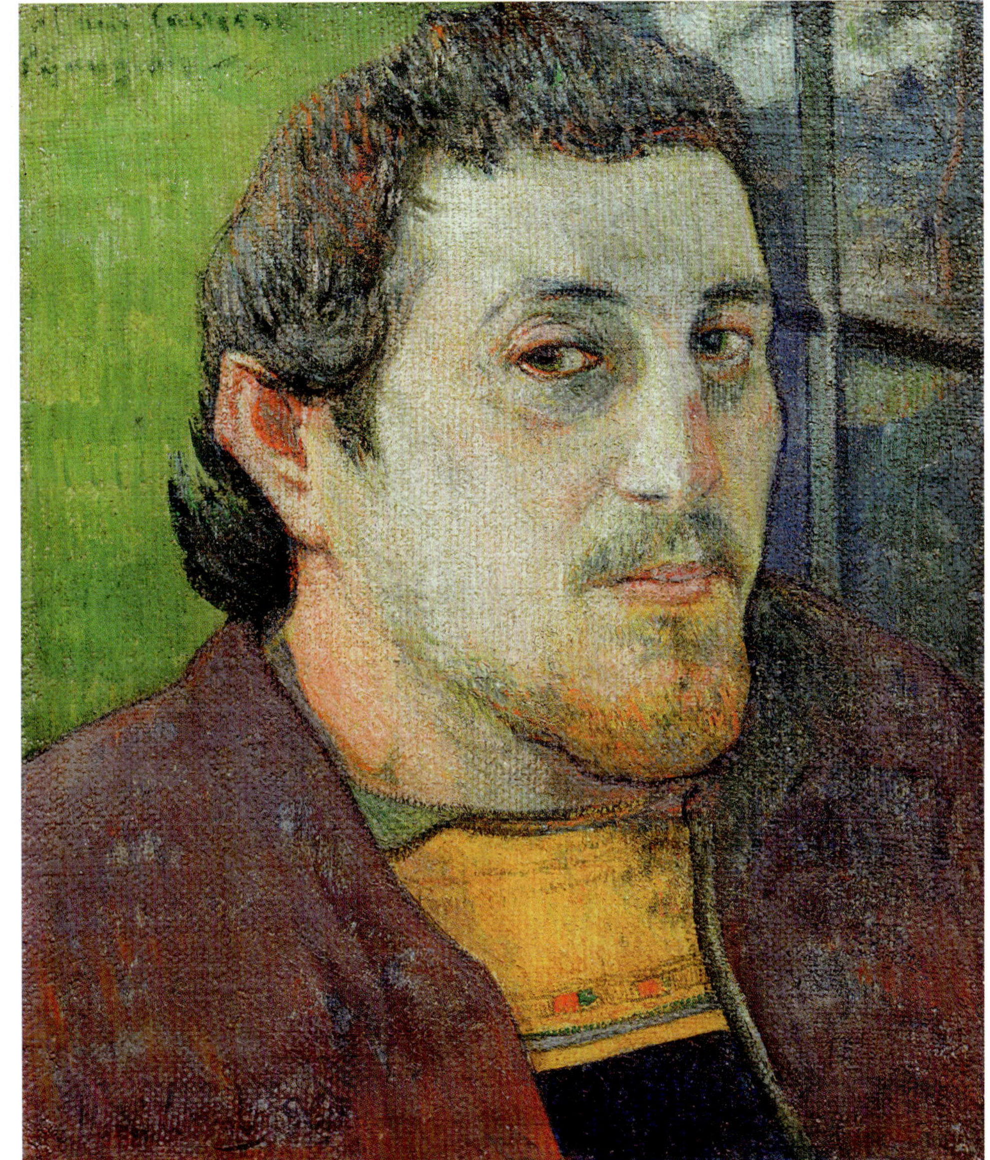

Self Portrait dedicated to Charles Laval (then to Eugène Carrière)

Autoportrait dédicacé à Charles Laval (puis à Eugène Carrière)

Selbstbildnis, Charles Laval gewidmet (später Eugène Carrière)

Autorretrato dedicatoria a Charles Laval (después a Eugène Carrière)

Autoritratto dedicato a Charles Laval (poi ad Eugène Carrière)

Zelfportret opgedragen aan Charles Laval (daarna aan Eugène Carrière)

1888, Oil on jute canvas/ Huile sur toile de jute, 46,5 × 38,6 cm, National Gallery of Art, Washington

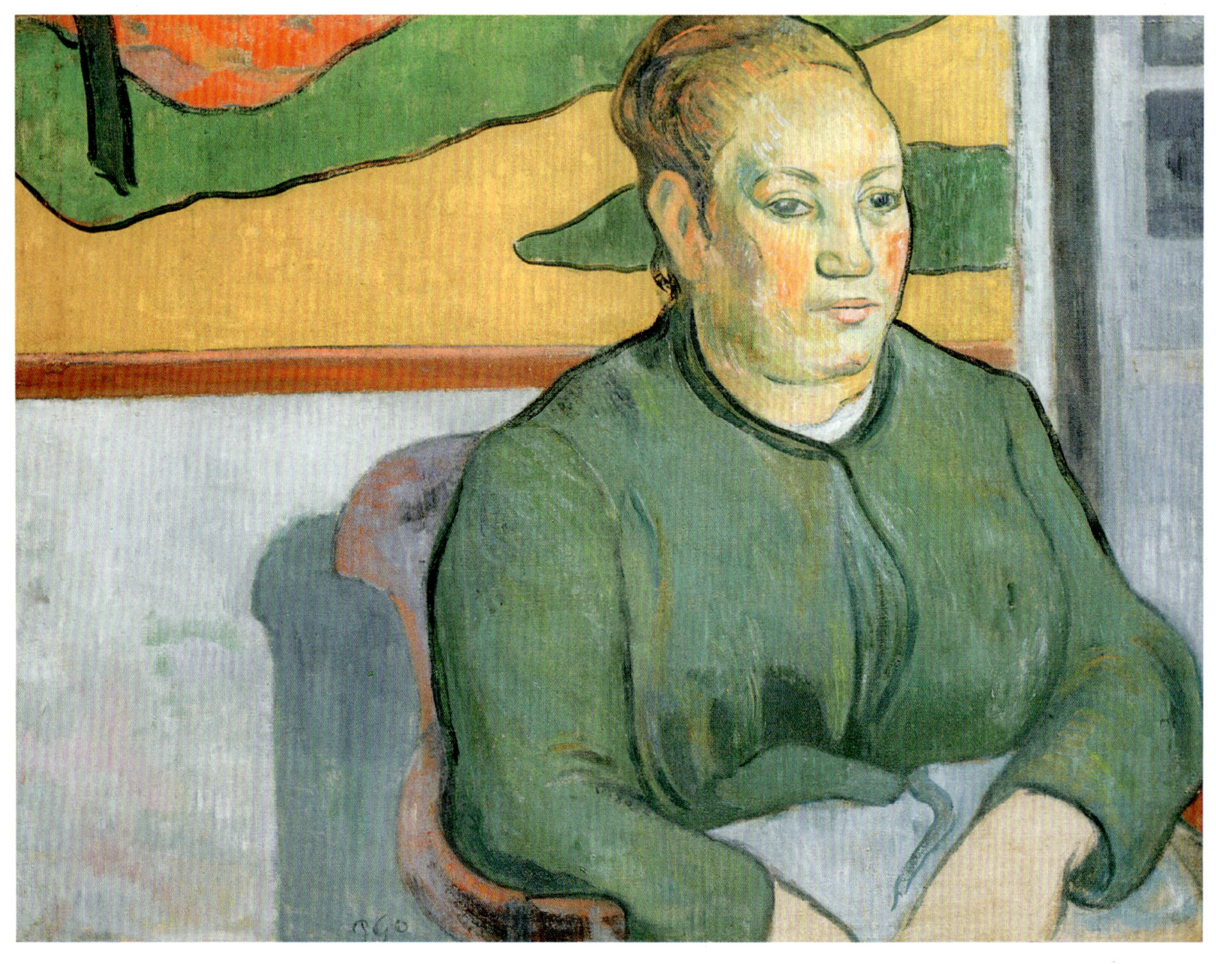

Madame Roulin

1888, Oil on canvas/Huile sur toile, 50,5 × 63,5 cm, Saint Louis Art Museum, Missouri

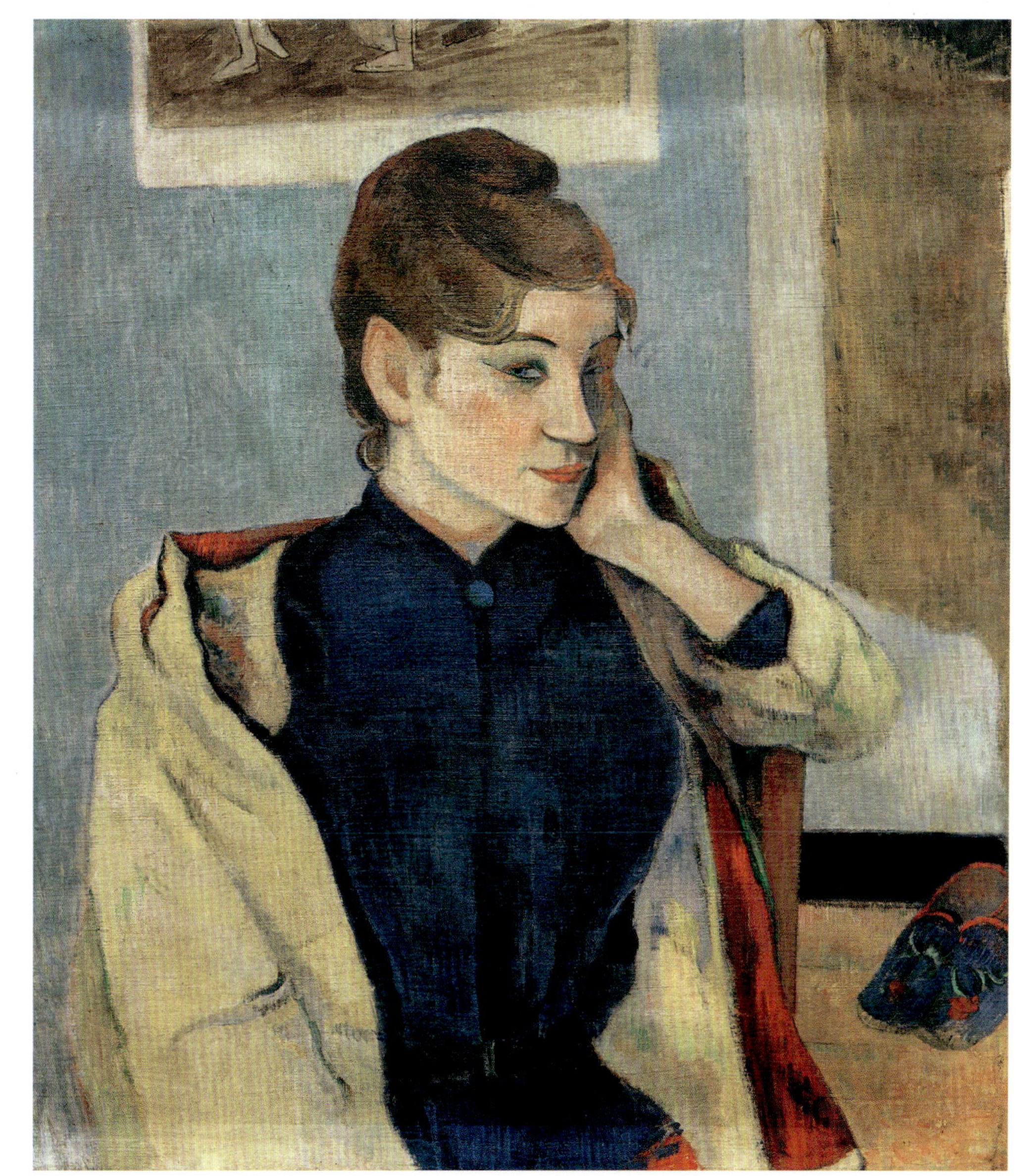

Madeleine Bernard

*1888, Oil on canvas/
Huile sur toile,
72 × 58 cm, Musée de
Grenoble, Grenoble*

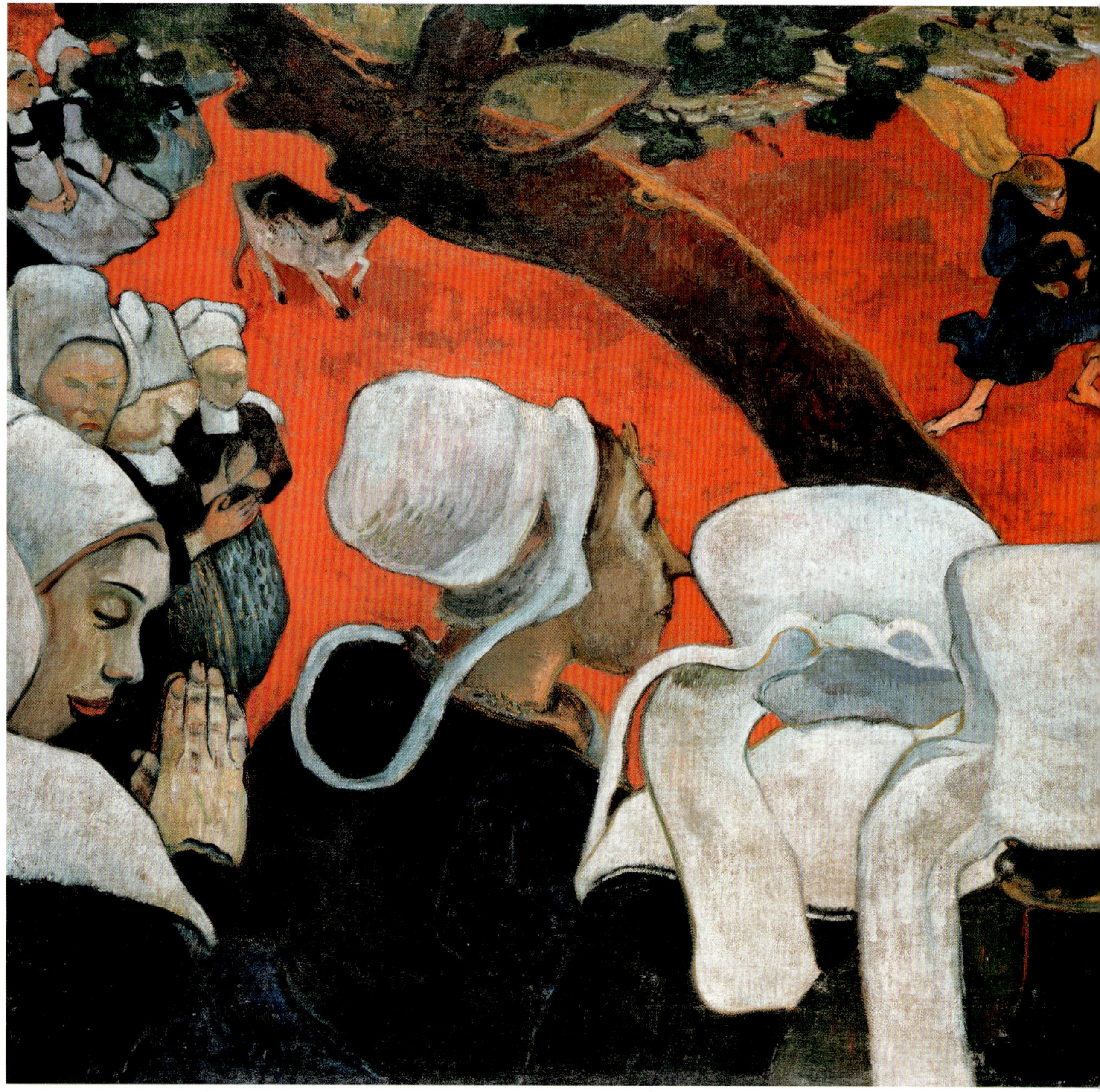

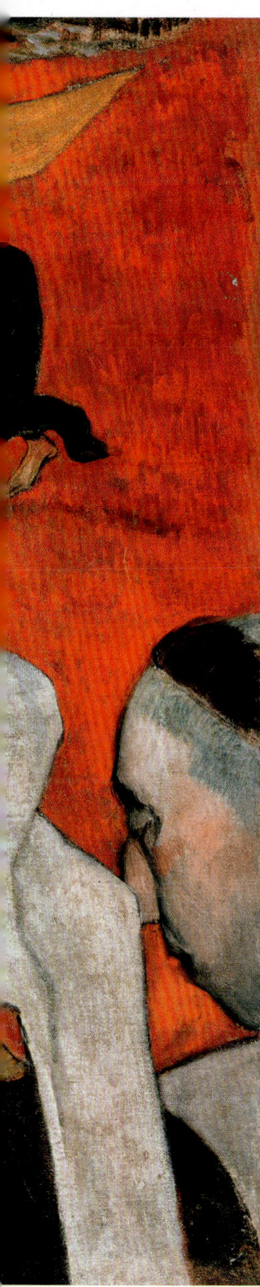

Vision of the Sermon (Jacob Wrestling with the Angel)

La Vision après le sermon (Jacob luttant avec l'ange)

Die Vision nach der Predigt (Der Kampf Jacobs mit dem Engel)

La visión tras el sermón (Jacob luchando con el ángel)

La visione dopo il sermone (Giacobbe lotta con l'angelo)

Het visioen na de preek (Jakob in gevecht met de engel)

1888, Oil on canvas/Huile sur toile, 72 × 91 cm, Scottish National Gallery of Modern Art, Edinburgh

In a letter written to Van Gogh in September 1888, the artist explains this revolutionary canvas, which quickly became an emblem of modern painting: "I believe to have achieved a great rustic and supernatural simplicity in this painting [...] The landscape and the struggle exist only in the imagination of the people praying after the sermon."

Dans une lettre écrite à Vincent Van Gogh en septembre 1888, l'artiste explique cette toile révolutionnaire, vite devenue un emblème de la peinture moderne : « Je crois avoir atteint dans les figures une grande simplicité rustique et superstitieuse dans ce tableau [...] Le paysage et la lutte n'existe que dans l'imagination des gens en prière par suite du sermon. »

In einem Brief, den er im September 1888 an Vincent van Gogh schreibt, erklärt der Künstler dieses revolutionäre Gemälde, das schnell zu einem Emblem der modernen Kunst geworden ist: „Ich glaube, ich habe in diesem Gemälde den Gestalten eine sehr rustikale und abergläubische Einfachheit gegeben [...] Landschaft und Kampf existieren nur in der Phantasie der Menschen im Gebet nach der Predigt."

En una carta escrita a Vincent van Gogh en septiembre de 1888, el artista explicó este lienzo revolucionario, que rápidamente se convirtió en un símbolo de la pintura moderna: "Creo haber alcanzado en los rostros una gran simplicidad rústica y supersticiosa en este cuadro [...] El paisaje y la lucha no existen más que en la imaginación de las personas que siguen el sermón."

In una lettera a Vincent van Gogh scritta nel mese di settembre 1888, l'artista spiega questo tessuto rivoluzionario, diventato rapidamente un emblema della pittura moderna: "Credo di aver raggiunto nelle figure una grande semplicità rustica e superstiziosa in questa tavolozza [...] Il paesaggio e la lotta non esistono che nella fantasia di persone in preghiera a seguito del sermone."

In een brief aan Vincent van Gogh in september 1888 geeft de kunstenaar uitleg bij dit revolutionaire doek dat al snel het symbool van de moderne schilderkunst wordt: "Ik denk dat ik op dit schilderij in de figuren een hoge mate van rustieke en bijgelovige eenvoud heb bereikt [...] Het landschap en het gevecht bestaan alleen in de verbeelding van de gelovigen die bidden na de preek."

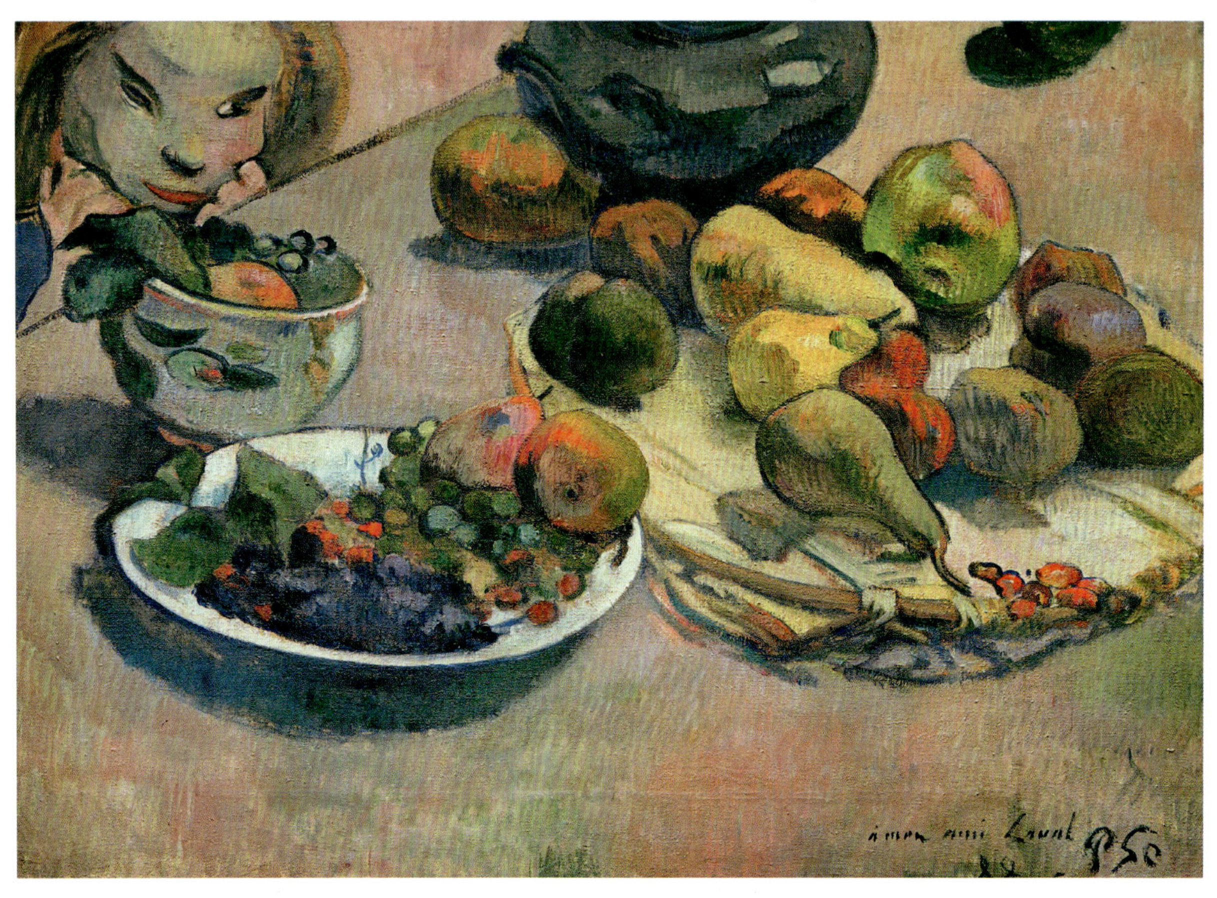

Still Life with Fruits

Nature morte aux fruits

Stillleben mit Früchten

Naturaleza muerta, frutas

Natura morta di frutta

Stilleven met vruchten

1888, Oil on canvas/Huile sur toile, 43 × 58 cm, Pushkin Museum, Moscow

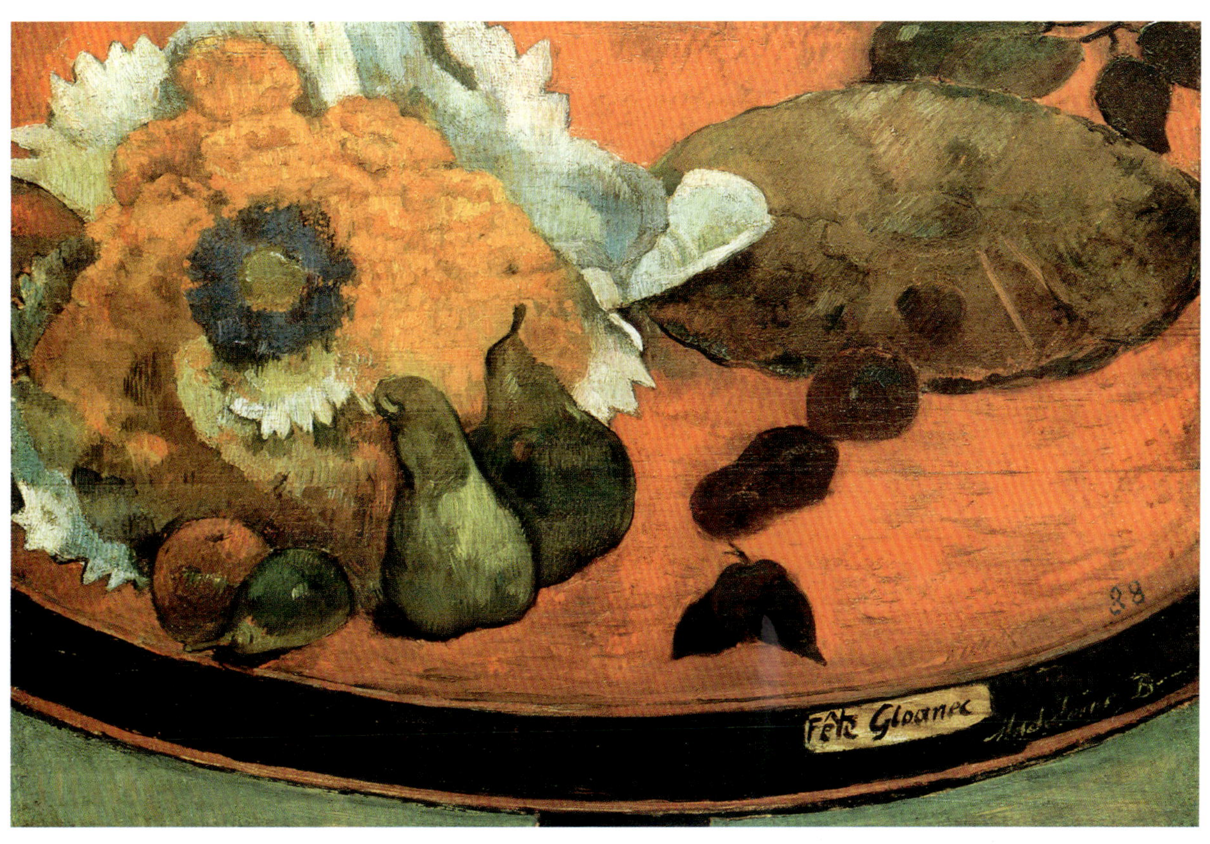

Still-Life, Fête Gloanec

Nature morte, fête Gloanec

Stillleben Fête Gloanec

Naturaleza muerta, fiesta Gloanec

Natura morta, festa di Gloanec

Stilleven, Fête Glouanec

1888, Oil on wood/Huile sur bois, 38 × 53 cm, Musée des Beaux-Arts, Orléans

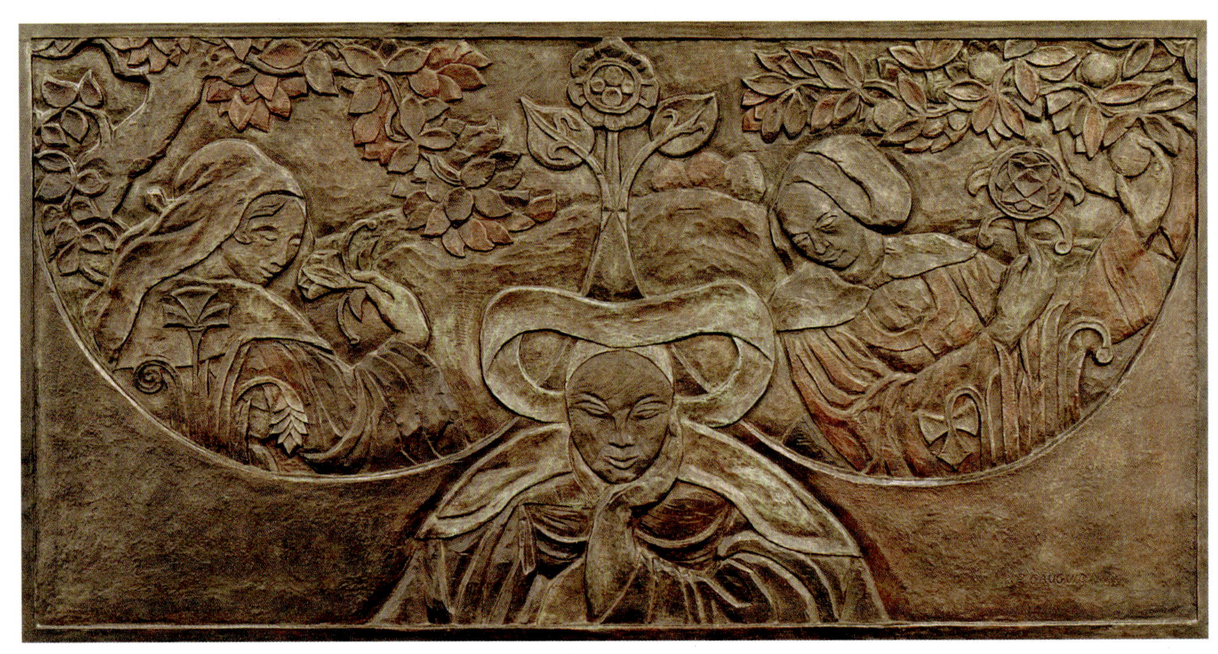

The Three Breton Girls

Les Trois Bretonnes

Drei Bretoninnen

Las tres bretonas

Le tre bretoni

Drie Bretonse vrouwen

1888, Bronze relief/Relief en bronze, 73 × 133 cm, Musée du Petit Palais, Genève

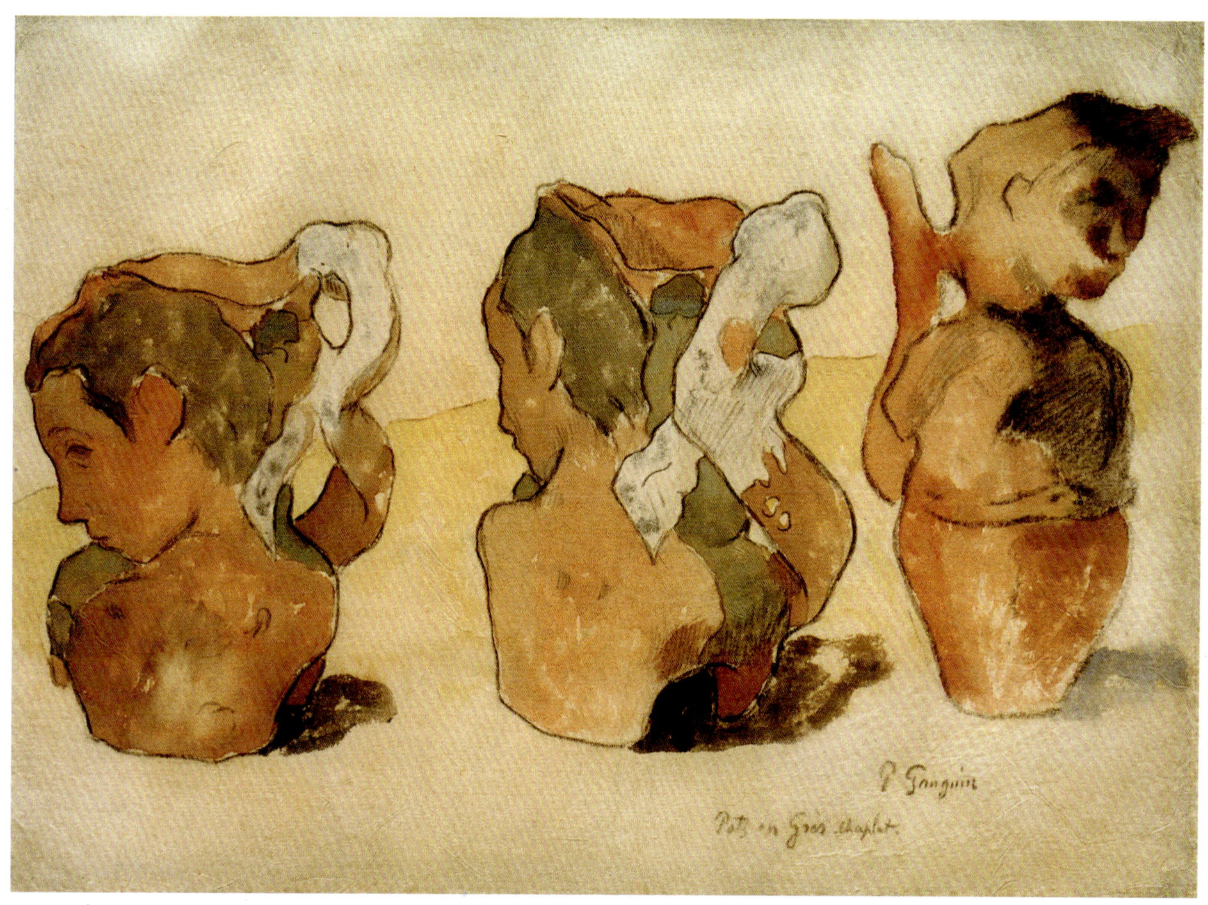

Three Stoneware Pots

Trois pots en grès

Drei Steinkrüge

Macetas de arenisca

Tre pentole in arenaria

Drie potten van gres

c. 1888, Gouache, watercolor and charcoal on Japanese paper/Gouache, aquarelle et fusain sur papier japonais,
30,4 × 40 cm, The Frances Lehman Loeb Art Center, Poughkeepsie, New York

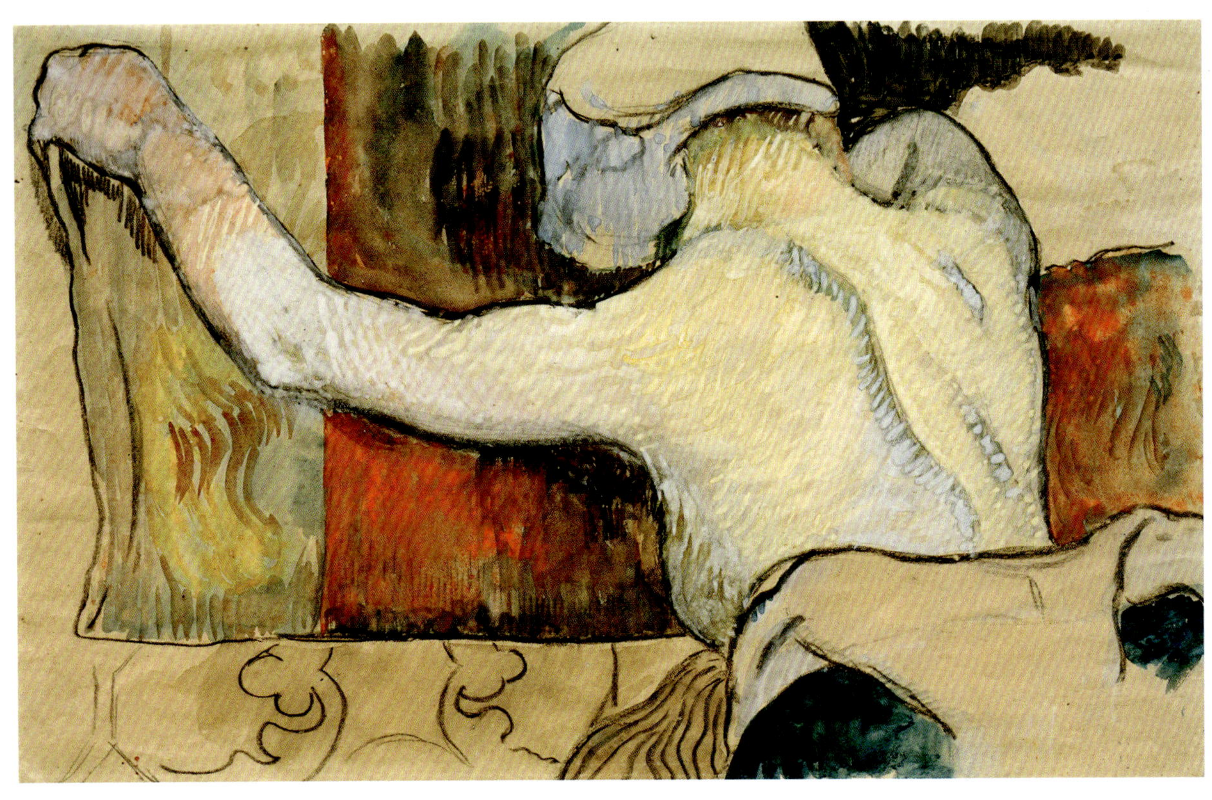

Woman in the Hay with Pigs: In the Full Heat of the Day

Étude pour *Dans le foin* ou *La Femme aux cochons, en pleine chaleur*

Studie zu *Im Heu* oder *Frau mit Schweinen in Mittagshitze*

Estudio para *En el heno* o *La mujer de los cerdos, en una tarde calurosa*

Studio per *Dentro il fieno* o *La donna dei maiali in pieno calore*

Studie voor *In het hooi* of *De vrouw met de varkens, in de hitte*

1888, Aquarelle/Aquarelle, 26 × 40 cm, Van Gogh Museum, Amsterdam

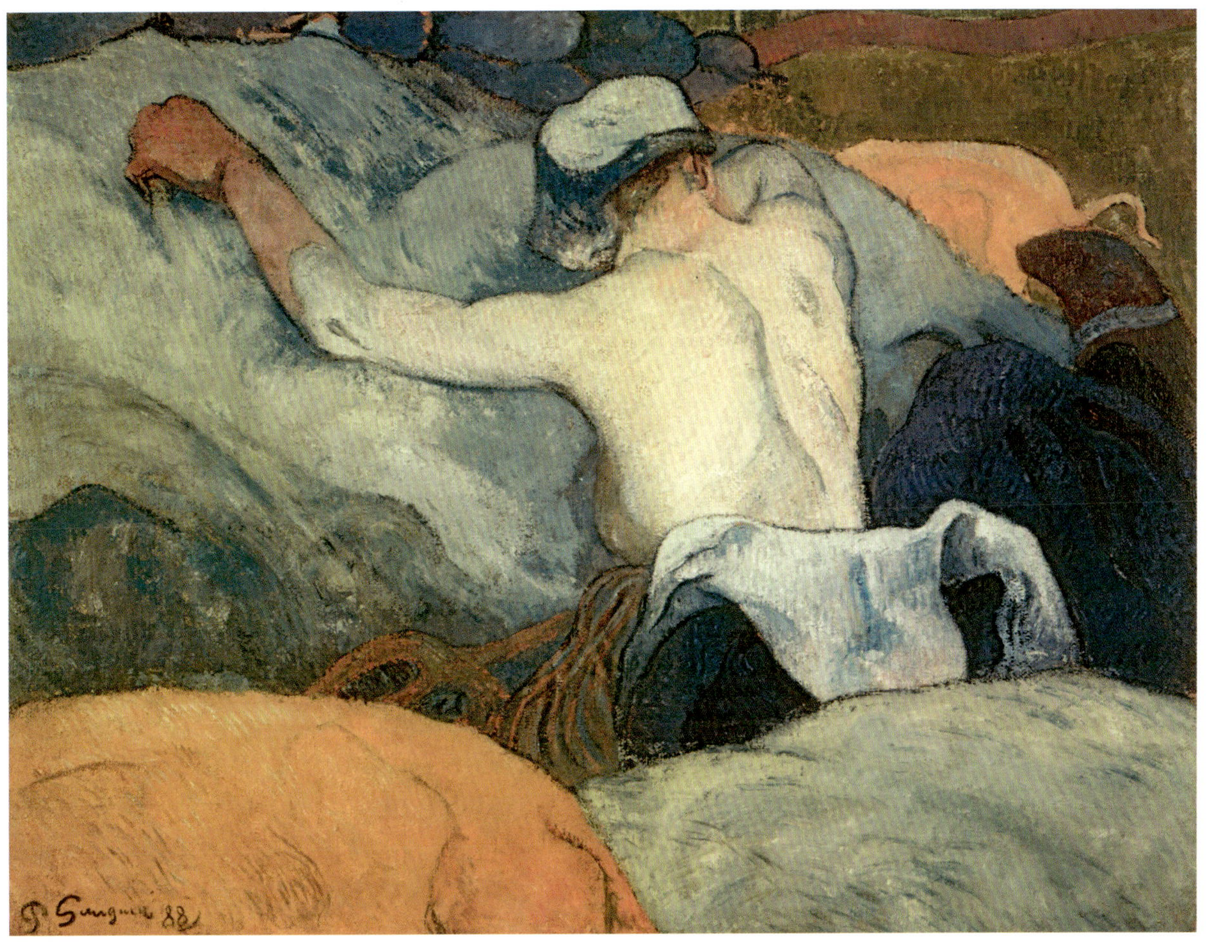

Woman in the Hay with Pigs: In the Full Heat of the Day

Dans le foin ou *La Femme aux cochons, en pleine chaleur*

Im Heu oder *Frau mit Schweinen in Mittagshitze*

En el heno o *La mujer de los cerdos, en una tarde calurosa*

Dentro il fieno o *La donna dei maiali in pieno calore*

In het hooi of *De vrouw met de varkens, in de hitte*

1888, Oil on Canvas/Huile sur toile, 73 x 92 cm, Private collection

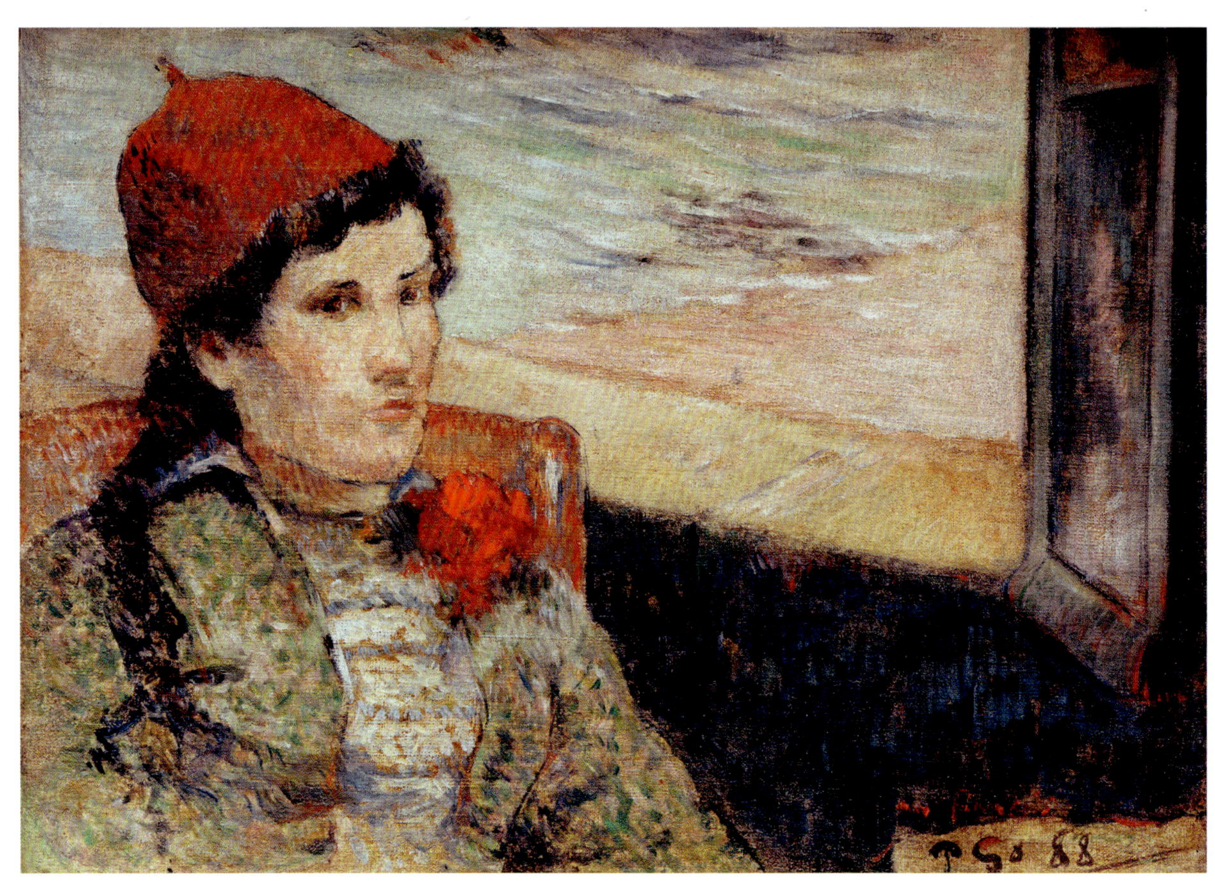

Girl in Front of Open Window or La Fiancee
Femme devant une fenêtre ouverte, dite *La Fiancée*
Frau vor einem geöffneten Fenster, genannt *Die Verlobte*
Mujer delante de una ventana abierta, llamada *La novia*
Donna davanti una finestra aperta, detta *La Fidanzata*
Vrouw voor het open raam, oftewel *De verloofde*

1888, Oil on canvas/Huile sur toile, 33,8 × 41 cm, Private collection

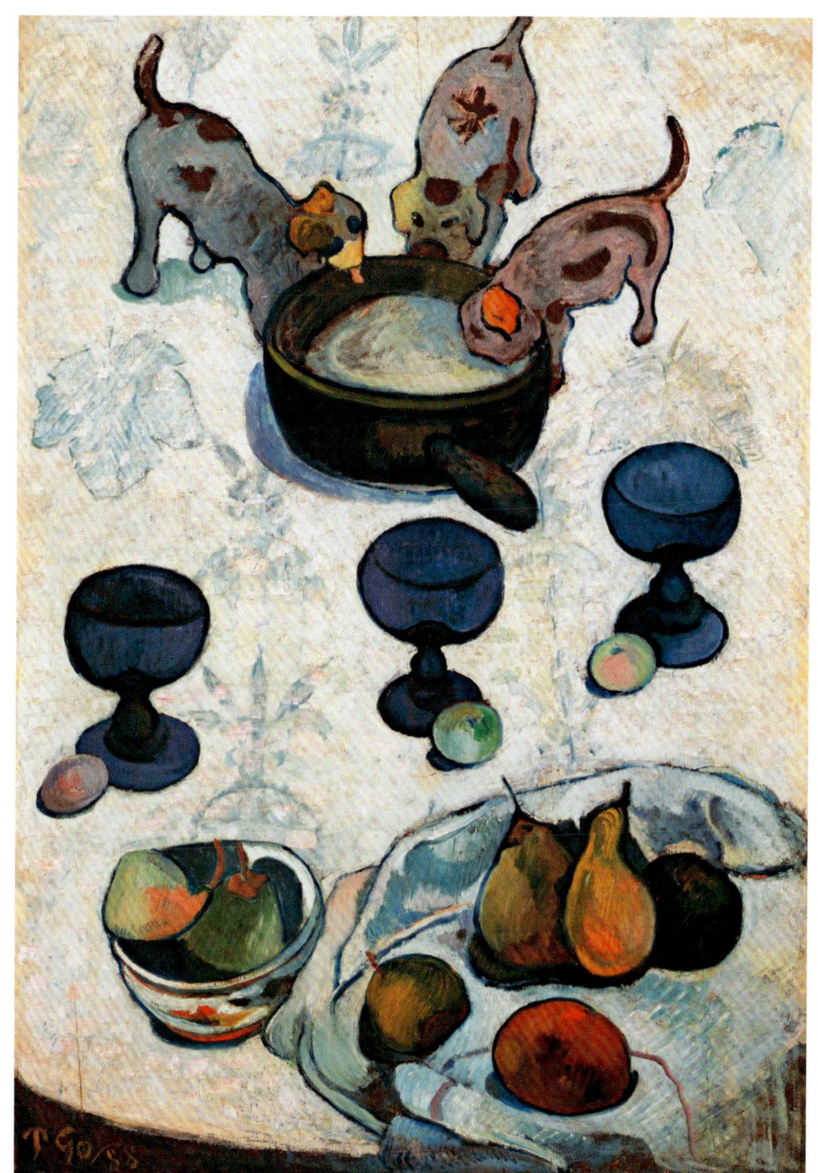

Still Life with Three Puppies
Nature morte aux trois petits chiens
Stillleben mit drei kleinen Hunden
Naturaleza muerta con tres perros pequeños
Natura morta con tre piccoli cani
Stilleven met drie hondjes
1888, Oil on wood/Huile sur bois, 91,8 × 62,6 cm,
Museum of Modern Art, New York

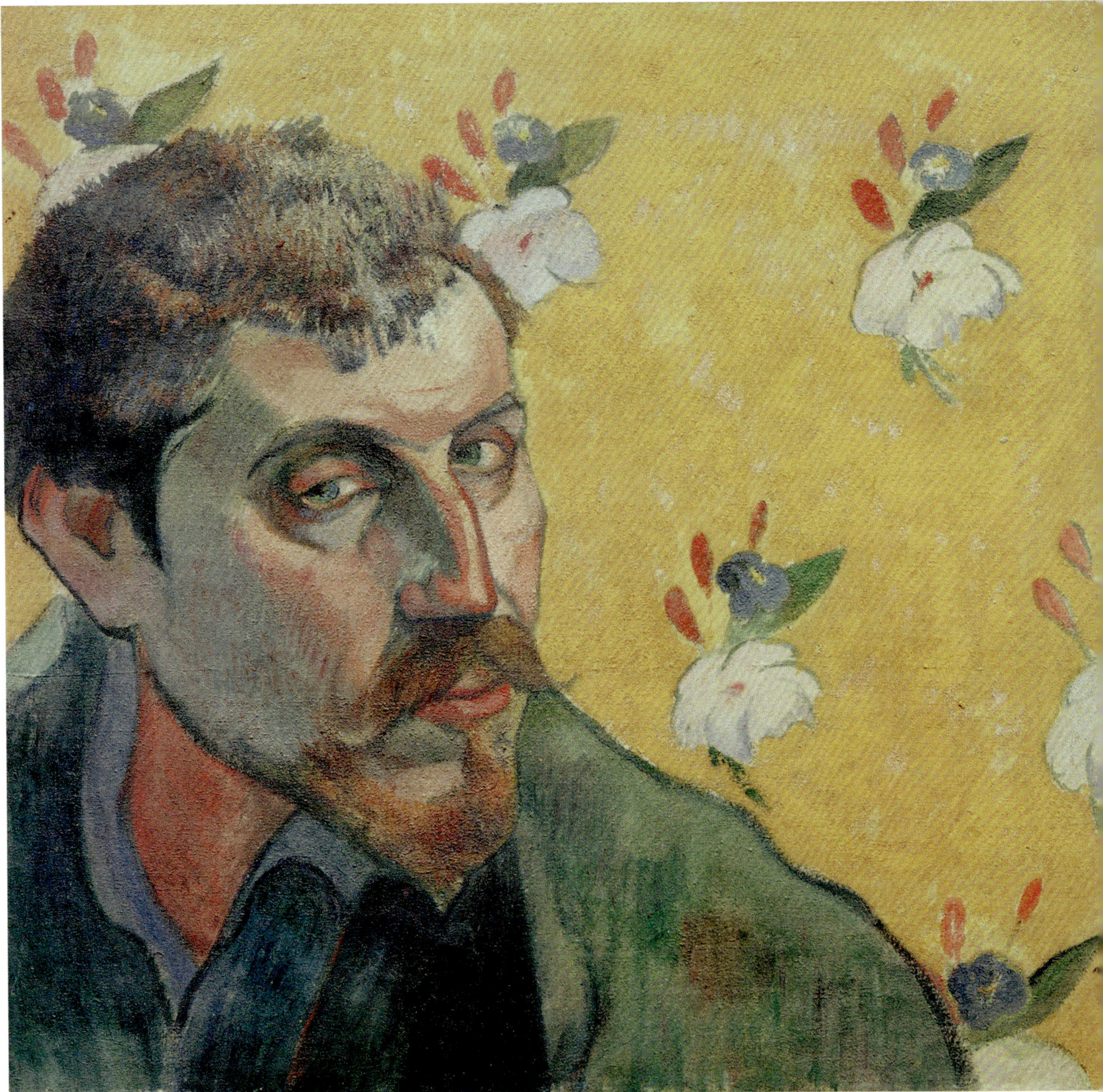

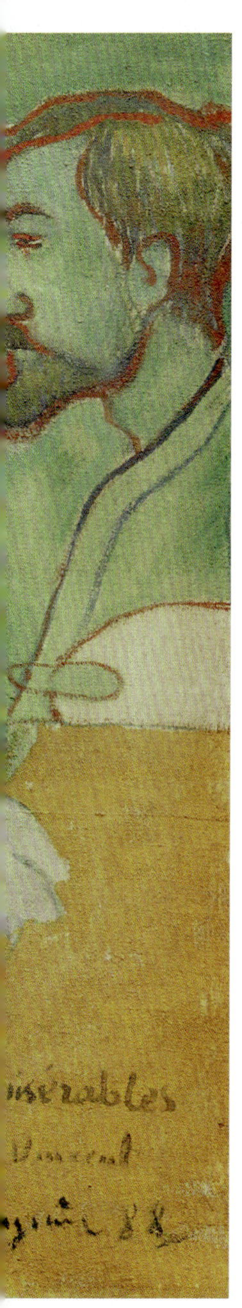

Self Portrait *Les Misérables*, Dedicated to Vincent van Gogh, with the Portrait of Émile Bernard

Autoportrait *Les Misérables*, dédié à Vincent Van Gogh, avec le portrait d'Émile Bernard

Selbstbildnis *Les Misérables*, Vincent van Gogh gewidmet, mit dem Porträt Bernards

Autorretrato *Los miserables*, dedicado a Vincent van Gogh, con el retrato de Émile Bernard

Autoritratto *I miserabili*, dedicato a Vincent van Gogh, con ritratto di Emile Bernanrd

Zelfportret *Les Misérables*, opgedragen aan Vincent van Gogh, met het portret van Émile Bernard

1888, Oil on canvas/Huile sur toile, 44,5 × 50,3 cm, Van Gogh Museum, Amsterdam

On the 8th of October 1888, Gauguin commented to the painter Émile Schuffenecker on this self-portrait made for Vincent van Gogh: "One of my best things; absolutely incomprehensible - such is its degree abstraction. The bandit's head at first [...] the eyes the mouth the nose are like Persian carpet flowers, also personifying the symbolic side."

Le 8 octobre 1888, Gauguin commente au peintre Émile Schuffenecker cet autoportrait fait pour Vincent van Gogh : « Une de mes meilleures choses ; absolument incompréhensible tellement il est abstrait. Tête de bandit au premier abord [...] les yeux la bouche le nez sont comme des fleurs de tapis persans personnifiant aussi le côté symbolique. »

Am 8. Oktober 1888 erläutert Gauguin dieses Selbstbildnis, das er für Vincent van Gogh geschaffen hat, dem Maler Émile Schuffenecker folgendermaßen: „Eines meiner besten Sachen; absolut unverständlich, so abstrakt wie ist es ist. Zuerst der Kopf des Banditen [...] die Augen, der Mund und die Nase sind wie Blumen auf einem persischen Teppich, sie personifizieren auch die symbolische Seite."

El 8 de octubre de 1888, Gauguin comentó al pintor Émile Schuffenecker sobre este autorretrato realizado por Vincent van Gogh: "Una de mis mejores cosas, absolutamente incomprensible por lo abstracto que es. Cabeza de bandido a primera vista [...] los ojos, la boca, la nariz son como flores de alfombras persas que personifican también la parte simbólica."

L'8 ottobre 1888, Gauguin commenta al pittore Émile Schuffeneckers questo autoritratto fatto per Vincent van Gogh: "Una delle mie migliori cose; assolutamente incomprensibile, tanto è astratto. Testa di bandito a primo acchito [...] gli occhi, il naso, la bocca sono come fiori di tappeti persiani che personificano anche il lato simbolico."

Op 8 oktober 1888 geeft Gauguin de schilder Émile Schuffenecker een toelichting bij dit zelfportret dat hij maakte voor Vincent van Gogh: "Een van mijn beste dingen; absoluut onbegrijpelijk, zo abstract is het. Op het eerste gezicht een schurkenkop [...] de ogen de mond de neus zijn als bloemen op een Perzisch tapijt en belichamen ook de symbolische kant."

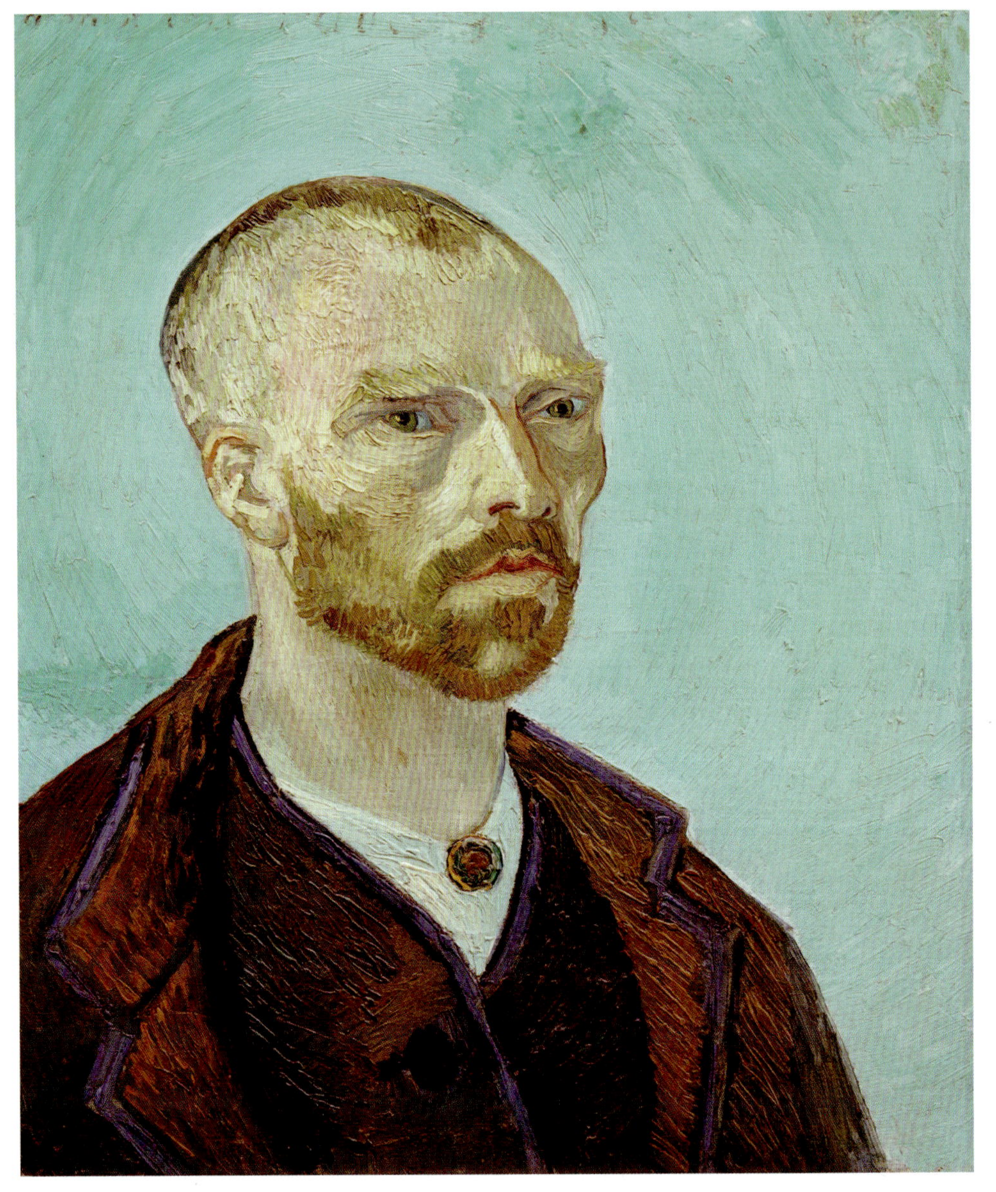

Vincent van Gogh (1853–1890)

Self Portrait dedicated to Paul Gauguin

Autoportrait dédicacé à Paul Gauguin

Selbstbildnis, Paul Gauguin gewidmet

Autorretrato dedicatoria a Paul Gauguin

Autoritratto dedicato a Paul Gauguin

Zelfportret opgedragen aan Paul Gauguin

1888, Oil on canvas/Huile sur toile, 61,5 × 50,3 cm, Fogg Art Museum, Cambridge

"The head is modelled in light-coloured thick impasto against a light-coloured background with almost no shadows. But I've slightly slanted the eyes in the Japanese manner", thus did Vincent van Gogh, in September 1888, describe to his brother Théo his self-portrait dedicated to Gauguin, which he had not yet sent to him.

« La tête est modelée en pleine pâte claire contre le fond clair sans ombres presque. Seulement j'ai obliqué un peu les yeux à la japonaise. », ainsi Vincent Van Gogh décrit-il à son frère Théo, en septembre 1888, son autoportrait dédicacé à Gauguin, qu'il ne lui a pas encore envoyé.

„Der Kopf ist ausschließlich mit dick aufgetragener heller Paste gegen den hellen Hintergrund modelliert, nahezu ohne Schatten. Nur die Augen habe ich ein wenig – auf die japanische Art – schräg gemalt", so beschreibt Vincent van Gogh seinem Bruder Théo im September 1888 das Gauguin gewidmete Selbstbildnis, das er ihm noch nicht geschickt hat.

"La cabeza está modelada en plena pasta clara contra el fondo claro casi sin sombras. Solo he pintado un poco en oblicuo los ojos, al estilo japonés", de este modo Vincent van Gogh describió a su hermano Théo, en septiembre de 1888, su autorretrato dedicatoria a Gauguin, que aún no le había enviado.

"La testa è modellata in tutto il corpo bianco contro lo sfondo luminoso, quasi senza ombre. Ho soltanto messo gli occhi in obliquo un po' alla giapponese". Vincent van Gogh descrive al fratello Theo nel Settembre 1888 il suo autoritratto dedicato a Gauguin, che ancora non gli ha inviato.

"Het hoofd is gemodelleerd in dikke heldere verflagen tegen de heldere achtergrond, bijna zonder schaduwen. Maar de ogen heb ik op z'n Japans een beetje scheef laten toelopen", schrijft Vincent zijn broer Theo in september 1888 over dit zelfportret dat hij opdroeg aan Gauguin, maar dat hij hem toen nog niet had gestuurd.

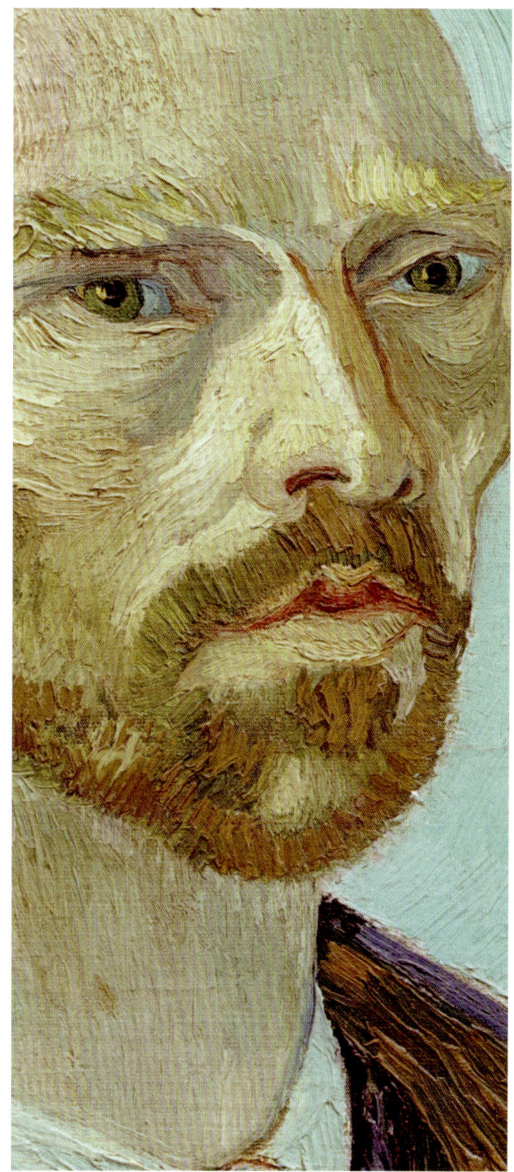

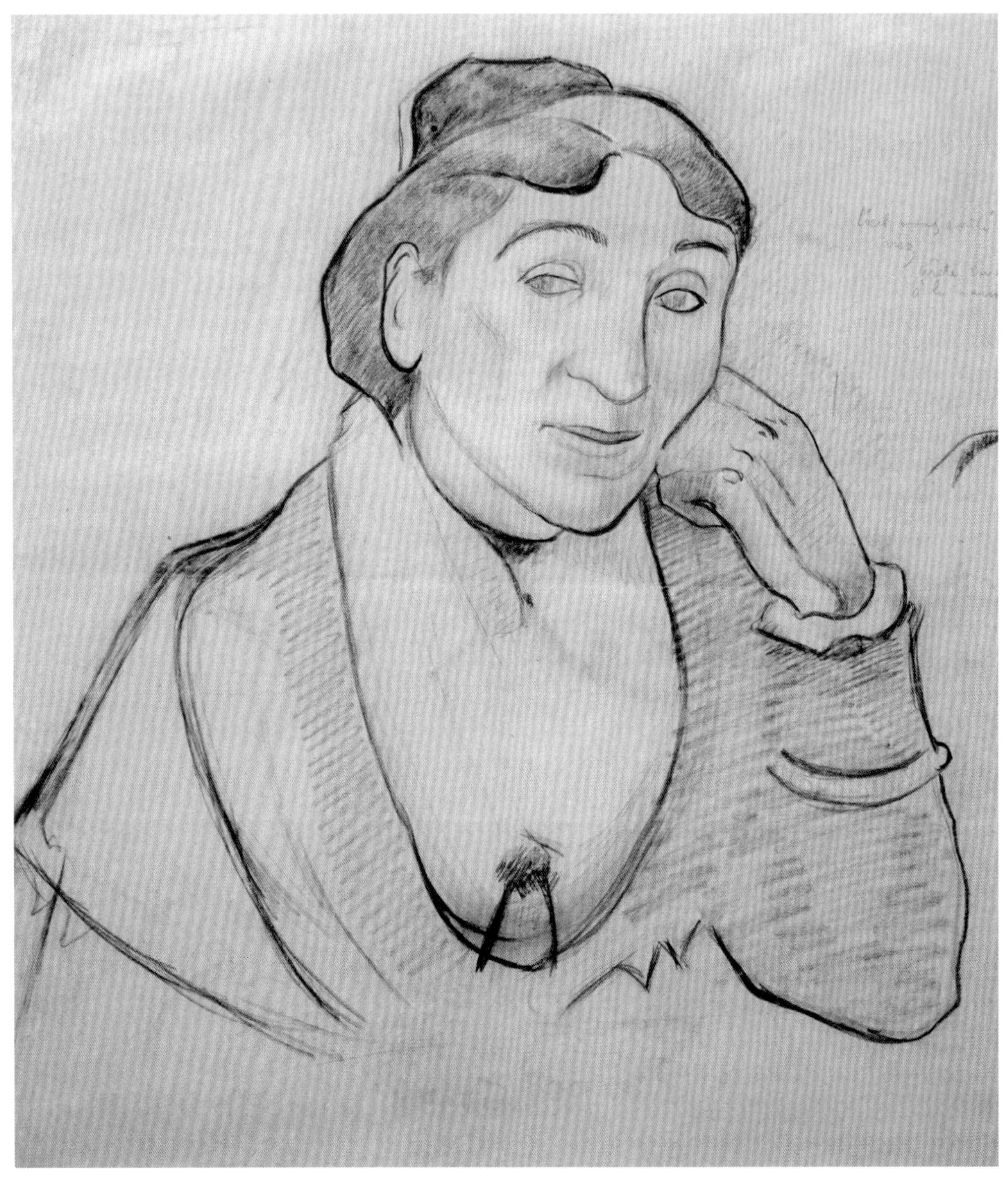

The Woman from Arles, Madame Ginoux

L'Arlésienne, Madame Ginoux

L'Arlésienne, Madame Ginoux

La arlesiana, señora Ginoux

L'Arlesiana, Madame Ginoux

L'Arlésienne, de vrouw uit Arles, Madame Ginoux

1888, Charcoal and chalk on paper/Fusain et craie sur papier, 56,1 × 49,2 cm, Fine Arts Museum, San Francisco

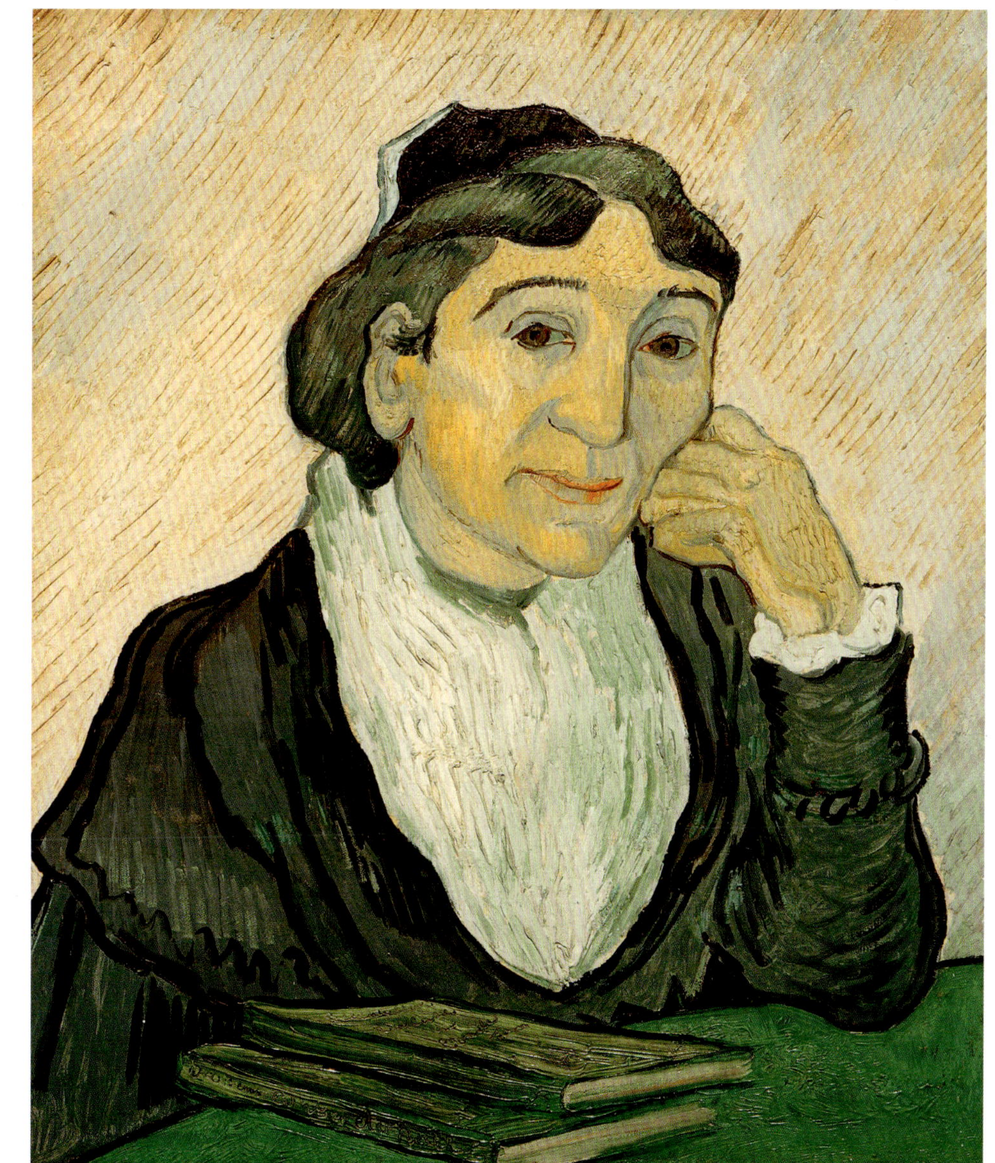

Vincent van Gogh

The Woman from Arles after Paul Gauguin

L'Arlésienne d'après Paul Gauguin

L'Arlésienne nach Paul Gauguin

La arlesiana según Paul Gauguin

L'Arlesiana secondo Paul Gaugin

De vrouw uit Arles, naar Paul Gauguin

1890, Oil on canvas/Huile sur toile, 60 × 50 cm, Galleria Nazionale d'Arte Moderna, Roma

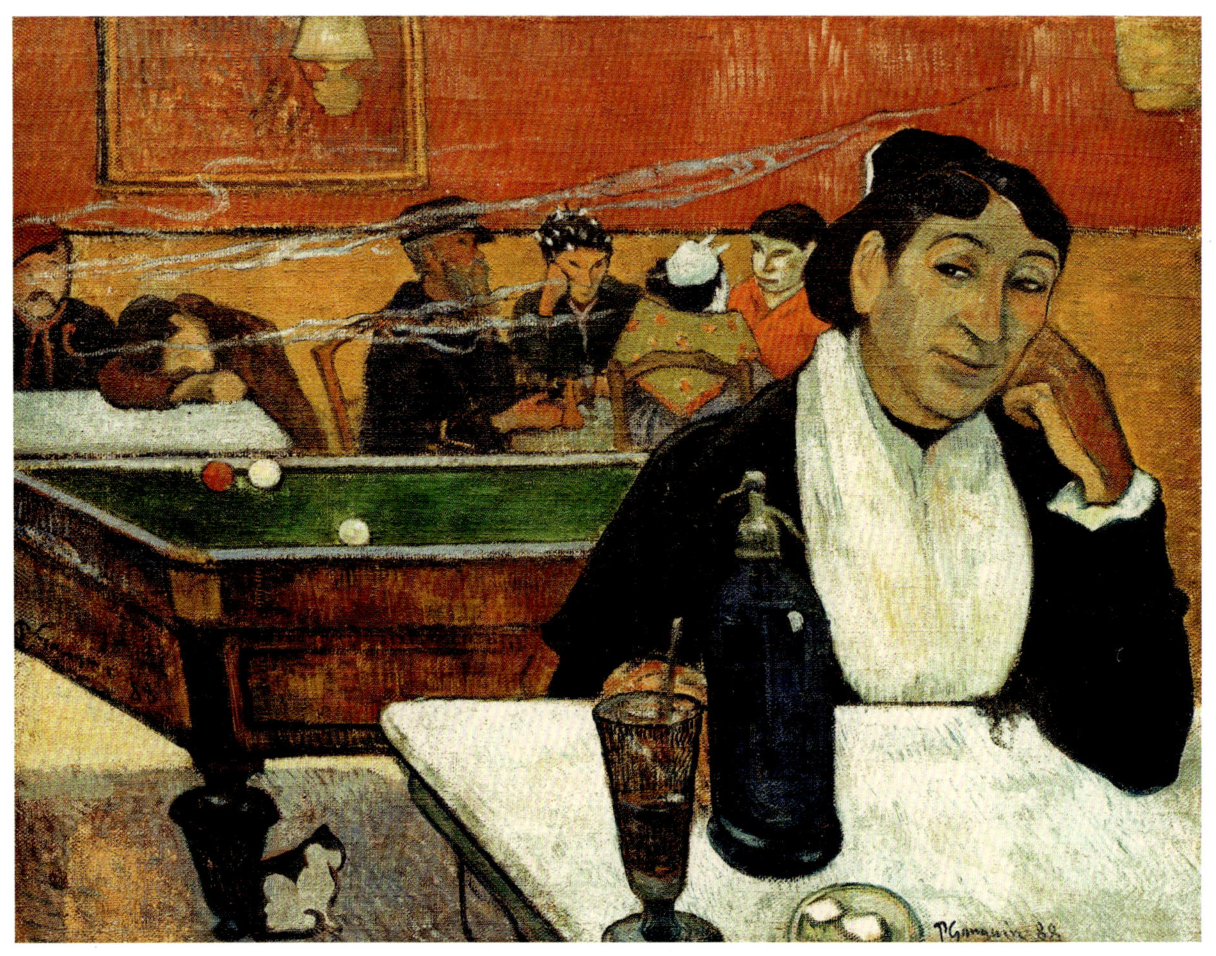

At the Café (Madame Ginoux)

Au café (Madame Ginoux)

Im Café (Madame Ginoux)

En el café (Señora Ginoux)

Al caffe' (Madame Ginoux)

In het café (Madame Ginoux)

1888, Oil on canvas/Huile sur toile, 72 × 92 cm, Pushkin Museum, Moscow

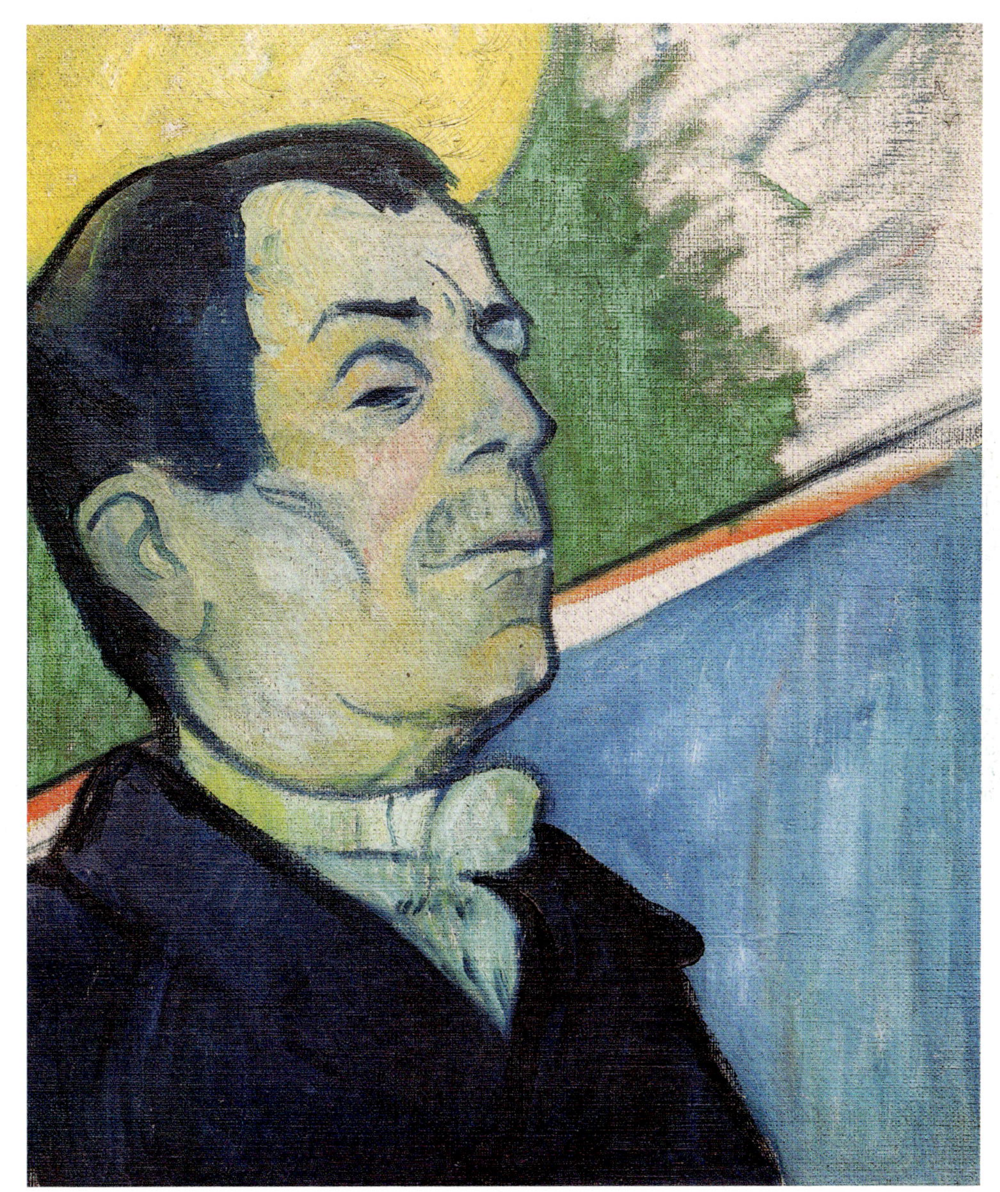

Monsieur Ginoux

1888, Oil on canvas/Huile
sur toile, 40,5 × 32 cm,
Van Gogh Museum,
Amsterdam

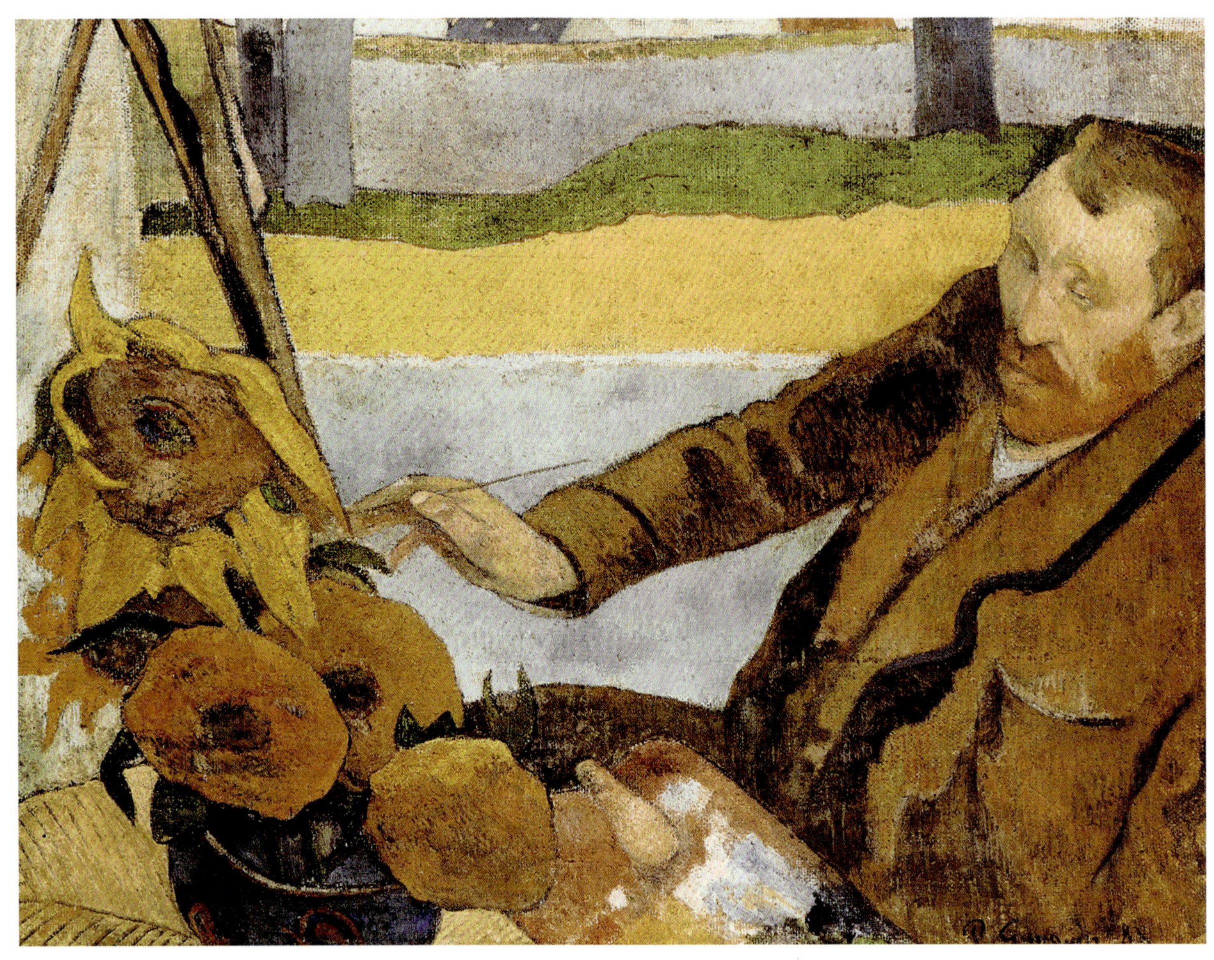

Vincent van Gogh Painting Sunflowers
Vincent Van Gogh peignant Les Tournesols
Vincent van Gogh, Sonnenblumen **malend**
Vincent van Gogh pintando Los girasoles
Vincent van Gogh che dipinge i Girasoli
Vincent van Gogh schildert De zonnebloemen

1888, Oil on canvas/Huile sur toile, 73 × 91 cm, Van Gogh Museum, Amsterdam

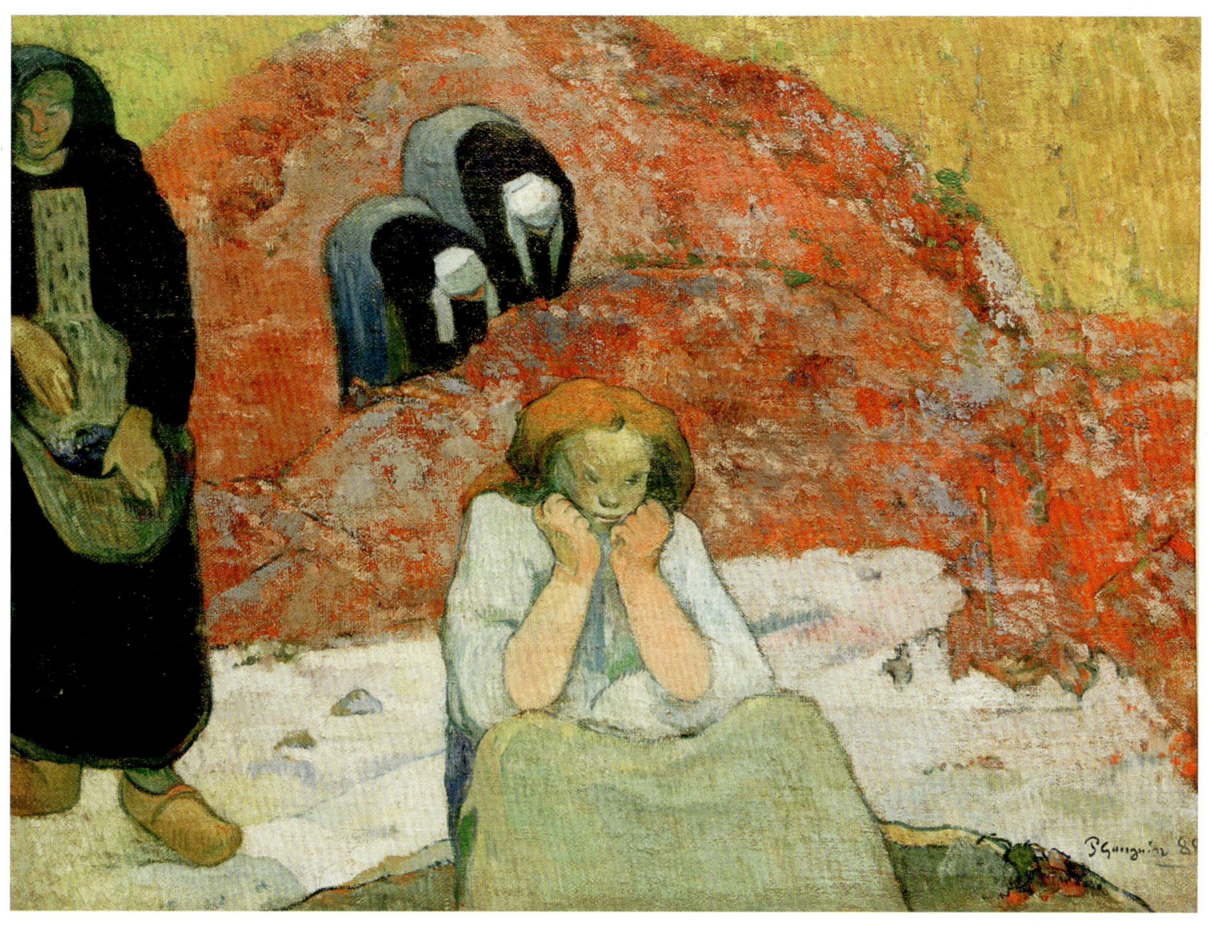

Human Misery or *The Wine Harvest* or *Poverty*

Misères humaines dite aussi *Les Vendanges* ou *La Pauvresse*

Menschliches Elend, auch genannt *Weinlese* oder *die Armut*

Miserias humanas llamado *La vendimia* o *La pobreza*

Miserie umane dette anche *Le vendemmie* o *La povertà*

Menselijk leed of *Oogst in Arles* of *De armoede*

1888, Oil on jute canvas/Huile sur toile de jute, 73,5 × 92 cm, Ordrupgaard, København

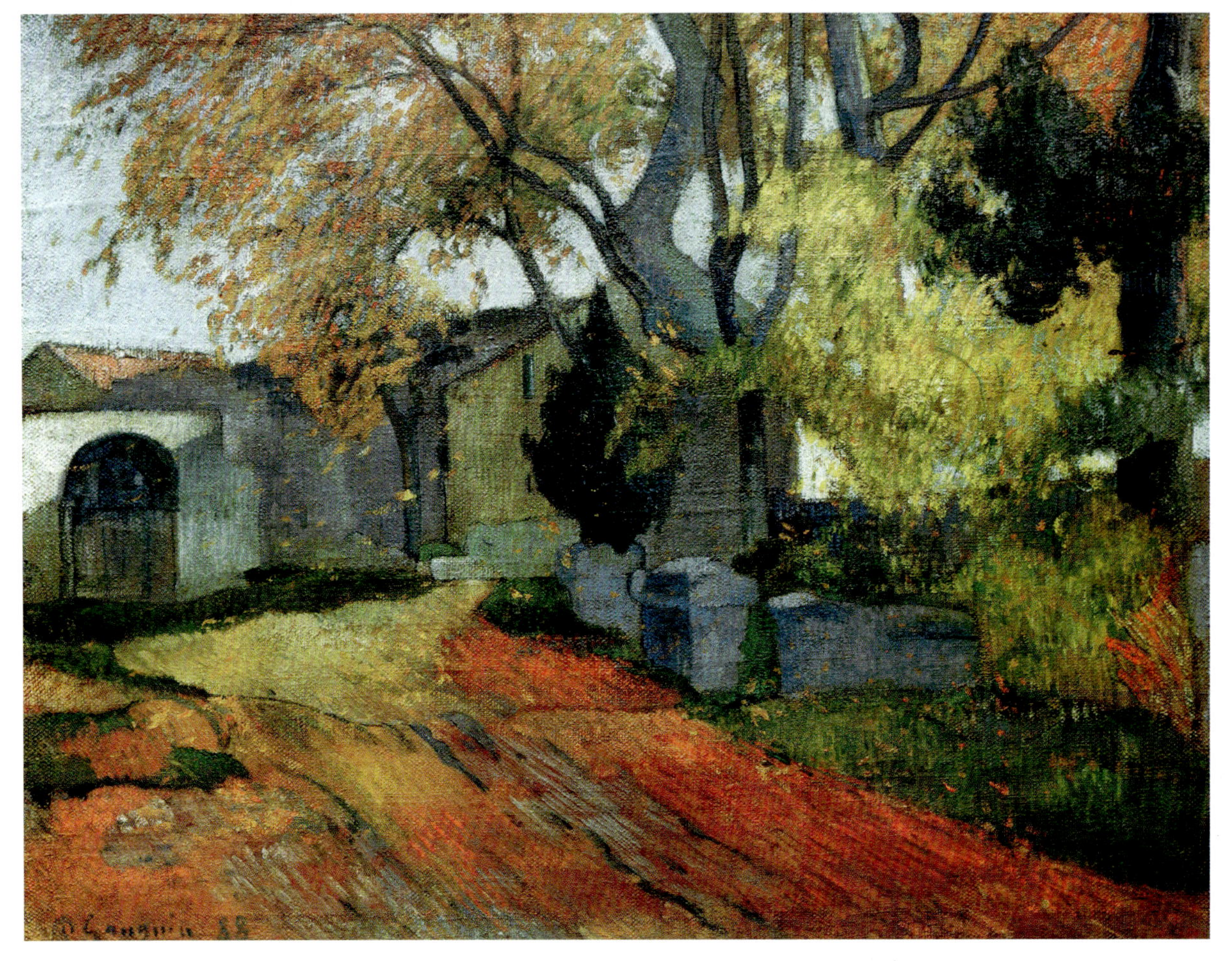

Les Alyscamps

1888, Oil on jute canvas/Huile sur toile de jute, 72,5 × 91,5 cm, Seiji Togo Memorial Sompo Japan Nipponkoa Museum of Art, Tokyo

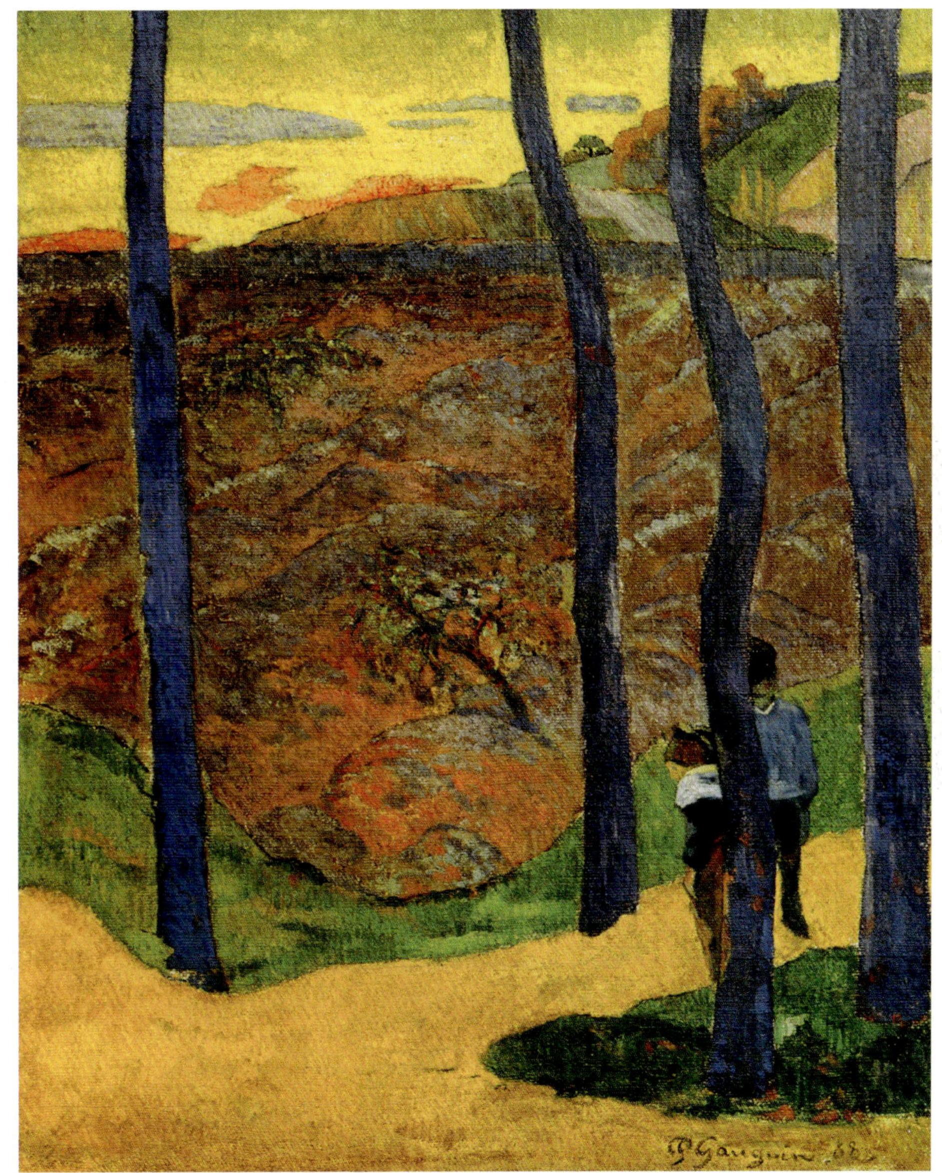

Blue Trees ("Your Turn Will Come, My Beauty!")

Les Arbres bleus (« Vous y passerez, la Belle ! »)

Die blauen Bäume („Deine Zeit wird kommen, meine Schöne")

Los árboles azules ("Pasarás por ellos, hermosa")

Gli alberi blu ("Voi ci passerete, oh Bella!")

De blauwe bomen ("Uw tijd zal komen, mijne schone!")

1888, Oil on canvas/Huile sur toile, 92 × 73 cm, Ordrupgaard, København

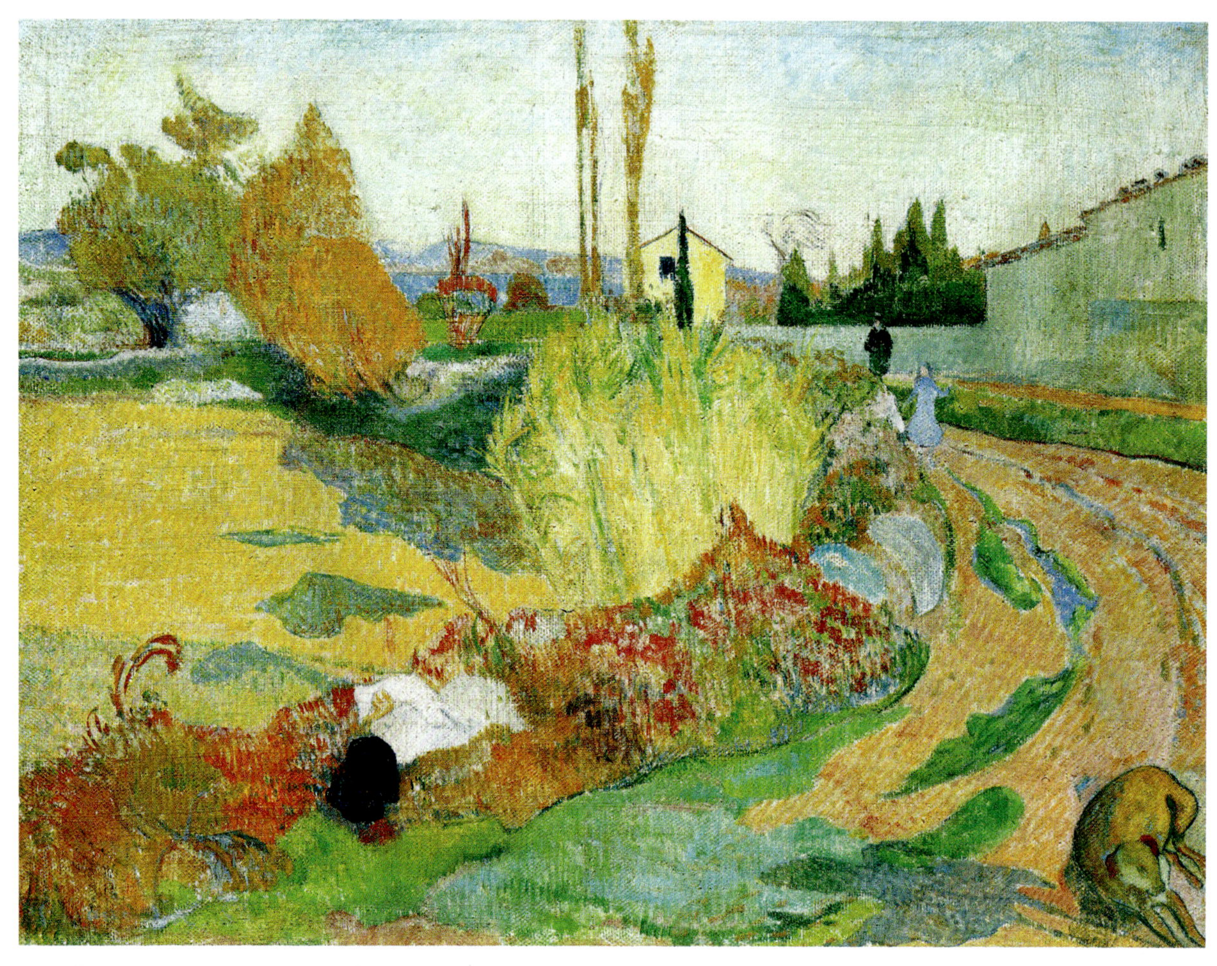

Landscape near Arles (Peace in the Roubine du Roi Canal)
Paysage près d'Arles (Paix dans la roubine du Roi Canal)
Landschaft bei Arles (Weg am Roubin-du-Roi-Kanal)
Paisaje cercano a Arlés (Paz en la Roubine du Roi Canal)
Paesaggi nei pressi di Arles (Pace alla foce di Roi Canal)
Lanschap bij Arles (Vrede aan het Roubine-du-Roi-kanaal)
1888, Oil on canvas/Huile sur toile, 72,5 × 92 cm, Nationalmuseum, Stockholm

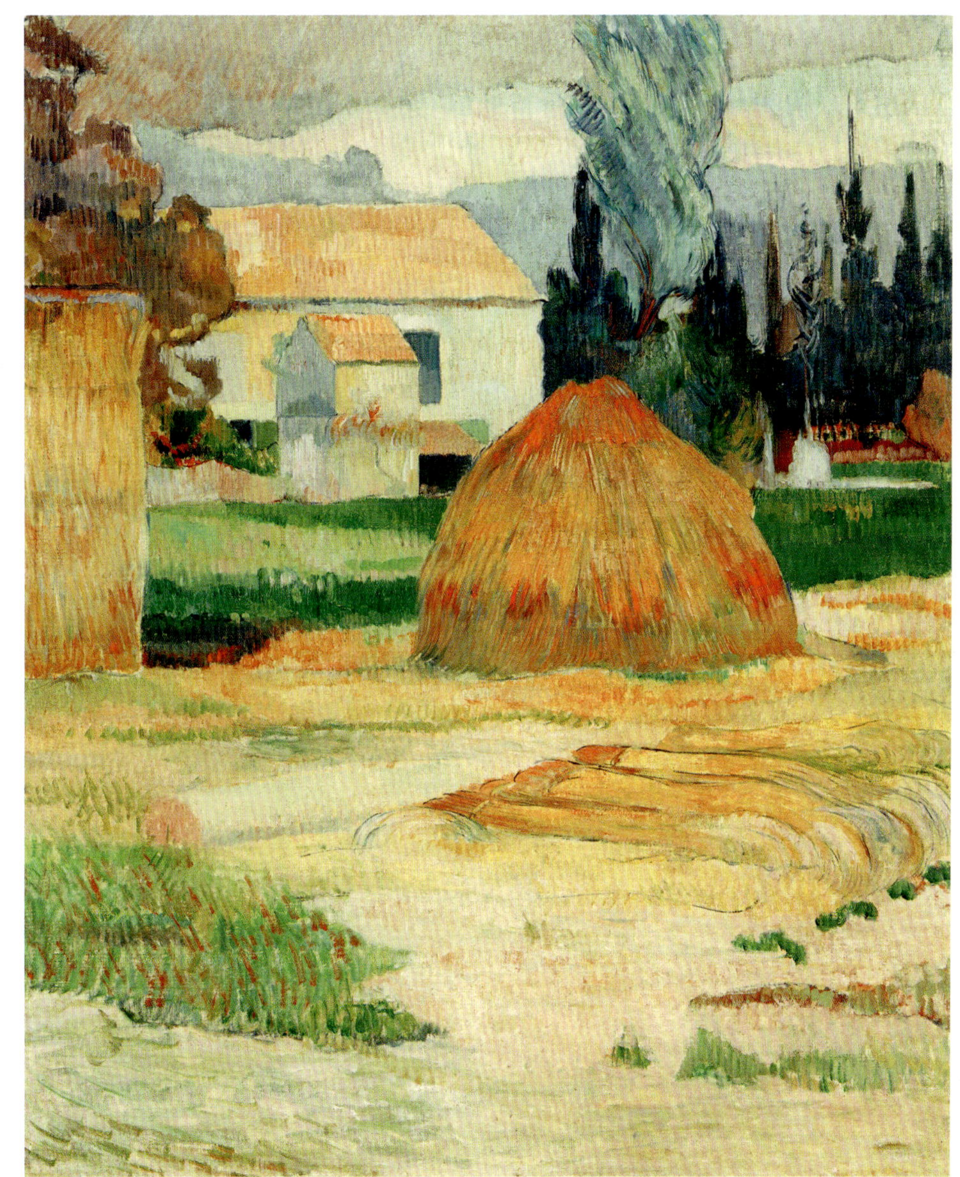

Mas, near Arles

Mas d'Arles

Bauernhaus in Arles

Mas d'Arles

Le cascine d'Arles

Boerenhuis in Arles

1888, Oil on canvas/Huile sur toile, 91 × 72 cm, Indianapolis Museum of Art, Indianapolis

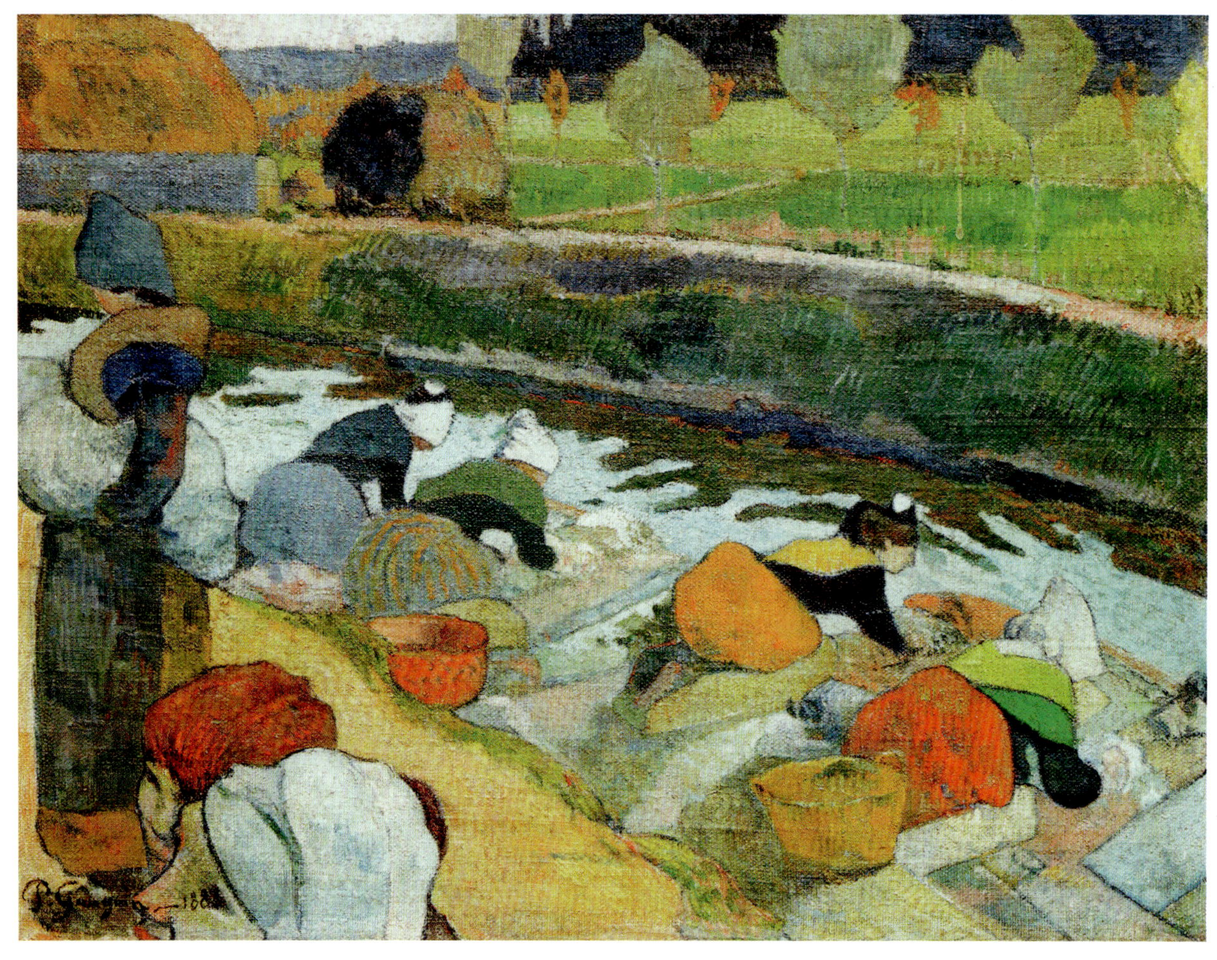

The Roubine du Roi Canal With Washerwomen

Laveuses à la roubine du Roi Canal

Wäscherinnen am Roubine-du-Roi-Kanal

Lavanderas en la Roubine du Roi Canal

Lavandaie alla foce di Roi Canal

Wasvrouwen aan het Roubine-du-Roi-kanaal

1888, Oil on jute canvas/Huile sur toile de jute, 75,9 × 92,1 cm, Museum of Modern Art, New York

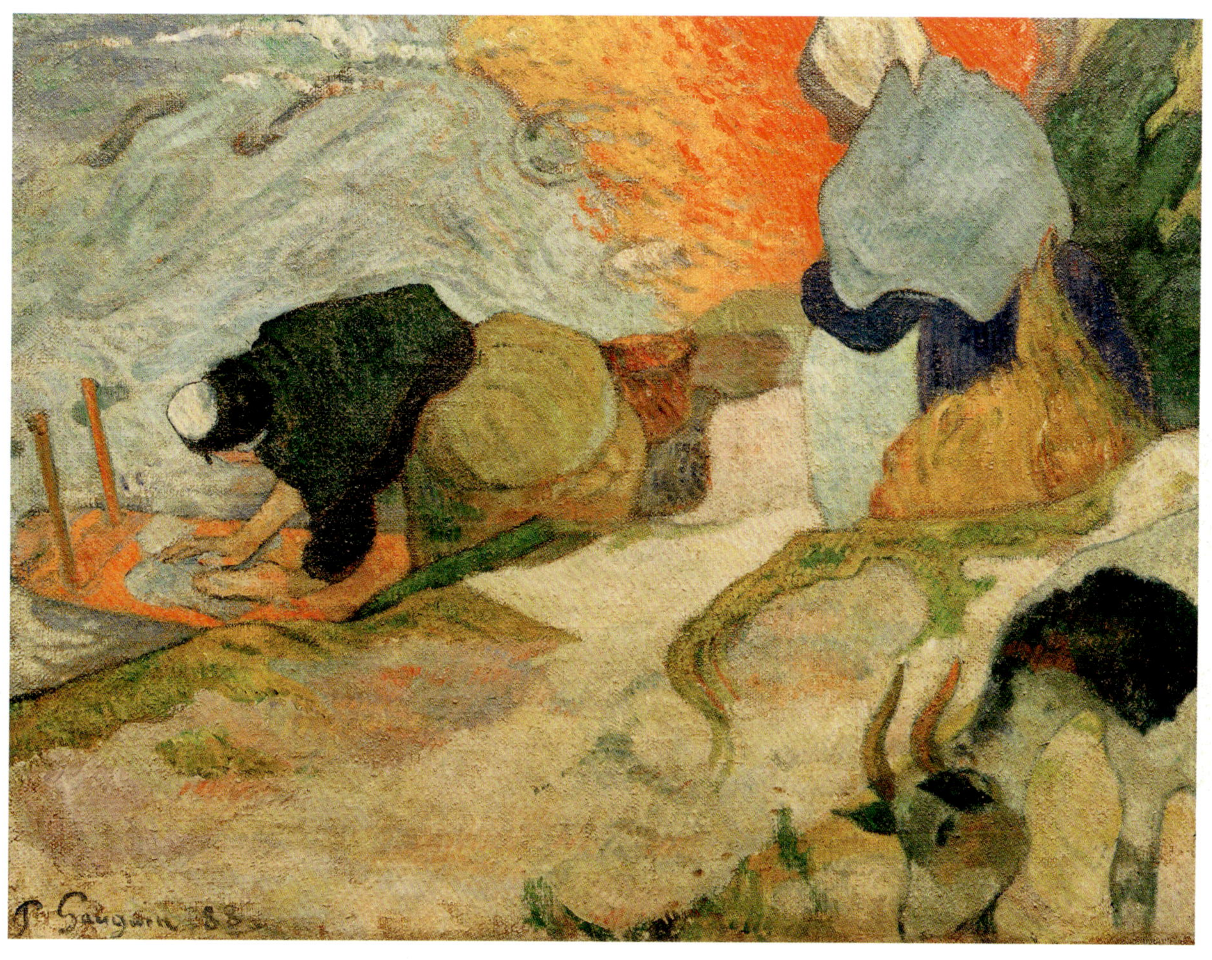

The Roubine du Roi Canal With Washerwomen

Laveuses à la roubine du Roi Canal

Wäscherinnen am Roubine-du-Roi-Kanal

Lavanderas en la Roubine du Roi Canal

Lavandaie alla foce di Roi Canal

Wasvrouwen aan het Roubine-du-Roi-kanaal

1888, Oil on canvas/Huile sur toile, 73 × 92 cm, Museo de Bellas Artes, Bilbao

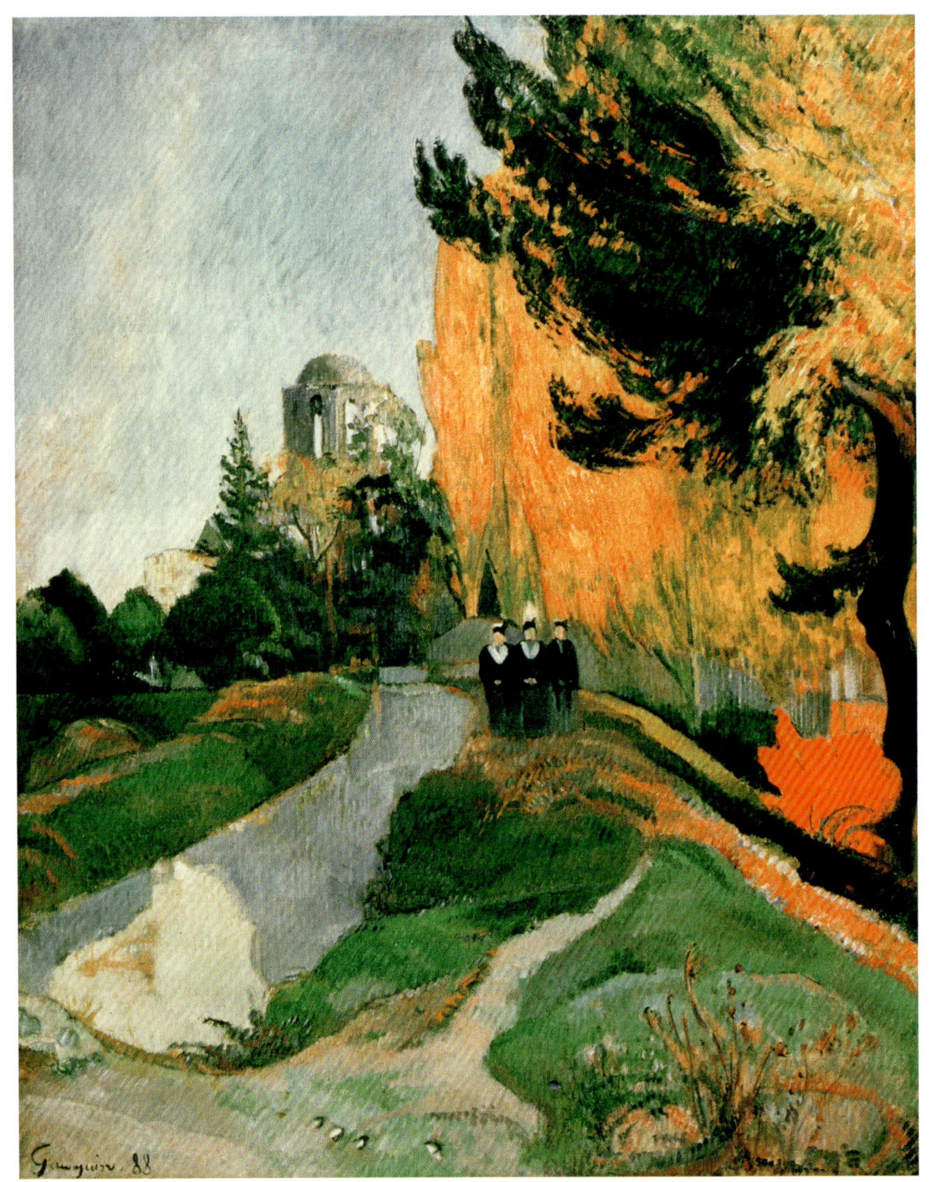

Les Alyscamps

1888, Oil on canvas/Huile sur toile, 91,5 × 72,5 cm, Musée d'Orsay, Paris

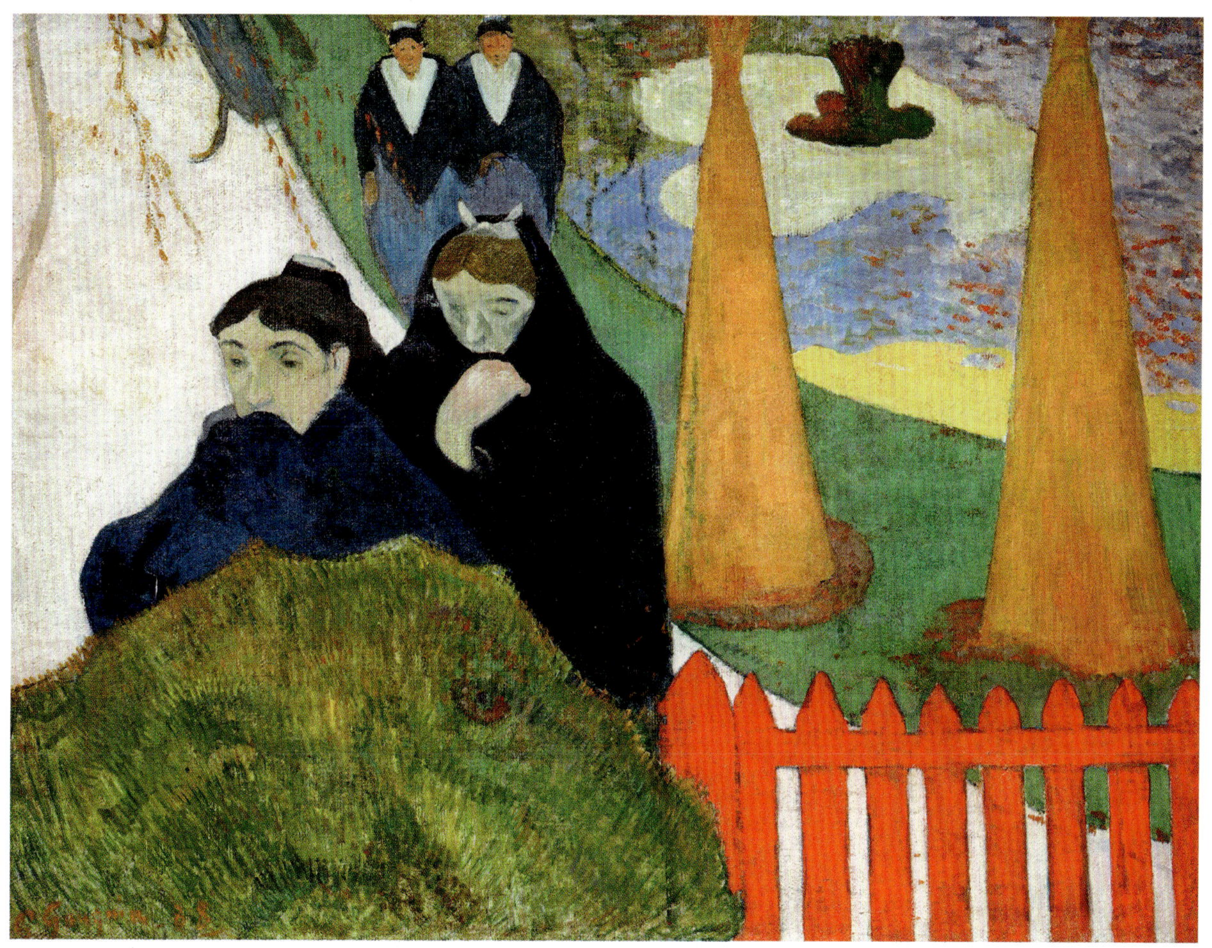

Women from Arles in the Public Garden (Mistral)

Arlésiennes (Mistral)

Frauen aus Arles (Mistral)

Arlesianas (Mistral)

Arlesiane (Mistral)

Vrouwen uit Arles (Mistral)

1888, Oil on canvas/Huile sur toile, 73 × 92 cm, Art Institute of Chicago, Chicago

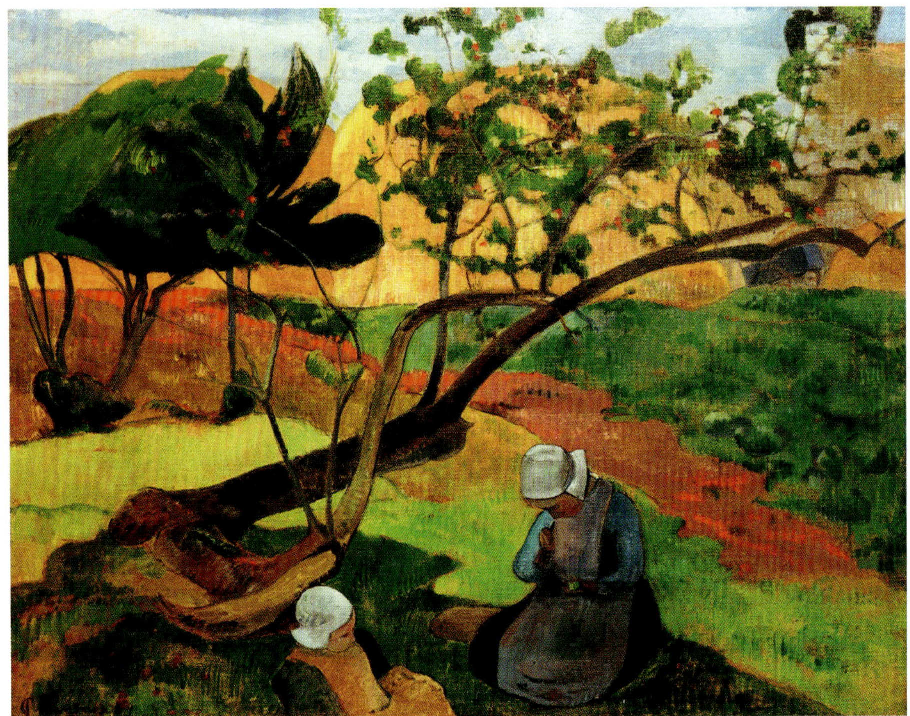

The Brittany studio,
between Pont-Aven and Le Pouldu

After having exhibited at Théo van Gogh's
Parisian gallery and then at the exhibition
of "Les XX" in Brussels in the spring of
1889, Gauguin withdrew to Brittany. He
stayed there until the autumn of 1890,
between Pont-Aven and the fishing
village of Le Pouldu. Reassured by a
growing visibility and critical acclaim, he
managed to find in the lands of Breton an
inspiration that Paris could not provide
for him.

In full possession of his capabilities,
the artist proclaimed loud and clear

L'atelier de Bretagne,
entre Pont-Aven et Le Pouldu

Après avoir exposé à la galerie parisienne
de Théo Van Gogh puis au Salon des
XX de Bruxelles, au printemps 1889,
Gauguin se retire en Bretagne. Il y reste
jusqu'à l'automne 1890, entre Pont-
Aven et le petit village de pêcheurs du
Pouldu. Rasséréné par une visibilité et
une fortune critique grandissantes, il
sait trouver en terres bretonnes une
inspiration que Paris ne peut lui donner.

En pleine possession de ses moyens,
l'artiste revendique haut et fort son
nouveau langage plastique fait de

Das Atelier in der Bretagne,
zwischen Pont-Aven und Le Pouldu

Im Frühjahr 1889, nach einer Ausstellung
in der Pariser Galerie Théo van Goghs
und im „Salon des XX" in Brüssel, zieht
sich Gauguin in die Bretagne zurück. Hier
bleibt er bis zum Herbst 1890 zwischen
Pont-Aven und dem kleinen Fischerdorf
Pouldu. Zuversichtlich durch wachsende
Bekanntheit und günstige Kritiken, findet
er in der bretonischen Landschaft die
Inspiration, die ihm in Paris fehlt.

Im Vollbesitz seiner Kräfte bekennt
sich der Künstler selbstbewusst zu
seiner neuen Formensprache, die auf

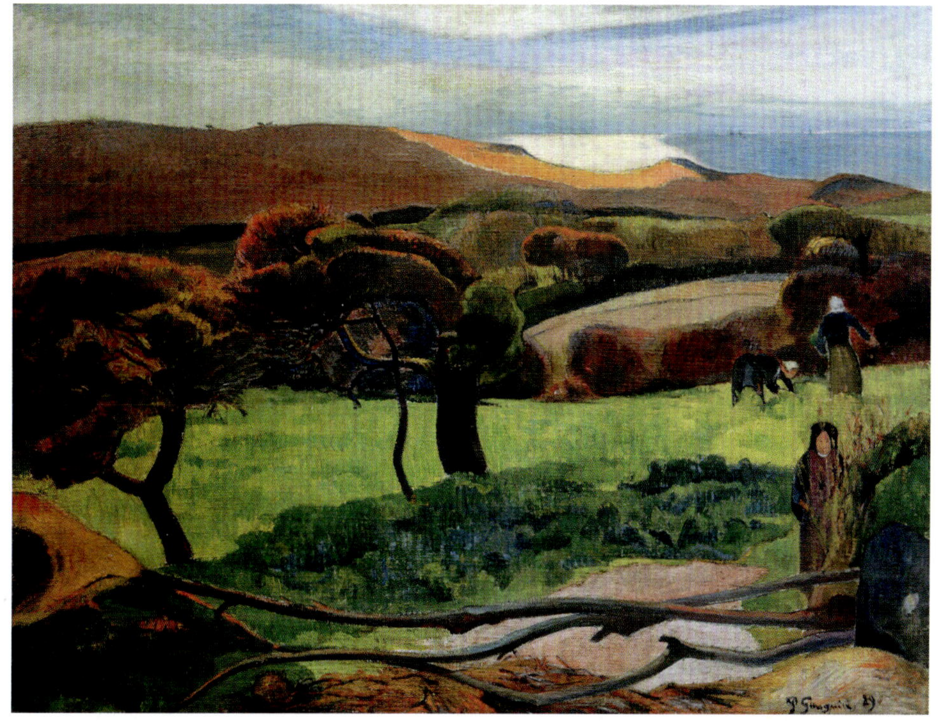

El taller de Bretaña, entre Pont-Aven y Le Pouldu

Después de haber expuesto en la galería parisina de Théo van Gogh y después en el "Salon des XX" en Bruselas, en la primavera de 1889, Gauguin se retiró a Bretaña. Allí se quedó hasta el otoño de 1890, entre Pont-Aven y el pequeño pueblo pesquero de Le Pouldu. Reconfortado por una visibilidad y una fortuna crítica en aumento, supo encontrar en tierras bretonas una inspiración que París no pudo darle.

En total posesión de sus facultades, el artista reivindicó alto y claro su

L'atelier bretone, tra Pont-Aven e Le Pouldu

Dopo aver esposto Presso la Galleria parigina di Theo van Gogh e poi al "Salon des XX" in Bruxelles nella primavera del 1889, Gauguin si ritira in Bretagna. Vi resta fino all'autunno 1890 tra Pont-Aven e il piccolo villaggio di pescatori di Pouldu. Rassicurato da una crescente visibilità e successo di critica, sa di poter trovare in Bretagna un'aspirazione che Parigi non può dargli.

In pieno possesso dei suoi mezzi, l'artista rivendica a gran voce il suo nuovo linguaggio plastico fatto di semplificazioni

Het atelier van Bretagne, tussen Pont-Aven en Le Pouldu

Na exposities in de Parijse kunstgalerie van Theo van Gogh en in het voorjaar van 1889 op de "Salon des XX" in Brussel trekt Gauguin zich terug in Bretagne. Hij blijft er tot het najaar van 1890, tussen Pont-Aven en het vissersdorpje Le Pouldu. Daar voelt hij zich gezien, en krijgt hij steeds lovender kritieken. Dat geeft hem innerlijke rust om in het Bretonse landschap de inspiratie te vinden die Parijs hem niet kan bieden.

Vol zelfvertrouwen claimt de kunstenaar luid en duidelijk zijn nieuwe

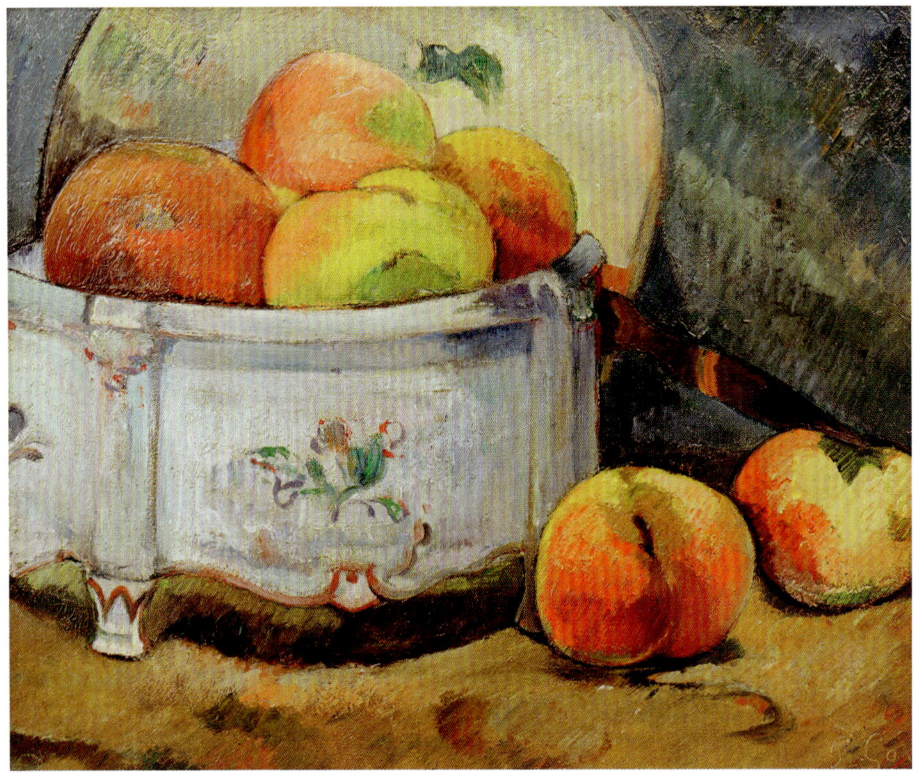

his new plastic language, made up of
simplified shapes, marked contours,
enhanced decorative lines, superimposed
planes of pure colour and growing
symbolism. The creations of this period
were marked by their primitivism and
syncretism, two of the orientations
characterising the whole of his work,
like the iconic *Yellow Christ* (inspired
by local statuary), *La Belle Angèle*
(figured with Peruvian pottery) and *Be
Mysterious* (low relief with decorative
whorls). Gauguin committed to memory

simplification des formes, de contours
cernés, de valorisation des lignes
décoratives et de superpositions
d'aplats de couleurs pures au
symbolisme grandissant. Les créations
de cette période se distinguent par leur
primitivisme et leur syncrétisme, deux
des orientations qui caractériseront
l'ensemble de son œuvre, à l'image des
iconiques *Le Christ jaune* (inspiré par la
statuaire locale), *La Belle Angèle* (figurée
avec une poterie péruvienne) et *Soyez
mystérieuses* (bas-relief tout en volutes

der Vereinfachung der Formungen
beruht, umrandeten Konturen, der
Aufwertung dekorativer Linien und
reiner, sich überlagernden Farbflächen
als Ausdruck eines wachsenden
Symbolismus. Die Werke dieser
Periode heben sich hervor durch
Primitivismus und Synkretismus – zwei
der Richtungen, die sein ganzes Werk
charakterisieren – wie beim Ikonenbild
Der gelbe Christus (inspiriert von der
lokalen Bildhauerkunst), *La Belle Angèle*
(abgebildet mit einer peruanischen

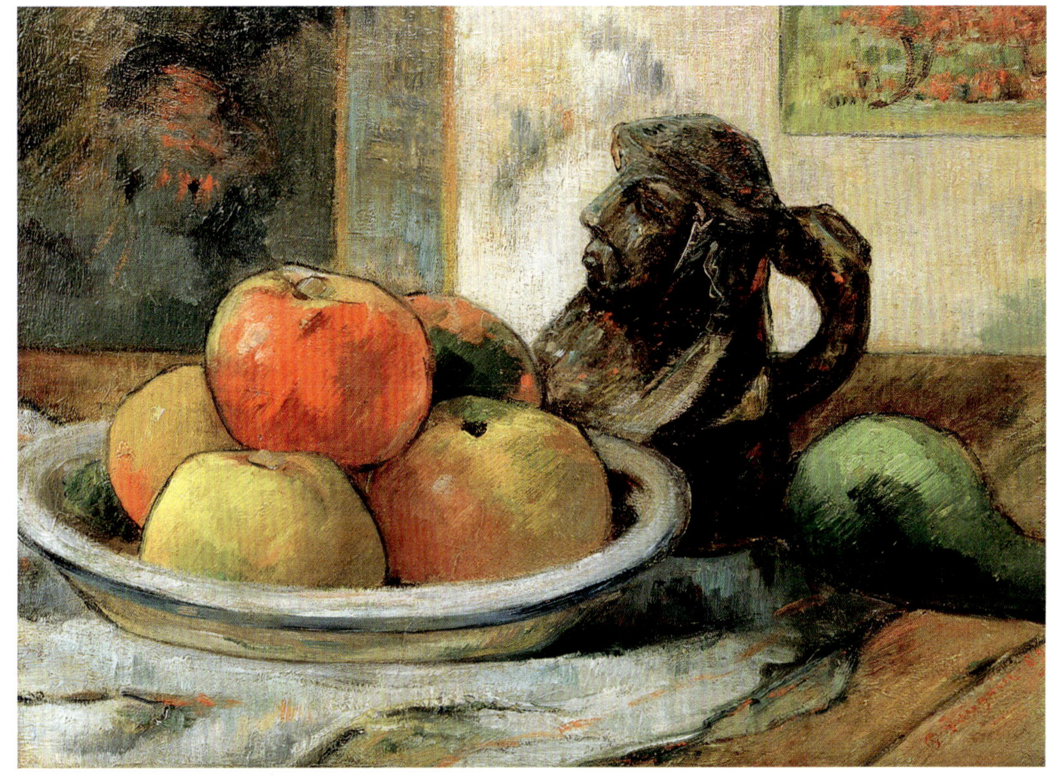

nueva expresión plástica formada por
la simplificación de formas, contornos
definidos, apreciación de las líneas
decorativas y superposición de colores
sólidos, puros del simbolismo creciente.
Las creaciones de este período se
distinguen por su primitivismo y su
sincretismo, dos de las orientaciones
que caracterizarían el conjunto de su
obra, a la imagen de los icónicos *El Cristo
amarillo* (inspirado por la talla local), *La
bella Angèle* (retratada con una pieza
de alfarería peruana) y *Sed misteriosas*

di forme, di contorni delineati, di
valorizzazioni delle linee decorative e di
sovrapposizioni piane di colori puri al
simbolismo crescente. Le creazioni di
questo periodo si caratterizzano per il
loro primitivismo e il loro sincretismo,
due orientamenti che caratterizzeranno
l'insieme della sua opera, dall'immagine
delle icone *Il Cristo giallo* (ispirato
dallo scultore locale), *La Belle Angèle*
(mostrata su Ceramica Peruviana)
e *Soyez mystérieuses* (basso rilievo
interamente fatto di riccioli decorativi).

plastische taal die zich kenmerkt door
vereenvoudigde vormen, donkere
contouren, een nadruk op decoratieve
lijnen en grote vlakken in zuivere
kleuren die steeds meer symbolische
waarde krijgen. Zijn werk uit die
periode draagt het stempel van zowel
het primitivisme als het syncretisme,
twee van de stromingen die zijn
gehele oeuvre zullen karakteriseren,
met als sprekendste voorbeelden
De gele Christus (geïnspireerd op
een plaatselijk kruisbeeld), *De mooie*

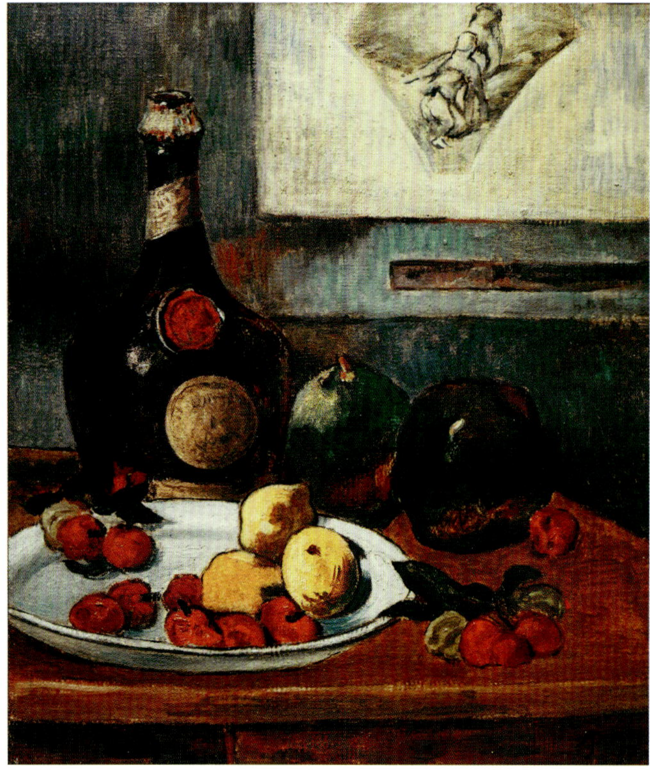

testimonials to Javanese, Polynesian, Cambodian, and Malagasy cultures, discovered (by him) during the 1889 World Exposition, which fuelled his taste for the exotic and which strengthened his resolve to build a "studio of the tropics", conducive to "making nothing but simple, very simple art".

décoratives). Gauguin garde en mémoire les témoignages des cultures javanaises, polynésiennes, cambodgiennes et malgaches découverts lors de l'exposition universelle de 1889 qui attisent son goût de l'exotique et le confortent dans son désir de fonder un « atelier des tropiques », propice à « ne faire que de l'art simple, très simple ».

Keramikfigur) und *Seid geheimnisvoll*. (Flachrelief verziert mit dekorativen Wellen). Gauguin erinnert sich lebhaft an die Zeugnisse der javanischen, polynesischen, kambodschanischen und madagassischen Kulturen, die er während der Weltausstellung von 1889 entdeckt hat und die seinen exotischen Geschmack anfachen, seinen Wunsch bestärken, ein „Atelier der Tropen" zu gründen, gerade richtig für „nichts anderes als einfache, sehr einfache Kunst".

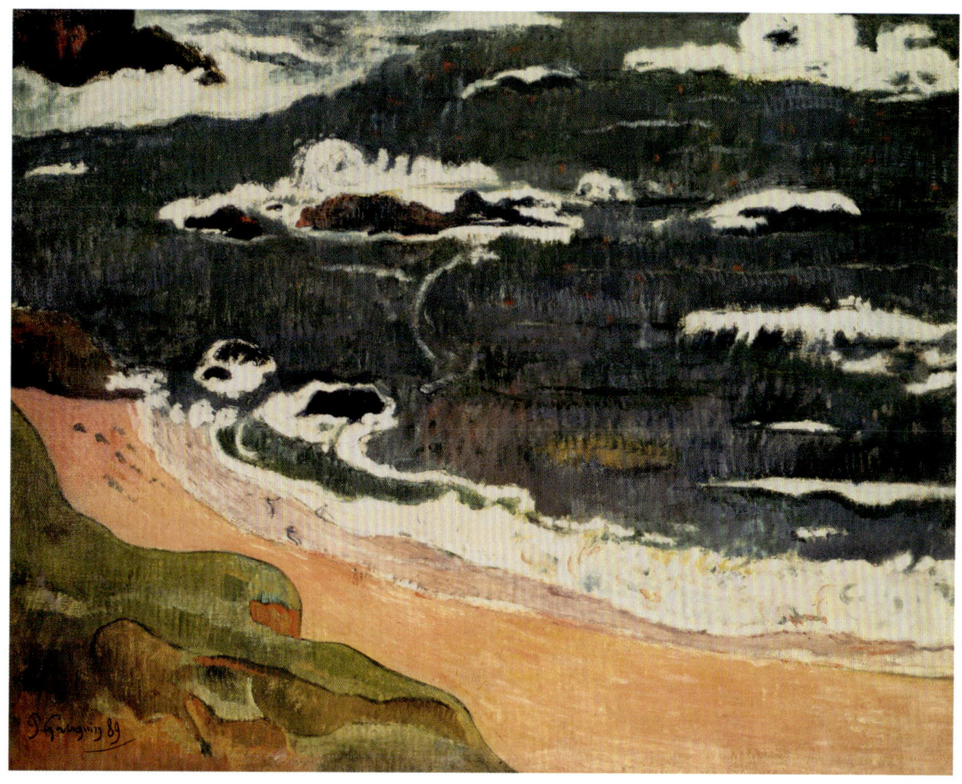

(bajorrelieve totalmente realizado en volutas decorativas). Gauguin recuerda los testimonios de las culturas javanesas, polinesias, camboyanas y malgaches descubiertas durante la exposición universal de 1889 que avivan su gusto por lo exótico y le reconfortan en su deseo de fundar un "taller de los trópicos", dispuesto a "crear solo arte sencillo, muy sencillo."

Gauguin si fa testimone delle culture giavanese, polinesiana, cambogiana e malgascia scoperte durante la mostra internazionale del 1889 che attira il suo gusto per l'esotico e conferma il suo desiderio di avviare un "Atelier dei Tropici" precipuo a "fare che dell'Arte semplice, molto semplice."

Angèle (poserend met een Peruviaanse aardewerken pot) en *Wees mysterieus* (bas-reliëf van uitsluitend decoratieve voluten). Gauguin heeft altijd de Javaanse, Polynesische, Cambodjaanse en Madagaskische kunstuitingen in zijn achterhoofd die hij tijdens de Wereldtentoonstelling van 1889 ontdekte. Zij stillen zijn honger naar exotisme en voeden zijn verlangen een "tropenatelier" te stichten waar hij "uitsluitend eenvoudige, zeer eenvoudige kunst kan maken".

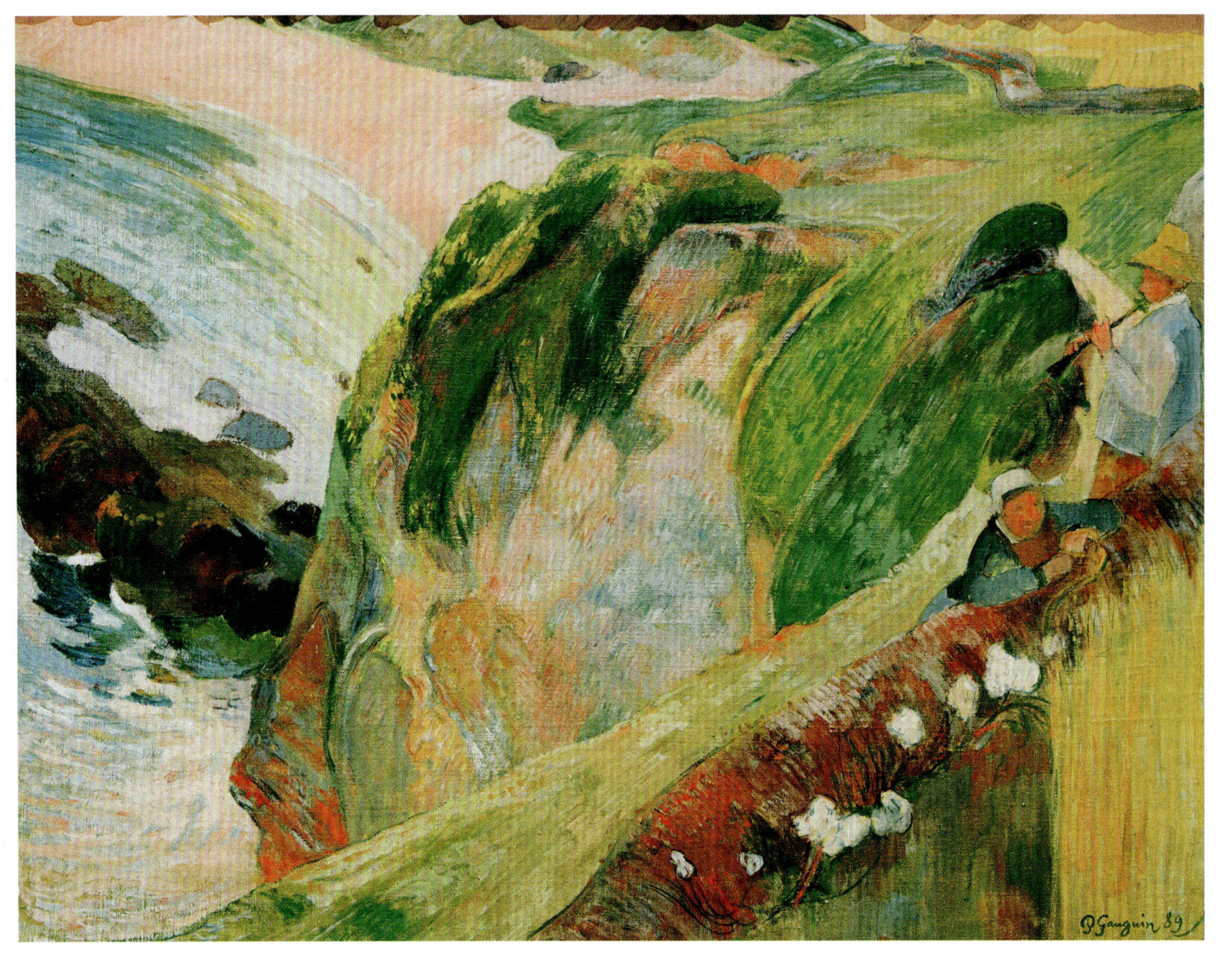

The Flageolet Player on the Cliff
Le Joueur de flûte sur la falaise
Flötenspieler auf den Klippen
El flautista al borde del acantilado
La gioia del flauto sulla falesia
De fluitist op de rots

1889, Oil on canvas/Huile sur toile, 73 × 92 cm, Indianapolis Museum of Art, Indianapolis

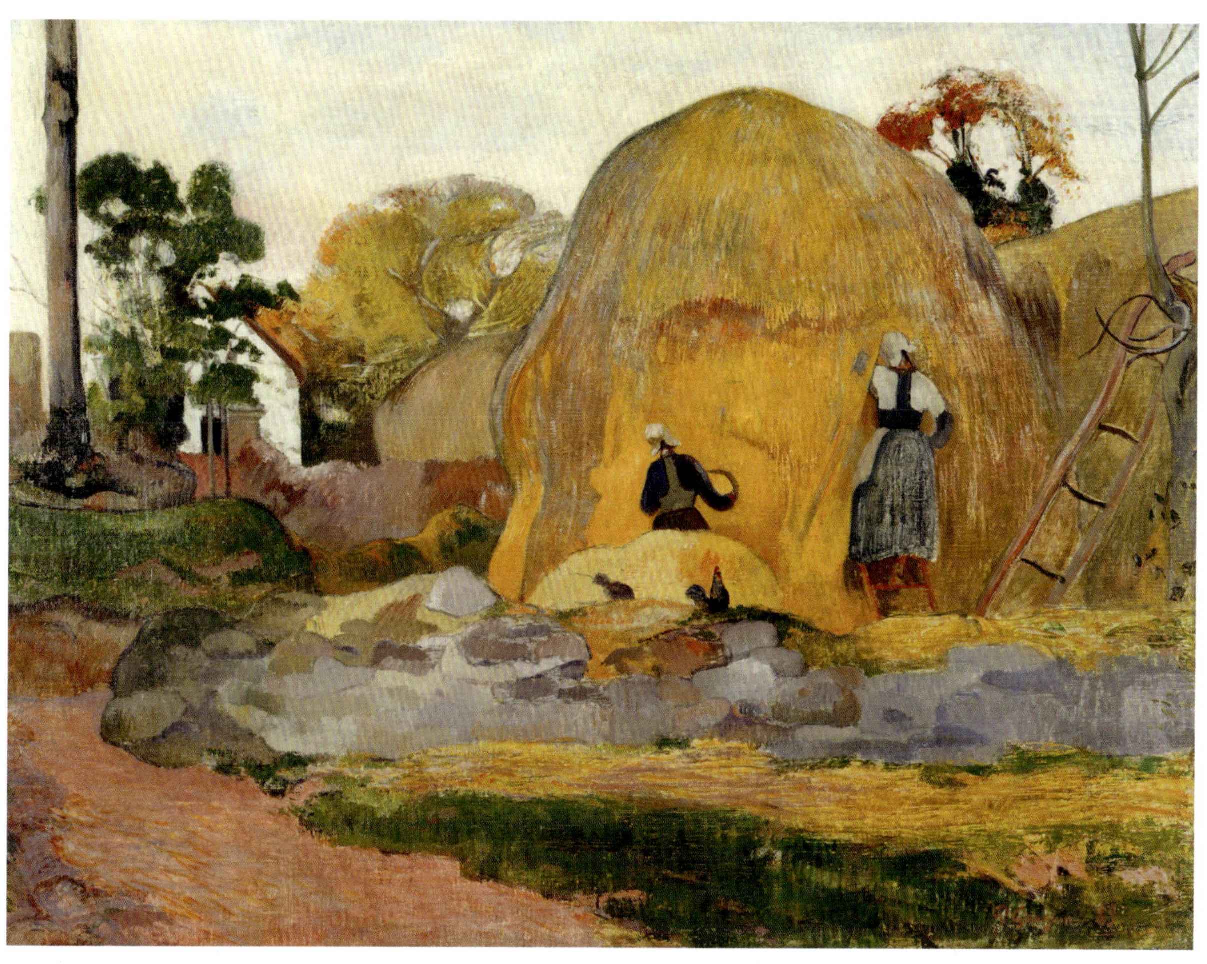

Yellow Haystacks or *The Golden Harvest*

Les Meules jaunes ou *La Moisson blonde*

Die gelben Heuschober oder *Goldene Ernte*

Almiar amarillo o *La siega en Bretaña*

Le macine gialle o *La Mola bionda*

De gele hooibergen of *De blonde oogst*

1889, Oil on canvas/Huile sur toile, 73 × 92,5 cm, Musée d'Orsay, Paris

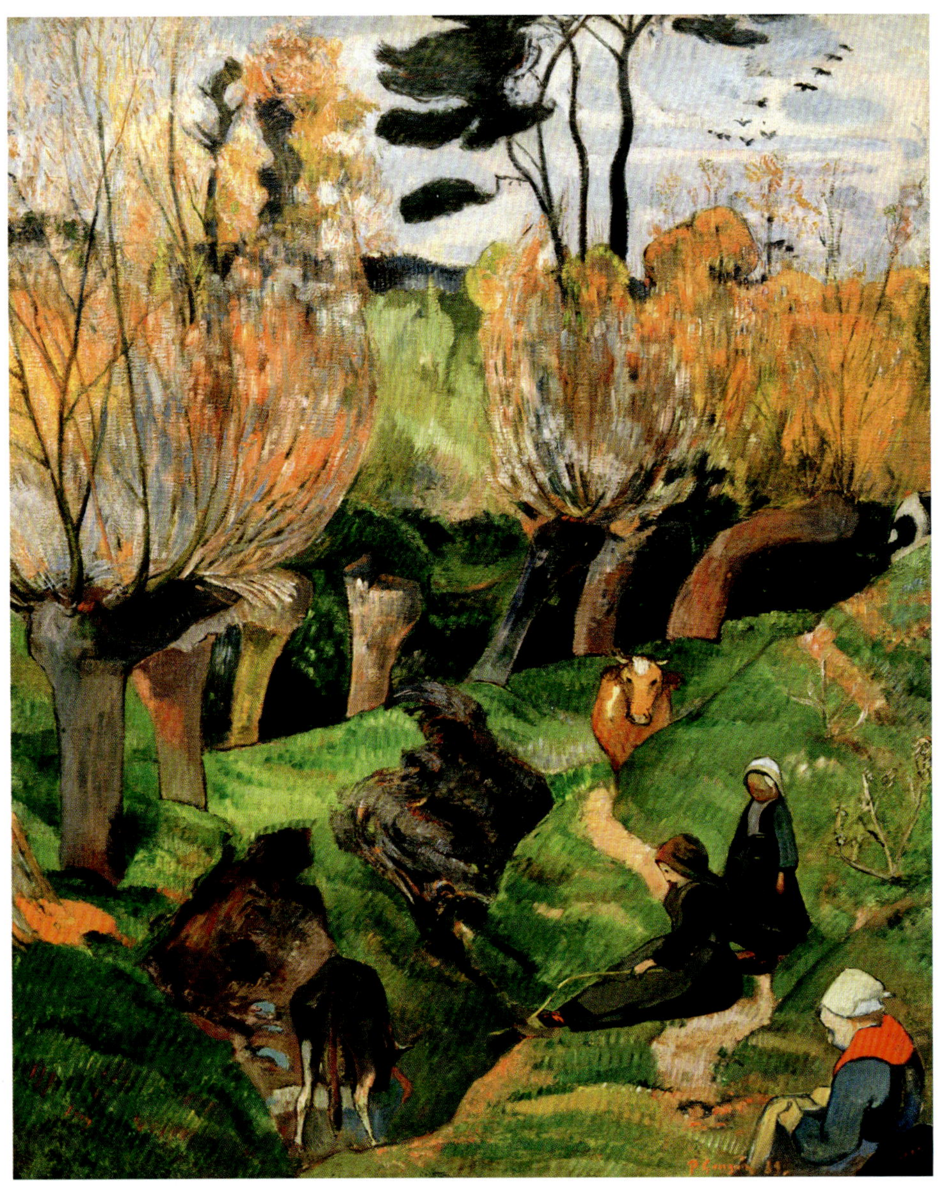

The Willows

Les Saules

Die Weiden

Los sauces

I salici

De wilgen

*1889, Oil on canvas/
Huile sur toile, 92 × 73 cm,
Nasjonalgalleriet, Oslo*

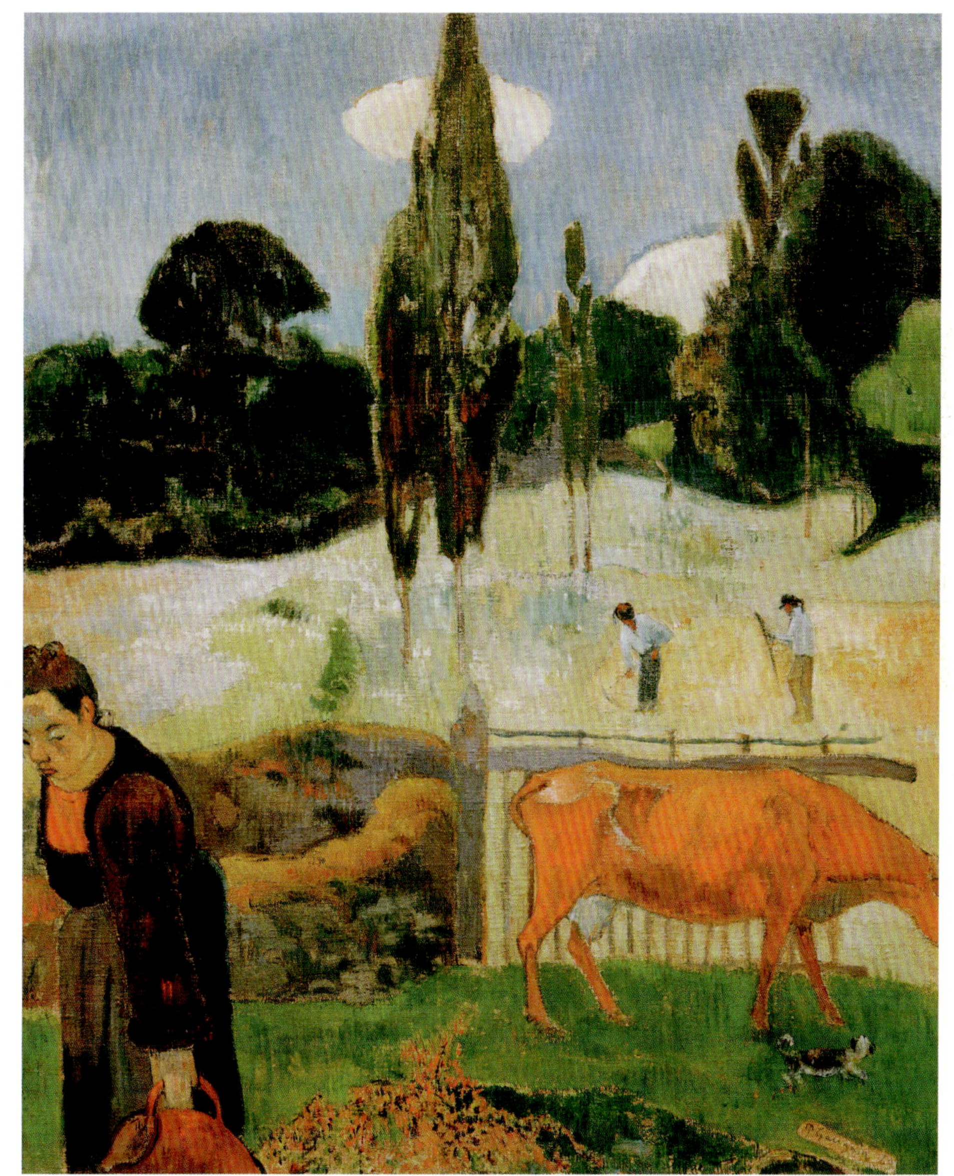

The Red Cow
La Vache rouge
Die rote Kuh
La vaca roja
La vacca Rossa
De rode koe

1889, Oil on canvas/Huile sur
toile, 92 × 73 cm, Los Angeles
County Museum of Art,
Los Angeles

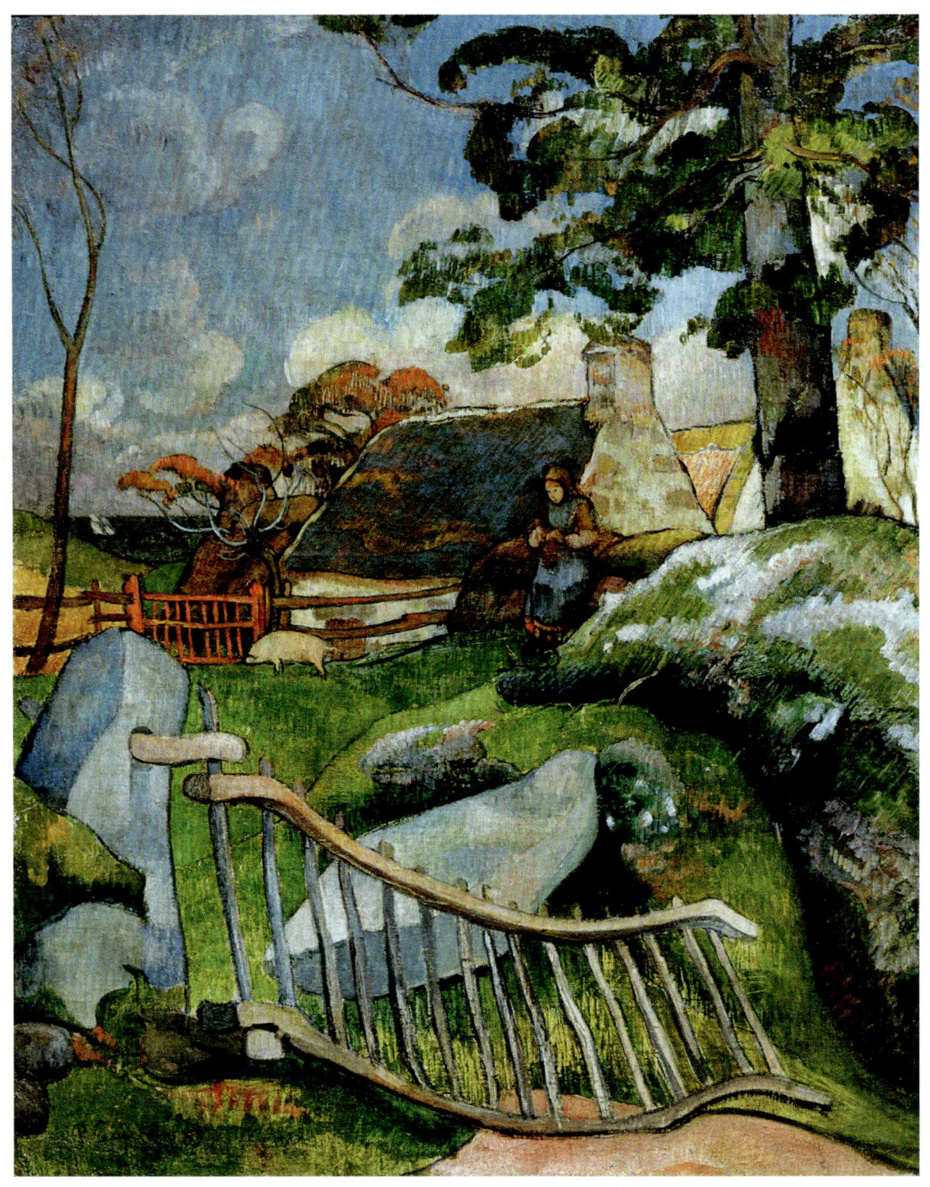

The Fence

La Barrière

Das Gatter

La barrera

La Barriera

Het hek

1889, Oil on canvas/Huile sur toile, 92,5 × 73 cm, Kunsthaus, Zürich

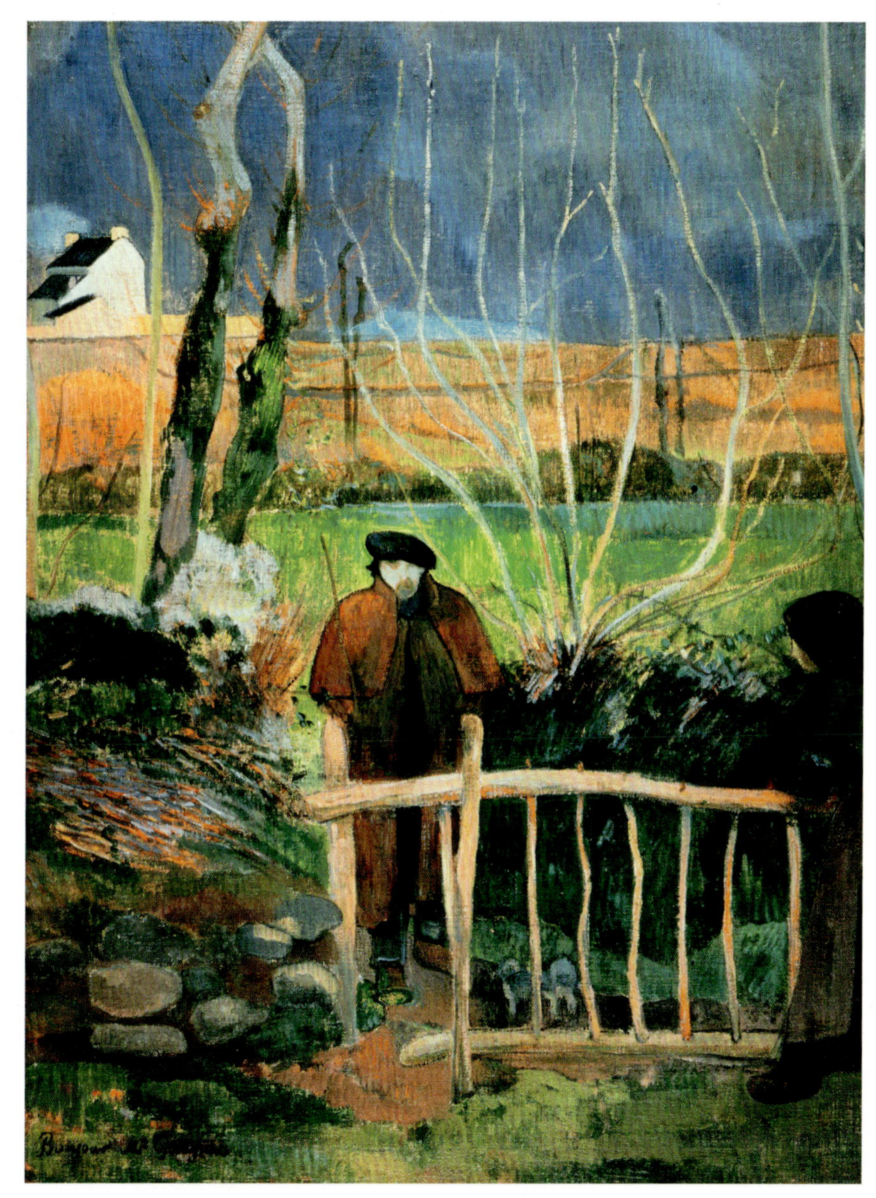

Bonjour Monsieur Gauguin !

*1889, Oil on canvas/Huile sur toile,
74,9 × 54,8 cm, Armand Hammer Museum
of Art, Los Angeles*

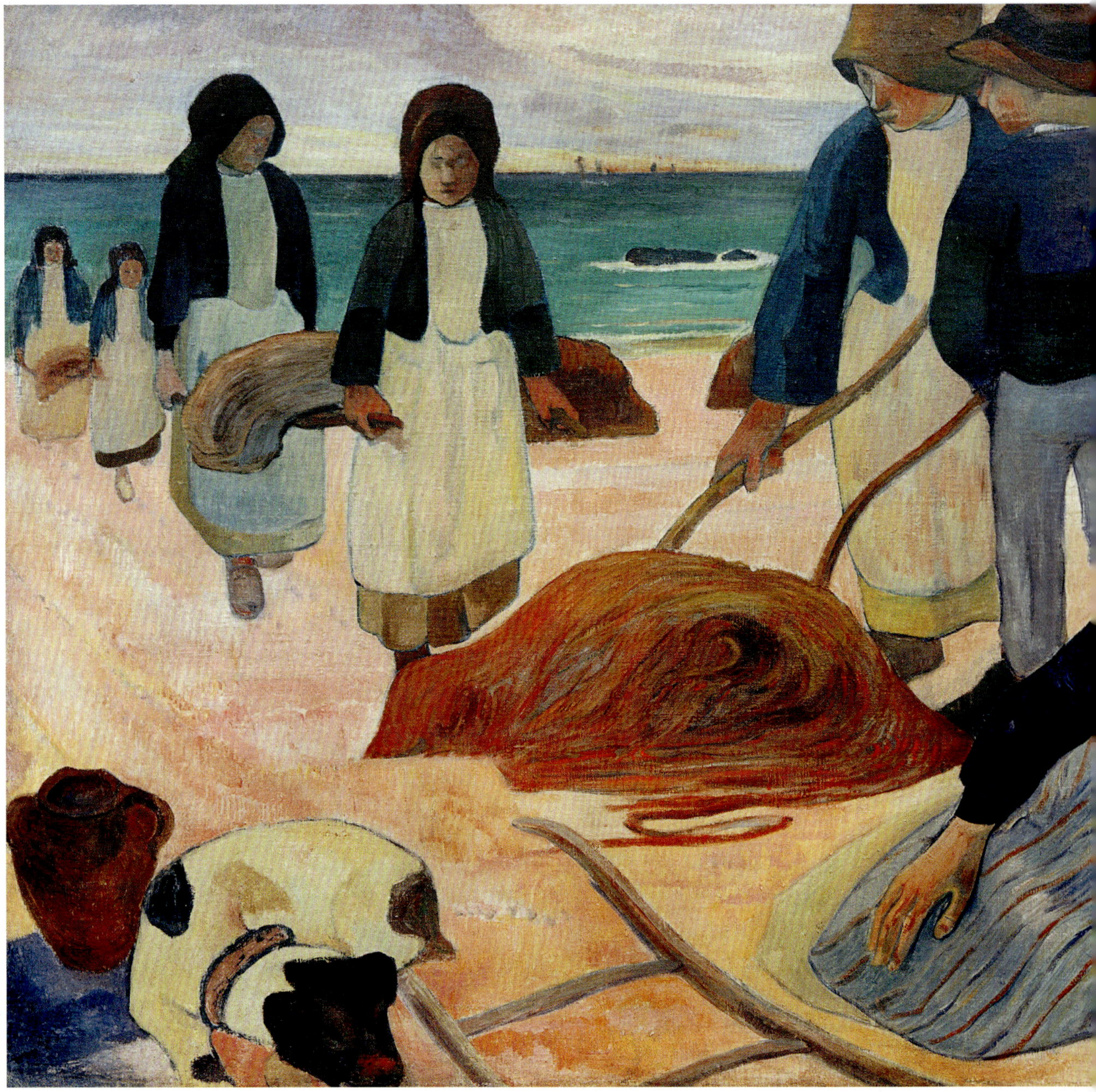

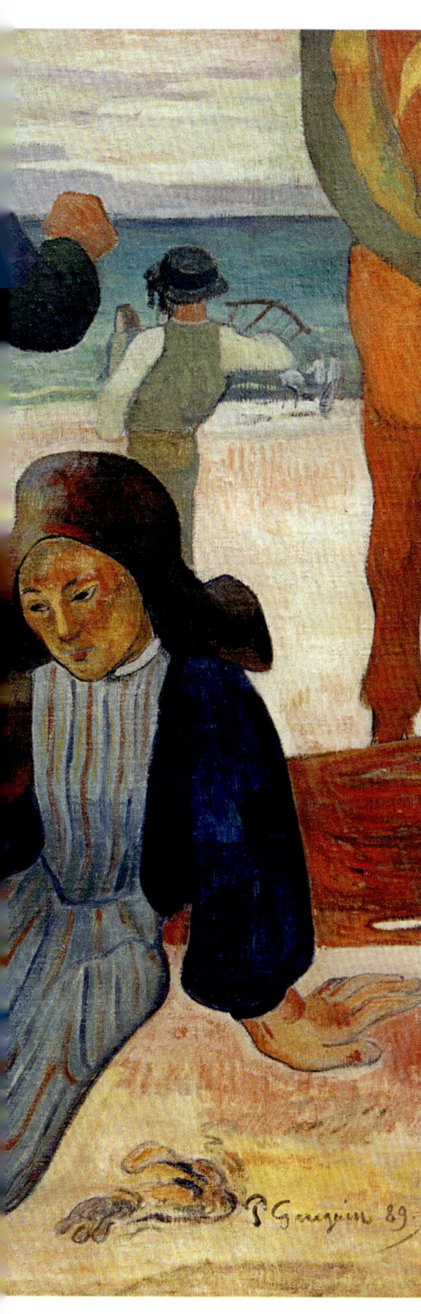

Kelp Gatherers

Les Ramasseuses de varech

Bretonische Tangsammlerinnen

Las remeras de varech

I raccoglitori di vareck

Bretonse vrouwen verzamelen zeewier

1889, Oil on canvas/Huile sur toile, 87 × 123,1 cm, Museum Folkwang, Essen

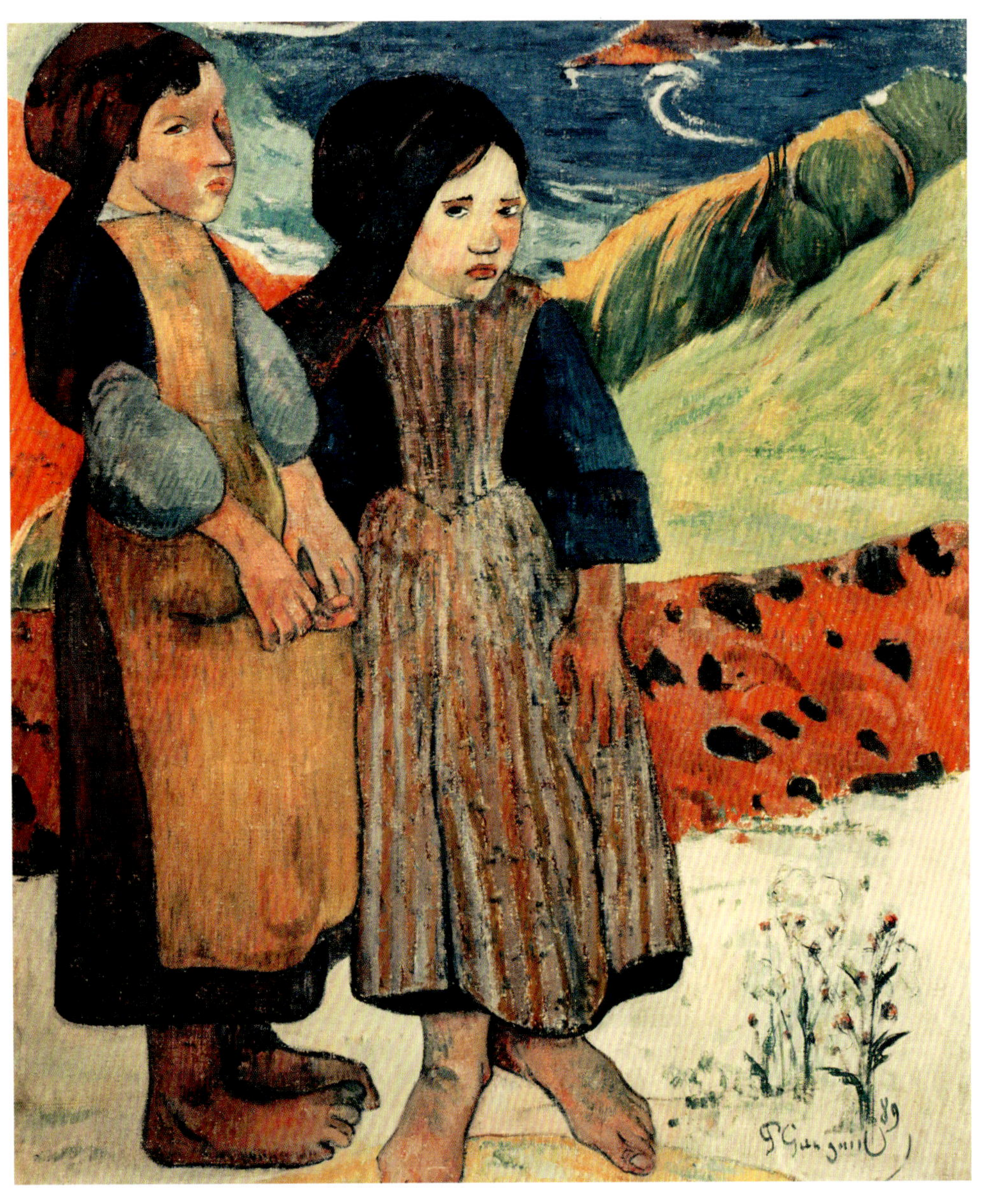

Breton Girls by the Sea

Petites Bretonnes devant la mer

Kleine bretonische Mädchen an der Küste

Pequeñas bretonas frente al mar

Piccoli bretoni davanti al mare

Bretonse meisjes voor de zee

1889, Oil on canvas/Huile sur toile, 92,5 × 73,6 cm, The National Museum of Western Art, Tokyo

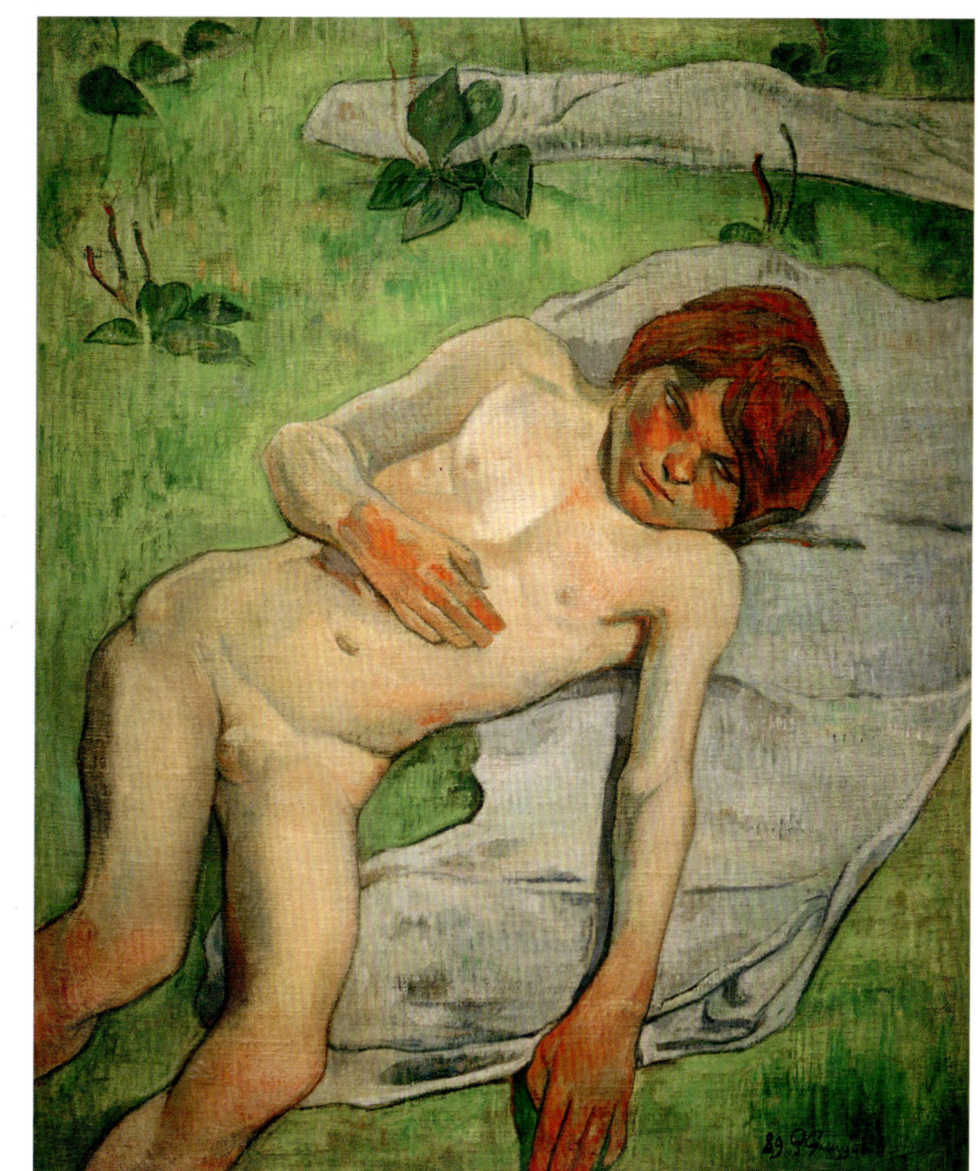

A Young Breton
Un Jeune Breton
Ein bretonischer Junge
Un joven bretón
Un giovane Bretone
Een jonge Breton

1889, Oil on canvas/Huile sur toile, 93 × 74,2 cm, Wallraf-Richartz-Museum & Fondation Corboud, Köln

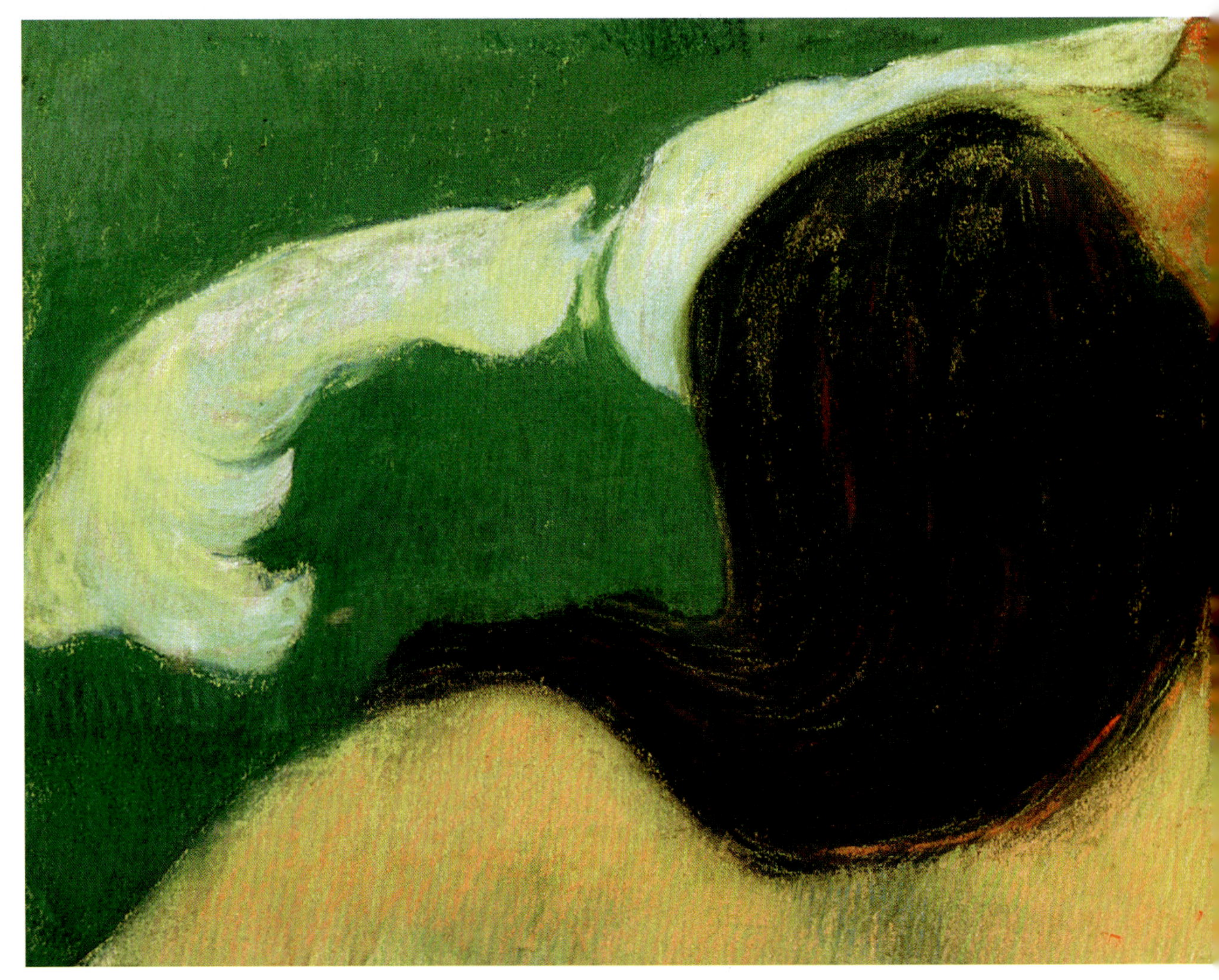

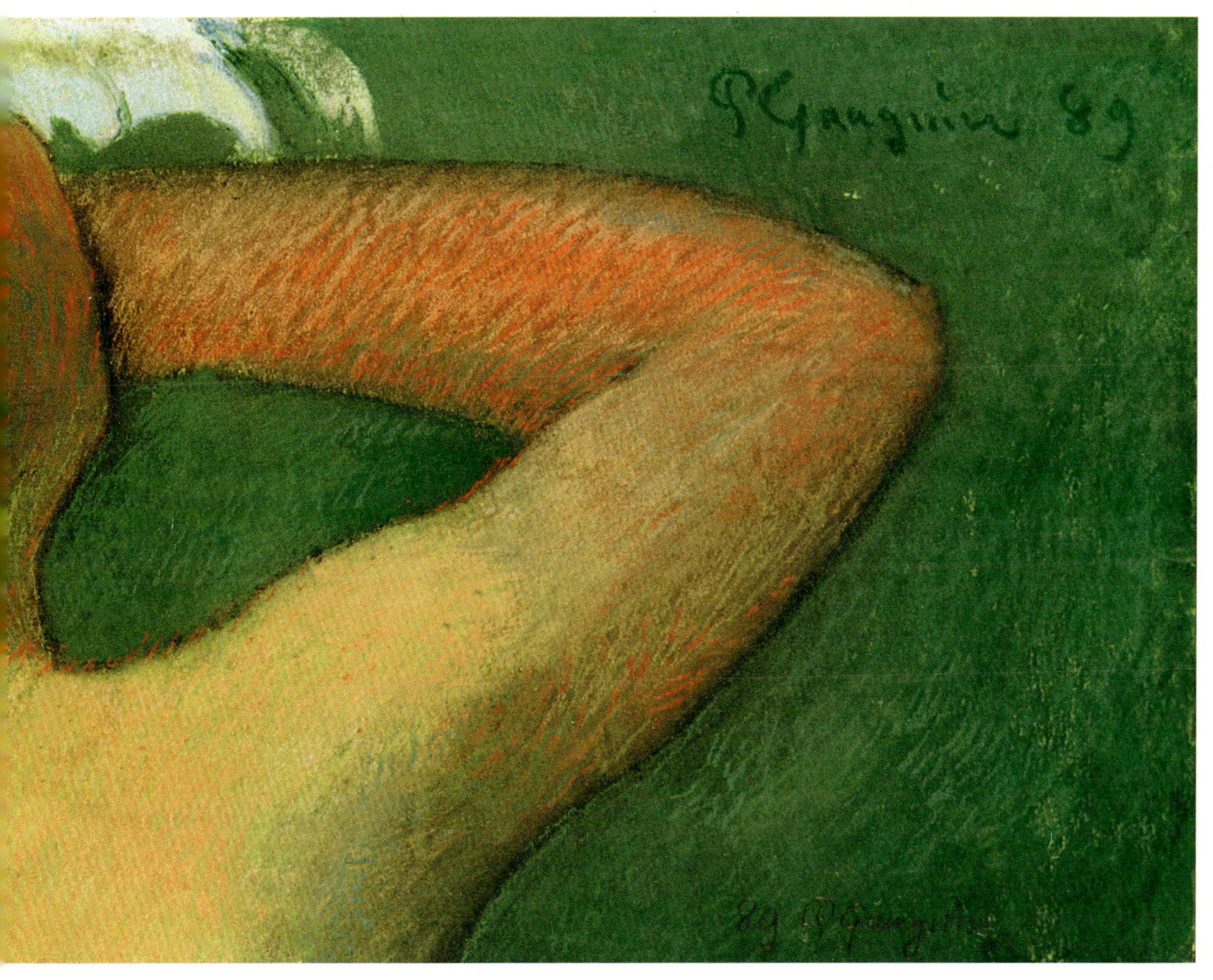

Woman in the Waves or *Ondine*
Femme dans les vagues ou *Ondine*

Frau in den Wellen oder *Undine*
Mujer entre las olas u *Ondine*

Donna tra le onde o *Ondina*
Vrouw in de golven of *Ondine*

1889, Pastel and gouache on vellum/Pastel et gouache sur papier vélin, 12 × 36,5 cm, Private collection

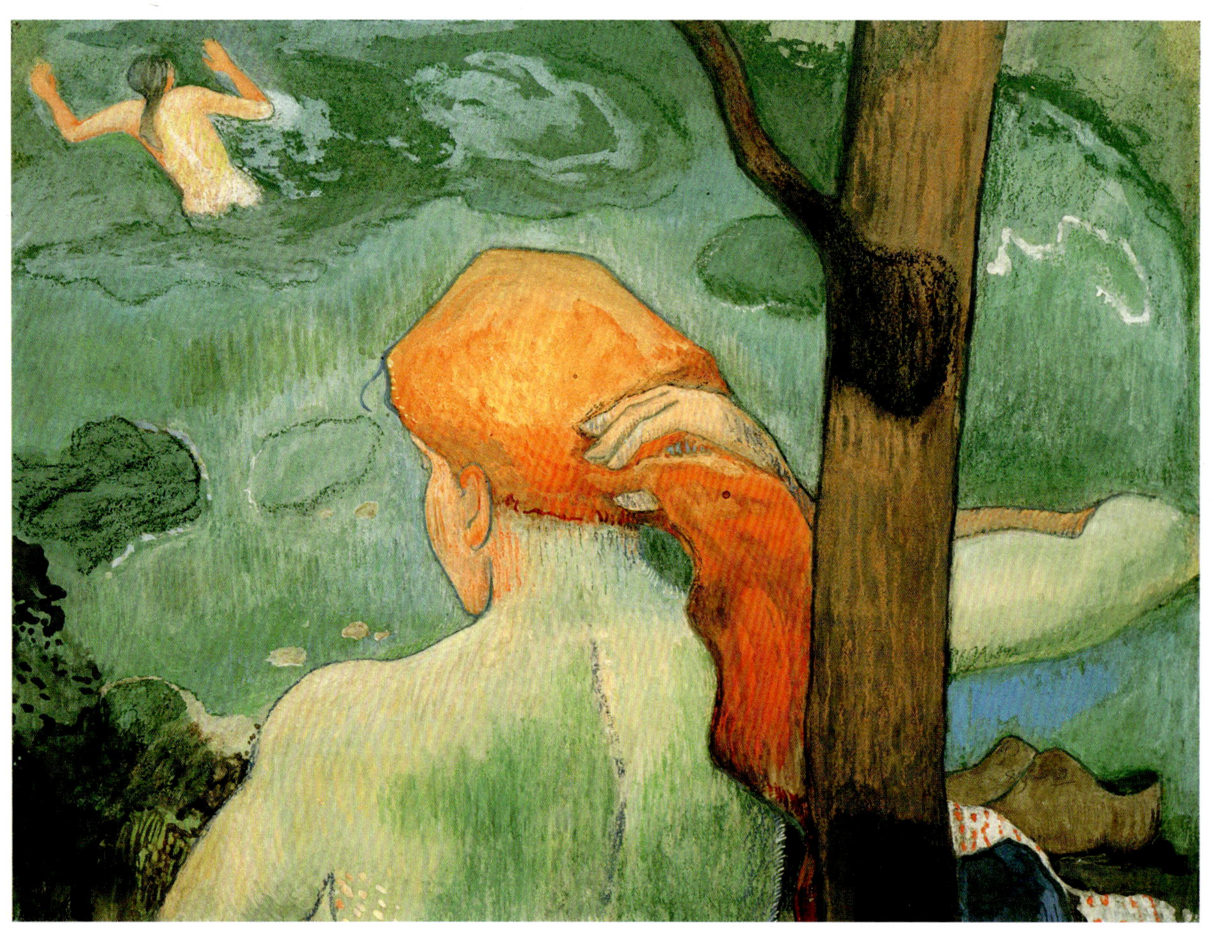

The Bathing Place

La Baignade

Badende

El baño

La bagnante

De zwempartij

1889, Gouache, watercolor, pastel and gold paint on vellum, marouflaged on wood/Gouache, aquarelle, pastel et peinture dorée sur vélin, marouflé sur bois, 34,5 × 45 cm, Private collection

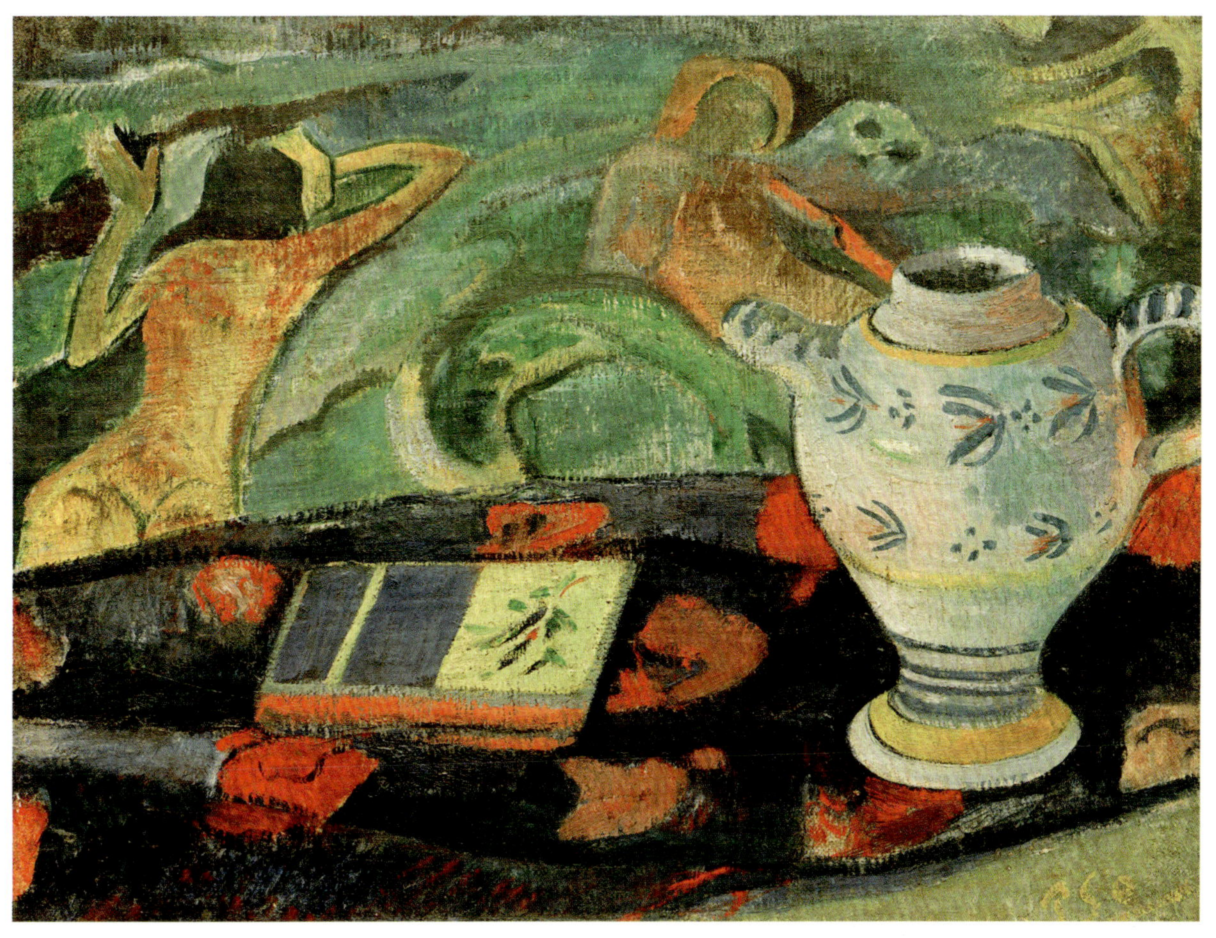

Still Life with Quimper Jug

Nature morte avec une cruche de Quimper

Stillleben mit Krug aus Quimper

Naturaleza muerta con una jarra de Quimper

Natura morta con una brocca di Quimper

Stilleven met een kruik uit Quimper

1889, Oil on canvas/Huile sur toile, 34,3 × 42 cm, Berkeley Art Museum, Berkeley

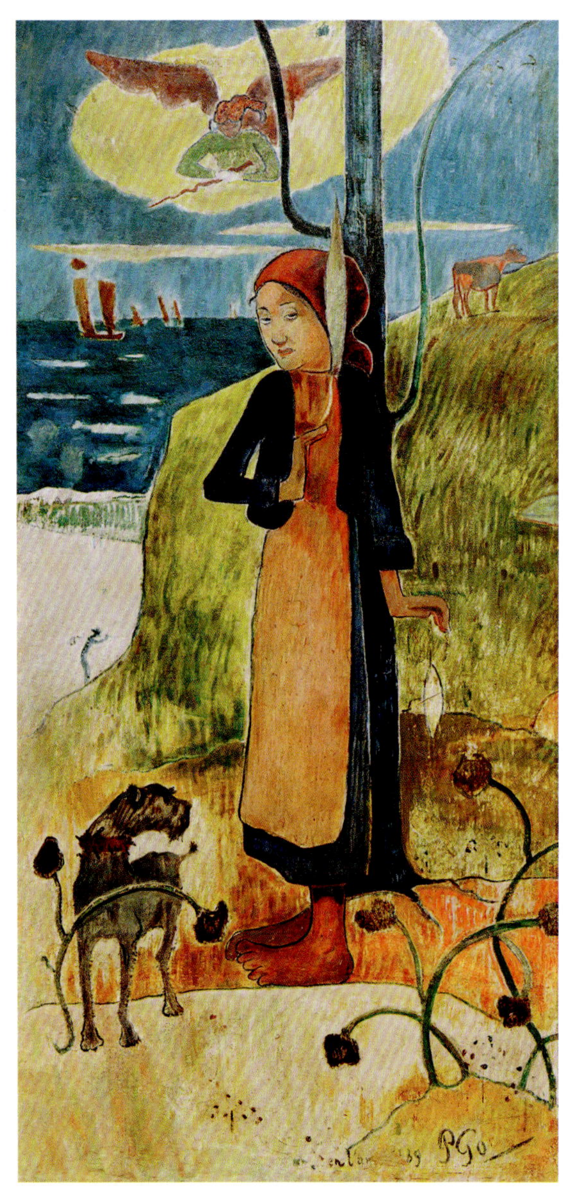

Breton Girl Spinning (Jeanne d'Orléans)
Jeune Bretonne filant (Jeanne d'Orléans)
Bretonisches Mädchen beim Spinnen (Johanna von Orléans)
Joven bretona hilando (Jeanne de Orléans)
Giovane bretone filante (Giovanna d'Orleans)
Bretons meisje bij het spinnen (Jeanne d'Orléans)

1889, Oil on plaster/Huile sur plâtre, 135 × 62 cm, Van Gogh Museum, Amsterdam

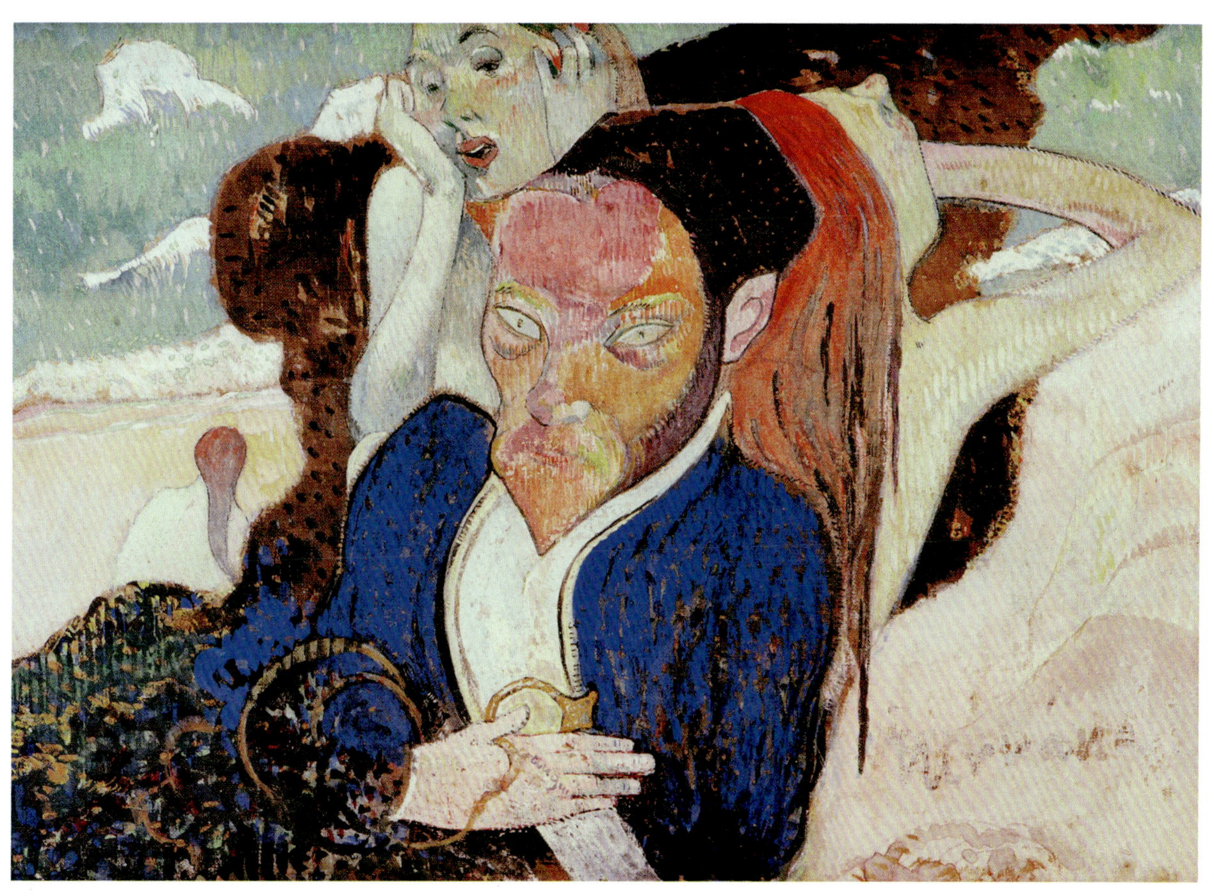

Meyer de Haan

c. 1889, Oil on silk/Huile sur soie, 20 × 29 cm, Wadsworth Atheneum Museum of Art, Hartford

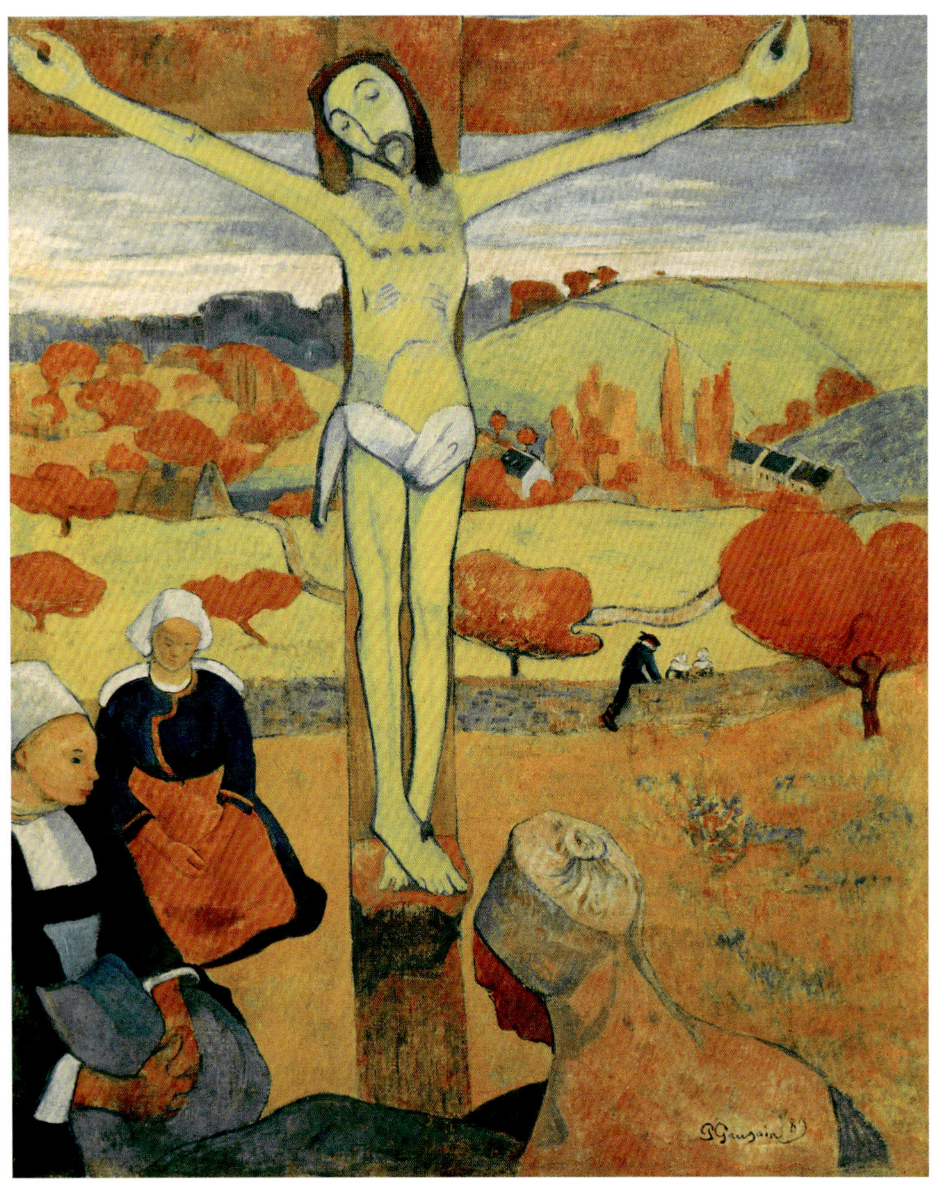

The Yellow Christ

Le Christ jaune

Der gelbe Christus

El Cristo amarillo

Il Cristo giallo

De gele Christus

1889, Oil on canvas/Huile sur toile, 91,1 × 73,4 cm, Albright-Knox Art Gallery, Buffalo

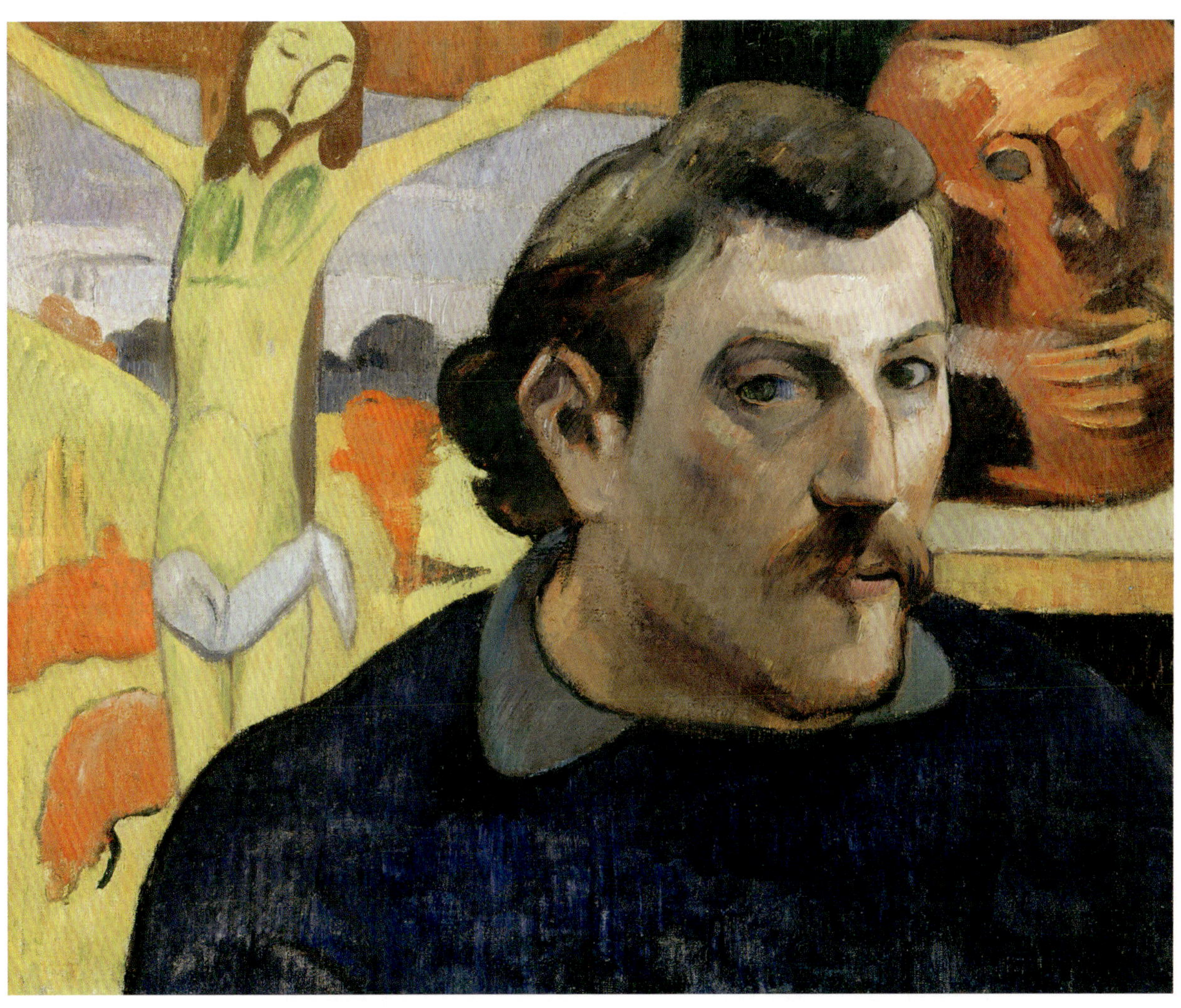

Portrait of the Artist with the Yellow Christ

Autoportrait au Christ jaune

Selbstbildnis mit Christus

Autorretrato con el Cristo amarillo

Autoritratto del Cristo giallo

Zelfportret met de gele Christus

c. 1890–91, Oil on canvas/Huile sur toile, 30 × 46 cm, Musée d'Orsay, Paris

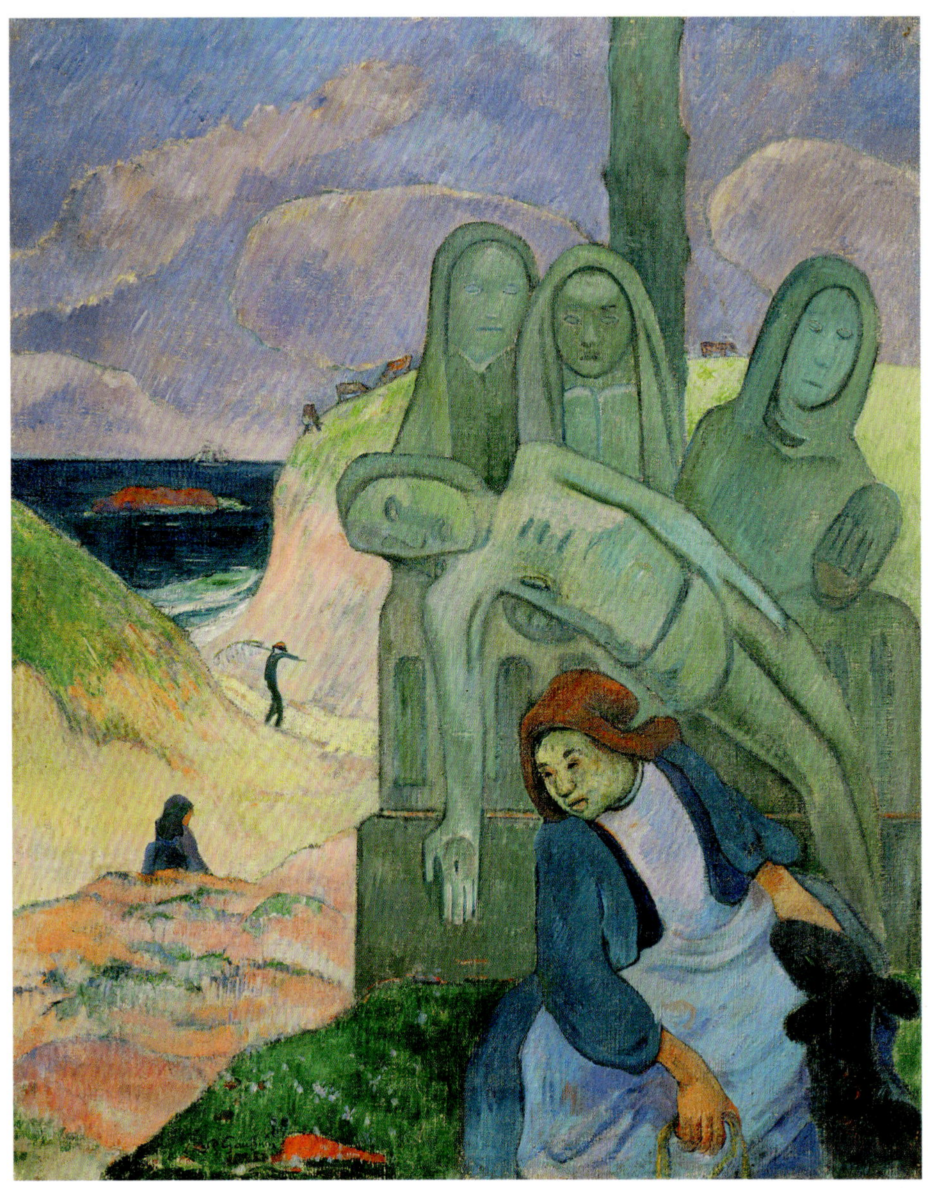

The Green Christ

Le Christ vert

Der grüne Christus

El Cristo verde

Il Cristo verde

De groene Christus

1889, Oil on canvas/Huile sur toile, 92 × 73,5 cm, Musées royaux des Beaux-Arts de Belgique, Bruxelles

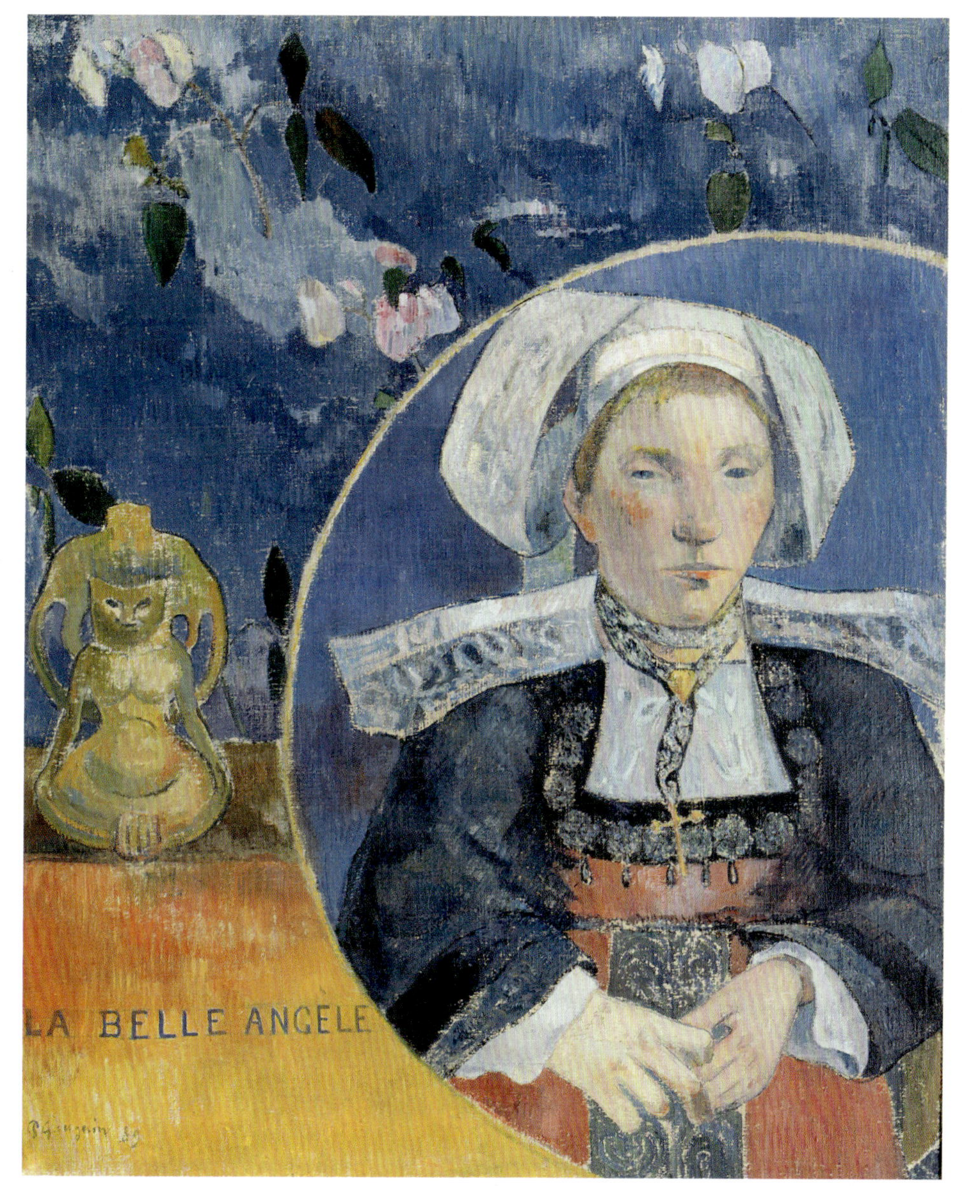

La Belle Angèle

1889, Oil on canvas/Huile
sur toile, 92 × 73 cm, Musée
d'Orsay, Paris

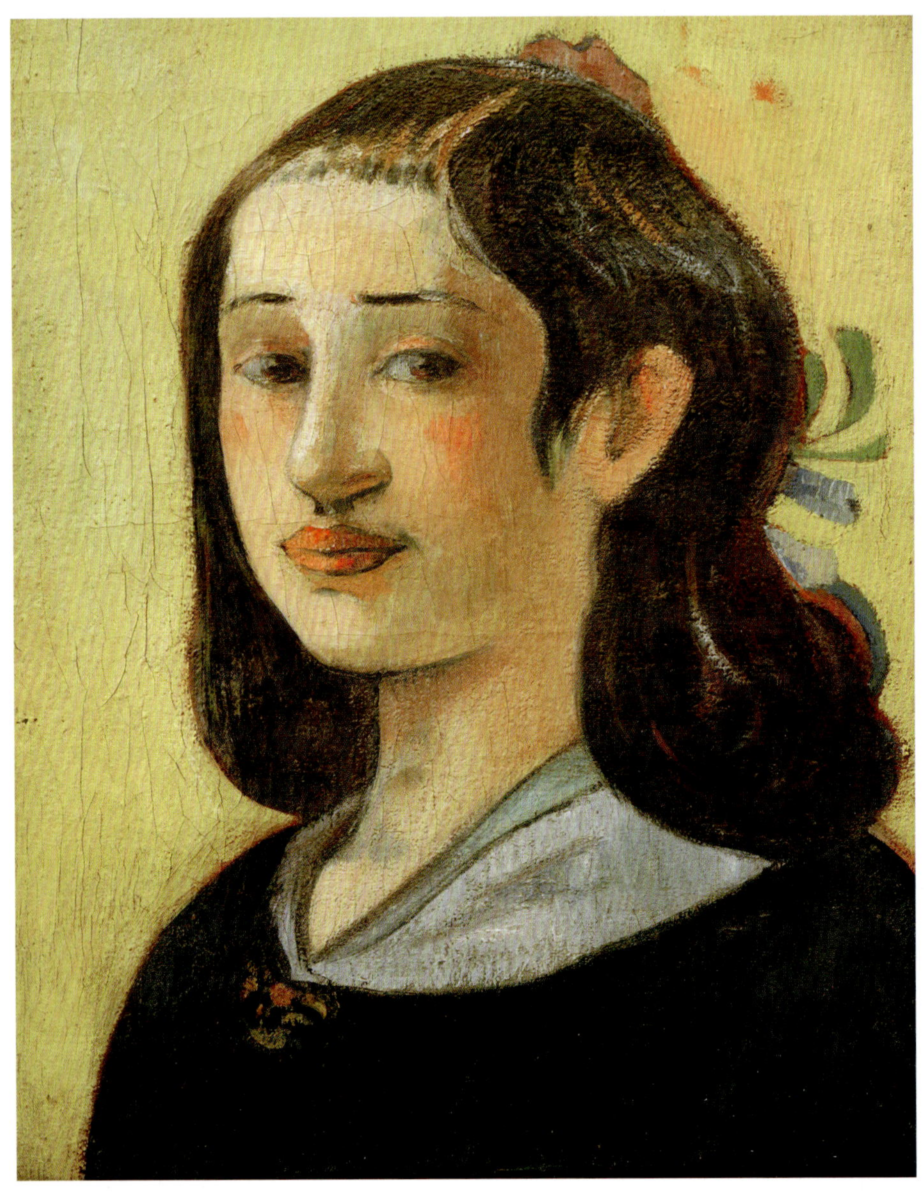

**Portrait of Aline Gauguin
(his mother)**

**Portrait de la mère de
l'artiste, Aline Gauguin**

**Bildnis der Mutter des
Künstlers, Aline Gauguin**

**Retrato de la madre del
artista, Aline Gauguin**

**Ritratto della moglie
dell'artista, Aline Gauguin**

**Portret van de moeder van de
kunstenaar, Aline Gauguin**

*c. 1890–93, Oil on wood/Huile sur
bois, 41 × 33 cm, Staatsgalerie,
Stuttgart*

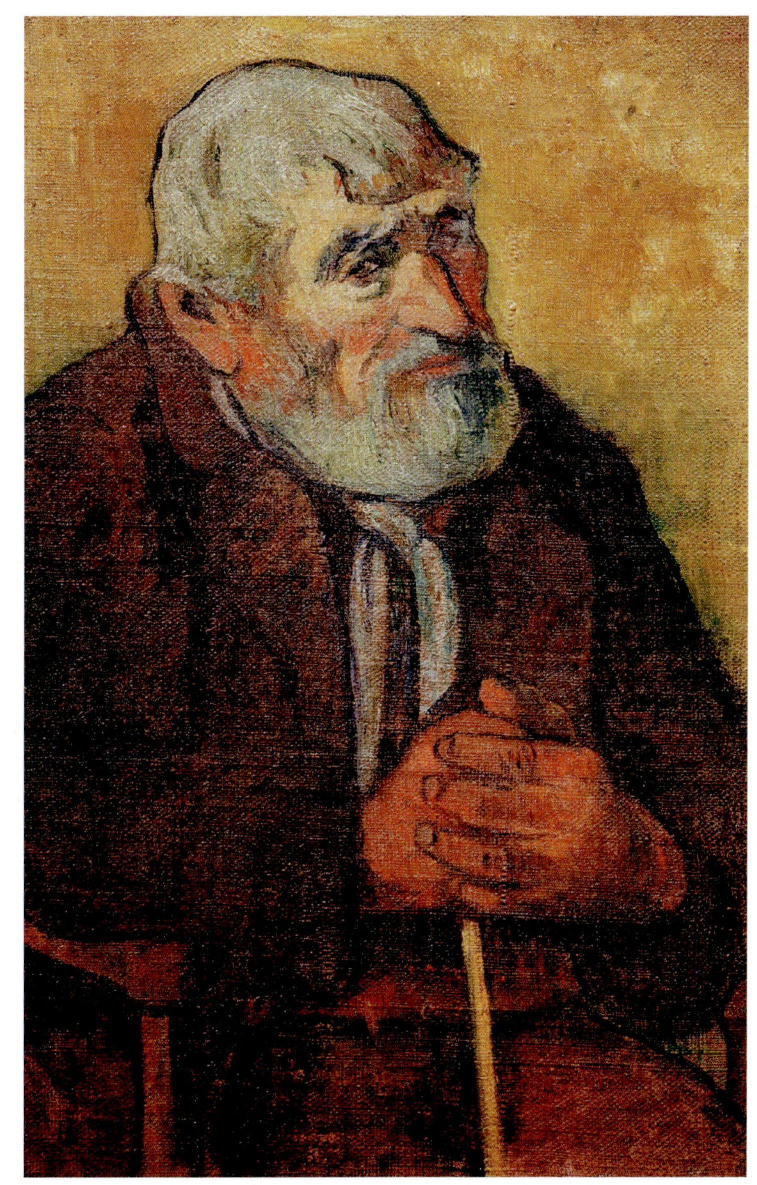

Old Man with a Cane
Vieil homme au bâton
Alter Mann mit Stock
Anciano con bastón
Uomo anziano con bastone
Oude man met stok

1889–90, Oil on canvas/Huile sur toile, 70 × 45 cm,
Petit Palais, Musée des Beaux-Arts de la ville de Paris, Paris

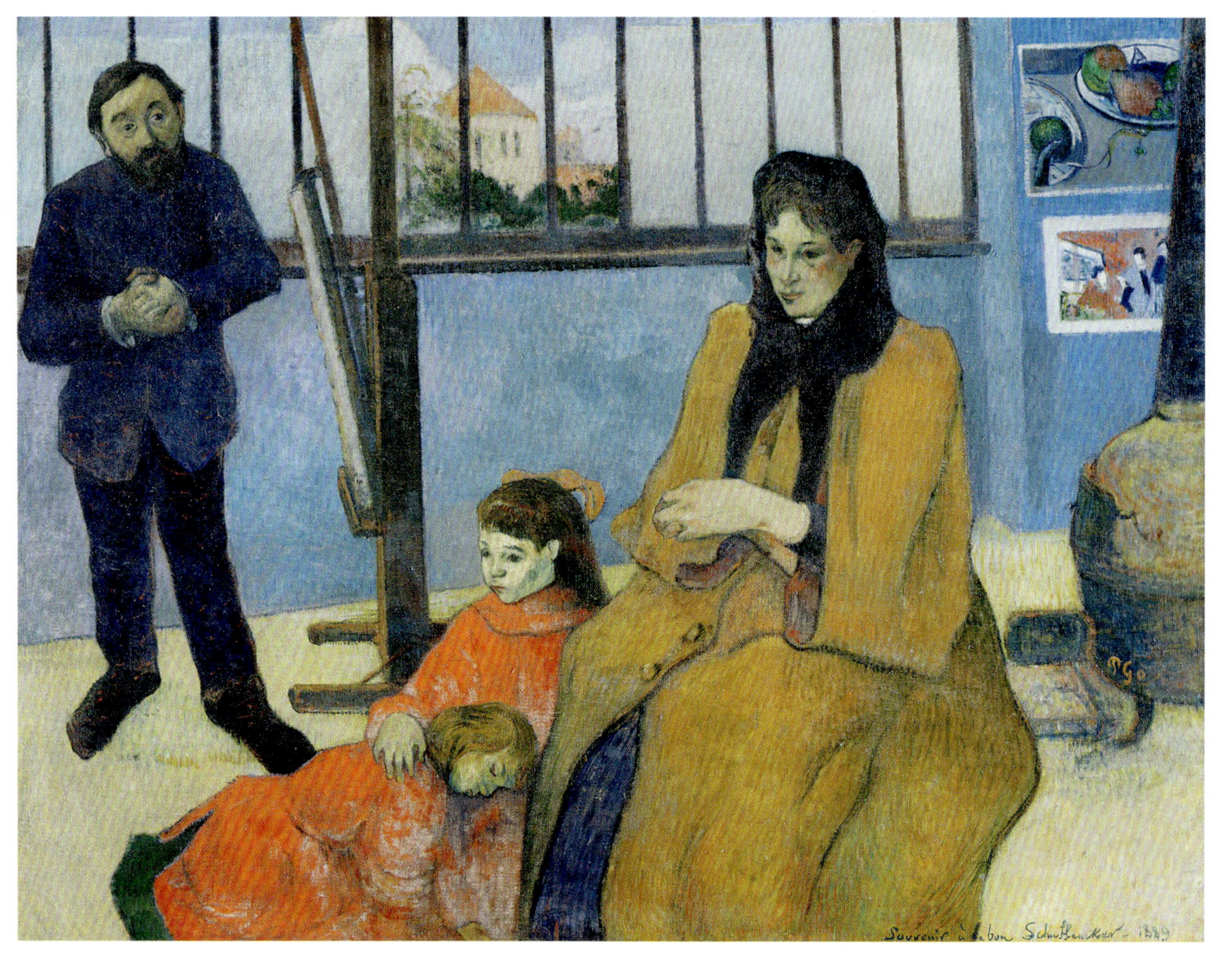

Schuffenecker's Studio

L'Atelier de Schuffenecker

Schuffeneckers Atelier

El taller de Schuffenecker

L'atelier di Schuffenecker

Het atelier van Schuffenecker

1889, Oil on canvas/Huile sur toile, 73 × 92 cm, Musée d'Orsay, Paris

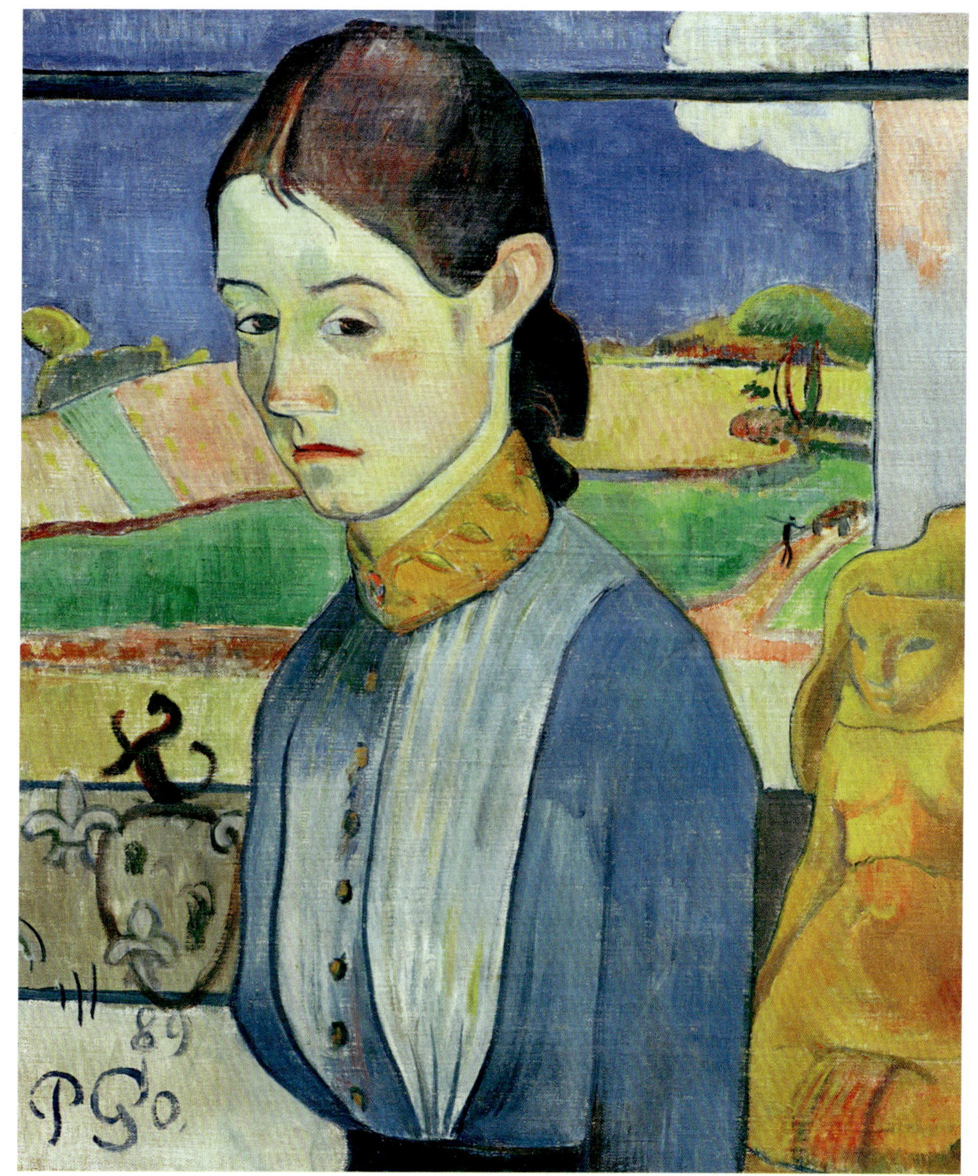

Young Breton Girl
Jeune Bretonne
Junge Bretonin
Una joven bretona
Giovane bretone
Jonge Bretonse vrouw

1889, Oil on canvas/Huile sur toile, 46 × 38 cm, Private collection

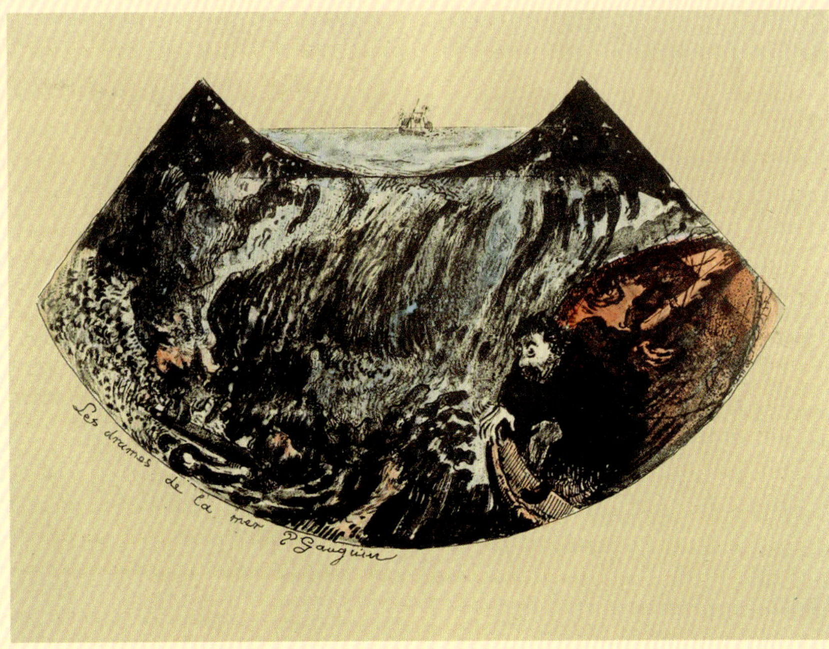

Dramas of the Sea or
A Descent into the Maelstrom

Les Drames de la mer ou
Une descente dans le maelstrom

Die Dramen des Meers oder
Ein Abstieg in den Strudel

Los dramas del mar o
Un descenso en la vorágine

I Drammi del mare o
Una discesa nel Maelstrom

De drama's van de zee of
Een afdaling in de draaikolk

1889, Colored zincography/Zincographie colorisée, 18,5 × 27,5 cm, Van Gogh Museum, Amsterdam

Gauguin the engraver

A polymorphic and inquisitive artist, Gauguin added at will the techniques and materials of artistic creation to his repertoire. Wood engraving is one of his favourite techniques, as witnessed by countless low relief pieces, statuettes, and xylographs. Artist and artisan, he likes to print his prints himself, often inspired by his own paintings, whose colours he accentuates and whose lines he frees up. Gauguin experiments with engraving techniques (etching, zincography, lithography, monotype) and even claimed to be the inventor of the "dessin-empreinte", of single-print engraving.

Gauguin graveur

Artiste polymorphe et curieux, Gauguin multiplie à l'envi les techniques et les matériaux de création. La gravure sur bois est l'une de ses techniques de prédilection, dont attestent quantité de bas-reliefs, statuettes et xylographies. Artiste-artisan, il se plaît à imprimer lui-même ses estampes, souvent inspirées de ses propres peintures, dont il accentue les couleurs et libère le trait. Gauguin expérimente toutes les techniques de gravures (eau-forte, zincographie, lithographie, monotype) et prétend même être l'inventeur de la technique du dessin-empreinte.

Gauguin, der Graveur

Vielseitig und neugierig wie er ist, verwendet der Künstler Gauguin nach Belieben weitere Techniken und Materialien für seine Werke. Die Gravur von Holz ist eine seiner bevorzugten Techniken, davon zeugen eine Vielzahl von Flachreliefs, kleinen Statuen und Xylographien. Künstler und Handwerker zugleich, vermag er seine eigenen Drucke anzufertigen, oft von seinen eigenen Gemälden inspiriert, mit akzentuierten Farben und freigestellter Linienführung. Gauguin experimentiert mit allen Ätztechniken (Radierung, Zinkografie, Lithografie) und behauptet sogar, der Erfinder der „dessin-empreinte" – einer einzigartigen Gravurtechnik – zu sein.

*1889, Zincography/Zincographie, 16,6 × 22,6 cm, Cleveland
Museum of Art, Cleveland*

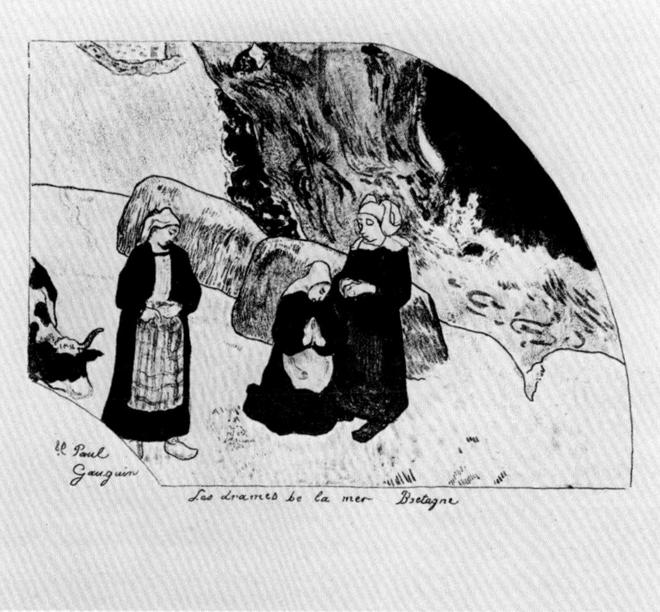

Gauguin grabador

Artista polimórfico y curioso, Gauguin replicó de manera envidiable las técnicas y los materiales de creación. Grabar la madera es una de sus técnicas predilectas, como bien atestiguan los numerosos bajorrelieves, estatuillas y xilografías. Artista y artesano, gustaba de imprimir él mismo sus estampas, inspiradas frecuentemente en sus propias pinturas, acentuando los colores y dando libertad al trazo. Gauguin experimentó con todas as técnicas de grabación (aguafuerte, zincografía, litografía, monotipo) e incluso quiso ser el inventor de la técnica "dessin-empreinte", la grabación única.

Gauguin incisore

Artista polimorfo e curioso, Gauguin moltiplica a piacimento le tecniche e il materiale di creazione. L'incisione del legno è una delle sue tecniche preferite, come attestano quantità di bassi rilievi, statue e xilografie. Artista-artigiano, gli piace stampare le proprie stampe, spesso ispirate dai suoi dipinti, in cui accentua i colori e rilascia la linea. Gauguin sperimenta tutte le tecniche di incisione (acquaforte, zincografia, litografia, monotipo) e addirittura sostiene di essere l'inventore della tecnica "dessin-empreinte", l'incisione unica.

Gauguin als etser

Gauguin is een veelzijdig en nieuwsgierig kunstenaar die voortdurend zijn arsenaal aan technieken en materialen uitbreidt. Houtgravure is een van zijn favoriete technieken, getuige het grote aantal bas-reliëfs, beeldjes en xylografieën. Als kunstenaar-ambachtsman drukt hij zijn prenten bij voorkeur zelf. Vaak zijn die geïnspireerd op zijn eigen schilderijen, met extra kleuraccenten en lossere penseelstreken. Gauguin experimenteert met alle etstechnieken (diepdruk, zinkdruk, steendruk, monotype) en pretendeert zelfs de uitvinder van de techniek "dessin-empreinte" te zijn.

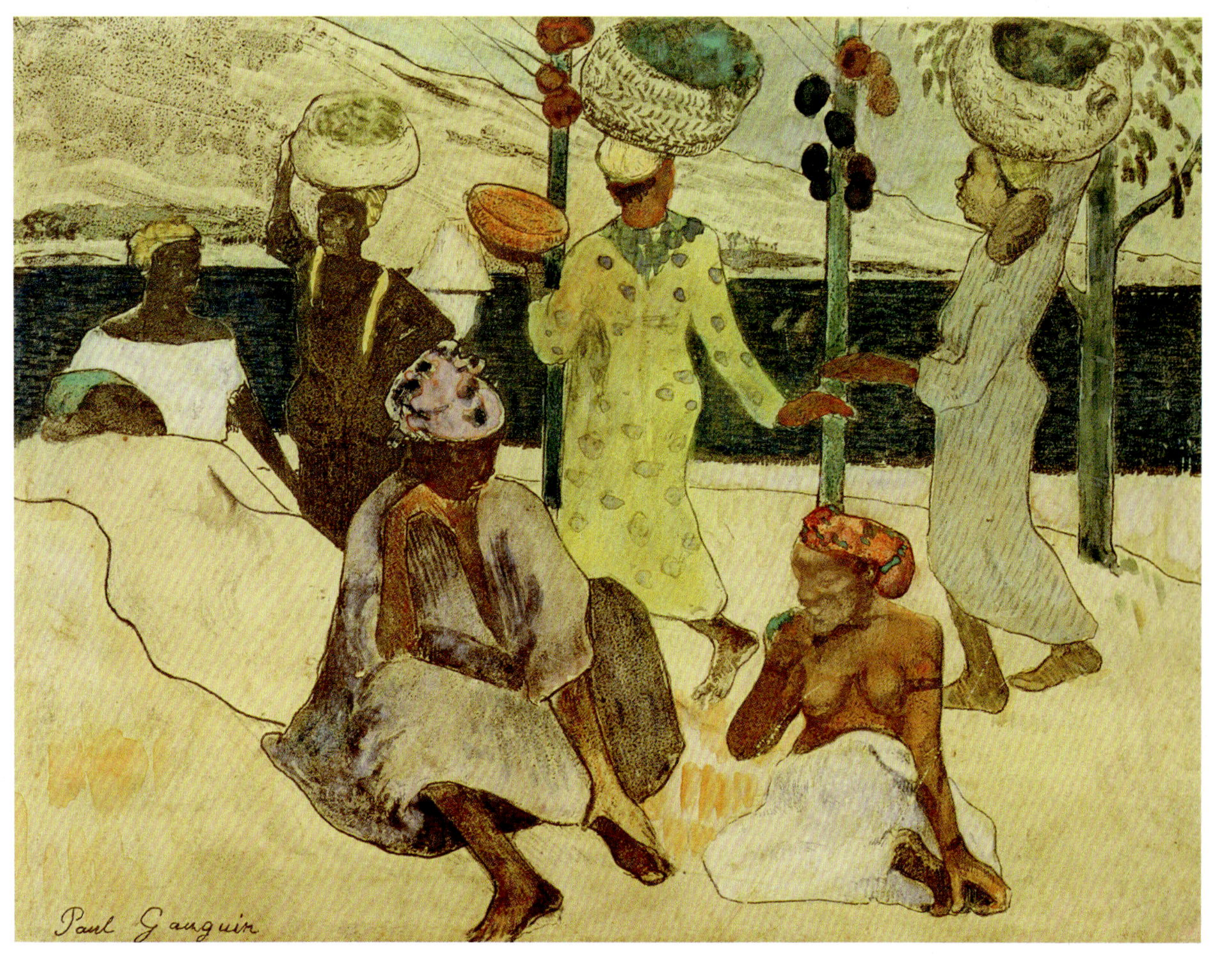

The Cicadas And The Ants

Les Cigales et les fourmis

Grillen und Ameisen

Las cigalas y las hormigas

Le cicale e le formiche

Krekels en mieren

1889, Colored zincography/Zincographie colorisée, 19,3 × 26,7 cm, Private collection

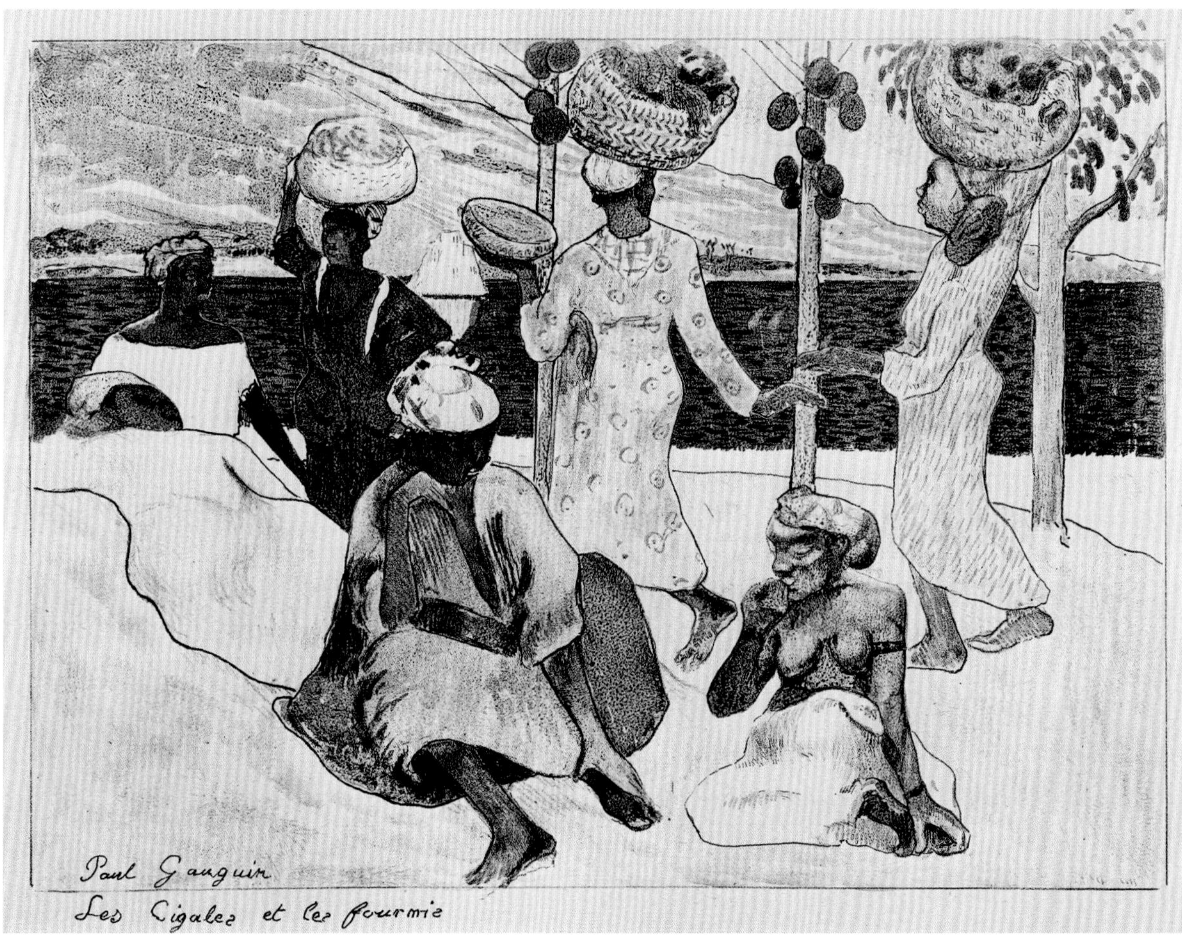

The Cicadas And The Ants

Les Cigales et les fourmis

Grillen und Ameisen

Las cigalas y las hormigas

Le cicale e le formiche

De krekels en de mieren

1889, Zincography/Zincographie, 20,4 × 26,2 cm, Cleveland Museum of Art, Cleveland

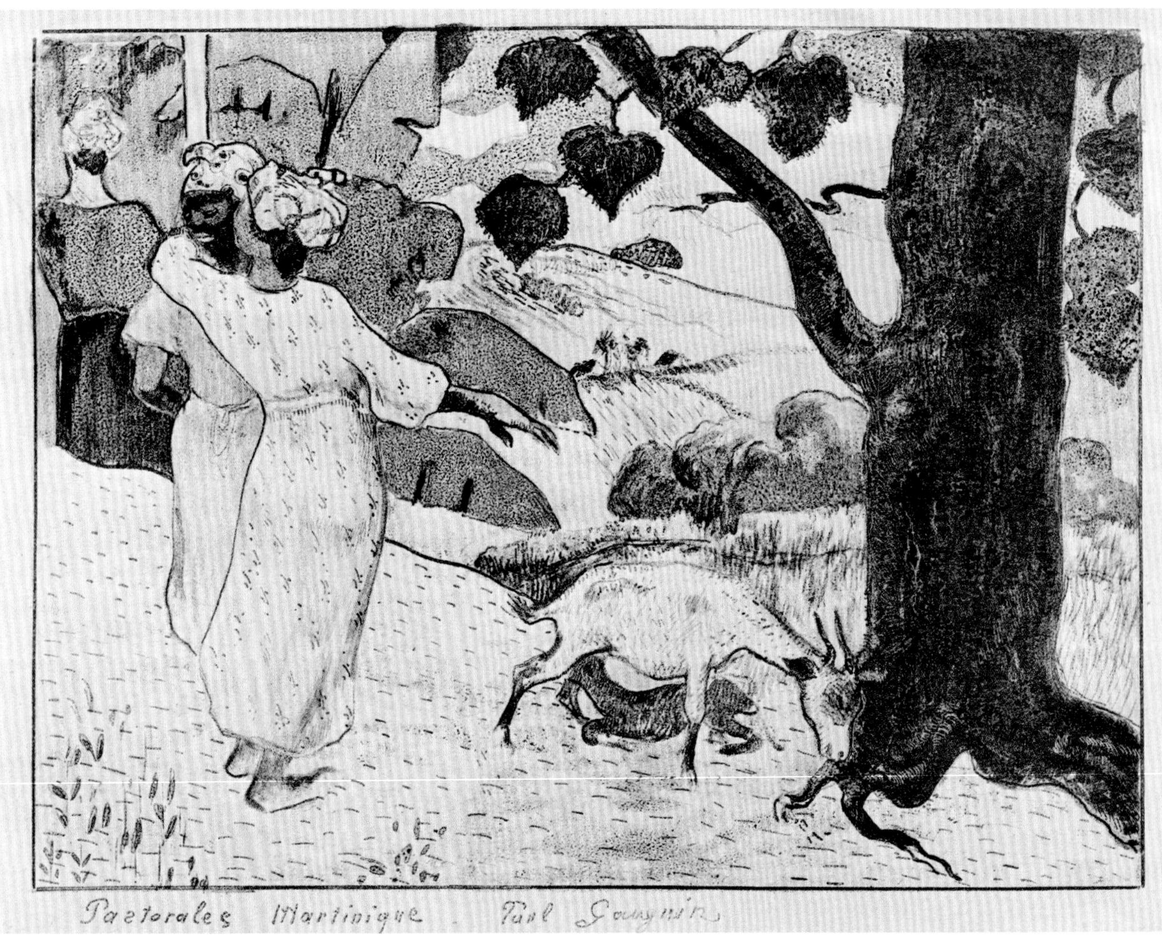

Pastoral in Martinique

Pastorale de Martinique

Pastorale auf Martinique

Pastoral de Martinica

Pastorale di Martinica

Pastorale op Martinique

1889, Zincography/Zincographie, 17,6 × 22,3 cm, Cleveland Museum of Art, Cleveland

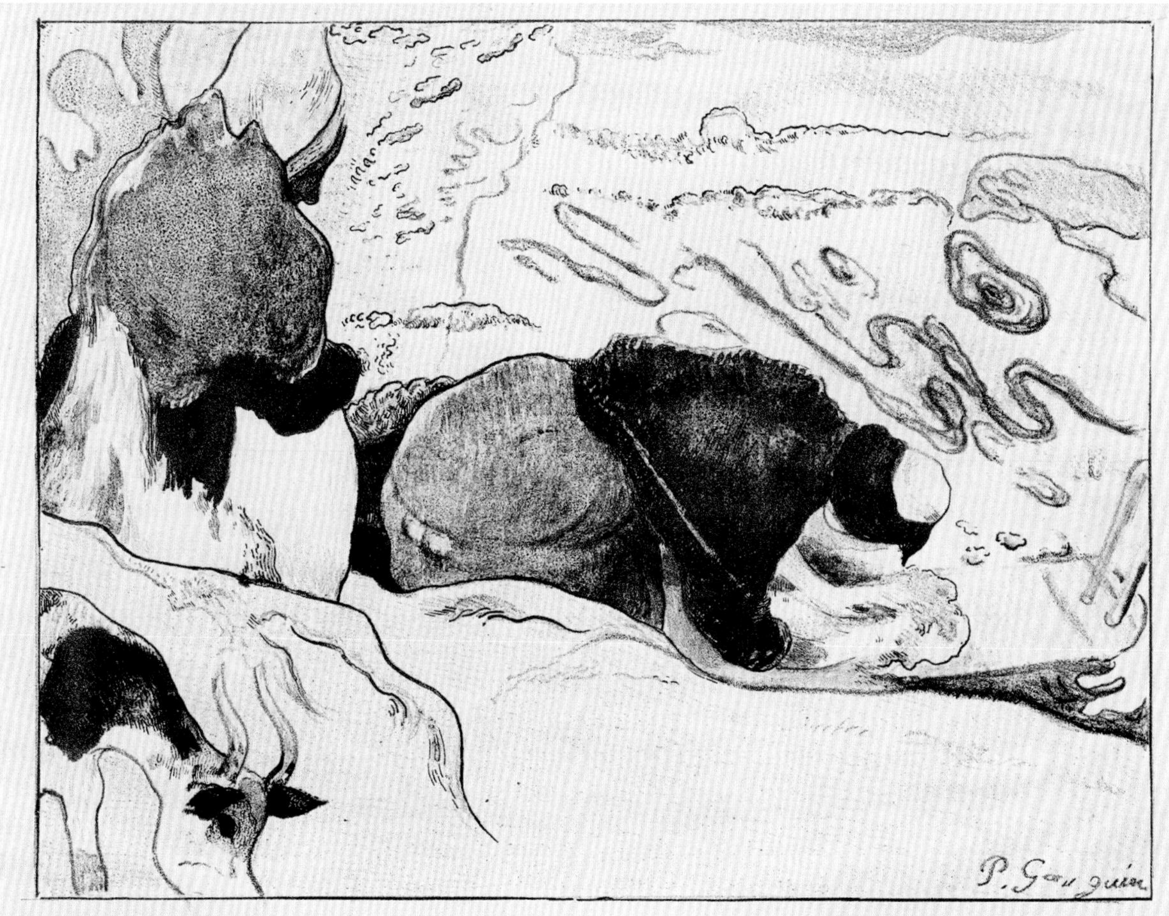

The Washerwomen

Les Laveuses

Die Wäscherinnen

Las lavanderas

Le lavandaie

De wasvrouwen

1889, Zincography/Zincographie, 20,3 × 26,1 cm, Cleveland Museum of Art, Cleveland

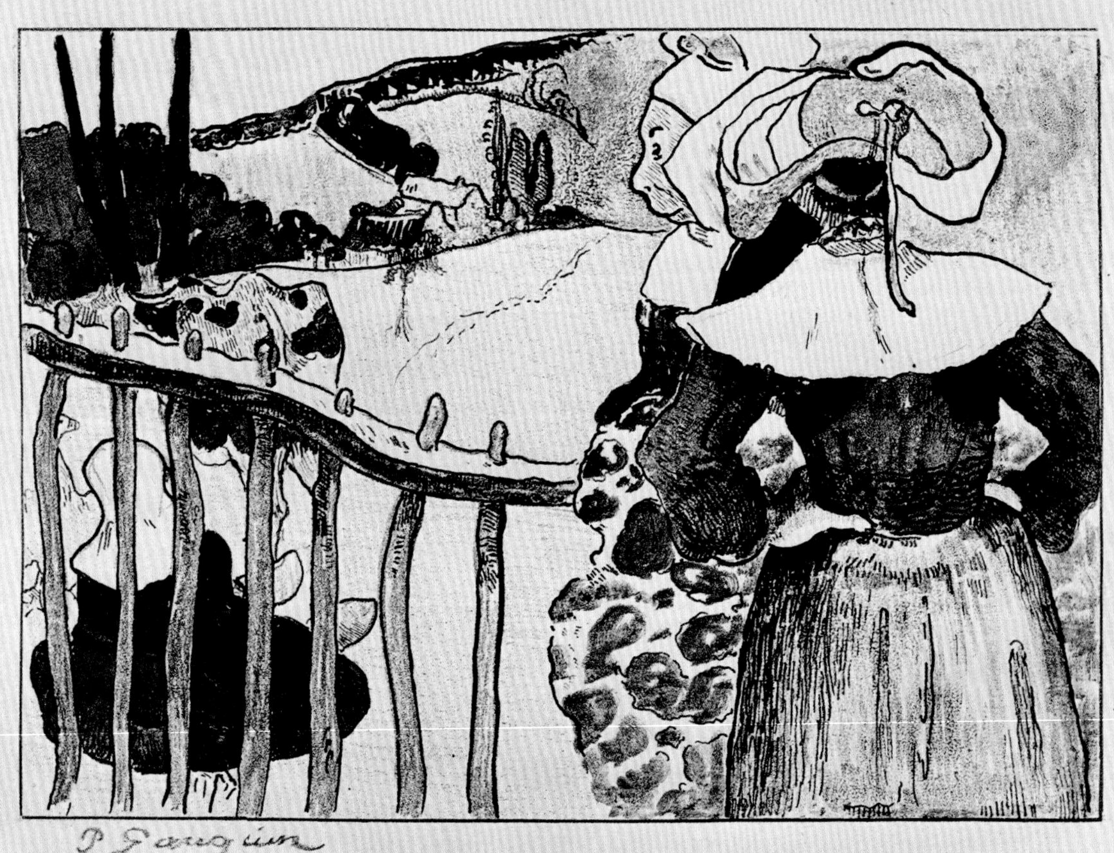

Breton Women at a Fence

Bretonnes à la barrière

Bretoninnen am Zaun

Bretonas en la barrera

Bretoni alla barriera

Bretonse vrouwen bij het hek

1889, Zincography/Zincographie, 28,4 × 23,3 cm, Cleveland Museum of Art, Cleveland

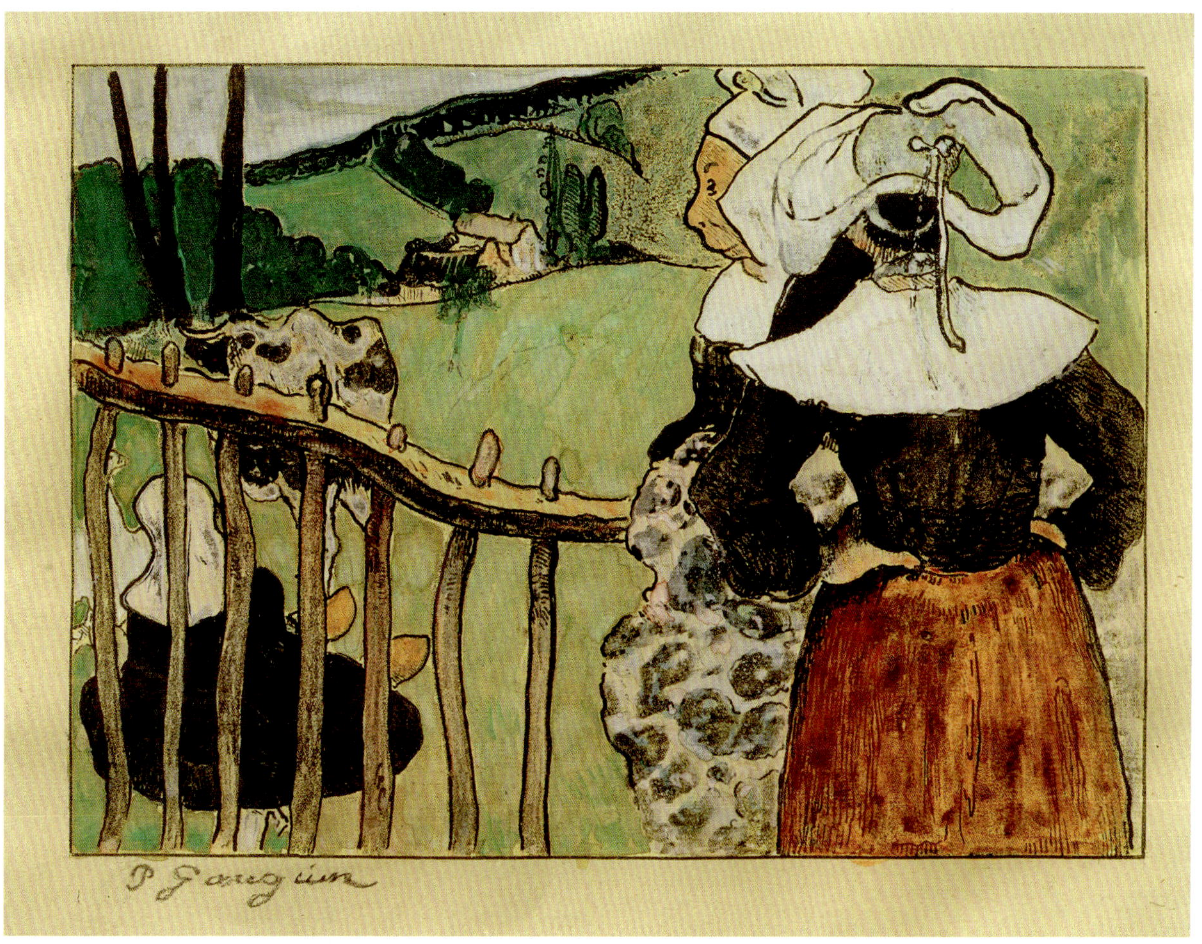

Breton Women at a Fence

Bretonnes à la barrière

Bretoninnen am Zaun

Bretonas en la barrera

Bretoni alla barriera

Bretonse vrouwen bij het hek

1889, Colored zincography/Zincographie colorisée, 27 × 31,5 cm, Private collection

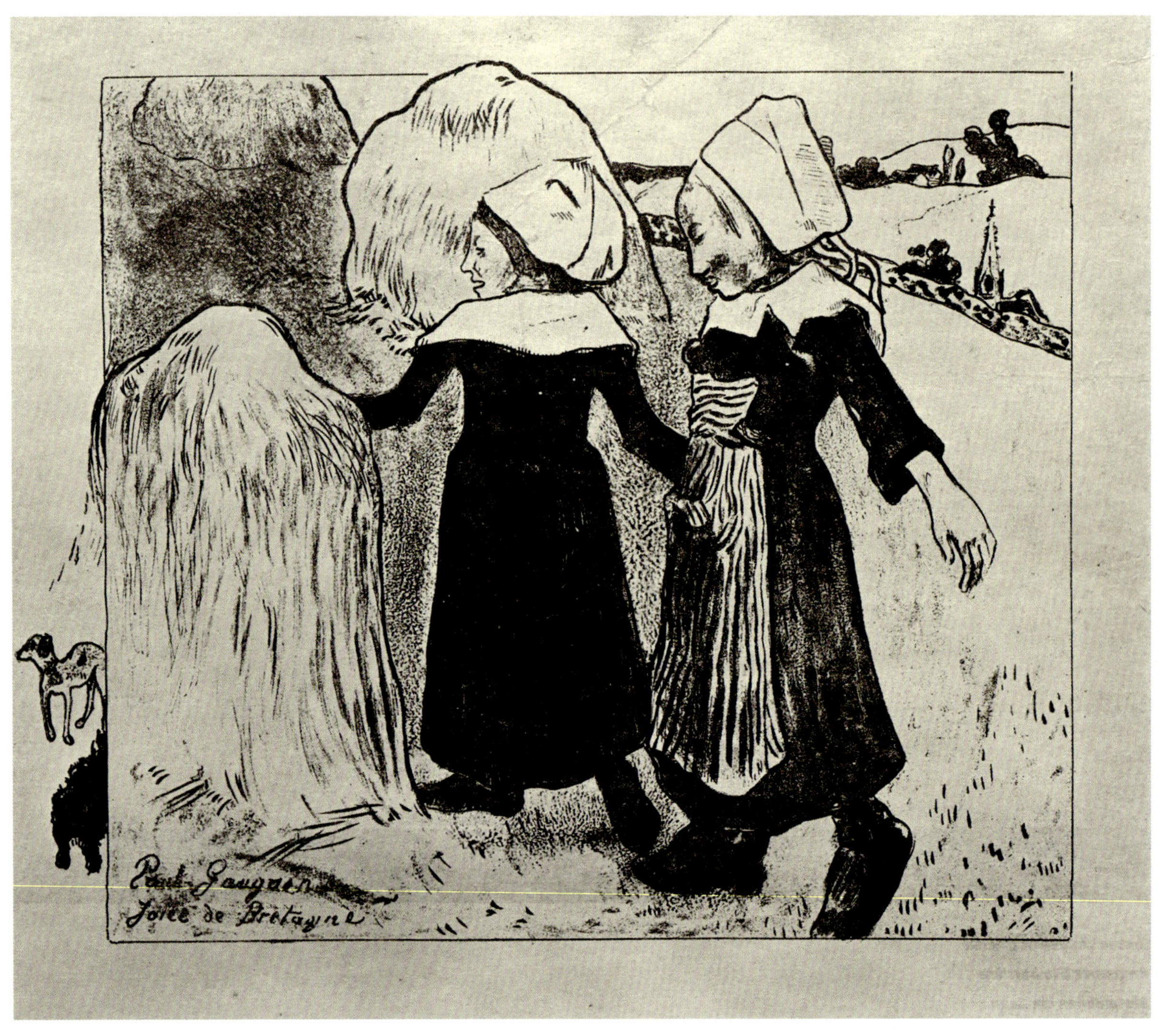

Joys of Brittany   **Freuden der Bretagne**   **Gioie di Bretagna**

Joies de Bretagne   **Alegrías de Bretaña**   **De vreugden van Bretagne**

1889, Engraving/Gravure, 32,2 × 36,1 cm, Kunsthalle, Bremen

122

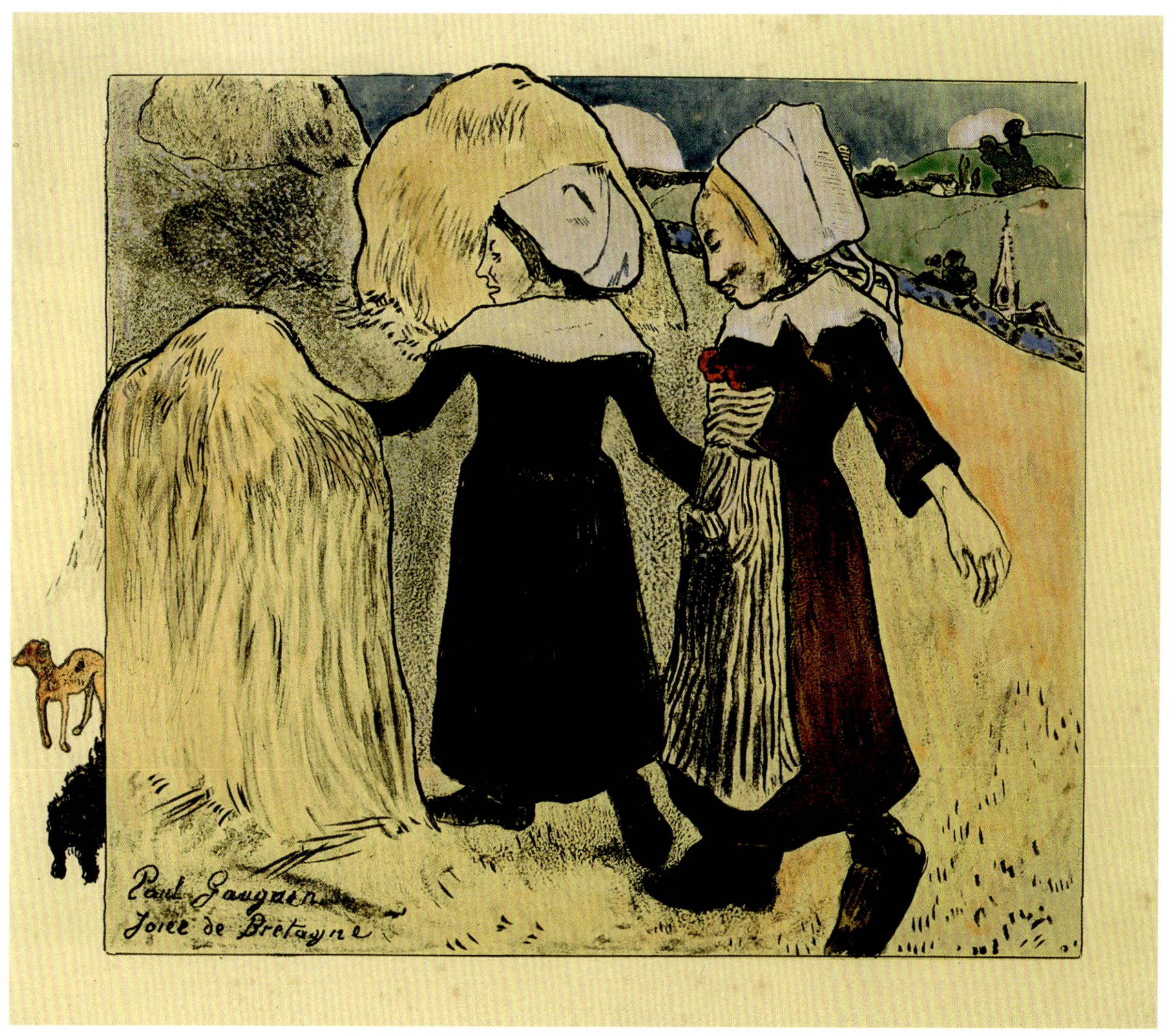

Joys of Brittany — **Freuden der Bretagne** — **Gioie di Bretagna**

Joies de Bretagne — **Alegrías de Bretaña** — **De vreugden van Bretagne**

1889, Colored zincography/Zincographie colorisée, 20,2 × 24,1 cm, Museum of Fine Arts, Boston

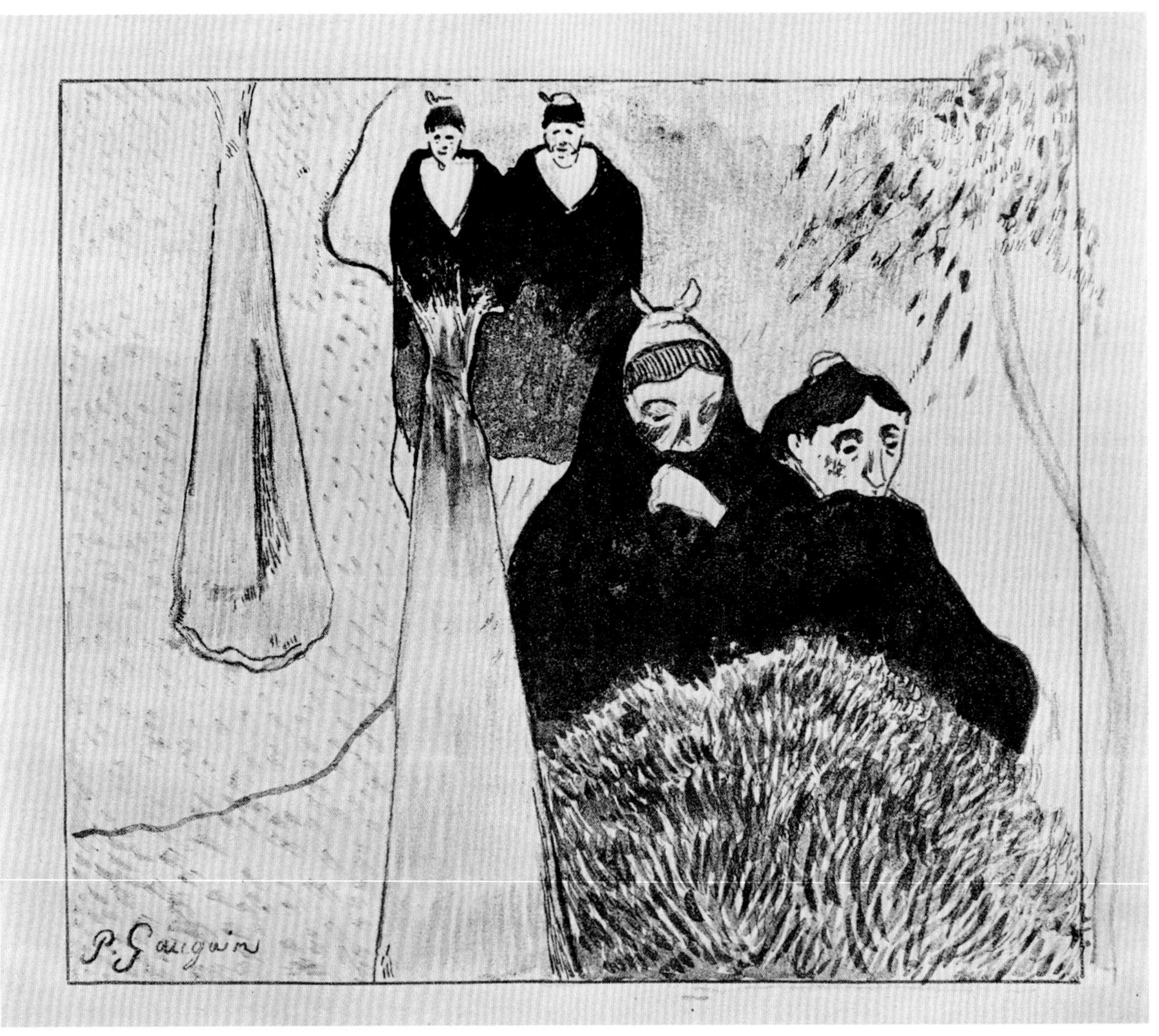

The Old Women (Arles)

Les Vieilles filles (Arles)

Die alten Jungfern (Arles)

Viejas (Arlés)

Le anziane donne (Arles)

De oude vrijsters (Arles)

1889, Zincography/Zincographie, 19,2 × 20,9 cm, Cleveland Museum of Art, Cleveland

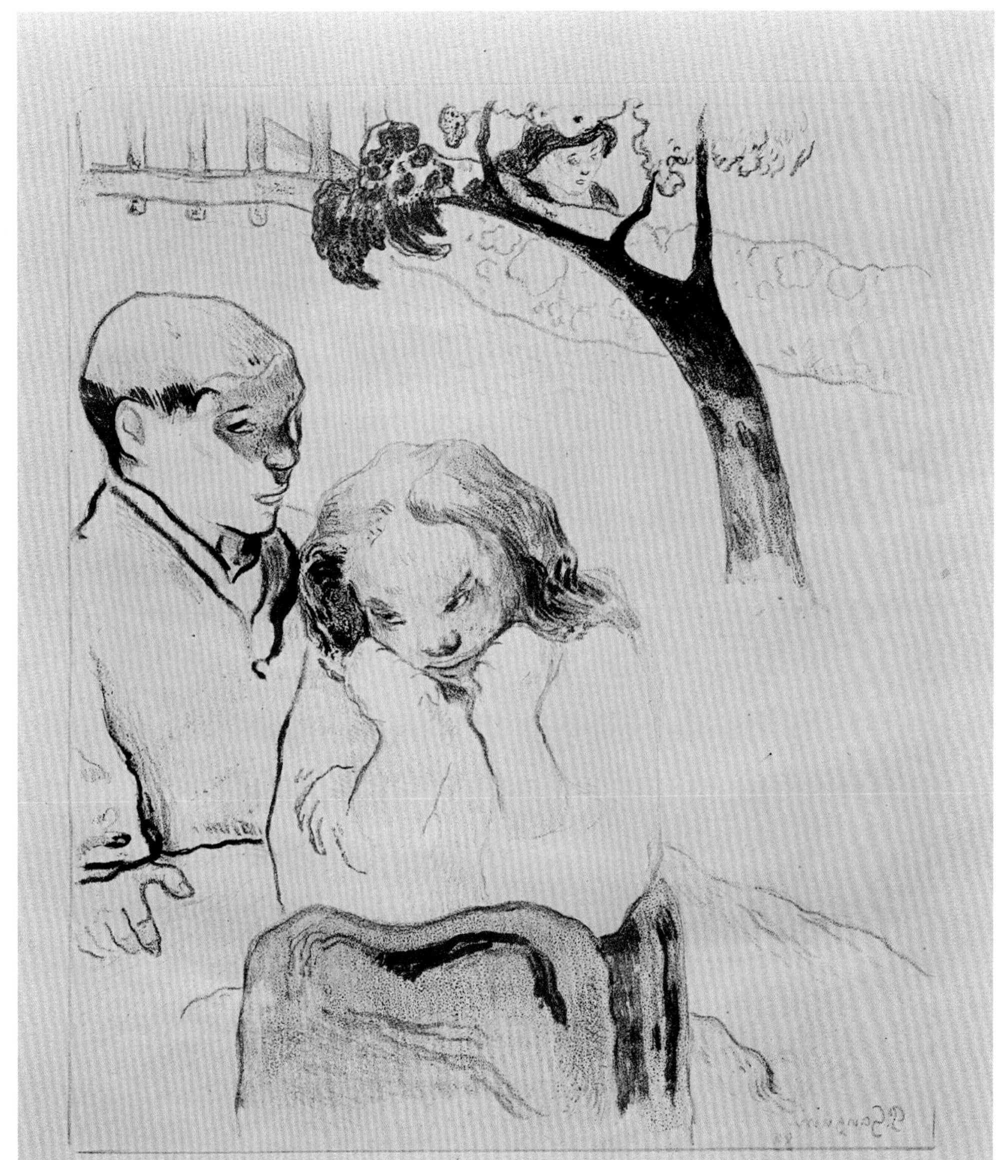

Women By a Gate

**Petits Bretons
à la barrière**

**Kleine Bretonen
am Zaun**

**Pequeños bretones
en la barrera**

**Piccoli bretoni
alla barriera**

**Jonge Bretons
bij het hek**

*1889, Zincography/
Zincographie,
16 × 21,5 cm, Cleveland
Museum of Art,
Cleveland*

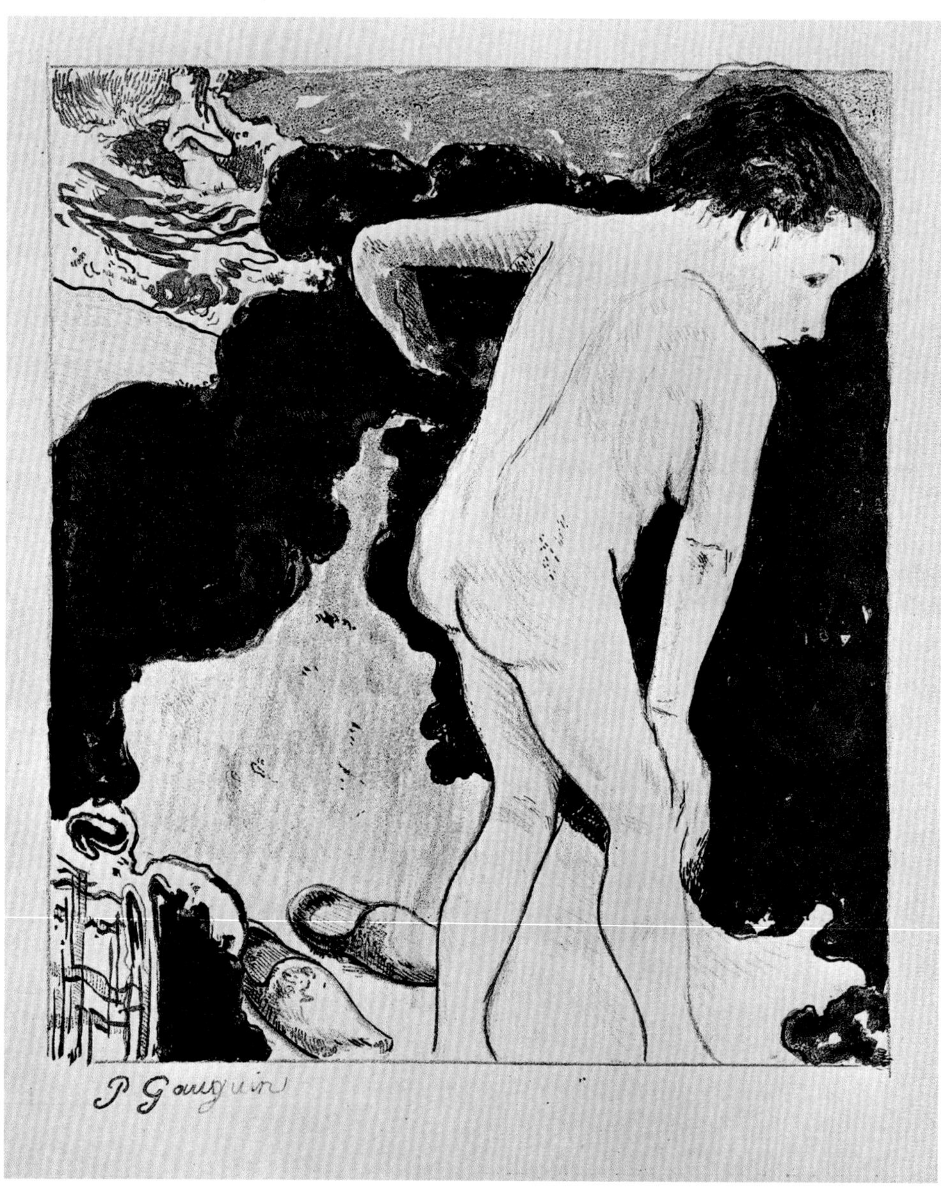

Breton Bathers

Baigneuses bretonnes

Badende Bretoninnen

Bañistas bretonas

Bagnanti bretoni

Bretonse baadsters

1889, Zincography/
Zincographie, 23,5 × 20 cm,
Van Gogh Museum,
Amsterdam

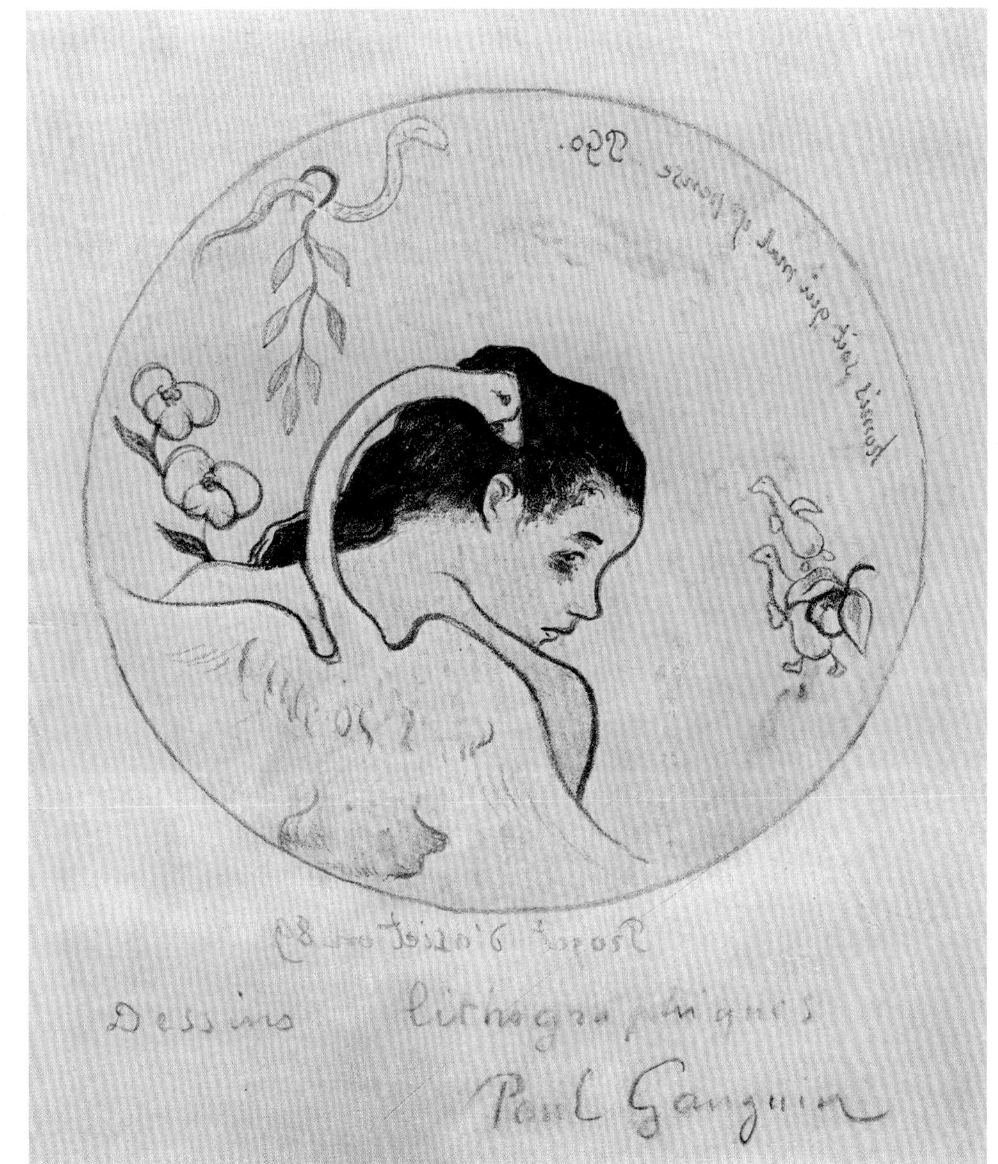

***Leda and the Swan,*
design for a plate**

***Léda et le cygne,*
projet d'assiette**

***Leda und der
Schwan,* Entwurf
für einen Teller**

***Leda y el cisne,*
proyecto de plato**

***Leda e il cigno,*
progetto su piatto**

***Leda en de zwaan,*
ontwerp voor een bord**

*1889, Zincography/
Zincographie,
20,2 × 20,3 cm, Cleveland
Museum of Art, Cleveland*

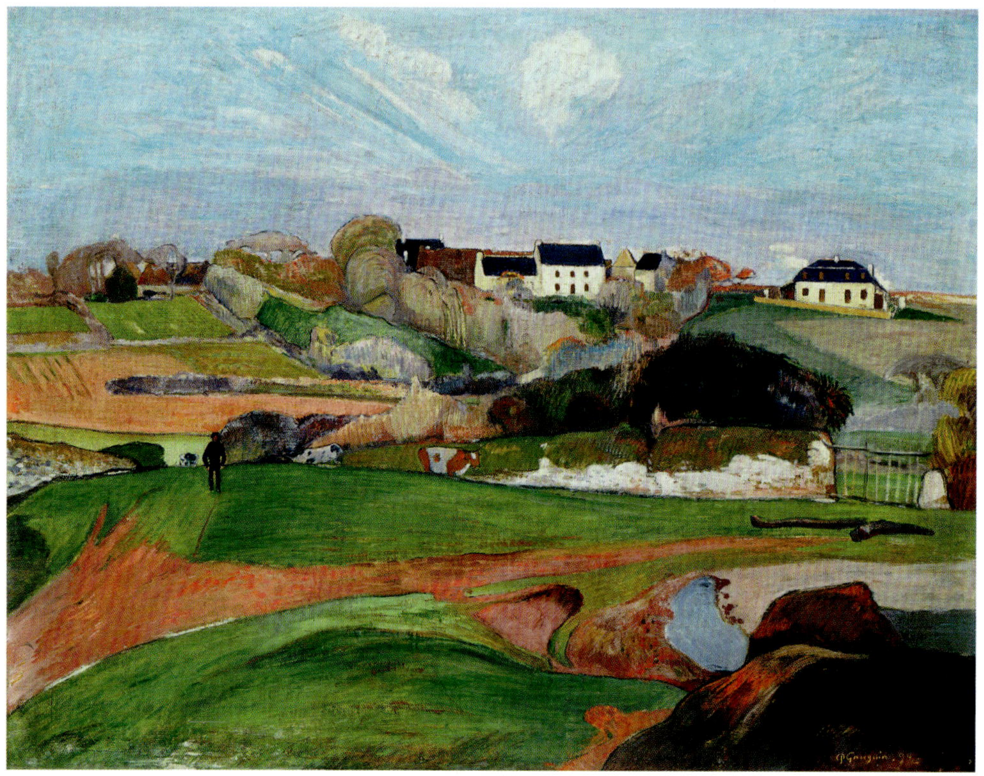

Preparing for the grand departure

During a number of months, the artist thought about the ideal location for this "studio of the tropics". Which far country could tear him from the "horrors of occidental civilisation" and respond to his artistic and existential aspirations? He knew that he "needed to re-immerse himself in virgin nature … without any other preoccupation than to render, as a child does, the conceptions of his brain, with the aid only of the primitive means of art, the only good, the only true ". His

Préparer le grand départ

L'artiste réfléchit à la localisation idéale de son « atelier des tropiques » durant des mois. Quelle contrée lointaine pourra l'arracher à « l'horreur de la civilisation occidentale » et répondre à ses aspirations existentielles et artistiques ? Lui sait avoir « besoin de [se] retremper dans la nature vierge […] sans autre préoccupation que de rendre, comme ferait un enfant, les conceptions de [son] cerveau, avec l'aide seulement des moyens d'art primitifs, les seuls bons,

Vorbereitungen für die große Reise

Monatelang denkt der Künstler über die ideale Lage seines „Ateliers der Tropen" nach. Welche fernen Länder könnten ihn von dem „Grauen der westlichen Zivilisation" losreißen und seinem existentiellen und künstlerischen Verlangen genügen? Er weiß, dass er „es braucht, in die unberührte Natur einzutauchen […] ohne jegliche Sorge, als ob man ein Kind wäre, nur in der eigenen Gedankenwelt lebend, einzig mithilfe der primitiven Kunst, nur

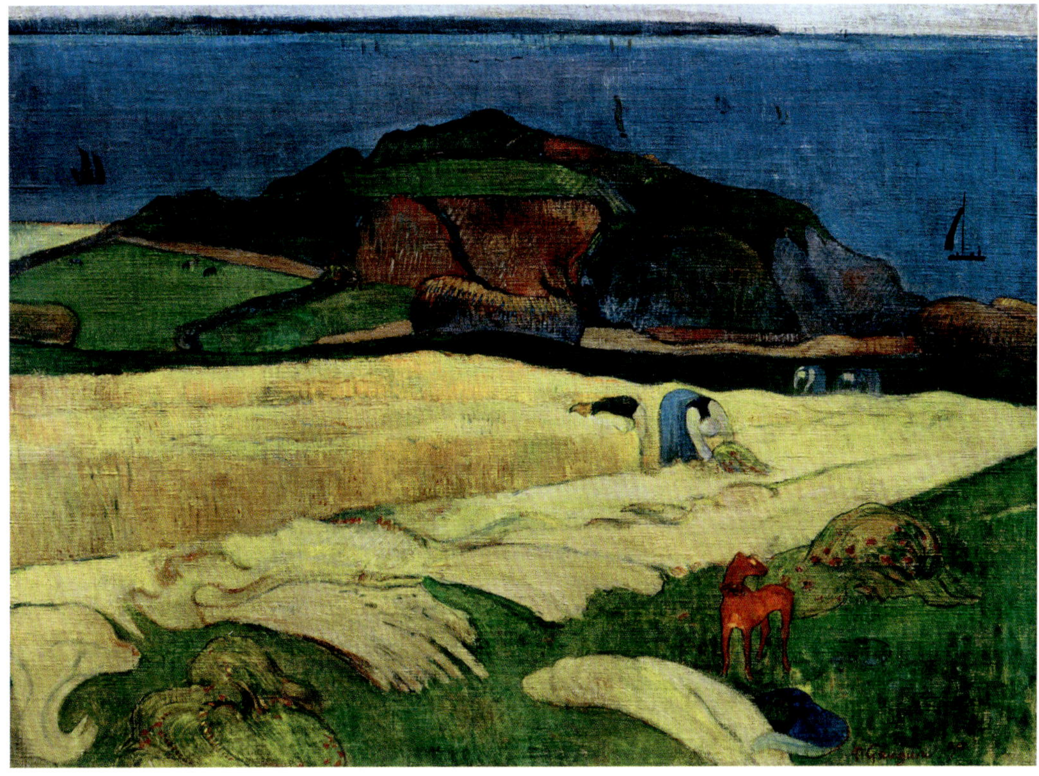

Preparar el gran adiós

El artista reflexionó sobre la ubicación ideal de su "taller de los trópicos" durante meses. ¿Qué lejano rincón podría arrancarle del "horror de la civilización occidental" y responder a sus aspiraciones existenciales y artísticas? Él supo "necesitar empaparse en la naturaleza virgen [...] sin otra preocupación que plasmar, como haría un niño, las concepciones de su cerebro, con la única ayuda de sus primitivos materiales artísticos, los únicos buenos,

Preparare la grande partenza

L'artista riflette sulla posizione ideale del suo "Atelier dei tropici" per mesi. Quanto lontano il paese lo strapperà da "l'orrore della civiltà occidentale" e risponderà alle sue aspirazioni esistenziali e artistiche? Egli sa di avere il "bisogno di ritemprare [se stesso] nel deserto [...] senza alcuna preoccupazione se non soltanto quella di creare, come farebbe un bambino, concezioni del [suo] cervello con il solo utilizzo di mezzi d'arte primitivi, i soli buoni, gli unici veri". Il suo progetto

De voorbereiding op de grote sprong

De kunstenaar denkt maandenlang na over de ideale locatie voor zijn "tropenatelier". Welke verre streek kan hem vrijwaren van "de verschrikkingen van de westerse beschaving" en zijn existentiële en artistieke ambities vervullen? Hij weet dat hij "behoefte [heeft] om op krachten te komen in ongerepte natuur [...] zonder zich om iets anders te bekommeren dan uitdrukking geven aan de ideeën van [zijn] hersenen, zoals een kind dat zou doen, en daarbij

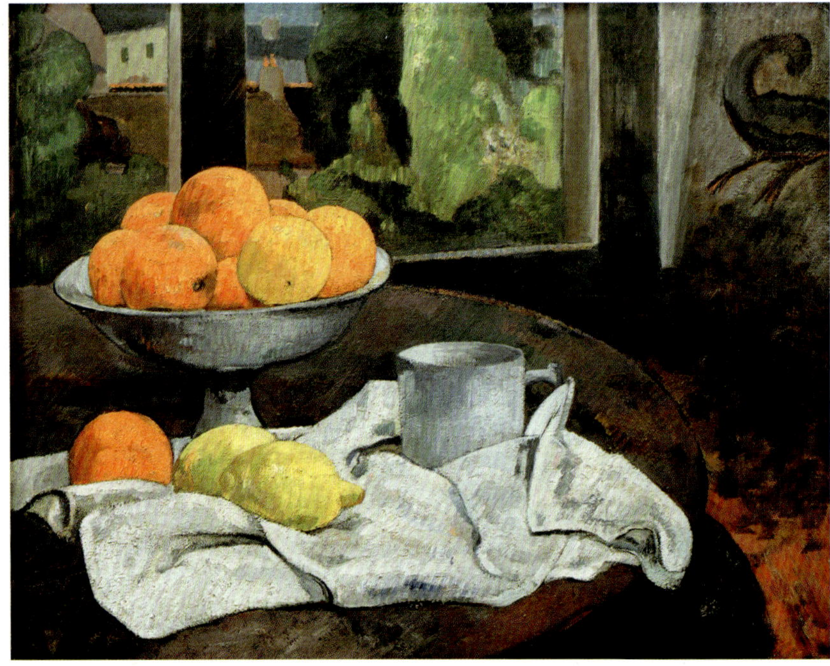

project was defined in terms of simplicity and authenticity – as he had already felt when clinging to traditional Breton society. "I leave in order to become calm, in order to be rid of the influence of our civilisation," he said, just before leaving for Polynesia in the spring of 1891.

After hesitating between Tonkin, Madagascar, and Tahiti, he settled for Oceania. But it was still necessary to finance such a voyage. Times were hard, his paintings did not sell well, even at ridiculous prices. He organised an auction of thirty paintings at the Hotel Drouot on 23 February, which brought him 9860 francs – enough for a ticket to Papeete. He bade farewell to his friends

les seuls vrais ». Son projet se définit en termes de simplicité et d'authenticité, comme il l'avait déjà ressenti en se coltinant à la société traditionnelle bretonne. « Je pars pour être tranquille, pour être débarrassé de l'influence de notre civilisation » affirme-t-il peu avant d'embarquer pour la Polynésie, au printemps 1891.

Après avoir hésité entre Le Tonkin, Madagascar et Tahiti, il se décide pour l'Océanie. Mais encore faut-il pouvoir financer un tel voyage. Les temps sont durs, ses tableaux se vendent mal, même à des prix dérisoires... Il organise une vente aux enchères de trente toiles à l'hôtel Drouot, le 23 février, qui lui

das ist gut, das einzig Wahre". Sein Projekt bestimmt sich in Begriffen wie Einfachheit und Authentizität, so wie er es schon empfand, als er sich mit der traditionellen bretonischen Gesellschaft beschäftigte. „Ich gehe fort, damit ich ungestört bin, befreit von den Einflüssen unserer Zivilisation", versichert er kurz vor der Einschiffung nach Polynesien im Frühjahr 1891.

Nachdem er zwischen Le Tonkin, Madagaskar und Tahiti geschwankt hat, entscheidet er sich für Ozeanien. Aber eine solche Reise muss man sich leisten können. Die Zeiten sind hart, seine Gemälde verkaufen sich schlecht, zu fast lächerlichen Preisen.

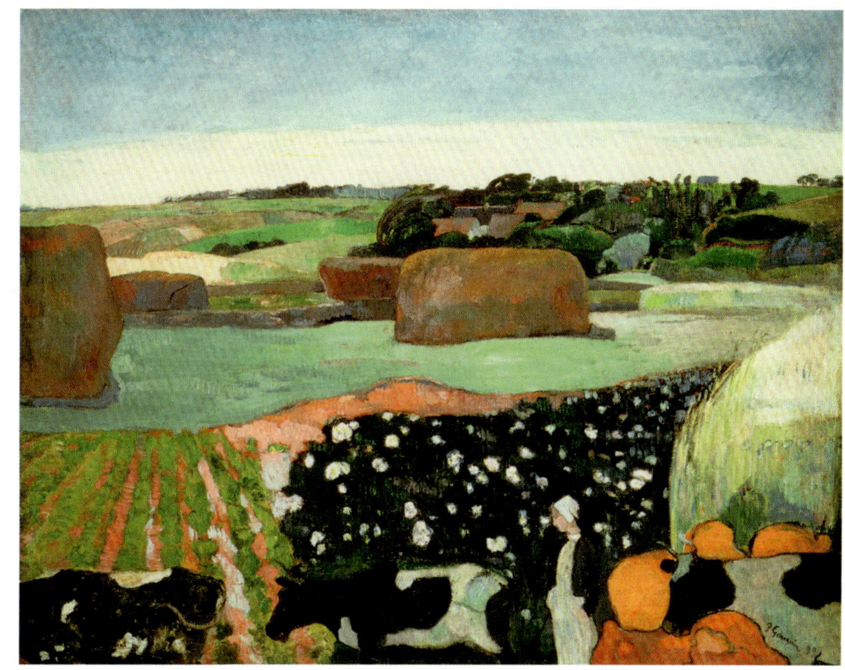

los únicos verdaderos". Su proyecto se define en términos de simplicidad y autenticidad, tal y como lo había sentido acercándose a la sociedad tradicional bretona. "Me marcho para estar tranquilo, para deshacerme de la influencia de nuestra civilización" afirmó algo antes de embarcarse hacia la Polinesia, en la primavera de 1891.

Tras dudar entre Le Tonkin, Madagascar y Tahití, se decidió por Oceanía. Aunque aún tenía que conseguir financiación para el viaje. Los tiempos fueron duros, sus cuadros se vendieron mal, incluso a precios irrisorios… Organizó una subasta de treinta lienzos en el hotel Drouot, el

è definito in termini di semplicità e genuinità, come aveva già sentito amalgamandosi alla società tradizionale bretone. "Parto per essere tranquillo, per sbarazzarmi dell'influenza della nostra civiltà", ha detto poco prima di imbarcarsi nella primavera del 1891 per la Polinesia.

Dopo aver esitato tra Tonkin, Madagascar e Tahiti, decide di stabilirsi in Oceania. Ma è necessario trovare i fondi per finanziare un tale viaggio. I tempi duri, i suoi dipinti stanno vendendo poco, anche a prezzi molto bassi. Organizza un'asta di trenta dipinti presso l'Hotel Drouot, il 23 febbraio e guadagna 9860 franchi. Abbastanza per comprare un biglietto per Papeete. Egli dirà addio ai

alleen gebruik te maken van de middelen die kunst weer primitief maken, de enige goede, de enige echte." Zijn plan laat zich het best beschrijven in termen van eenvoud en authenticiteit, net als toen hij deel werd van de traditionele Bretonse maatschappij. "Ik vertrek om rustig te worden, om te worden bevrijd van de invloed van onze beschaving", verklaart hij kort voordat hij in het voorjaar van 1891 inscheept voor de reis naar Polynesië.

Aarzelend tussen Tonkin, Madagaskar en Tahiti, besluit hij uiteindelijk naar Oceanië te gaan. Maar hij moet de lange reis wel kunnen betalen! Het zijn moeilijke tijden; zijn schilderijen verkopen slecht, ook al vraagt hij er spotprijzen voor…

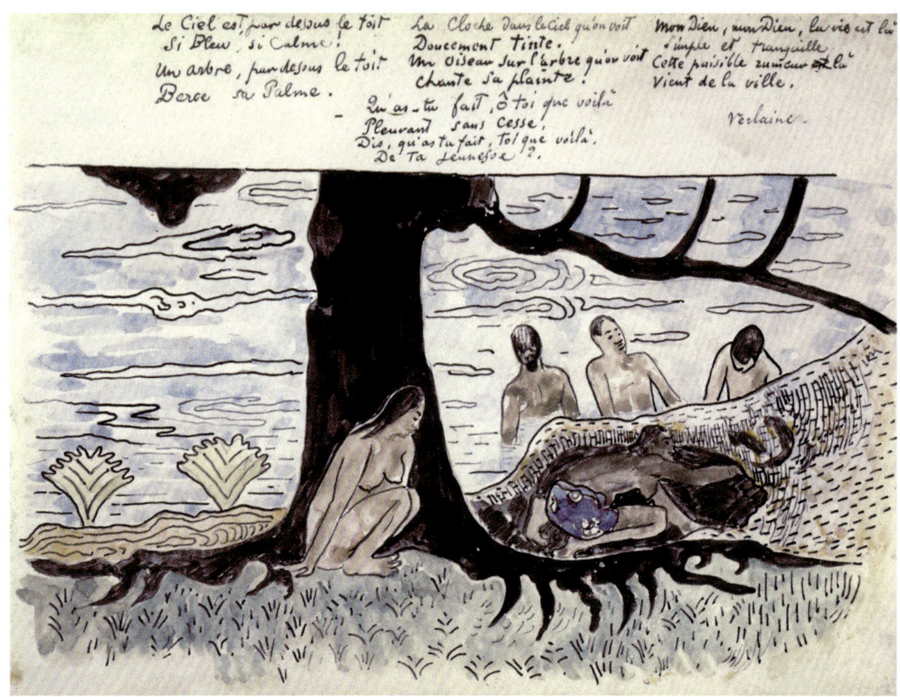

Bathers (illustrating a poem by Verlaine)

Baigneuses (illustrant un poème de Verlaine)

Badende (Illustration zu einem Gedicht von Verlaine)

Bañistas (ilustrando un poema de Verlaine)

Bagnanti (illustranti una poesia di Verlaine)

Baadsters (illustratie bij een gedicht van Verlaine)

c. 1888, Watercolor/Aquarelle, Private collection

at the café Voltaire on 23 April, at a banquet presided by Stéphane Mallarmé, who declared in his toast "to admire this superb consciousness which, in the brilliance of his talent, exiled him in order to retreat, into the distance and into oneself." Gauguin leaves for Marseille on 1 April 1891, carried by his dream of a new Cythera.

rapporte 9860 francs. Assez pour se payer un billet pour Papeete. Il fait ses adieux à ses amis le 23 avril, au café Voltaire, lors d'un banquet présidé par Stéphane Mallarmé, qui déclare dans son toast « admirer cette conscience superbe qui, en l'éclat de son talent, l'exile, pour se retremper, vers les lointains et vers soi-même ». Gauguin embarque à Marseille, le 1er avril 1891, porté par son rêve vers la nouvelle Cythère.

Am 23. Februar organisiert er eine Versteigerung von dreißig Gemälden im Hotel Drouot, die 9860 Francs einbringt. Genug für eine Überfahrt nach Papeete. Er verabschiedet sich am 23. April im Café Voltaire von seinen Freunden mit einem Festessen unter dem Vorsitz von Stéphane Mallarmé; dieser erklärt in seinem Trinkspruch: „Ich bewundere dieses großartige Bewusstsein Gauguins, das ihn mit seinem strahlenden Talent in die Ferne und zu sich selbst ins Exil schickt, um noch stärker zu werden." Am 1. April 1891 geht Gauguin in Marseille an Bord, getragen von seinem Traum des neuen Kythira.

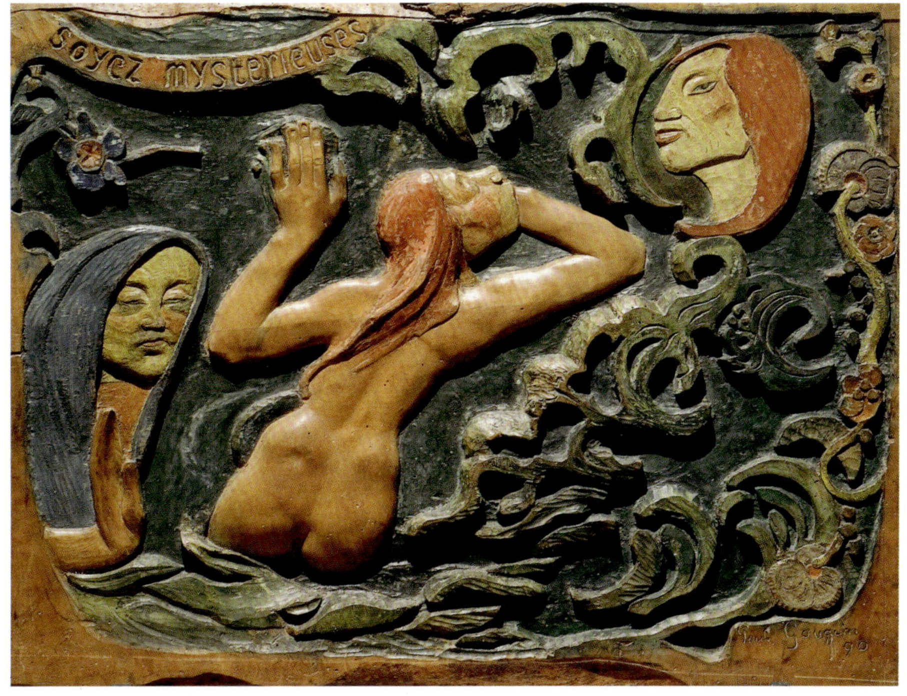

Be Mysterious
Soyez mystérieuses
Seid geheimnisvoll
Sed misteriosas
Siate misteriosi
Wees mysterieus

1890, Polychrome lime wood/Bois
de tilleul polychrome, 73 × 95 cm,
Musée d'Orsay, Paris

23 de febrero que le reportó 9860 francos. Lo suficiente para pagarse un billete para Papeete. Se despidió de sus amigos el 23 de abril, en el café Voltaire, en un banquete presidido por Stéphane Mallarmé, quien declaró en su brindis "admirar esta soberbia conciencia que, en la explosión de su talento, le exilia, para fortalecerse, hacia lo lejos y hacia sí mismo". Gauguin se embarcó en Marsella el 1 de abril de 1891, guiado por su sueño hacia la nueva Citera.

suoi amici il 23 aprile al Cafe Voltaire, a un banchetto presieduto da Stéphane Mallarmé, che nel suo brindisi disse "per ammirare questa superba coscienza, nello splendore del suo talento, spinto all'esilio per immergere se stesso verso lontano e verso se stesso. " Gauguin si imbarca a Marsiglia, 1 aprile 1891, guidato dal suo sogno verso la nuova Cythère.

Op 23 februari organiseert hij in Hôtel Drouot een veiling van dertig doeken, die hem 9860 frank oplevert. Genoeg voor een ticket naar Papeete. Op 23 april neemt hij in Café Voltaire afscheid van zijn vrienden, tijdens een diner dat Stéphane Mallarmé voor hem organiseert. Als de dichter een toast op Gauguin uitbrengt, spreekt hij zijn "bewondering [uit] voor dit superbe geweten dat hem, in de weerschijn van zijn talent, in ballingschap voert, om op krachten te komen, naar verre oorden en naar zichzelf". Gauguin scheept zich op 1 april 1891 in Marseille in voor de reis naar het nieuwe Kythira, zijn droom achterna.

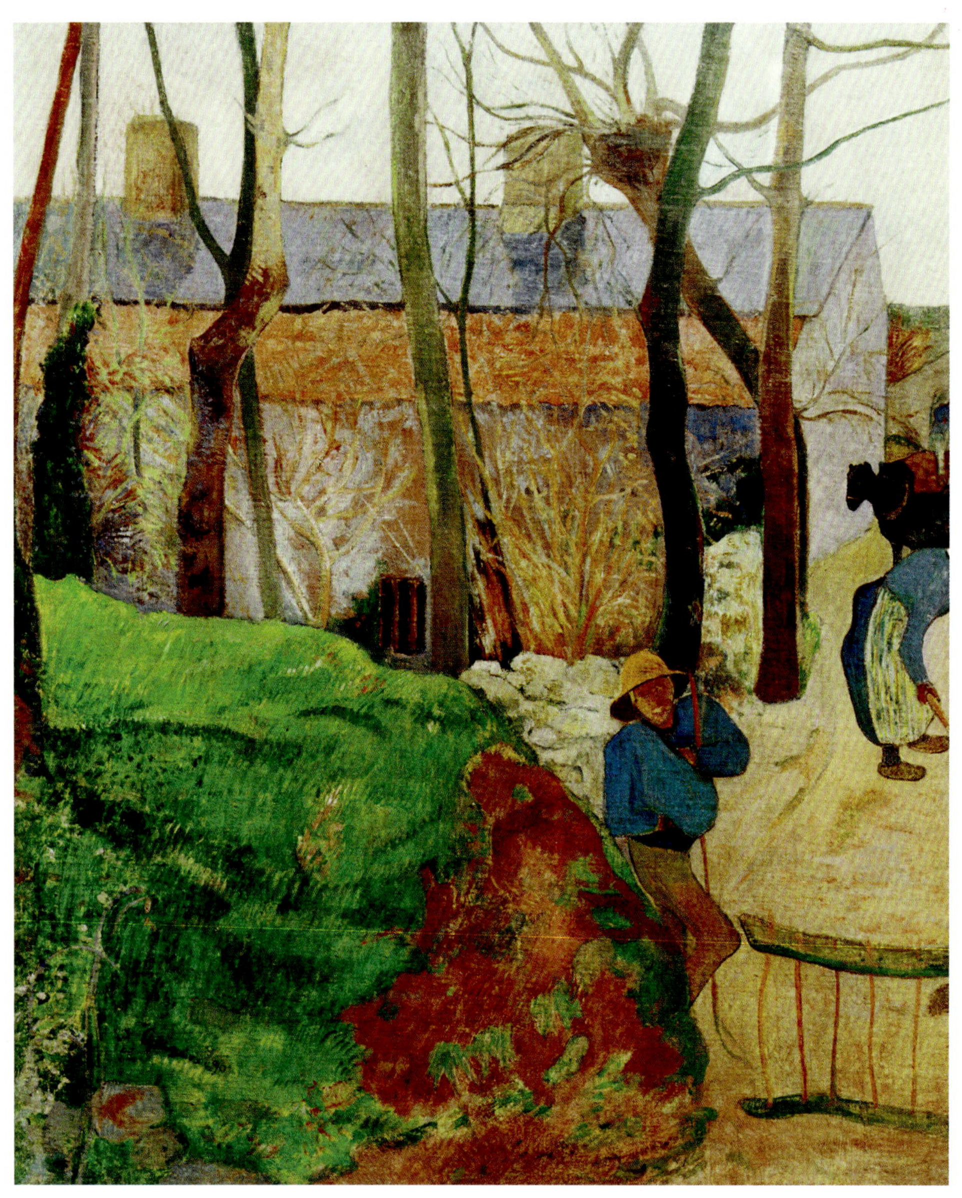

Cottage at Le Pouldu

Entrée de ferme au Pouldu

Hoftor in Le Pouldu

**Entrada a una
granja en Pouldu**

**Entrata di fattoria
a Pouldu**

**Ingang van een
boerderij in Le Pouldu**

*1890, Oil on canvas/Huile sur
toile, 92 × 73 cm, Staatliche
Kunsthalle, Karlsruhe*

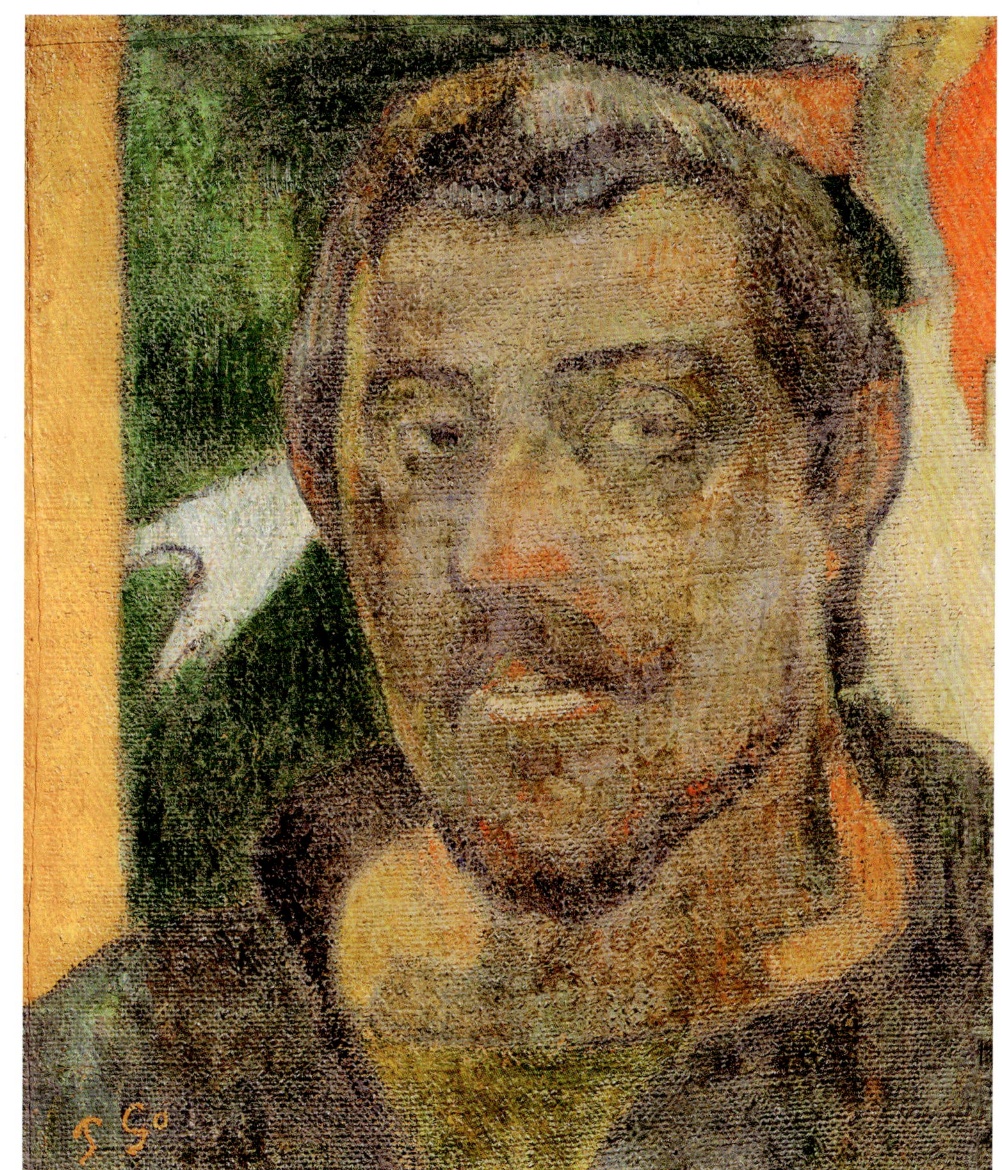

Self Portrait

Autoportrait

Selbstbildnis

Autorretrato

Autoritratto

Zelfportret

c. 1890–94, Oil on canvas/Huile sur toile, 46 × 37 cm, Pushkin Museum, Moscow

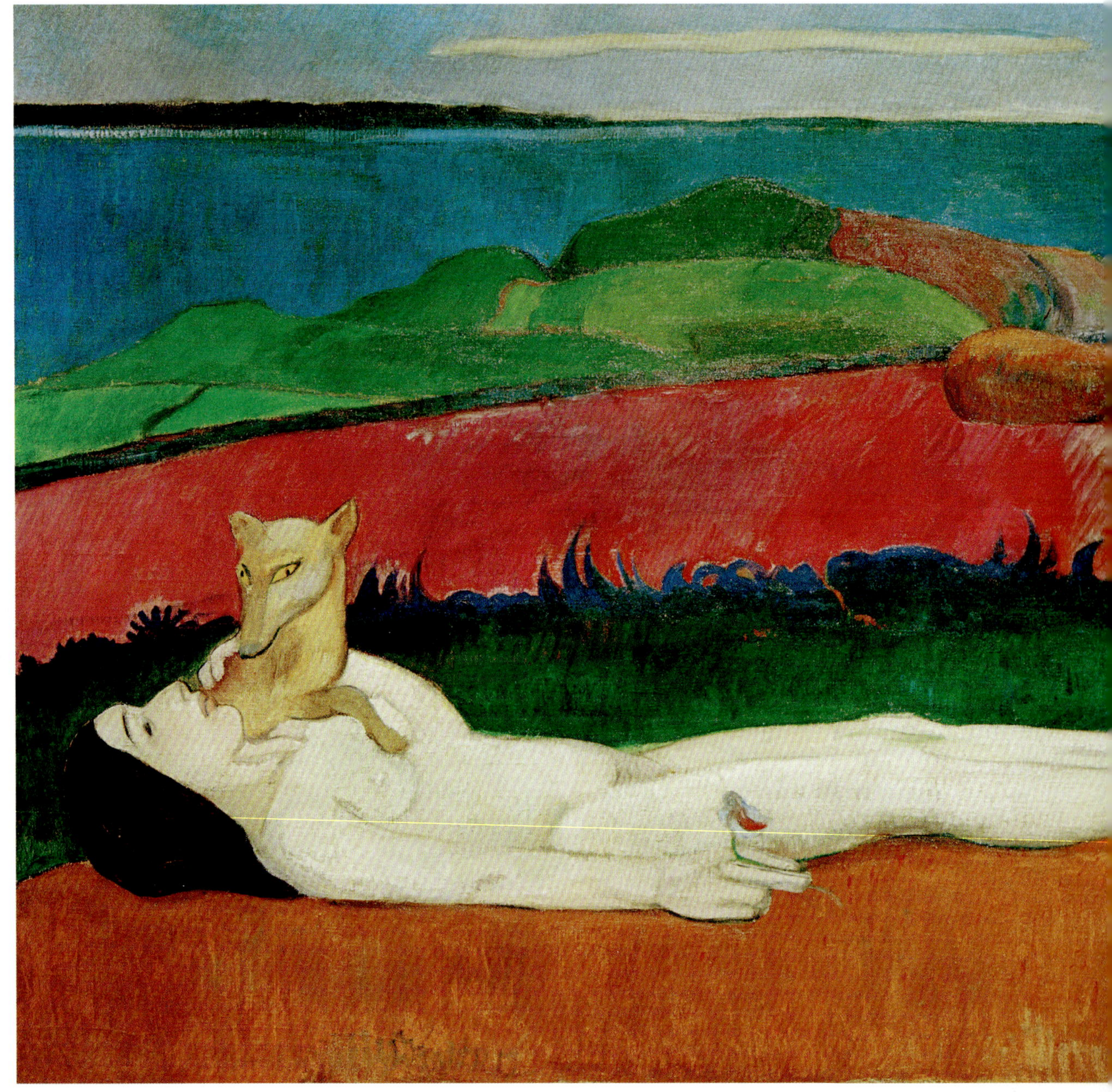

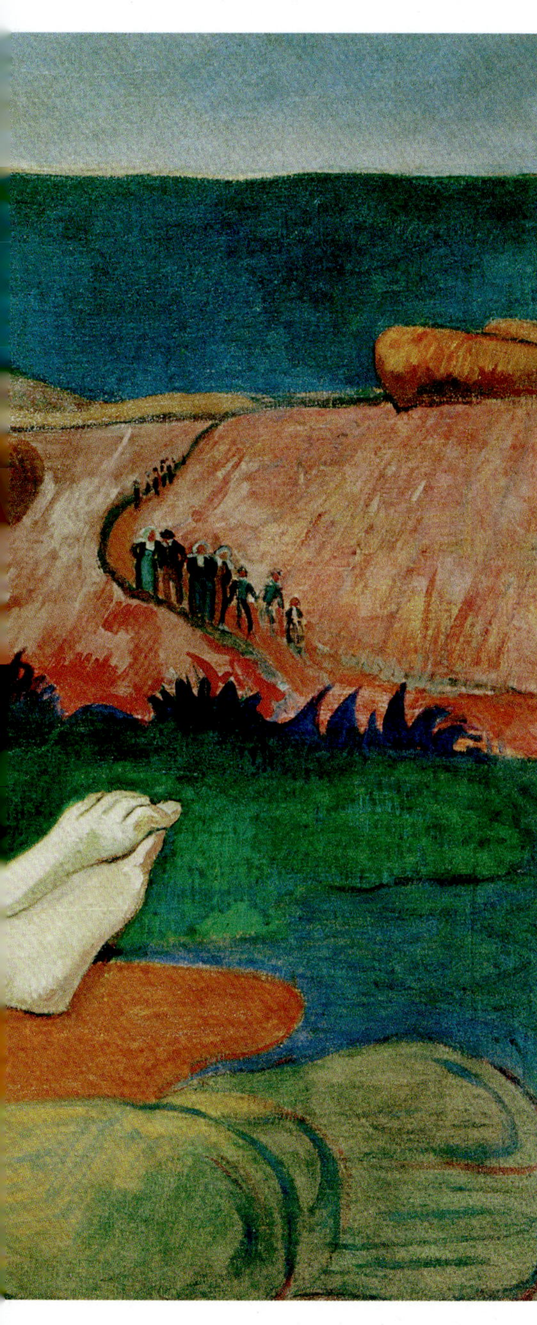

The Loss of Virginity or *Awakening of Spring*
La Perte du pucelage ou *L'Éveil du printemps*
Der Verlust der Unschuld oder *Frühlingserwachen*
La pérdida de la virginidad o *El demonio de la primavera*
La perdita della verginità o *Il Risveglio della primavera*
Het verlies van de onschuld of *Het ontwaken van de lente*
1890–91, Oil on canvas/Huile sur toile, 90 × 130 cm, Chrysler Museum of Art, Norfolk

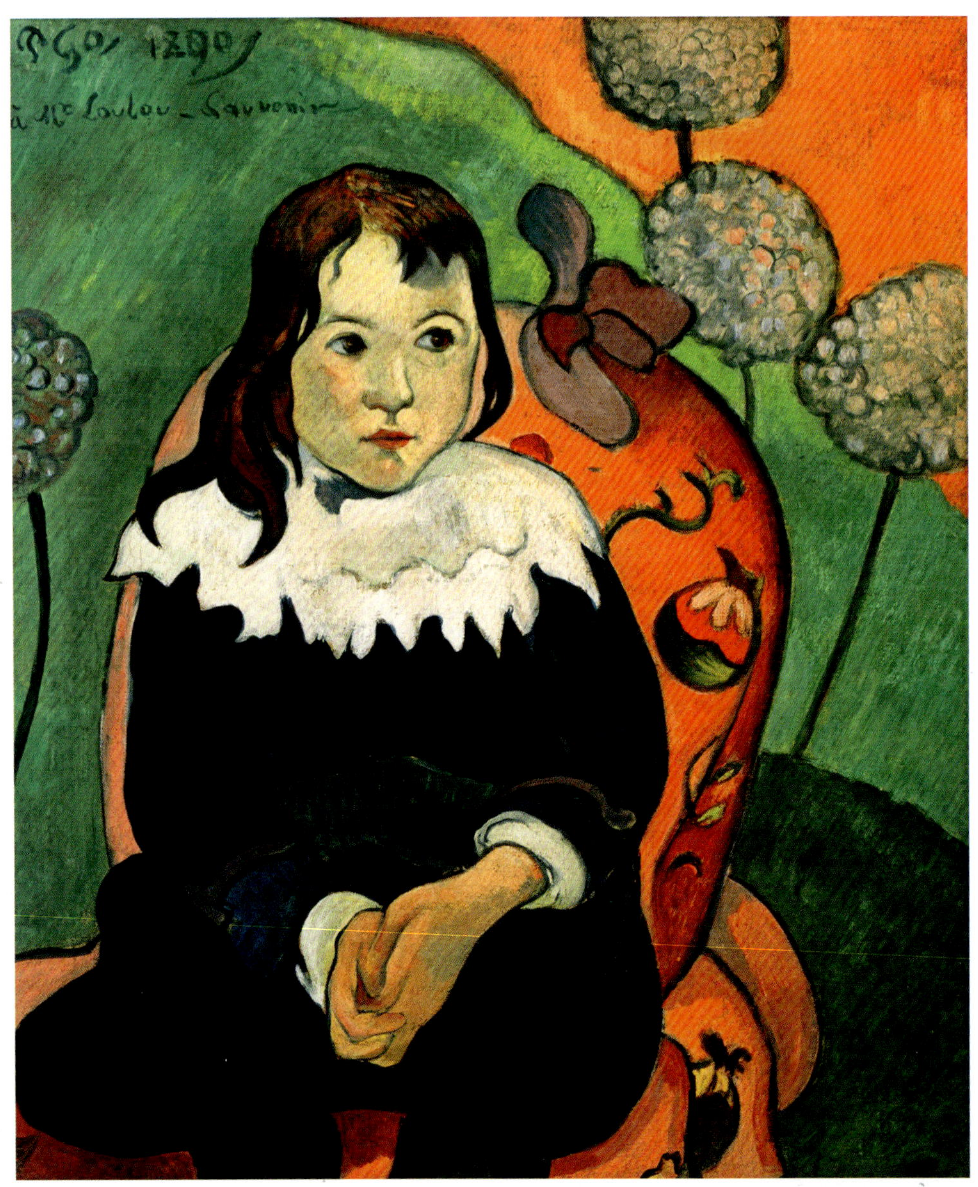

Mr Loulou (Louis Le Ray)

1890, Oil on canvas/Huile sur toile, 55,2 × 46,4 cm, The Barnes Collection, Philadelphia

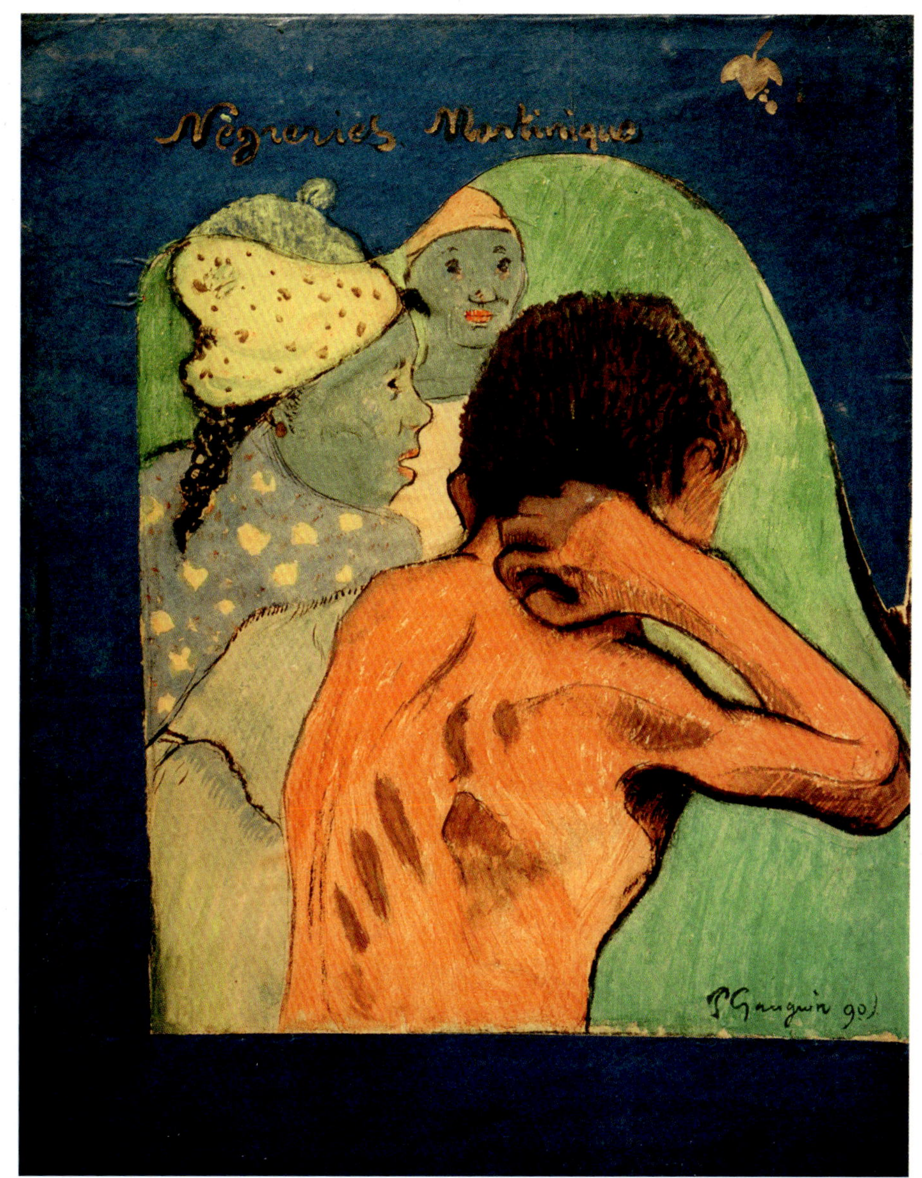

Nègreries Martinique

1890, Gouache, watercolor, black ink, gilded painting and collage/ Gouache, aquarelle, encre noire, peinture dorée et collage, 33,2 × 24,8 cm, Private collection

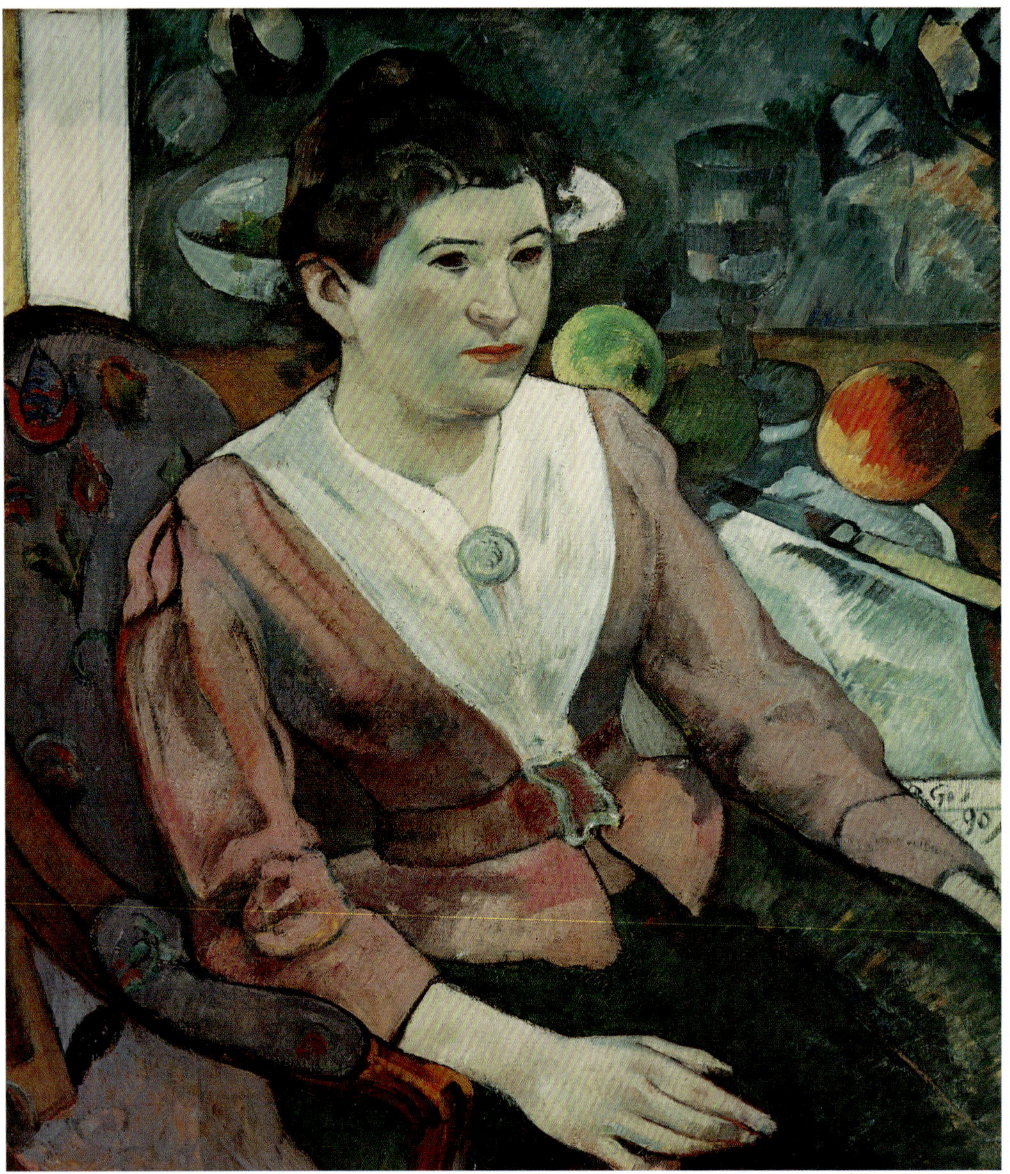

Portrait of a Woman in Front of a Still Life by Cézanne (Marie Derrien with the still life of Cézanne)

Portrait de femme devant une nature morte de Cézanne (Marie Derrien à la nature morte de Cézanne)

Frau vor einem Stillleben Cézannes (Marie Derrien vor einem Stillleben Cézannes)

Retrato de mujer frente a una naturaleza muerta de Cézanne (Marie Derrien con naturaleza muerta de Cézanne)

Ritratto di donna davanti una natura morta di Cezanne (Marie Derrien nella natura morta di Cezanne)

Vrouwenportret voor een stilleven van Cézanne (Marie Derrien voor een stilleven van Cézanne)

1890, Oil on canvas/ Huile sur toile, 65,3 × 54,9 cm, Art Institute of Chicago, Chicago

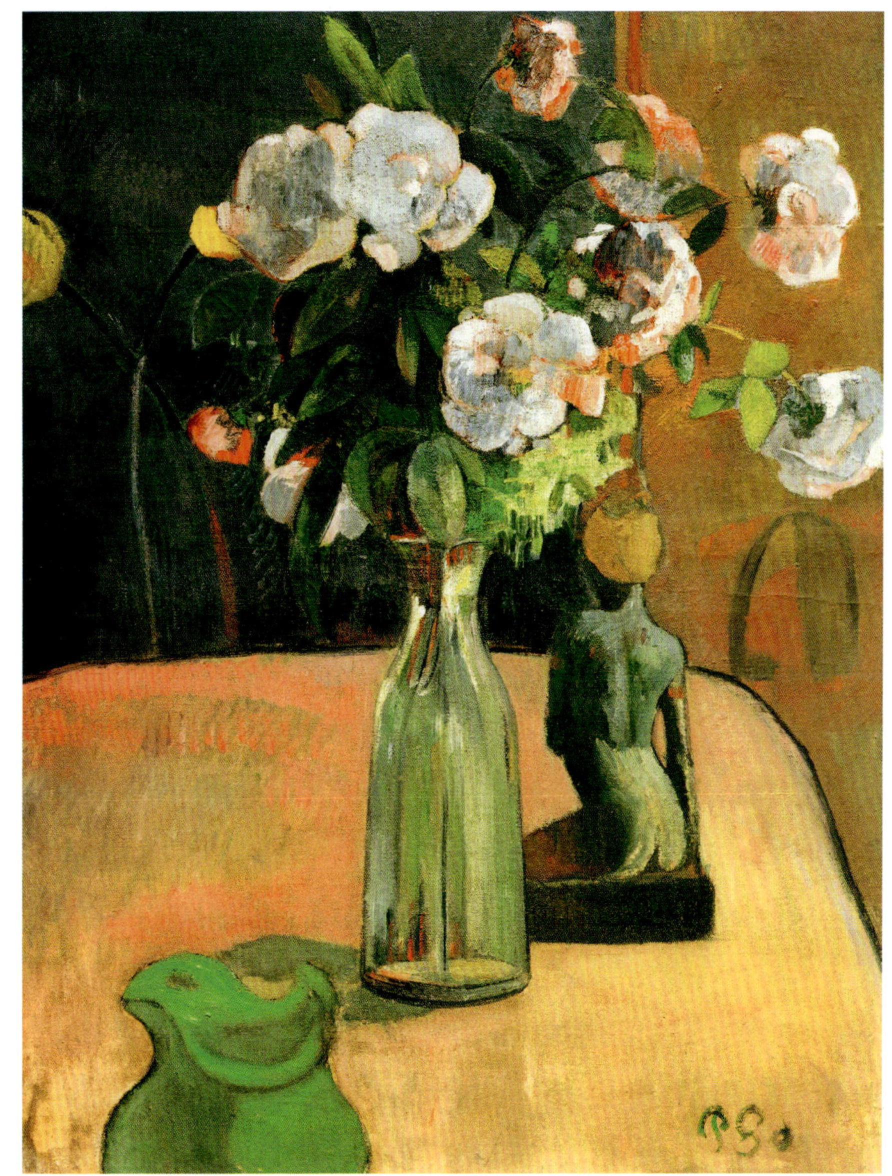

Roses and Statuette
Roses et statuette
Rosen und Statuette
Rosas y estatuilla
Rosa e statuetta
Rozen en beeldje

*1890, Oil on canvas/Huile sur toile,
73 × 54 cm, Musée des Beaux-Arts,
Reims*

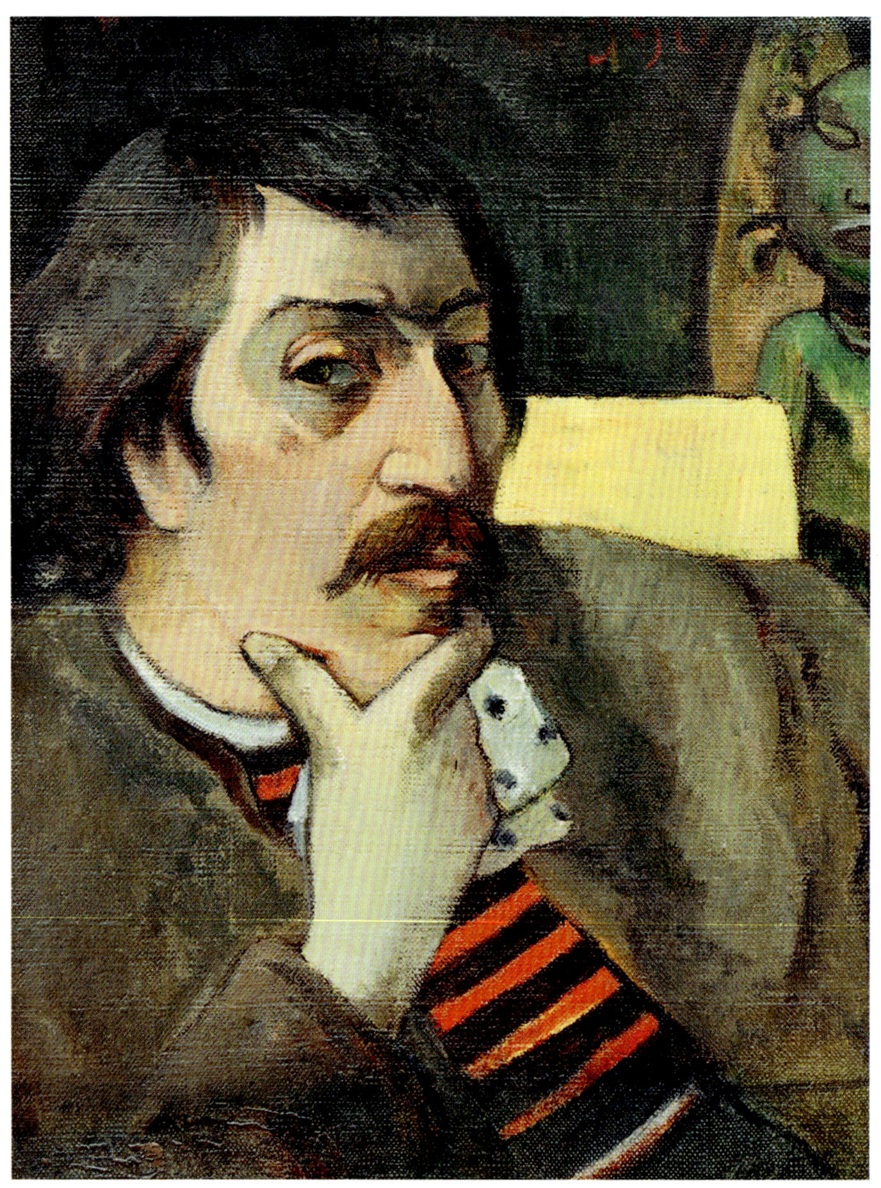

Self Portrait with the Idol

Autoportrait à l'idole

Selbstbildnis mit Idol

Autorretrato con ídolo

Autoritratto con idolo

Zelfportret met afgodsbeeld

*c. 1891–93, Oil on canvas/Huile sur toile,
46 × 33 cm, McNay Art Museum,
San Antonio*

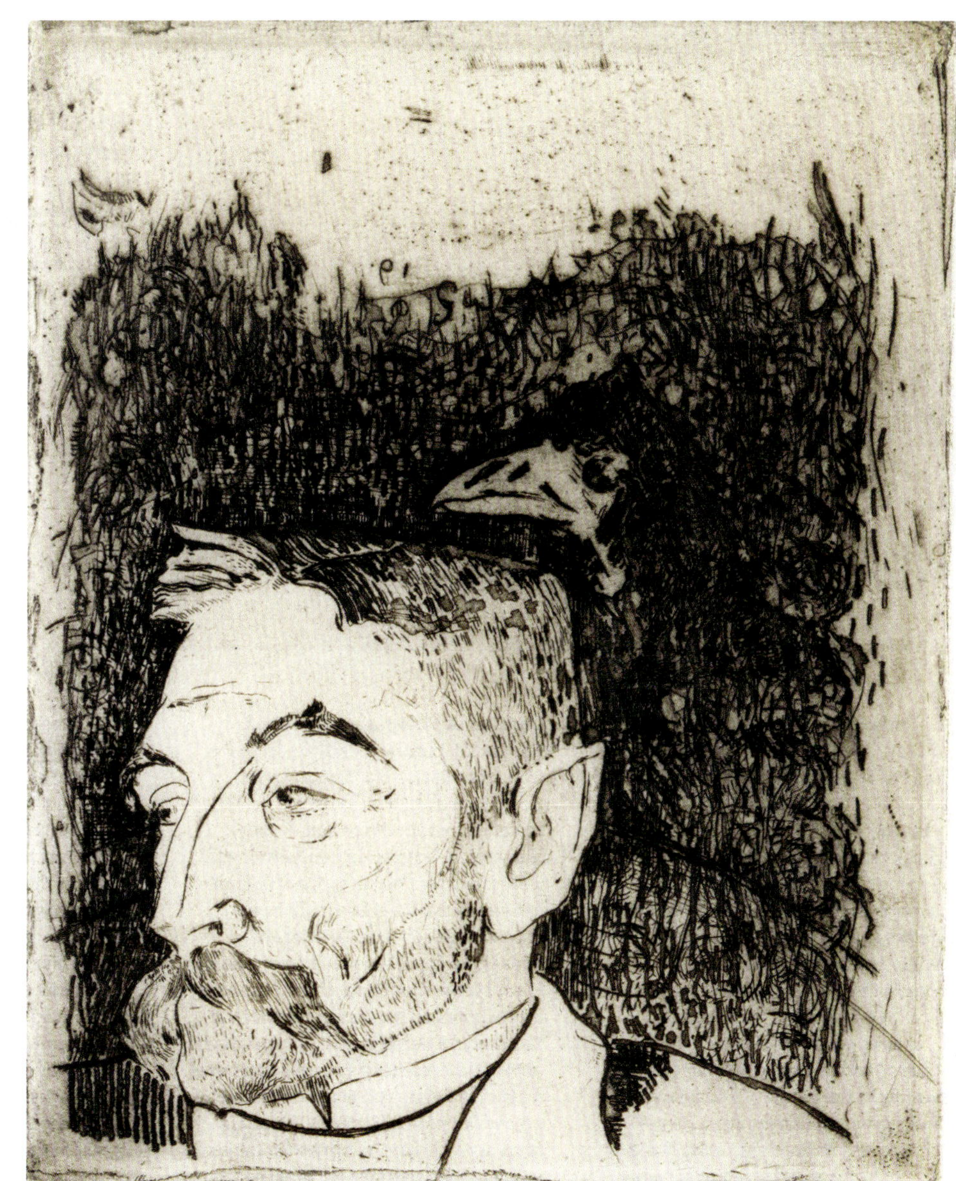

Stéphane Mallarmé

1891, Test on laid paper (etching and dry point on copper)/Épreuve sur vergé (gravure à l'eau-forte et pointe sèche sur cuivre), 18,2 × 14,3 cm, Musée départemental Stéphane-Mallarmé, Vulaines-sur-Seine

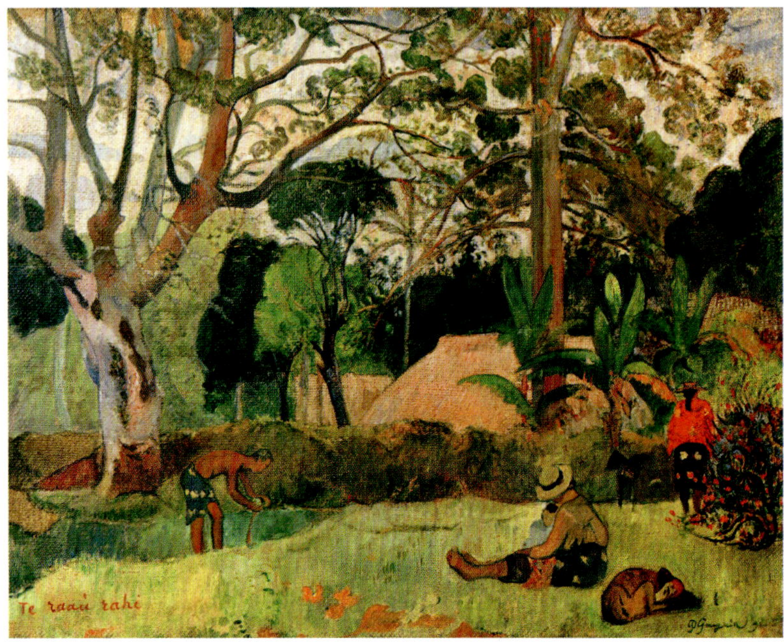

Te raau rahi
(The Big Tree)
(Le Grand Arbre)
(Der große Baum)
(El gran árbol)
(Il grande albero)
(De grote boom)

1891, Oil on canvas/Huile sur toile, 73 × 91,5 cm,
Art Institute of Chicago, Chicago

The "studio of the tropics" at Tahiti

Gauguin arrived in Papeete on 9 June 1891, holding in his pocket an assignment from the ministry of Fine Arts and some letters of recommendation. Upon his arrival, he encountered none of what he came for: his imagined Eden existed no more as a result of Christianisation and the modernisation of Tahitian society imposed by colonisation. Fleeing worldly life and the "aggravating species of colonial snobbery," he moved 45 kilometres south of Papeete in the autumn, and settled in an indigenous dwelling in the village of Mataiea, a small corner of lush paradise on the Pacific coast. He learned Tahitian and met Teha'amana who quickly became

L'atelier des tropiques de Tahiti

Gauguin débarque à Papeete le 9 juin 1891, une mission du ministère des Beaux-Arts et quelques lettres de recommandation en poche. À son arrivée, il ne trouve rien de ce qu'il est venu chercher : l'éden qu'il a fantasmé n'existe plus suite à la christianisation et à la modernisation de la société tahitienne imposées par la colonisation. Fuyant la vie mondaine et les « espèces aggravantes du snobisme colonial », à l'automne, il déménage à 45 kilomètres au sud de Papeete. Il s'installe dans une maison indigène du village de Mataiea, un petit coin de paradis luxuriant au bord du Pacifique. Il apprend le tahitien et fait la connaissance de Teha'amana,

Das „Atelier der Tropen" auf Tahiti

Gauguin geht am 9. Juni 1891 in Papeete an Land mit einem Auftrag des Ministeriums der Schönen Künste und einigen Empfehlungsschreiben in der Tasche. Bei seiner Ankunft findet er nichts von dem vor, wofür er gekommen ist: Den Garten Eden, den er sich erträumt hat, gibt es nicht mehr, Folge von Christianisierung und Modernisierung der tahitischen Gesellschaft im Zuge der Kolonialisierung. Er flüchtet im Herbst vor dem mondänen Leben und den „wachsenden Ausprägungen des kolonialen Snobismus" und zieht weiter. 45 Kilometer südlich von Papetee lässt er sich im Dorf Mataiea nieder, einem

*1891, Oil on canvas/Huile sur toile, 72,6 × 92,3 cm,
The Israel Museum, Jerusalem*

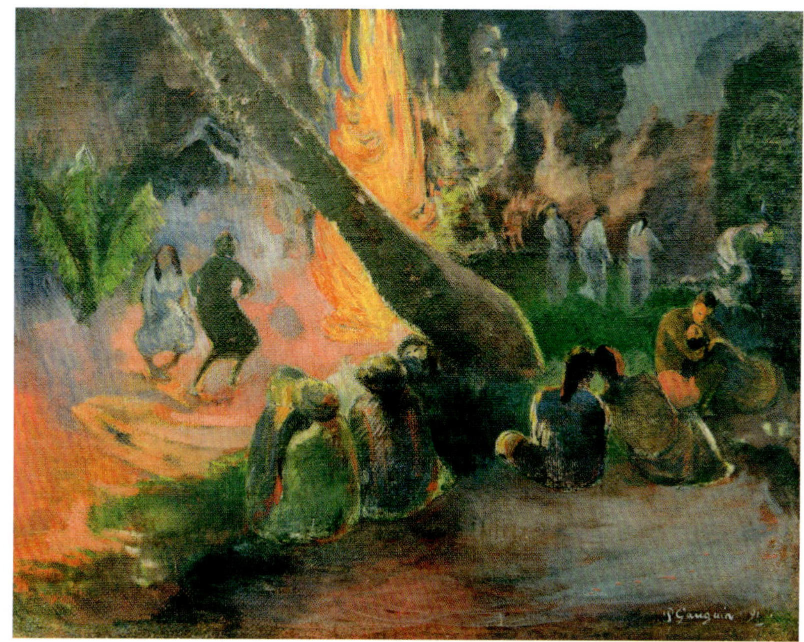

El "taller de los trópicos" de Tahití

Gauguin desembarcó en Papeete el
9 de junio de 1891, con una misión del
ministerio de Bellas Artes y algunas
cartas de recomendación en el bolsillo.
A su llegada, no encontró nada de lo
que iba buscando: el edén que imaginó
ya no existe como consecuencia de la
cristianización y la modernización de
la sociedad tahitiana impuestas por
la colonización. Huyendo de la vida
mundana y las "especies agravantes
del esnobismo colonial", en otoño, se
mudó 45 kilómetros al sur de Papeete.
Se instaló en una casa indígena del
pueblo de Mataiea, un pequeño rincón
de ese exuberante paraíso a orillas del
Pacífico. Aprendió tahitiano y conoció

"L'atelier dei tropici" di Tahiti

Gauguin arriva a Papeete il 9 Giugno 1891,
una missione del Dipartimento di Belle
Arti e alcune lettere di raccomandazione
in tasca. Al suo arrivo, non trova nulla
di ciò per cui è giunto: l'eden di cui ha
fantasticato non esiste più dopo la
cristianizzazione e la modernizzazione
della società Tahitiana imposta dalla
colonizzazione. In fuga dalla vita
mondana e dalle "specie aggravanti
dello snobismo coloniale" in autunno,
si trasferisce a 45 chilometri a sud di
Papeete. Si stabilisce in una casa indigena
di Mataiea, piccolo gioiello lussureggiante
ai limiti del Pacifico. Impara il Tahitiano e
conosce Teha'amana, che presto diviene
il suo modello e sua vanità. In questo

Het "tropenatelier" op Tahiti

Gauguin komt op 9 juni 1891 in Papeete
aan, met een missie van het ministerie
van Schone Kunsten en een aantal
aanbevelingsbrieven op zak. Bij
aankomst vindt hij niets van wat hij is
komen zoeken: als gevolg van de door
de kolonisatie opgelegde kerstening
en de modernisatie van de Tahitiaanse
maatschappij bestaat zijn gedroomde
paradijs niet meer. Hij vlucht voor het
mondaine leven en de "steeds vreselijkere
gedaanten van het koloniale snobisme"
en betrekt in het najaar 45 kilometer
ten zuiden van Papeete een authentiek
Tahitiaans huis in het dorpje Mataiea, een
weelderig begroeid, paradijselijk hoekje
aan de Stille Oceaan. Hij leert Tahitiaans

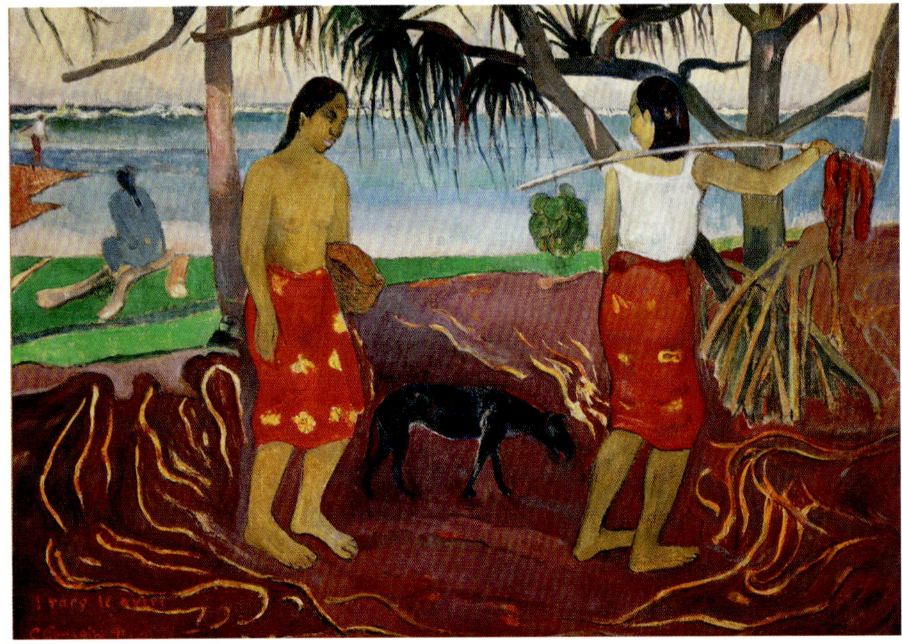

I raro te oviri

(Under the Pandanus)

(Sous les pandanus)

(Unter dem Pandanusbaum)

(Bajo los pandanus)

(Sotto le pandanus)

(Onder de pandanus)

1891, Oil on canvas/Huile sur toile, 67,3 × 90,8 cm, Dallas Museum of Art, Dallas

his model and his wahine. At her side he led a simple life, unfortunately quickly undermined by his fragile health, which compelled him to stay at the hospital and then return to the metropolis in the early summer of 1893.

During that first Tahitian stay, the artist produced sixty paintings, drawings, and sculptures, particularly statues of idols which he designated as "ultra wild". A part of this production portrayed the disillusioned vision that he had of Tahitian society. He would never cease denouncing the acculturation suffered by the local populations. As for the remaining works, they celebrate a lost primitive world and an imagined golden age, in the vein of his watercolor

qui devient vite son modèle et sa vahiné. À ses côtés, il mène une vie simple, malheureusement vite mise à mal par sa santé fragile, qui le contraint à séjourner à l'hôpital puis à regagner la métropole au début de l'été 1893.

Durant ce premier séjour tahitien, l'artiste crée une soixantaine de toiles, des dessins et des sculptures, notamment des statuettes d'idoles, qu'il qualifie d'« ultra-sauvages ». Une partie de cette production livre la vision désabusée qu'il porte sur la société tahitienne. Il n'aura de cesse de dénoncer l'acculturation dont souffrent les populations locales. Quant au reste des œuvres, elles célèbrent un monde primitif perdu et un âge d'or fantasmé,

üppigen paradiesischen Flecken am Pazifik, und bezieht ein einheimisches Haus. Er lernt die Landessprache und begegnet Teha'amana, die bald sein Modell und seine „Vahiné" wird. An ihrer Seite führt er ein einfaches Leben, doch unglücklicherweise wird es bald durch seine angeschlagene Gesundheit untergraben. Er muss ins Krankenhaus und ist dann im Frühsommer 1893 zur Rückkehr in die Metropole gezwungen.

Während dieses ersten Aufenthalts auf Tahiti erschafft der Künstler ungefähr 60 Gemälde, Zeichnungen und auch Skulpturen, vor allem Statuetten mit Götzenbildern, die er als „ultrawild" bezeichnet. Ein Teil dieses Schaffens spiegelt sein desillusioniertes Bild der

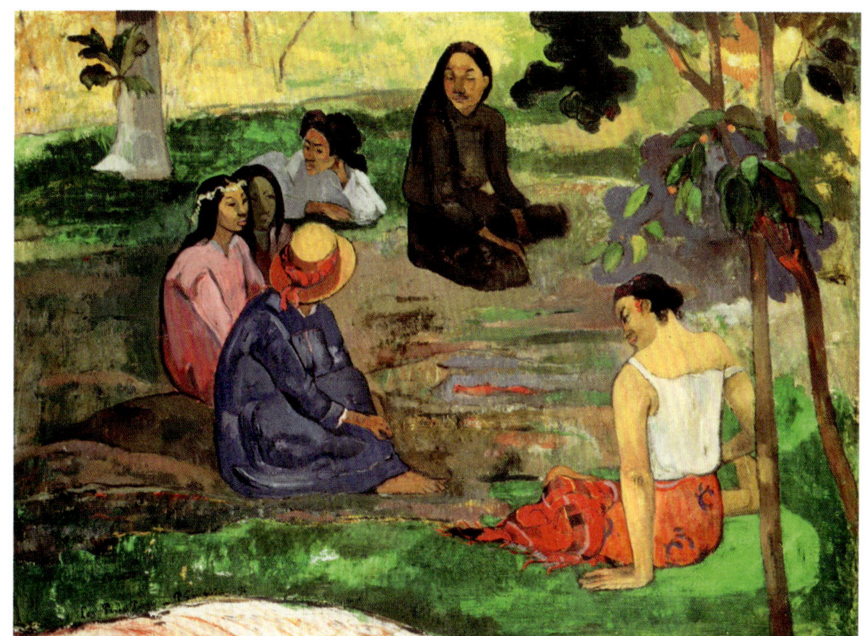

Les parau parau
(Conversation)
(Gespräch)
(Conversación)
(Conversazione)
(Het gesprek)

1891, Oil on canvas/Huile sur toile,
70,5 × 90,3 cm, State Hermitage Museum,
St. Petersburg

a Teha'amana, quien rápidamente se convirtió en su modelo y vahiné (mujer en tahitiano). A su lado, su vida era sencilla, que desgraciadamente pronto se vio saboteada por su mala salud, que le llevo a permanecer en el hospital y después a volver a la metrópolis a comienzos del verano de 1893.

Durante esta primera estancia en Tahití, el artista creó unos sesenta lienzos, dibujos y esculturas, principalmente estatuillas de ídolos, que calificó de "ultrasalvajes". Parte de su producción se libra de la imagen desengañada que se llevó de la sociedad tahitiana. No cesó de denunciar la aculturación sufrida por la población local. En lo relativo al resto de sus

frangente, conduce una vita semplice, purtroppo rapidamente minata dalla sua cattiva salute, che lo costringe a rimanere in ospedale per poi ritornare alla metropoli all'inizio dell'estate 1893.

Durante questo primo soggiorno a Tahiti, l'artista crea una sessantina di dipinti, disegni e sculture, tra cui statue di idoli, che descrive come "ultra-selvagge". Una parte di questa produzione rispecchia la visione disincantata che egli porta sulla società di Tahiti. Egli non cesserà di denunciare la necessità di acculturazione di cui soffrono la mancanza le popolazioni locali. Quanto al resto delle opere, celebrano un mondo primitivo perduto e un periodo d'oro fantasticato, a

en maakt kennis met Teha'amana. Zij wordt al snel zijn model en zijn vahine, zijn Tahitiaanse vrouw. Naast haar leeft hij een eenvoudig leven, dat helaas al snel wordt verstoord door zijn broze gezondheid, die hem dwingt om na een verblijf in het ziekenhuis in de zomer van 1893 naar Frankrijk terug te keren.

Tijdens zijn eerste verblijf op Tahiti maakt de kunstenaar een zestigtal schilderijen, tekeningen en sculpturen, vooral afgodenbeeldjes die hij 'superwilden' noemt. Een deel van zijn werk illustreert zijn ontgoochelde kijk op de Tahitiaanse maatschappij. Waar hij kan, stelt hij de acculturatie aan de kaak waaronder de lokale bevolking lijdt. De rest van zijn oeuvre is een lofzang

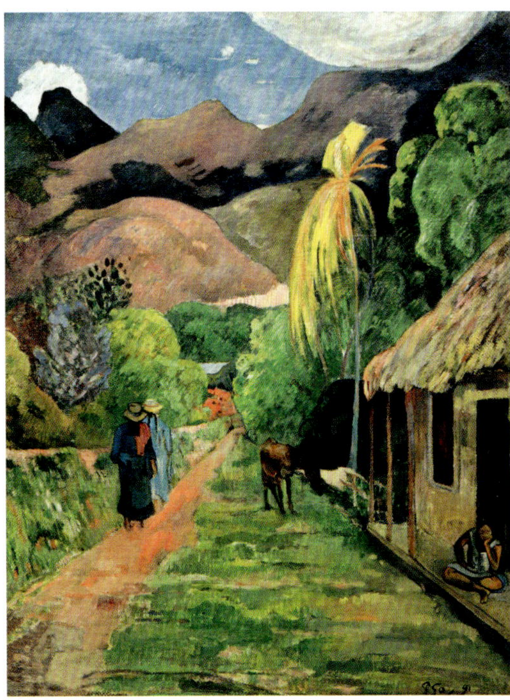

notebook entitled *Ancient Maori Cults*. Imbibed with the techniques and styles of local artists, Gauguin became the archaeologist and the ethnologist with the heavy burden of resurrecting Maori mythology and culture. In good times and bad, he created by the force of his art, a paradise of calm and voluptuousness.

à l'image de son cahier d'aquarelles intitulé *Ancien Culte Mahorie*. Imprégné des techniques et du style des artistes locaux, Gauguin se fait l'archéologue et l'ethnologue à qui incombe la lourde charge de ressusciter la mythologie et la culture maories. Bon an mal an, à la force de son art, il crée un paradis de calme et de volupté.

tahitischen Gesellschaft wider. Er wird nicht müde, den Akkulturationsdruck anzuprangern, unter dem die lokale Bevölkerung leidet. Andere Werke verklären eine verlorengegangene primitive Welt und ein erträumtes goldenes Zeitalter, wie dargestellt in einem Aquarellheft betitelt *Ancien Culte Mahorie*. Beeinflusst von Techniken und Stil der einheimischen Künstler entwickelt sich Gauguin zum Archäologen und Ethnologen, dem die schwere Aufgabe zufällt, Mythologie und Kultur der Maori wiederzuerwecken. Alles in allem schafft er mit der Kraft seiner Kunst ein Paradies der Stille und der Lust.

1891, Oil on canvas/Huile sur toile, 92,5 × 72,2 cm, Szépművészeti Múzeum, Budapest

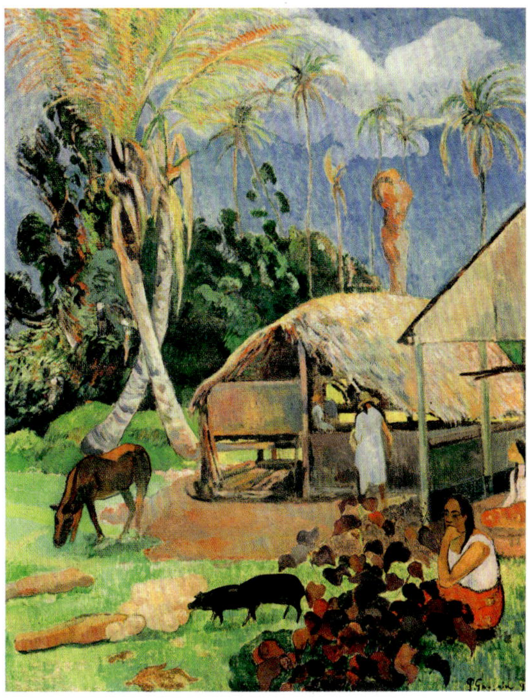

obras, en ellas se celebra un mundo primitivo perdido y una edad de oro imaginada, como resemblanza de su cuaderno de acuarelas titulado *Antiguo Culto Mahorí*. Impregnado de las técnicas y del estilo de los artistas locales, Gauguin se nombró arqueólogo y etnólogo asumiendo la pesada carga de resucitar la mitología y la cultura maoríes. Año tras año, gracias a su arte, creó un paraíso de calma y voluptuosidad.

immagine del suo libro di acquerelli intitolato Antico culto Mahori. Intriso di tecniche e stile degli artisti locali, Gauguin è un archeologo e antropologo che ha l'onere di far rivivere la mitologia e la cultura Maori. Anno dopo anno, la forza della sua arte, crea un paradiso di calma e voluttà.

op de verloren primitieve wereld en de niet bestaande glorietijd, in de sfeer van zijn schetsboek met aquarellen getiteld *De oude Mahorie-cultus*. Gauguin raakt in de ban van de technieken en de stijl van de plaatselijke kunstenaars en werpt zich als de archeoloog en ethnoloog op wie de zware taak rust de mythologie en de cultuur van de Maori's weer tot leven te wekken. Met zijn kunst creëert hij jaar in jaar uit een paradijs van rust en wellust.

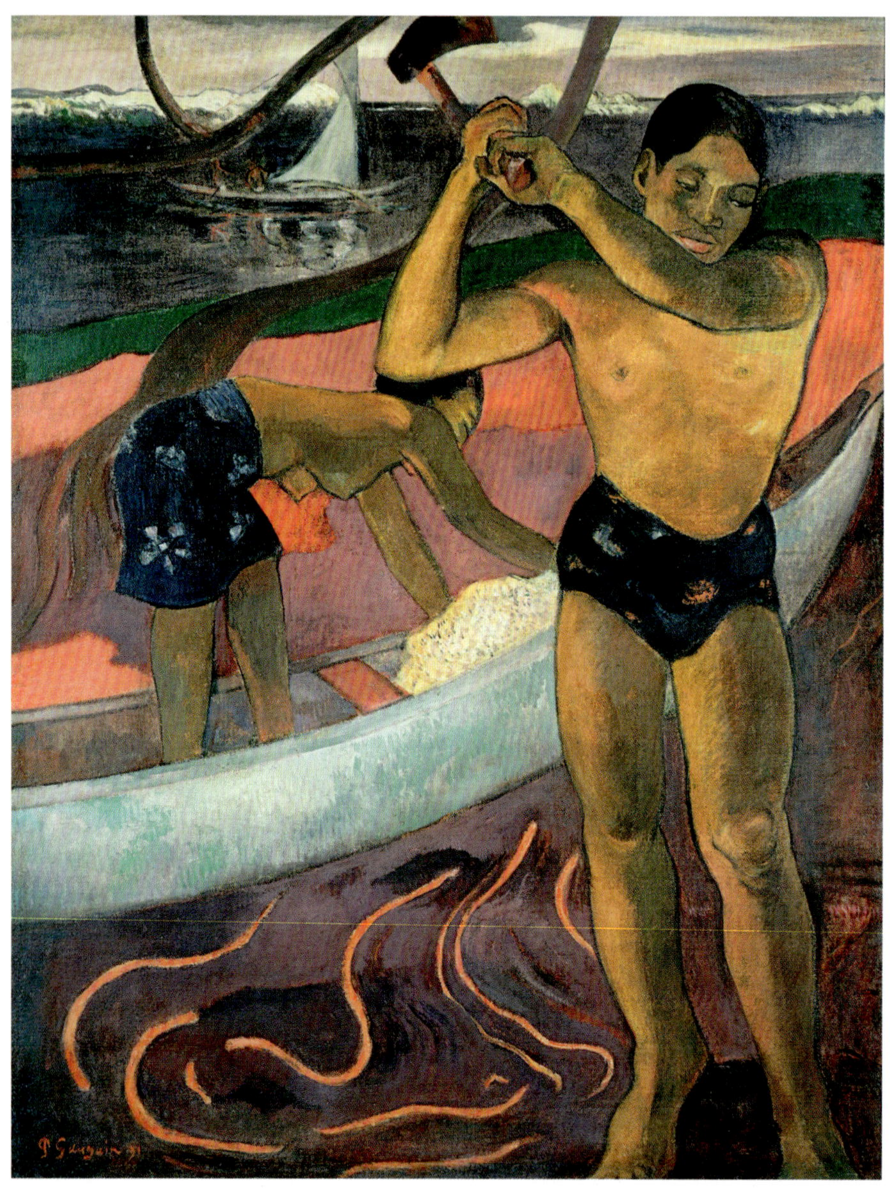

Man With an Ax

L'Homme à la hache

Der Mann mit der Axt

El hombre del hacha

L'uomo con l'ascia

De man met de bijl

*1891, Oil on canvas/Huile sur toile,
92,7 × 70 cm, Private collection*

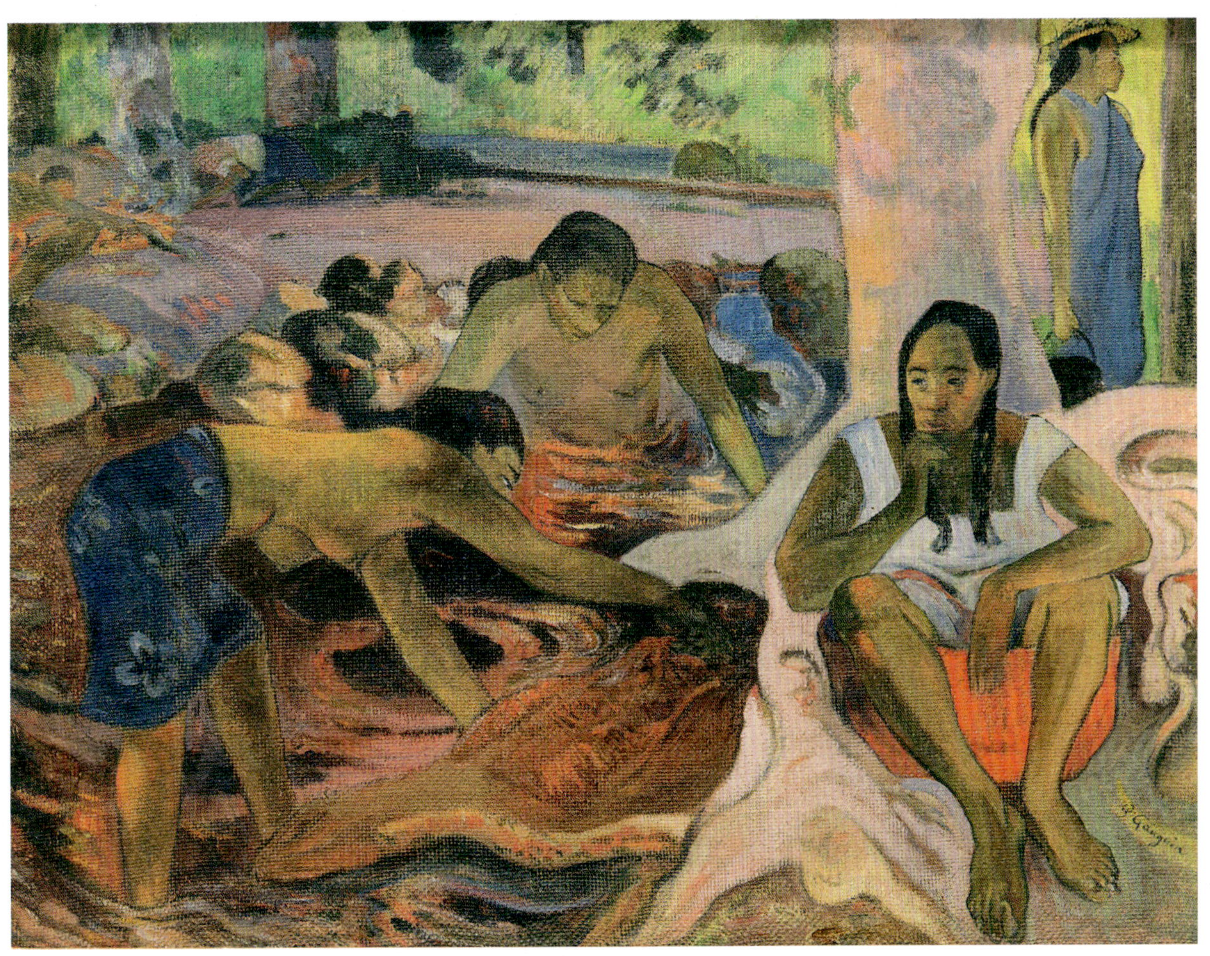

The Fisherwomen of Tahiti

Pêcheuses tahitiennes

Tahitische Fischerinnen

Pescadoras tahitianas

Pescatori taitiani

Tahitiaanse vissersvrouwen

1891, Oil on canvas/Huile sur toile, 71 × 90 cm, Nationalgalerie, Berlin

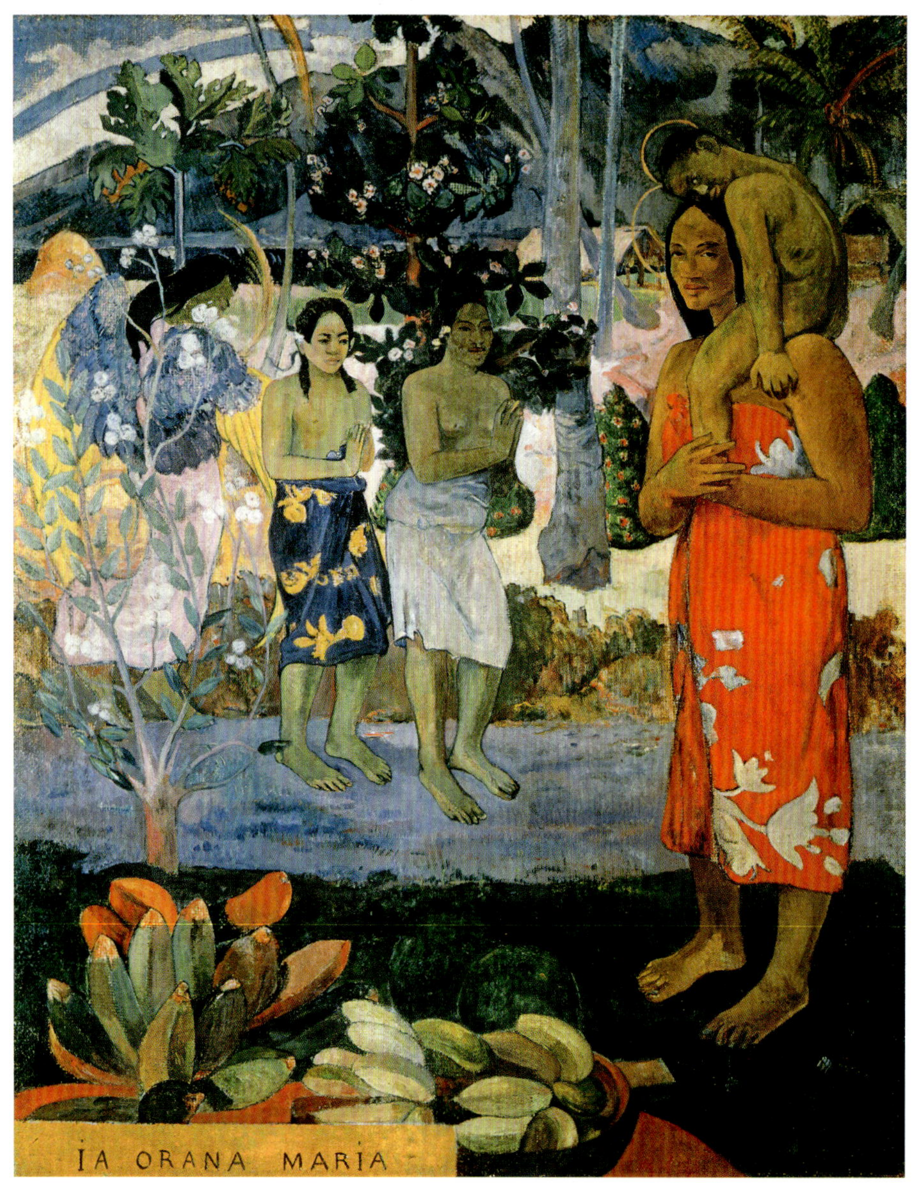

Ia orana Maria
(Hail Mary)
(Je vous salue Marie)
(Gegrüßet seist du, Maria)
(Yo te saludo, María)
(Vi saluto Maria)
(Wees gegroet Maria)

1891, Oil on canvas/Huile sur toile, 113,7 × 87,6 cm, Metropolitan Museum of Art, New York

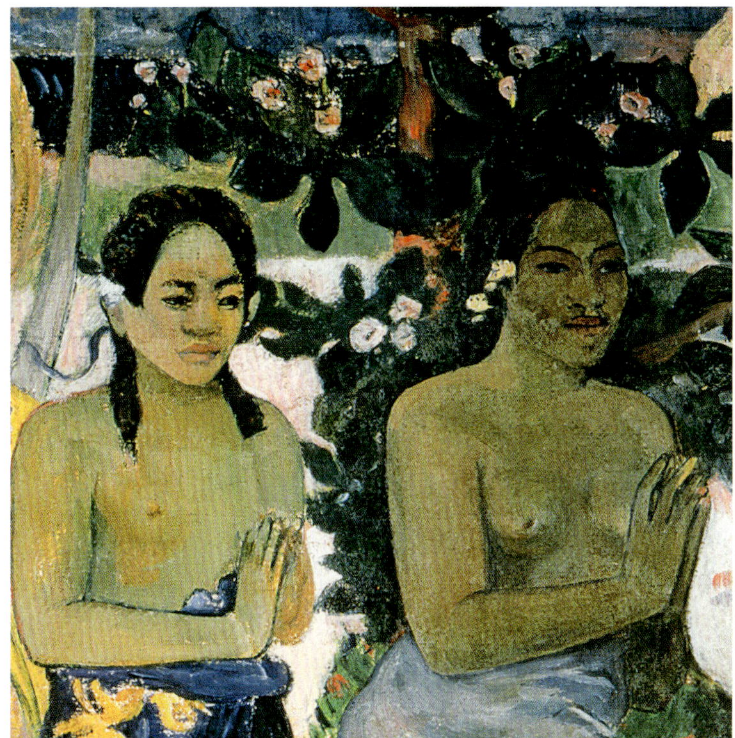 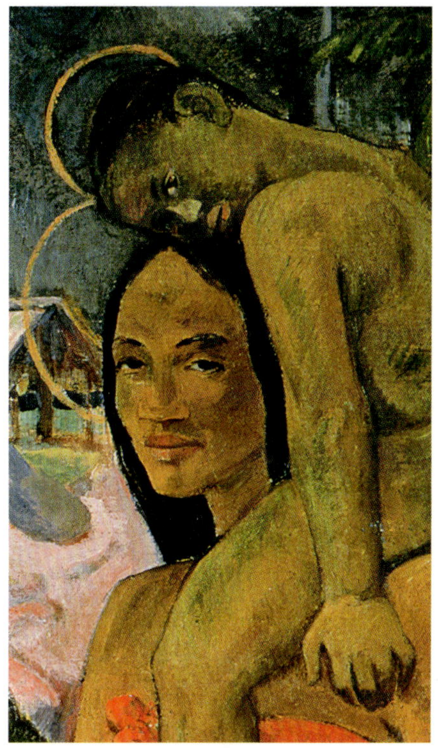

Painted like an ex-voto after a hospitalisation in Papeete, this masterpiece of syncretism entitled *Hail Mary* portrays an amazing Polynesian maternity, far from traditional Christian iconography and combines still life, landscape, scenes of daily life, and religious references.

Peint comme un ex-voto après une hospitalisation à Papeete, ce chef-d'œuvre de syncrétisme intitulé *Je vous salue Marie* propose une étonnante maternité polynésienne, bien loin de l'iconographie chrétienne traditionnelle, qui combine nature morte, paysage, scène de vie quotidienne et références religieuses.

Wie eine Votivtafel gemalt und entstanden nach einem Krankenhausaufenthalt in Papeete zeigt dieses Meisterwerk des Synkretismus mit dem Titel *Je vous salue Marie* (Gegrüßet seist du Maria) ein erstaunliches polynesisches Madonnenbild, weit entfernt von der traditionellen christlichen Ikonographie – eine Mischung von Stillleben, Landschaftsmalerei und Alltagsszene mit religiösem Bezug.

Pintado como una ofrenda tras una hospitalización en Papeete, esta obra maestra de sincretismo titulada *Yo te saludo, María* propone una sorprendente maternidad polinesia, muy alejada de la iconografía cristiana tradicional, que combina naturaleza muerta, paisaje, escena de vida cotidiana y referencias religiosas.

Dipinto come ex-voto dopo il ricovero a Papeete, questo capolavoro di sincretismo intitolato *Io vi saluto Maria* propone una straordinaria maternità polinesiana, ben lontana dall'iconografia cristiana tradizionale, che combina natura morta, paesaggio, scena di vita quotidiana e riferimenti religiosi.

Dit meesterwerk van syncretistische kunst getiteld *Wees gegroet Maria* schilderde Gauguin als een ex-voto na een verblijf in het ziekenhuis in Papeete: een Polynesische moeder met kind, die ver afstaat van de traditionele christelijke iconografie, een combinatie van stilleven, landschap, dagelijks leven en religieuze verwijzingen.

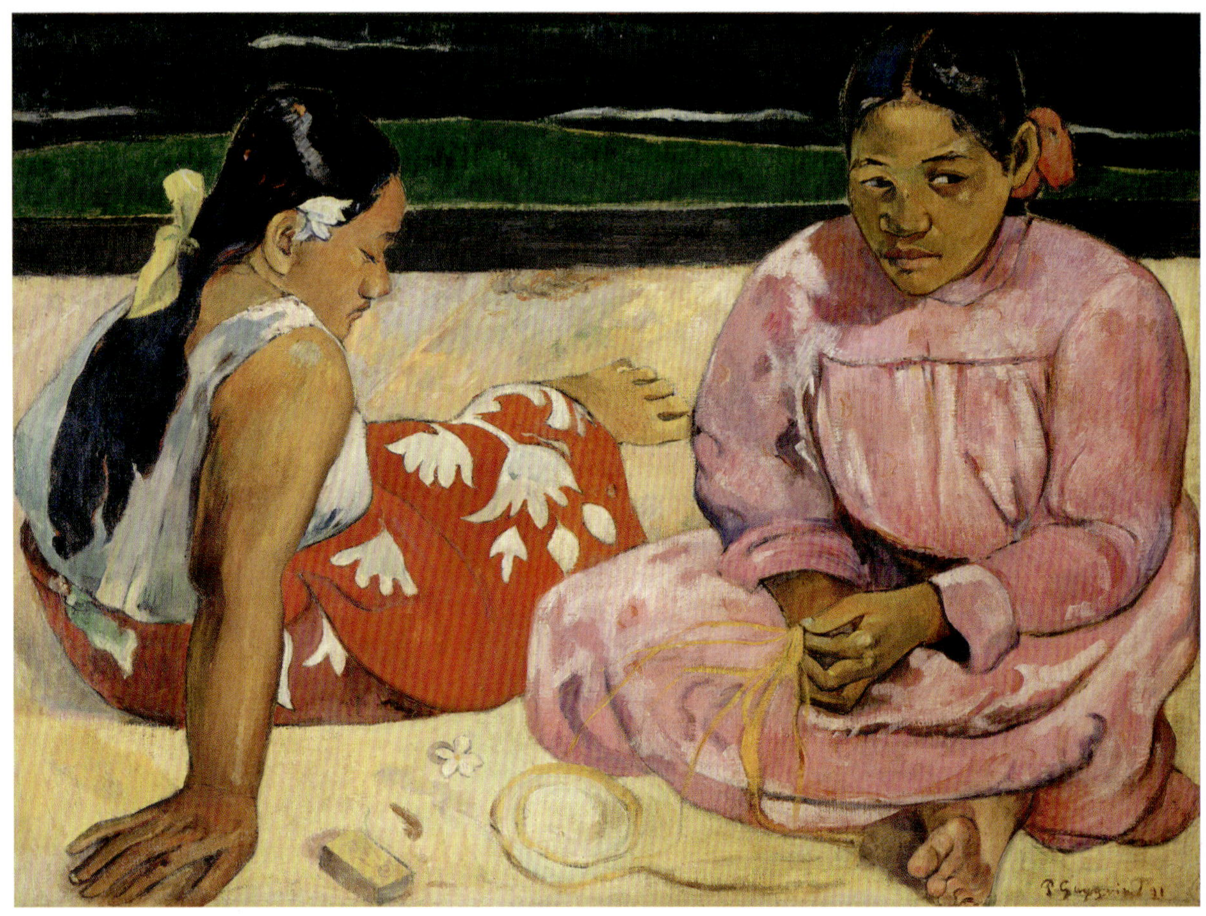

Tahitian Women

Femmes de Tahiti

Frauen auf Tahiti

Mujeres de Tahití

Donne di Tahiti

Vrouwen van Tahiti

1891, Oil on canvas/Huile sur toile, 69 × 91,5 cm, Musée d'Orsay, Paris

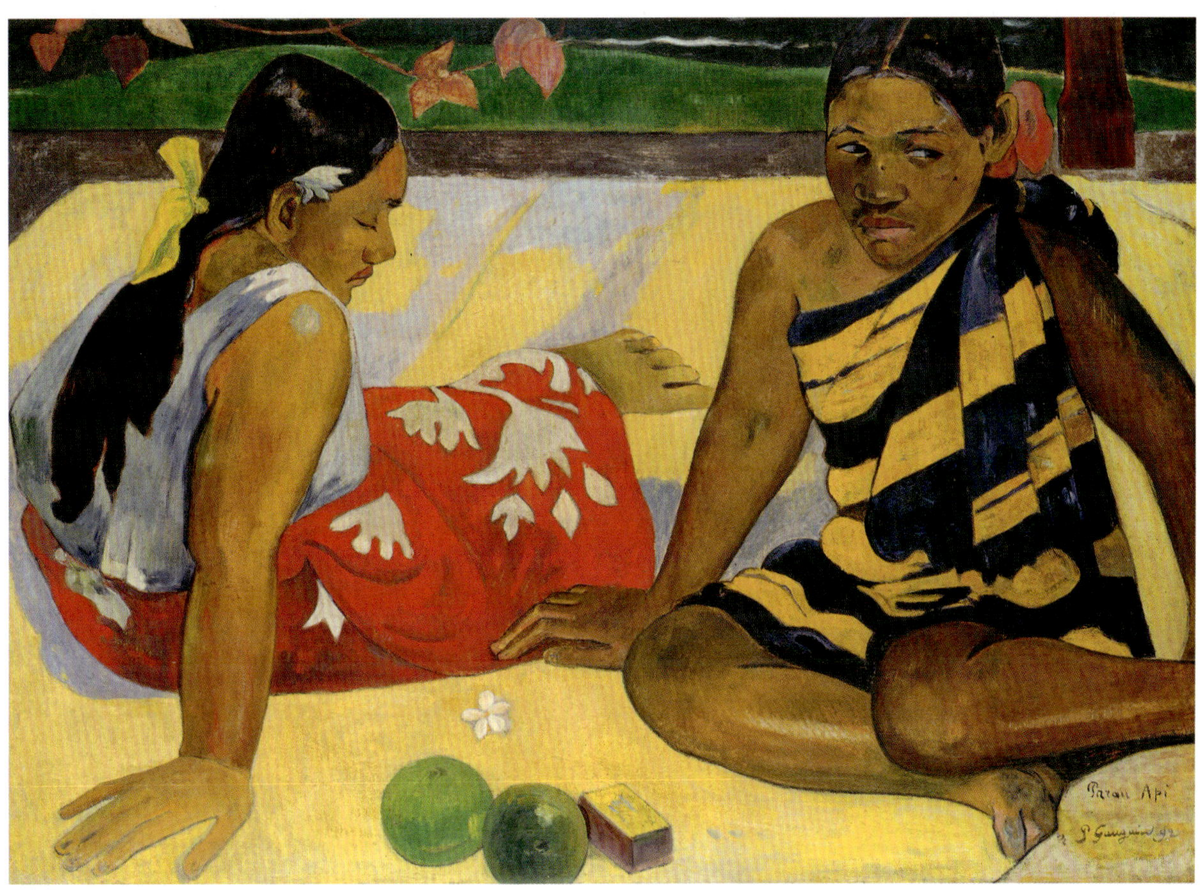

Parau api

(What's New?)

(Quoi de neuf ?)

(Was gibt es Neues?)

(¿Qué hay de nuevo?)

(Che c'è di nuovo)?

(Nog nieuws?)

1892, Oil on canvas/Huile sur toile, 67 × 92 cm, Galerie Neue Meister, Dresden

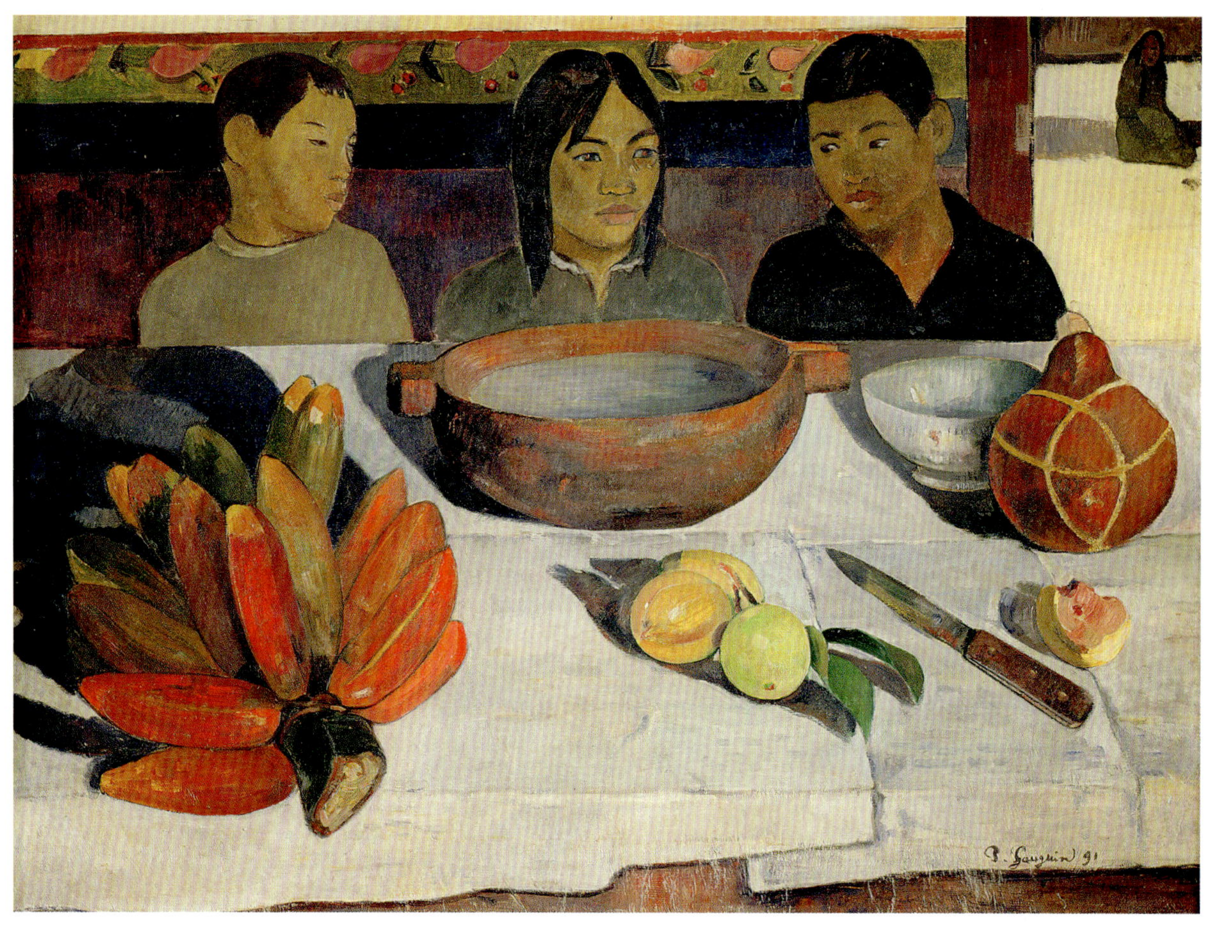

The Meal or *The Bananas*
Le Repas ou *Les Bananes*
Die Mahlzeit oder *Die Bananen*
La comida o *Los plátanos*
Il pasto o *Le Banane*
De maaltijd of *De bananen*

1891, Oil on paper marouflaged on canvas/Huile sur papier marouflé sur toile, 73 × 92 cm, Musée d'Orsay, Paris

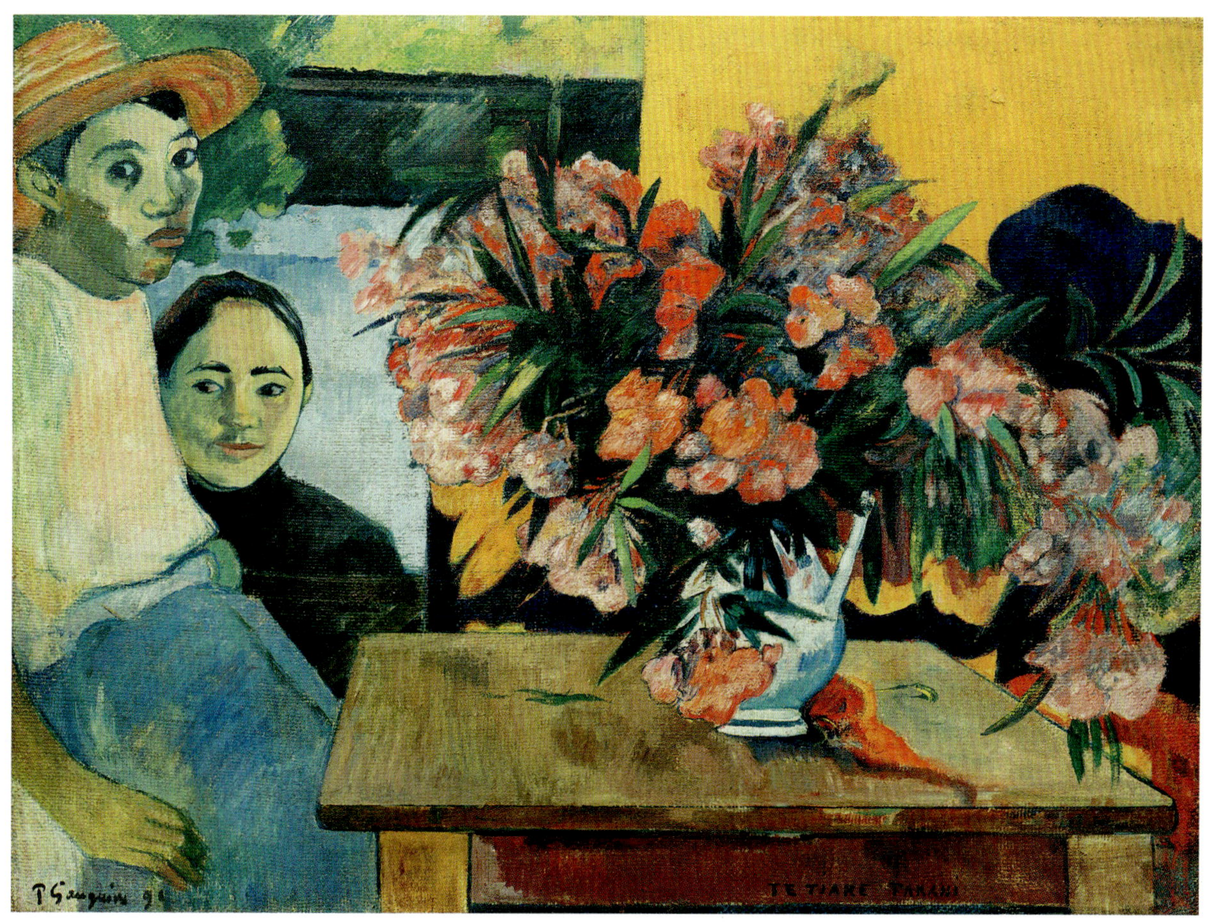

Te tiare farani

(The Flowers of France)

(Les Fleurs de France)

(Die Blumen Frankreichs)

(Las flores de Francia)

(I fiori di Francia)

(Bloemen uit Frankrijk)

1891, Oil on canvas/Huile sur toile, 72 × 92 cm, Pushkin Museum, Moscow

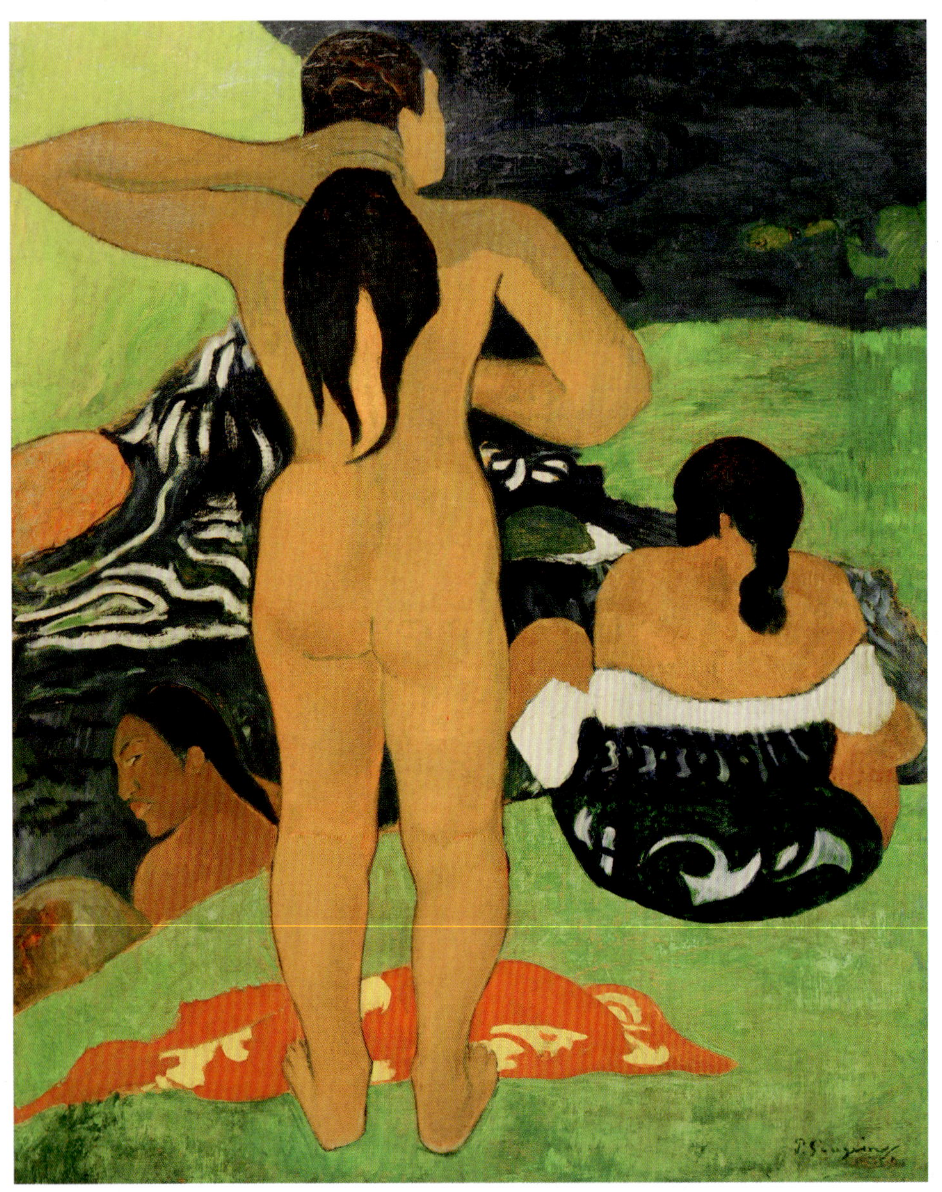

Bathers at Tahiti

Baigneuses tahitiennes

Badende Tahitianerinnen

Bañistas tahitianas

Bagnanti taitiane

Tahitiaanse baadsters

1891–92, Oil on paper marouflaged on canvas/Huile sur papier marouflé sur toile, 110 × 89 cm, Metropolitan Museum of Art, New York

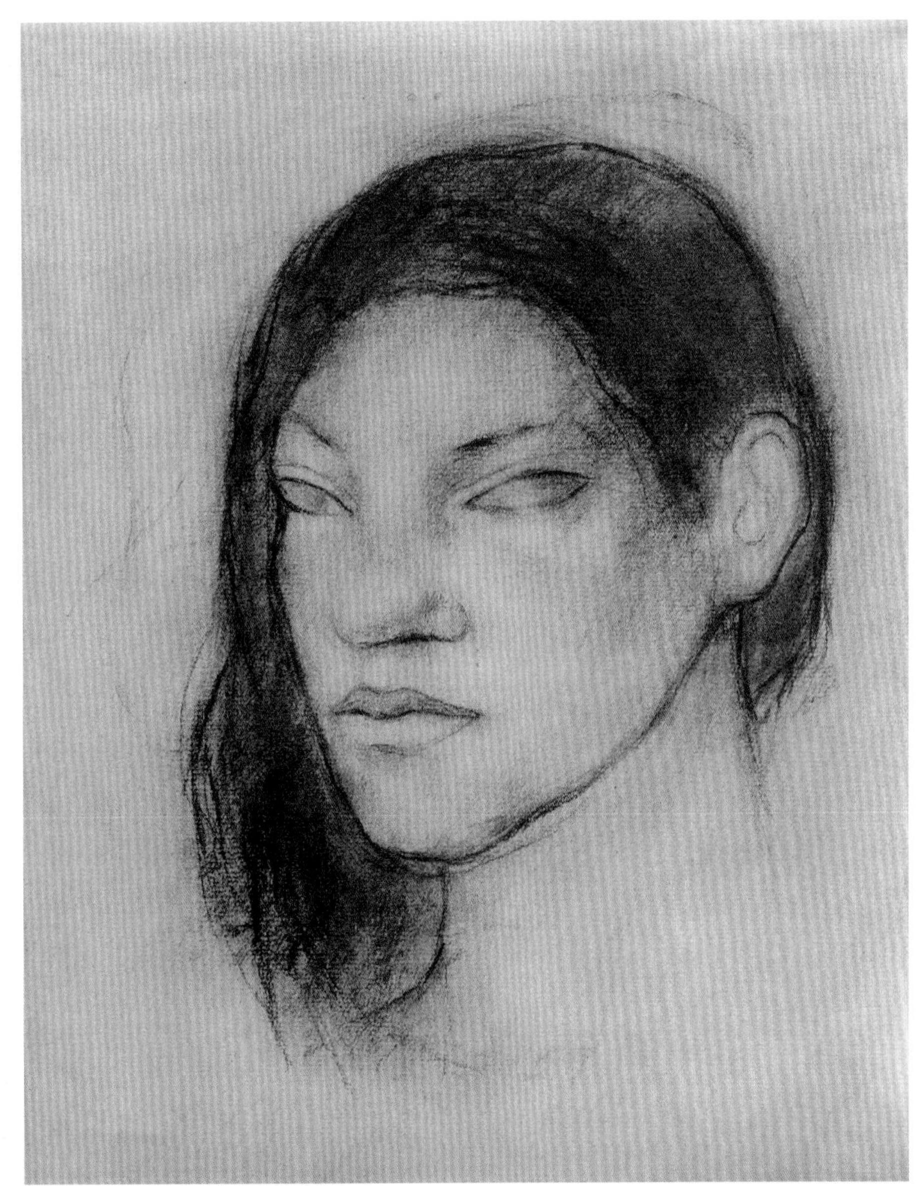

Portrait of a Woman of Tahiti
Portrait de tahitienne
Porträt einer Tahitianerin
Retrato de tahitiana
Ritratto di taitiana
Portret van een Tahitiaanse vrouw

c. 1891, 34 × 26,5 cm,
Private collection

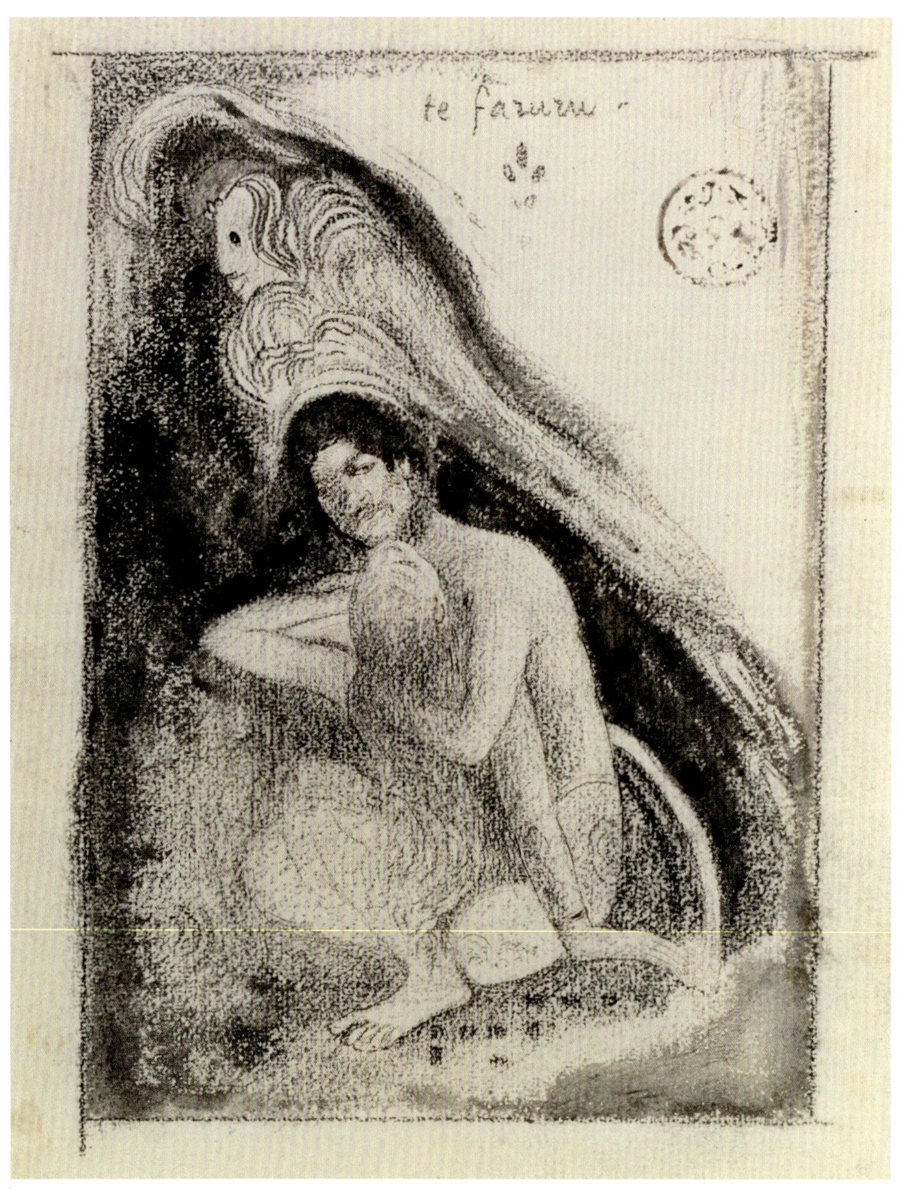

Te faruru
(Here We Make Love)
(Ici on fait l'amour)
(Liebesakt)
(Aquí hacemos el amor)
(Qui si fa l'amore)
(Hier wordt de liefde bedreven)
Private collection

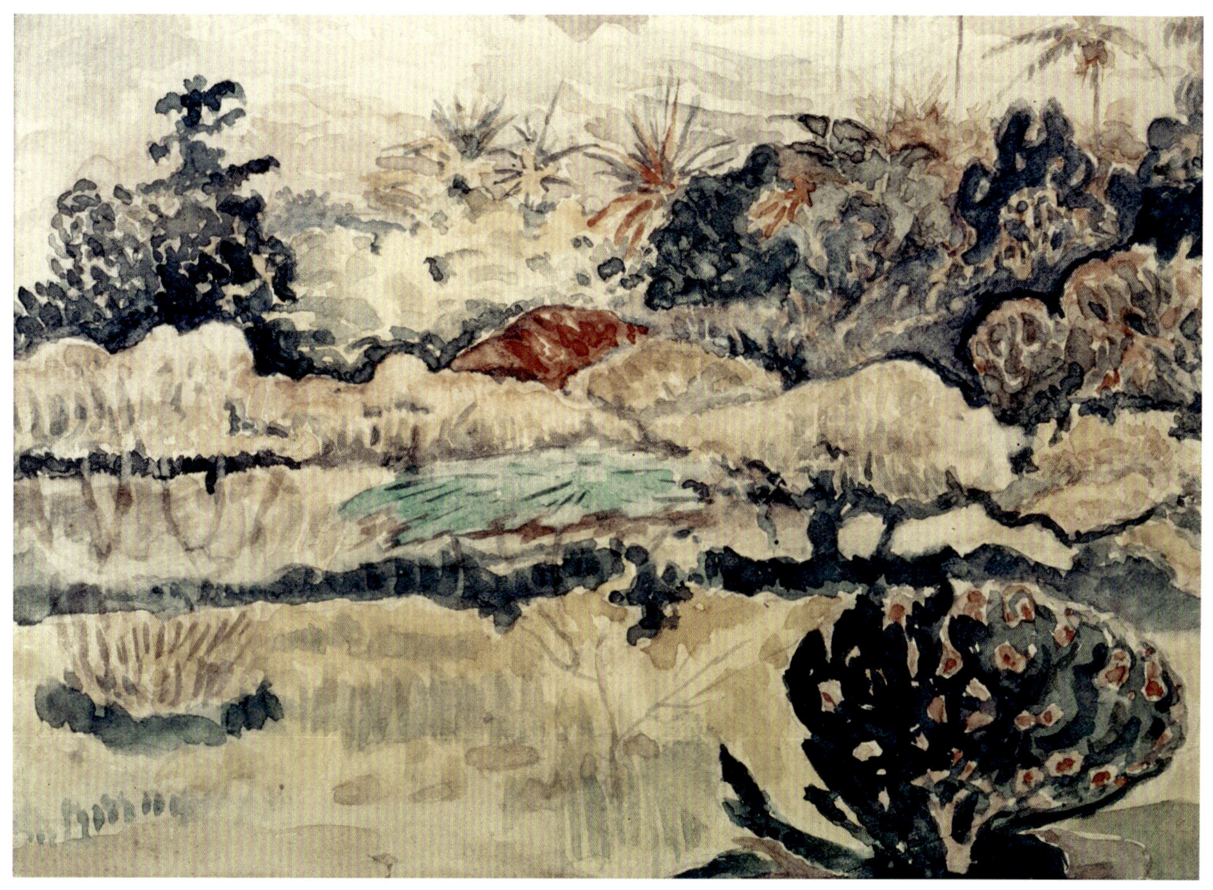

Tahitian Landscape

Paysage tahitien

Tahitische Landschaft

Paisaje tahitiano

Paesaggio taitiano

Tahitiaans landschap

c. 1891, Watercolor on paper/Aquarelle sur papier, 23 × 29 cm, Private collection

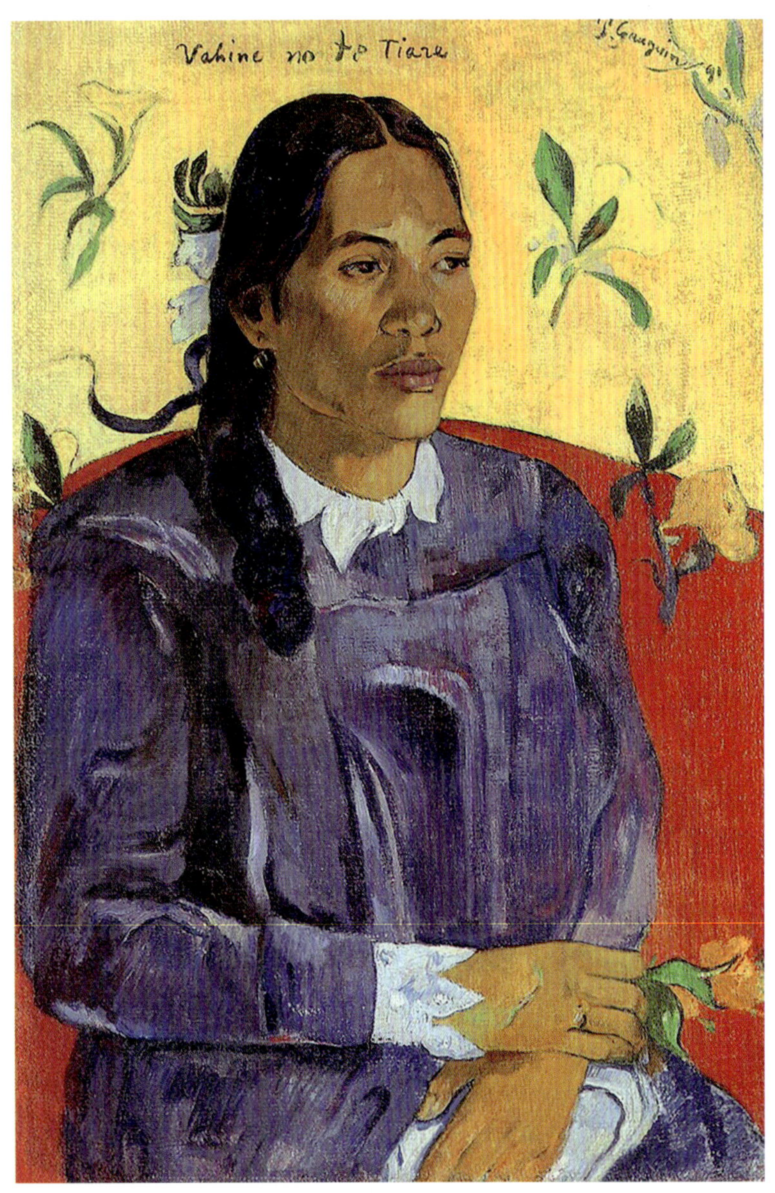

Vahine no te tiare

(Woman with Flower)

(Tahitienne à la fleur)

(Tahitianerin mit einer Blume)

(Tahitiana con flor)

(Taitiana con fiore)

(Tahitiaanse met de bloem)

*1891, Oil on canvas/Huile sur toile, 70,5 × 46,5 cm,
Ny Carlsberg Glyptotek, København*

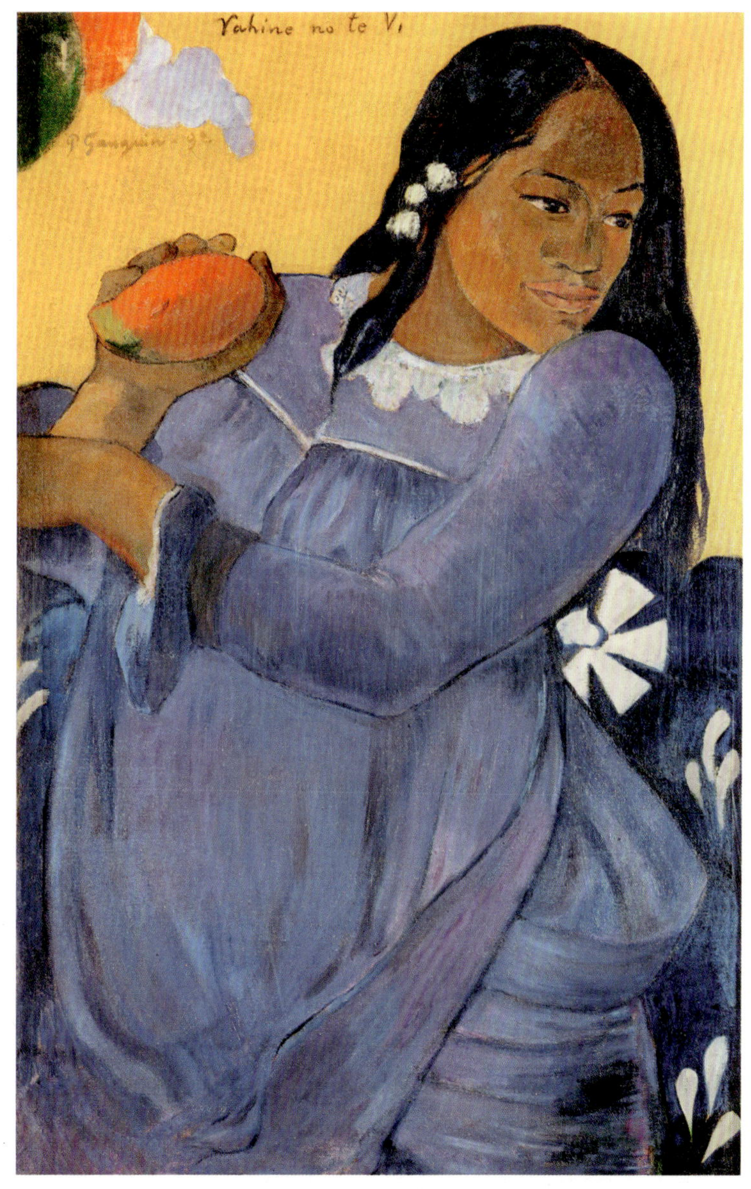

Vahine no te vi
(Woman of the Mango)
(Tahitienne à la mangue)
(Tahitianerin mit Mango)
(Tahitiana con mango)
(Taitiana con il mango)
(Tahitiaanse met de mango)
1892, Oil on canvas/Huile sur toile, 72,7 × 44,5 cm,
Baltimore Museum of Art, Baltimore

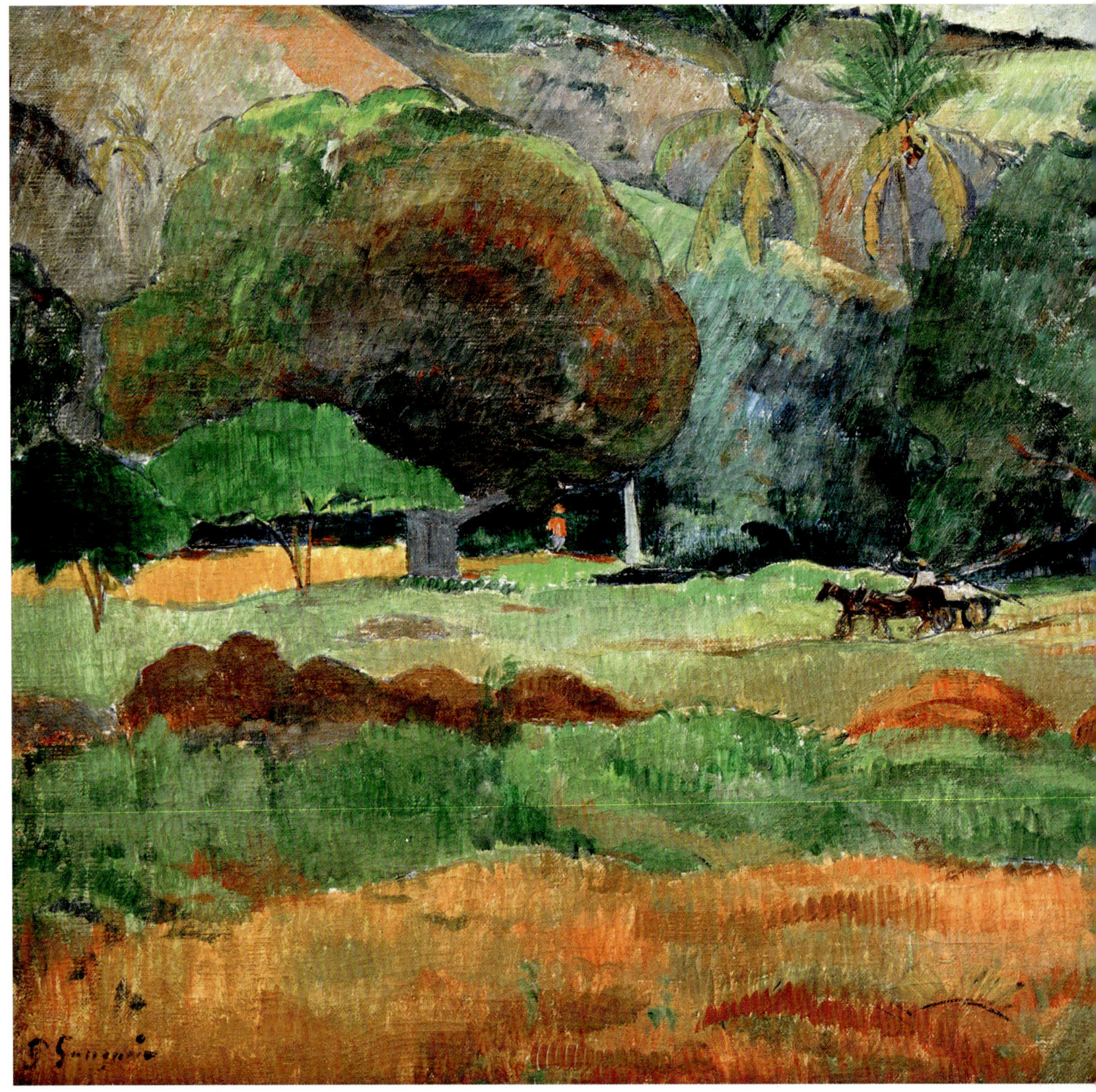
P Gauguin

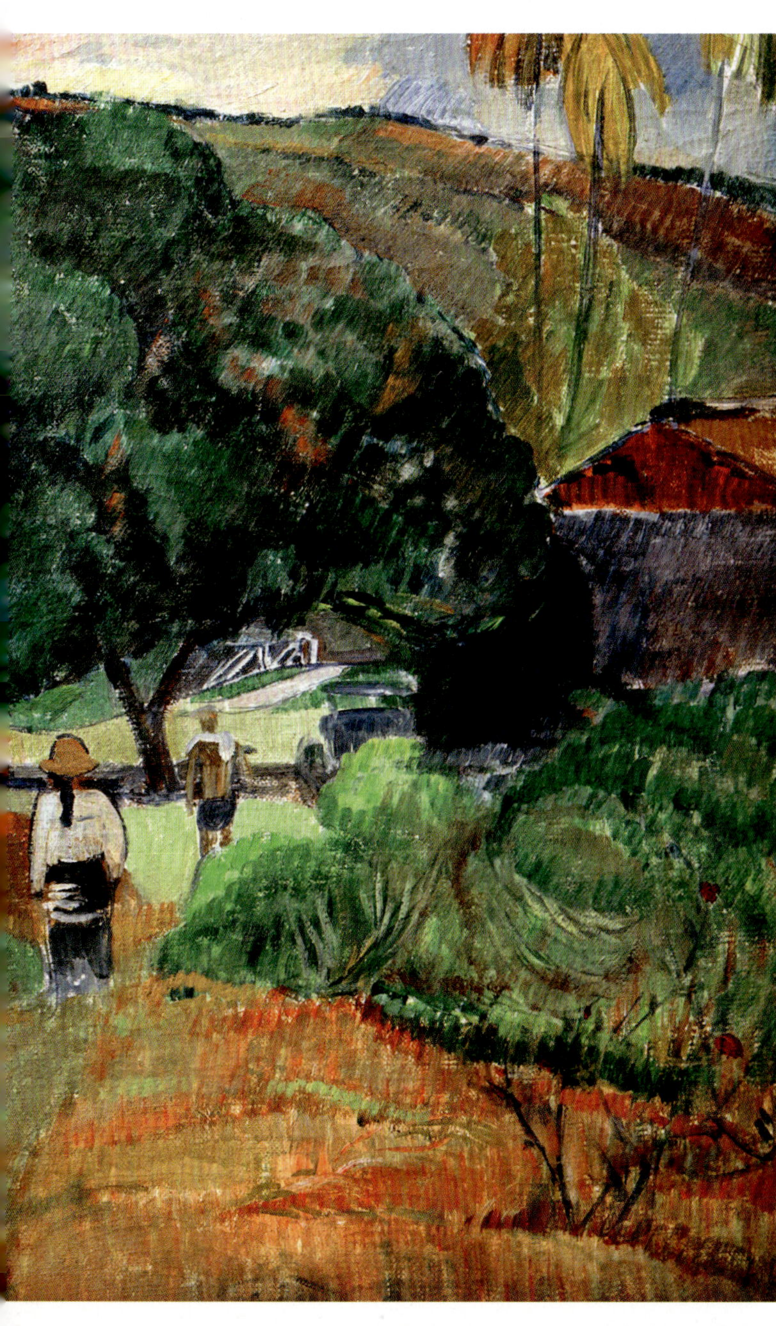

The Little Valley

Le Vallon

Das kleine Tal

El valle

La piccola valle

Het dalletje

1891–92, Oil on canvas/Huile sur toile, 41,7 × 67 cm,
Private collection

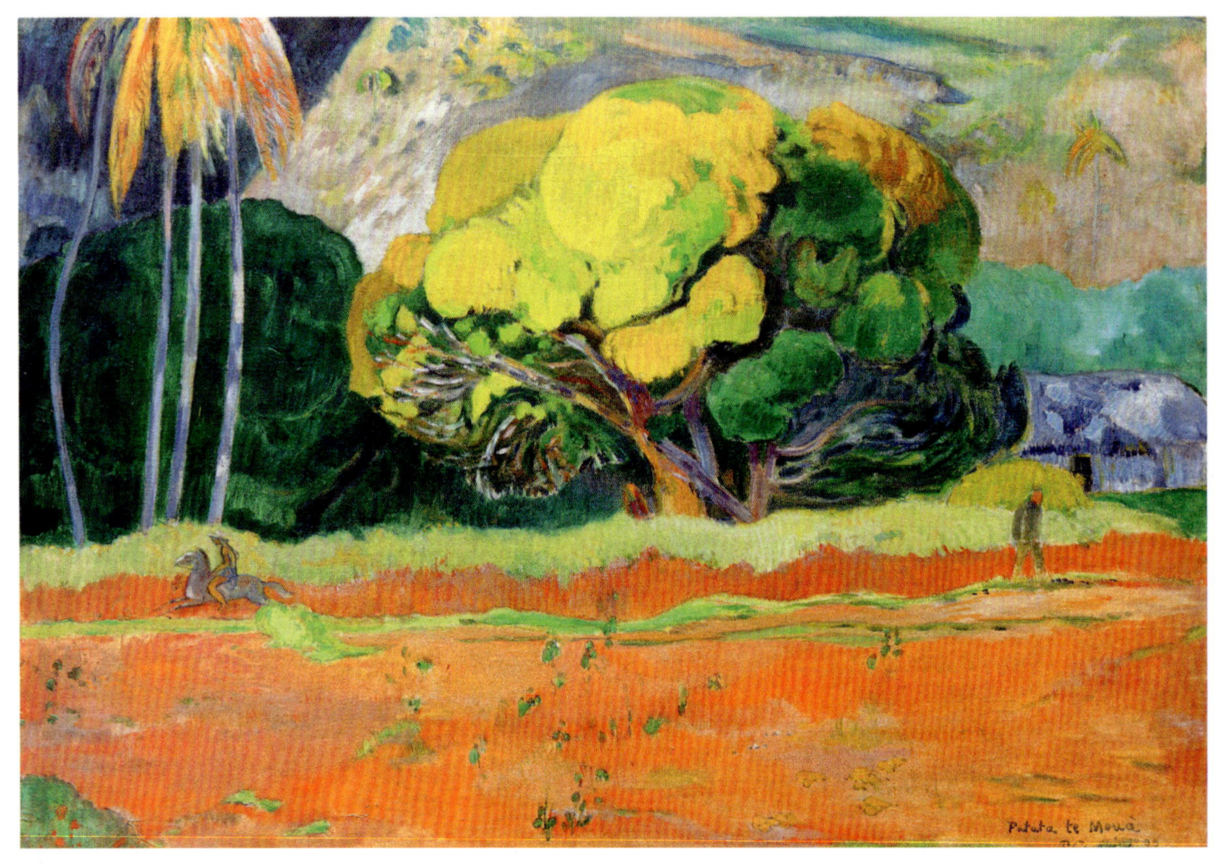

Fatata te moua

(At the Foot of a Mountain)

(Au pied de la montagne)

(Am Fuß des Berges)

(Al pie de la montaña)

(Ai piedi della montagna)

(Aan de voet van de berg)

1892, Oil on canvas/Huile sur toile, 68 × 92 cm, State Hermitage Museum, St. Petersburg

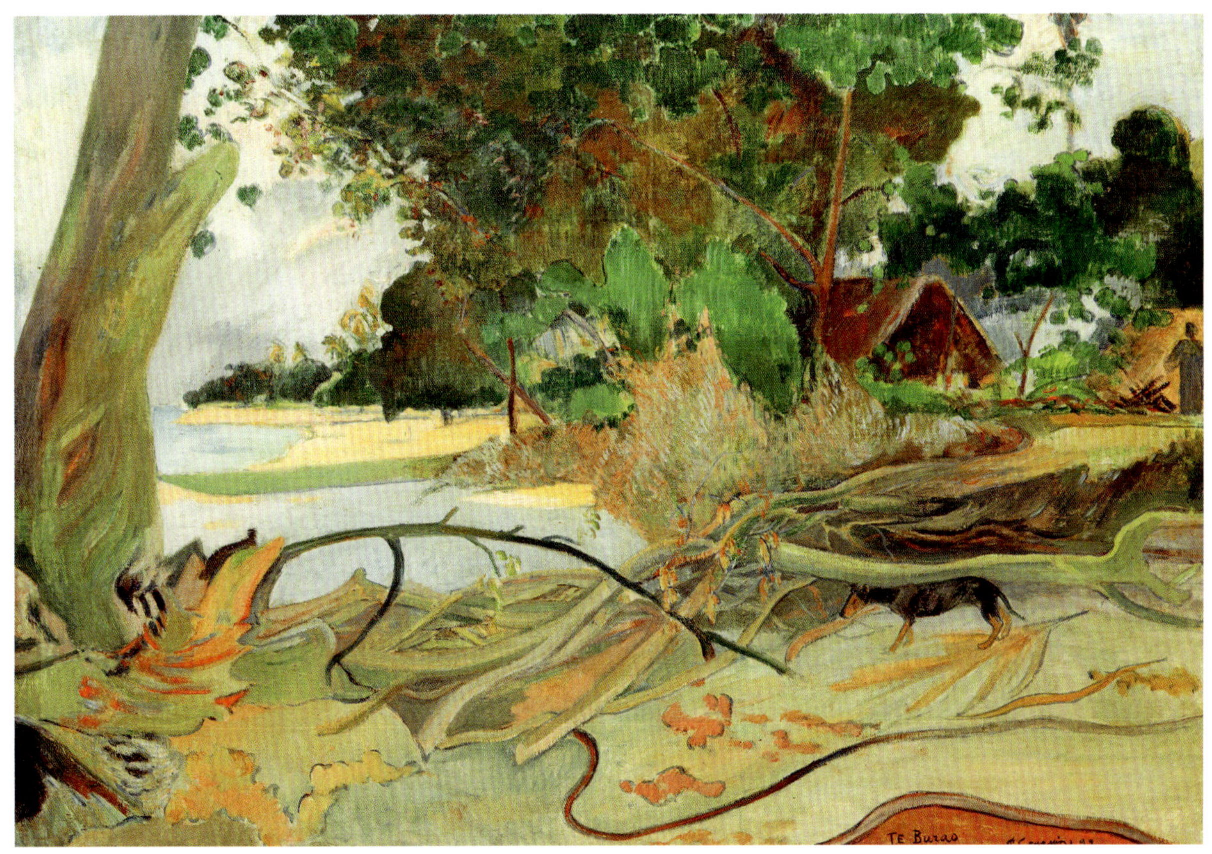

Te burau
(The Hibiscus Tree)
(L'Hibiscus)
(Der Hibiskusbaum)
(El Hibisco)
(L'Hibiscus)
(De hibiscus)

1892, Oil on canvas/Huile sur toile, 68 × 90,7 cm, Art Institute of Chicago, Chicago

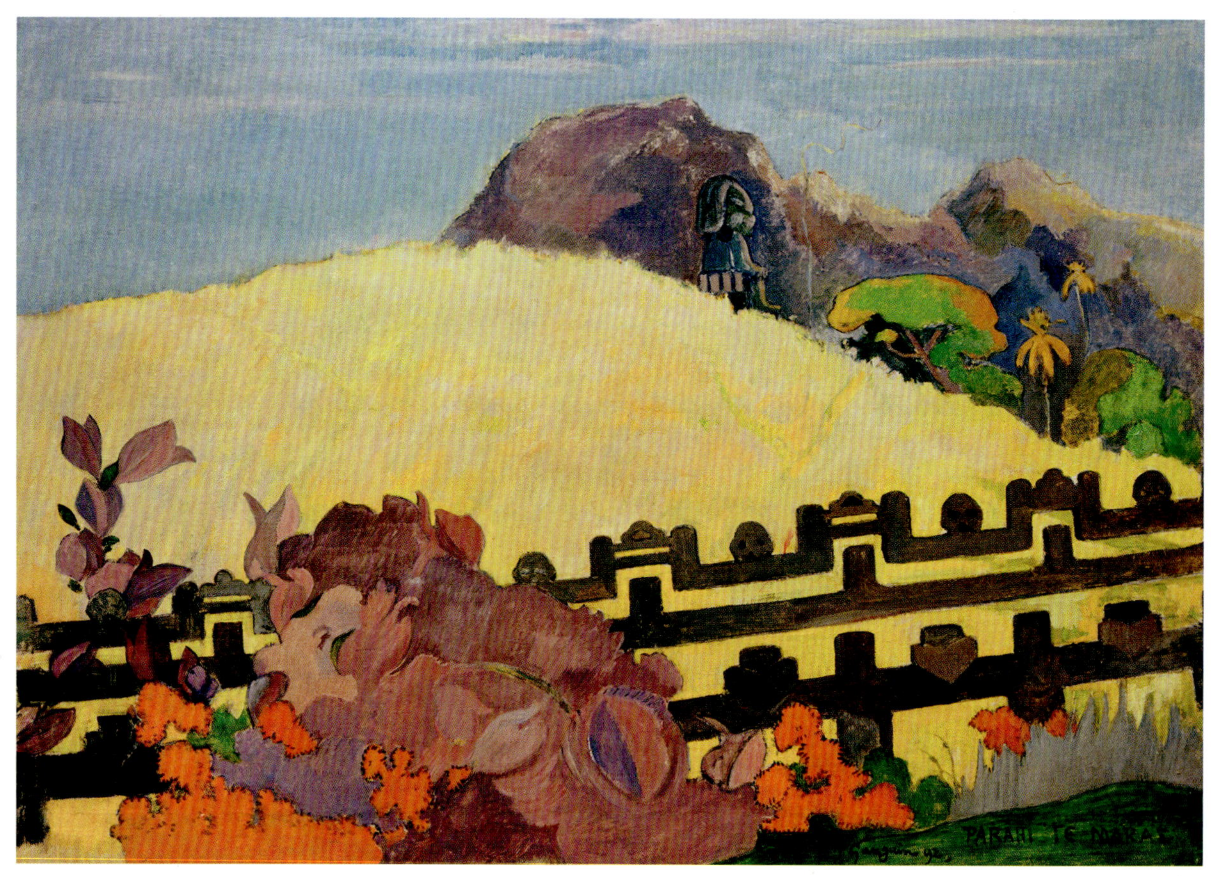

Parahi te marae
(There is the Temple)
(Ici est le temple)
(Hier ist der Tempel)
(Aquí está el templo)
(Qui è il tempio)
(Daar is de tempel)

1892, Oil on canvas/Huile sur toile, 66 × 88,9 cm, Philadelphia Museum of Art, Philadelphia

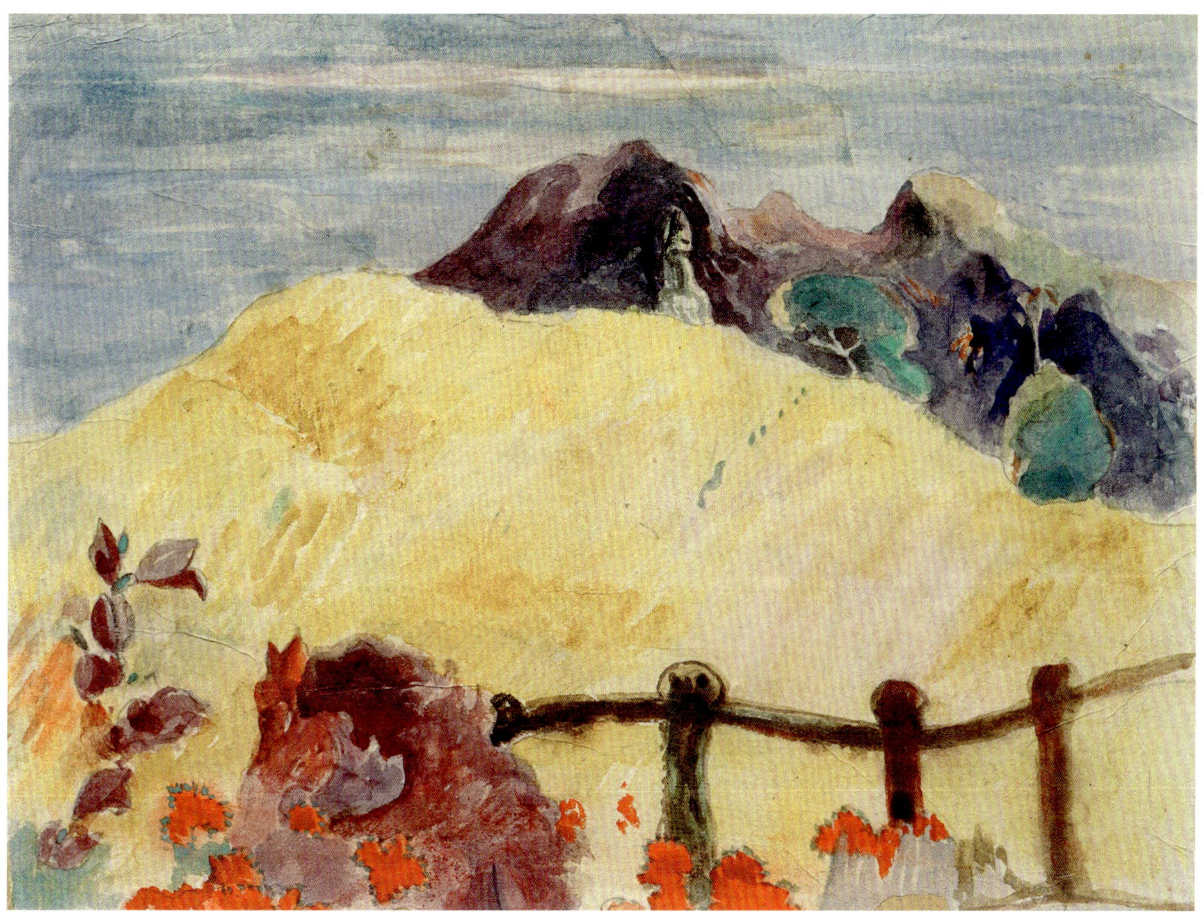

Parahi te marae

(There is the Temple)

(Ici est le temple)

(Hier ist der Tempel)

(Aquí está el templo)

(Qui è il tempio)

(Daar is de tempel)

c. 1892, Watercolor and graphite on Japanese paper/Aquarelle et graphite sur papier japonais, 18,5 × 22,9 cm, Fogg Art Museum, Cambridge

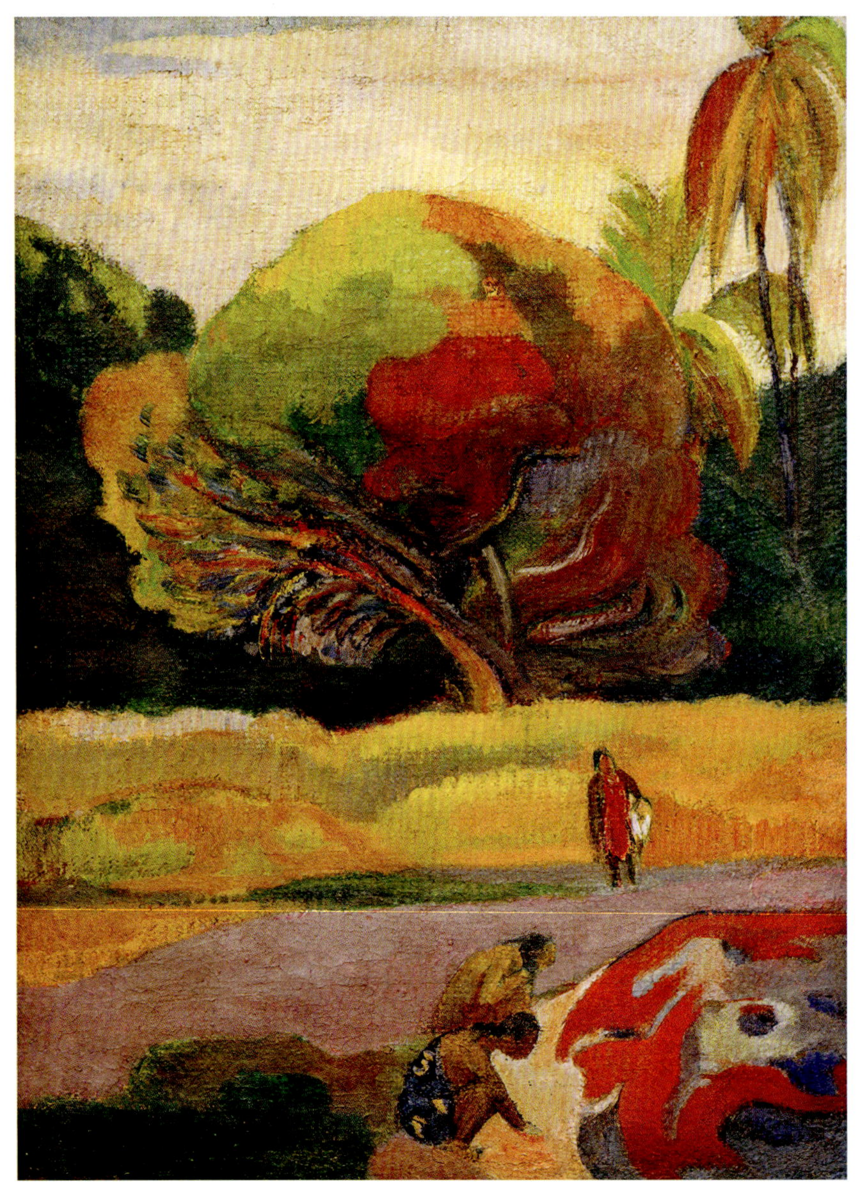

Women at the River
Femmes à la rivière
Frauen am Fluss
Mujeres en el río
Donne in riviera
Vrouwen aan de rivier

*1892, Oil on canvas/Huile sur toile,
43 × 31 cm, Van Gogh Museum, Amsterdam*

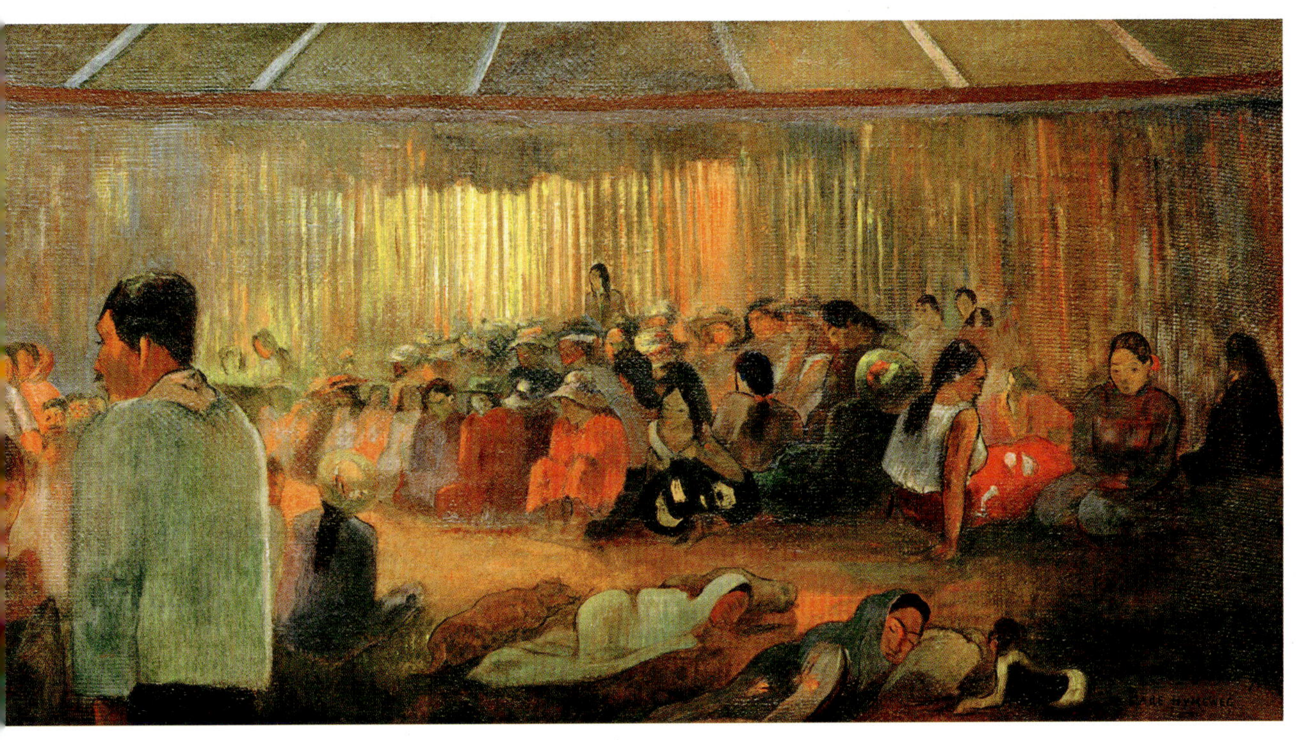

Te fare hymenee
(The House of Songs)
(La Maison des chants)
(Die Hütte der Gesänge)
(La casa de los himnos)
(La casa dei canti)
(De hut van de gezangen)

1892, Oil on canvas/Huile sur toile, 51 × 90,4 cm, Meadows Museum, Dallas

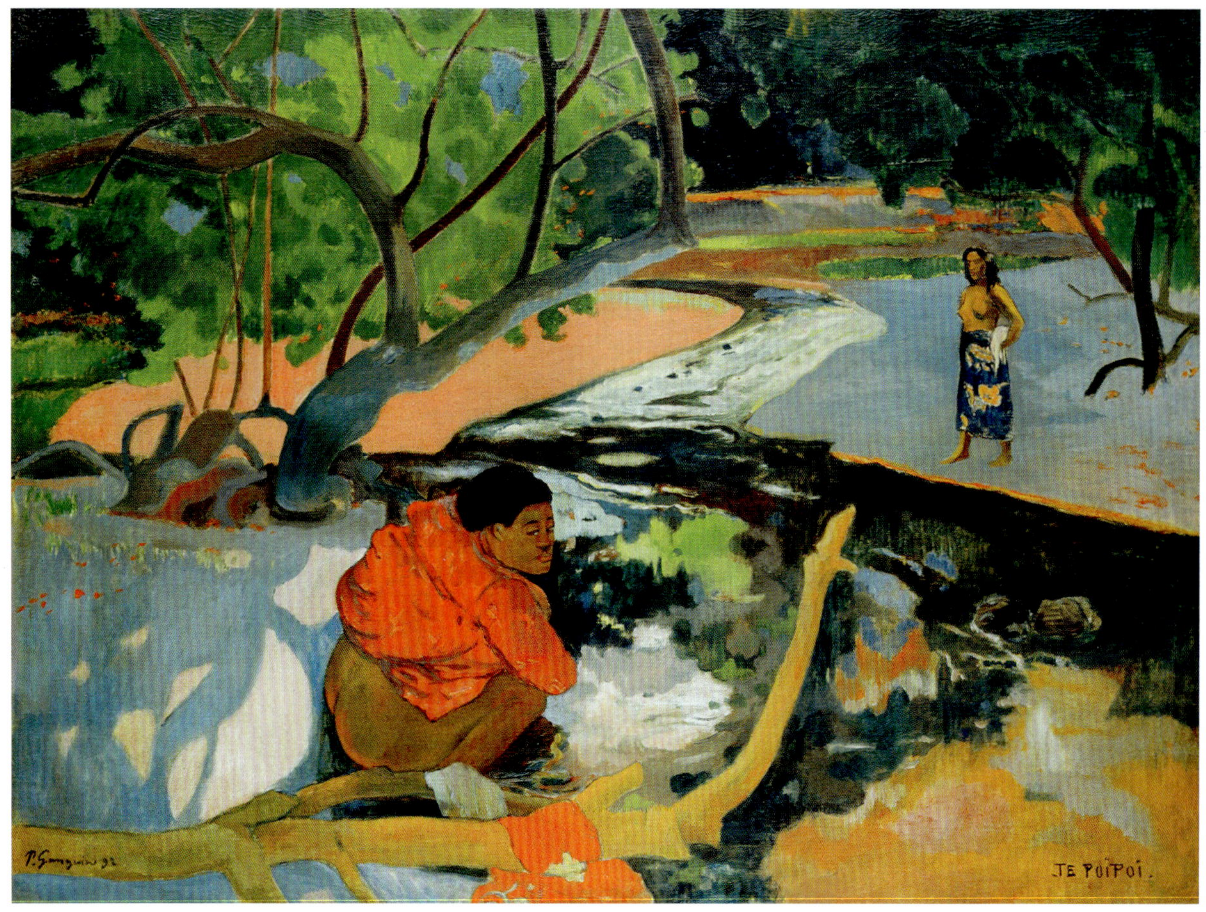

Te poipoi

(The Morning)

(Le Matin)

(Der Morgen)

(La mañana)

(Il Mattino)

(De ochtend)

1892, Oil on canvas/Huile sur toile, 68 × 92 cm, Private collection

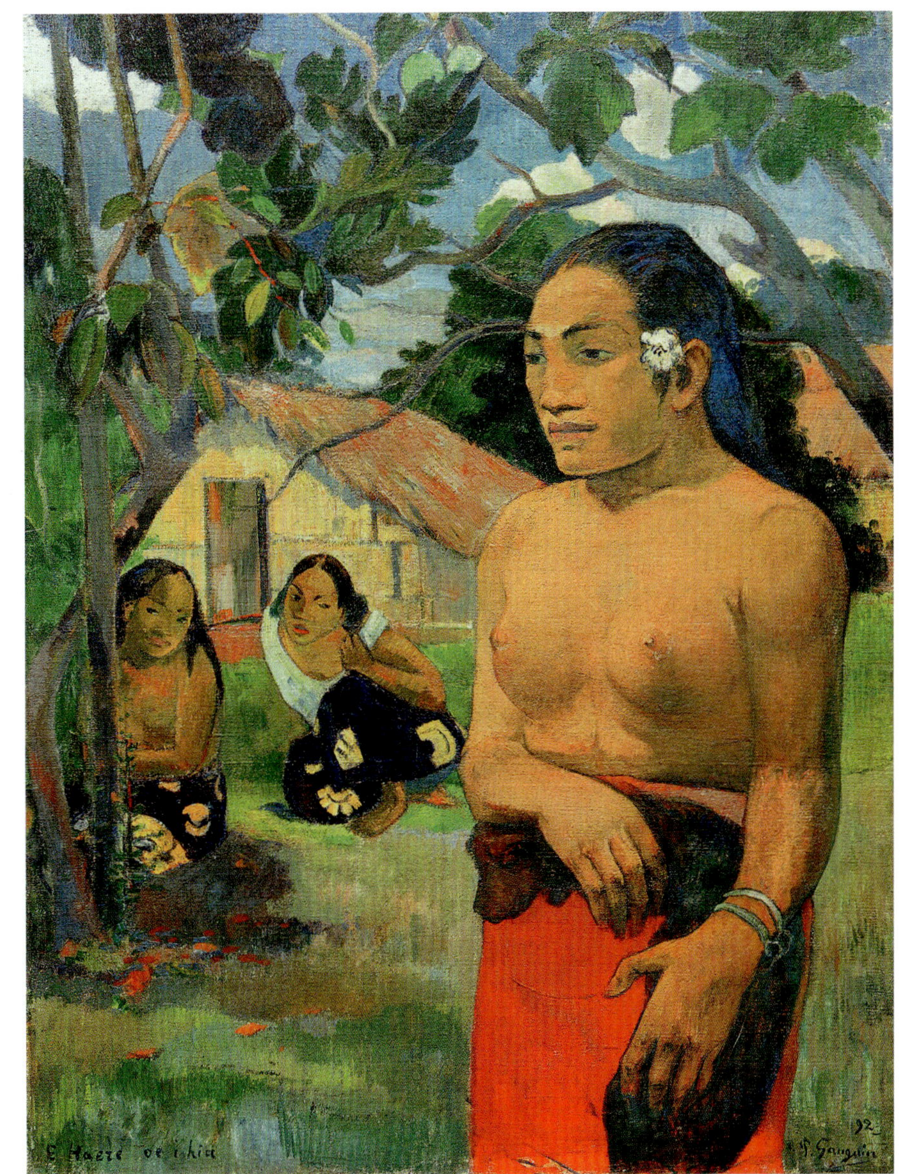

E Haere oe i hia
(Where Are You Going)
(Où vas-tu ?)
(Wohin gehst du?)
(¿A dónde vas?)
(Dove vai tu)?
(Waar ga je heen?)

1892, Oil on canvas/Huile sur toile,
96 × 69 cm, Staatsgalerie, Stuttgart

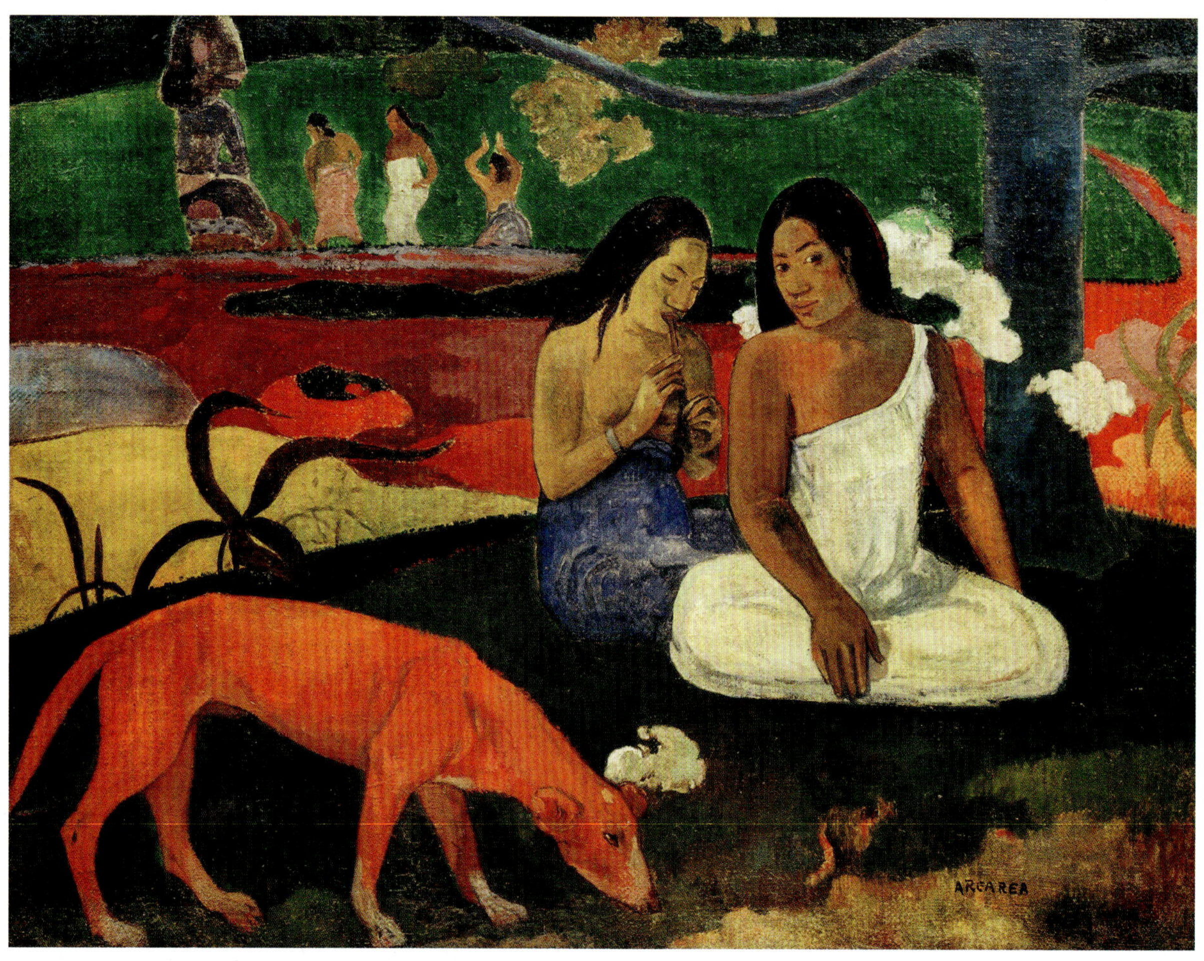

Arearea

(Joyousness)   *(Heiterkeit)*   *(Gaiezze)*

(Joyeusetés)   *(Bromas)*   *(Vrolijkheid)*

1892, Oil on canvas/Huile sur toile, 75 × 94 cm, Musée d'Orsay, Paris

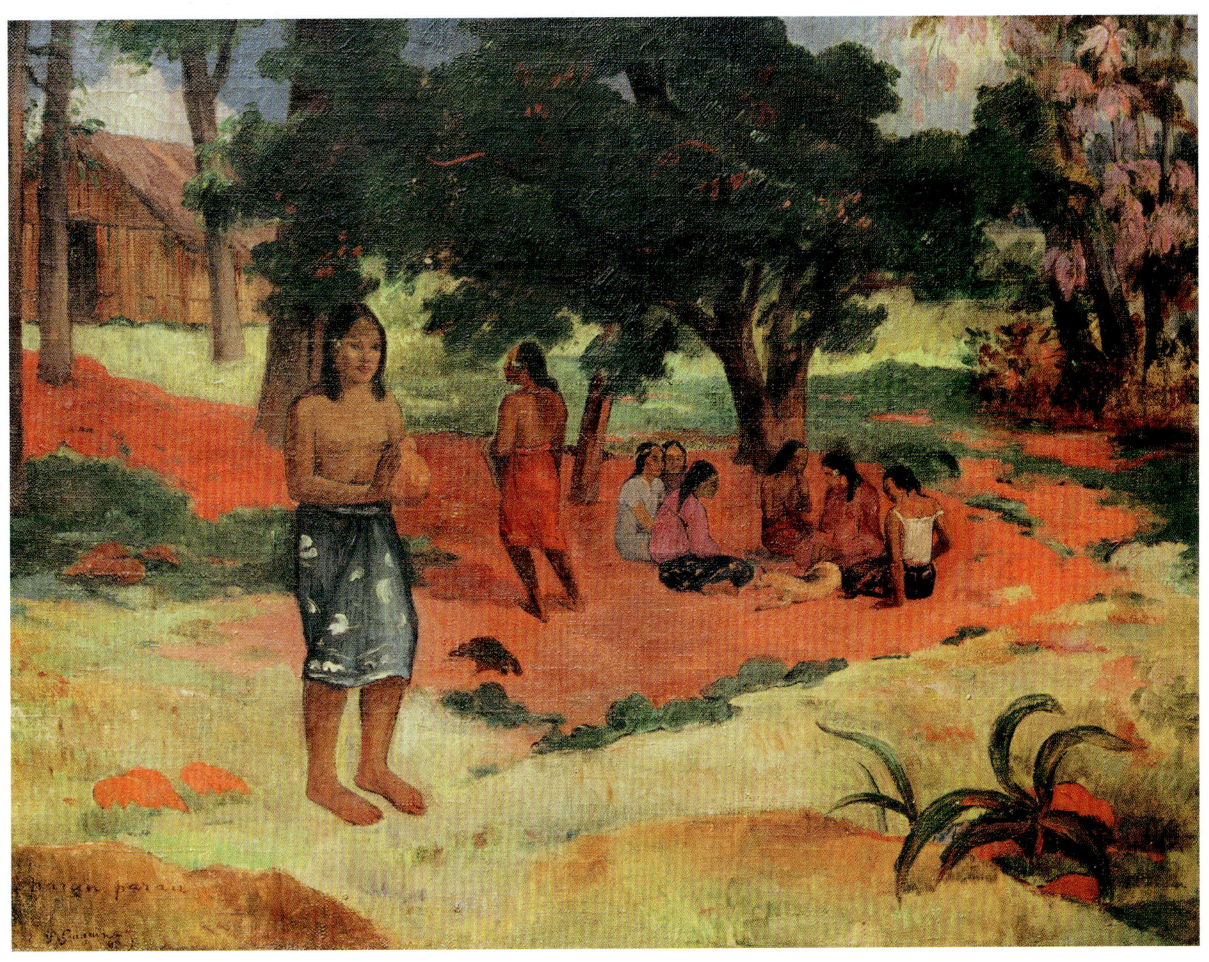

Parau parau

(Whispered Words)　　*(Die geflüsterten Worte)*　　*(Parole parole)*

(Paroles paroles)　　*(Palabras palabras)*　　*(Gefluisterde woorden)*

1892, Oil on canvas/Huile sur toile, 77,1 × 96,5 cm, Yale University Art Gallery, New Haven

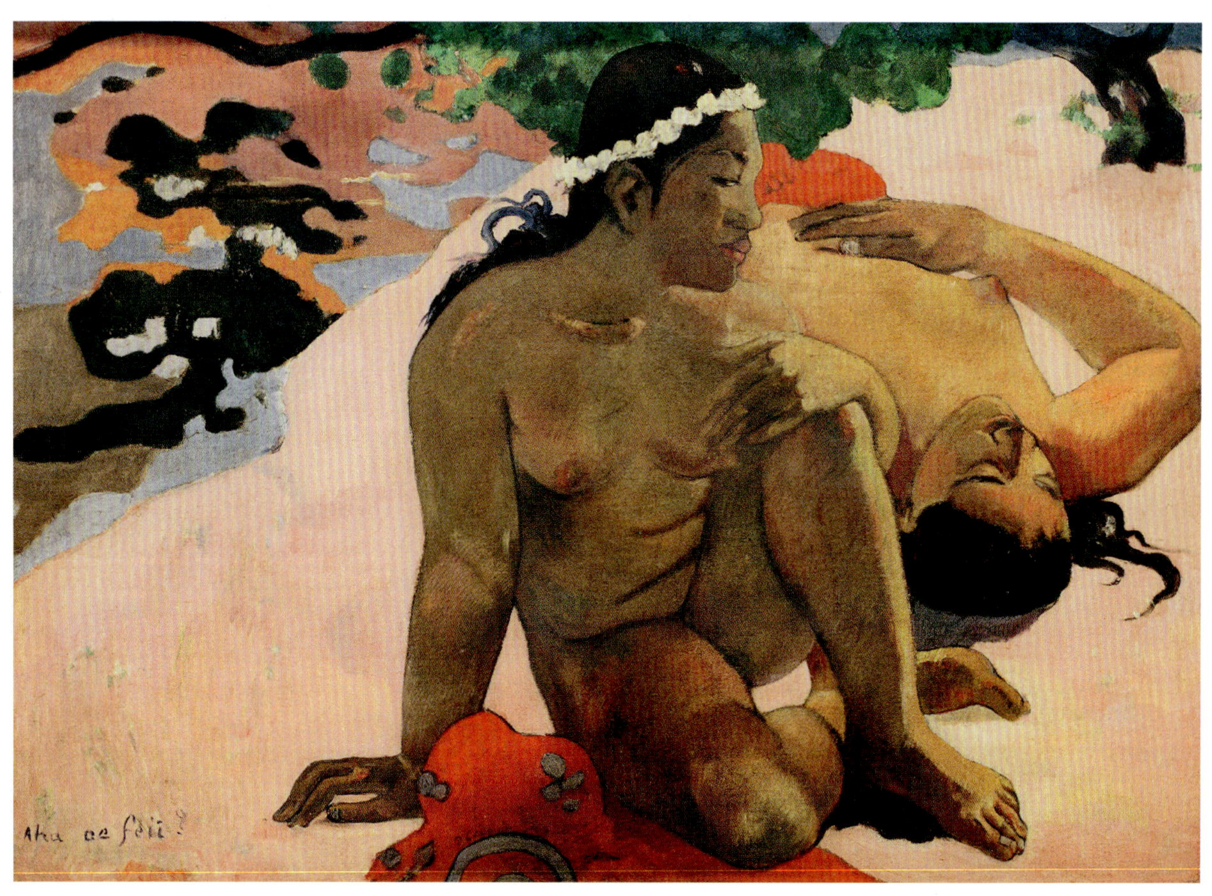

Aha oe feii ?

(What! Are You Jealous?)

(Eh quoi ! Tu es jalouse ?)

(Bist du eifersüchtig?)

(¡Y qué! ¿Estás celosa?)

(Eh con ciò? Tu sei gelosa?)

(Wat nou! Ben je soms jaloers?)

1892, Oil on canvas/Huile sur toile, 66 × 89 cm, Pushkin Museum, Moscow

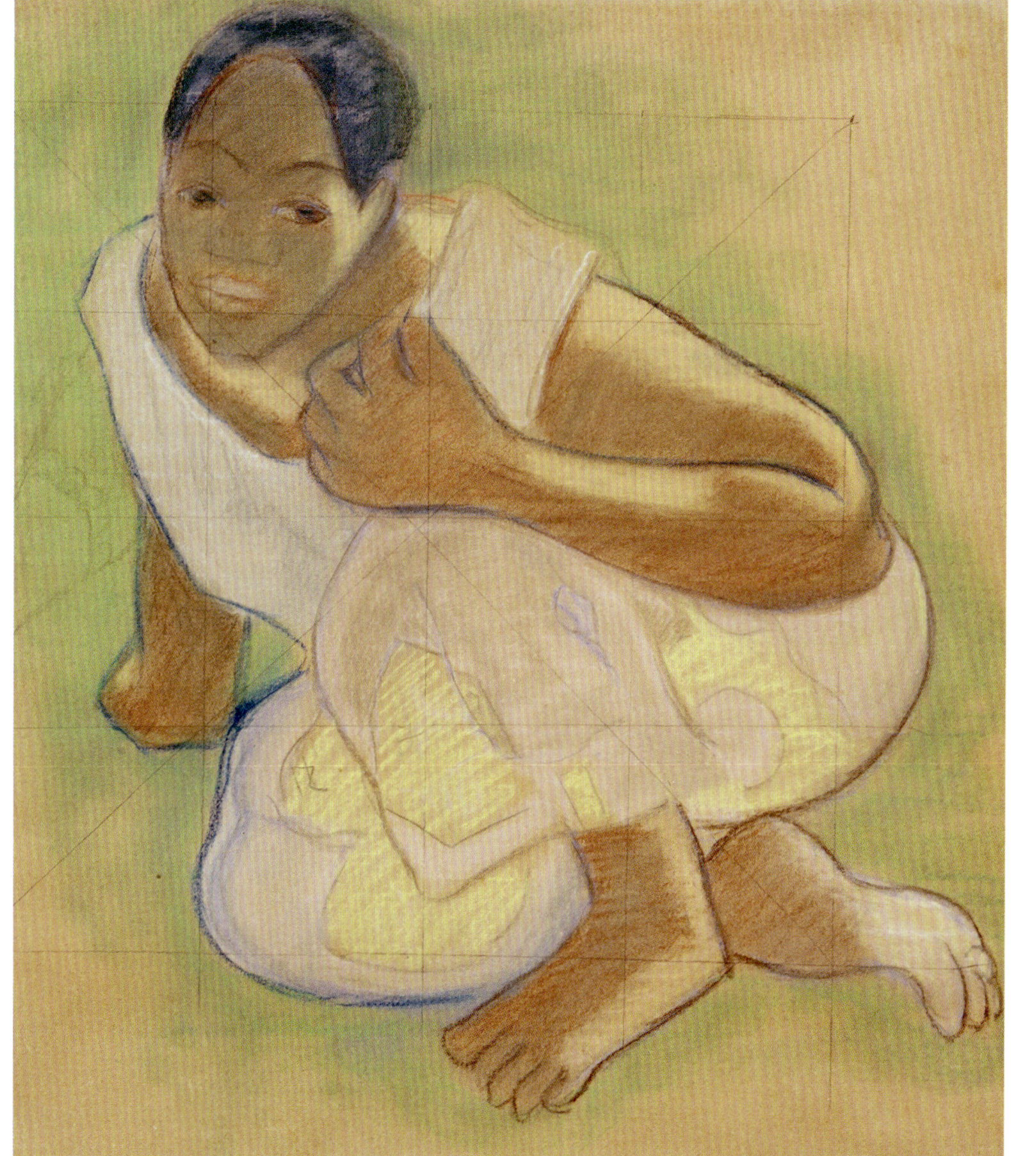

Seated Woman, sketch for Nafea Faa Ipoipo (When Will You Marry?)

Femme assise, étude pour Nafea faa ipoipo (Quand te maries-tu ?)

Kauernde Tahitianerin, Studie zu Nafea faa ipoipo (Wann heiratest du?)

Mujer sentada, estudio para Nafea faa ipoipo (¿Cuándo te casas?)

Donna seduta, studio per Nafea faaa ipoipo (Quando ti sposi?)

Zittende vrouw, studie voor Nafea faa ipoipo (Wanneer ga je trouwen?)

1892, Pastel and charcoal on paper/ Pastel et fusain sur papier, 55,5 × 48 cm, Art Institute of Chicago, Chicago

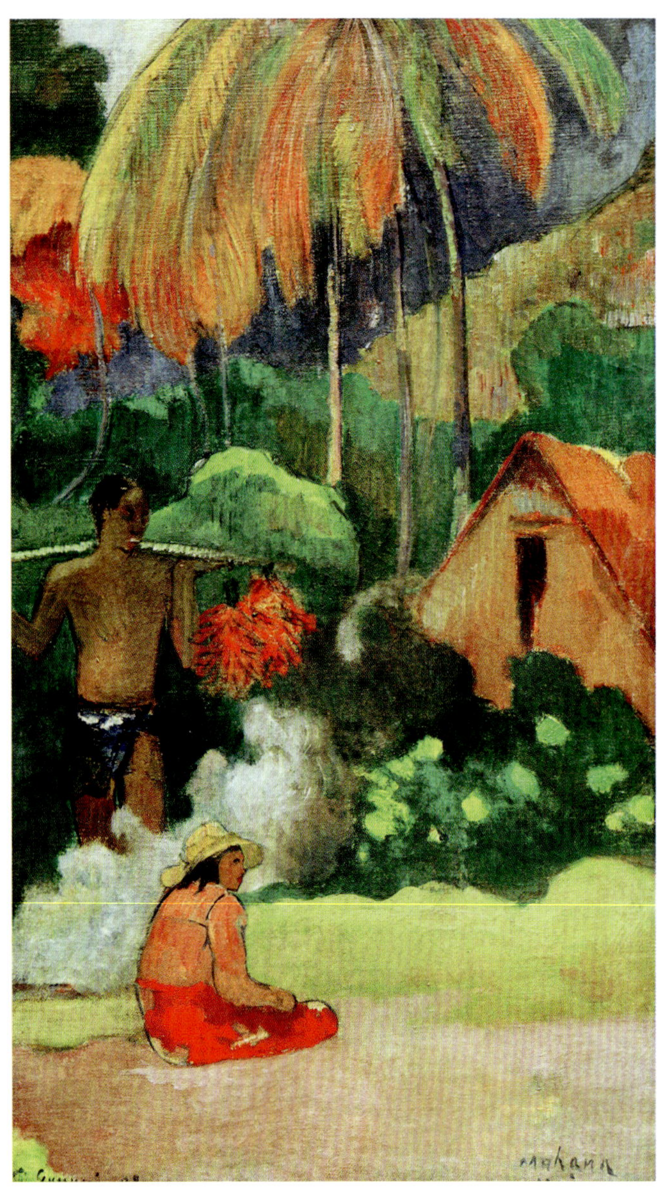

Mahana maa II
(The Moment of Truth II)
(Le Jour de vérité)
(Tag der Wahrheit)
(El día de la verdad)
(Il giorno della verità)
(De dag van de waarheid)
1892, Oil on canvas/Huile sur toile, 45 × 31 cm, Ateneum, Helsinki

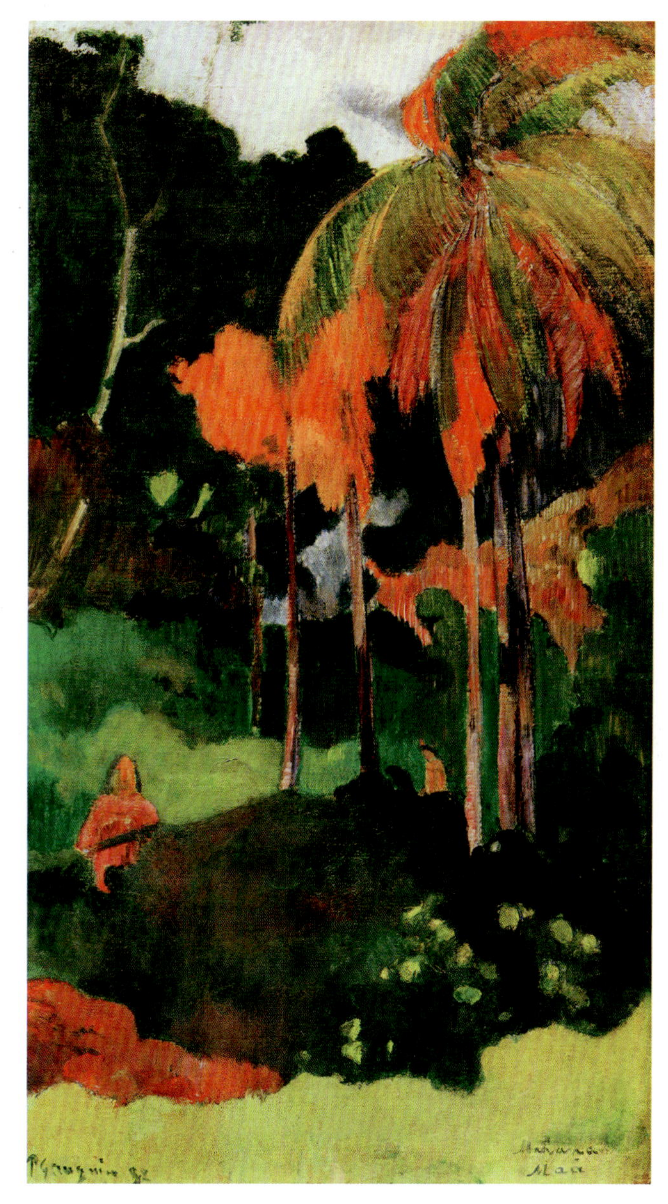

Mahana maa I
1892, Oil on canvas/Huile sur toile, 55,2 × 30 cm, Cincinnati Art Museum, Cincinnati

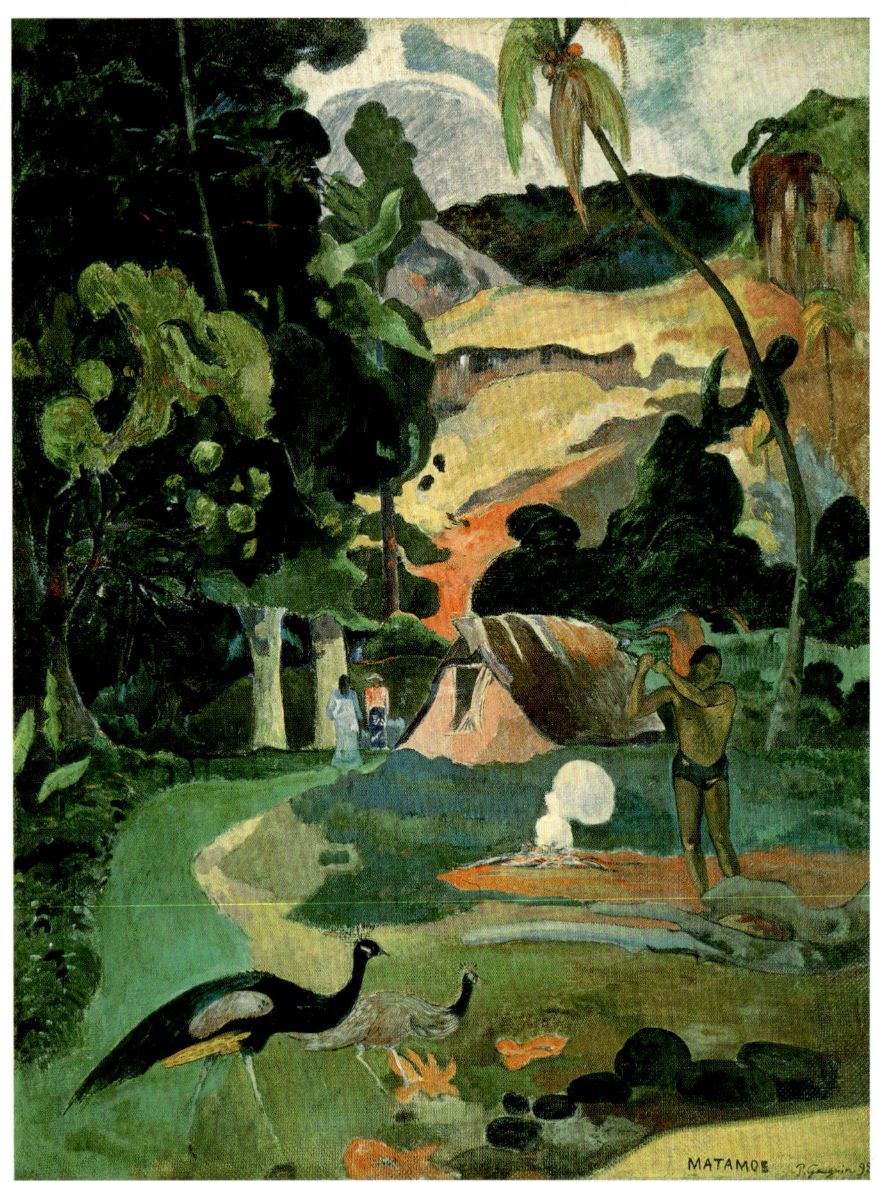

Matamoe

(Landscape with Peacocks)

(Paysage aux paons)

(Landschaft mit Pfauen)

(Paisaje con pavos reales)

(Paesaggio con pavoni)

(Landschap met pauwen)

*1892, Oil on canvas/Huile sur toile,
115 × 86 cm, Pushkin Museum, Moscow*

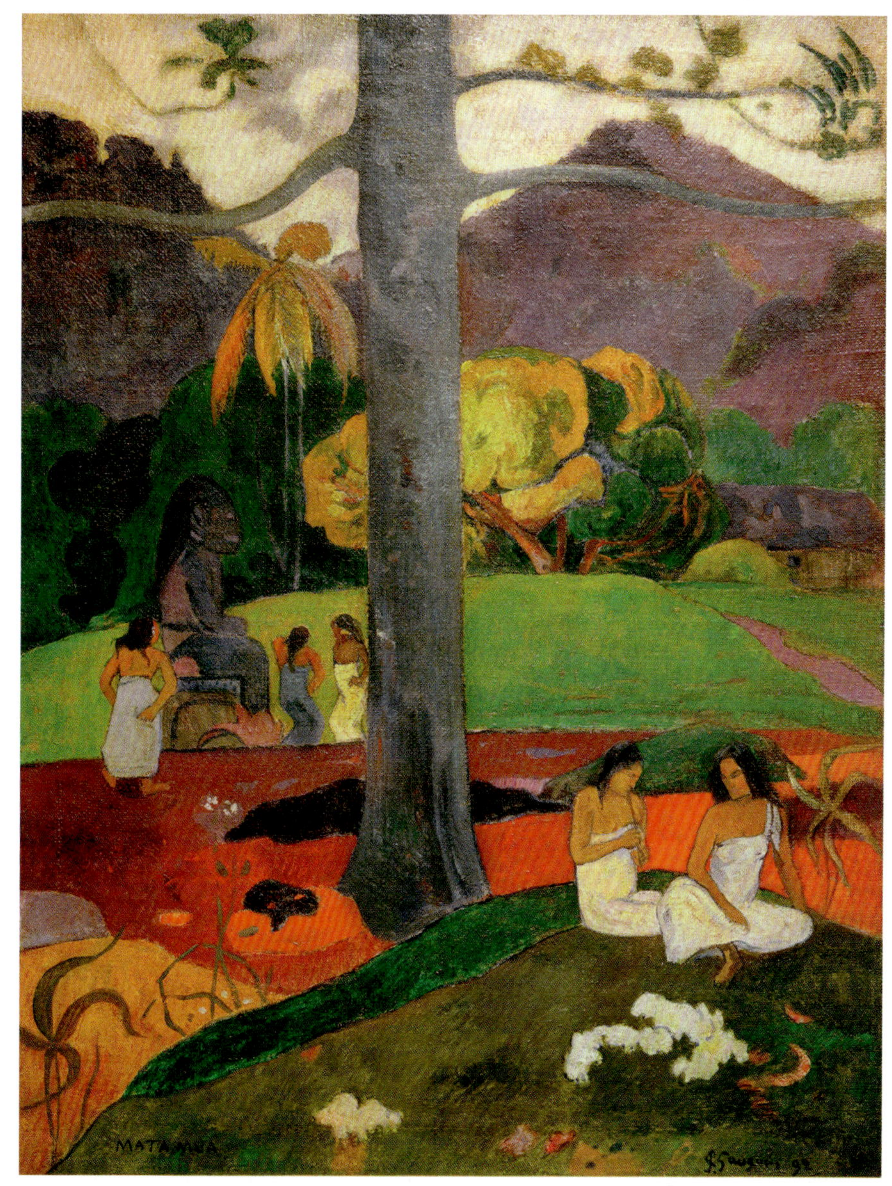

Matamua
(In Olden Times)
(Dans l'ancien temps)
(Es war einmal)
(En la antigüedad)
(Ai tempi antichi)
(Er was eens)

*1892, Oil on canvas/Huile sur toile,
91,5 × 68,5 cm, Museo Thyssen-
Bornemisza, Madrid*

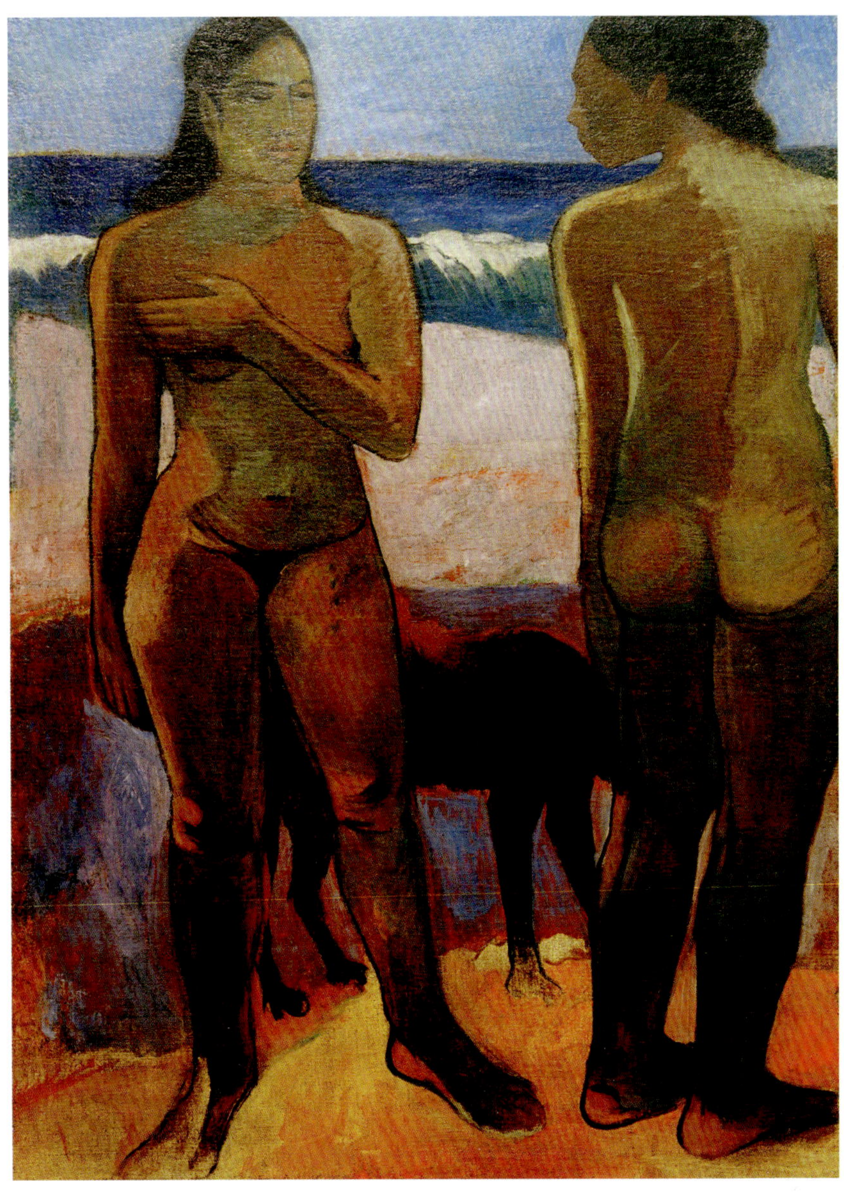

Tahitian Women on the Beach

Tahitiennes sur la plage

Zwei Tahitianerinnen am Strand

Tahitianas en la playa

Tahitiani sulla spiaggia

Tahitiaanse vrouwen op het strand

1892, Oil on canvas/Huile sur toile,
91 × 64 cm, Honolulu Museum of Art,
Honolulu

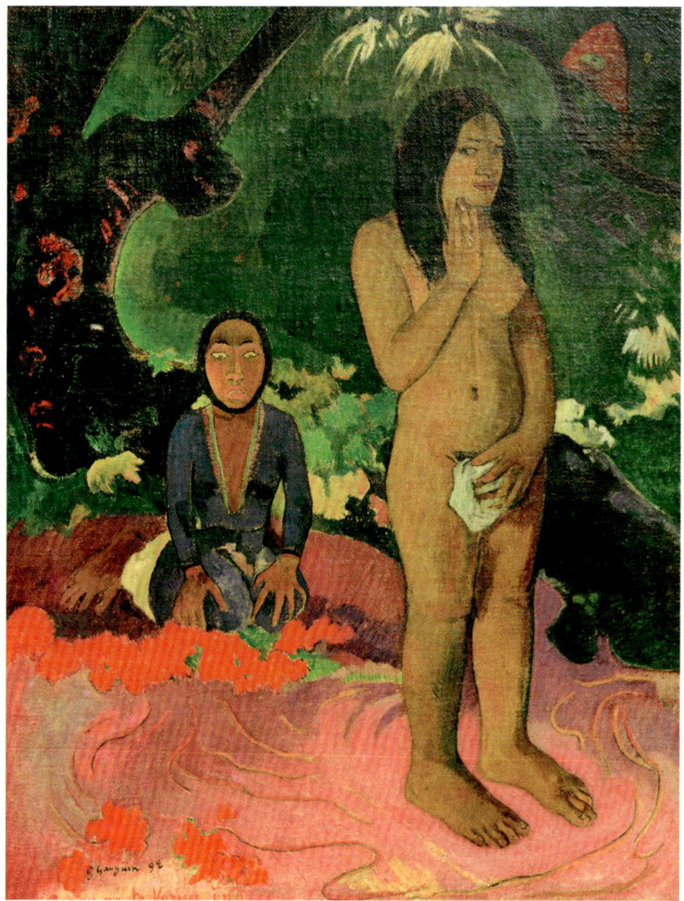

Parau na te varua ino
(Words of the Devil)
(Mots du diable)
(Worte des Teufels)
(Palabras del diablo)
(Parole del diavolo)
(Woorden van de duivel)

1892, Oil on canvas/Huile sur toile, 91,7 × 68,5 cm, National Gallery of Art, Washington

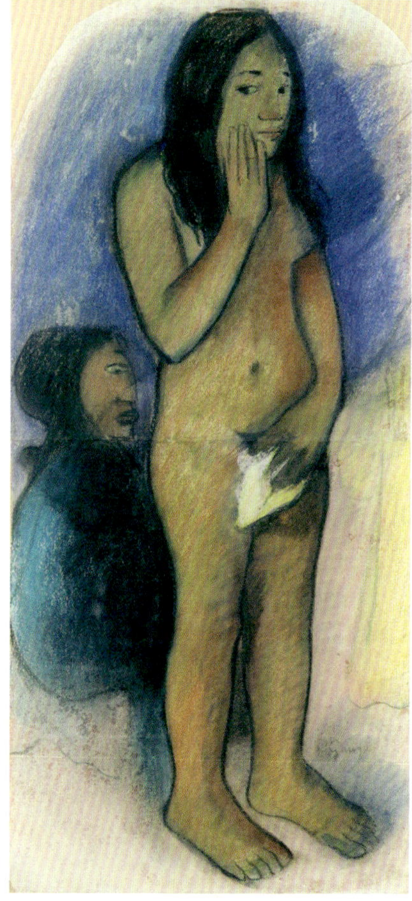

Tahitian Woman**, sketch for **Parau Na Te Varua Ino
Tahitienne**, étude pour **Parau na te varua ino
Tahitianerin**, Studie zu **Parau na te varua
Tahitiana**, estudio para **Parau na te varua ino
Taitiana**, studio per **Parau na te varua ino
Tahitiaanse vrouw**, studie voor **Parau na te varua ino

1892, Pastel on paper/Pastel sur papier,
76,5 × 34,5 cm, Kunstmuseum, Basel

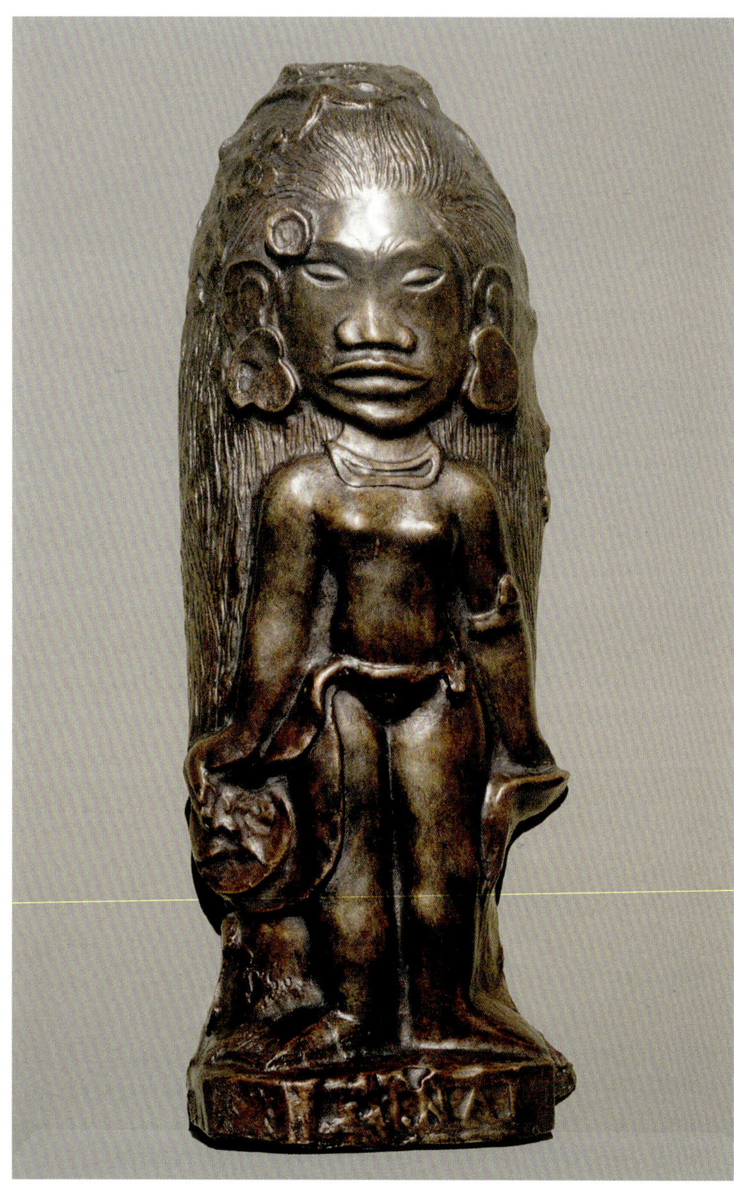

Hina, copy of the wooden original
Hina, copie de l'original en bois
Hina, Kopie nach dem Original in Holz
Hina, copia del original en madera
Hina, copia dell'originale in legno
Hina, kopie van het origineel in hout
Bronze, 36 × 13 × 6,2 cm, Private collection

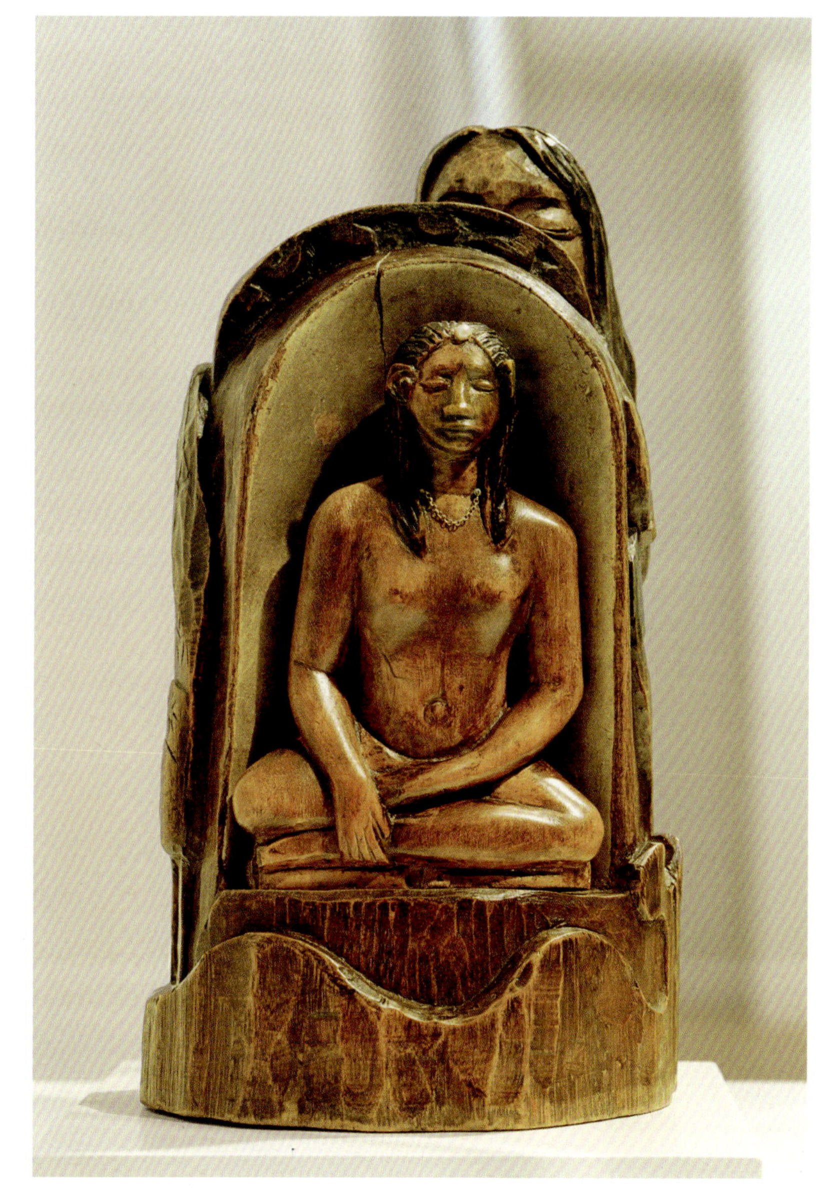

Tii with a Pearl
Tii à la perle
Tii mit Perle
Tii en la perla
Tii con la perla
Tii met de parel
c. 1892, 23,7 × 12,6 × 11,4 cm, Musée d'Orsay, Paris

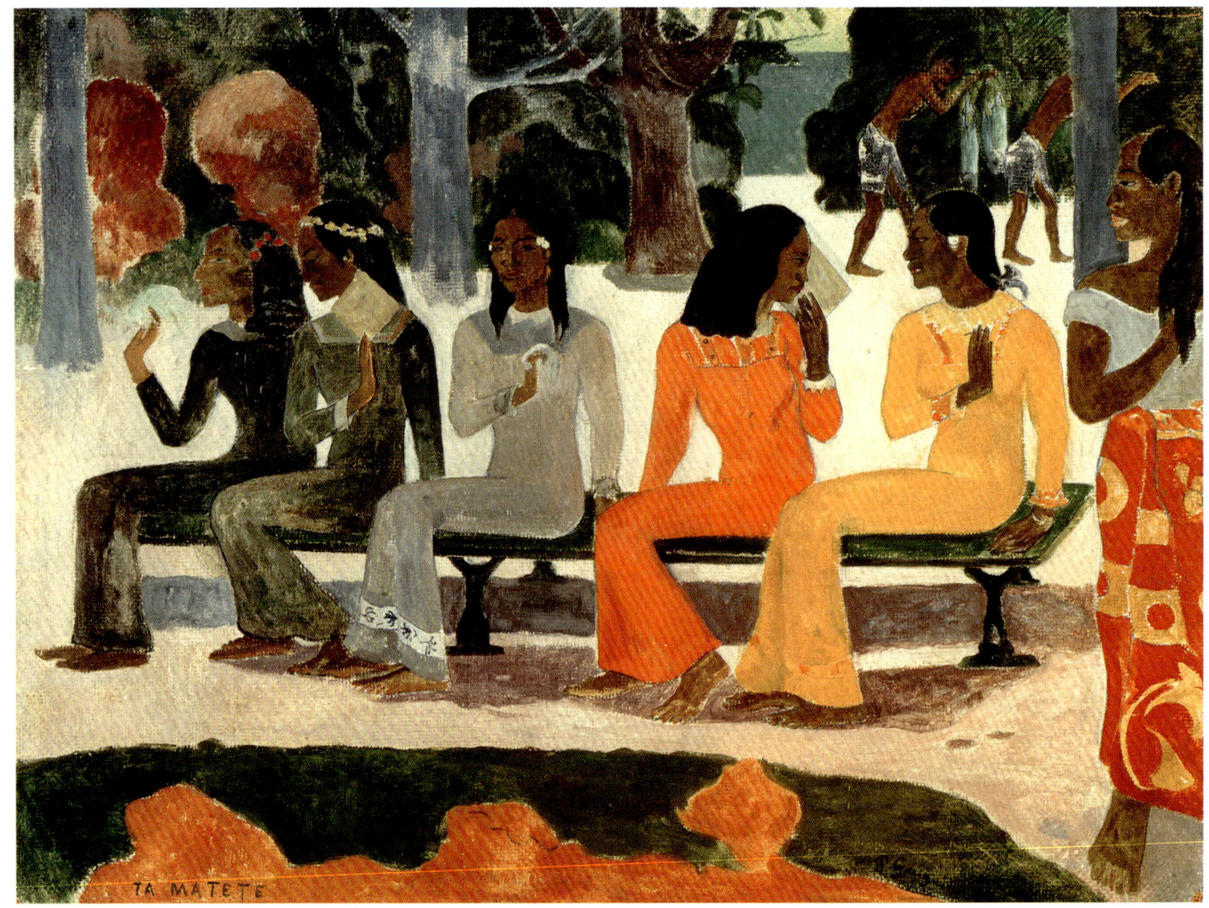

Ta matete

(The Market)

(Le Marché)

(Der Markt)

(El mercado)

(Il Mercato)

(De markt)

1892, Tempera on canvas/Tempera sur toile, 73 × 92 cm, Kunstmuseum, Basel

186

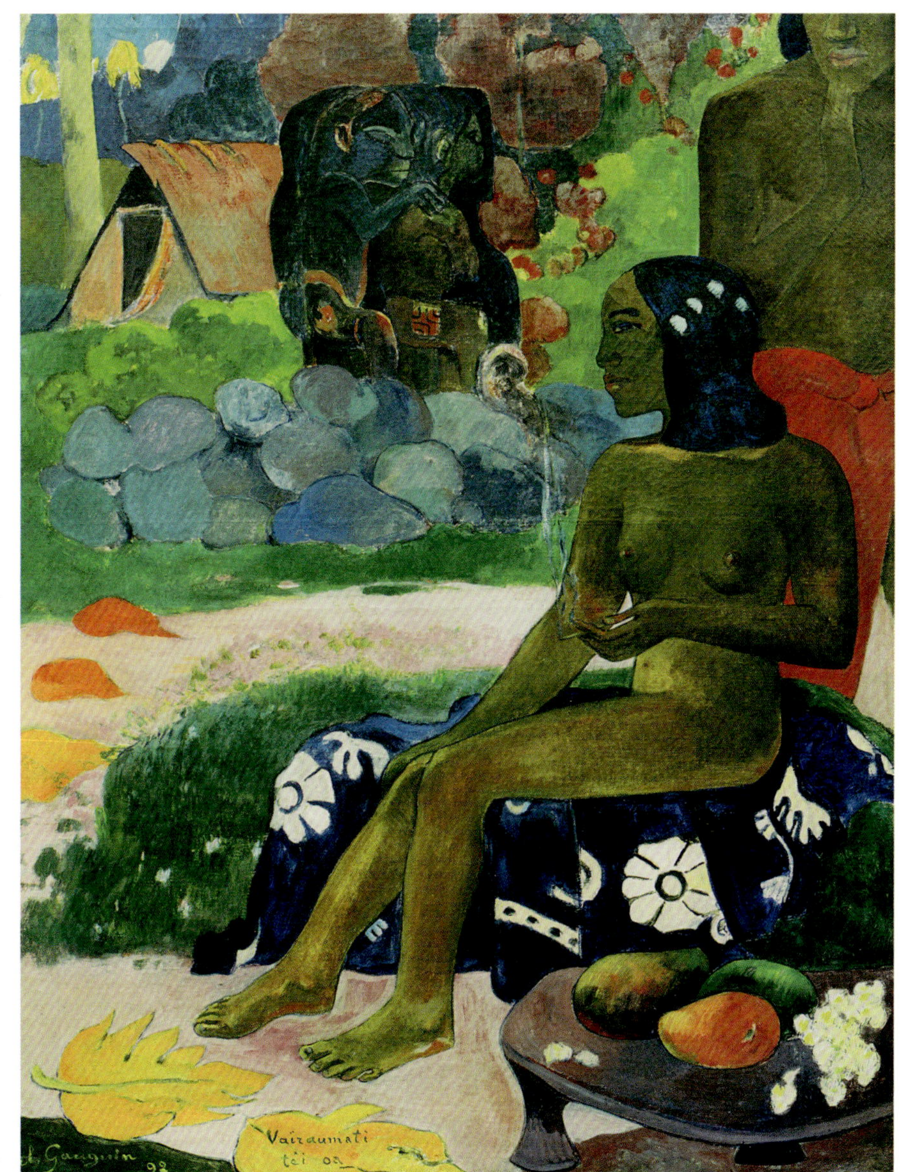

Vairaumati tei oa

(Her Name is Vairaumati)

(Son nom est Vairaumati)

(Ihr Name ist Vairaumati)

(Su nombre es Vairaumati)

(Il suo nome è Vairaumati)

(Haar naam is Vairaumati)

1892, Oil on canvas/Huile sur toile,
91 × 68 cm, Pushkin Museum, Moscow

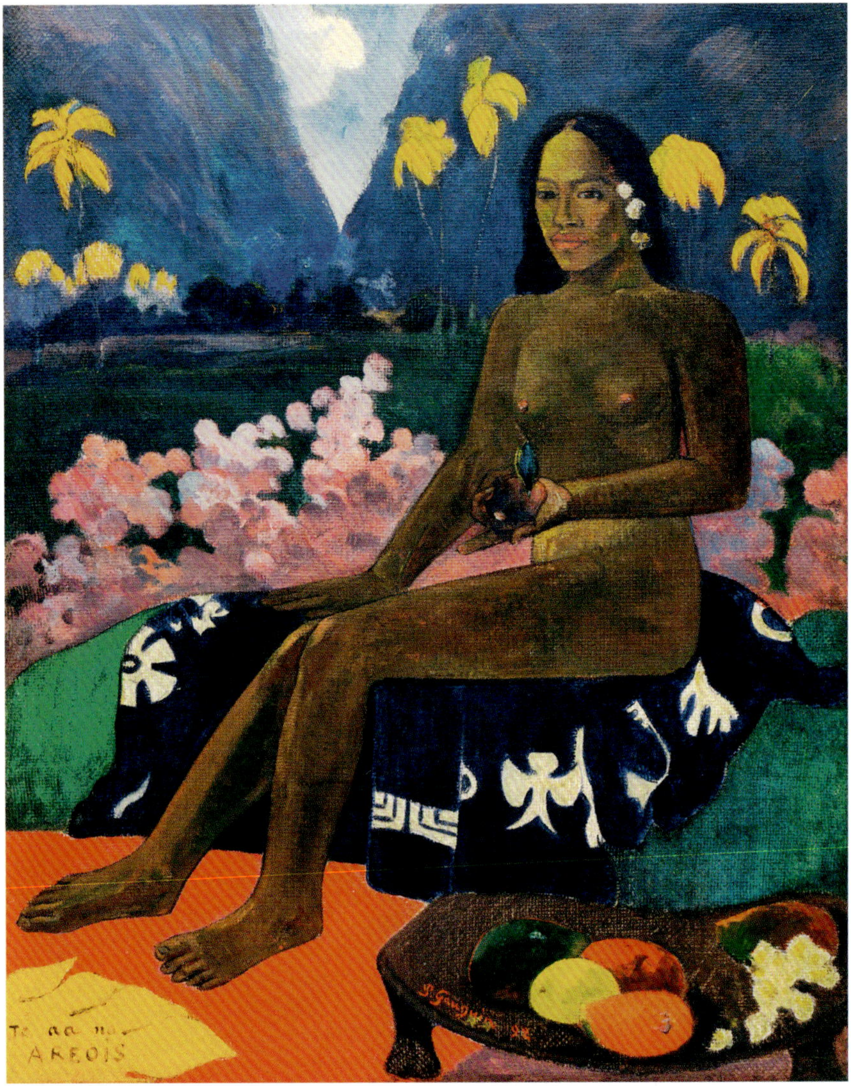

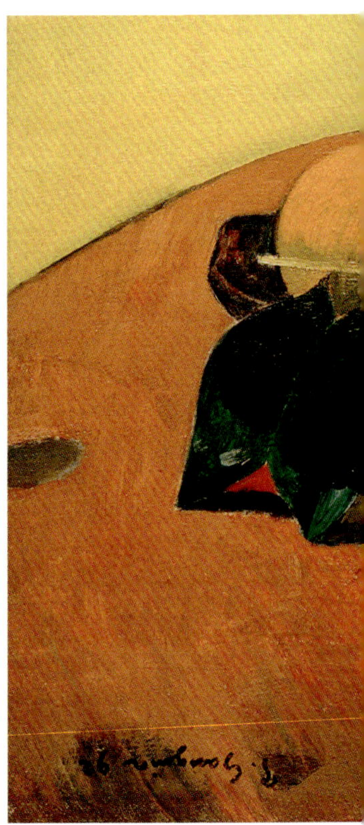

Te aa no Areois

1892, Oil on canvas/Huile sur toile, 92,1 × 72,1 cm, Museum of Modern Art, New York

188

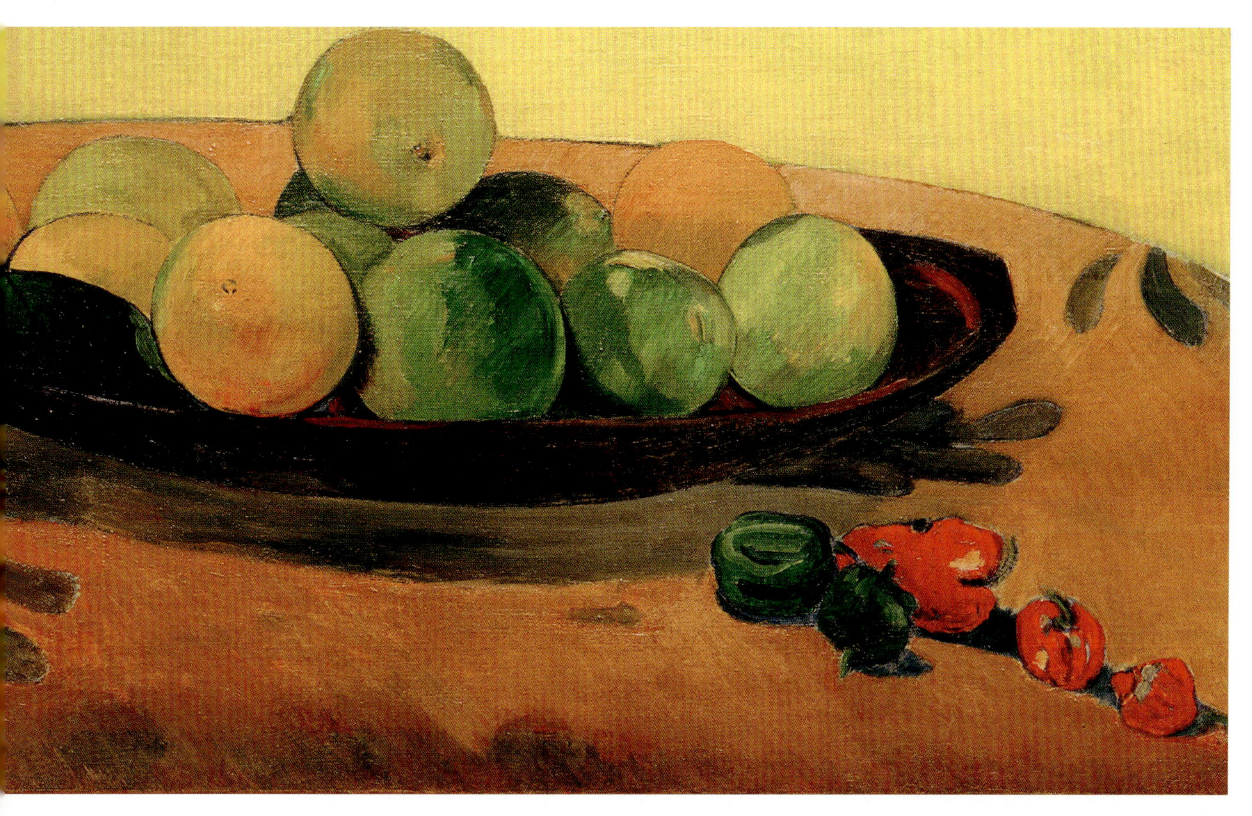

Still Life with Fruit and Peppers
Nature morte aux fruits et piments
Stillleben mit Früchten und Gewürzen
Naturaleza muerta con frutas y pimientos
Natura morta con frutti e pimenti
Stilleven met vruchten en pepers
1892, Oil on canvas/Huile sur toile, 31,7 × 66 cm, Private collection

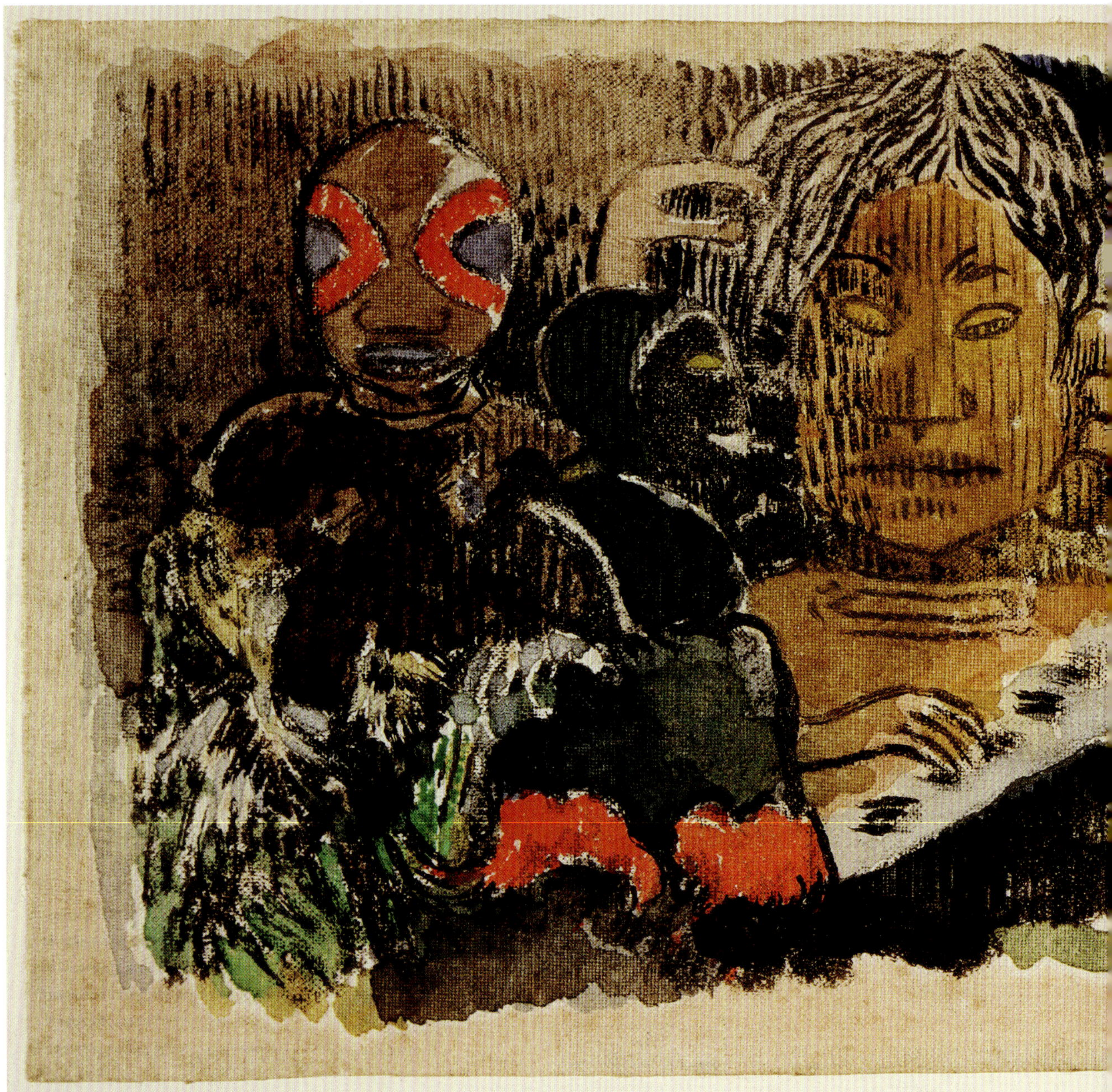

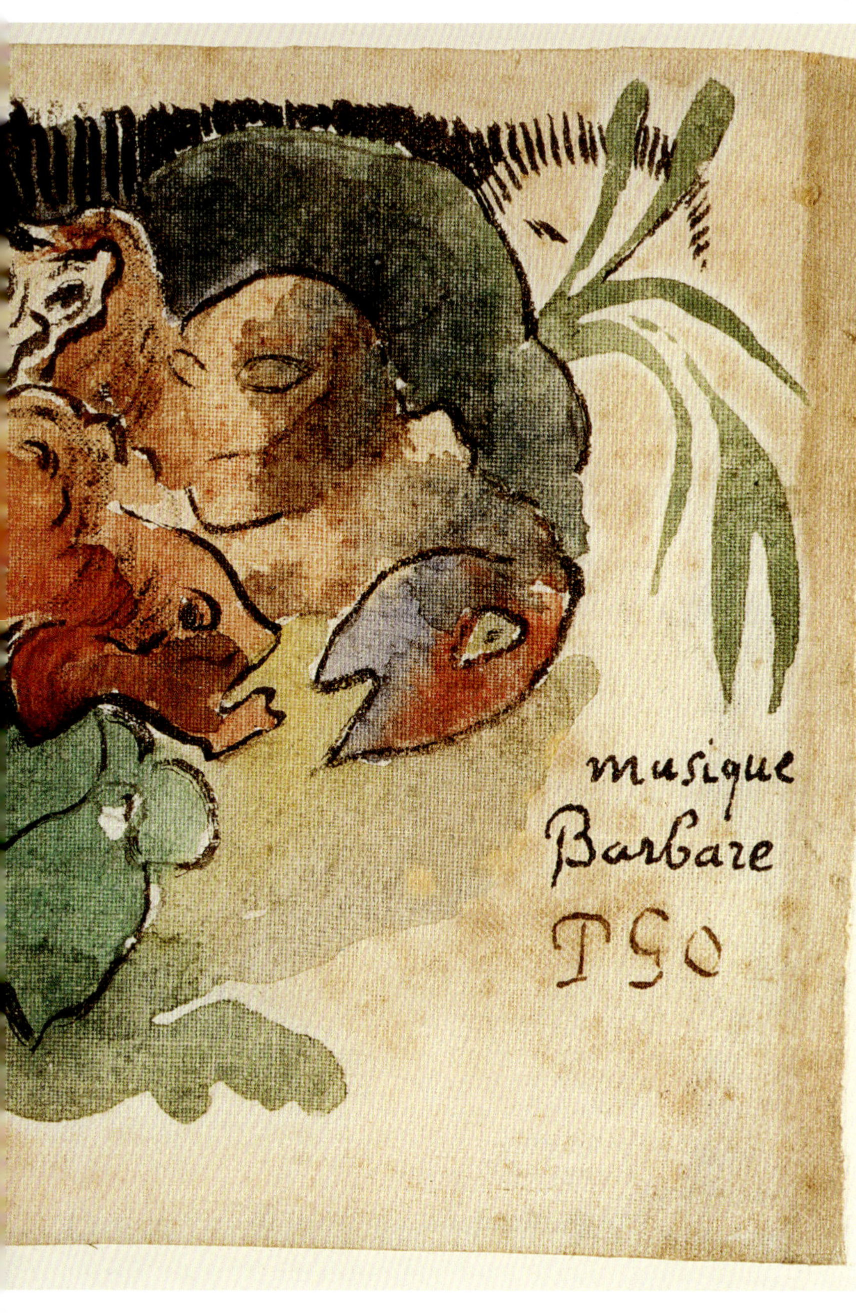

Barbarian Music
Musique barbare
Barbarenmusik
Música bárbara
Musica barbara
Barbaarse muziek

1892, 11,4 × 20 cm, Kunstmuseum, Basel

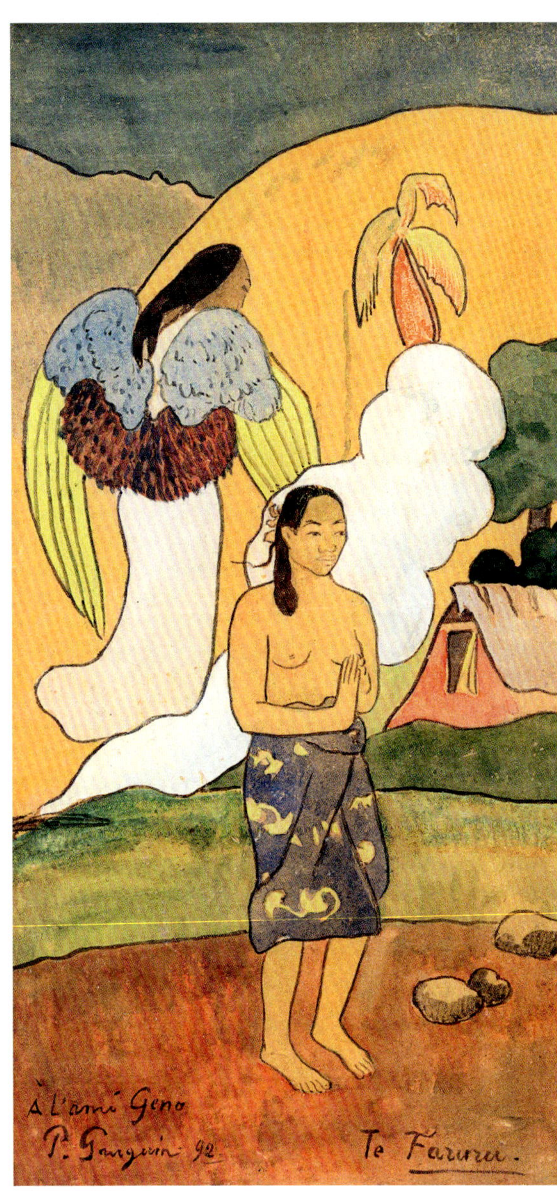

Te faruru
(Here we make love)
(Ici on fait l'amour)
(Der Liebesakt)
(Aquí hacemos el amor)
(Qui si la l'amore)
(Hier wordt de liefde bedreven)

1892, Oil and gouache on paper/Huile et gouache sur papier, 40 × 21 cm, Michele and Donald D'Amour Museum of Fine Arts, Springfield

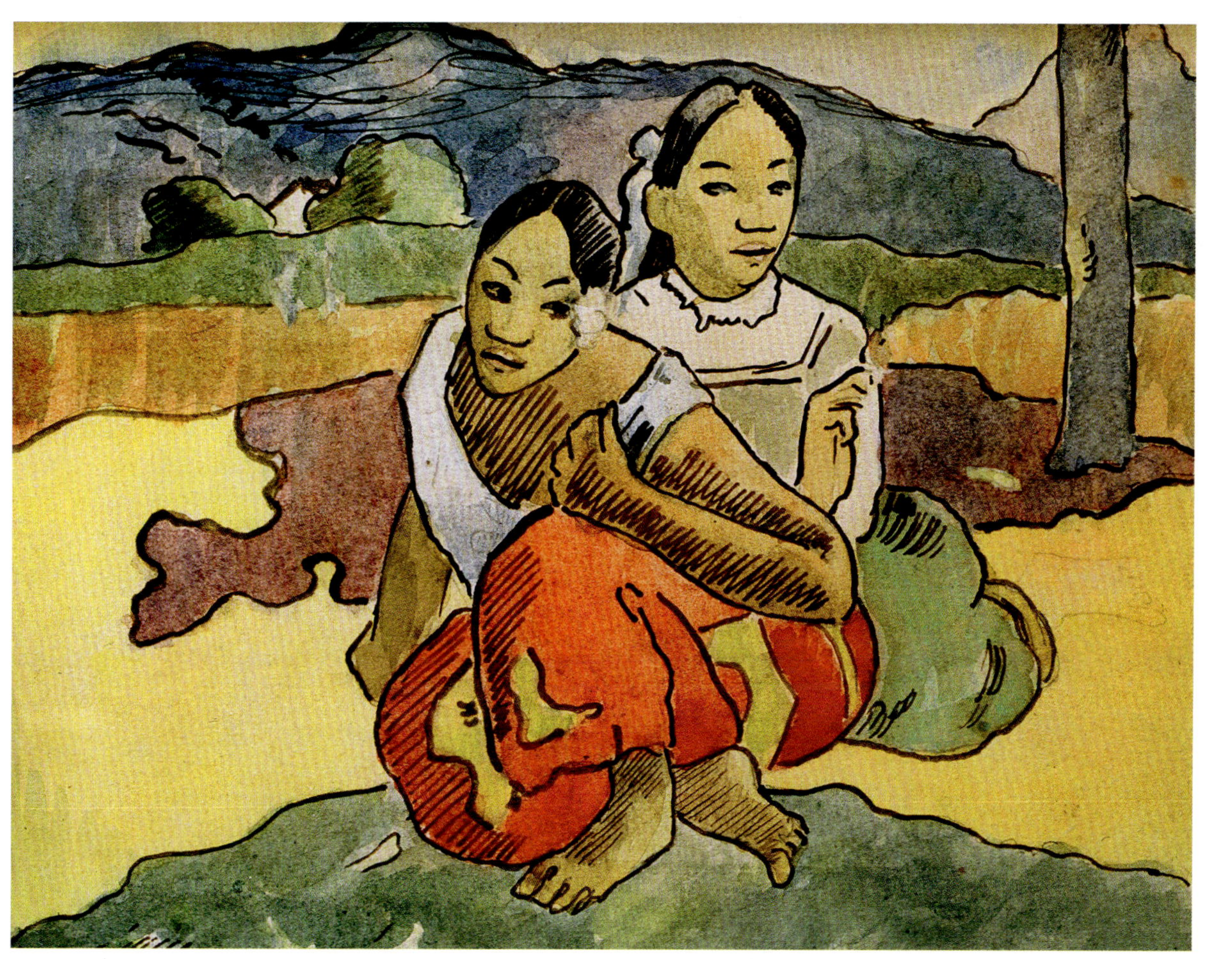

Sketch for *Nafea Faa Ipoipo (When Will You Marry?)*

Étude pour Nafea faa ipoipo (Quand te maries-tu ?)

Studie zu *Nafea faa ipoipo (Wann heiratest du?)*

Estudio para *Nafea faa ipoipo (¿Cuándo te casas?)*

Studio per *Nafea faa ipoipo (Quando ti sposi?)*

Studie voor *Nafea faa ipoipo (Wanneer ga je trouwen?)*

1892, Watercolor/Aquarelle, 13 × 15 cm, Private collection

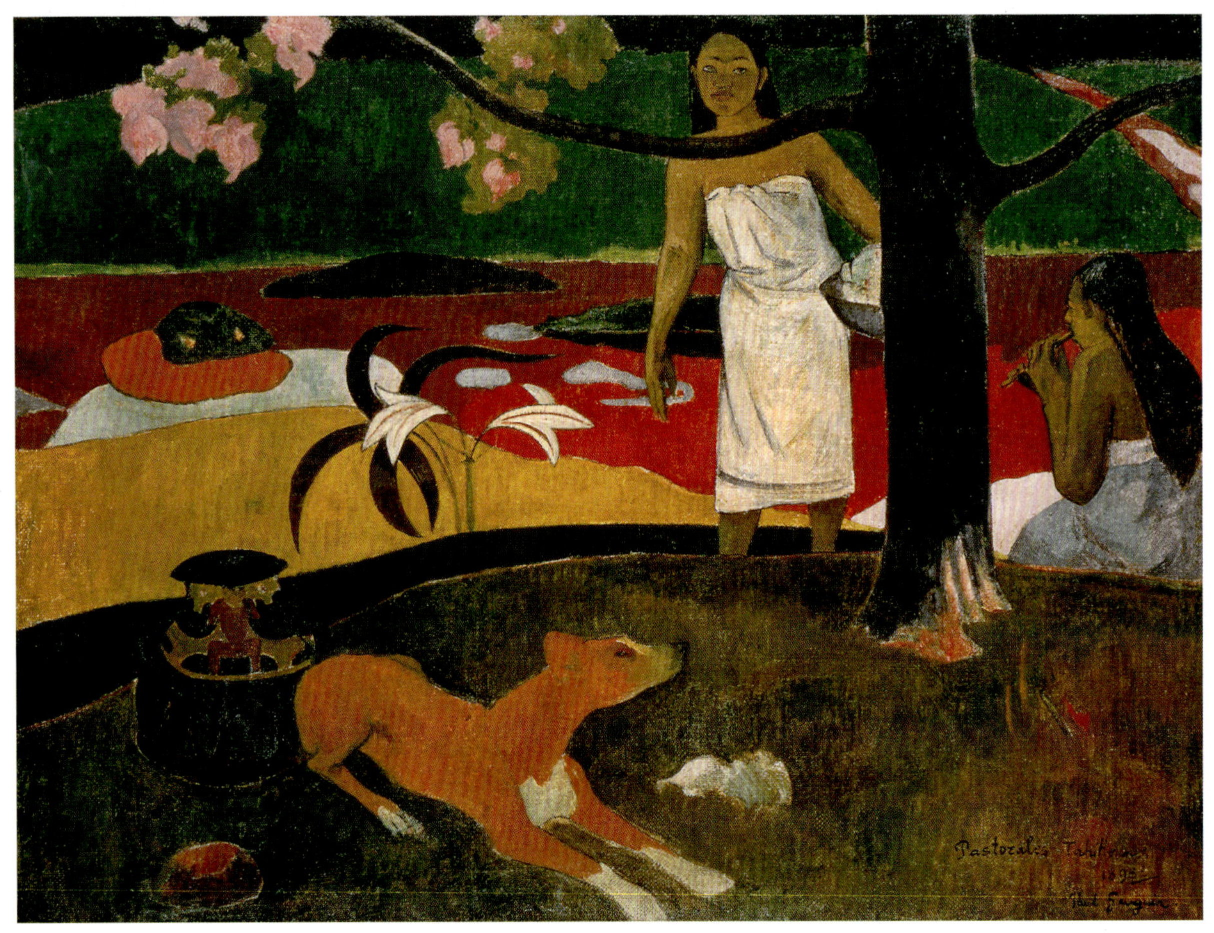

Tahitian Pastoral

Pastorales Tahitiennes

Zwei Tahitianerinnen mit Hund

Pastorales tahitianas

Pastorali Taitiani

Twee Tahitiaanse vrouwen met hond

1892, Oil on canvas/Huile sur toile, 87,5 × 113,7 cm, State Hermitage Museum, St. Petersburg

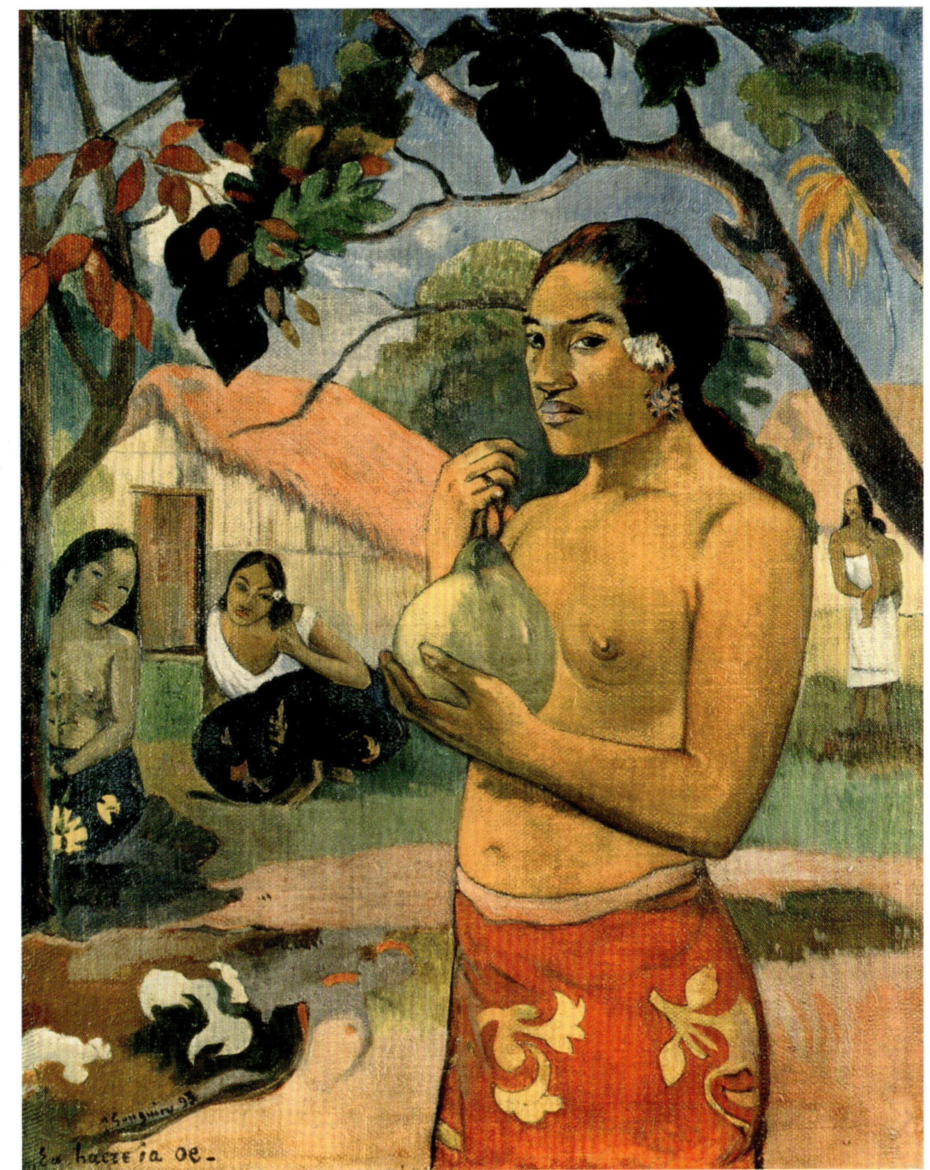

Eu haere ia oe

(Where are you Going?) or ***Woman Holding a Fruit***

(Où vas-tu ?) ou ***Femme tenant un fruit***

(Wohin gehst Du?) oder ***Tahitianerin mit Frucht***

(¿A dónde vas?) o ***Mujer sujetando una fruta***

(Dove vai tu)? o ***Donna che tiene un frutto***

(Waar ga je heen?) of ***Vrouw met een vrucht***

1893, Oil on canvas/Huile sur toile, 92,5 × 73,5 cm, State Hermitage Museum, St. Petersburg

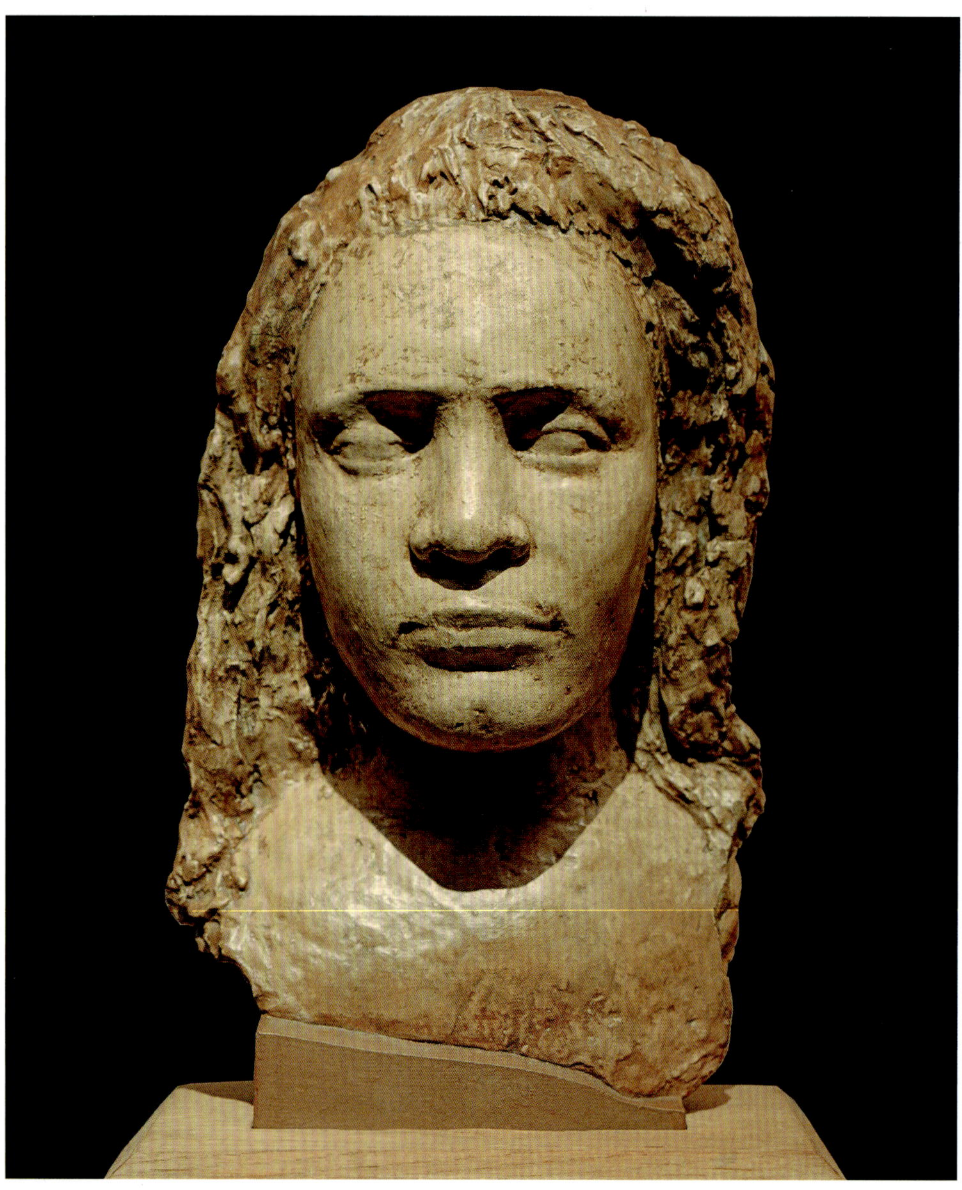

Mask of a Woman
Masque de femme
Maske einer Frau
Máscara de mujer
Maschera di donna
Masker van een vrouw

c. 1893–95, Painted plaster/Plâtre verni, Private collection

Tehura, copy of the wooden original

Tehura, copie de l'original en bois

Tehura, Kopie nach dem Original in Holz

Tehura, copia del original en madera

Tehura, copia dell'originale in legno

Tehura, kopie van het origineel in hout

Bronze, 20,7 × 17 × 10 cm, Saarlandmuseum, Saarbrücken

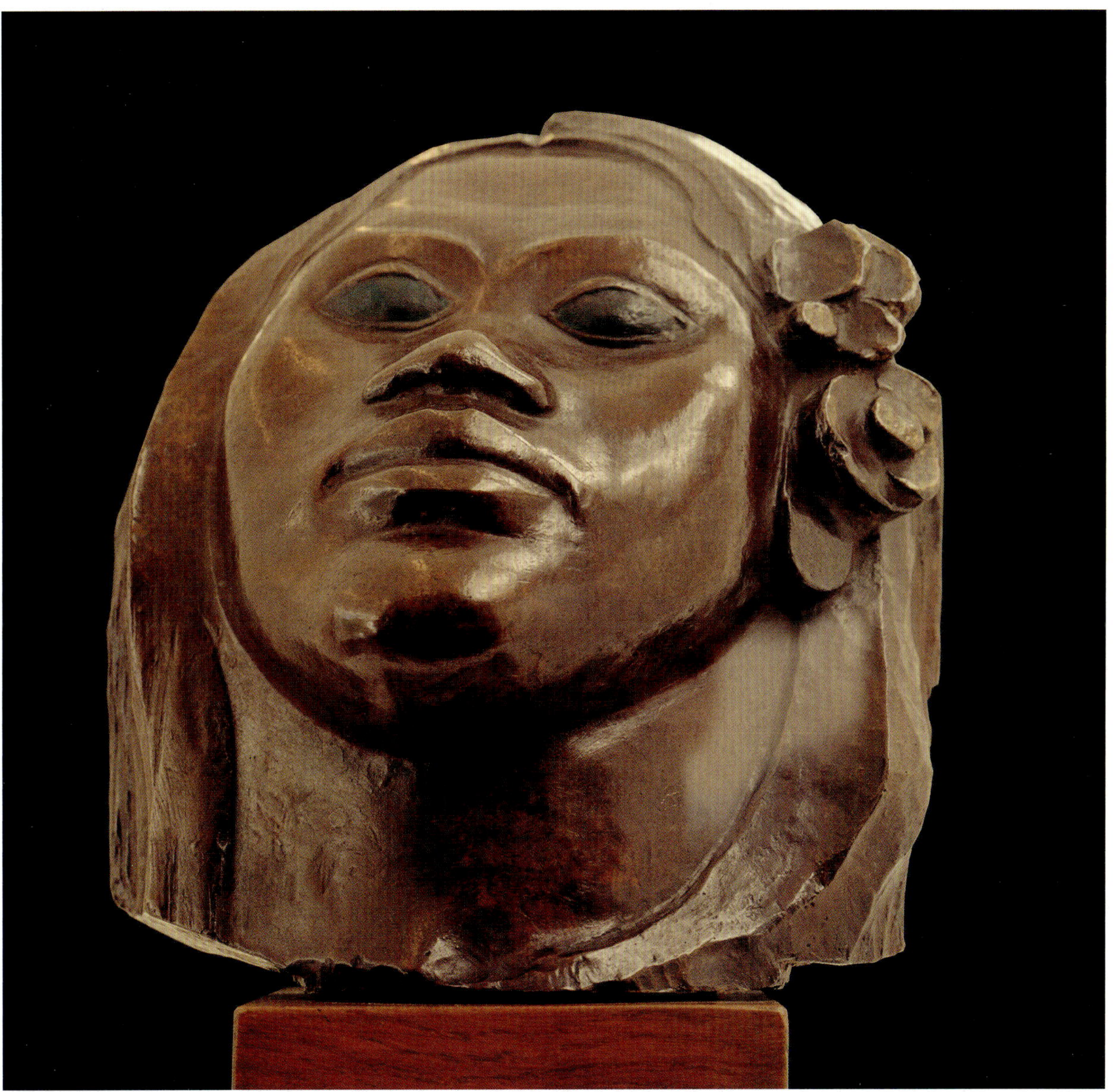

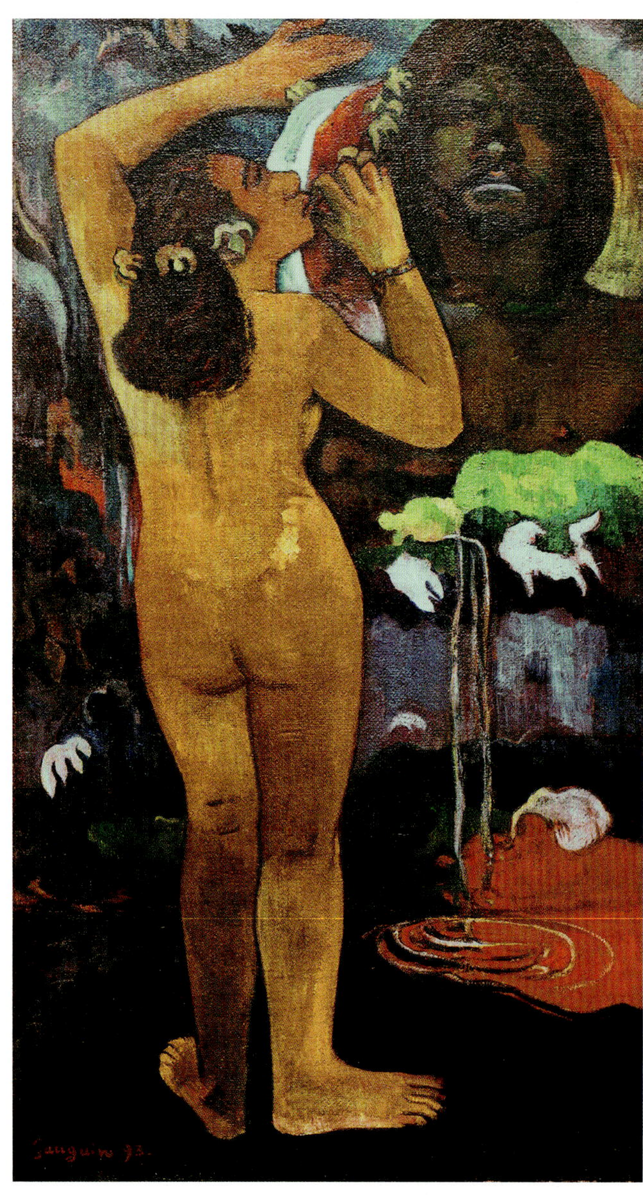

Hina Te Fatou

(The Moon and the Earth)

(La Lune et la Terre)

(Der Mond und die Erde)

(La Luna y la Tierra)

(La luna e la terra)

(De maan en de aarde)

1893, Oil on jute canvas/Huile sur toile de jute, 114,3 × 62,2 cm, Museum of Modern Art, New York

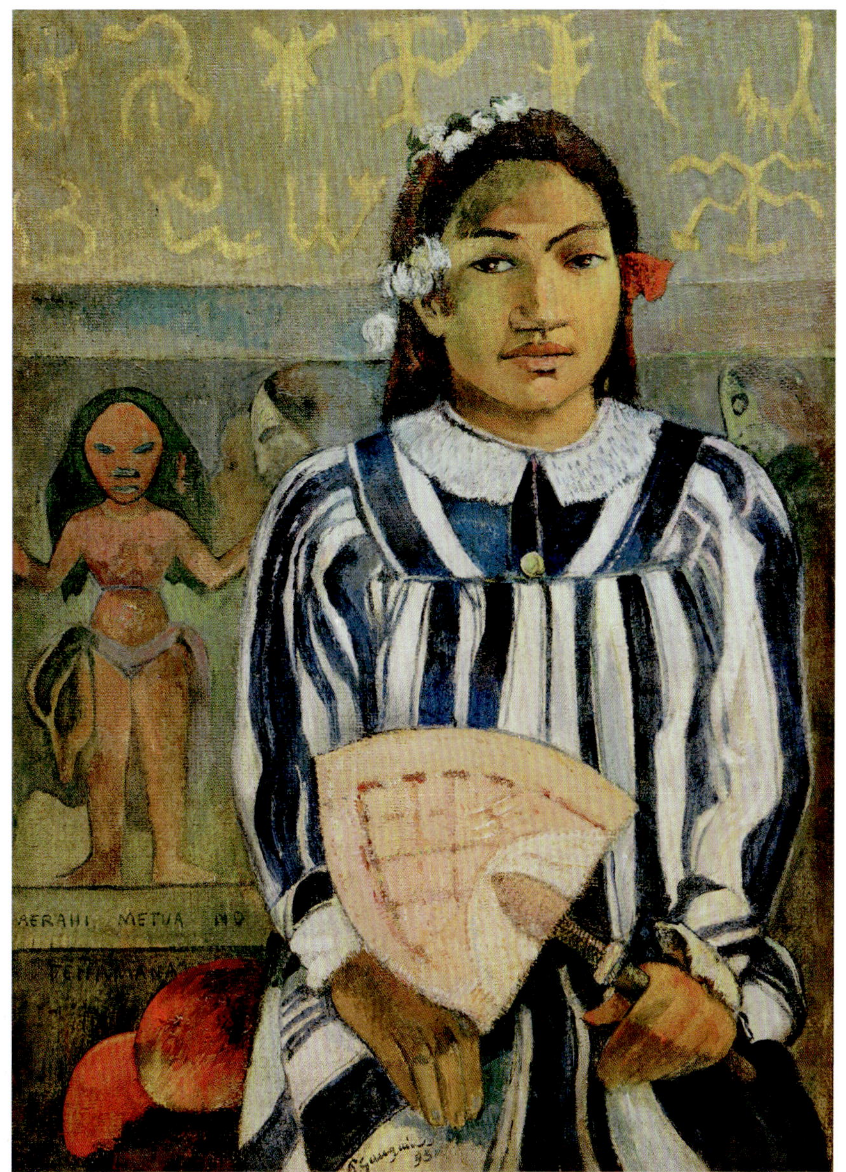

Merahi metua no Tehamana

(The Ancestors Of Tehamana)
or *The Woman with the Fan*

(Les Ancêtres de Tehamana)
ou *La Femme à l'éventail*

(Tehamana hat viele Ahnen) oder
Die Frau mit dem Fächer

(Los ancestros de Tehamana)
o *Mujer con abanico*

(Gli Antenati di Tehamama)
o *la Donna col ventaglio*

(De voorouders van Tehamana)
of *De vrouw met de waaier*

*1893, Oil on canvas/Huile sur
toile, 76,3 × 54,3 cm, Art Institute
of Chicago, Chicago*

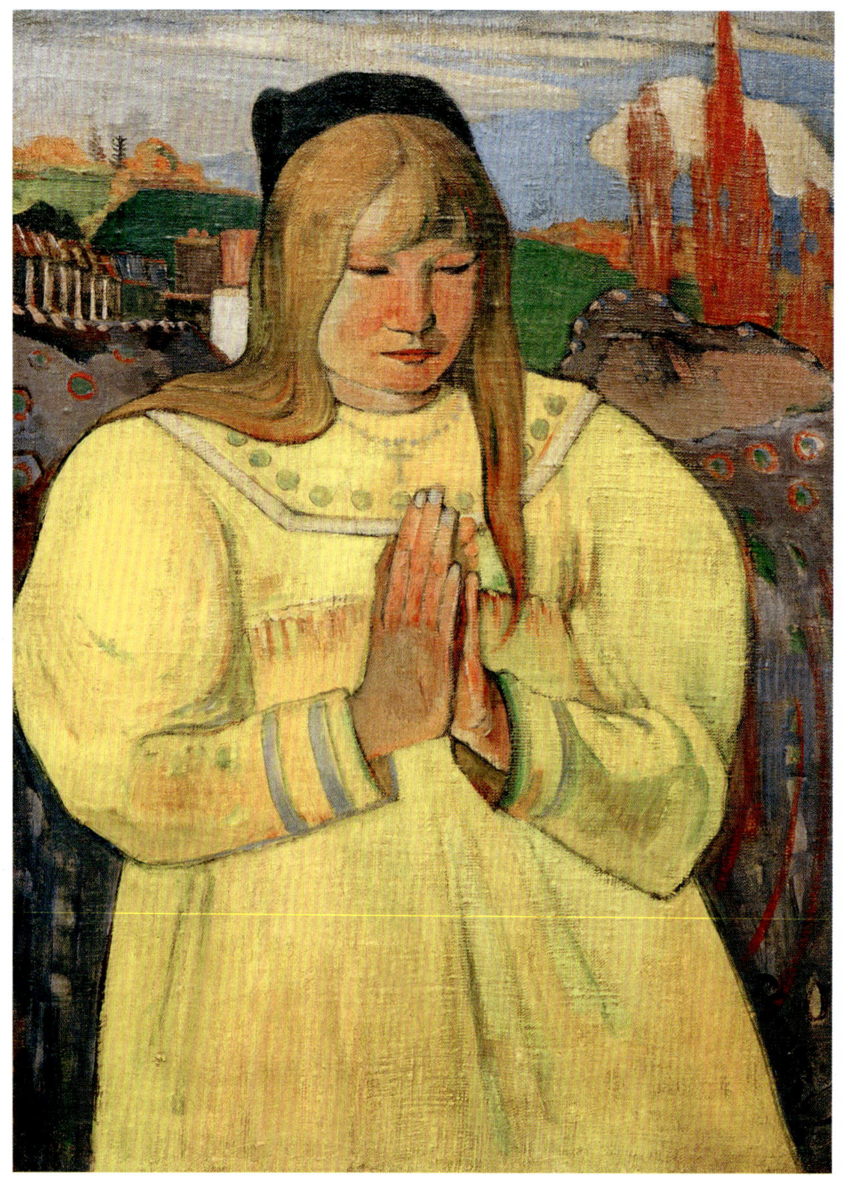

Young Christian Girl
Jeune Chrétienne
Junge Christin
Joven cristiana
Giovane Cristiana
Jonge christin

*1894, Oil on canvas/Huile sur toile,
65,3 × 46,7 cm, The Clark, Williamstown*

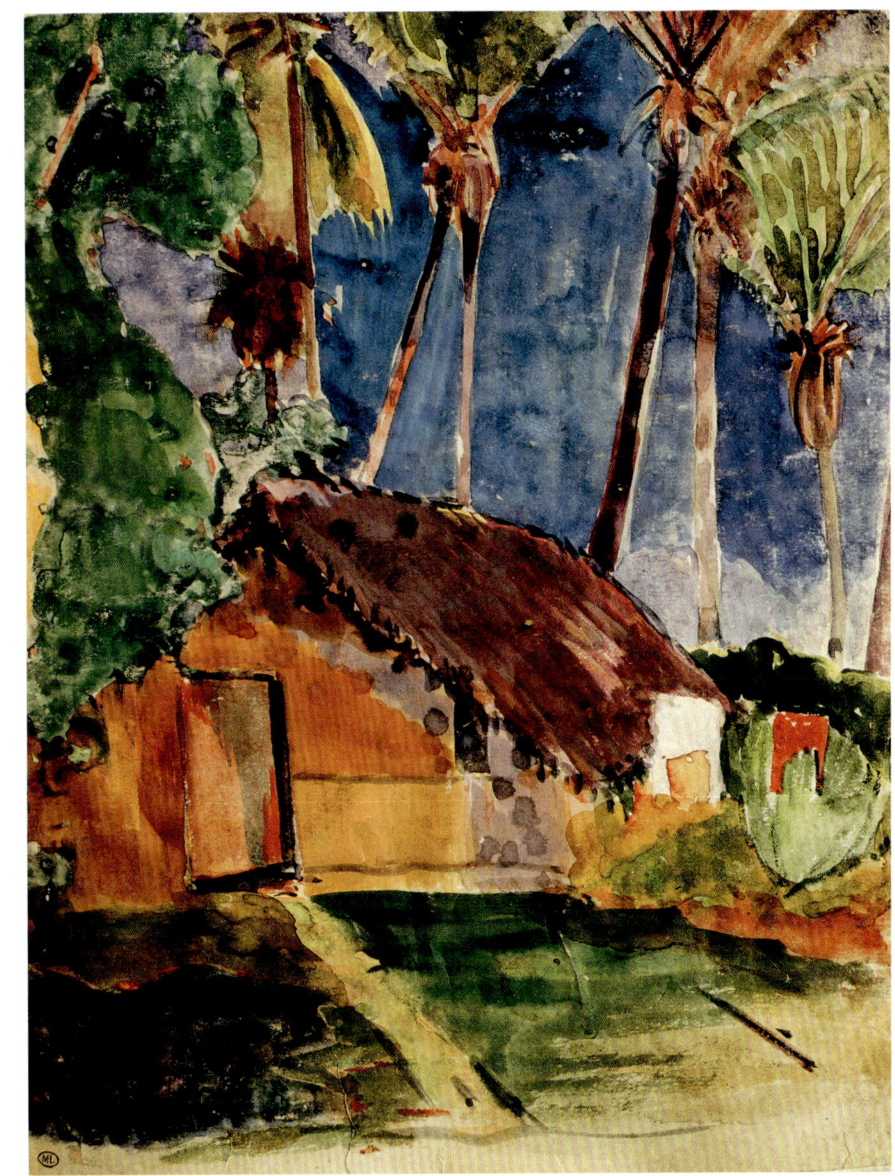

Tahitian Landscape
Paysage tahitien
Landschaft auf Tahiti
Paisaje tahitiano
Pessaggio taitiano
Tahitiaans landschap

c. 1894–97, Watercolor/Aquarelle,
30,4 × 22,8 cm, Musée du Louvre, Paris

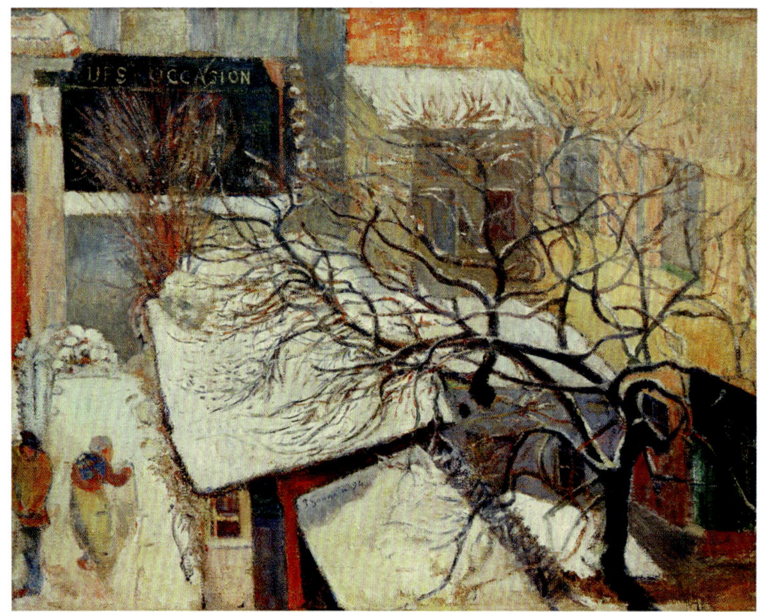

The rejection by France

Gauguin returned to the metropolis on 30 August 1893. In spite of some favourable reviews and some purchases made by Degas, the exposition of Tahitian works at the Durand-Ruel gallery did not garner the expected success. Aided by the poet Charles Morice (1860–1919), he embarked on a recitation of his Tahitian adventure, entitled *Noa Noa*, for which he would produce ten wooden engravings in February 1894. Thanks to a providential inheritance in that year, he settled in a studio called *Te faruru* (here one makes love) at 6 rue Vercingétorix, where he received his artist friends. In his exotic costume, flanked by his young mistress Annah, the Javanese, and his small

Le rejet de la France

Gauguin regagne la métropole le 30 août 1893. Malgré quelques critiques favorables et des achats de Degas, l'exposition de ses œuvres tahitiennes à la galerie Durand-Ruel n'obtient pas le succès escompté. Aidé par le poète Charles Morice (1860–1919), il se lance dans le récit de son aventure tahitienne, *Noa Noa*, pour lequel il réalisera dix bois gravés en février 1894. Cette année-là, grâce un héritage providentiel, il s'installe dans un atelier bariolé intitulé *Te faruru* (Ici on fait l'amour), au 6 rue Vercingétorix, où il reçoit ses amis artistes. Dans son costume exotique, flanqué de sa jeune maîtresse Annah la Javanaise et de son petit singe de compagnie,

Die Ablehnung Frankreichs

Am 30. August 1893 kehrt Gauguin zurück nach Paris. Trotz einiger günstiger Kritiken und Ankäufe durch Degas hat die Ausstellung seiner tahitischen Werke in der Galerie Durand-Ruel nicht den erhofften Erfolg. Unterstützt durch den Dichter Charles Morice (1860–1919) beginnt er mit der Dokumentation seines Tahiti-Abenteuers *Noa Noa*, für die er im Februar 1894 zehn Holzschnitte anfertigt. In diesem Jahr wird ihm eine segensreiche Erbschaft zuteil und er lässt sich in einer kunterbunten Werkstatt nieder, genannt *Te faruru* (Hier machen wir die Liebe), in der Rue Vercingétorix 6, in der er seine Künstlerfreunde empfängt. In exotischem Kostüm, an der Seite seiner jungen Geliebten Annah,

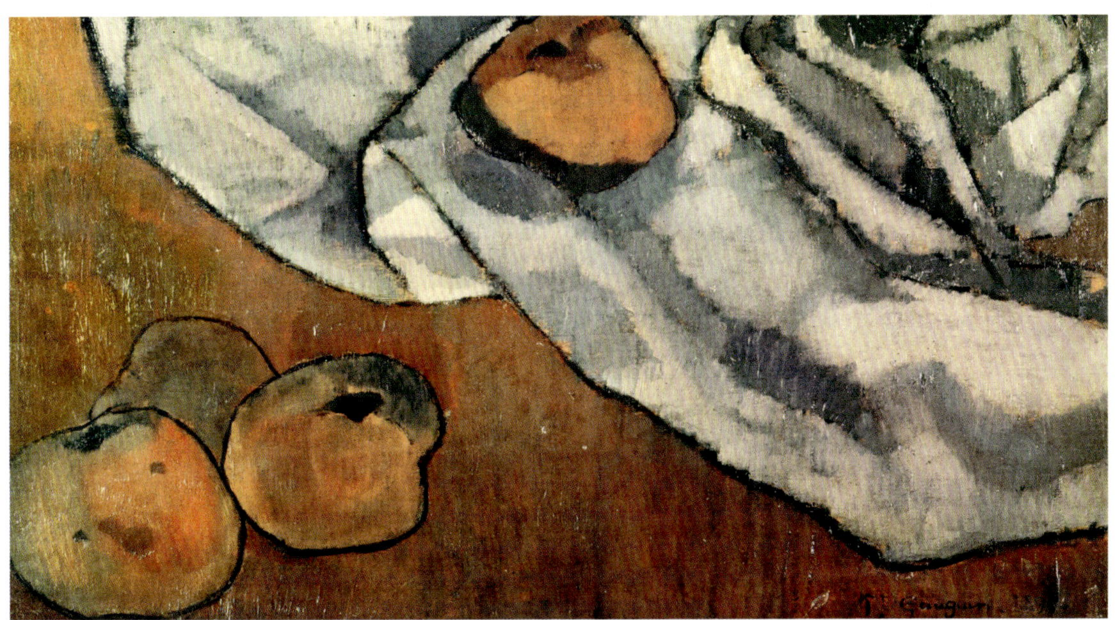

El rechazo de Francia

Gauguin regresó a la metrópolis
el 30 de agosto de 1893. A pesar de
algunas críticas favorables y de las
compras de Degas, la exposición de sus
obras tahitianas en la galería Durand-
Ruel no obtuvo el éxito esperado.
Ayudado por el poeta Charles Morice
(1860–1919), se embarcó en la redacción
de su aventura tahitiana, *Noa Noa*, para
el que realizó diez maderas grabadas
en febrero de 1894. Aquel año, gracias
a una herencia providencial, se instaló
en un colorista taller conocido como *Te
faruru* (Aquí hacemos el amor), en 6 rue
Vercingétorix, donde recibía a sus amigos
artistas. Con su vestimenta exótica,
flanqueado por su joven amante Annah
la Javanesa y de su pequeño mono de

Il rigetto della France

Gauguin ritorna alla città il 30 agosto
1893. Nonostante alcune recensioni
favorevoli e l'assistenza di Degas, la
mostra delle sue opere tahitiane alla
Galerie Durand-Ruel non ottiene il
successo desiderato. Aiutato dal poeta
Charles Morice (1860–1919), si lancia nel
racconto della sua avventura a Tahiti,
Noa Noa, per la quale realizzerà dieci
xilografie nel febbraio 1894. Quell'anno,
grazie ad un'eredità provvidenziale, si
insedia in un atelier colorato dal titolo
Te faruru (Qui facciamo l'amore), al
numero 6 di rue Vercingetorix, dove
riceve i suoi amici artisti. Nel suo costume
esotico, affiancato dalla sua giovane
amante giavanese Annah e la sua piccola
scimmietta, non passa certo inosservato!

Adieu la France

Gauguin keert op 30 augustus 1893 in
Frankrijk terug. Ondanks een aantal
positieve kritieken en aankopen door
Degas brengt de expositie van zijn
Tahitiaanse schilderijen in galerie
Durand-Ruel niet het verwachte succes.
Met hulp van de dichter Charles Morice
(1860–1919) stort hij zich op een vertelling
van zijn Tahitiaanse avontuur, *Noa Noa*,
een bundel waarvoor hij in februari 1894
tien houtgravures maakt. Hij neemt
dat jaar zijn intrek in een kakelbont
atelier genaamd *Te faruru* (Hier wordt
de liefde bedreven) op nummer 6 in de
rue Vercingétorix, waar hij zijn vrienden-
kunstenaars ontvangt. In exotische kledij,
vergezeld van zijn aapje en met zijn jonge
maîtresse Annah la Javanaise aan zijn

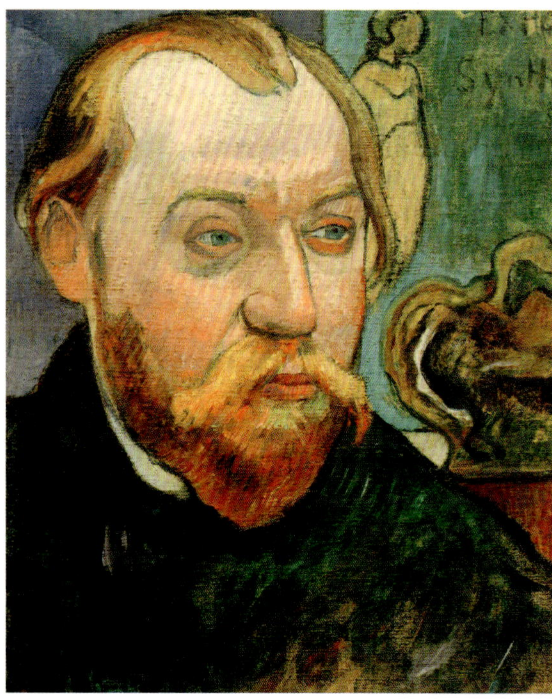

Portrait of Louis Roy

Portrait de Louis Roy

Bildnis Louis Roy

Retrato de Louis Roy

Ritratto di Loius Roy

Portret van Louis Roy

1893, Oil on canvas/Huile sur toile, 40,5 × 32,5 cm, Private collection

companion monkey, he could not go unnoticed! With her he also stayed at Pont-Aven and at Le Pouldu, for what would be his last Breton sojourn.

Back in Paris, the artist had only one idea in mind: to definitely leave the "rotten Occident" and recover Pacific bliss. He organised one last auction, which was disastrous, but which nevertheless was good enough for a simple one-way fare to Papeete. After leaving on 28 June, 1895, he would never set foot again in France, and not even in Europe.

il ne passe pas inaperçu ! Avec elle, il séjourne aussi à Pont-Aven et au Pouldu, pour ce qui sera son dernier séjour breton.

De retour à Paris, l'artiste n'a plus qu'une idée en tête : quitter définitivement cet « Occident pourri » et retrouver la douceur du Pacifique. Il organise une ultime vente aux enchères, désastreuse, mais qui lui permet néanmoins d'acheter un aller simple pour Papeete. Parti le 28 juin 1895, il ne remettra plus jamais les pieds en France, ni même en Europe.

der Javanerin mit ihrem kleinen Affen als Gesellschaftstier, ist er nicht zu übersehen! Mit ihr besucht er auch Pont-Aven und Pouldu – sein letzter Aufenthalt in der Bretagne.

Zurück in Paris hat der Künstler nur eines im Sinn: dauerhaft diesen „verdorbenen Westen" zu verlassen und die Sanftheit Ozeaniens wiederzufinden. Er organisiert eine letzte, desaströs verlaufende Versteigerung; aber sie erlaubt ihm den Kauf einer einfachen Überfahrt nach Papeete. Nach einer Abschiedsfeier am 28. Juni 1895 setzt er nie wieder in Frankreich oder sonst wo in Europa einen Fuß auf den Boden.

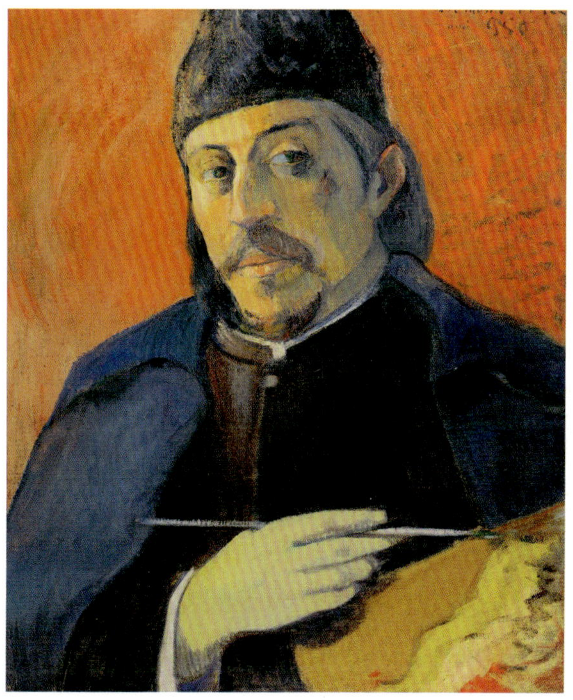

compañía, no pasaba desapercibido. Con ella, también residió en Pont-Aven y en Pouldu, en la que sería su última estancia bretona.

De regreso en París, el artista solo tenía una idea en la cabeza: abandonar definitivamente este "Occidente podrido" y recuperar la dulzura del Pacífico. Organizó una última subasta, desastrosa, pero que le permitió comprar un billete de ida a Papeete. Se marchó el 28 de junio de 1895, y no volvió a poner sus pies en Francia, ni siquiera en Europa.

Con lei, rimane anche a Pont-Aven e Pouldu, per quello che sarà il suo ultimo soggiorno bretone.

Di ritorno a Parigi, l'artista ha una sola cosa in mente: di lasciare definitivamente questo "marcio Occidente" e ritrovare la dolcezza del Pacifico. Organizza un'asta finale, disastrosa, ma che gli permette di comprare un biglietto di sola andata a Papeete. Partito il 28 Giugno 1895, non metterà più piede in Francia, né in Europa.

zijde, is hij een opvallende verschijning. Met haar brengt hij ook nog enige tijd in Pont-Aven en in Le Pouldu door, tijdens wat zijn laatste verblijf in Bretagne zal zijn.

Terug in Parijs wil de kunstenaar nog maar één ding: voor altijd weg, weg uit dit "verrotte Westen", terug naar het goede leven op Tahiti. Hij organiseert nog één keer een veiling. Die levert bedroevend weinig op, maar wel voldoende om een enkele reis Papeete ter kopen. Gauguin vertrekt op juni 1895 en zal nooit meer een voet in Frankrijk noch in Europa zetten.

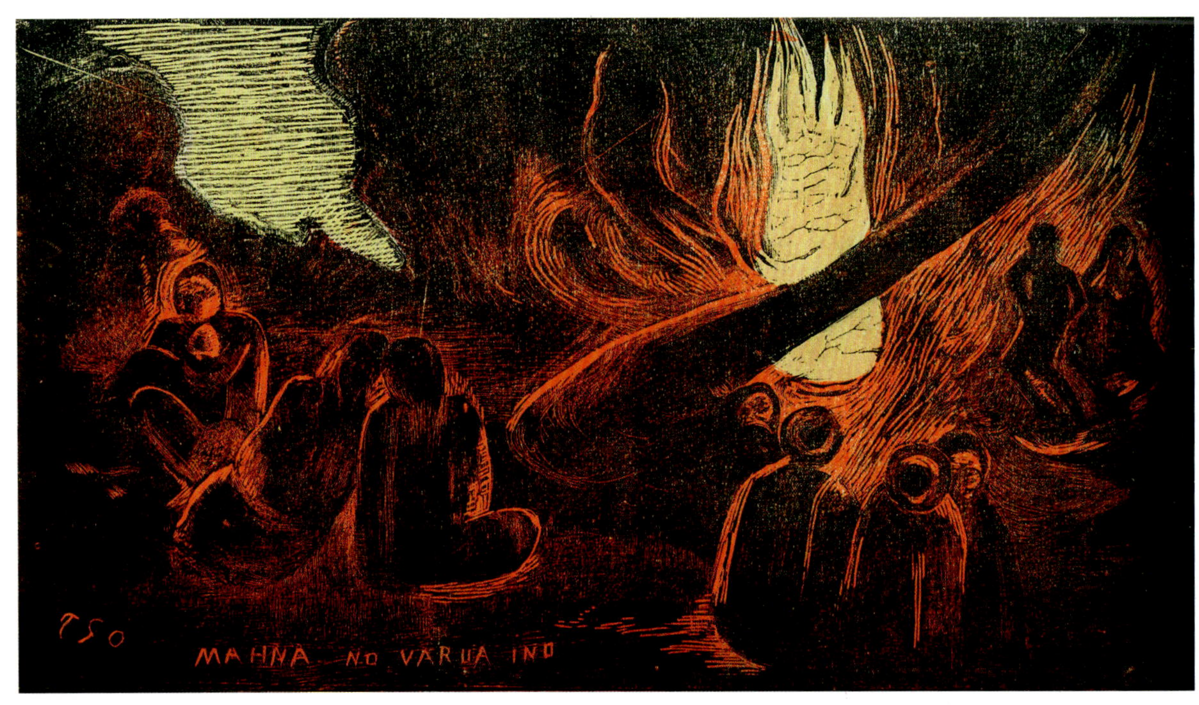

Mahna no varua ino

(The Devil Speaks), **extract of the album** *Noa Noa*

(Le Diable parle), **extrait de l'album** *Noa Noa*

(Der Teufel spricht), **aus der Mappe** *Noa Noa*

(El diablo habla), **extracto del álbum** *Noa Noa*

(Il diavolo parla), **estratto dall'album** *Noa Noa*

(De duivel spreekt), **fragment uit Gauguins dagboek** *Noa Noa*

1893–94, Engraving on wood/Gravure sur bois, 20,2 × 35,6 cm, Private collection

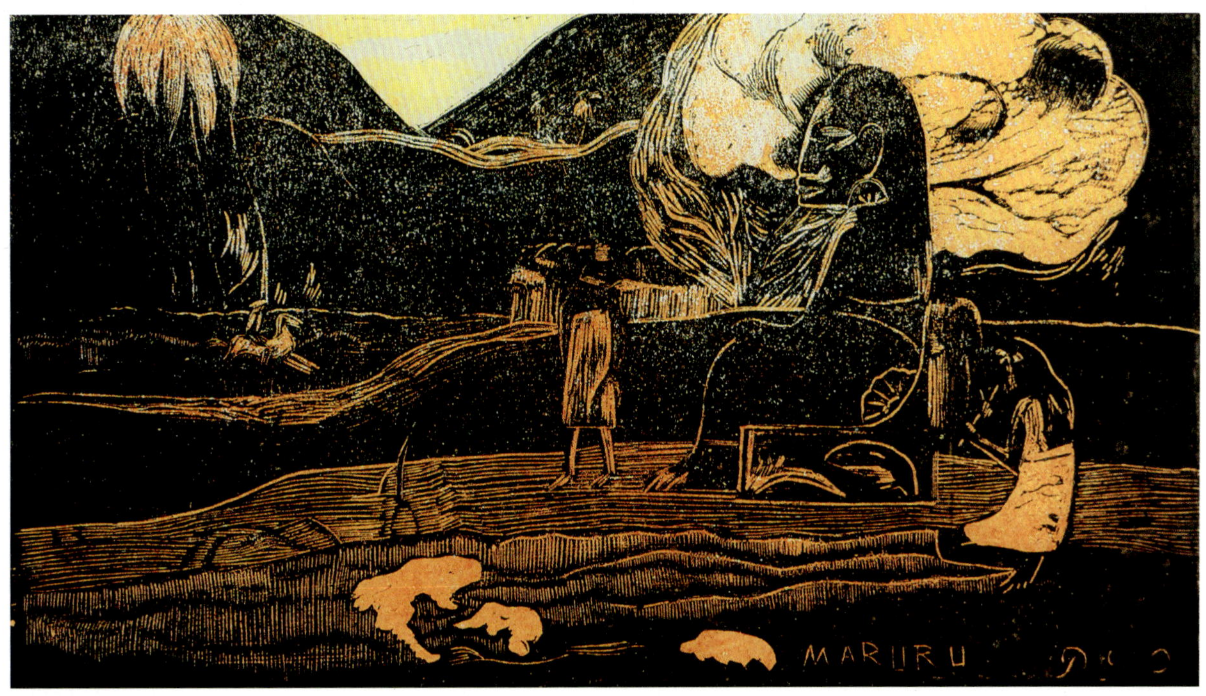

Maruru

(Offerings of Gratitude)

(Satisfait)

(Danksagung)

(Satisfecha)

(Soddisfatto)

(Voldaan)

1893–94, Engraving on colored wood/Gravure sur bois colorisée, 20,5 × 35,5 cm, Private collection

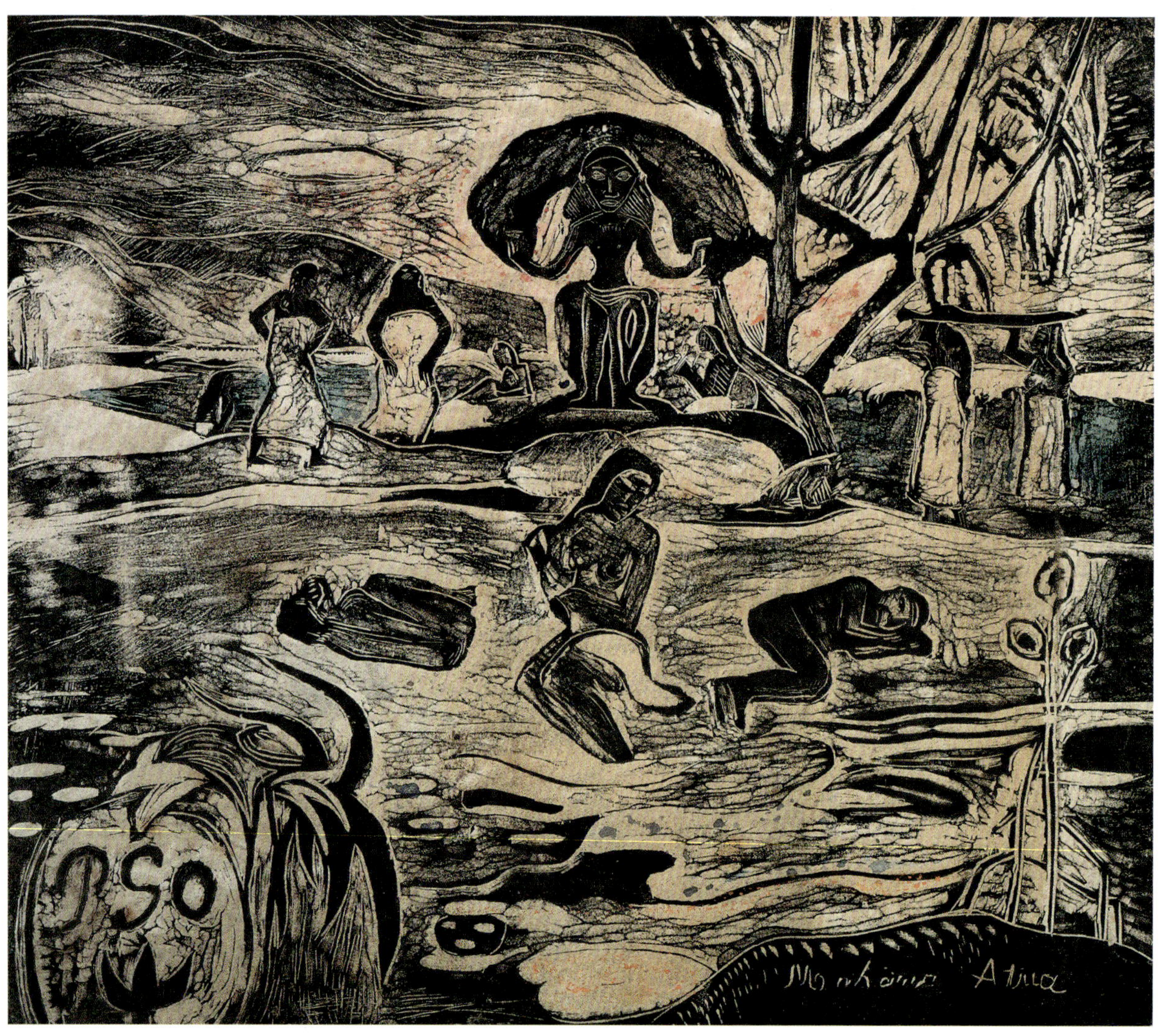
Mahana Atua

Mahana atua

(Day of the God)

(Le Jour de Dieu)

(Der Tag Gottes)

(El día de Dios)

(Il Giorno di Dio)

(De dag Gods)

1894–95, Wood engraving, black ink print on China paper/Gravure sur bois, tirage à l'encre noire sur papier de Chine, 18,2 × 20,3 cm, Art Institute of Chicago, Chicago

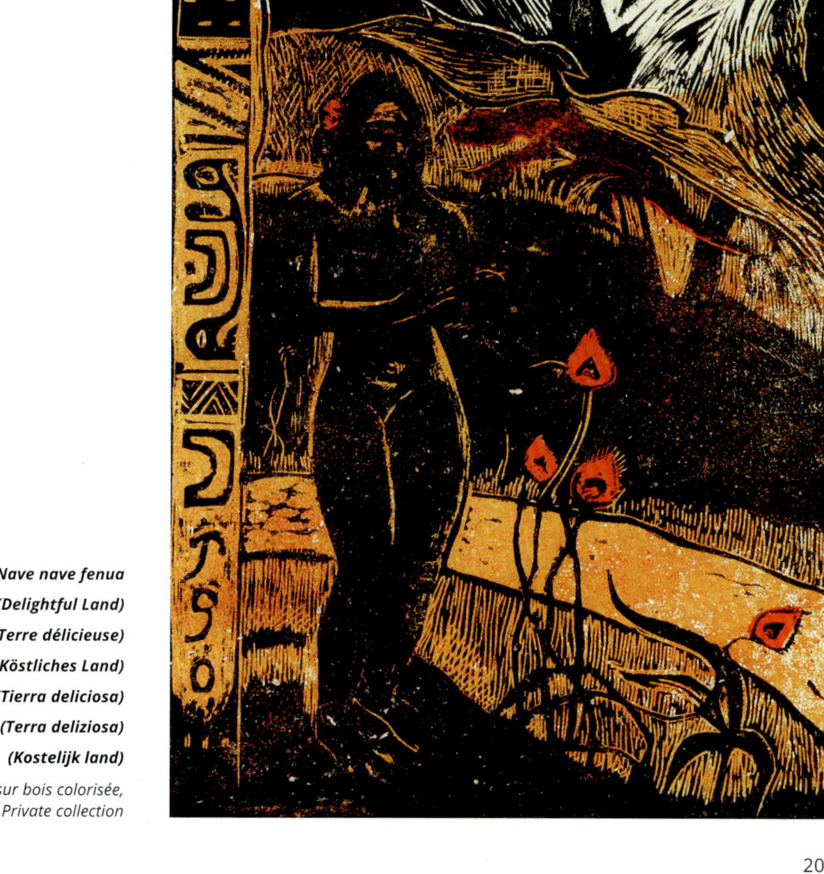

Nave nave fenua

(Delightful Land)

(Terre délicieuse)

(Köstliches Land)

(Tierra deliciosa)

(Terra deliziosa)

(Kostelijk land)

1893–94, Engraving on colored wood/Gravure sur bois colorisée, 35,6 × 20,3 cm, Private collection

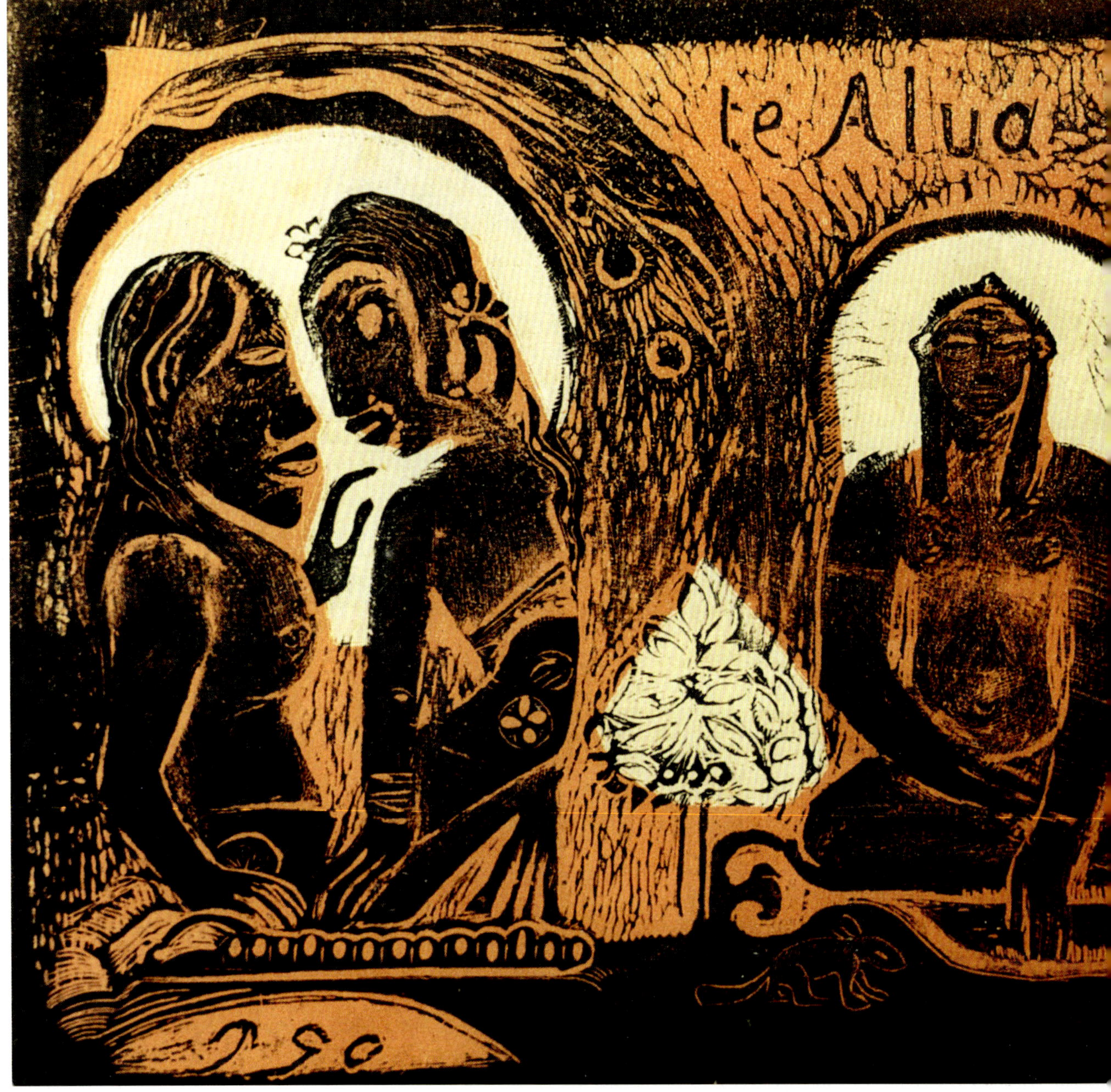
te Atua

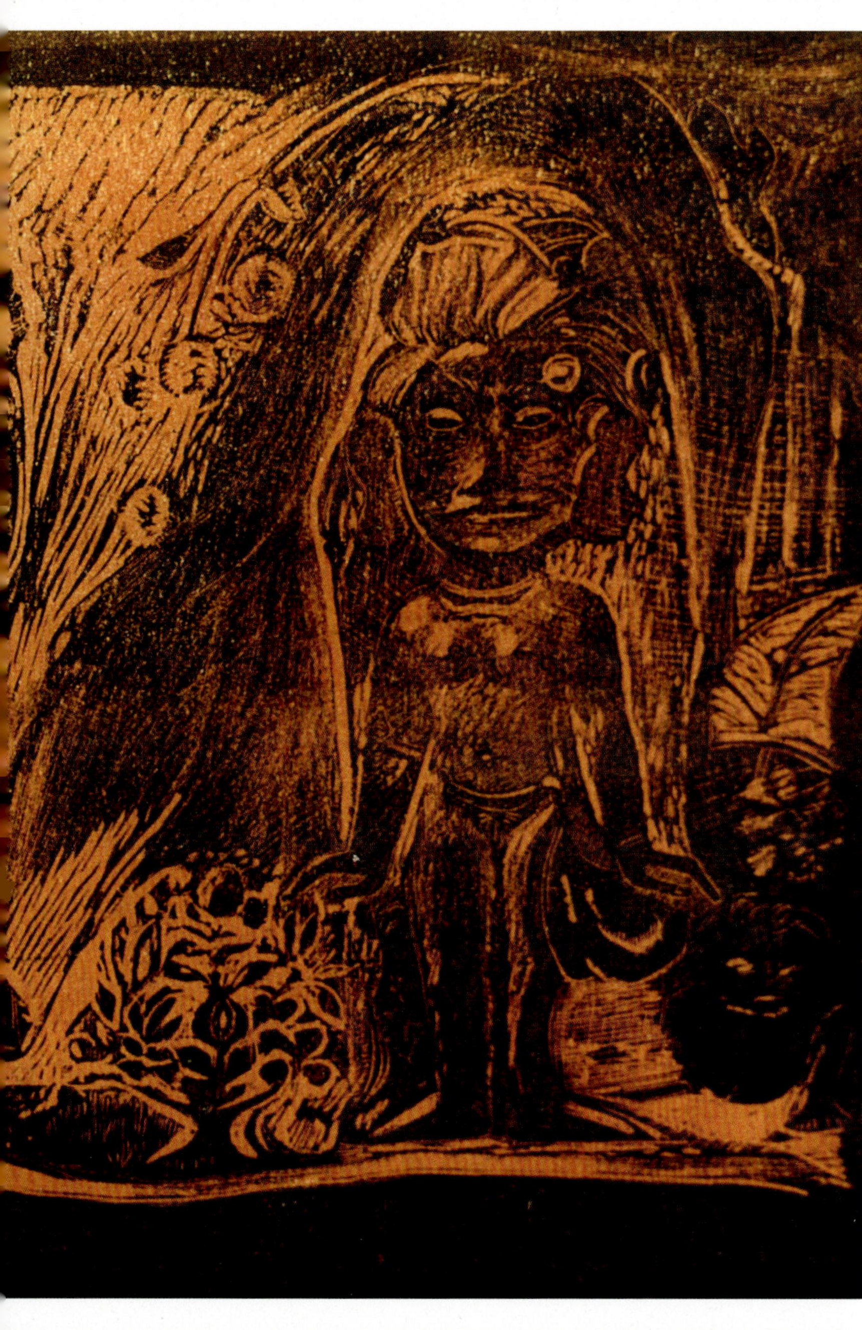

Te Atua

(The Gods)

(Les Dieux)

(Die Götter)

(Los Dioses)

(Gli Dei)

(De goden)

1894, Engraving on colored wood/Gravure sur bois colorisée, 20,4 × 35,5 cm, Private collection

211

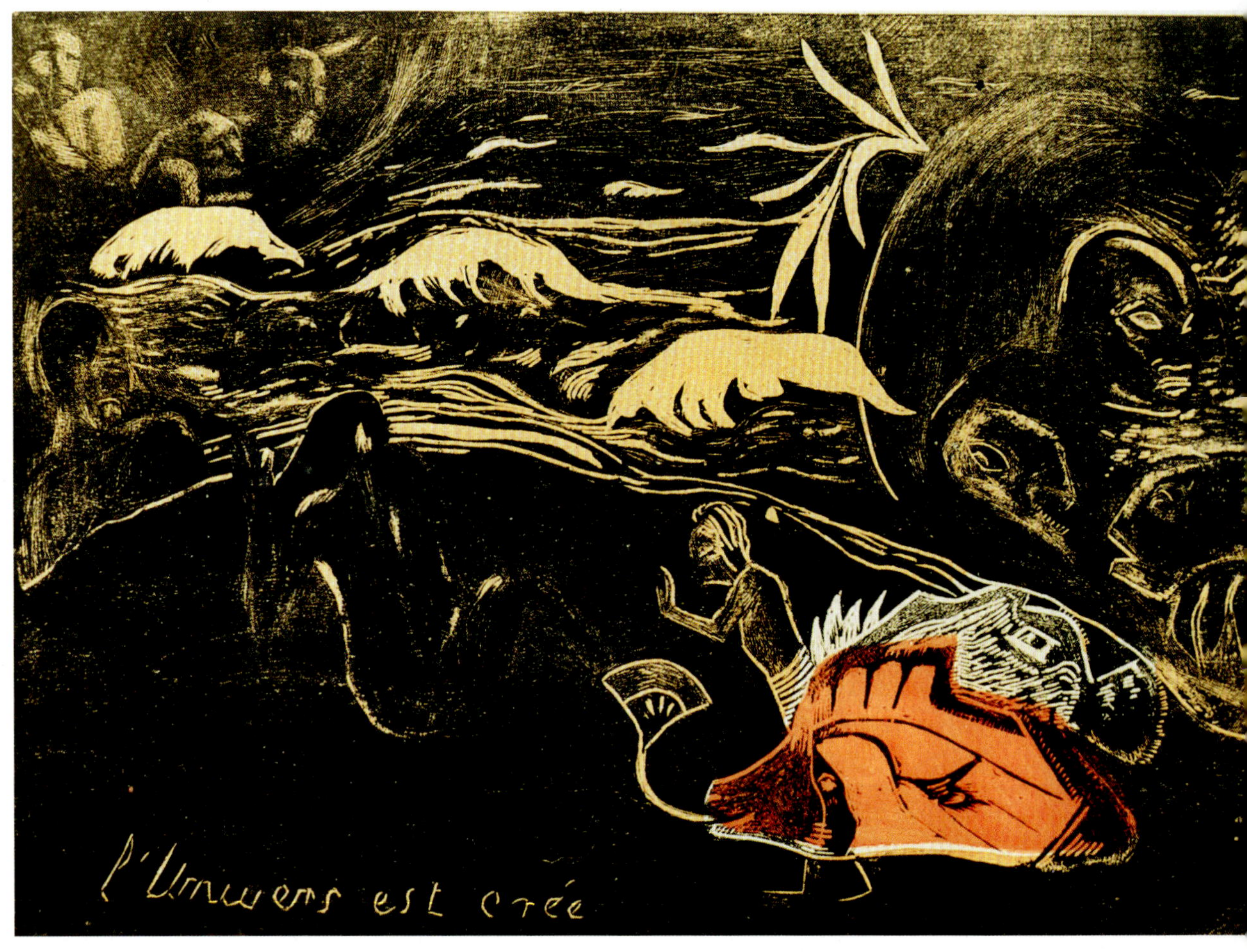

The Creation of the Universe

L'univers est créé

Die Welt ist erschaffen

El universo ha sido creado

L'universo è creato

Het universum is geschapen

1893–94, Engraving on colored wood/Gravure sur bois colorisée, 20,5 × 35,5 cm, Private collection

212

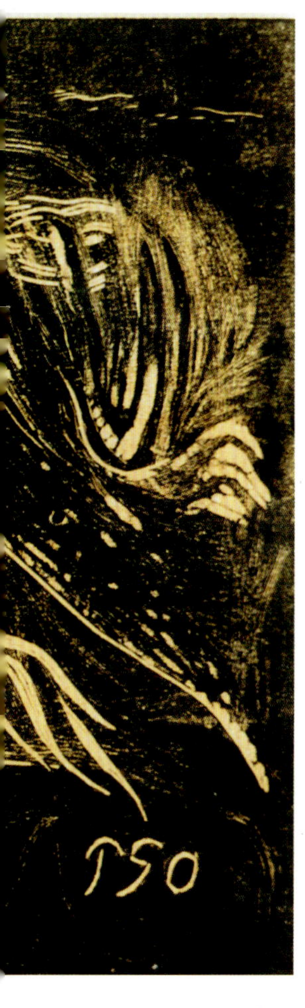

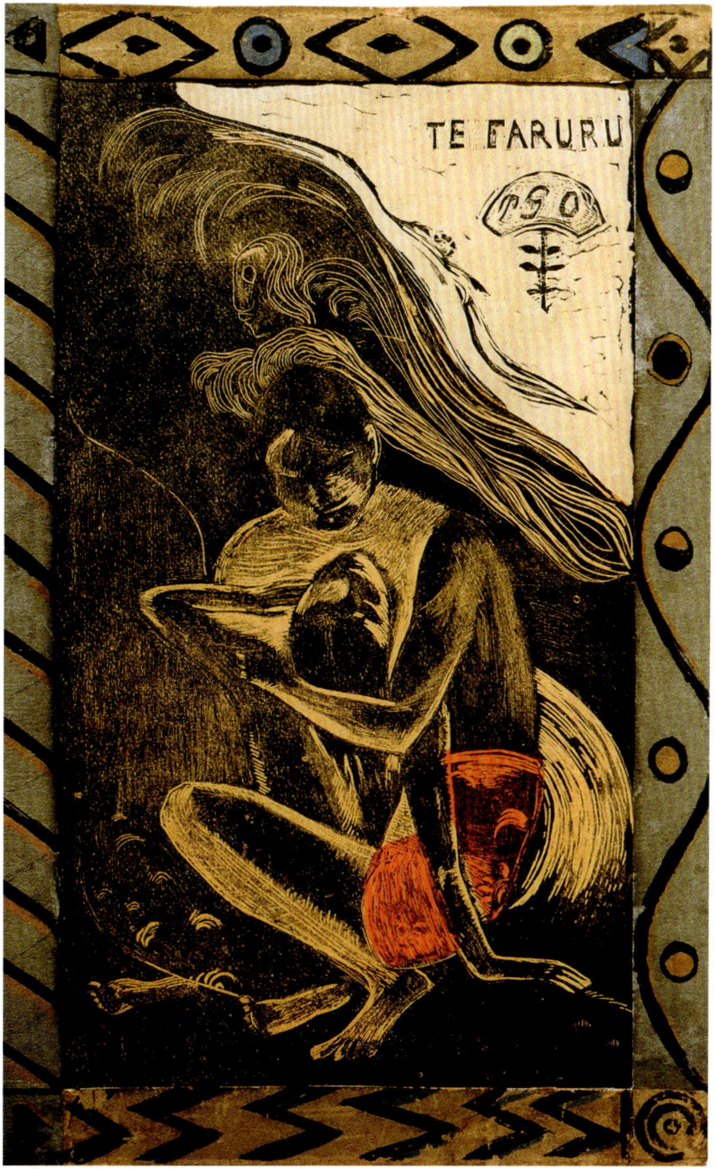

Te Faruru

(Here We Make Love)

(Ici on fait l'amour)

(Liebesakt)

(Aquí hacemos el amor)

(Qui si fa l'amore)

(Hier bedrijven we de liefde)

1894, Engraving on colored wood/ Gravure sur bois colorisée, 35,6 × 20,3 cm, Private collection

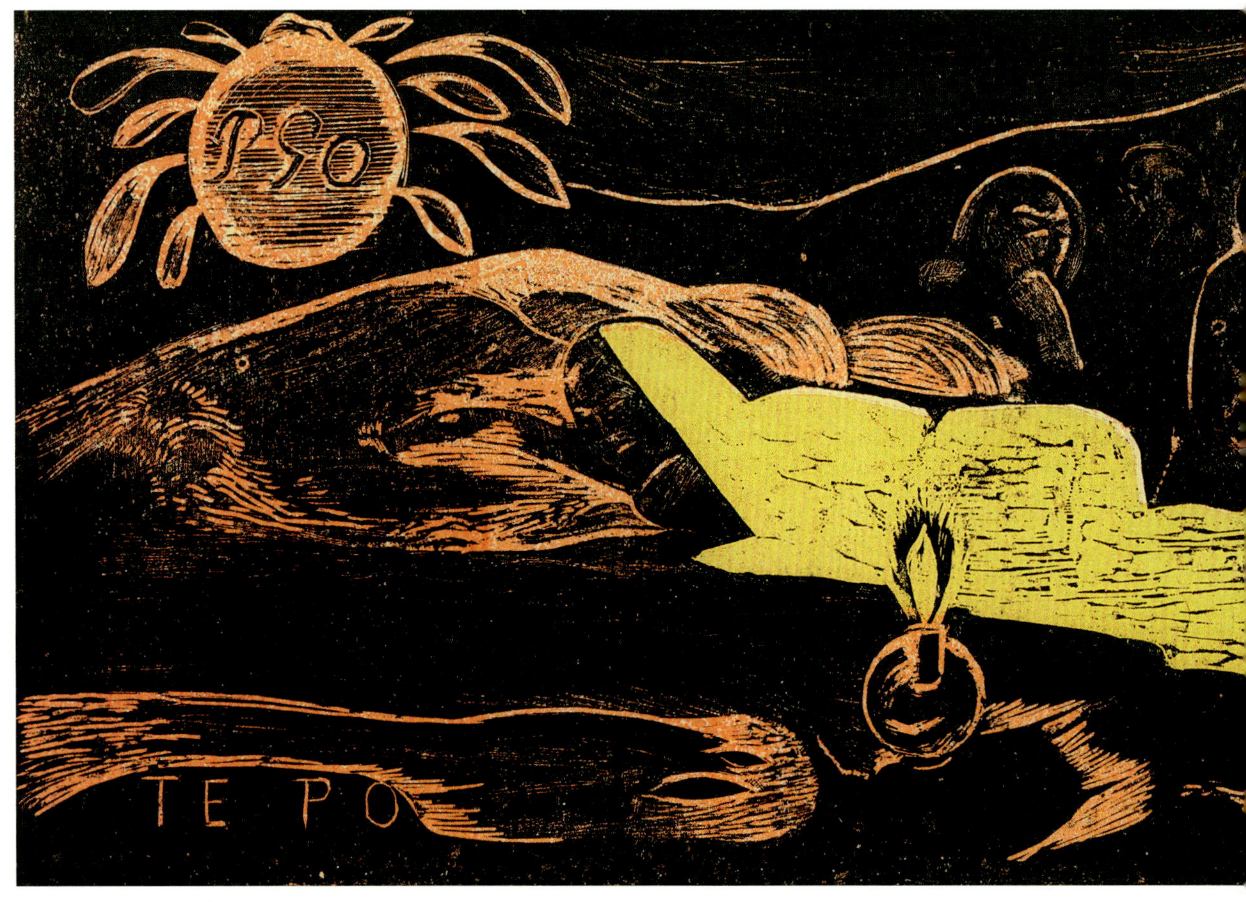

Te Po
(Eternal Night)
(La Grande Nuit)
(Die große Nacht)
(La gran noche)
(La Grande notte)
(De grote nacht)

1893–94, Wood engraving, print in black, yellow and orange on Japanese paper/Gravure sur bois, tirage en noir, jaune et orange sur papier japon, 20,5 × 35,6 cm, Ulmer Museum, Ulm

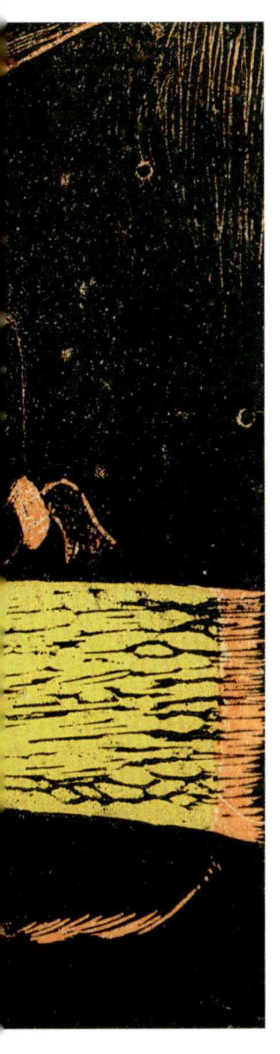

***Noa Noa,*
the Album's Cover**

***Noa Noa,*
couverture de l'album**

***Noa Noa,*
Umschlag des Albums**

***Noa Noa,*
cubierta del álbum**

***Noa Noa,*
copertina dell'album**

***Noa Noa,*
omslag van het dagboek**

*1894, Engraving on colored
wood/Gravure sur bois
colorisée, 35,8 × 20,4 cm,
Private collection*

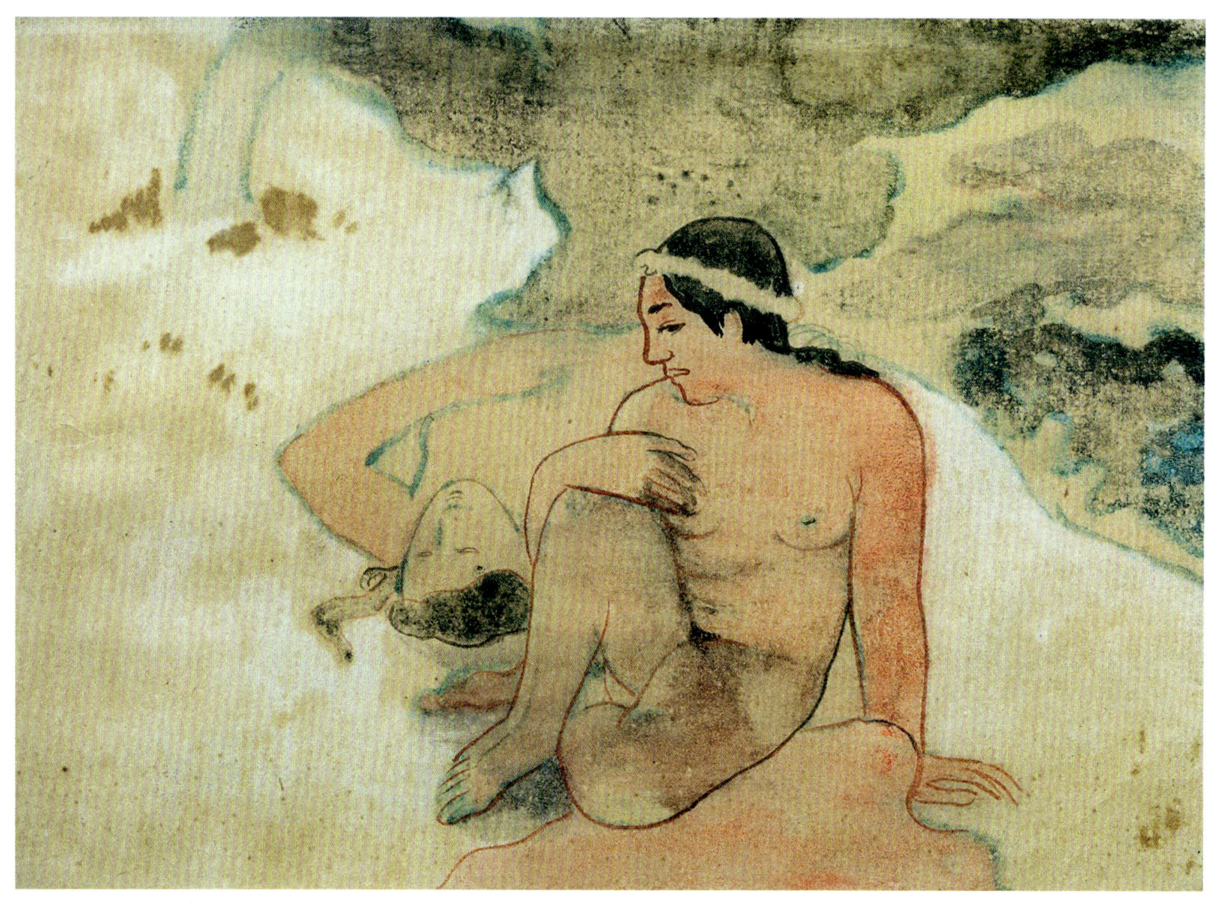

Aha oe feii ?

(What! Are You Jealous?)

(Pourquoi es-tu rancunière ?)

(Warum bist du eifersüchtig?)

(¿Por qué eres rencorosa?)

(Perché sei rancorosa?)

(Ben je soms jaloers?)

1894, Watercolour done in "dessin-empreinte" technique on Japan paper, with coloured highlights in water, brown ink and white chalk/Dessin-empreinte à l'aquarelle sur papier japon, avec rehauts de couleurs à l'eau, d'encre brune et de craie blanche, 19,5 × 23,2 cm, Art Institute of Chicago, Chicago

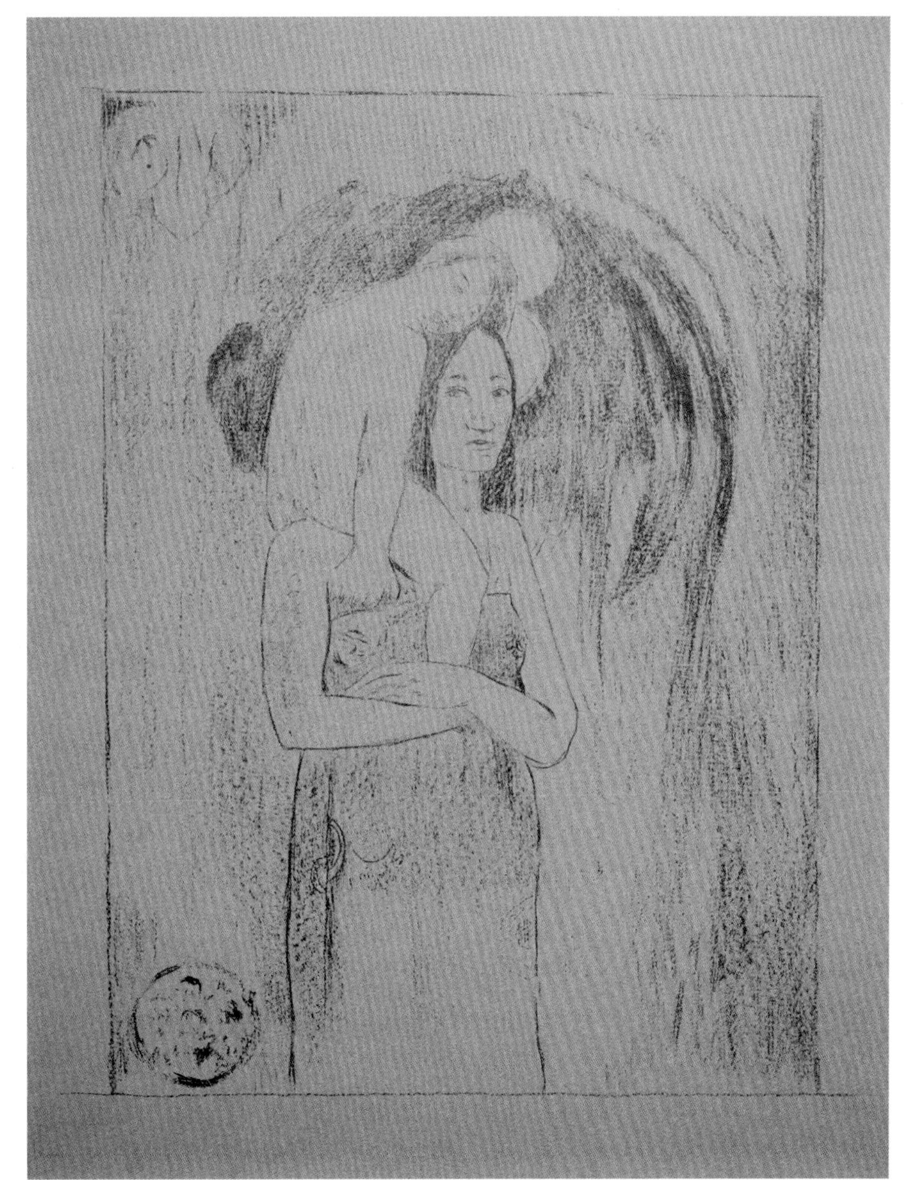

Ia Orana Maria
(Hail Mary)
(Je vous salue Marie)
(Gegrüßet seist du, Maria)
(Yo te saludo, María)
(Vi saluto Maria)
(Wees gegroet Maria)
1894–95, Zincography/zincographie,
37,3 × 27,9 cm, Private collection

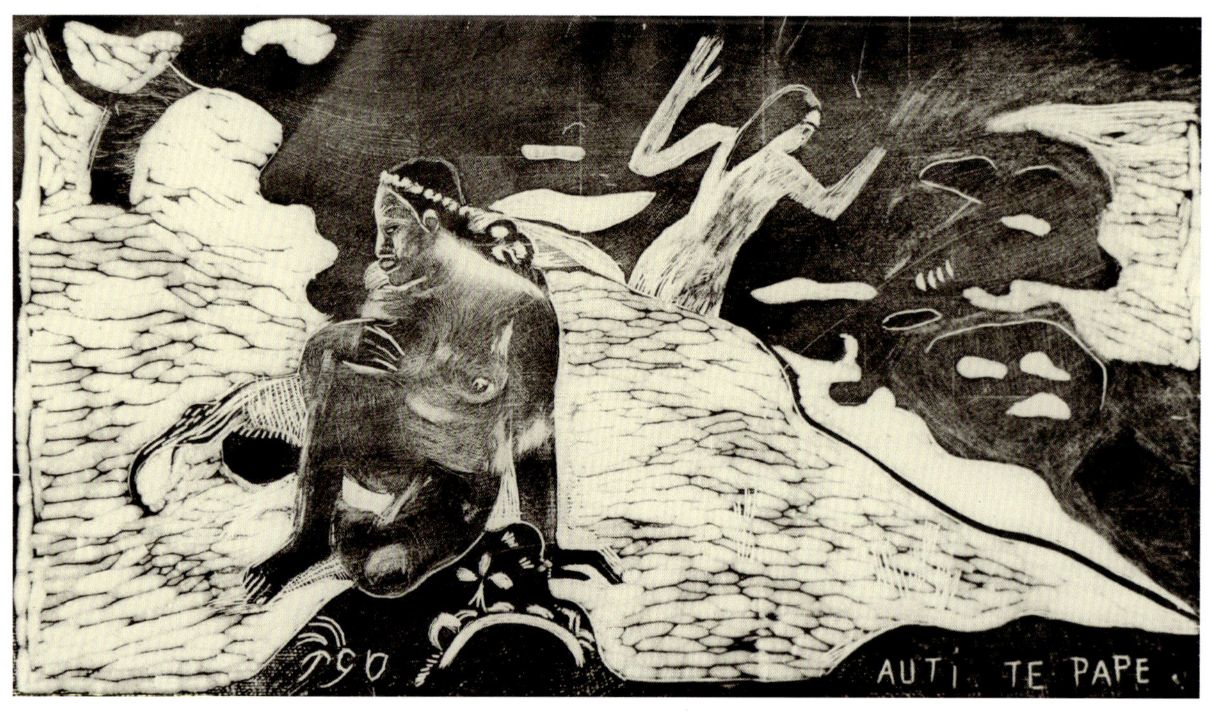

Auti te pape
(Women at the River)
(Les Femmes à la rivière)
(Frauen am Fluss)
(Las mujeres en el río)
(Le Donne alla riviera)
(Vrouwen bij de rivier)

1893/94, Engraving on wood/Gravure sur bois, 20,3 × 35,6 cm, Private collection

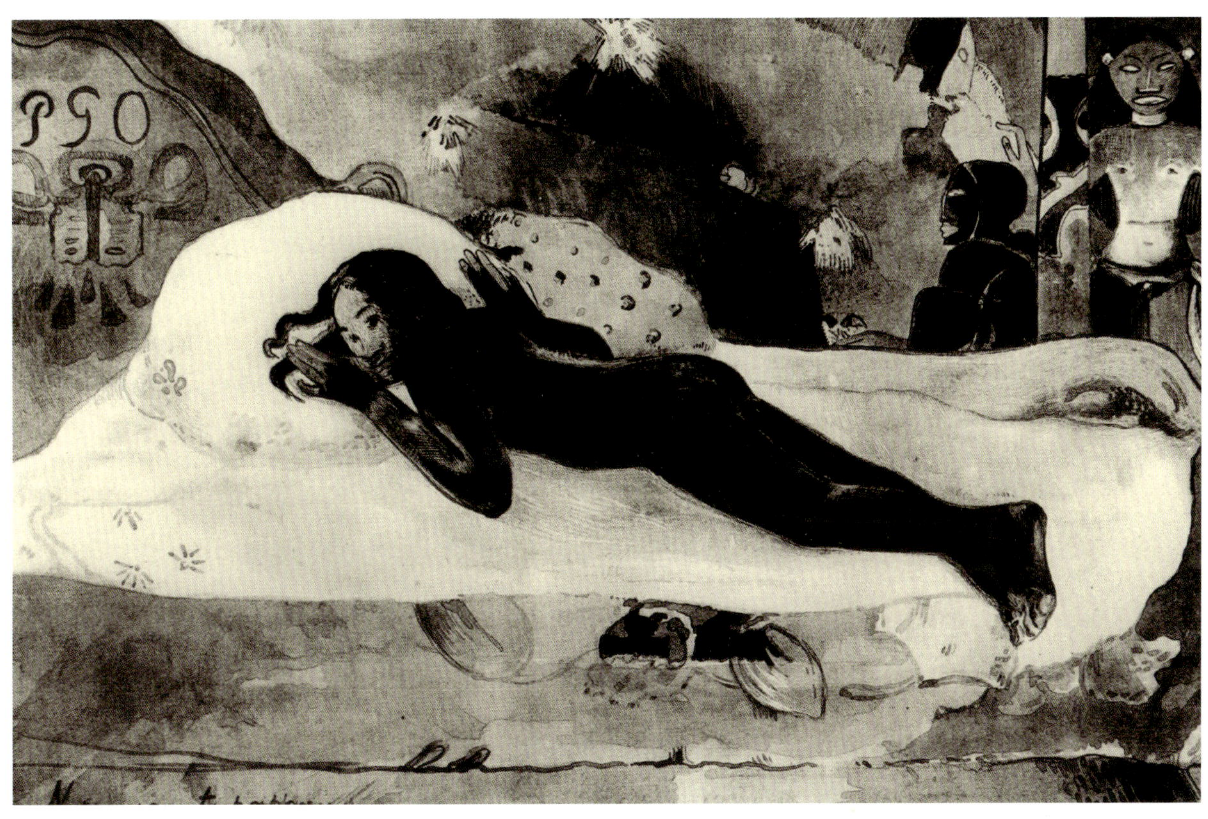

Manao Tupapau
(The Spirit of the Dead Keep Watch)
(L'Esprit des morts veille)
(Der Geist der Ahnen)
(El espíritu de los muertos vigila)
(Lo spirito dei vecchi morti)
(De geest van de doden waakt)
c. 1894, Lithography/Lithographie, 18 × 27,1 cm, Kunsthalle, Hamburg

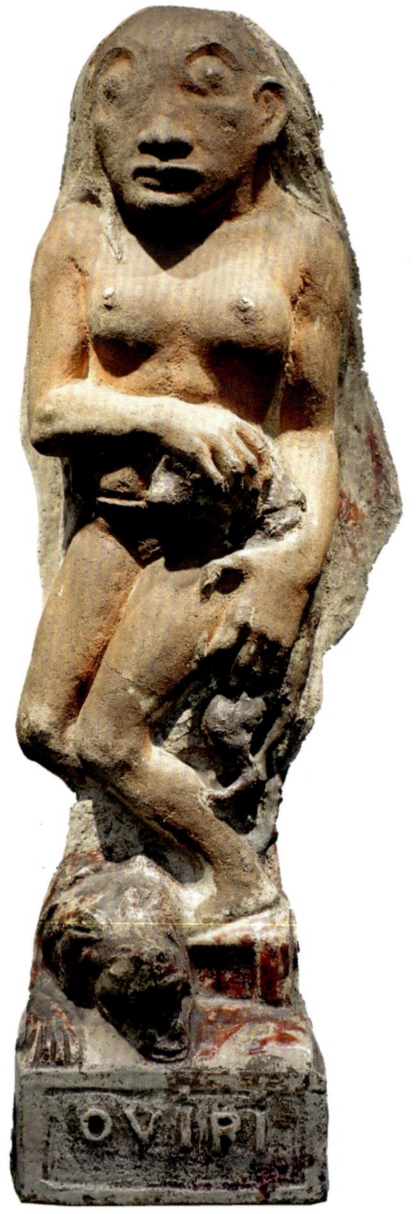

Oviri

1894, Partially enameled stoneware/Grès partiellement émaillé, 75 × 19 × 27 cm, Musée d'Orsay, Paris

The last sculpture made in Paris, in Ernest Chaplet's studio, this statue named *Oviri* (meaning "savage" in Tahitian) and nicknamed "The Murderess" by the artist, portrays an androgynous being in the act of slaying wolves. Emblematic of Gauguin's thinking, this allegory of death, of regeneration into the "savage" is so precious to his eyes that he had said to Daniel de Monfried: "If it is not sold, I would like to retake it in order to place it on my tomb."

Dernière sculpture réalisée à Paris, dans l'atelier d'Ernest Chaplet, cette statue dénommée *Oviri* (qui signifie « sauvage » en tahitien) et surnommée « La Tueuse » par l'artiste figure un être androgyne en train d'égorger des loups. Emblématique de la pensée de Gauguin, cette allégorie de la mort, de la régénérescence par le « sauvage » est si précieuse à ses yeux qu'il dit à George-Daniel de Monfreid : « Si elle n'est pas vendue, je désire la récupérer pour la mettre sur ma tombe. »

Diese letzte in Paris geschaffene Skulptur, entstanden im Atelier von Ernest Chaplet, heißt *Oviri* (was auf tahitisch „wild" bedeutet) und bekam von Gauguin den Beinamen „Die Mörderin". Sie stellt ein androgynes Wesen dar, das Wölfen die Kehle durchschneidet. Sinnbildlich für die Gedankenwelt Gauguins, ist diese bildhafte Darstellung des Todes und der Erneuerung durch das „Primitive" in seinen Augen so kostbar, dass er zu George-Daniel de Monfreid sagt: „Wenn sie nicht verkauft wird, möchte ich sie behalten und auf mein Grab stellen lassen."

Última escultura realizada en París, en el taller de Ernest Chaplet, esta estatua llamada *Oviri* (que significa "salvaje" en tahitiano) y apodada "La victimaria" por el artista representa a un ser andrógino tratando de matar a los lobos. Representativa del pensamiento de Gauguin, esta alegoría de la muerte, de la regeneración por el "salvaje" es tan valioso a sus ojos que le dijo a George-Daniel de Monfreid: "Si no se vende, deseo recuperarla para ponerla sobre mi tumba."

Ultima scultura fatta a Parigi nella bottega di Ernest Chaplet, questa statua chiamata *Oviri* (che significa "selvaggio" in tahitiano) e soprannominata "La Cacciatrice" dall'artista, raffigura un essere androgino che cerca di uccidere dei lupi. Emblematica del pensiero di Gauguin, questa allegoria della morte, della rigenerazione da parte del "selvaggio" è così preziosa ai suoi occhi, che dice a George-Daniel de Monfreid "Se non verrà venduta, desidero recuperarla per metterla sulla mia tomba."

Oviri (Tahitiaans voor 'wilde'), bijgenaamd De "moordenares", het laatste beeld dat Gauguin in Parijs in het atelier van Ernest Chaplet maakt, stelt een androgyne figuur voor die wolven de keel doorsnijdt. Deze voor Gauguin kenmerkende gedachte, deze allegorie op de dood, op de herschepping door 'het wilde', is voor hem van zoveel waarde dat hij tegen George-Daniel de Monfreid zegt: "Als het niet wordt verkocht, dan wil het terug om het op mijn graf te zetten."

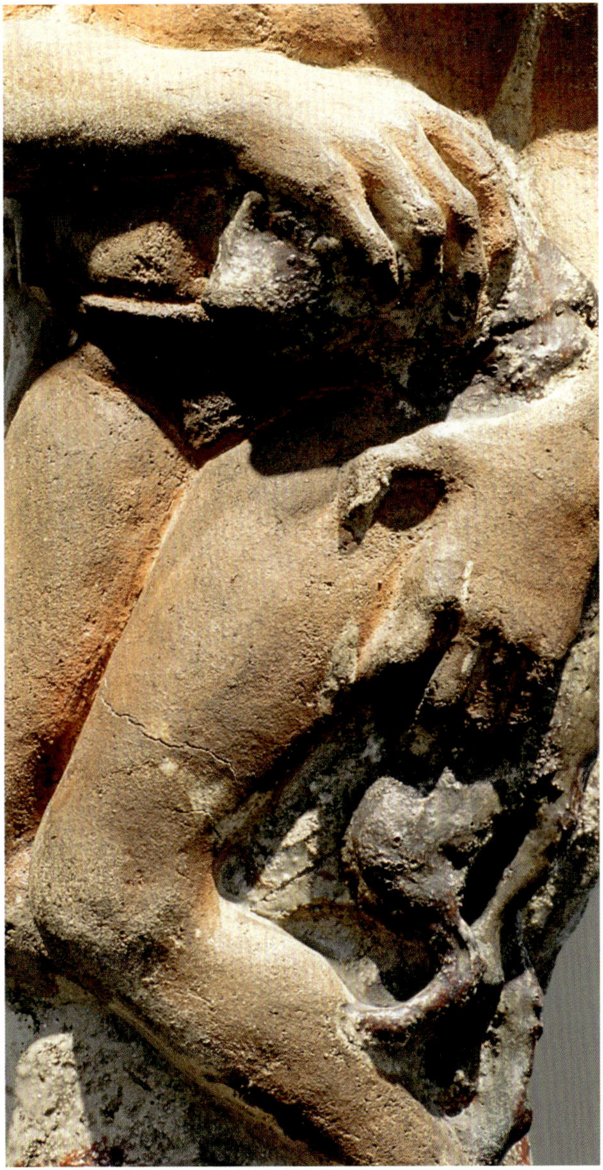

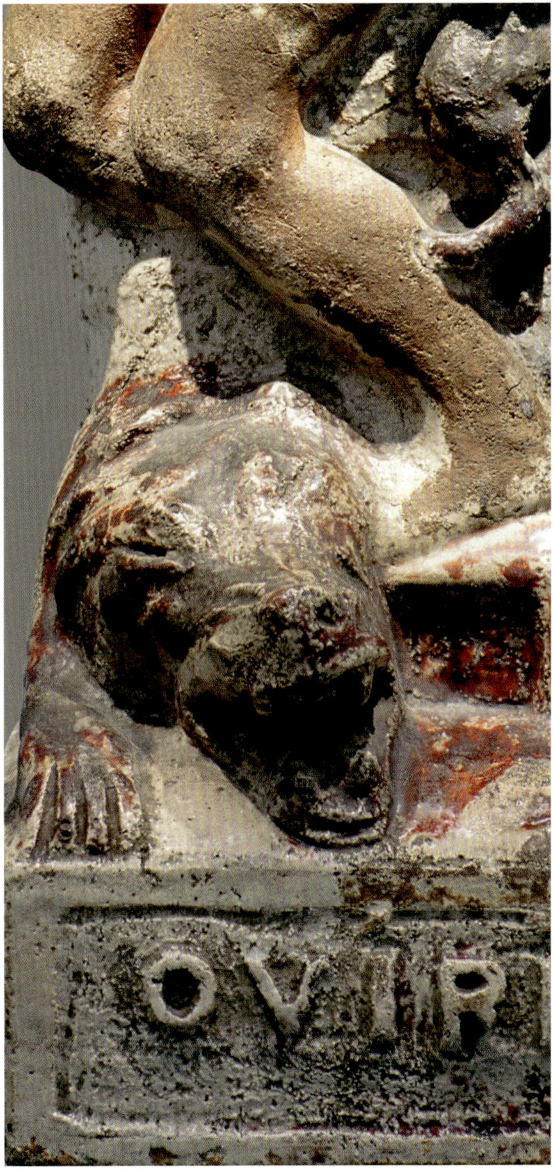

OVIR

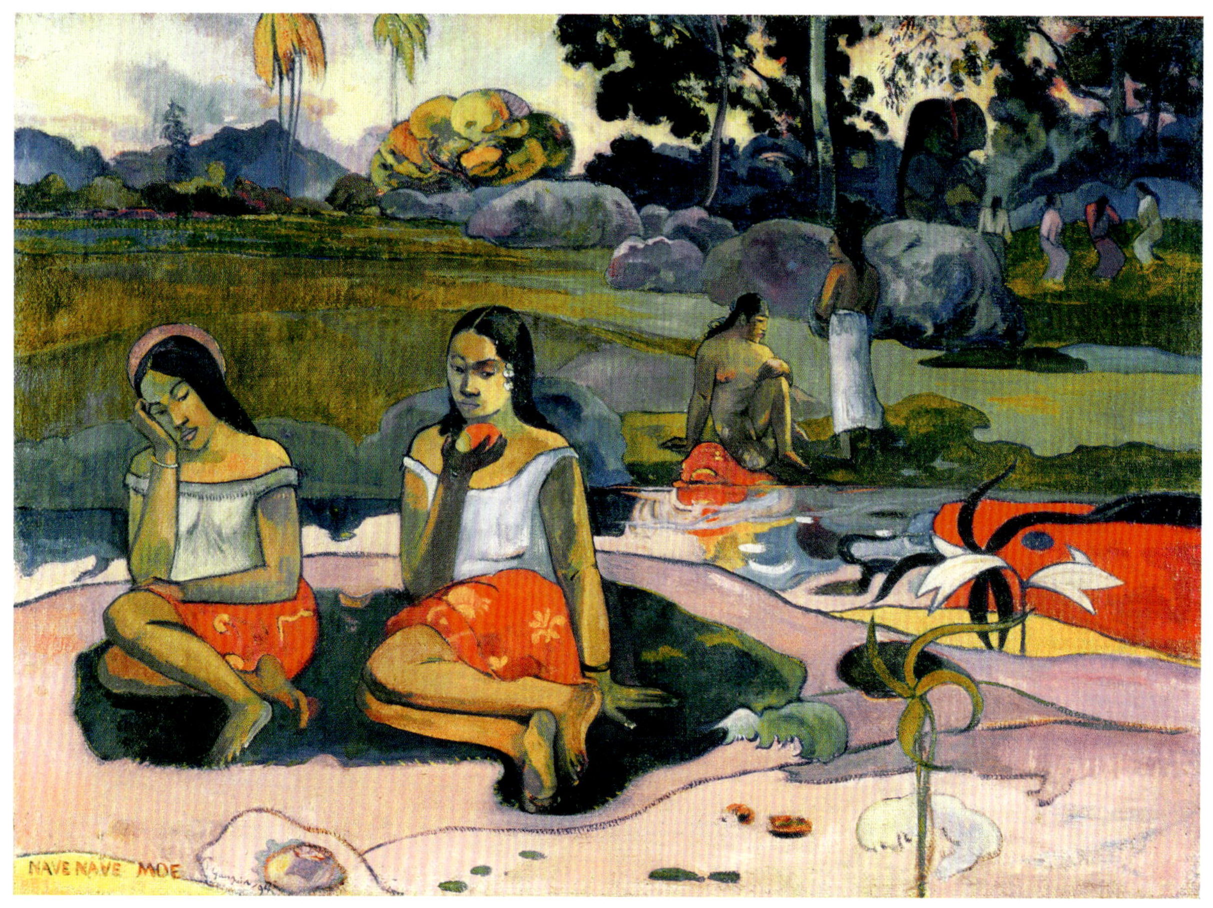

Nave nave moe

(Sacred Spring, Sweet Dreams)

(Délicieux mystère)

(Köstliches Geheimnis)

(Delicioso misterio)

(Delizioso mistero)

(Heerlijk geheimenis)

1894, Oil on canvas/Huile sur toile, 74 × 100 cm, State Hermitage Museum, St. Petersburg

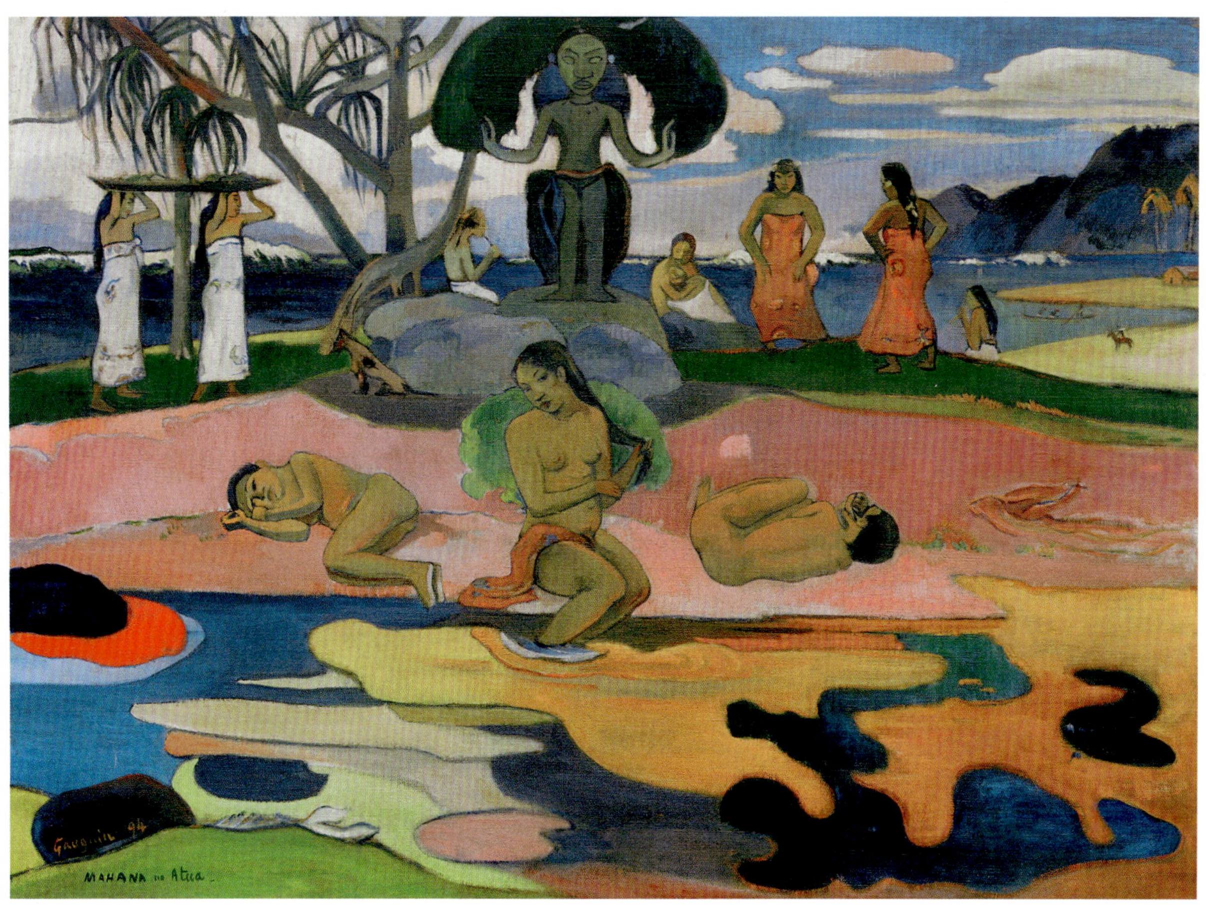

Mahana no Atua
(Day of the God)
(Le Jour de Dieu)
(Der Tag Gottes)
(El día de Dios)
(Il giorno di Dio)
(De dag Gods)

1894, Oil on canvas/Huile sur toile, 68,3 × 91,5 cm, Art Institute of Chicago, Chicago

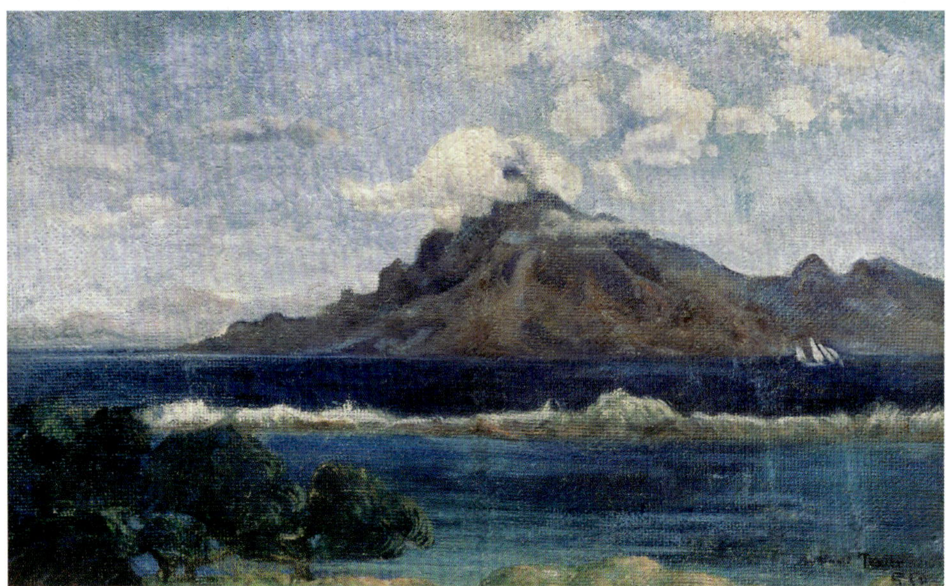

Landscape of Te Vaa

Paysage de Te Vaa

Landschaft von Te Vaa

Paisaje de Te Vaa

Paesaggio di Te Vaa

Landschap van Te Vaa

1896, Oil on canvas/Huile sur toile, 46,4 × 74,4 cm, Musée d'art moderne André Malraux, Le Havre

Polynesia rediscovered

After a stopover in Auckland, New Zealand, Gauguin arrived in Tahiti on 9 September 1895. Short of financial resources and suffering from a leg injury he falls into such a depression, in the spring of 1896, that the lush compositions bursting with colour and serene prints that he paints at the time, can hardly be imagined.

The various ills he suffered, the solitude, the misery and alcohol dragged him into a terrible depression —further aggravated by the news of his daughter Aline's death in 1897— which led him to attempt to put an end to his life. Having surmounted this tribulation, he resumes creative work, elaborating on the symbolical vein of the theme of lost paradise in his paintings, in a "program"

La Polynésie retrouvée

Après avoir fait une escale à Auckland, en Nouvelle-Zélande, Gauguin arrive à Tahiti le 9 septembre 1895. À court de ressources, souffrant d'une blessure à la jambe, il entre, au printemps 1896, dans une déprime, que les somptueuses compositions éclatantes de couleurs et empreintes de sérénité qu'il peint alors ne laissent pas imaginer.

Les divers maux dont il souffre, la solitude, la misère et l'alcool, l'entraînent dans une terrible dépression – qu'aggravera encore l'annonce du décès de sa fille Aline, en 1897 – et le conduiront à tenter de mettre fin à ses jours. Cette épreuve surmontée, il se remet à créer, approfondissant la veine symboliste du thème de l'éden perdu dans des tableaux « à programme » qui livrent sa vision très

Die Wiederentdeckung Polynesiens

Nach einem Zwischenhalt in Auckland (Neuseeland) kommt Gauguin am 9. September 1895 auf Tahiti an. Trotz ausreichender Einkünfte überfällt ihn, leidend an einer Beinverletzung, im Frühjahr 1896 Niedergeschlagenheit. Er malt Bilder mit üppigen, strahlenden Farben, die Heiterkeit ausstrahlen und seine wahre Gemütsverfassung nicht erkennen lassen.

Die verschiedenen Krankheiten, die Einsamkeit, das Elend und der Alkohol stürzen ihn in eine schwere Depression – die sich durch die Nachricht des Todes seiner Tochter Aline im Jahre 1897 noch verschlimmern wird – und treiben ihn schließlich in einen Selbstmordversuch. Nach dieser schweren Prüfung findet er wieder

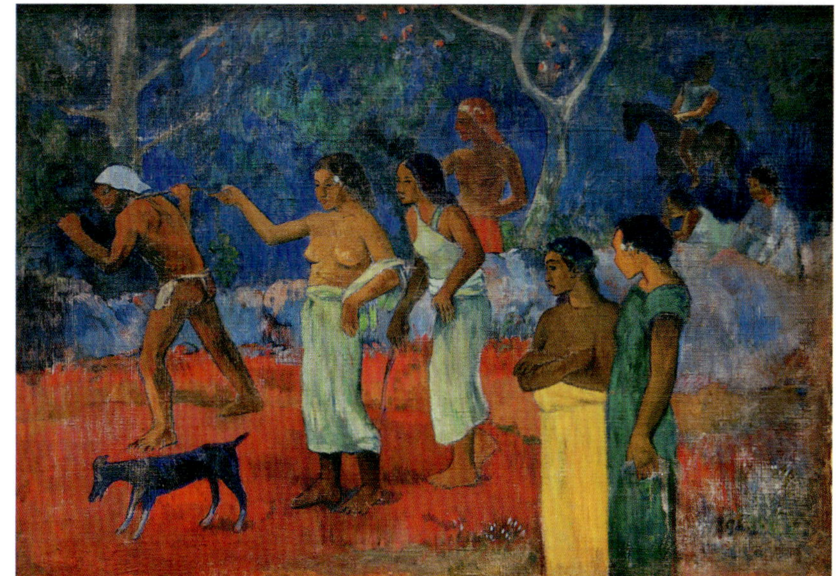

La recuperación de la Polinesia

Después de hacer escala en Auckland, Nueva Zelanda, Gauguin llegó a Tahití el 9 de septiembre de 1895. Al límite de sus fuerzas, sufriendo de una herida en su pierna, llegó en la primavera de 1896, con una depresión que las suntuosas y brillantes composiciones de colores e imágenes de serenidad que pintó allí, no dejan entrever.

Los diferentes males que sufría, la soledad, la miseria y el alcohol, le llevaron a una terrible depresión, que se vio agravada aún más tras el anuncio del fallecimiento de su hija Aline, en 1897, y le llevaron a intentar poner fin a sus días. Una vez superada esta prueba, volvió a crear, profundizando en la corriente simbolista del tema del edén perdido en sus cuadros "de forma programada"

La Polinesia ritrovata

Dopo aver fatto una sosta a Auckland, Nuova Zelanda, Gauguin arriva a Tahiti il 9 settembre 1895. A corto di risorse, soffre di un infortunio alla gamba, e nella primavera 1896 cade in depressione, nonostante le sontuose e vivaci composizioni di colori e le impronte di serenità che dipinge non lascino immaginare nulla.

I vari mali di cui soffre, la solitudine, la miseria e l'alcool, lo avviano ad una terribile depressione – che si aggraverà con l'annuncio della morte della figlia Aline, nel 1897 – e che lo portano a tentare di porre fine alla sua vita. Superata questa prova, si rimette a creare, approfondendo la vena simbolista del tema del paradiso perduto nelle tavole "a programma" che offrono la

Terug in Polynesië

Na een tussenstop in Auckland, Nieuw-Zeeland, komt Gauguin op 9 september 1895 op Tahiti aan. Bijna blut en met een beenblessure krijgt hij in het voorjaar van 1896 een inzinking, al is dat niet af te zien aan de overdadige schilderijen in felle kleuren die hij in die periode maakt en die een en al rust en kalmte uitstralen.

Als gevolg van zijn kwalen, de eenzaamheid, de ellende en de alcohol raakt hij in een diepe depressie – die nog dieper wordt als hij in 1897 bericht krijgt dat zijn dochter Aline is overleden – en probeert hij zelfs een eind aan zijn leven te maken. Hij komt de crisis te boven en begint weer te schilderen. Hij diept het symbolistische thema van het verloren paradijs verder uit in 'programmaschilderijen', die zijn zeer

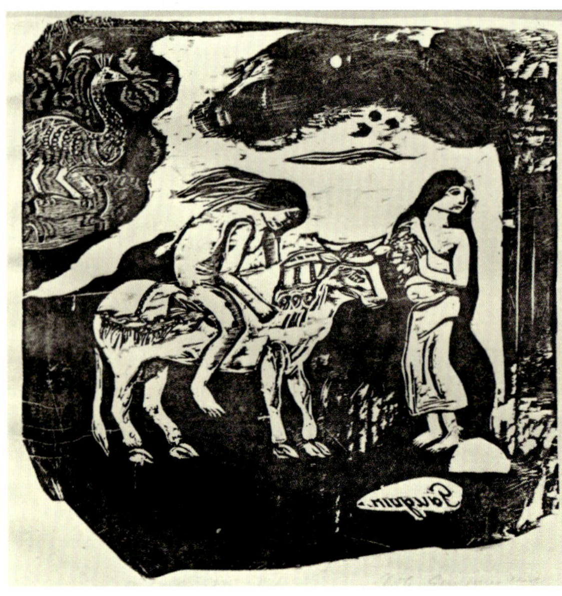

The Abduction of Europa

L'Enlèvement d'Europe

Die Entführung der Europa

El secuestro de Europa

La Rimozione d'Europa

De ontvoering van Europa

*c. 1896–98, Engraving on wood/Gravure sur bois, 24,2 × 23 cm,
Kupferstichkabinett, Berlin*

that sets forth his very disillusioned vision of the world and humanity. In 1899, he relinquished pencils and brushes in order to focus on his assignments as collaborator in, and then editor of, the newspaper *Les Guêpes* (politically committed against the Protestant clan), and as a creator of *Sourire* [Smile], a satirical leaflet illustrated with his wood engravings.

Following a providential offer made by Ambroise Vollard at the start of March in 1901—to remunerate him with 300 francs per month for the annual production of some 20 paintings—he moved to the Marquesas in the summer, realising an old dream.

désabusée du monde et de l'humanité. En 1899, il délaisse crayons et pinceaux, pour se concentrer sur ses missions de collaborateur puis de rédacteur au journal *Les Guêpes* (politiquement engagé à l'encontre du clan protestant) et de créateur du *Sourire*, feuille satyrique illustrée de ses bois gravés.

Suite à l'offre providentielle faite début mars 1901 par Ambroise Vollard – de le rémunérer 300 francs mensuels contre la production annuelle d'une vingtaine de toiles –, il part s'installer aux Marquises dans l'été, réalisant un vieux rêve.

zu seinem Schaffen zurück. Er vertieft die symbolistische Ader des Themas vom verlorenen Paradies in „programmatischen" Bildern, die seine tief desillusionierte Sicht der Verlorenheit von Welt und Menschheit widerspiegeln. 1899 legt er Farbstifte und Pinsel zur Seite und widmet sich seiner Aufgabe als Mitarbeiter, später Redakteur, der Zeitschrift *Les Guêpes* (politisch engagiert gegen den protestantischen Clan) und als Gründer des mit seinen Holzschnitten illustrierten Satireblatts *Sourire*.

Nachdem ihm Anfang März 1901 Ambroise Vollard anbietet, 300 Francs monatlich für die jährliche Produktion von 20 Gemälden zu zahlen, reist er im Sommer ab, um sich auf den Marquesas-Inseln niederzulassen. Er verwirklicht damit einen alten Traum.

c. 1896–97, Engraving on wood/Gravure sur bois, 10,5 × 9 cm, Private collection

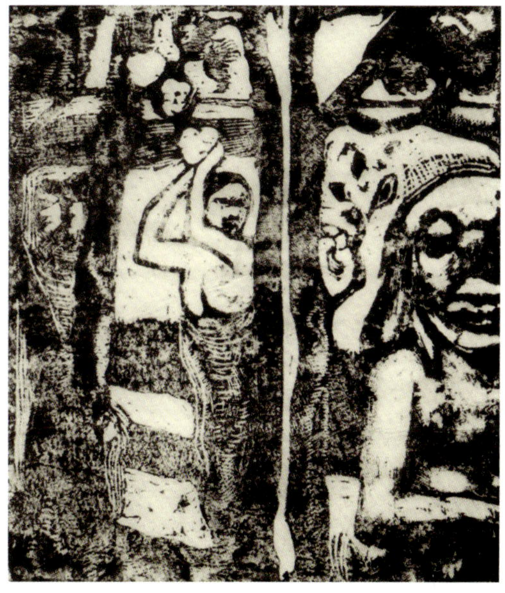

que se libran de la imagen desengañada del mundo y de la humanidad. En 1899, abandona sus lápices y pinceles, para concentrarse en sus misiones de colaborador y después redactor en el periódico *Les Guêpes* (comprometido políticamente contra el clan protestante) y de creador del *Sourire*, folletín satírico ilustrado por sus maderas grabadas.

Después de la oferta providencial realizada a comienzos de marzo de 1901 por Ambroise Vollard, de remunerarle con 300 francos mensuales por la producción anual de unos veinte lienzos, se marchó para instalarse en Marquises ese verano, haciendo realidad un viejo sueño.

sua visione molto disillusa del mondo e dell'umanità. Nel 1899, abbandona matite e pennelli, per concentrarsi sulle sue missioni di collaboratore e poi redattore del quotidiano *Les Guêpes* (politicamente impegnato all'incontro con i gruppi protestanti) e creatore del *Sourire*, foglio illustrato delle sue xilografie.

Dopo l'offerta provvidenziale fatta nei primi di marzo 1901 da Ambroise Vollard – di pagargli 300 franchi al mese per la produzione annuale di venti dipinti – si trasferisce a Marquises in estate, realizzando un vecchio sogno.

gedesillusioneerde kijk op de wereld en de mensheid verbeelden. In 1899 legt hij potlood en penseel neer om zich te wijden aan zijn taak van medewerker en later redacteur bij het politiek geëngageerde en tegen de protestantse clan schrijvende dagblad *Les Guêpes* en als producent van *Sourire*, een satirisch blad dat met zijn houtgravures wordt geïllustreerd.

Wanneer Ambroise Vollard hem begin maart 1901 een als door de voorzienigheid beschikt aanbod doet – een honorarium van 300 frank per maand voor de productie van een twintigtal schilderijen per jaar –, kan een oude droom in vervulling gaan: die zomer verruilt hij Tahiti voor de Marquesas-eilanden.

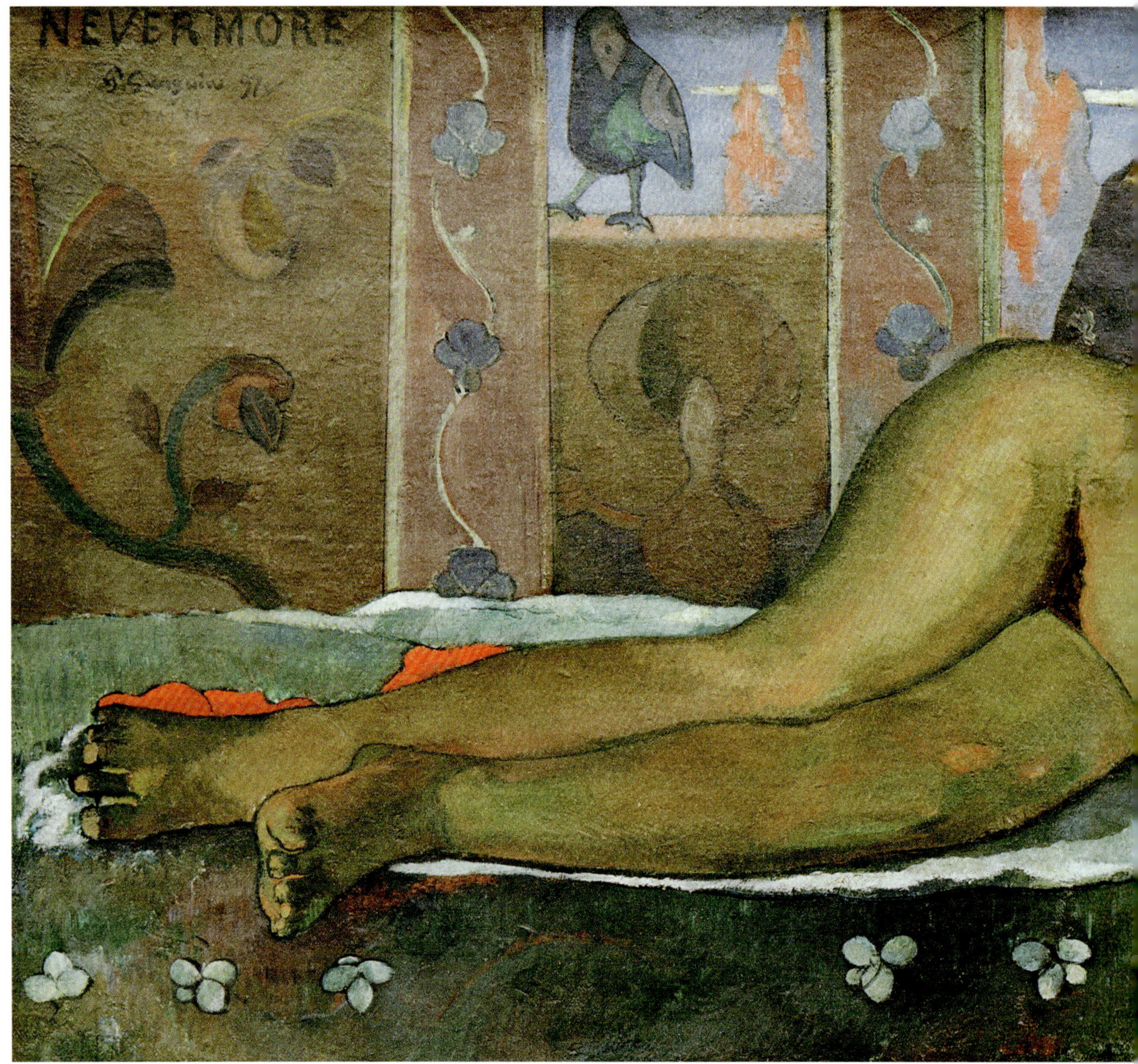

NEVERMORE
P Gauguin 97

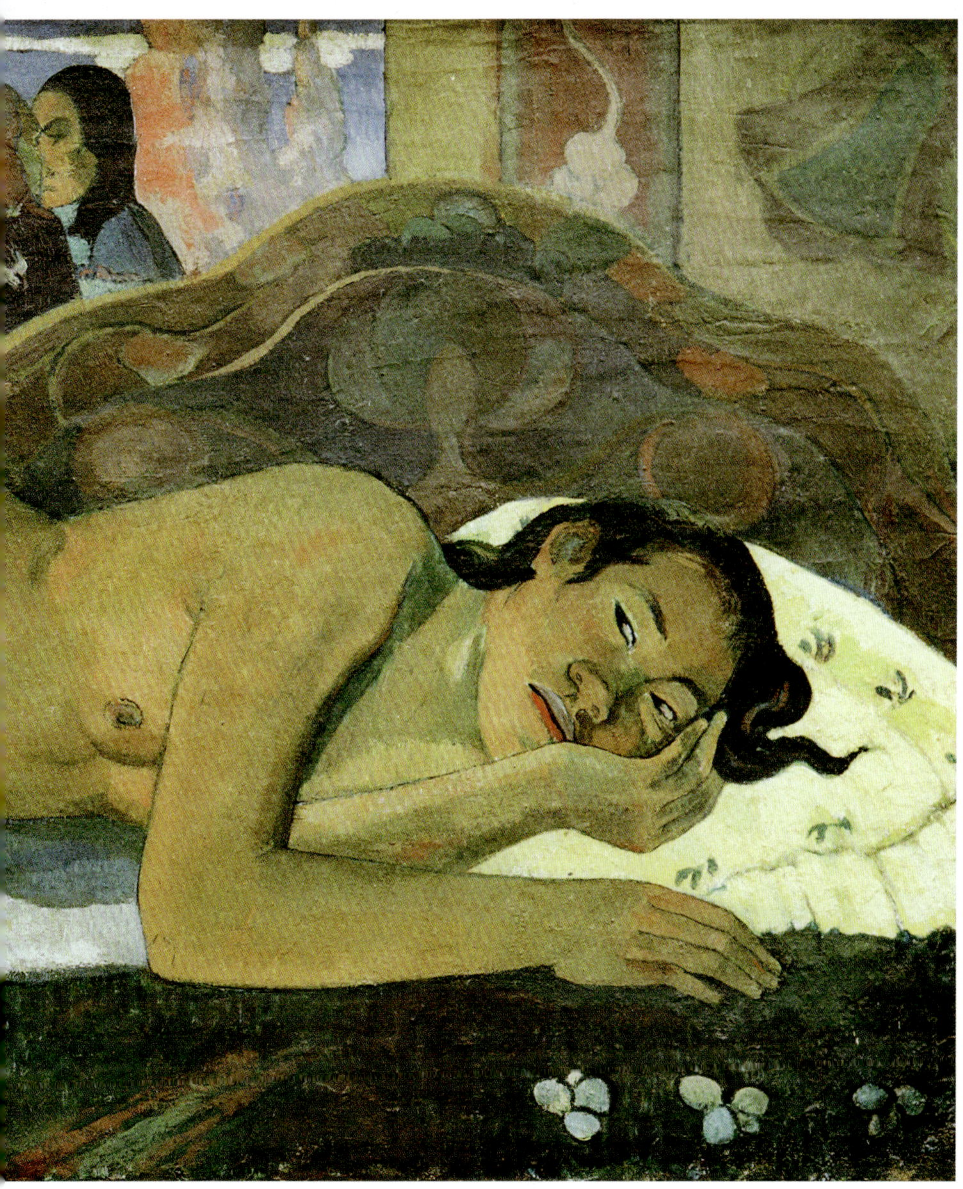

Nevermore

*1897, Oil on canvas/Huile sur
toile, 60,5 × 116 cm, Courtauld
Institute of Art, London*

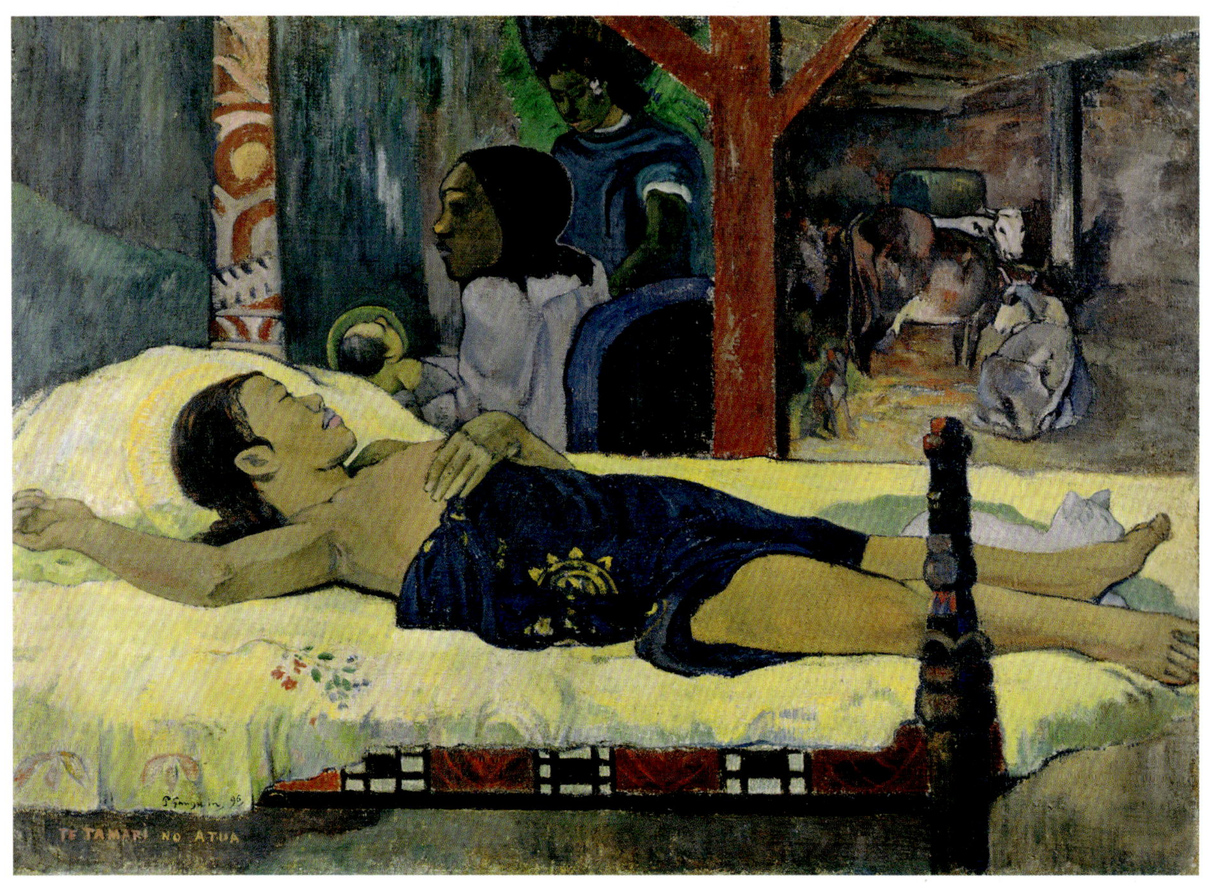

Te tamari no atua

(Birth of Christ)

(La Naissance du Christ)

(Die Geburt Christi)

(El nacimiento de Cristo)

(La Nascita del Cristo)

(De geboorte van de Christus)

1896, Oil on canvas/Huile sur toile, 96 × 131,1 cm, Neue Pinakothek, München

230

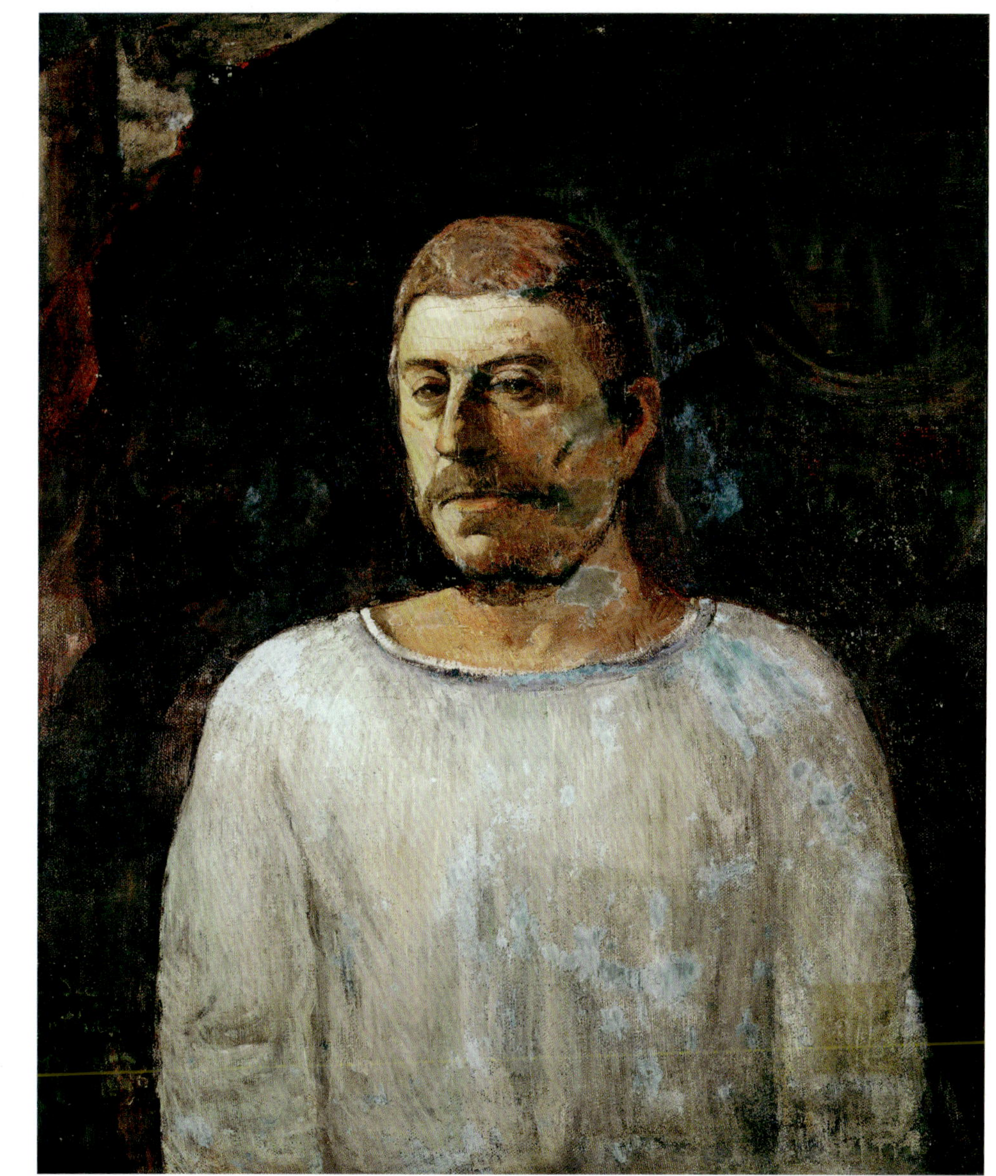

Self Portrait
Autoportrait
Selbstbildnis
Autorretrato
Autoritratto
Zelfportret

1896, Oil on canvas/Huile sur toile, 76 × 64 cm, Museu de Arte de São Paulo, São Paulo

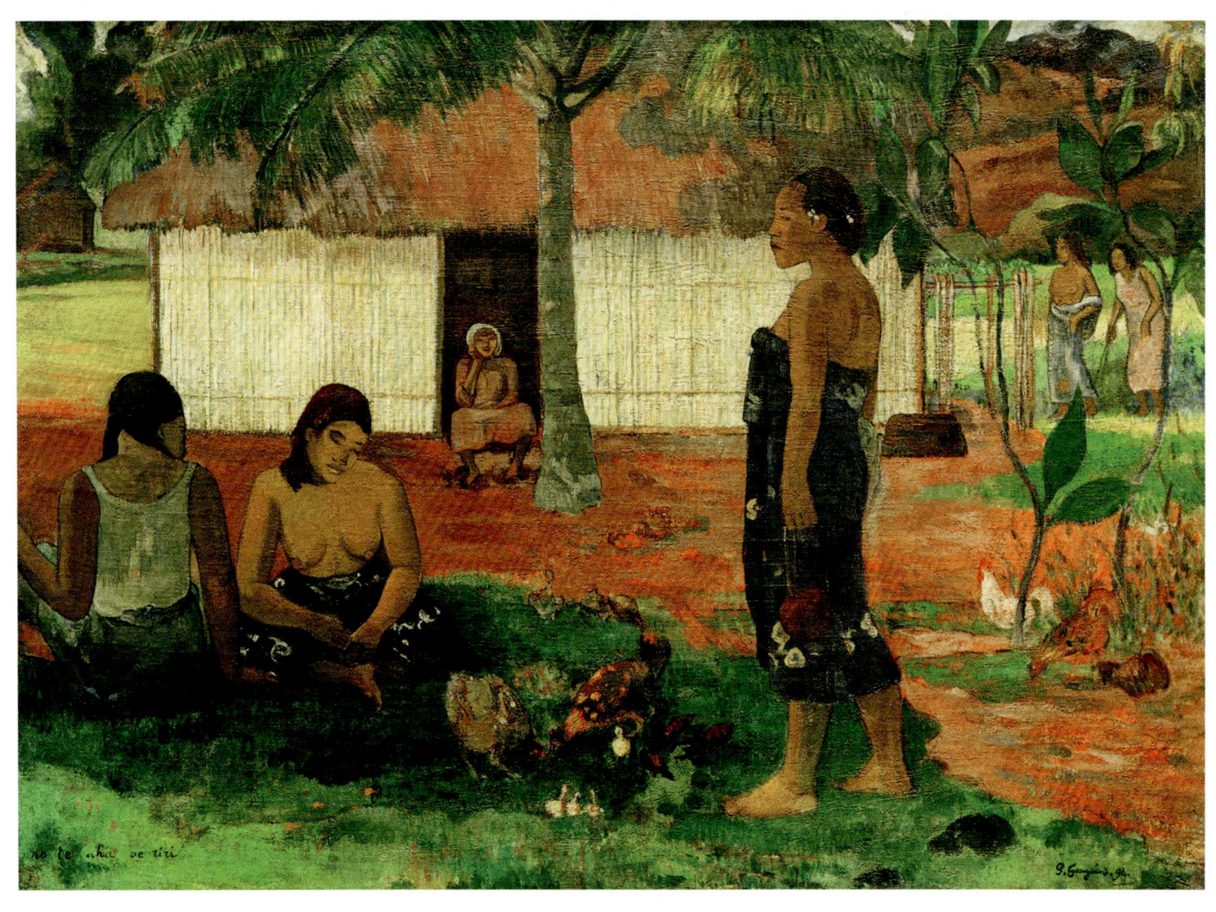

No Te Aha Oe Riri
(Why Are You Angry?)
(Pourquoi es-tu en colère ?)
(Warum bist du ärgerlich?)
(¿Por qué estás enfadada?)
(Perché sei tu in collera)?
(Ben je soms boos?)

1896, Oil on canvas/Huile sur toile, 95,3 × 130,5 cm, Art Institute of Chicago, Chicago

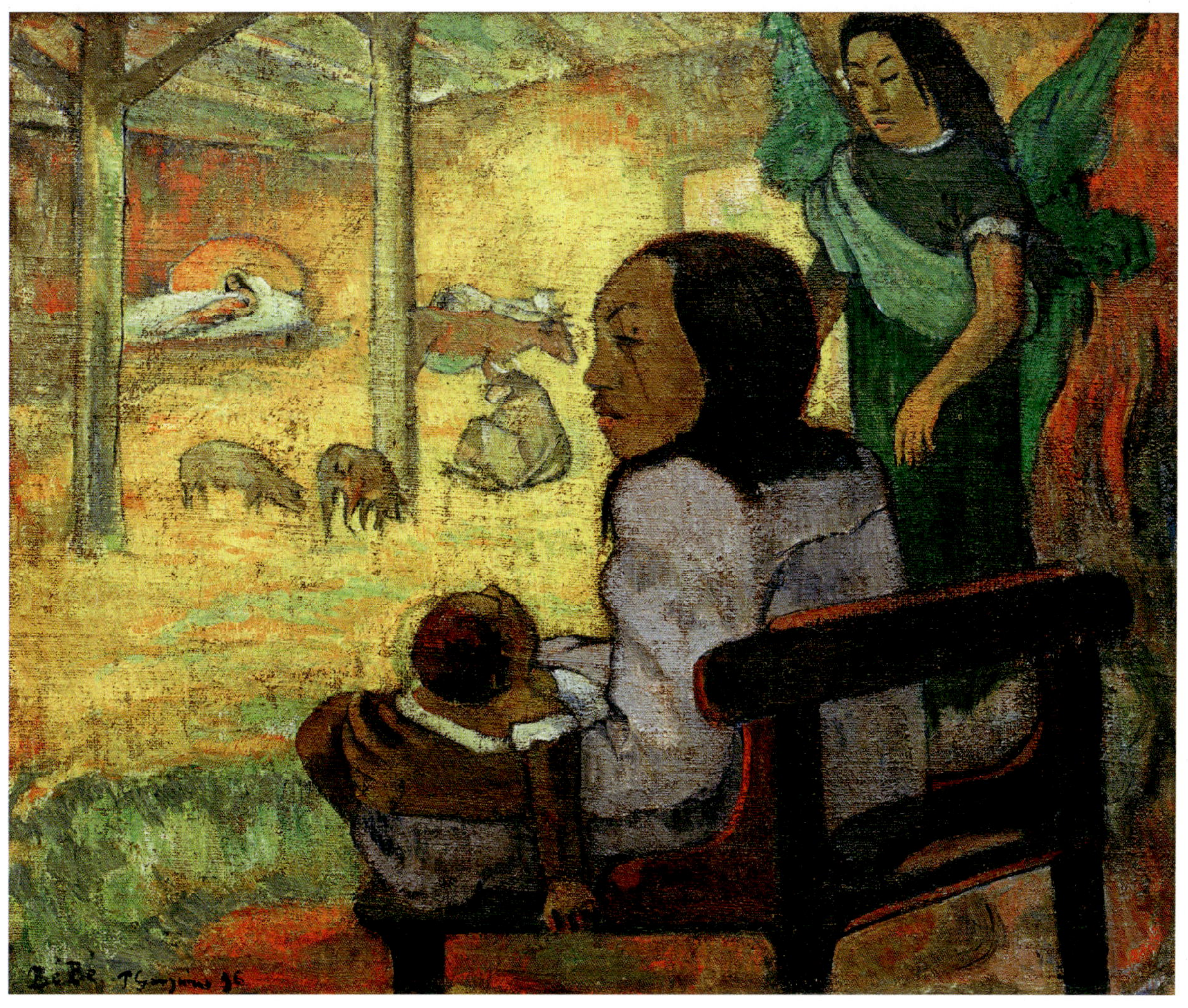

Be Be

(The Nativity)   ***(Die Geburt)***   ***(La Natività)***

(La Nativité)   ***(La Natividad)***   ***(Christus' geboorte)***

1896, Oil on canvas/Huile sur toile, 67 × 76,5 cm, State Hermitage Museum, St. Petersburg

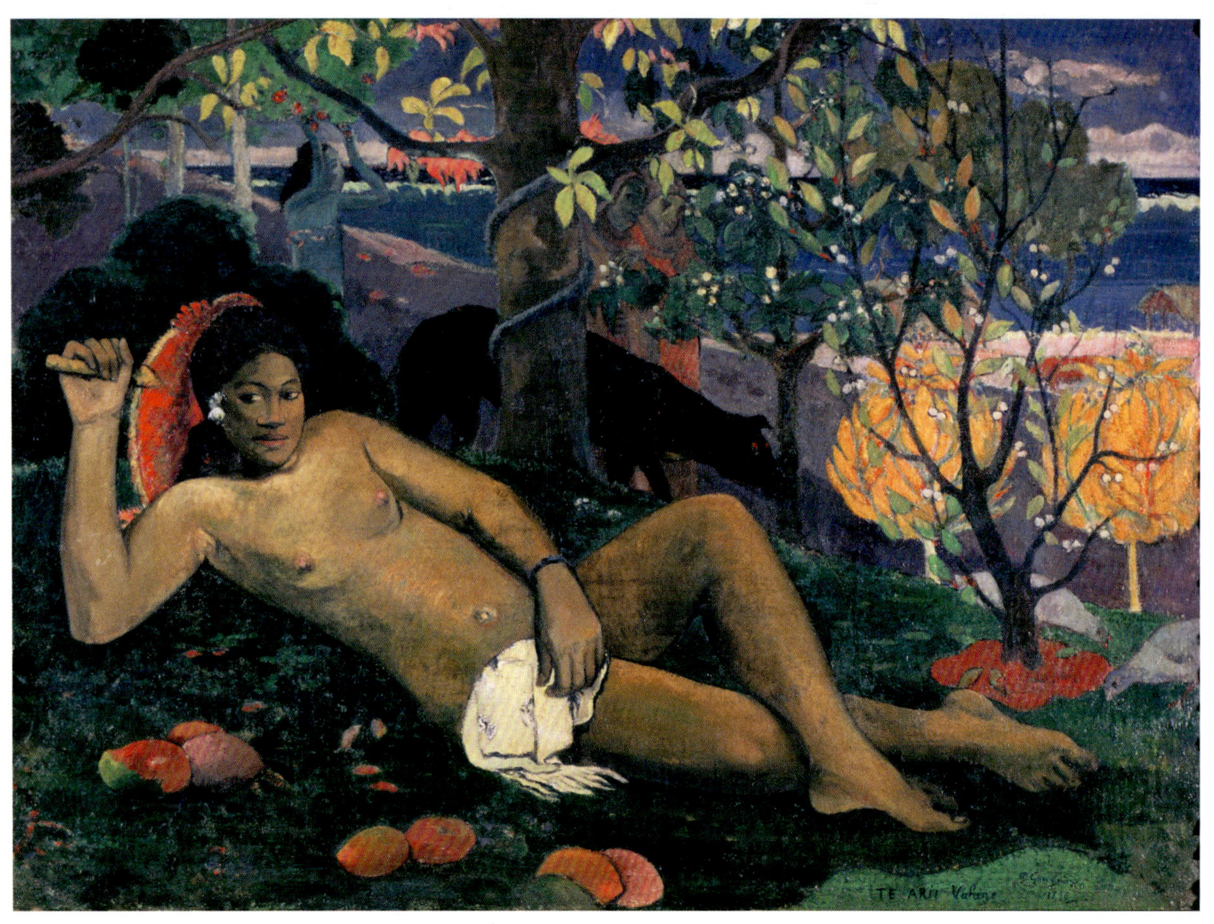

Ne Arii Vahine

(The Queen, the King's Wife)

(L'Épouse du roi)

(Die königliche Braut)

(La esposa del rey)

(La Sposa del re)

(De echtgenote van de koning)

1896, Oil on canvas/Huile sur toile, 97 × 130 cm, Pushkin Museum, Moscow

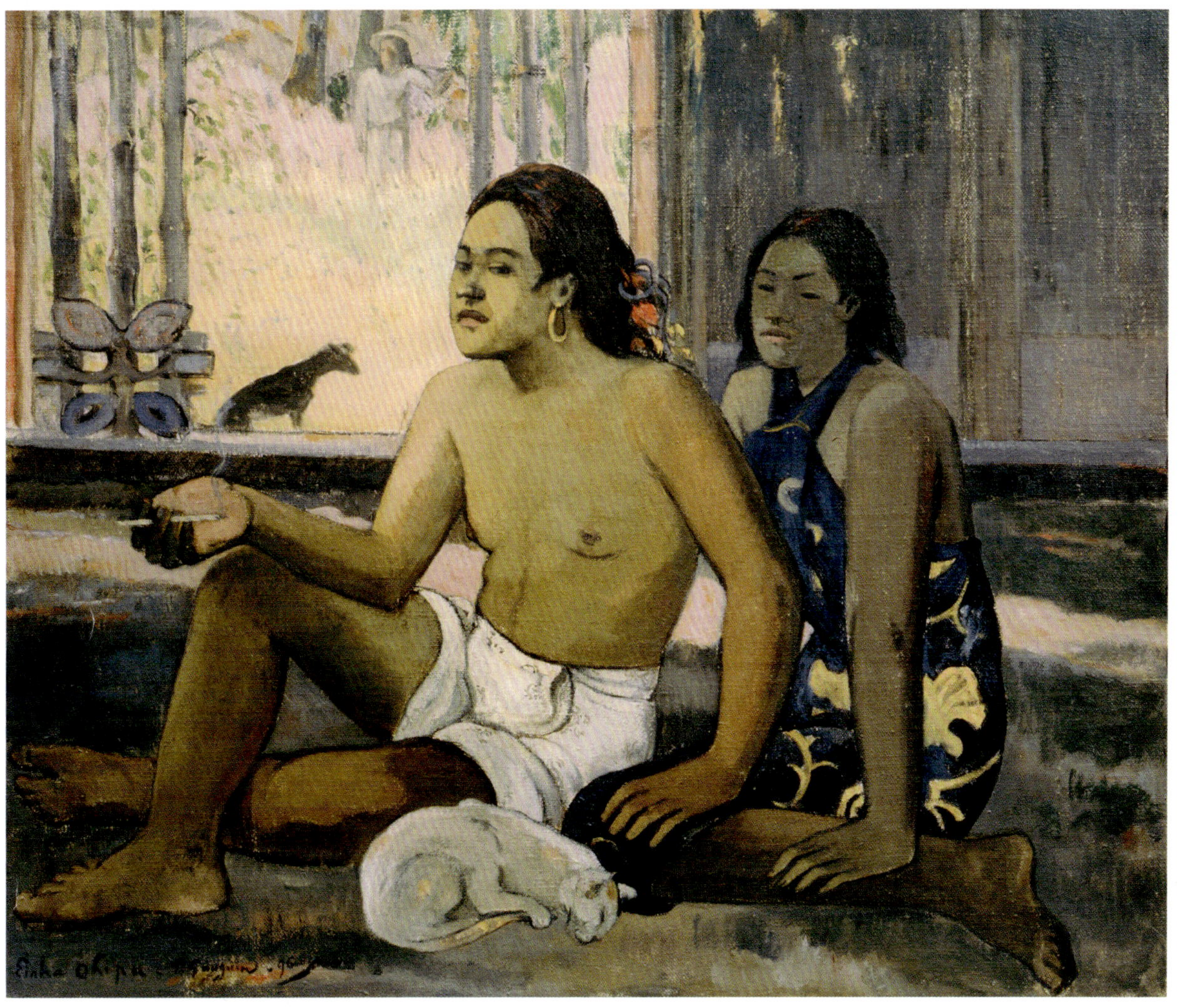

Eiaha Ohipa

(Tahitians in a Room) **(Tahitianer in einem Zimmer)** **(taitiani in una camera)**

(Tahitiens dans une chambre) **(Tahitianas en una habitación)** **(Tahitianen in een kamer)**

1896, Oil on canvas/Huile sur toile, 65 × 75 cm, Pushkin Museum, Moscow

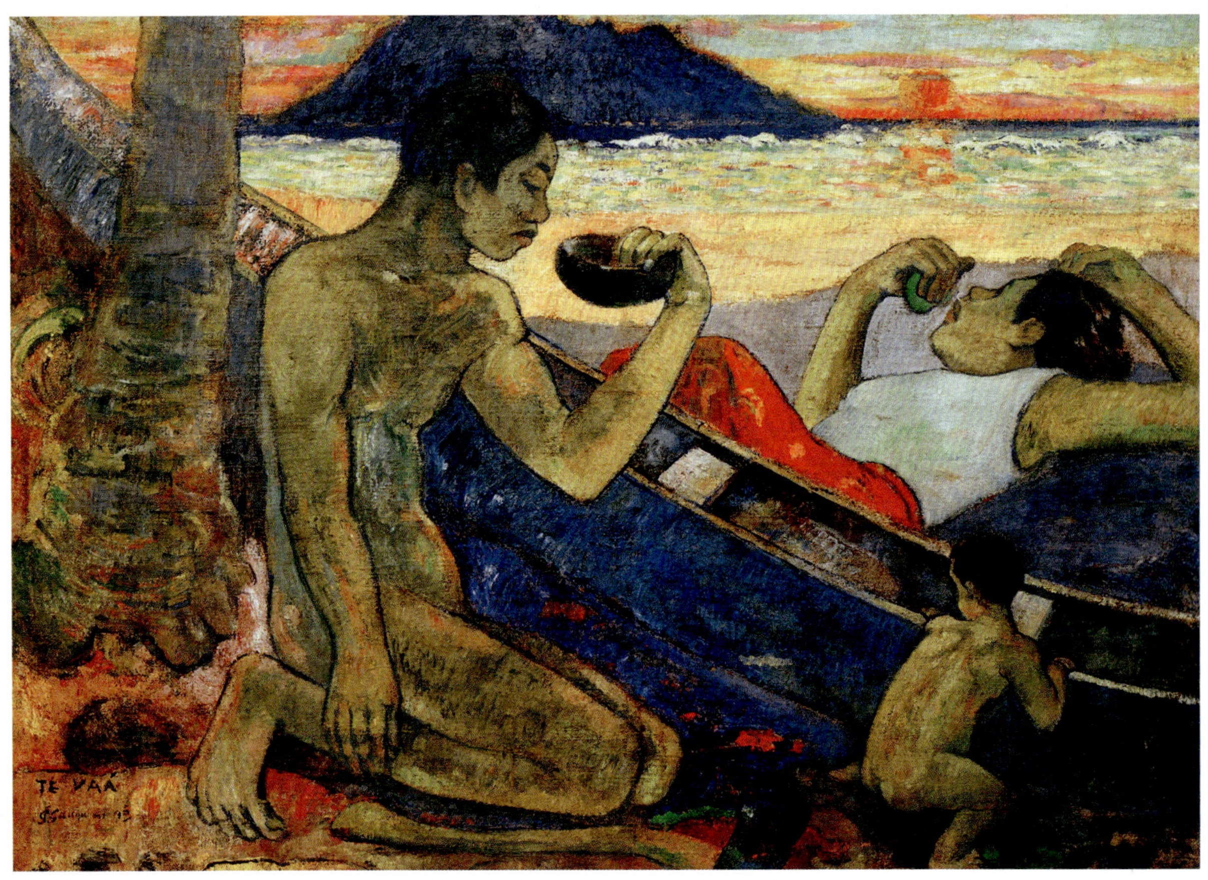

Te vaa

(The Canoe)

(Le Canoë)

(Der Einbaum)

(La canoa)

(Le Canoe)

(De kano)

1896, Oil on canvas/Huile sur toile, 95,5 × 131,5 cm, State Hermitage Museum, St. Petersburg

236

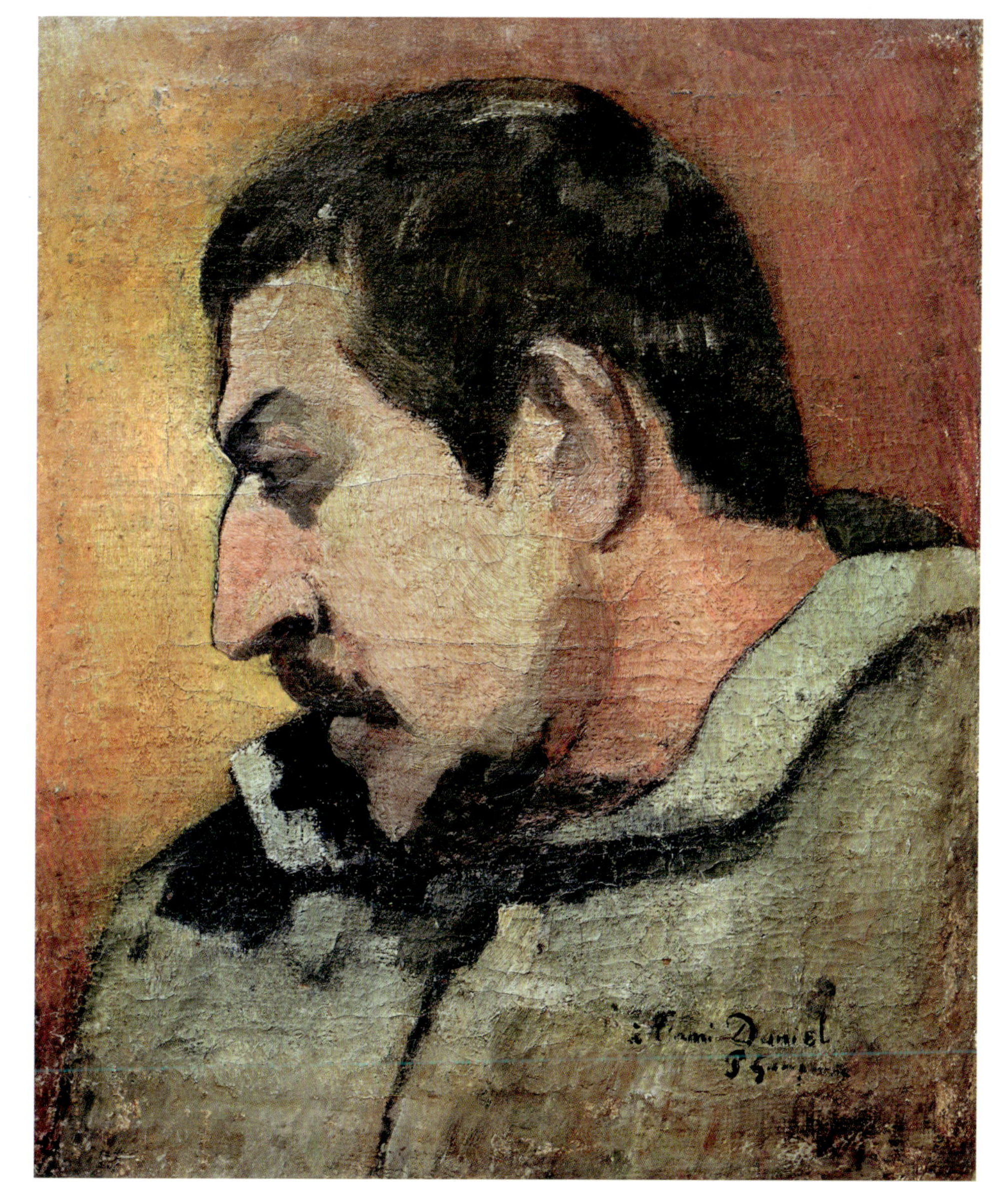

Portrait of the Artist
Portrait de l'artiste
Bildnis des Künstlers
Retrato del artista
Ritratto dell'artista
Portret van de kunstenaar

1896, Oil on canvas/Huile sur toile, 40 × 32 cm, Musée d'Orsay, Paris

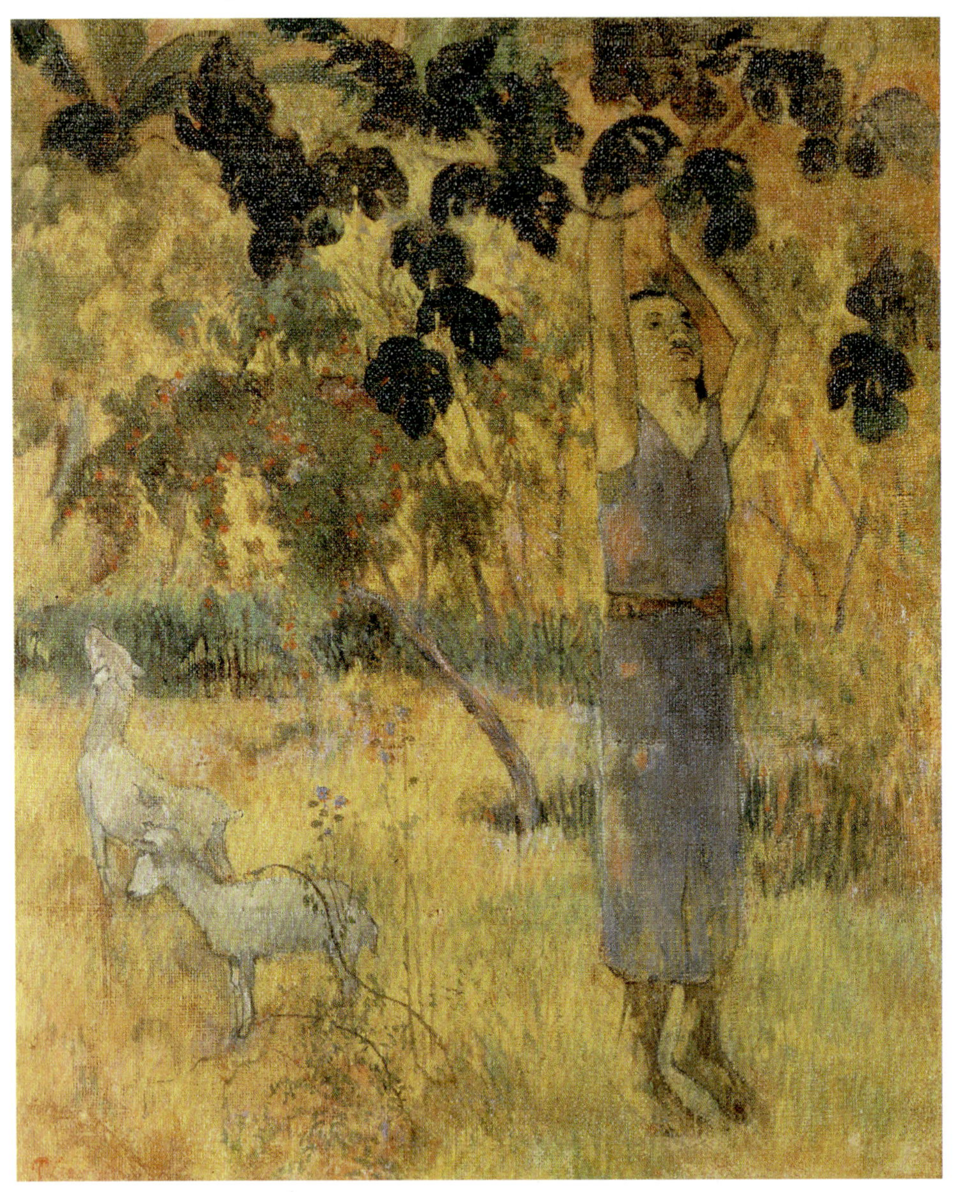

**Man Picking Fruit
from a Tree**

Homme ceuillant un fruit

Mann beim Obstpflücken

**Hombre cosechando
un fruto**

Uomo che coglie un frutto

Man bij de fruitoogst

*1897, Oil on canvas/Huile
sur toile, 92,5 × 73,3 cm,
State Hermitage Museum,
St. Petersburg*

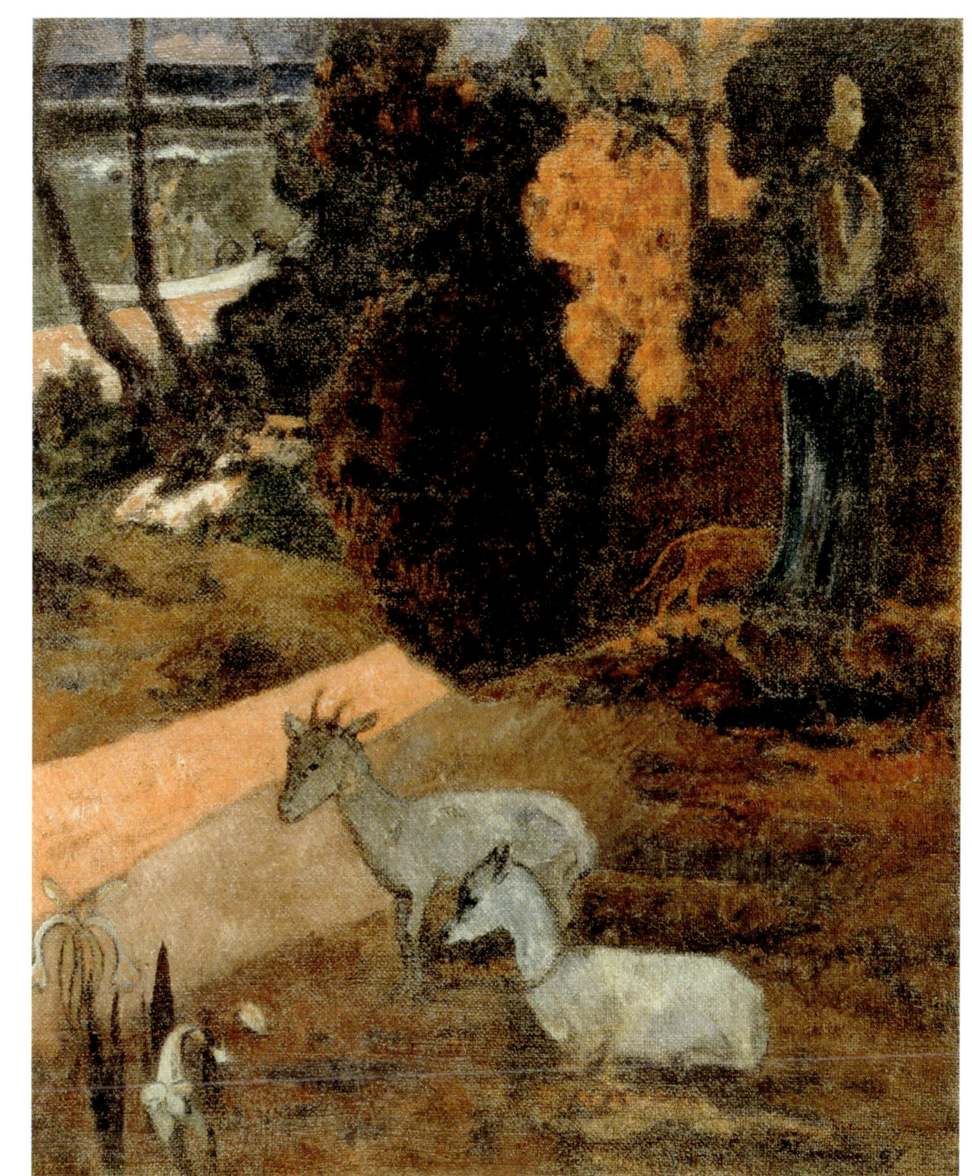

Tarari Maruru
(Landscape with Two Goats)
(Paysage aux deux chèvres)
(Landschaft mit zwei Ziegen)
(Paisaje con dos cabras)
(Paesaggio con due capre)
(Landschap met twee geiten)

1897, Oil on canvas/Huile sur toile, 92,5 × 73 cm, State Hermitage Museum, St. Petersburg

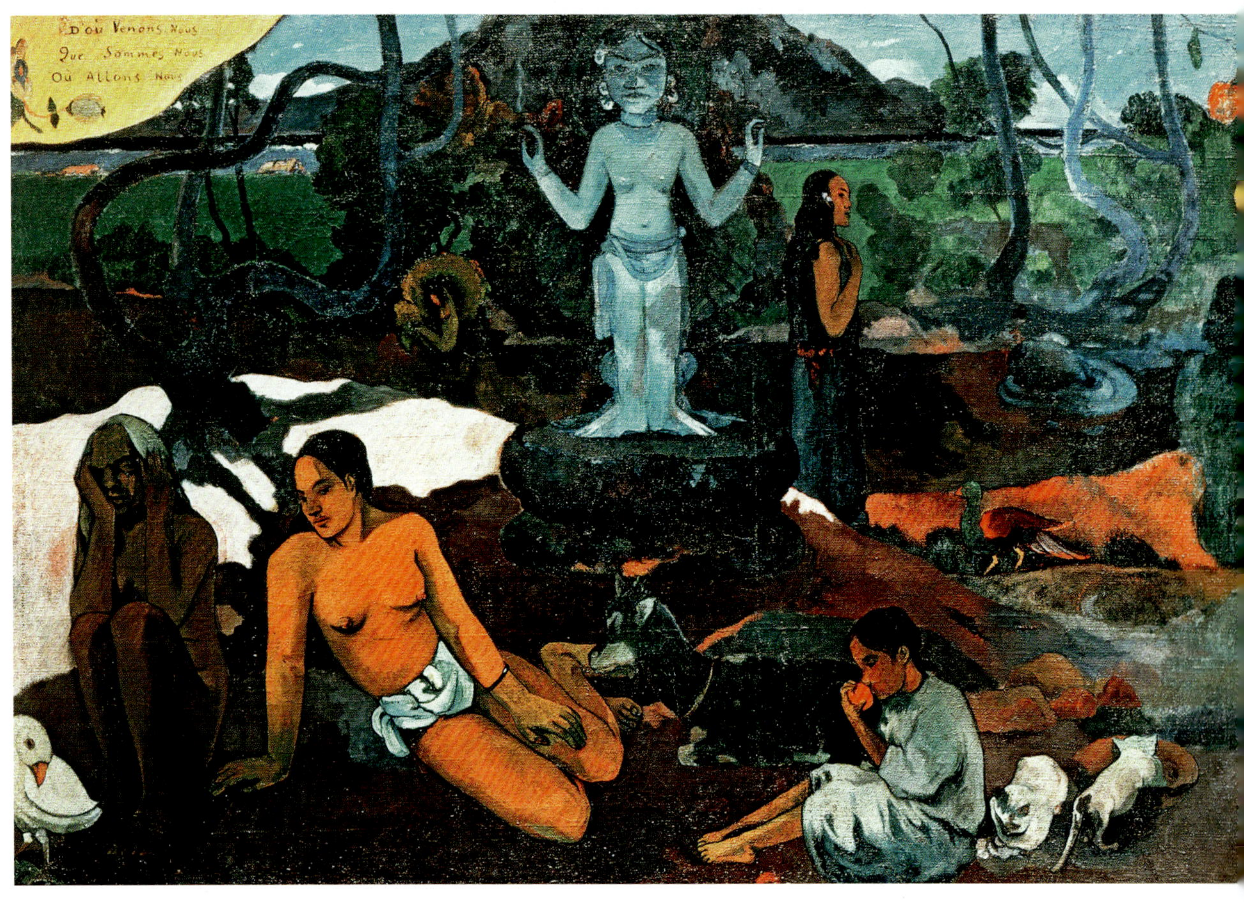

This particularly ambitious metaphysical frieze—conceived by the painter whilst in the depth of his depression—is a summary of existential questions that had plagued him. His artistic testament, as he had confided to Monfried: "I believe this painting does not just surpass in value all of the preceding ones. I have put all of my energy into it, a painful passion in terrible circumstances, with a vision so clear that haste disappears and life arises from it."

Particulièrement ambitieuse, cette frise métaphysique – conçue par le peintre alors qu'il est au plus profond de sa dépression – est un condensé des questions existentielles qui le tourment. Son testament artistique, comme il le confie à Monfreid : « Je crois que non seulement cette toile dépasse en valeur toutes les précédentes. J'y ai mis là avant de mourir toute mon énergie, une telle passion douloureuse dans des circonstances terribles, et une vision tellement nette sans corrections, que le hâtif disparaît, et que la vie en surgit. »

Dieser metaphysische Fries ist besonders ambitioniert. Vom Maler am Tiefpunkt seiner Depression entworfen ist es eine Verdichtung der ihn quälenden existenziellen Fragen. Sein künstlerisches Testament, wie er Monfreid anvertraut: „Ich glaube, dass dieses Werk nicht nur alle seine Vorgänger übertrifft. Ich habe in dieses Gemälde meine ganze Energie gesteckt, bevor ich sterbe, eine derart schmerzliche Leidenschaft in verheerenden Umständen und solch eine deutliche Vision ohne Korrekturen, dass jegliche Eile verschwindet, und das Leben daraus aufersteht."

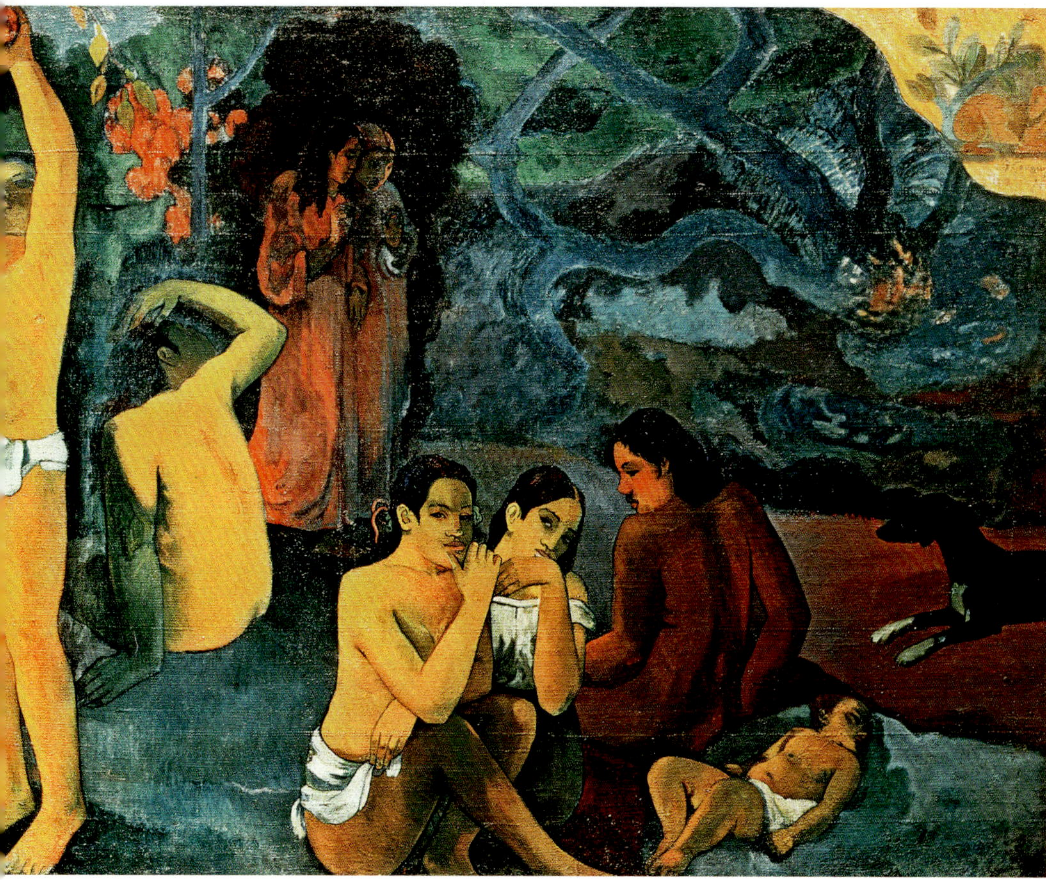

Particularmente ambiciosa, esta pieza metafísica, concebida por el pintor cuando se hallaba en lo más profundo de su depresión, es una condensación de estas cuestiones existenciales que le atormentan. Su testamento artístico, tal y como le confiesa a Monfreid: "No solo creo que este lienzo sobrepasa en valor a todos los anteriores. Antes de morir he plasmado en él mi energía, una pasión tan dolorosa en estas circunstancias terribles y una visión tan limpia sin correcciones, que la prisa desaparece y a vida resurge."

Particolarmente ambizioso, questo fregio metafisico – disegnato dal pittore quand'egli è nella profondità della sua depressione – è un condensato di domande esistenziali che lo tormentano. La sua eredità artistica, come confidò a Monfreid: "Io credo che non solo questo dipinto superi ogni valore precedente. Ho messo via prima di morire tutta la mia energia, una tale passione dolorosa in circostanze terribili, e una visione così chiara e senza correzione, che l'avventato scompare, e la vita spunta fuori. "

Dit uitzonderlijk ambitieuze metafysische fries – dat de schilder op het dieptepunt van zijn depressie maakt – is een beknopte weergave van de existentiële vragen die hem benauwen. Zijn artistieke testament, vertrouwt hij Monfreid toe: "Ik denk dat dit schilderij al de voorgaande niet alleen in waarde overtreft. Ik heb er voordat ik overlijd al mijn energie in gestoken, zo'n pijnlijke passie in vreselijke omstandigheden, en zo'n duidelijke visie zonder correcties, dat het haastige verdwijnt en het leven eruit opspringt."

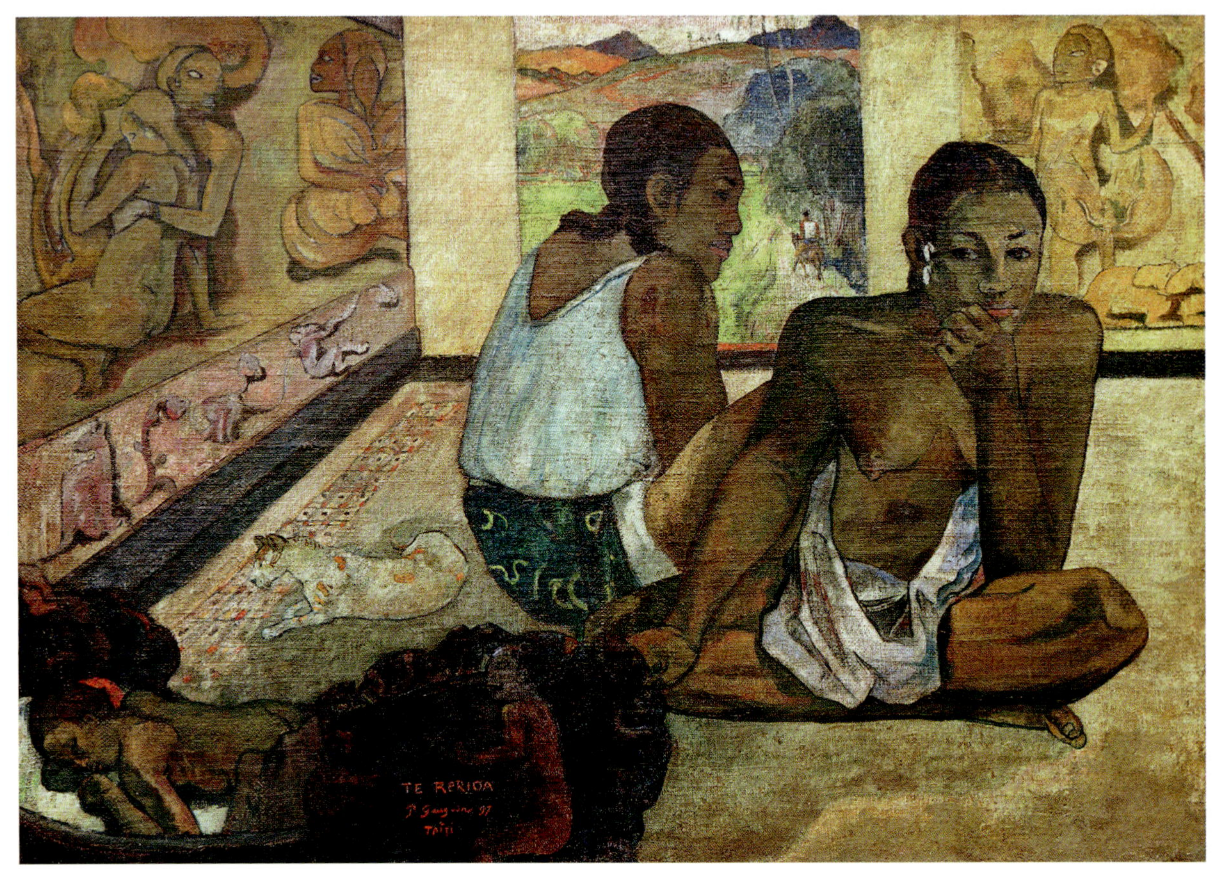

Te rerioa

(The Dream)

(Le Rêve)

(Der Traum)

(El sueño)

(Il Sogno)

(De droom)

1897, Oil on canvas/Huile sur toile, 95,1 × 130,2 cm, Courtauld Institute of Art, London

242

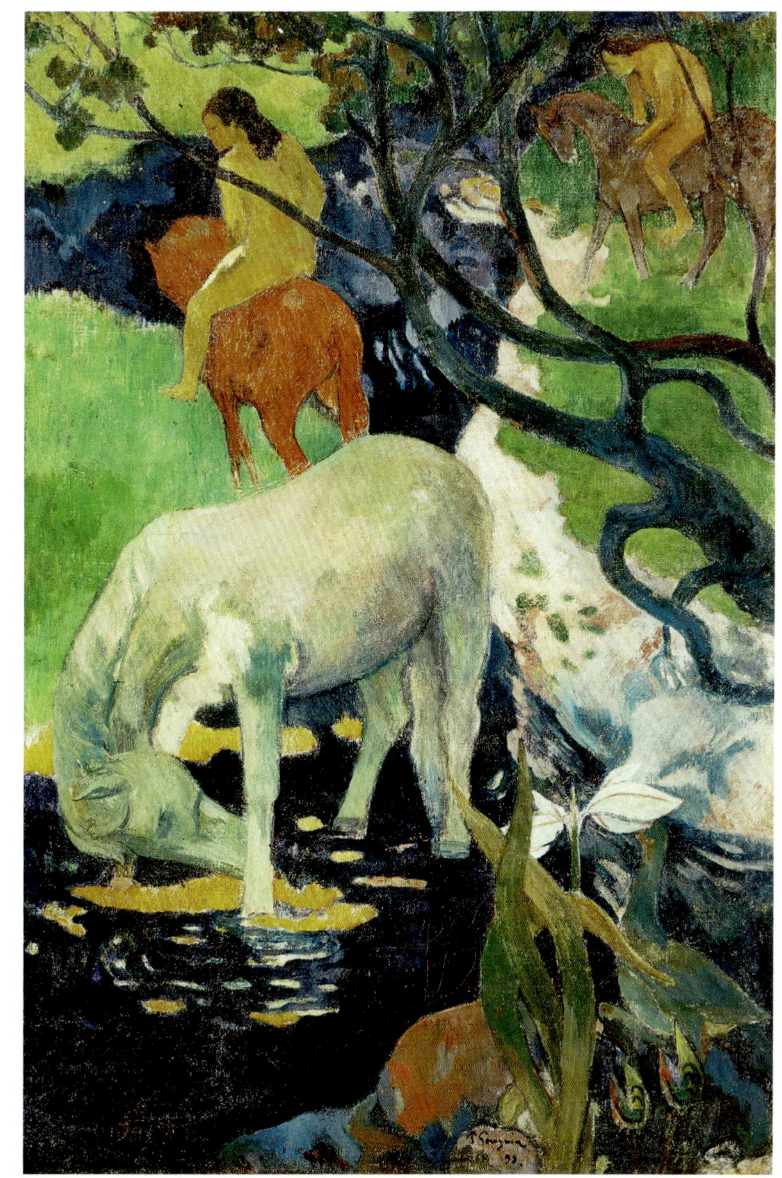

The White Horse

Le Cheval blanc

Der Schimmel

El caballo blanco

Il Cavallo bianco

De schimmel

1898, Oil on canvas/Huile sur toile, 140,5 × 92 cm,
Musée d'Orsay, Paris

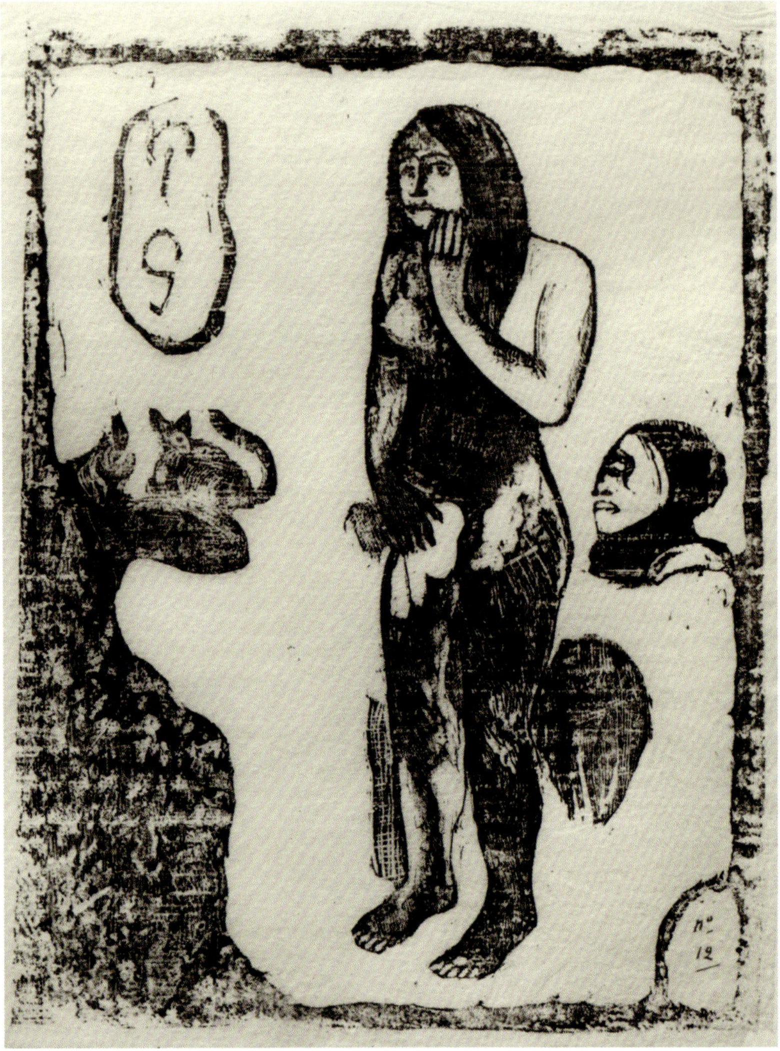

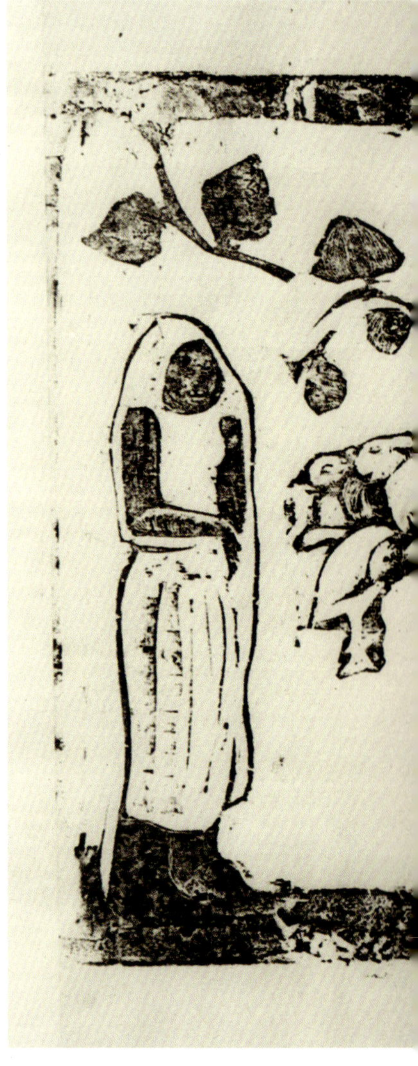

Ève

1898–99, Engraving on wood/Gravure sur bois, 28,3 × 21,5 cm, Private collection

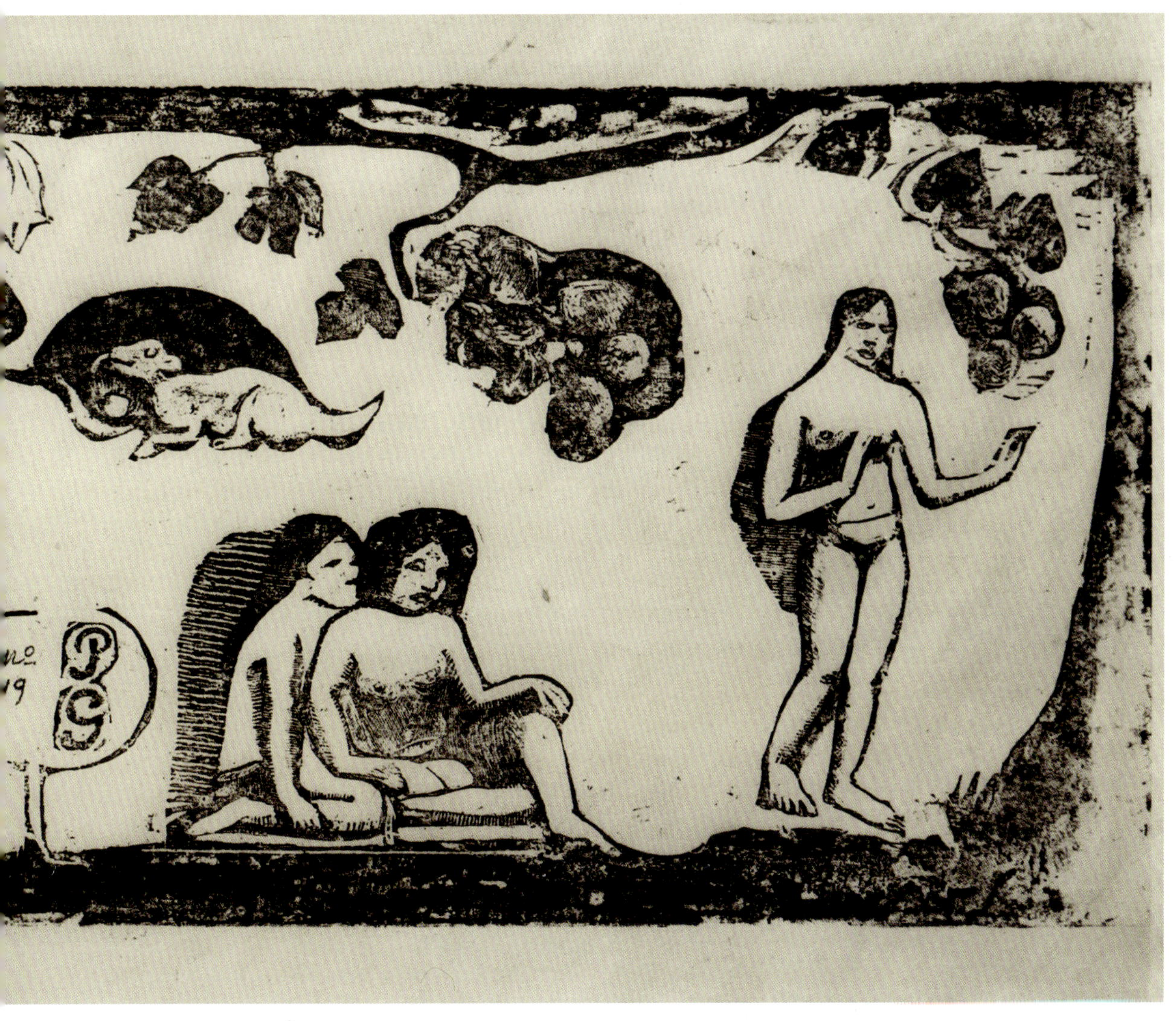

Women, Animals and Foliage　　　**Frauen, Tiere und Blattwerk**　　　**Donne, animali e fogliame**

Femmes, animaux et feuillages　　　**Mujeres, animales y hojas**　　　**Vrouwen, dieren en gebladerte**

1898, Engraving on wood/Gravure sur bois, 16,5 × 33,5 cm, Private collection

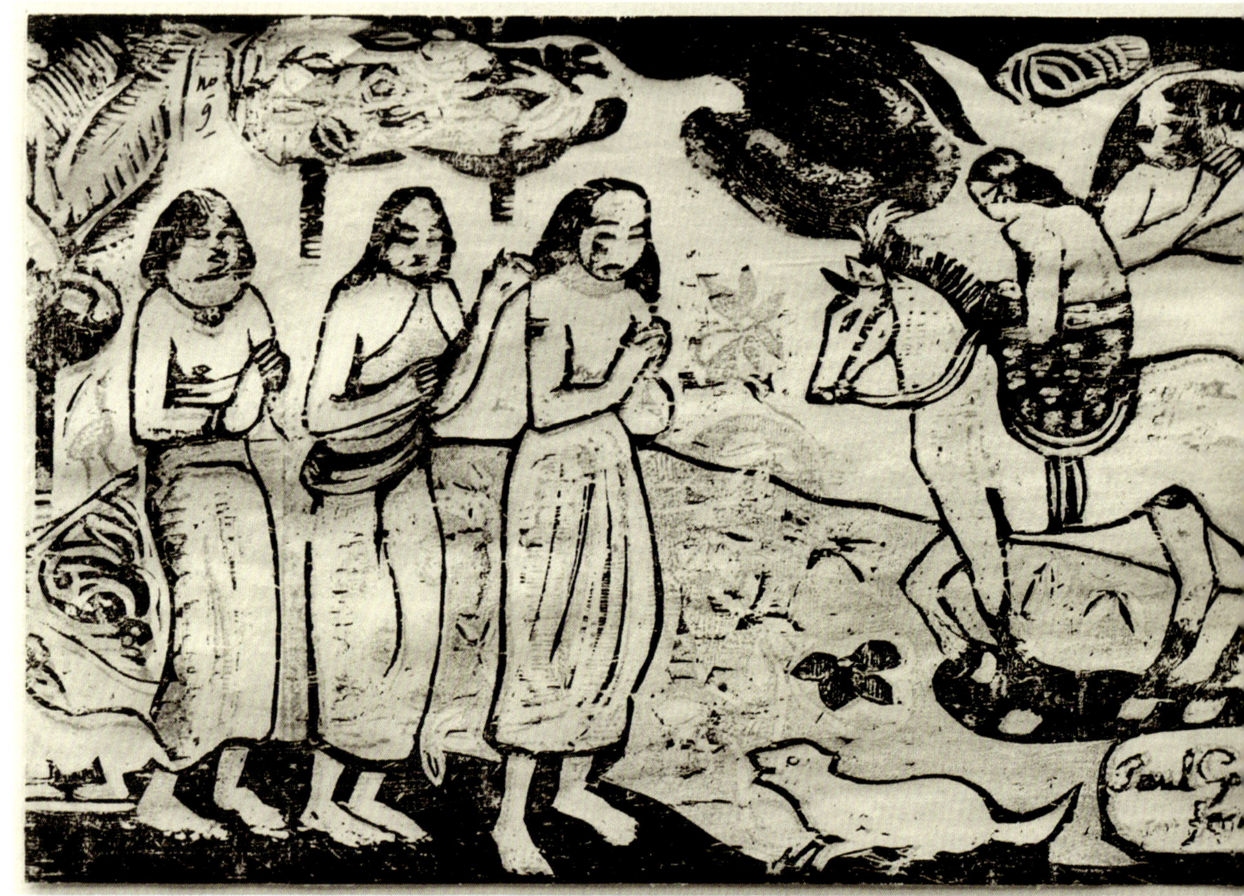

Change of Residence

Changement de résidence

Umzug

Cambio de residencia

Cambiamento di residenza

Verhuizing

1899, Engraving on wood/Gravure sur bois, 16 × 30,1 cm, Private collection

246

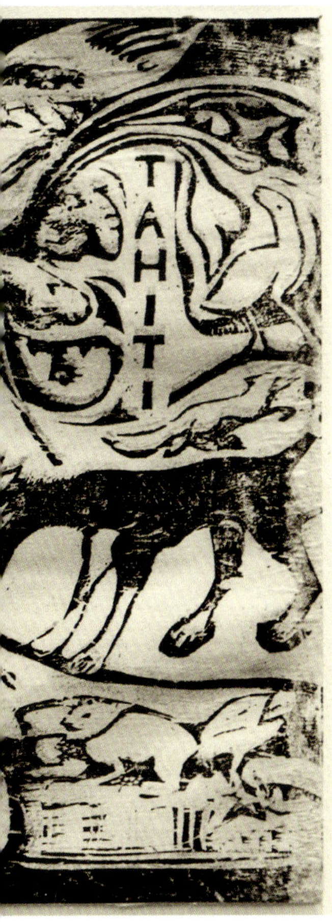

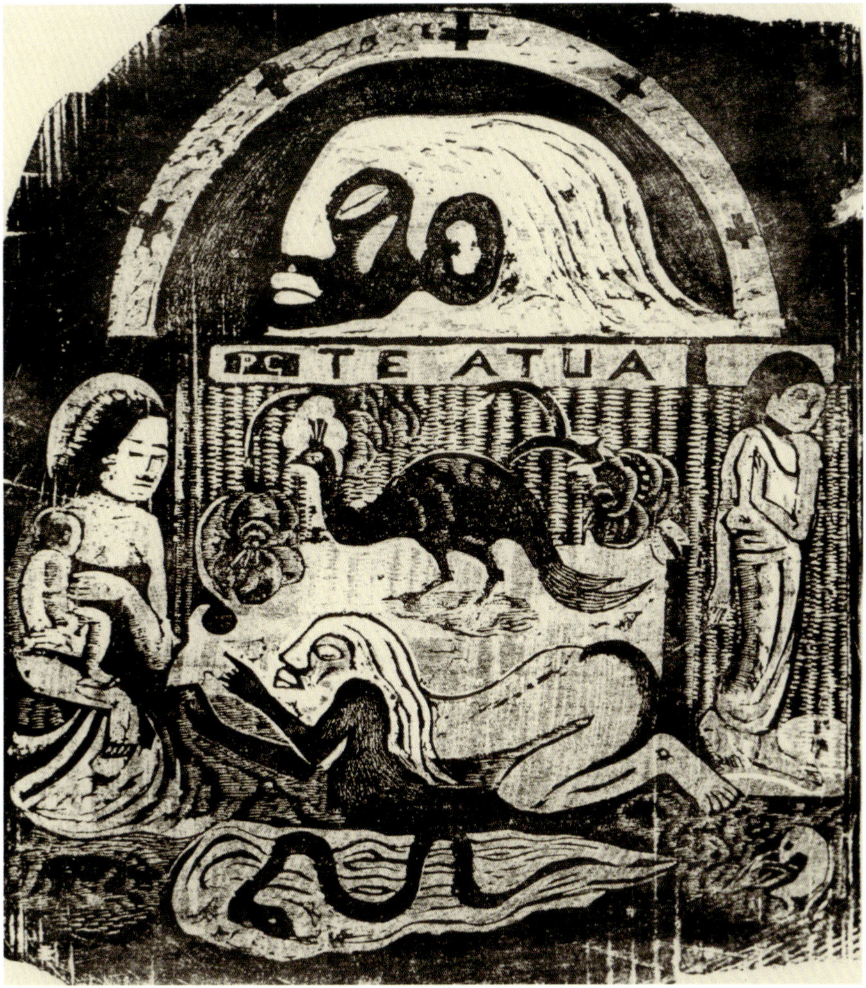

Te Atua

(The God)	*(Gott)*	*(Il Dio)*
(Le Dieu)	*(El Dios)*	*(De god)*

1899, Engraving on wood/Gravure sur bois, 24,4 × 22,7 cm, Private collection

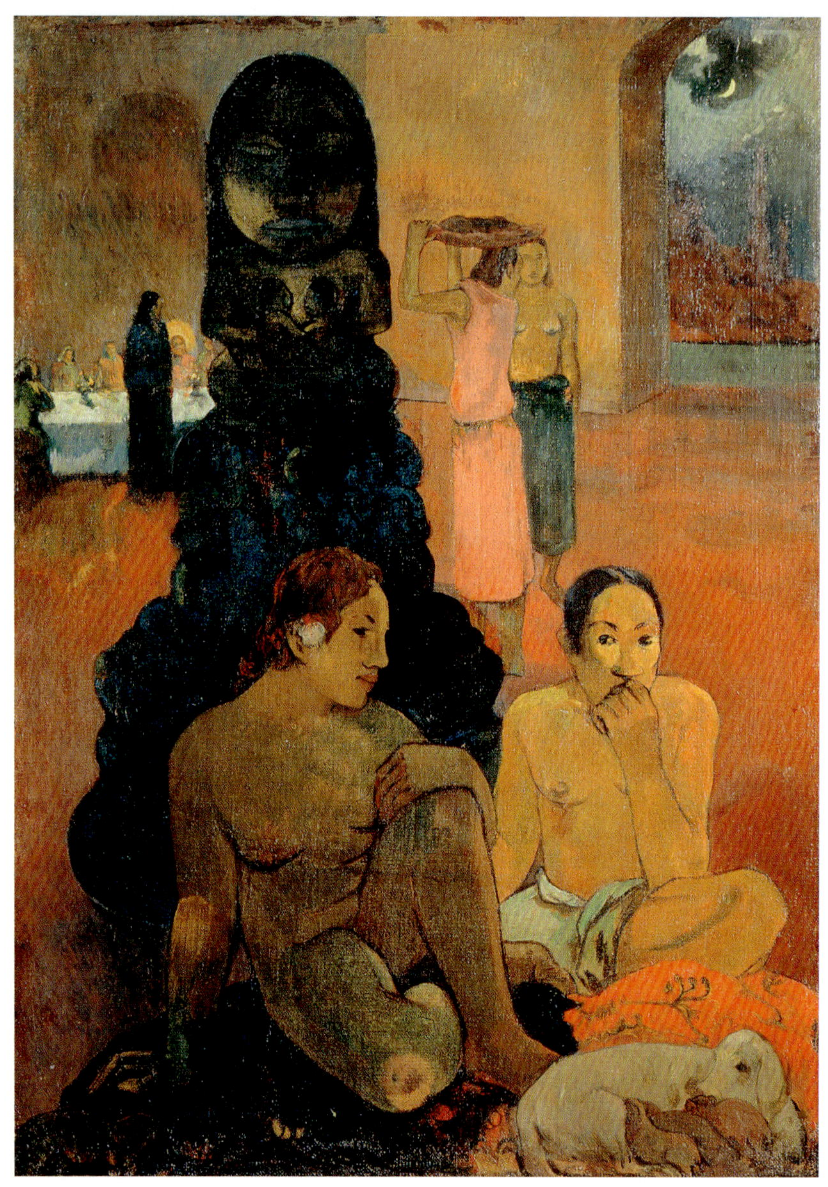

The Great Buddha
Le Grand Bouddha
Der große Buddha
El Gran Buda
Il Grande Budda
De grote Boeddha

1899, Oil on canvas/Huile sur toile, 134 × 95 cm,
Pushkin Museum, Moscow

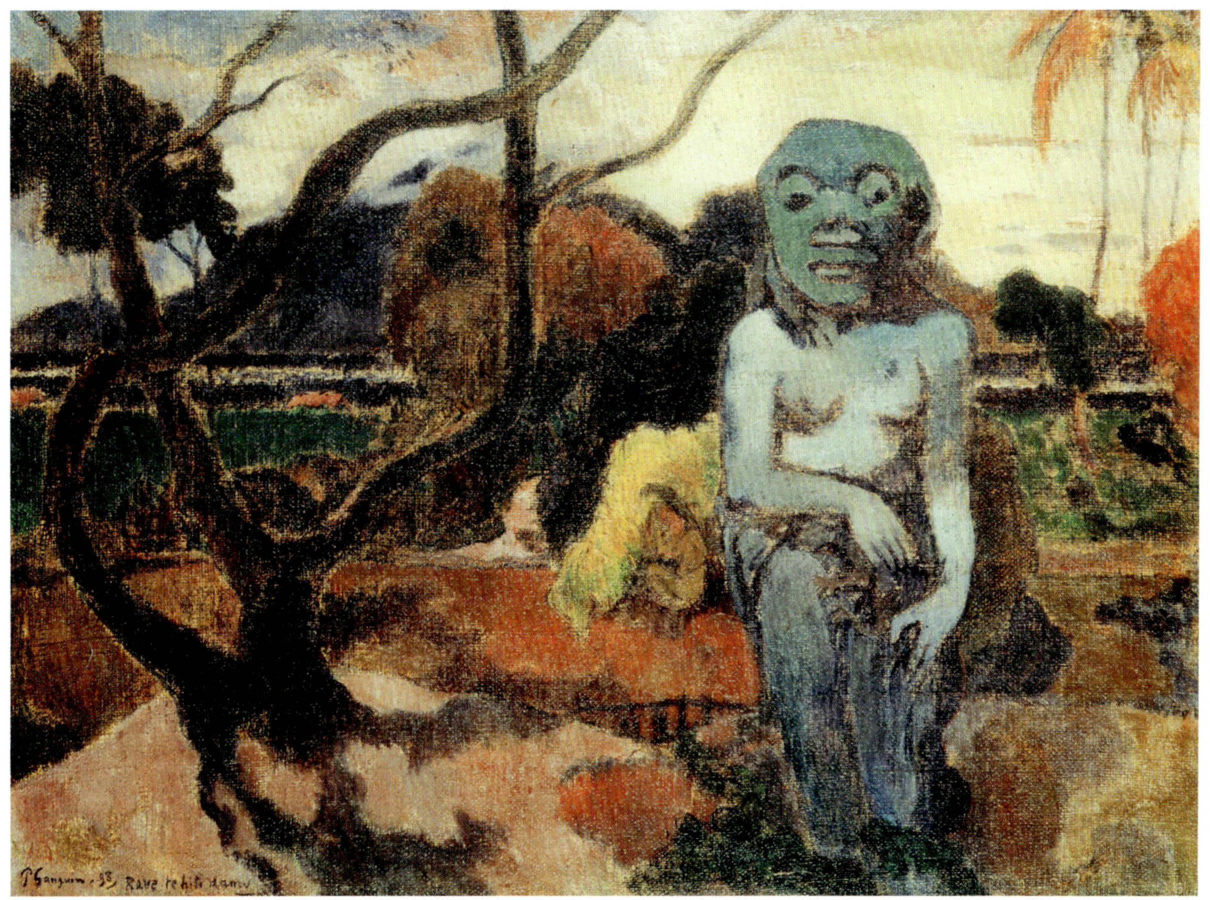

Rave Te Hiti Aamu

(The Idol)

(L'Idole)

(Götterfigur)

(El ídolo)

(L'Idolo)

(Het afgodsbeeld)

1898, Oil on canvas/Huile sur toile, 73,5 × 92 cm, State Hermitage Museum, St. Petersburg

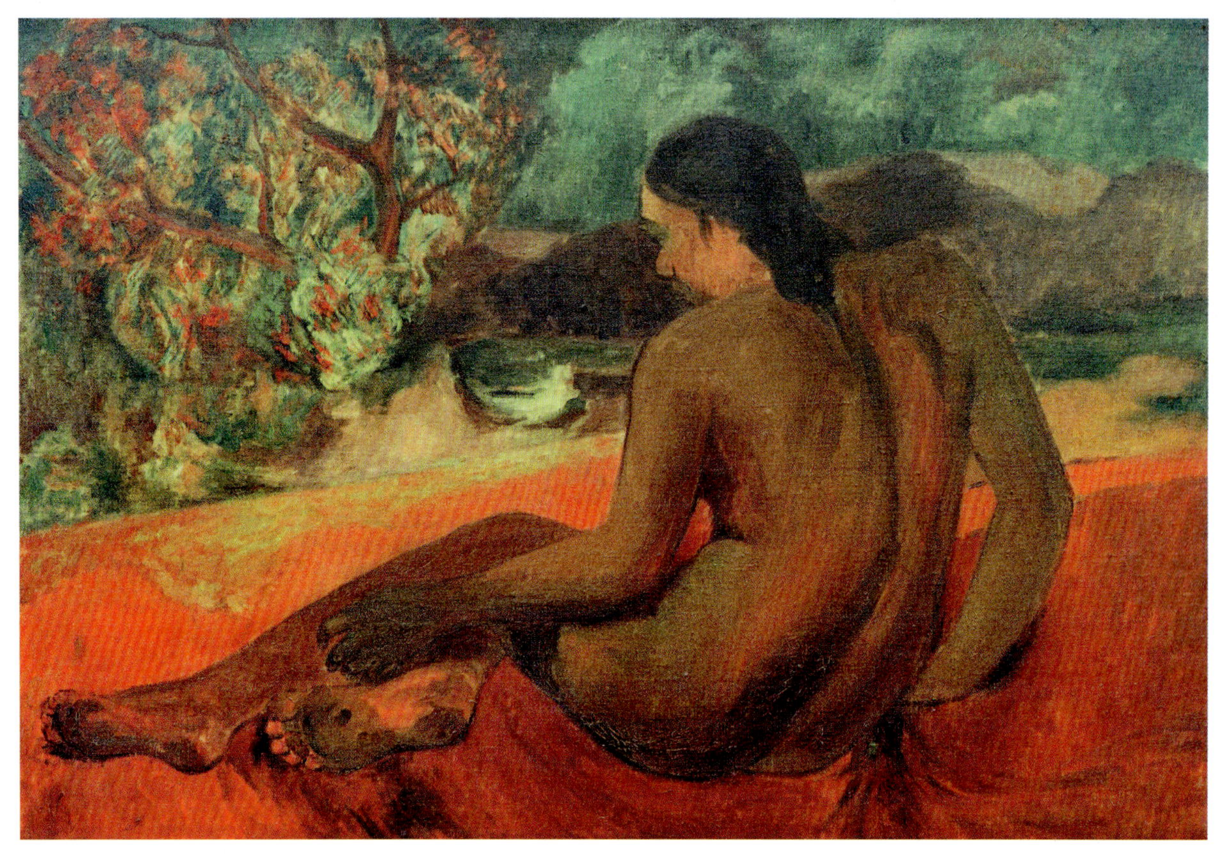

Tahitian Woman

Tahitienne

Tahitische Frau

Tahitiana

Tahitiana

Tahitiaanse vrouw

1898, Oil on canvas/Huile sur toile, 93,5 × 130 cm, Narodni muzej, Beograd

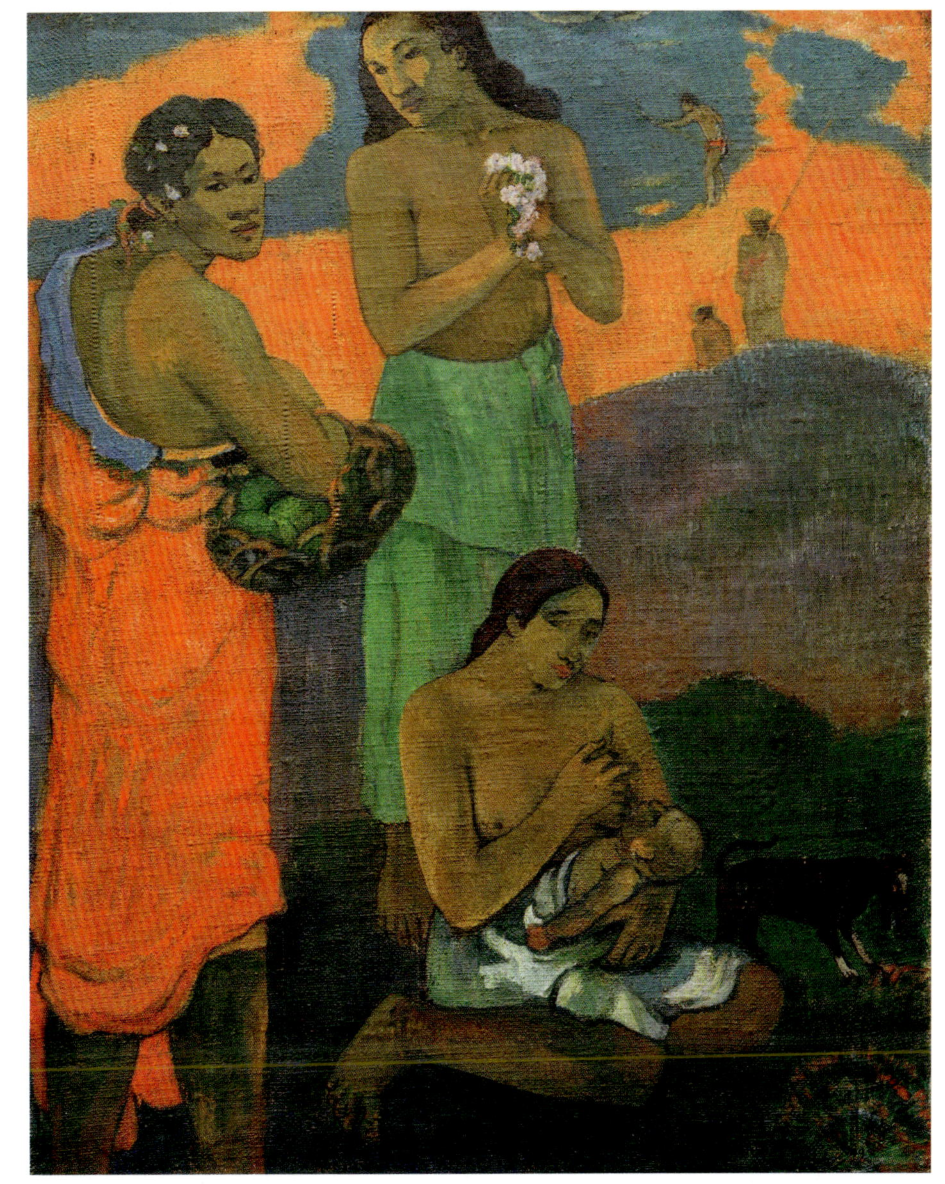

Women on the Seashore (Maternity)

Femmes au bord de la mer (Maternité)

Frauen am Meeresufer (Mutterschaft)

Mujeres a la orilla del mar (Maternidad)

Donne sul bordo del mare (Maternità)

Vrouwen aan de kust (Moederschap)

1899, Oil on canvas/Huile sur toile, 95,5 × 73,5 cm, State Hermitage Museum, St. Petersburg

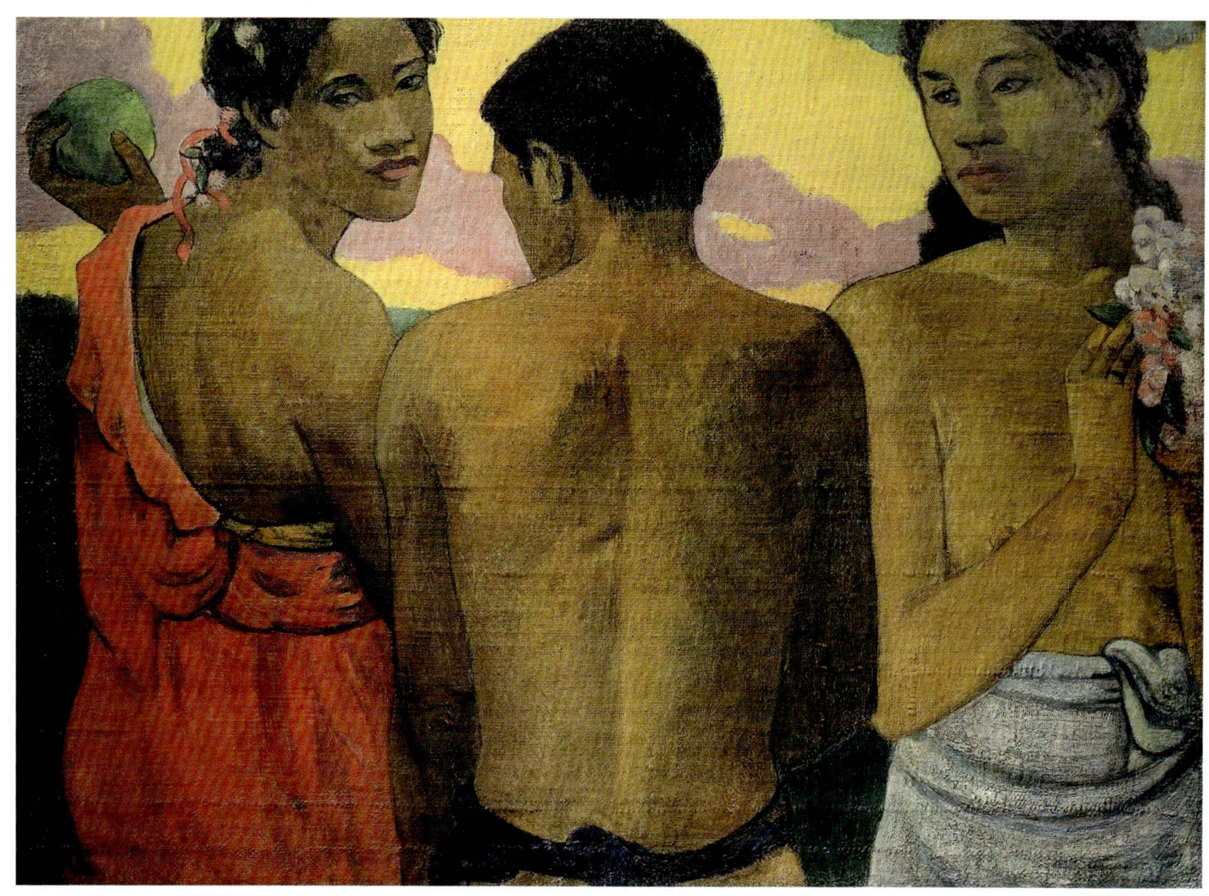

Three Tahitians

Trois Tahitiens

Drei Tahitianer

Tres tahitianas

Tre Tahitiani

Drie Tahitianen

1898, Oil on canvas/Huile sur toile, 73 × 93 cm, Scottish National Gallery of Modern Art, Edinburgh

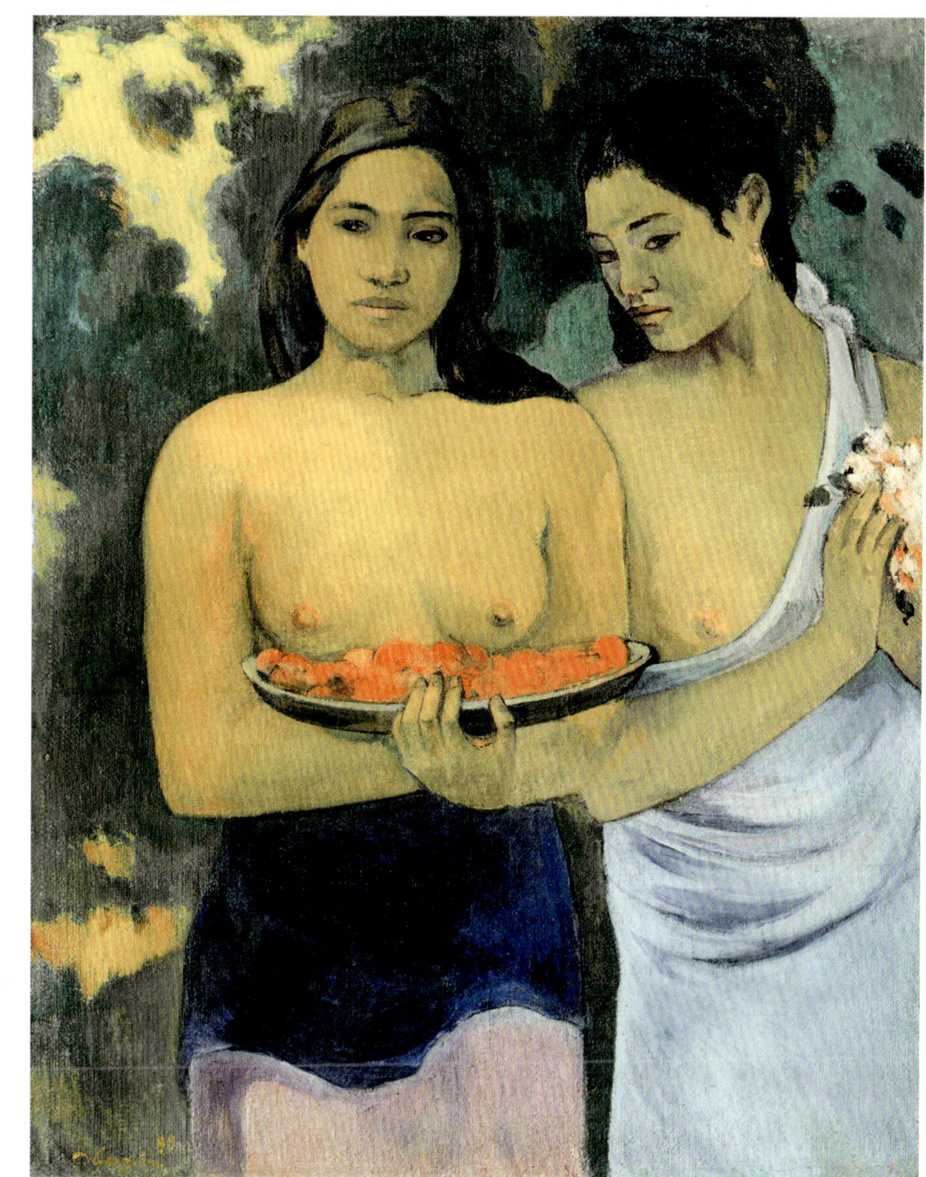

Two Tahitian Women or
Bosoms with Red Flowers

Deux Tahitiennes ou
Les Seins aux fleurs rouges

Zwei Tahitianerinnen oder
Brüste mit roten Blumen

Dos tahitianas o
Los senos con flores rojas

Due Tahitiane o
I Seni dai fiori rossi

*Twee Tahitiaanse
vrouwen* of *De borsten
met de rode bloemen*

*1899, Oil on canvas/Huile
sur toile, 94 × 72,4 cm,
Metropolitan Museum of Art,
New York*

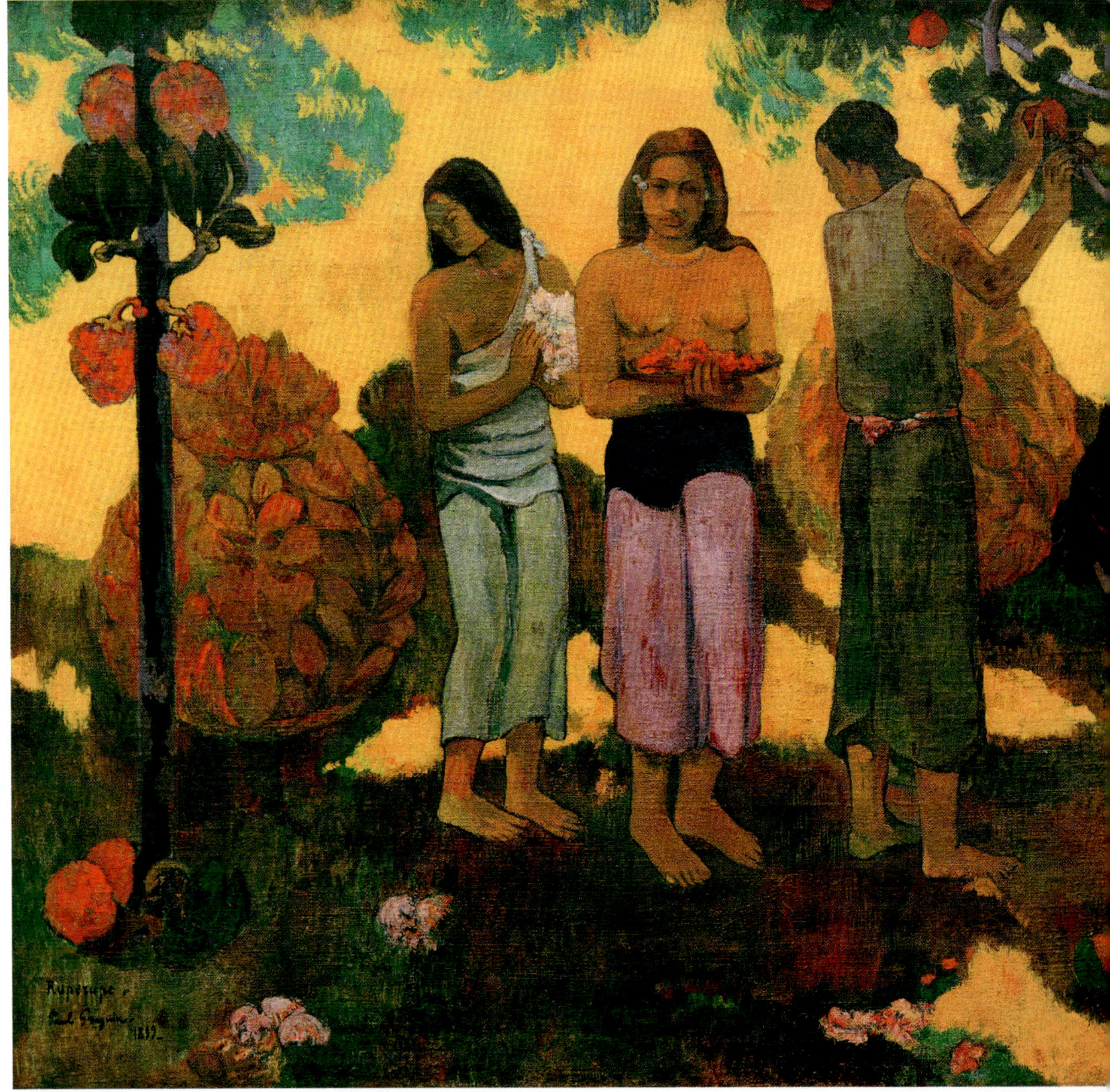
Ruperupe
Paul Gauguin
1899

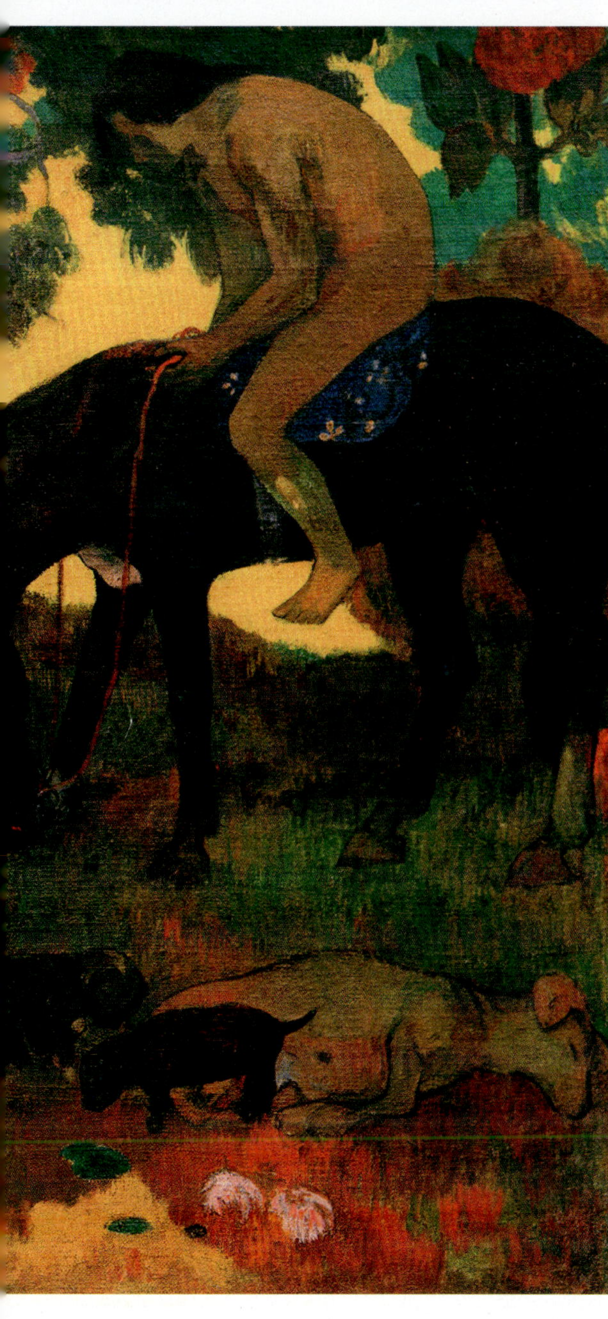

Rupe Rupe
(The Fruit Harvest)
(La Cueillette des fruits)
(Obsternte)
(La cosecha de las frutas)
(La raccolta della frutta)
(De fruitoogst)
1899, Oil on canvas/Huile sur toile, 128 × 190 cm, Pushkin Museum, Moscow

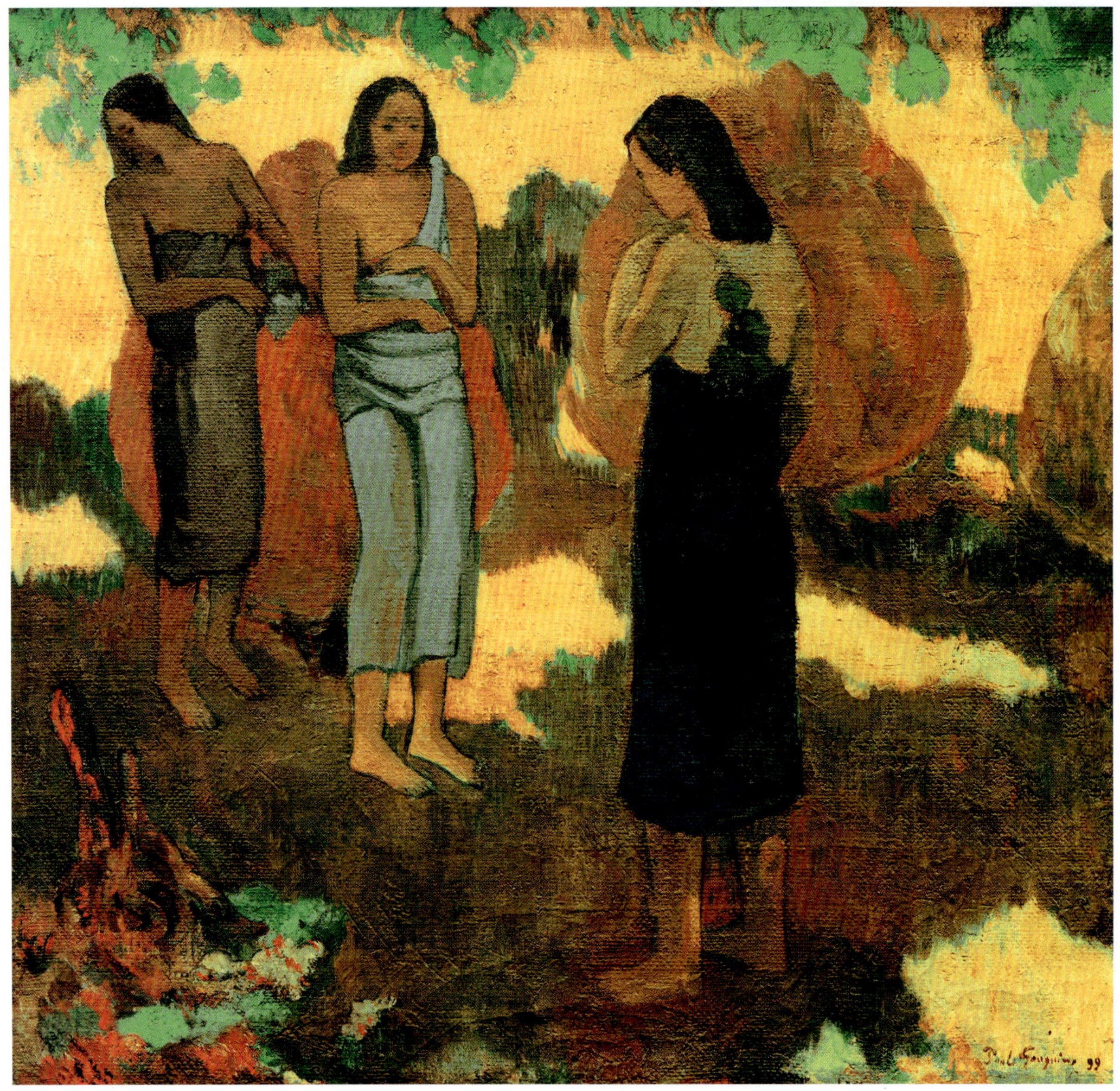

*Three Tahitian Women
against a Yellow Background*

*Trois Tahitiennes sur
un fond jaune*

*Drei Tahitianerinnen
vor gelbem Grund*

*Tres tahitianas sobre
fondo amarillo*

Tre Tahitiane su fondo giallo

*Drie Tahitiaanse vrouwen
tegen een gele achtergrond*

*1899, Oil on canvas/Huile sur
toile, 68 × 73,5 cm,
State Hermitage Museum,
St. Petersburg*

Te avae no Maria

(The Month of Mary)

(Le Mois de Marie)

(Marienmonat Mai)

(El mes de María)

(Il mese di Maria)

(De Maria-maand mei)

*1899, Oil on canvas/Huile
sur toile, 96 × 74,4 cm,
State Hermitage Museum,
St. Petersburg*

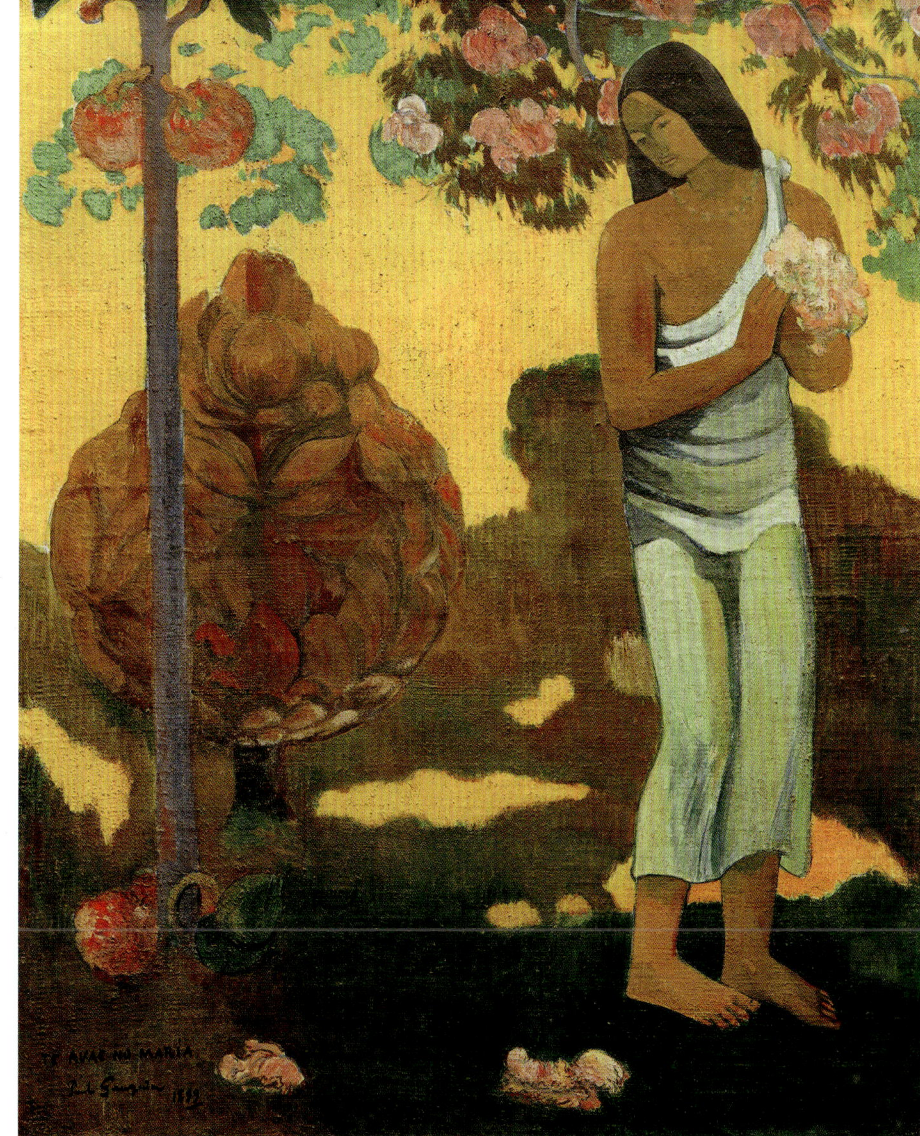

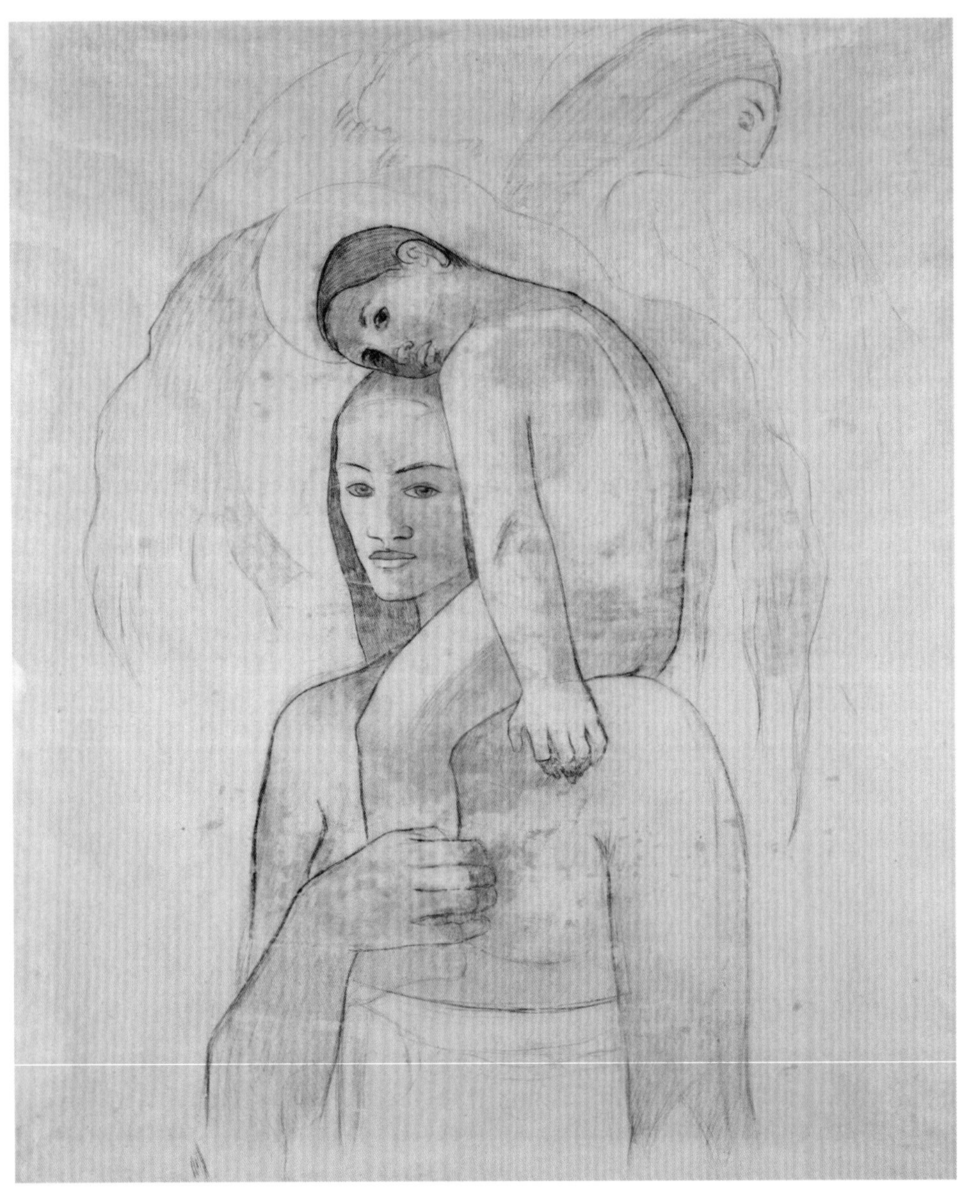

Ia orana Maria

(Hail Mary)

(Je vous salue Marie)

(Gegrüßet seist du, Maria)

(Yo te saludo, María)

(Vi saluto Maria)

(Wees gegroet Maria)

1899–1900, Pencil on paper/Crayon sur papier, 63,5 × 51,2 cm, Private collection

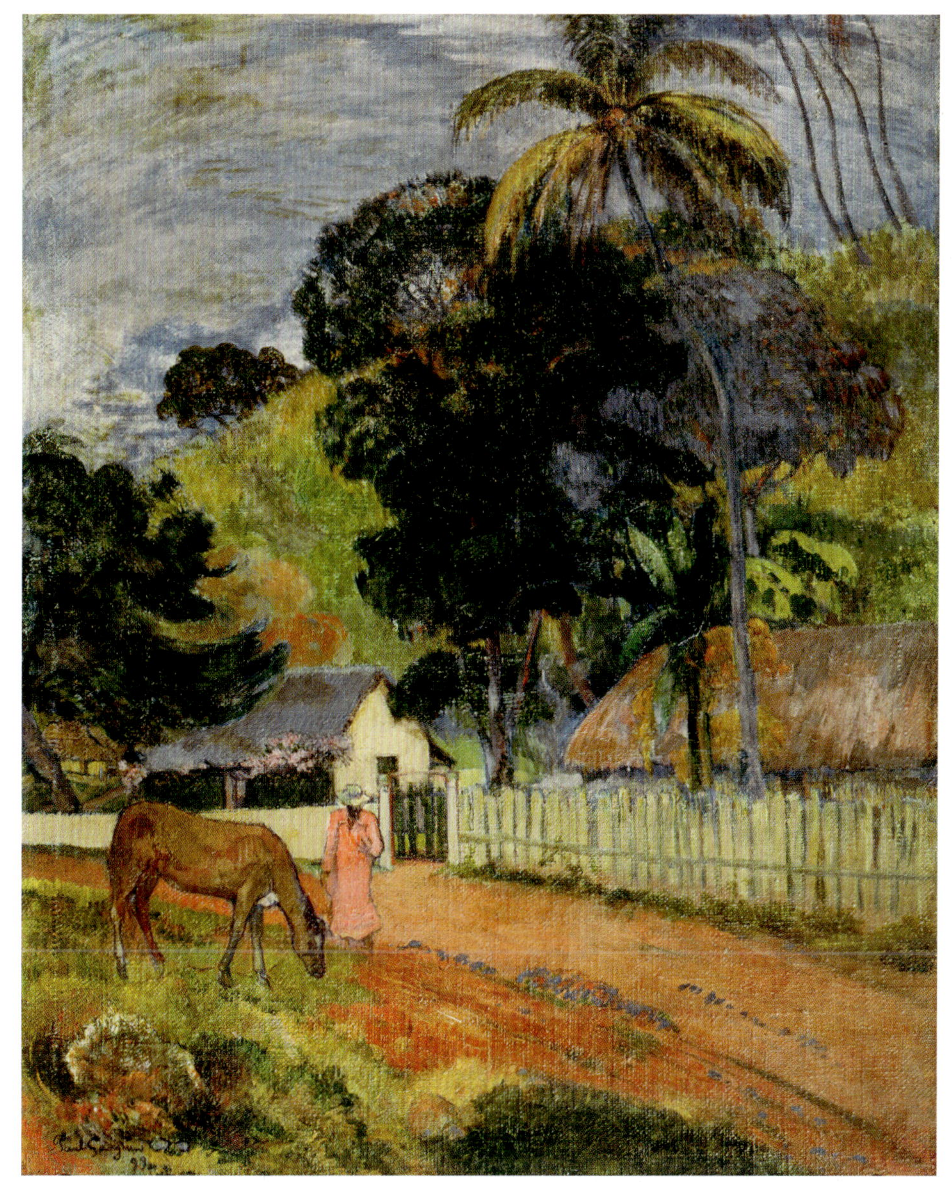

Horse on Road

Le Cheval sur le chemin

Pferd auf dem Weg

El caballo en el camino

Il cavallo sul sentiero

Het paard op het pad

1899, Oil on canvas/Huile sur toile, 94 × 73 cm, Pushkin Museum, Moscow

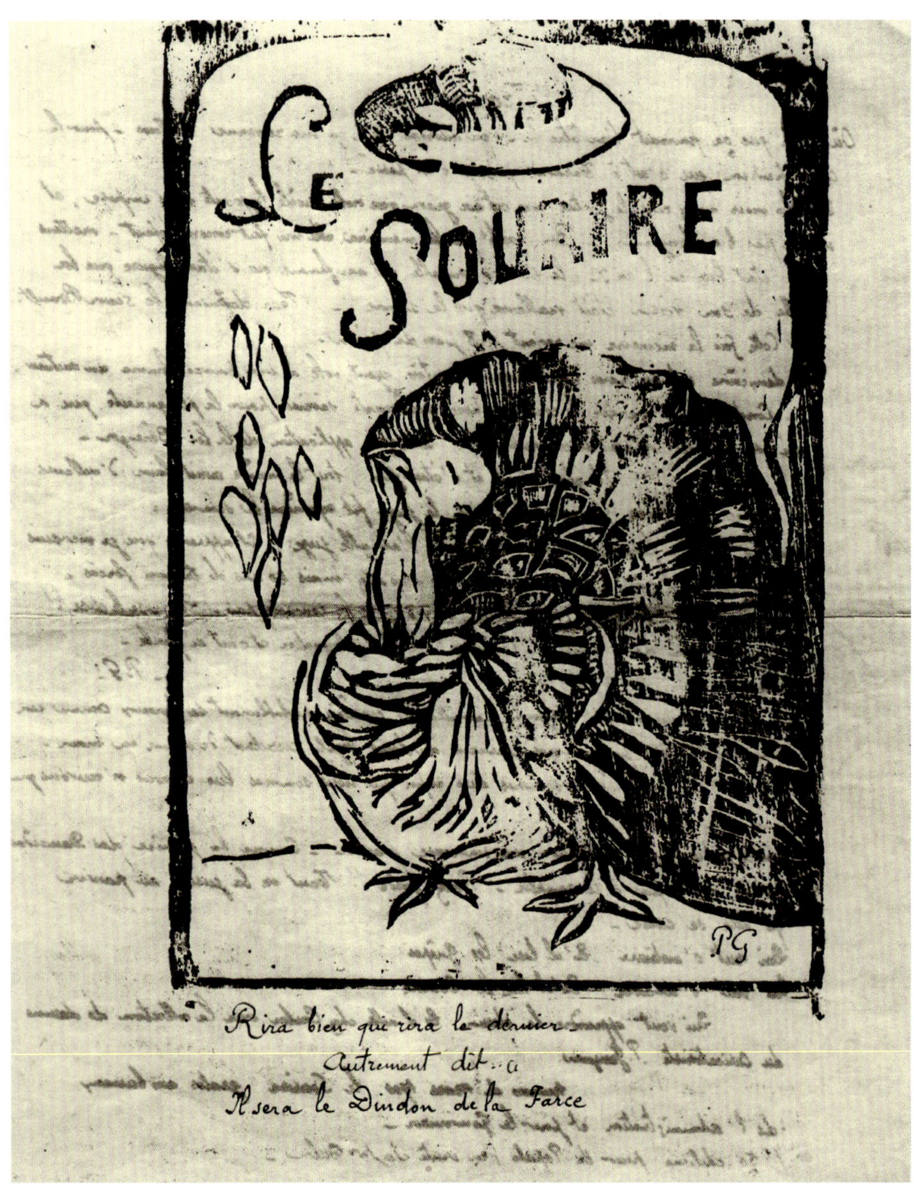

Le Sourire, **title page**

Le Sourire, **page de titre**

Le Sourire, **Titelblatt**

Le Sourire, **página de título**

Le Sourire, **frontespizio**

Le Sourire, **titelpagina**

1900, Engraving on wood/Gravure sur bois, 26 × 16 cm, Private collection

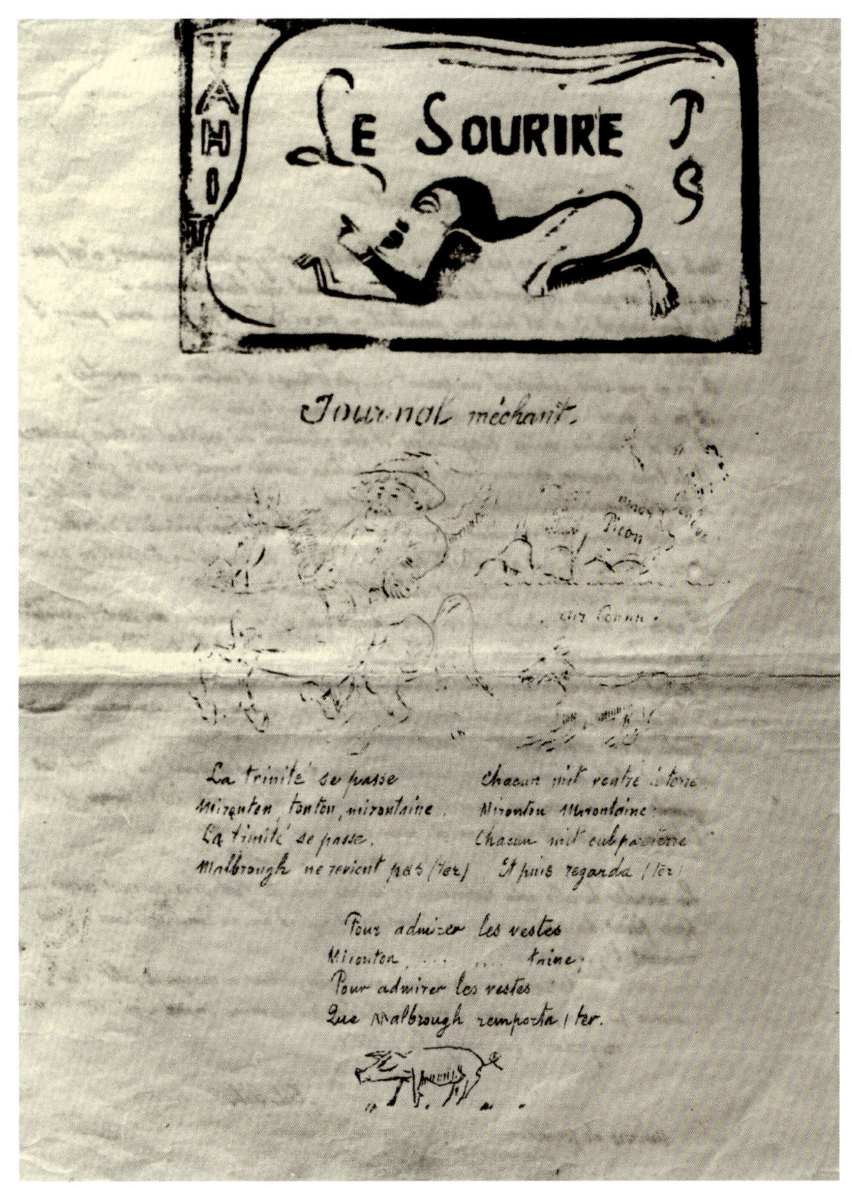

Le Sourire

1900, Engraving on wood/Gravure sur bois,
9,7 × 16,5 cm, Private collection

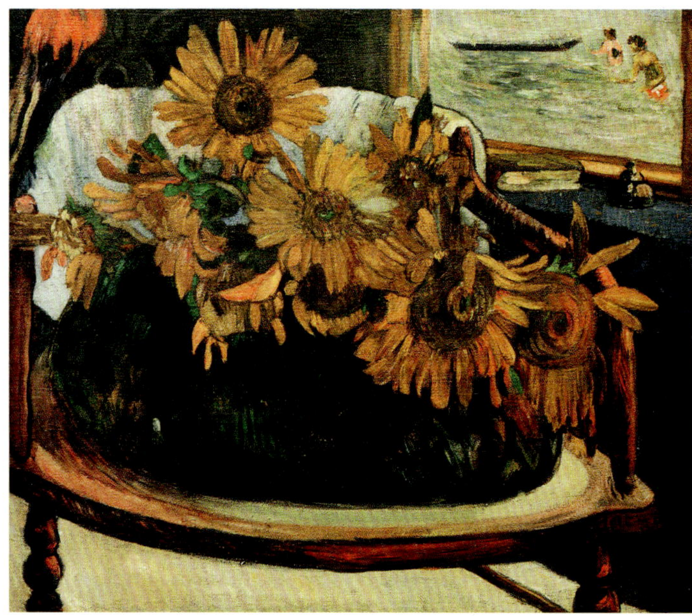

Sunflowers in a Chair
Tournesols sur un fauteuil
Sonnenblumen auf einem Sessel
Girasoles sobre un sillón
Girasoli su una sedia
Zonnebloemen op een stoel

*1901, Oil on canvas/Huile sur toile, 68 × 75,5 cm,
Private collection*

The last residence at the Marquesas

In 1901, Gauguin set sail for the Marquesas, one of the most isolated archipelagos of the Pacific. He settled in the village of Atuona on the isle of Hiva-Oa where was warmly received by the Marquesans who had heard of his political encounter against the central administration! In November he wrote to Monfried: "I have all that a modest artist could dream of … I only ask for a couple of healthy years and not too many money hassles in order that I may reach a certain maturity in my art." This was exactly the time he had left to live!

Entitled "House of Enjoyment", his hut is decorated with wooden bas-reliefs decorated with interwoven patterns

L'ultime demeure des Marquises

En 1901, Gauguin met le cap sur les Marquises, un des archipels les plus isolés du Pacifique. Il s'installe dans le village d'Atuona, sur l'île d'Hiva-Oa, où il est chaleureusement accueilli par des Marquisiens qui ont eu vent de son engagement politique à l'encontre de l'administration centrale ! En novembre, il écrit à Monfreid : « J'ai tout ce qu'un artiste modeste peut rêver. […] Je demande seulement deux années de santé et pas trop de tracas d'argent […] pour arriver à une certaine maturité dans mon art. » Exactement le temps qu'il lui reste à vivre !

Intitulée la « Maison du Jouir », sa case est ornée de bas-reliefs en bois ornés de motifs entrelacés et d'inscriptions

Der letzte Aufenthalt auf den Marquesas-Inseln

1901 setzt Gauguin Segel in Richtung der Marquesas-Inseln, einem der entlegensten Archipele des Pazifiks. Er lässt sich in dem Dorf Atuona auf der Insel Hiva-Oa nieder, wo ihn die Bewohner, die von seinem politischen Engagement gegen die Zentralregierung gehört haben, herzlich willkommen heißen. Im November schreibt er an Monfreid: „Ich habe alles, was sich ein bescheidener Künstler träumen lässt. […] Alles, was ich mir wünsche, sind zwei gesunde Jahre und nicht allzu viele Geldsorgen […], damit ich mit meiner Kunst eine gewisse Reife erlange." Damit benennt er genau die Zeitspanne, die ihm noch zum Leben bleibt.

*1901, Oil on canvas/Huile sur toile, 73 × 92,3 cm,
State Hermitage Museum, St. Petersburg*

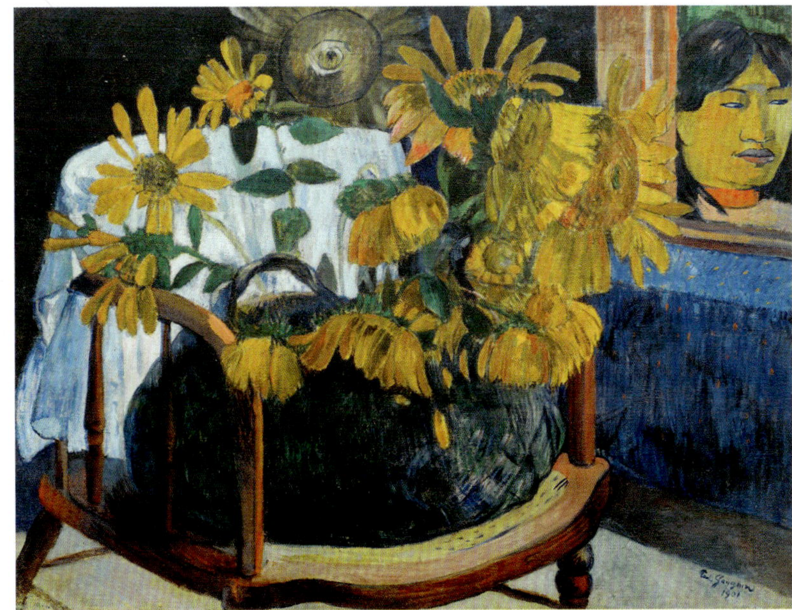

La última estancia en Marquises

En 1901, Gauguin pone rumbo a
Marquises, uno de los archipiélagos más
aislados del Pacífico. Se instaló en el
pueblo de Atuona, en la isla de Hiva-Oa,
donde recibe una calurosa bienvenida
por los marquisinos, conocedores
de su compromiso político contra la
administración central. En noviembre
escribió a Monfreid: "Tengo todo lo que
un modesto artista puede soñar. [...]
Tan solo pido dos años de salud y no
demasiadas apreturas económicas [...]
para alcanzar cierta madurez en mi arte".
¡Exactamente el tiempo que le quedaba
de vida!

Titulado la "Casa del gozo", su casa
está decorada con bajorrelieves en
madera adornados con motivos

L'ultima dimora a Marquises

Nel 1901, Gauguin salpa per Marquises,
una delle isole più remote del Pacifico.
Si stabilisce nel villaggio di Atuona
sull'isola di Hiva Oa, dove è accolto
calorosamente dagli abitanti che hanno
avuto sentore del suo impegno politico
contro il governo centrale. Nel mese di
novembre, scrive a Monfreid: "Ho tutto
ciò che un artista modesto può sognare.
[...] Chiedo solo due anni di salute e
non troppi problemi di soldi [...] per
raggiungere una certa maturità nella
mia arte." Esattamente il tempo che gli
resterà da vivere.

Chiamata la "casa della gioia", la
scatola è decorata da basso rilievi in
legno decorati con motivi intrecciati
e iscrizioni che sono altrettanto degli

Laatste woonplaats: de Marquesas-eilanden

In 1901 vertrekt Gauguin naar de
Marquesas-eilanden, een van de
meest afgelegen archipels in de
Stille Oceaan. Hij gaat wonen in het
dorpje Atuona, op het eiland Hiva-Oa,
waar hij hartelijk wordt ontvangen
door de eilandbewoners die al lucht
hadden gekregen van zijn politieke
betrokkenheid en afkeer van het
centrale bestuur! In november schrijft
hij Monfreid: "Ik heb alles wat een
bescheiden kunstenaar zich kan wensen.
[...] Het enige wat ik nog vraag zijn
twee jaar gezondheid en niet te veel
geldzorgen [...] om een zekere artistieke
rijpheid te bereiken." Precies de tijd die
hij nog te leven zou hebben!

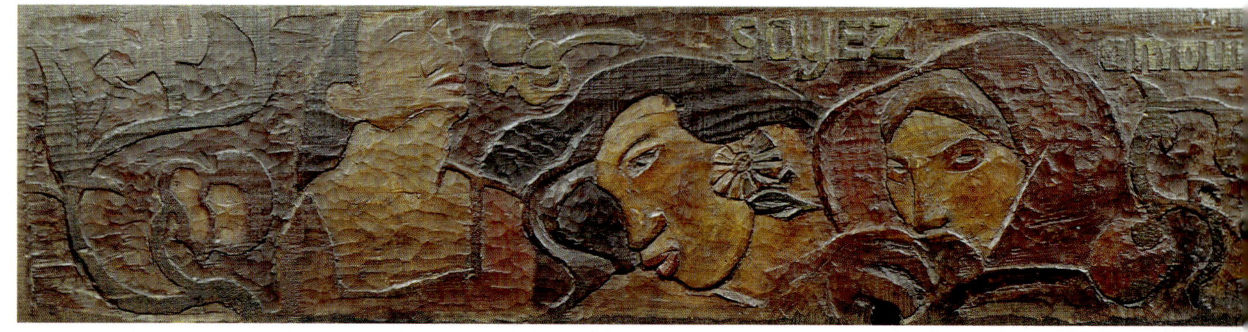

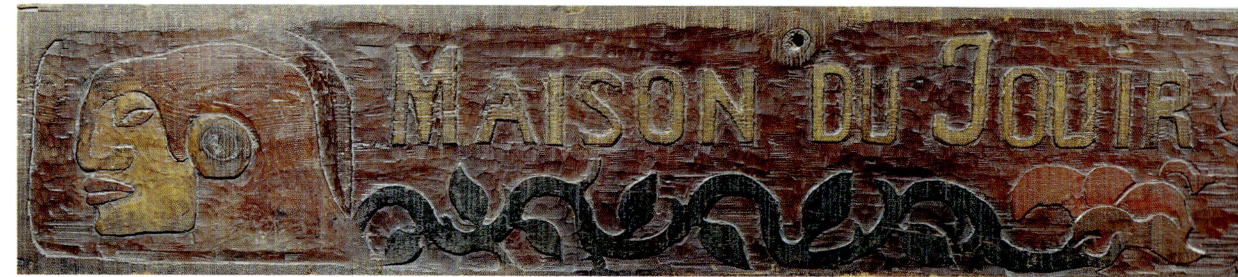

and inscriptions acting as invitations: "Be in love and you will be happy, Be mysterious!" In it he paints sumptuous inhabited landscapes traversed by enigmatic horsemen. Done with quick brush strokes and incredibly coloured, they feature simplified shapes and little allegorical content. These last two years were equally literary. The artist edits *Racontars de rapins* and *Avant et après* which combine aesthetic elements and mementos. He died at age 54 on 8 May 1903, and was buried in the village cemetery.

qui sont autant d'invites : « Soyez amoureuses et vous serez heureuses, Soyez mystérieuses ! » Il y peint de somptueux paysages habités, parcourus de cavaliers énigmatiques. Rapidement brossés et incroyablement colorés, ils arborent des formes simplifiées et peu de contenu allégorique. Ces deux dernières années sont également littéraires. L'artiste rédige *Racontars de rapins* et *Avant et après* qui mêlent considérations esthétiques et souvenirs. Décédé le 8 mai 1903 à l'âge de 54 ans, il est enterré dans le cimetière du village.

Seine Hütte, „Haus der Freude" getauft, ist mit Flachreliefs aus Holz verziert, mit verschachtelten Mustern und Inschriften, die sich an Besucher richten: „Seid verliebt und seid glücklich, seid geheimnisvoll!". Hier malt er üppige, bewohnte Landschaften, von rätselhaften Reitern durchquert. Rasch gepinselt und unglaublich farbenprächtig, zeigen sie vereinfachte Formen und wenig allegorischen Gehalt. Diese beiden letzten Jahre sind auch schriftstellerisch von Bedeutung. Der Künstler redigiert *Racontars de rapins* und *Avant et après* – Werke, die ästhetische Erwägungen und Erinnerungen verbinden. Am 8. Mail 1903 stirbt Gauguin im Alter von 54 Jahren. Er wird auf dem Dorffriedhof begraben.

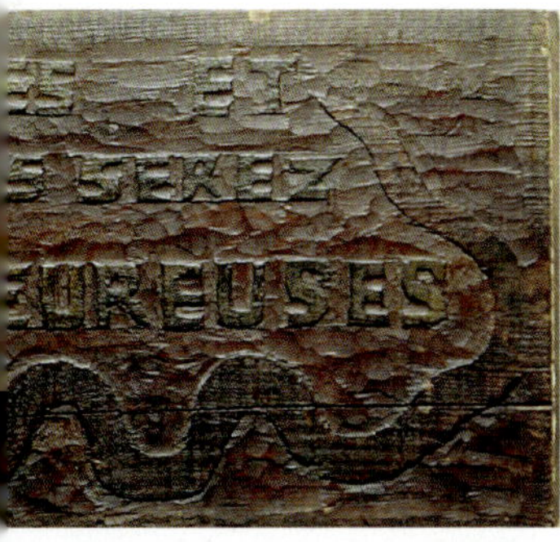

Be In Love and You Will Be Happy

Soyez amoureuses et vous serez heureuses

Seid verliebt und ihr werdet glücklich sein

Sed amorosas y sed felices, sed misteriosas

Siate innamorati e voi sarete felici

Wees verliefd en je zult gelukkig zijn

1901–1902, Bas-relief in polychrome gigantea sequoia wood/Bas-relief en bois de séquoia gigantea polychrome, 45 × 204,5 × 2,2 cm, Musée d'Orsay, Paris

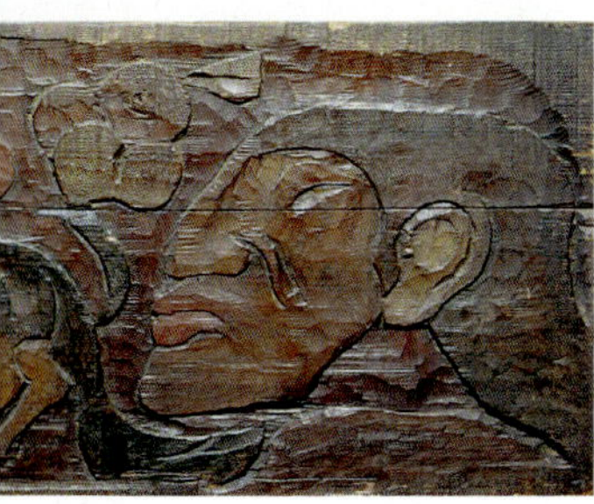

House of Pleasure

Maison du Jouir

Haus der Wonnen

Casa del gozo

Casa della Gioia

Lustenhuis

1901, Sculpted panel in polychrome gigantea sequoia wood/Panneau sculpté, bois de séquoia polychrome, Musée d'Orsay, Paris

entrelazados e inscripciones que son a su vez instrucciones: "¡Sed amorosas y sed felices, sed misteriosas!" Allí pintó suntuosos paisajes habitados, paseos y caballeros enigmáticos. Rápidamente pincelados e increíblemente coloridos, muestran formas simplificadas y escaso contenido alegórico. Estos dos últimos años son igualmente literarios. El artista redactó *Habladurías de un pintamonas* y *Antes y después* que mezclan consideraciones estéticas y recuerdos. Falleció el 8 de mayo de 1903 a los 54 años de edad, siendo enterrado en el cementerio del pueblo.

inviti: "Siate innamorati e sarete felici, siate misteriosi!" Vi dipinge paesaggi sontuosi percorsi da cavalieri enigmatici. Rapidamente dipinti e incredibilmente colorati, sono dotati di forme semplificate e un po' di contenuto allegorico. Questi ultimi due anni sono anche letterari. L'artista scrive *Racontars de rapins* e *Avant et après* che mescolano considerazioni estetiche e ricordi. Muore l'8 Maggio 1903 all'età di 54 anni, ed è sepolto nel cimitero del paese.

Zijn hut, het "Lustenhuis", is versierd met houten bas-reliëfs die zijn verfraaid met verstrengelde motieven en inscripties die evengoed stille wenken zijn: 'Wees verliefd en je zult gelukkig zijn' en 'Wees mysterieus'! Hij schildert er weelderig bewoonde landschappen waardoor raadselachtige ruiters dwalen. De doeken zijn snel geschetst en ongelooflijk kleurig; de vormen zijn vereenvoudigd en de allegorische betekenis is gering. Die laatste twee jaar zijn ook literair. De kunstenaar schrijft *Racontars de rapins* en *Avant et après*, een mix van esthetische beschouwingen en memoires. Paul Gauguin overlijdt op 8 mei 1903, 54 jaar oud en hij wordt op de dorpsbegraafplaats van Atuona begraven.

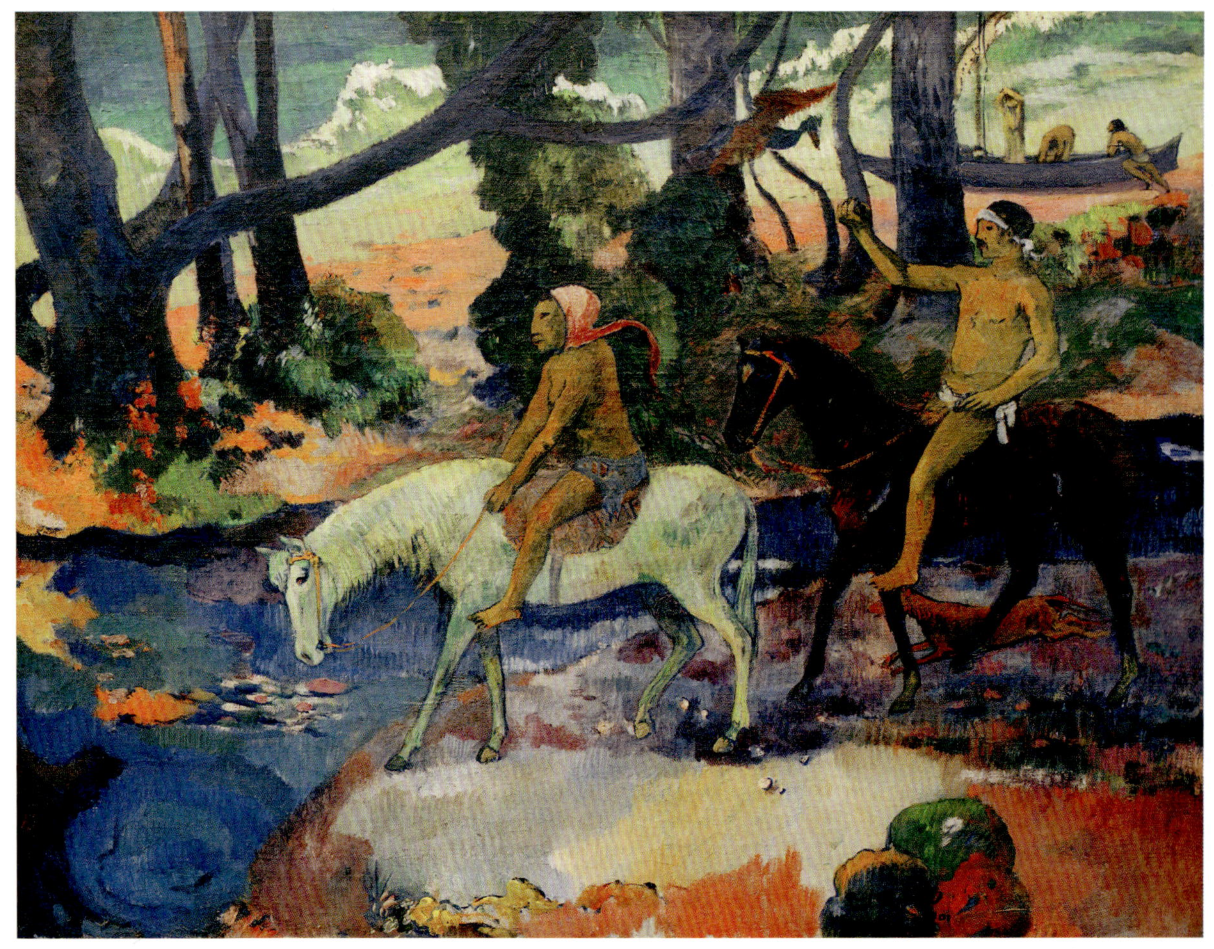

The Ford** or **Flight

*Le Gué **ou** La Fuite*

*Die Furt **oder** Die Flucht*

*El vado **o** La huida*

*Il Guè **o** Il Volo*

*De doorwaadbare plaats **of** De vlucht*

1901, Oil on canvas/Huile sur toile, 76 × 95 cm, Pushkin Museum, Moscow

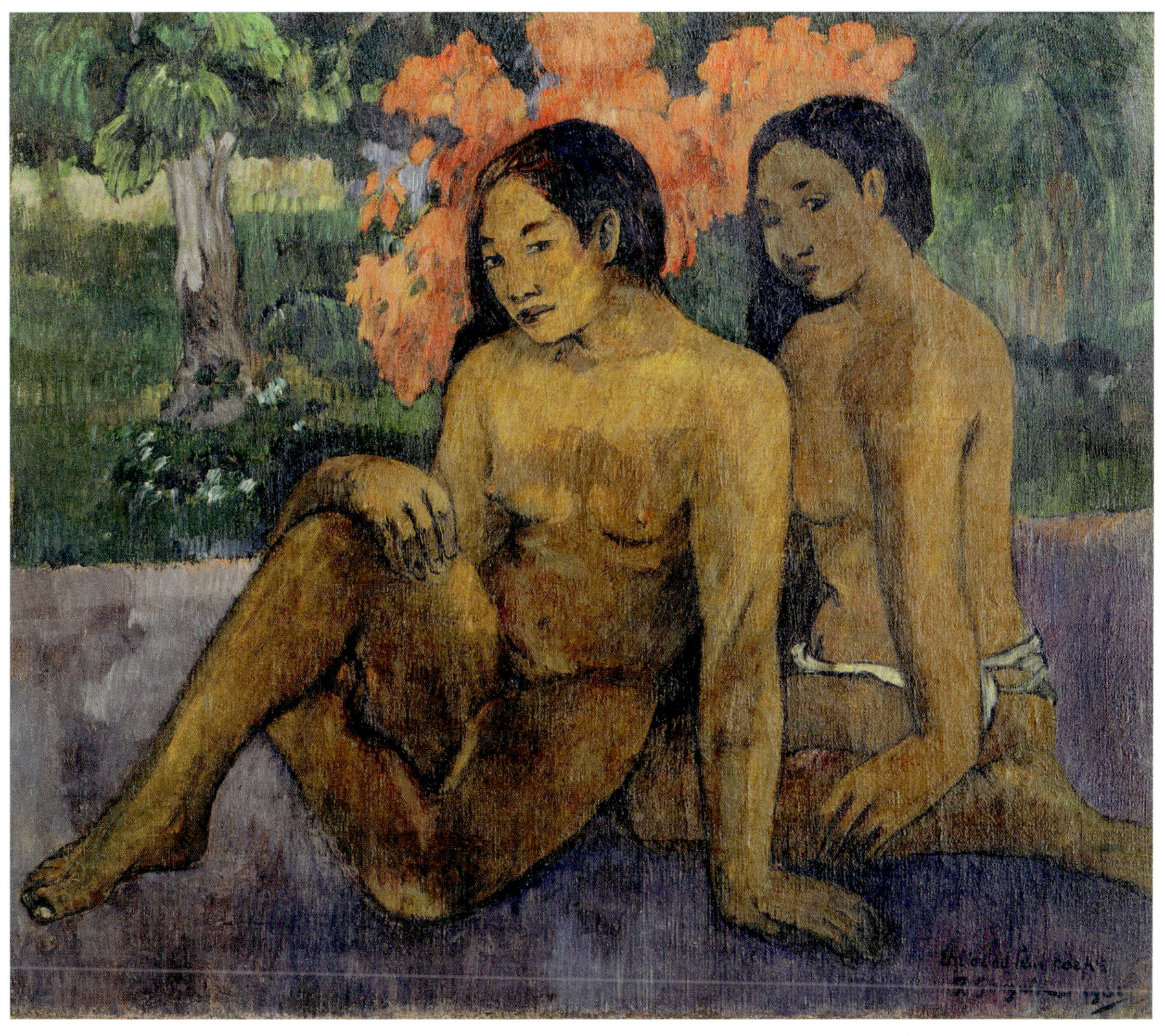

And the Gold of Their Bodies *Und das Gold ihrer Körper* *E l'oro dei loro corpi*

Et l'or de leur corps *Y el oro de su cuerpo* *En het goud van hun lichaam*

1901, Oil on canvas/Huile sur toile, 67 × 76,5 cm, Musée d'Orsay, Paris

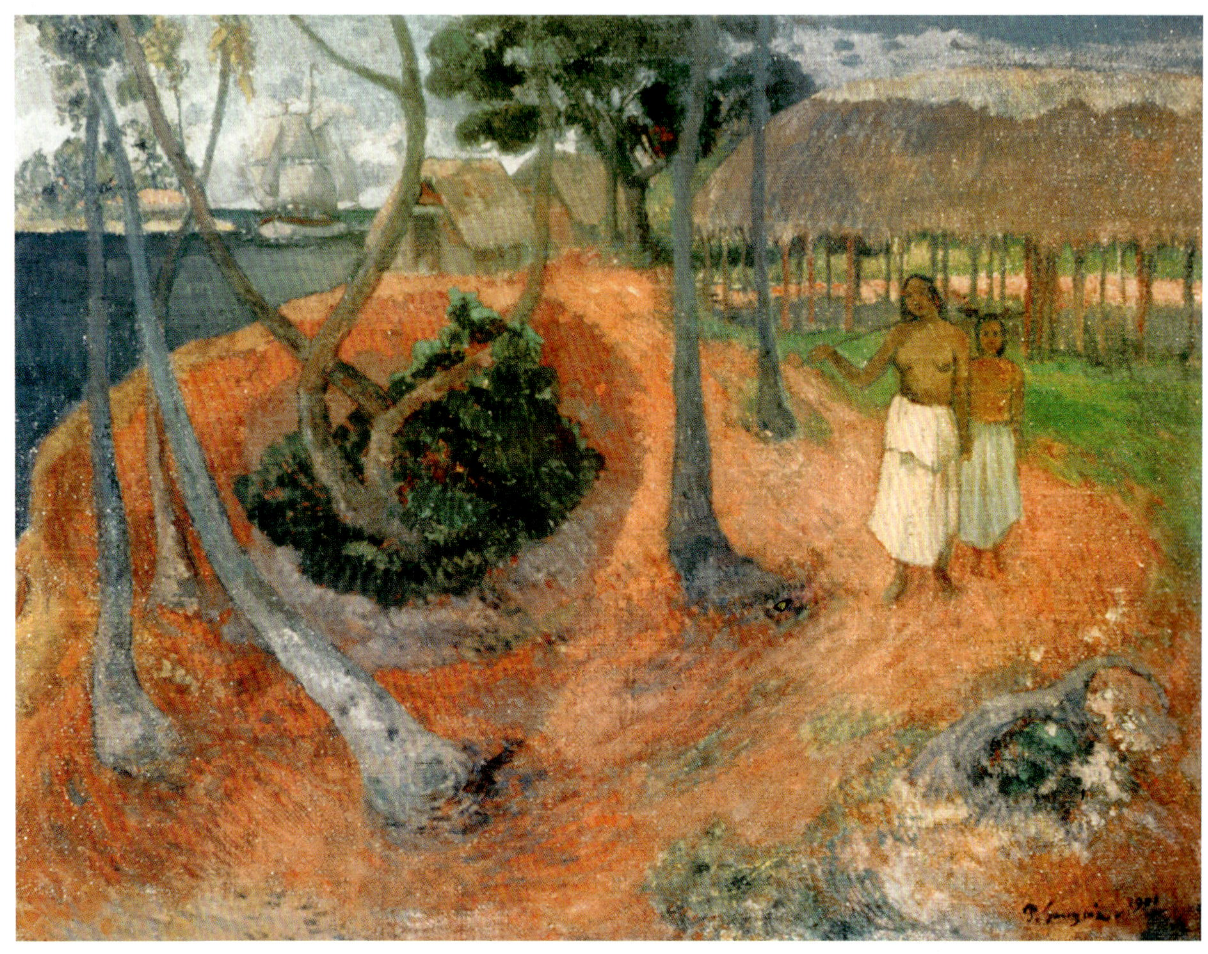

Idyll in Tahiti

Idylle à Tahiti

Idyll auf Tahiti

Idilio en Tahití

Idillio a Tahiti

Idylle op Tahiti

1901, Oil on canvas/Huile sur toile, 74,5 × 94,5 cm, Private collection

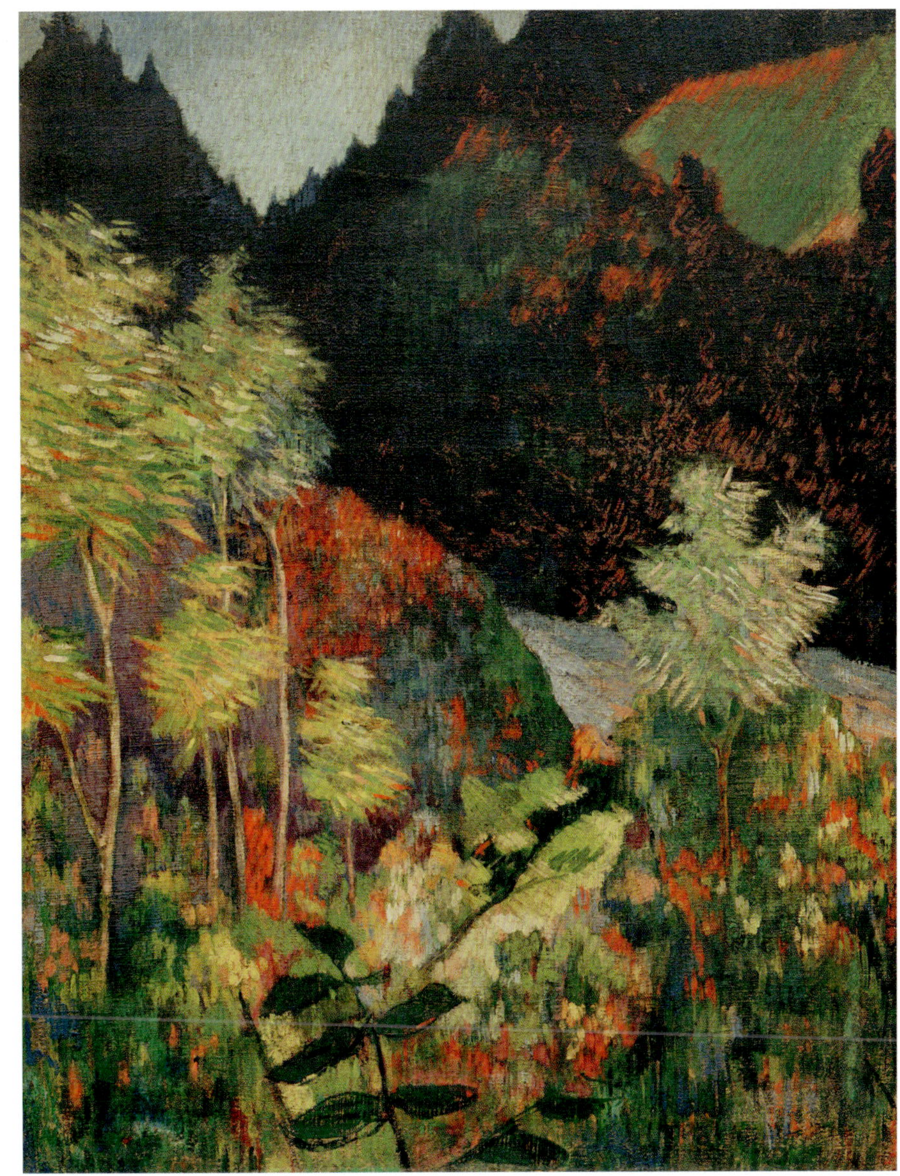

Attributed to/Attribué
à Paul Gauguin

Landscape

Paysage

Landschaft

Paisaje

Paesaggio

Landschap

Oil on canvas/Huile sur toile,
65 × 50 cm, Musée Picasso, Paris

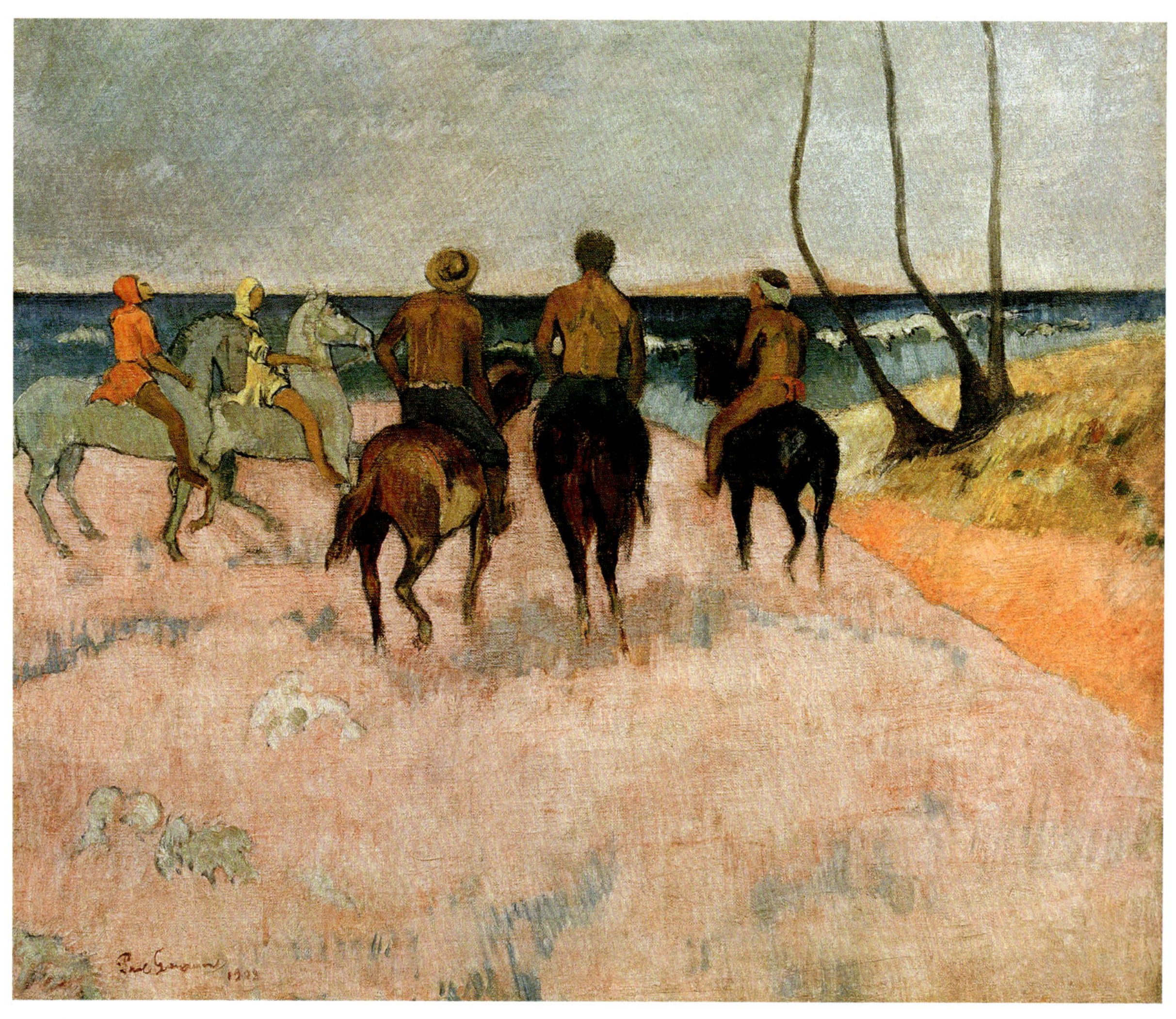

Horsemen On The Beach **Reiter am Strand** *Cavalieri sulla spiaggia*

Cavaliers sur la plage **Caballeros en la playa** **Ruiters op het strand**

1902, Oil on canvas/Huile sur toile, 65,6 × 75,9 cm, Museum Folkwang, Essen

270

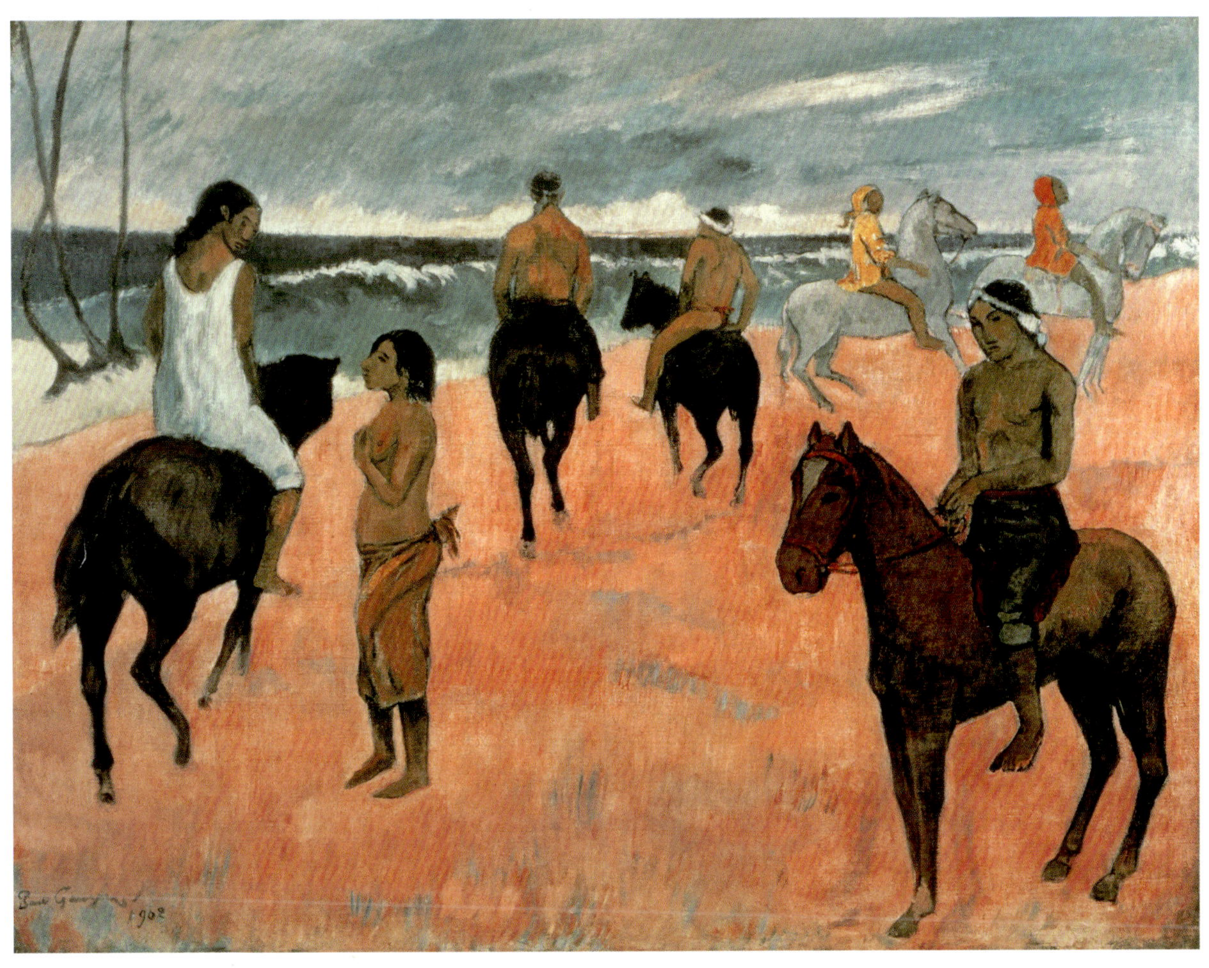

Horsemen On The Beach   **Reiter am Strand**   *Cavalieri sulla spiaggia*

Cavaliers sur la plage   **Caballeros en la playa**   **Ruiters op het strand**

1902, Oil on canvas/Huile sur toile, 73 × 92 cm, Private collection

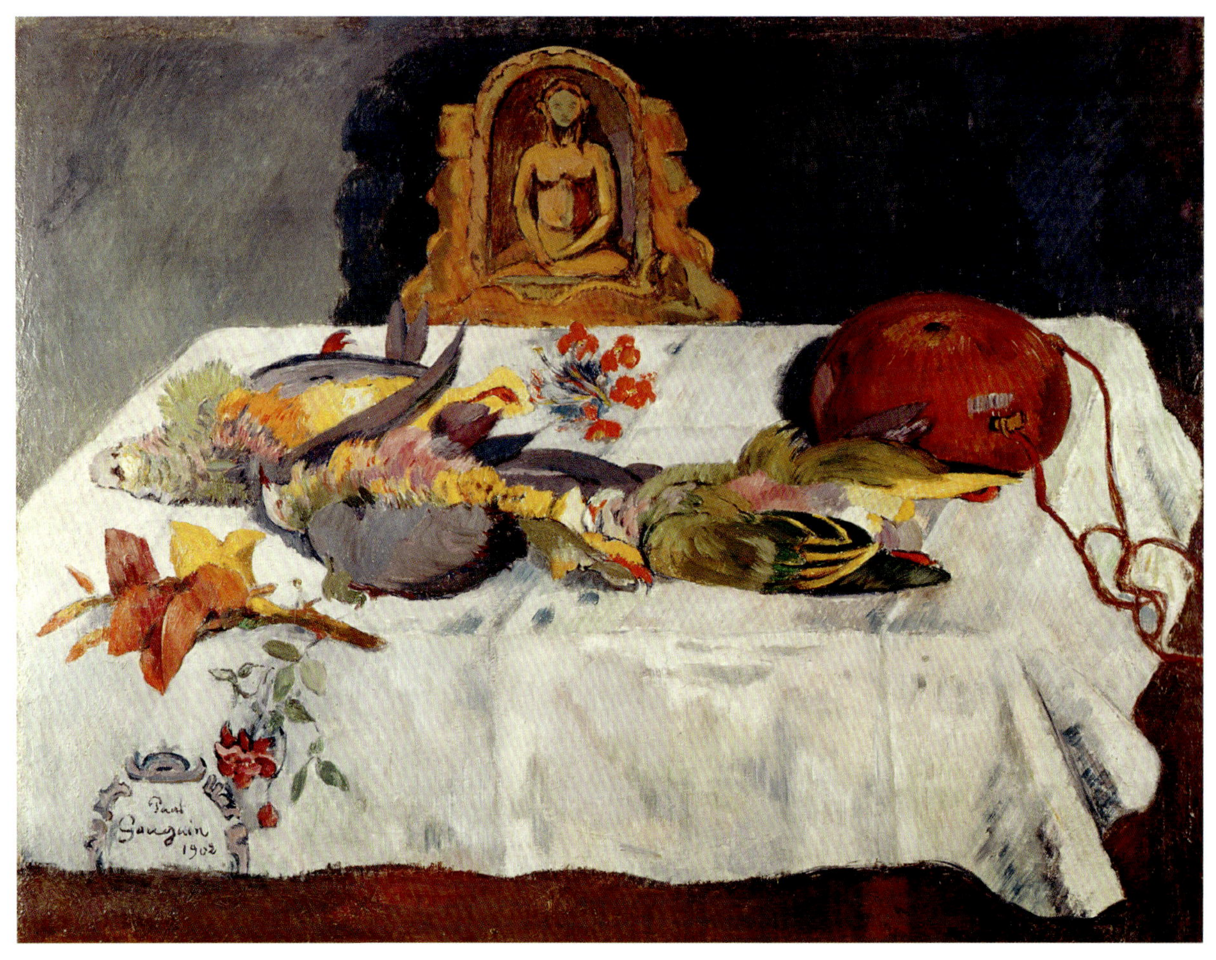

Still Life with Parrots

Nature morte aux perroquets

Stillleben mit Papageien

Naturaleza muerta con periquitos

Natura morta con pappagalli

Stilleven met papegaaien

1902, Oil on canvas/Huile sur toile, 62 × 76 cm, Pushkin Museum, Moscow

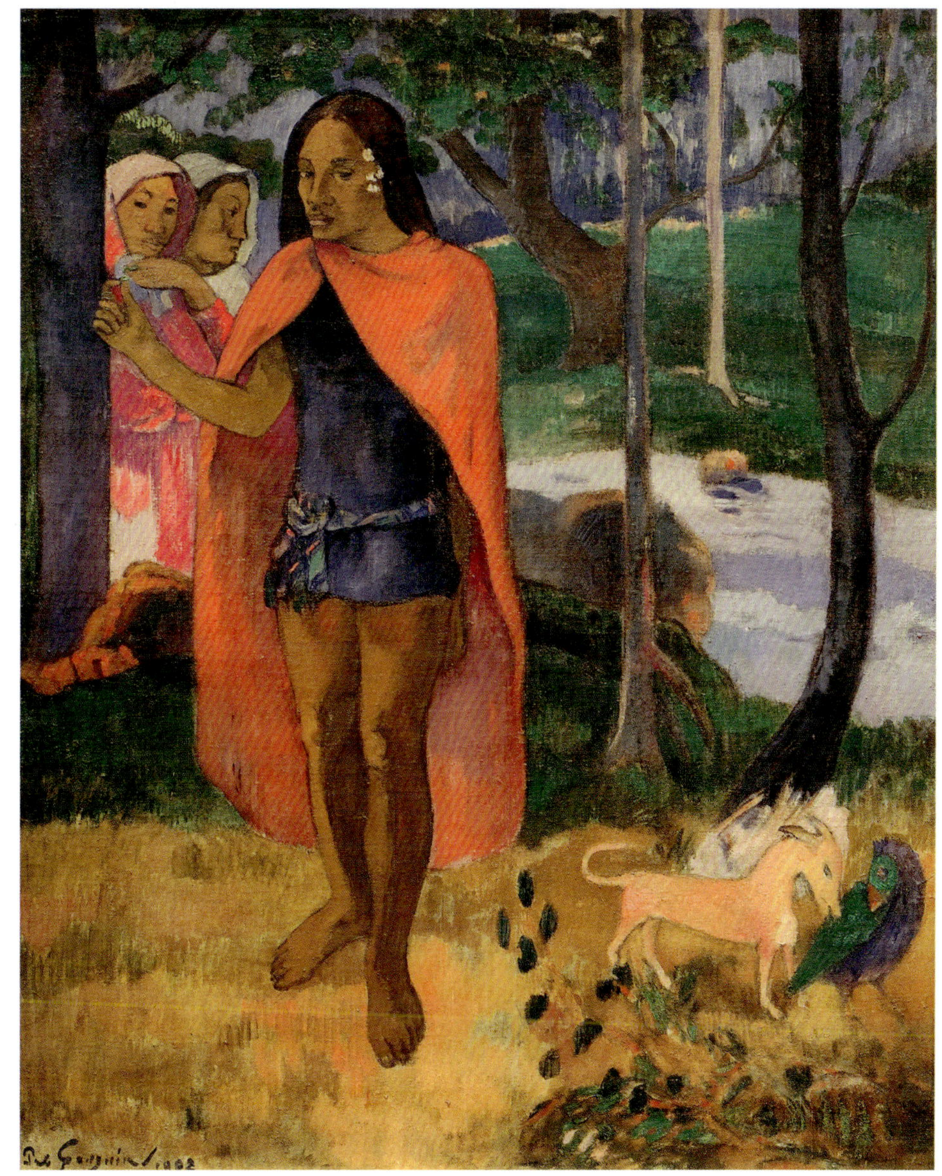

The Sorcerer of Hiva Oa or Marquesan Man in the Red Cape

Le Sorcier d'Hiva Oa ou Le Marquisien à la cape rouge

Der Zauberer von Hiva Oa oder Mann von den Marquesas-Inseln mit rotem Umhang

El brujo de Hiva Oa o El marquesano con la capa roja

Lo Stregone d'Hiva Oa o Il Marquisien dalla testa rossa

De tovenaar van Hiva Oa of De Marquesas-eilandbewoner met de rode cape

1902, Oil on canvas/Huile sur toile, 92 × 73 cm, Musée d'art moderne et d'art contemporain, Liège

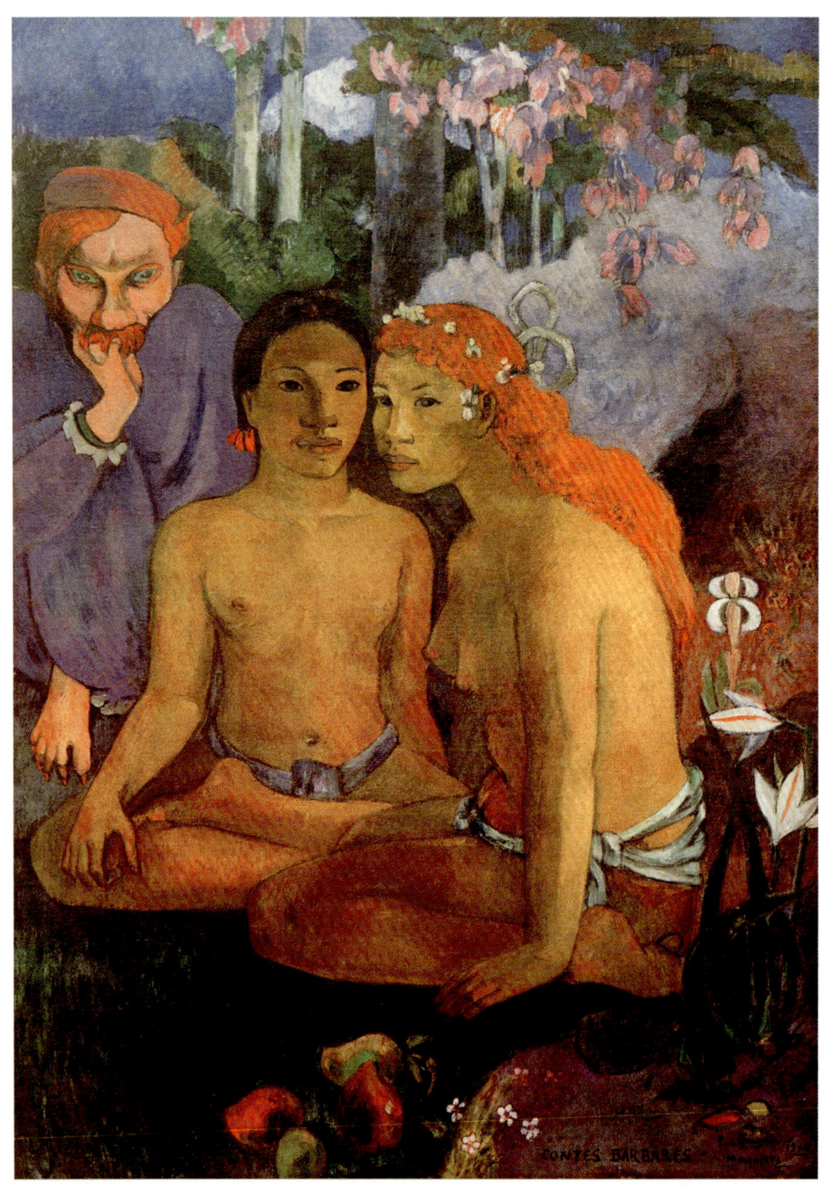

Barbarian Tales

Contes barbares

Barbarische Erzählungen

Cuentos bárbaros

Racconti barbari

Barbaarse vertellingen

*1902, Oil on canvas/Huile sur toile,
131,5 × 90,5 cm, Museum Folkwang, Essen*

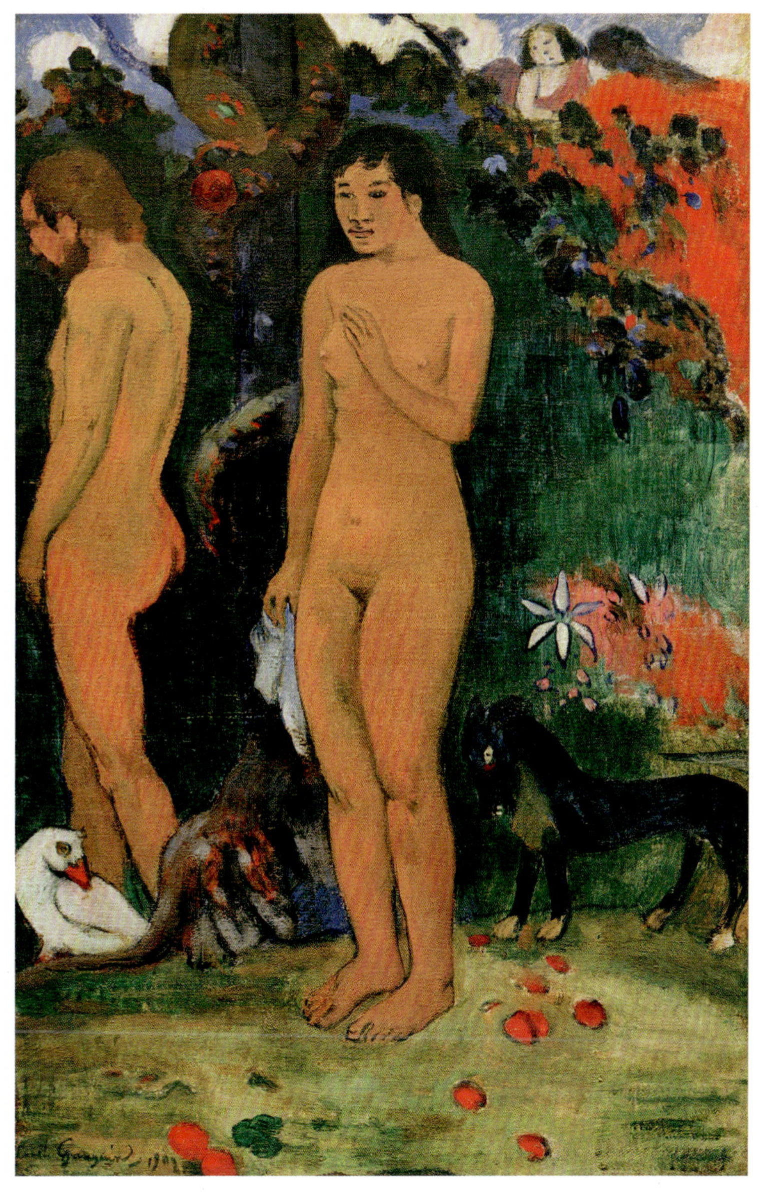

Adam and Eve
Adam et Ève
Adam und Eva
Adán y Eva
Adamo e Eva
Adam en Eva

*1902, Oil on canvas/Huile sur toile, 59 × 38 cm,
Ordrupgaard, København*

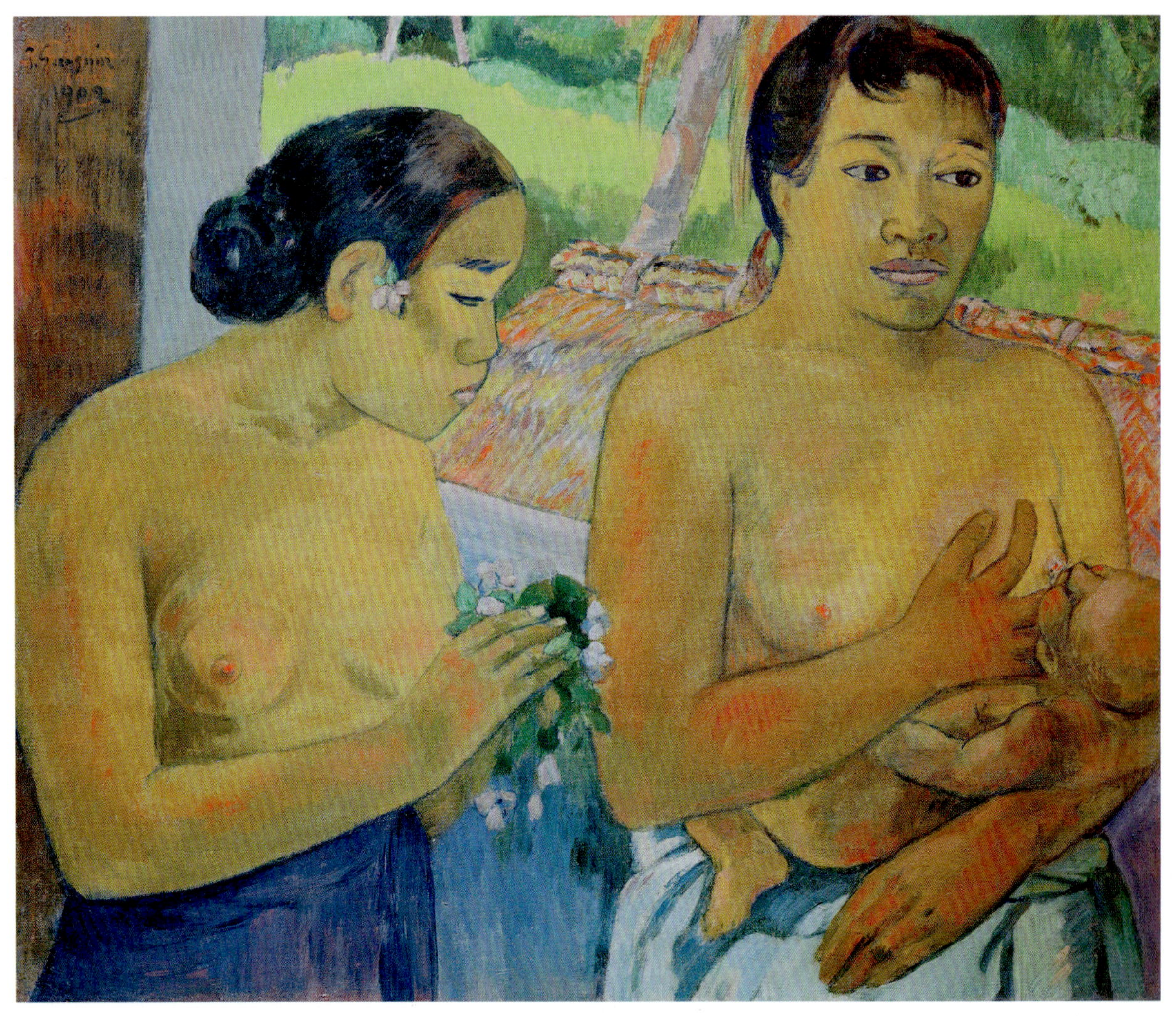

The Offering
L'Offrande

Die Opfergabe
La ofrenda

L'Offerta
De offerande

1902, Oil on canvas/Huile sur toile, 68,5 × 78,5 cm, Private collection

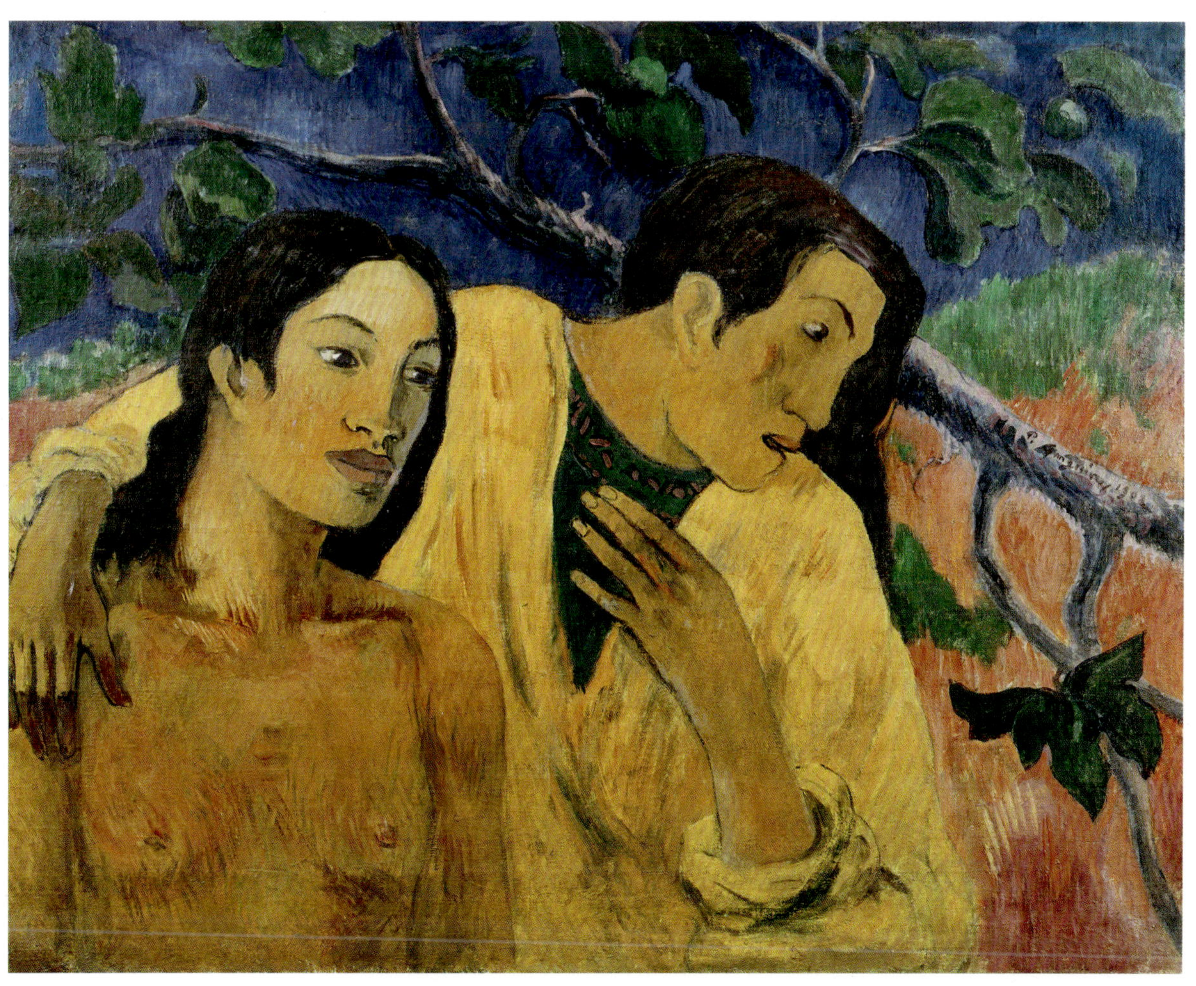

The Lovers **Liebespaar** **Gli Amanti**

Les Amants **Los amantes** **Liefdespaar**

1902, Oil on canvas/Huile sur toile, 72,5 × 92,5 cm, Národní galerie, Praha

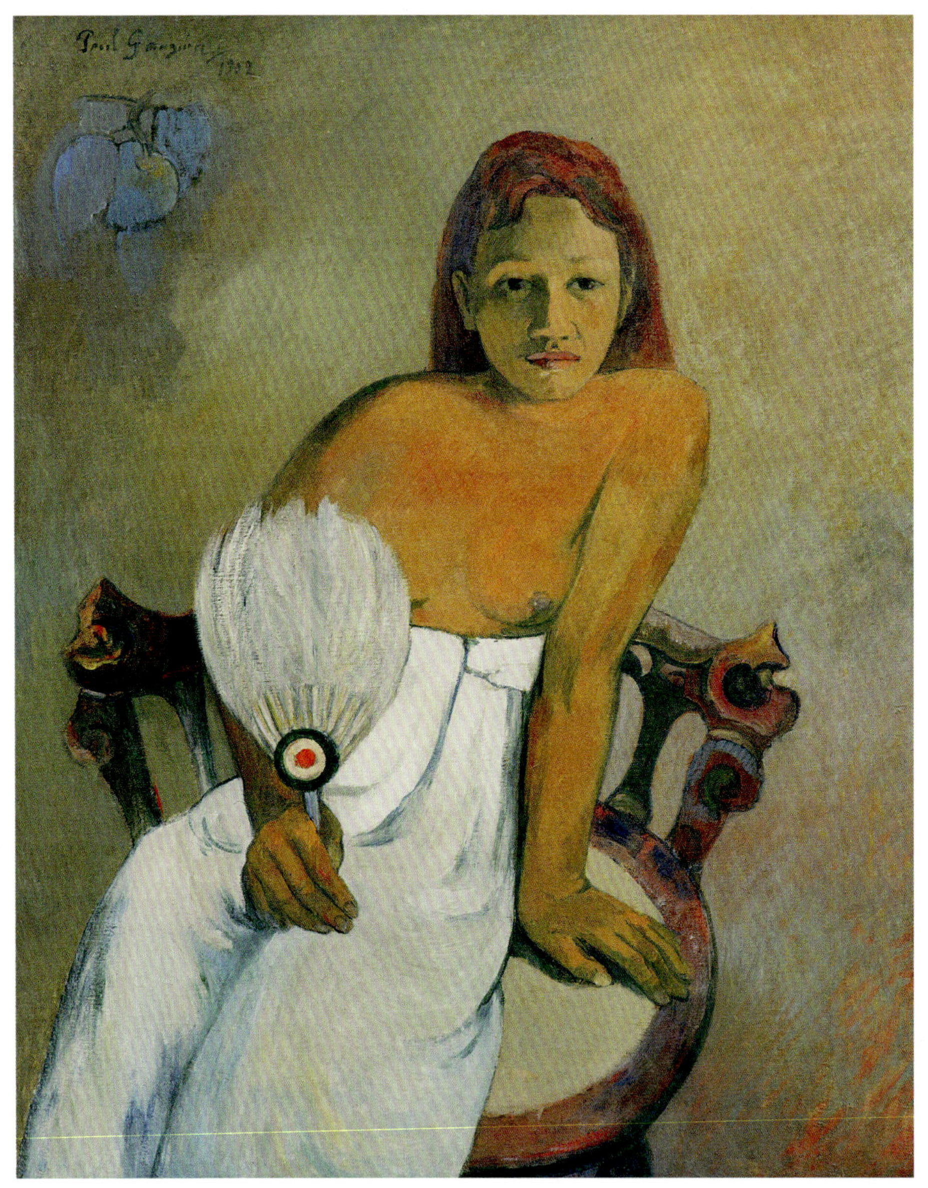

Young Tahitian Girl with a Fan

Jeune Tahitienne à l'éventail

Junge Tahitianerin mit Fächer

Joven tahitiana con abanico

*Giovane Tahitiana
col ventaglio*

*Jonge Tahitiaanse
met de waaier*

*1902, Oil on canvas/Huile sur
toile, 91,9 × 73 cm, Museum
Folkwang, Essen*

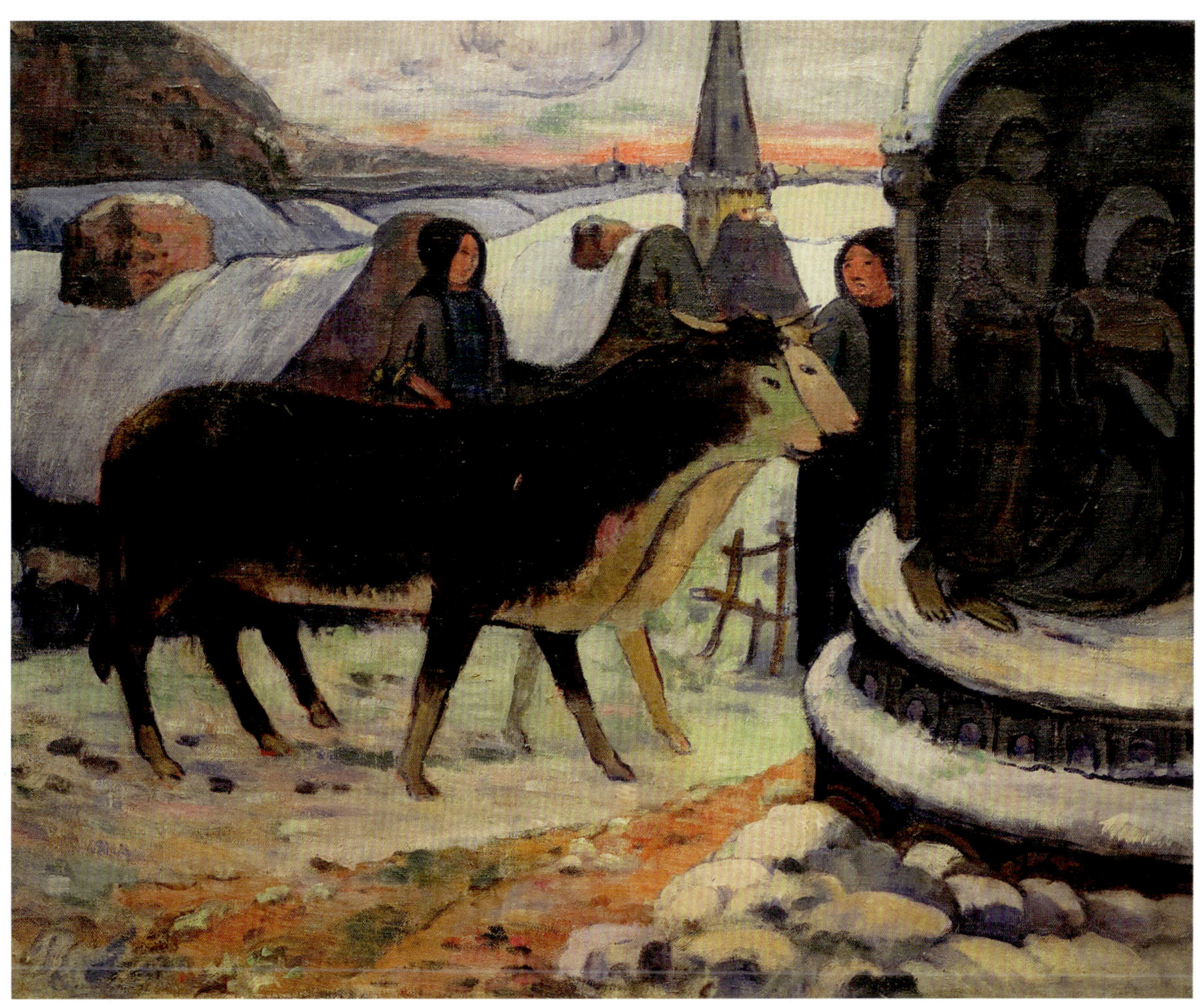

Christmas Night** or *The Blessing of the Oxen ***Heilige Nacht** oder *Segnung der Ochsen*** ***Notte di natale** o *la benedizione dei buoi***
Nuit de Noël ou *La Bénédicition des bœufs* ***Noche de Navidad** o *La bendición de los bueyes*** ***Kerstnacht** of *De zegening van de ossen***
c. 1902–1903, Oil on canvas/Huile sur toile, 71 × 82,5 cm, Indianapolis, Museum of Art, Indianapolis

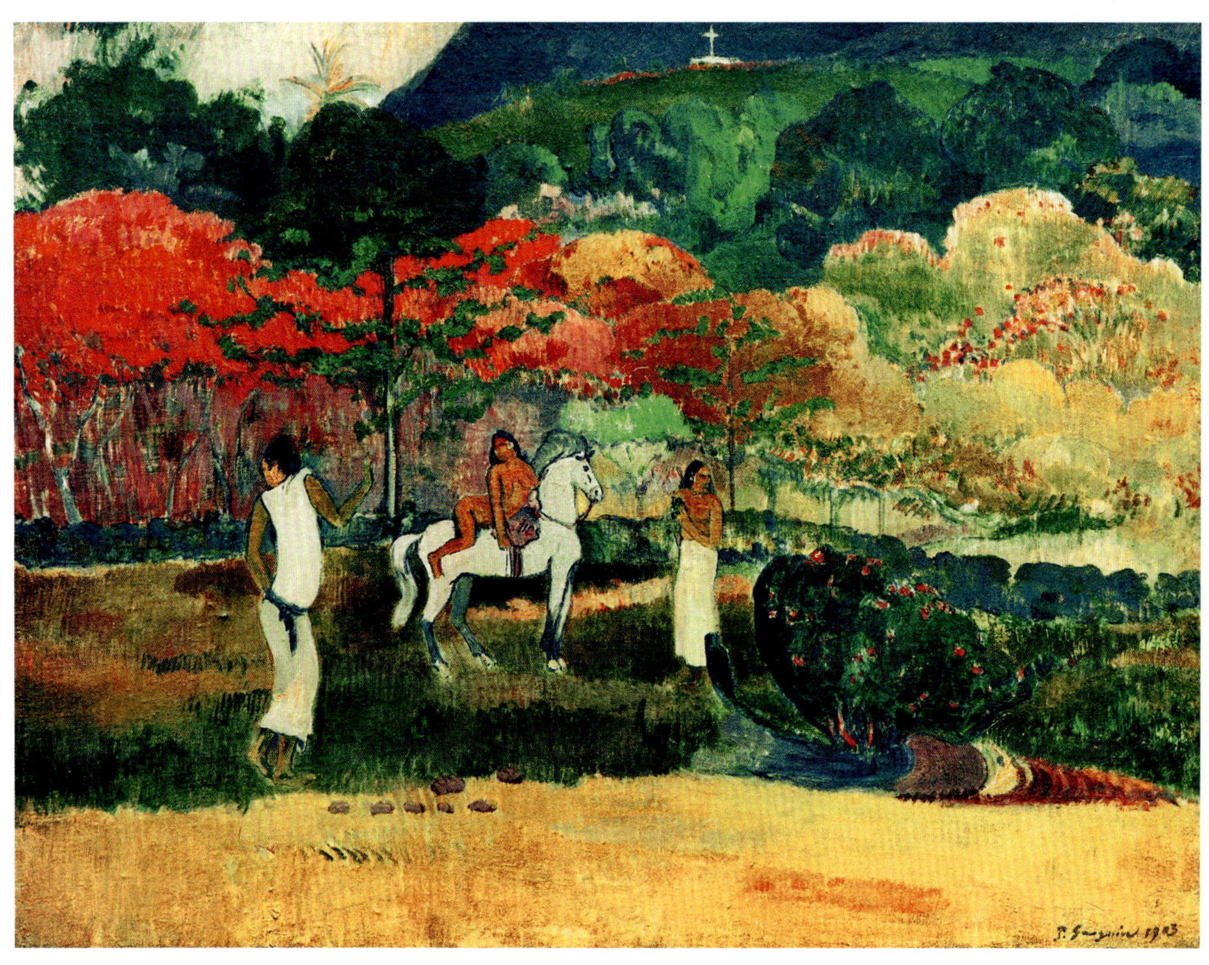

Women and a White Horse

Femmes et cheval blanc

Frauen mit weißem Pferd

Mujeres y caballo blanco

Donne e cavallo bianco

Vrouwen en wit paard

1903, Oil on canvas/Huile sur toile, 73,3 × 91,7 cm, Museum of Fine Arts, Boston

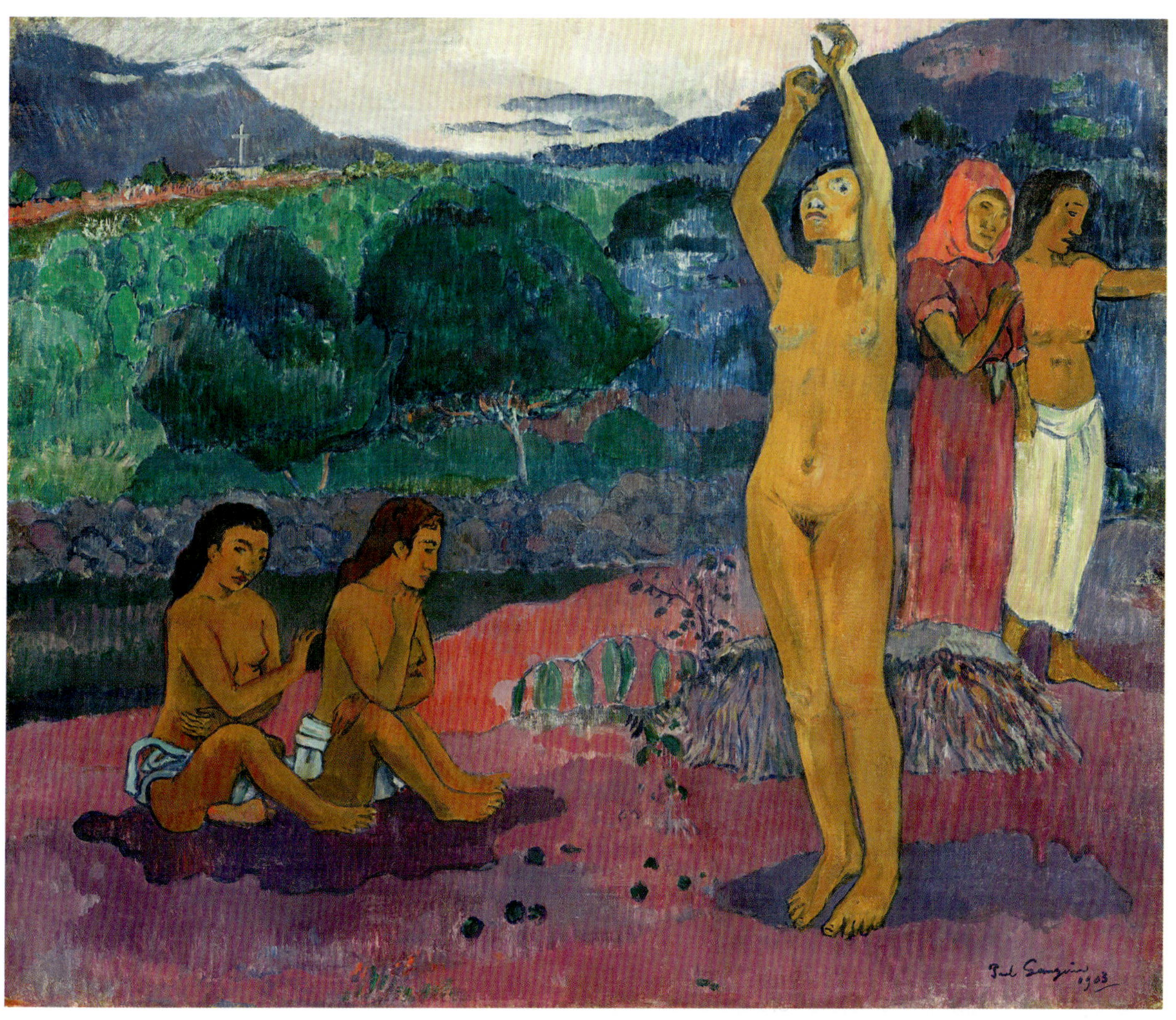

The Invocation   *Anrufung*   *L'Invocazione*

L'Invocation   *La invocación*   *De aanroeping*

1903, Oil on canvas/Huile sur toile, 65,5 × 75,6 cm, National Gallery of Art, Washington

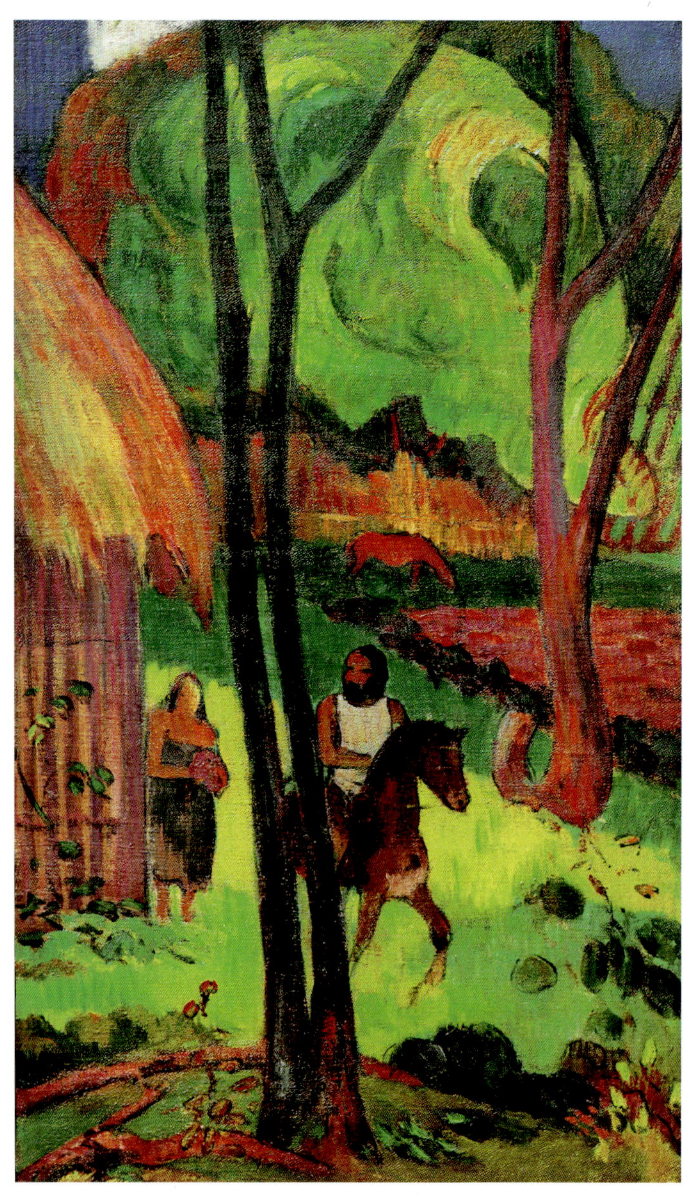

The Rider in Front of the Hub
Cavalier devant la case
Reiter vor der Hütte
Caballero frente a la choza
Cavaliere davanti alla capanna
Ruiter voor de hut

1902, Oil on canvas/Huile sur toile, 58 × 34 cm, Private collection

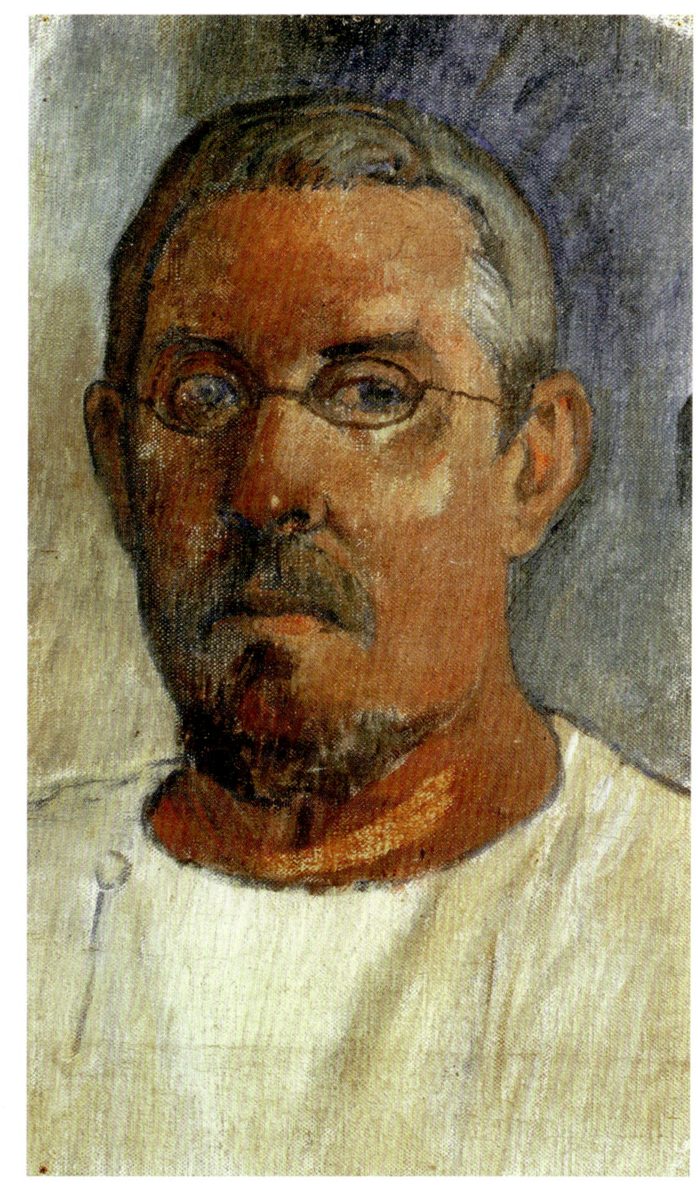

Self Portrait
Autoportrait
Selbstbildnis
Autorretrato
Autoritratto
Zelfportret

1903, Oil on canvas/Huile sur toile, 41,4 × 23,5 cm,
Kunstmuseum, Basel

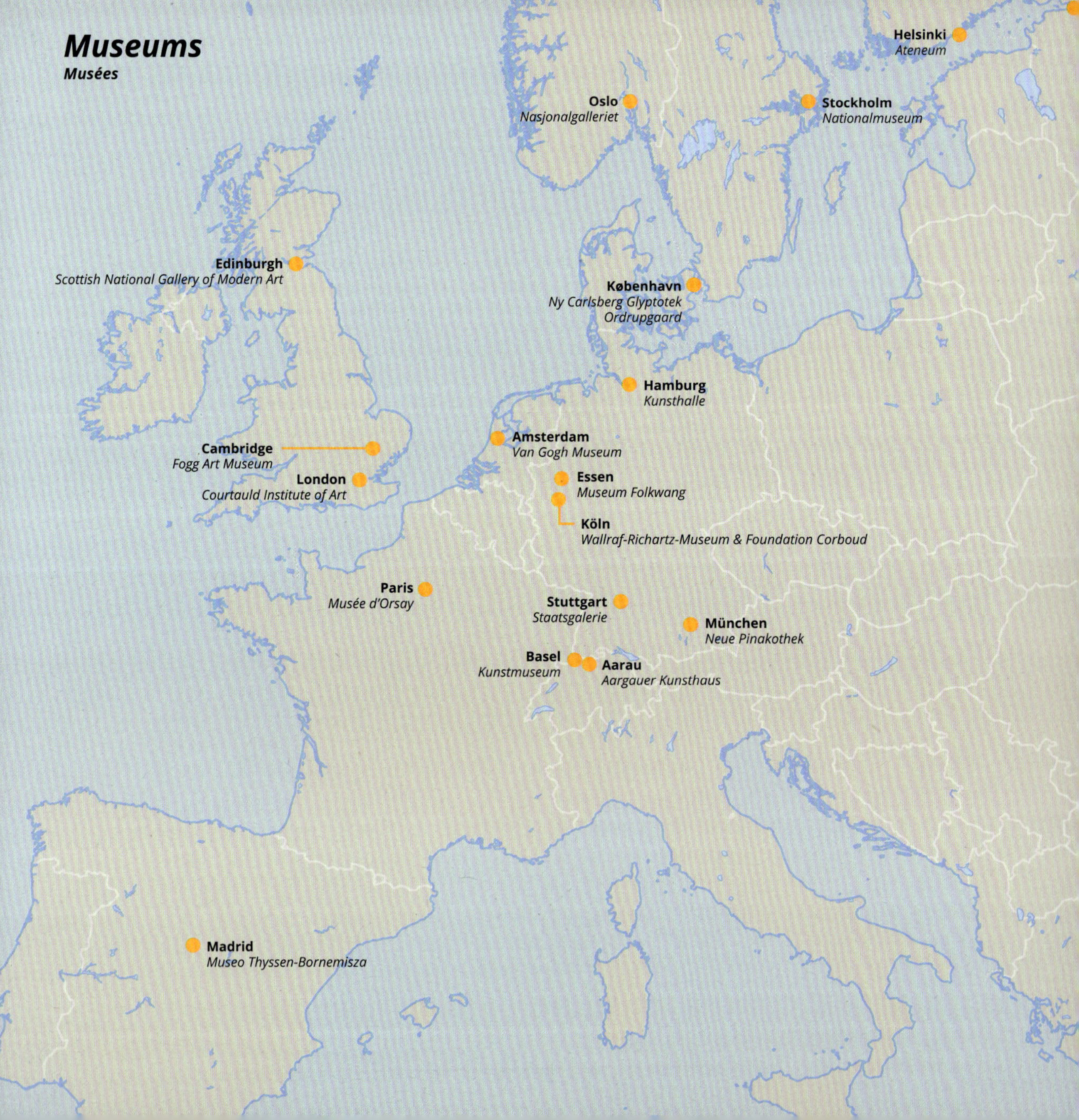

Museums
Musées

Helsinki
Ateneum

Oslo
Nasjonalgalleriet

Stockholm
Nationalmuseum

Edinburgh
Scottish National Gallery of Modern Art

København
Ny Carlsberg Glyptotek
Ordrupgaard

Hamburg
Kunsthalle

Cambridge
Fogg Art Museum

Amsterdam
Van Gogh Museum

London
Courtauld Institute of Art

Essen
Museum Folkwang

Köln
Wallraf-Richartz-Museum & Foundation Corboud

Paris
Musée d'Orsay

Stuttgart
Staatsgalerie

München
Neue Pinakothek

Basel
Kunstmuseum

Aarau
Aargauer Kunsthaus

Madrid
Museo Thyssen-Bornemisza

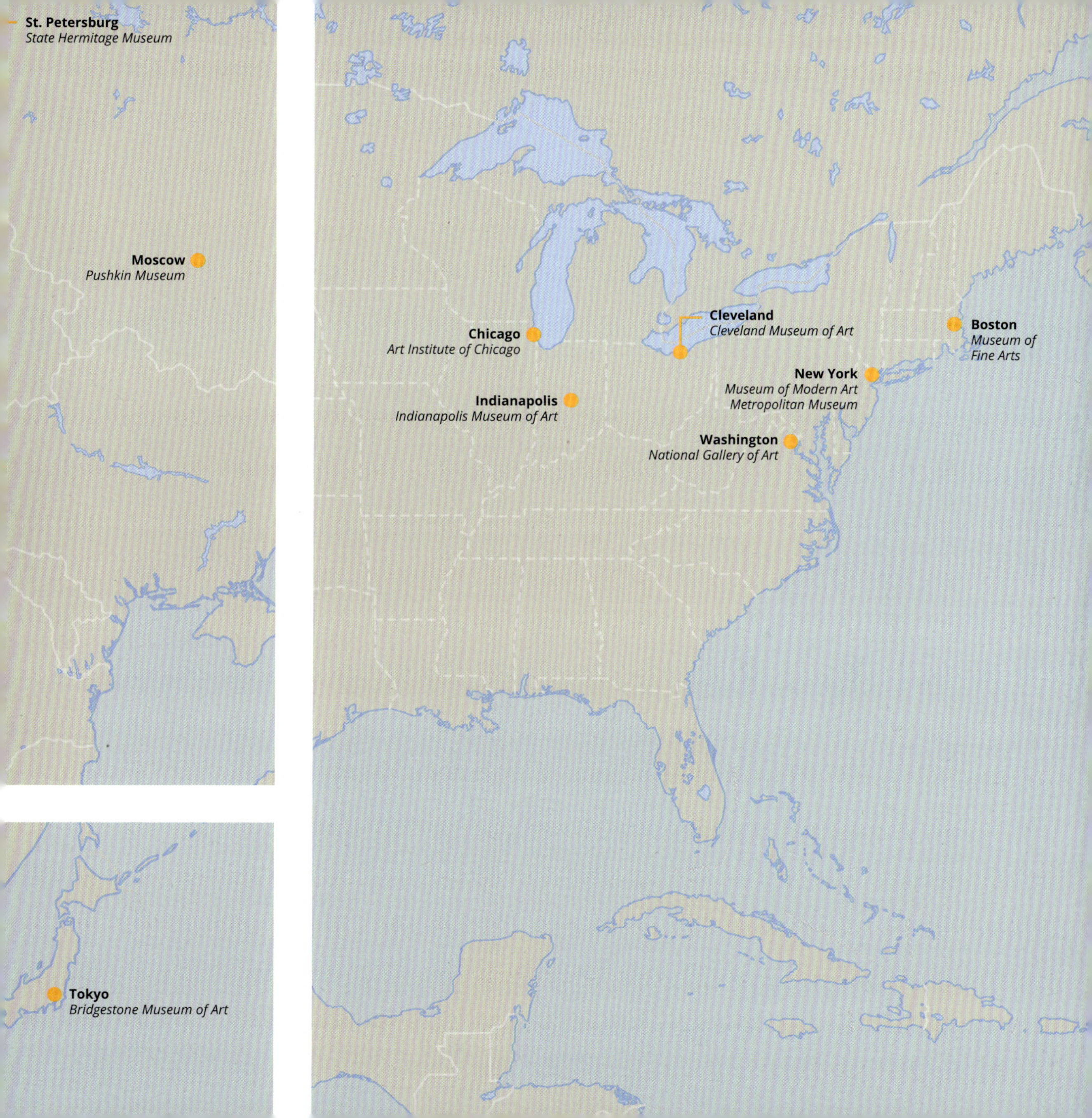

St. Petersburg
State Hermitage Museum
Moscow
Pushkin Museum
Chicago
Art Institute of Chicago
Indianapolis
Indianapolis Museum of Art
Cleveland
Cleveland Museum of Art
New York
Museum of Modern Art
Metropolitan Museum
Washington
National Gallery of Art
Boston
Museum of
Fine Arts
Tokyo
Bridgestone Museum of Art

Curriculum Vitae

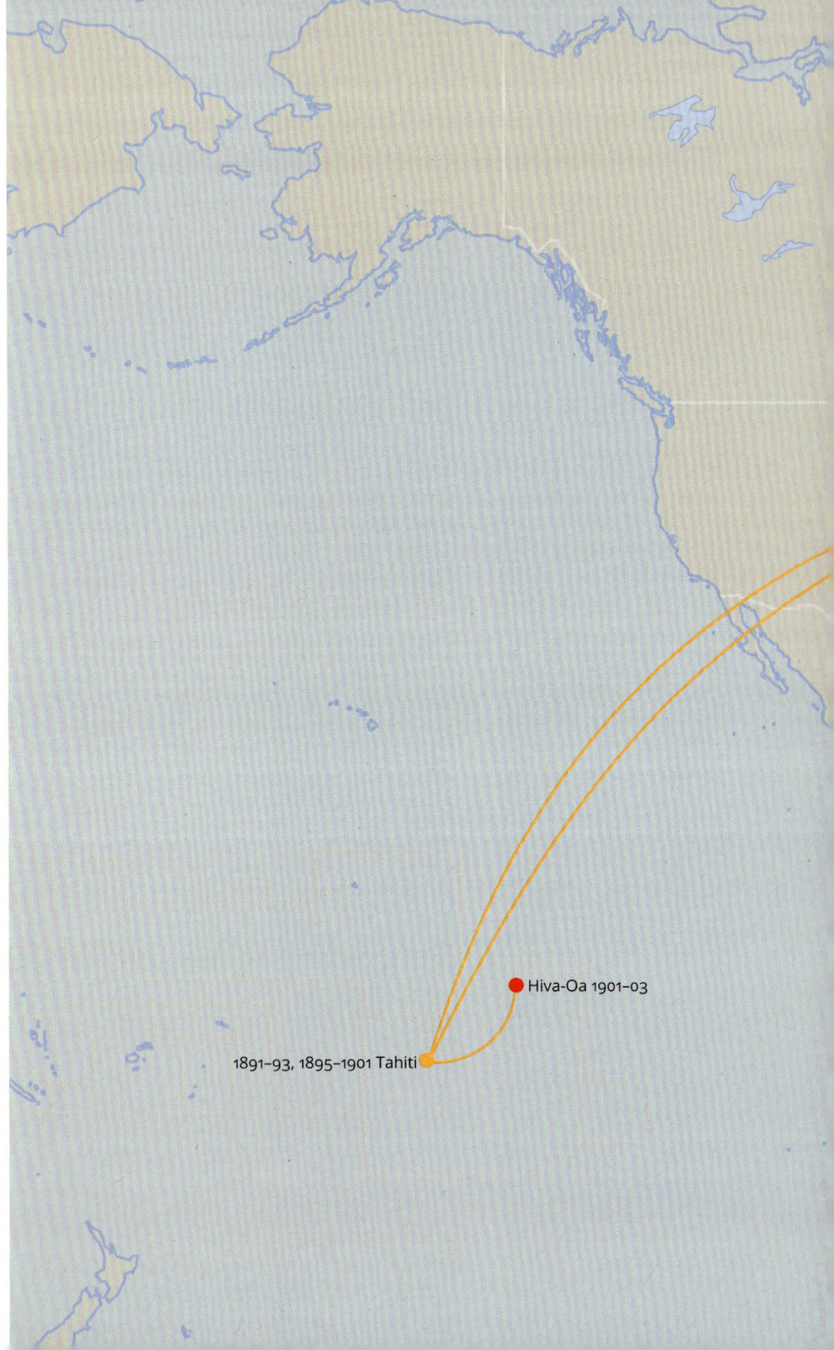

* 1848 Paris
  1849 Lima
  1854 Orléans
  1861 Paris
1865–1866 Paris, Rio de Janeiro
1866–1867 Paris, Martinique,
          Iquique, Mollendo,
          Arica, Carrizal Bajo,
          Valparaíso, Cardiff
1868–1871 Venezia, Trieste,
          Corfu, Bastia, Paris,
          København, Gdańsk,
          London, Peterhead,
          Bergen, Tromsø
  1872 Paris
  1884 Rouen, København
  1885 Paris
  1886 Pont-Aven, Paris
  1887 Martinique
  1888 Pont-Aven, Arles
  1889 Paris, Pont-Aven,
       Le Pouldu
  1891 Paris, Tahiti
  1893 Tahiti, Paris
  1894 Paris, Le Pouldu
  1895 Paris, Tahiti
  1901 Hiva-Oa
† 1903 Hiva-Oa

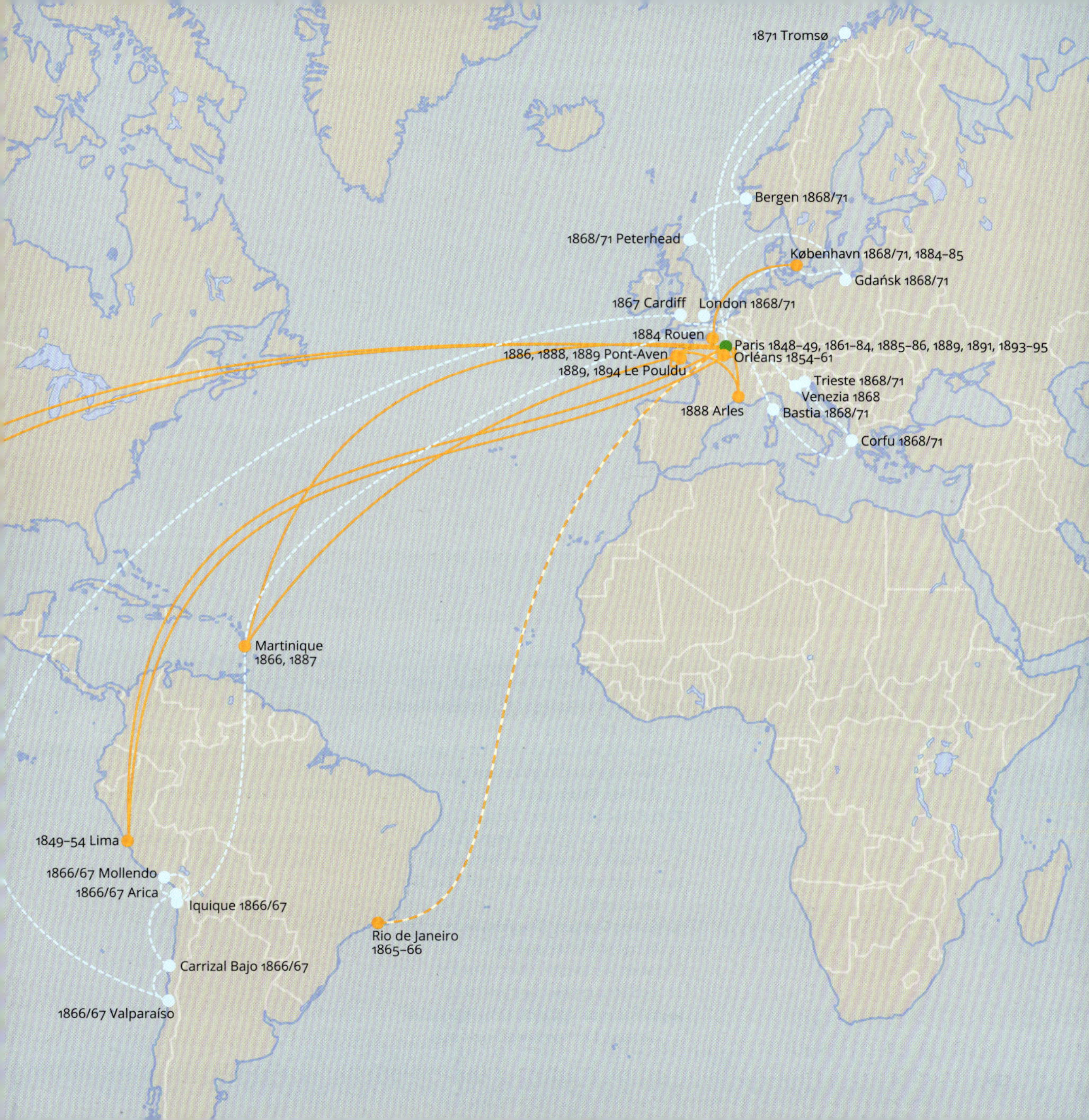

1871 Tromsø
Bergen 1868/71
1868/71 Peterhead
København 1868/71, 1884–85
Gdańsk 1868/71
1867 Cardiff
London 1868/71
1884 Rouen
1886, 1888, 1889 Pont-Aven
1889, 1894 Le Pouldu
Paris 1848–49, 1861–84, 1885–86, 1889, 1891, 1893–95
Orléans 1854–61
Trieste 1868/71
Venezia 1868
Bastia 1868/71
1888 Arles
Corfu 1868/71
Martinique
1866, 1887
1849–54 Lima
1866/67 Mollendo
1866/67 Arica
Iquique 1866/67
Carrizal Bajo 1866/67
1866/67 Valparaíso
Rio de Janeiro
1865–66

Recommended Literature
Fabrizio Dori, *Gauguin: The Other World*,
    London 2017
Starr Figura, Elizabeth C. Childs, *Gauguin:
    Metamorphoses*, New York 2014

Littérature recommandée
Françoise Cachin, *Gauguin*, Paris 1988
André Cariou, *Gauguin et l'école de Pont-
    Aven*, Paris 2015
Douglas W. Druick, Peter Kort Zegers,
    Van Gogh et Gauguin, l'atelier du midi,
    Chicago, Paris 2001
Claire Frèches-Thory, George T. M.
    Schackelford (dir.), *Gauguin Tahiti,
    l'atelier des tropiques*, Paris 2003
Paul Gauguin, Charles Morice, *Noa Noa*,
    Paris 1966
Stéphane Guégan, *Gauguin, le sauvage
    imaginaire*, Paris 2003
Laurence Madeline, *Ultra-sauvage.
    Gauguin sculpteur*, Paris 2002
Jean-François Staszack, *Géographies de
    Gauguin*, Rosny-sous-Bois 2003

Literaturempfehlungen
Raphaël Bouvier, *Paul Gauguin*,
    Berlin 2015
Elizabeth Prelinger, Tobia Bezzola,
    Paul Gauguin: Das druckgrafische Werk,
    München 2012
Ludwig Harig, *Gauguins Bretagne*,
    Hamburg 1998
Eckhard Hollmann, *Gauguin und seine
    Zeit*, Leipzig 2014